AF521933

HOLDING SPACE

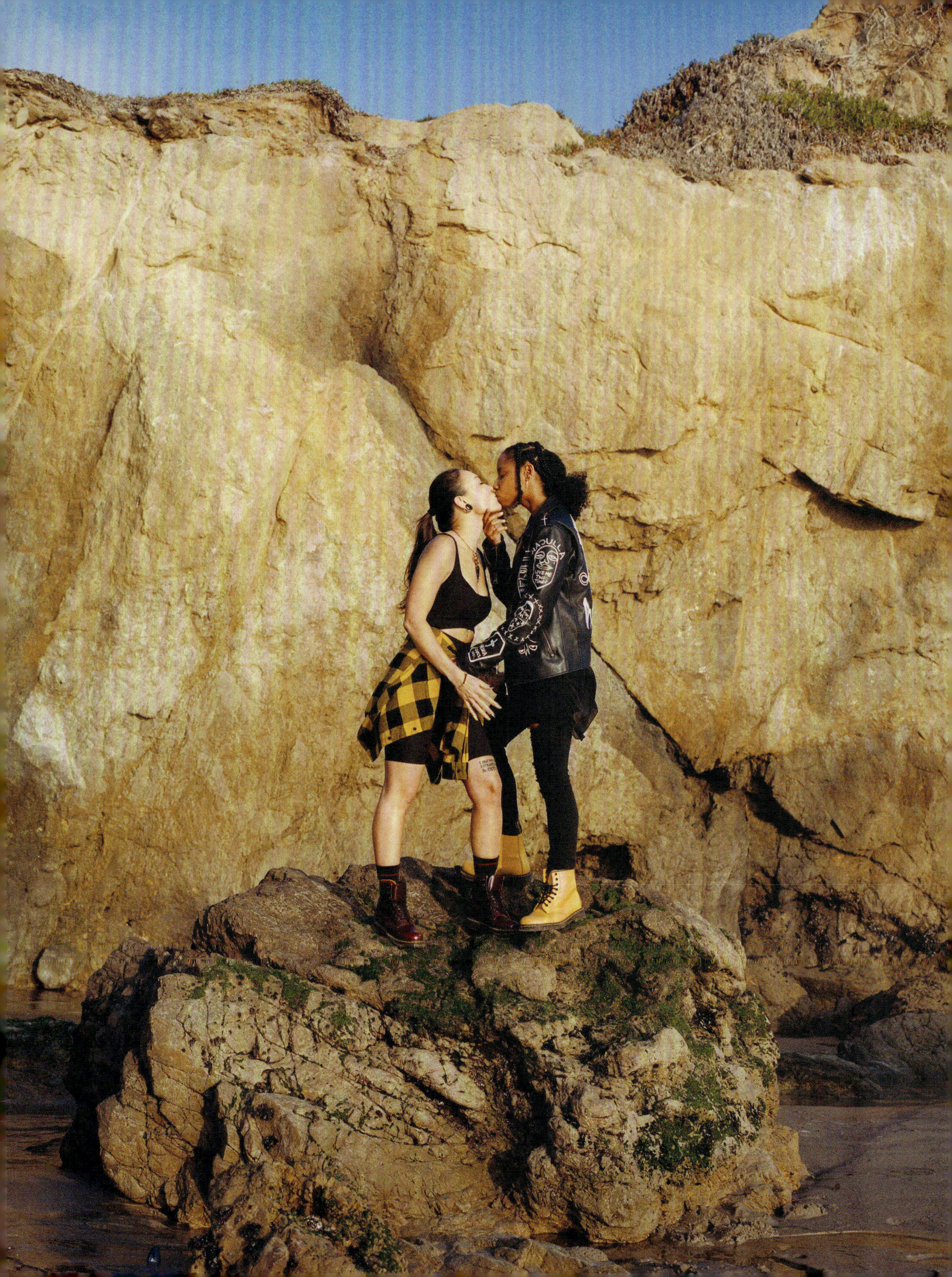

HOLDING SPACE

Life and Love Through a Queer Lens

Ryan Pfluger

Foreword by Janicza Bravo

PRINCETON ARCHITECTURAL PRESS · NEW YORK

Contents

Foreword

JANICZA BRAVO

> I must find an apartment high up, around the twentieth floor,
> where the sun will come flooding in in the morning and I won't
> awaken inside a deep shaft of gloom. Then I will be able to
> think and see clearly, about how integration came into style.
> And people getting along for a while…
>
> —KATHLEEN COLLINS, from *Whatever Happened to Interracial Love?*

The first man I ever loved loved, not familial love, but bed love, was my stepfather. He loved me back but not like that. He was Latin. Six foot two, six foot three. A giraffe. He was the Tom Selleck of his group. There wasn't a mom who wasn't in on him. I can still name his smell. After him, my next great love was a friend. A girlfriend. We met young. I can't place who led it or who started it. But I know we both participated in continuing it. Our time together remained sealed behind the doors of a two-bedroom in a second-floor walkup. Her mother taught me how to make dumplings. I would never learn enough to do it on my own. In the period after my father and before my friend there were many a romance. All of them I kept to myself. All of them an array of faces and hues. And when I got to college every infatuation got further and further away from what I call home. I was terrified of what my mother and father would think. Disappointing them was not an option I could live with. It wasn't until I was in my thirties and my parents were visiting me in Los Angeles that I told them I had a white partner. A white Jewish partner. I waited to tell them the night before they arrived. I've always been terrible at timing and deadlines.

They forgot he was Jewish, which served me because they are born-again Christian. The knot in my stomach. They went in a direction I wasn't expecting. They got high on the possibility of a mixed-race baby. "There's a lot of potential in mixing it up. The kid could be very beautiful. Or it could not work out at all. You've seen it when it doesn't work." We rode out on a 50/50 chance of a promising child. My parents had more acceptance in them than I had known. When we separated, I realized that every space I was walking into now without him on my arm meant having to provide context. Our union had brought me a certain cachet that meant I could walk a dog late at night without anyone crossing a street. Of course, it had also meant if we held hands in certain neighborhoods, people over fifty seemed to take it personally. One summer we drove cross-country in a green van with our dog, Janet. I did most of the driving. There wasn't a single diner between Nevada and Ohio that allowed us the privilege of invisibility.

I met Ryan a couple years ago. I'd heard about him from a group of friends we share. The little bits I'd gotten were always warm. A constant overlap of how tender he was and generous. I don't go into the business of being photographed too often. I prefer a spot comfortably behind the lens. I sat for him on a frenzied day that doesn't allow for much connection or exchange. Though he'd been one of many he was the first and only to take a moment with me before and after taking my portrait. Our interaction was brief but it allowed me to drop my shoulders and be as I was. To be held. To be seen. To be shared.

A year after our initial meet I'd had an opportunity to be photographed alongside one of my collaborators. It was for a fancy publication. I was allowed to put forward names for who I would want to sit for, which is rare, and without hesitation Ryan's name leapt off my tongue. This session was longer than our first. He chose the place. I chose the day. We started a back and forth of images that inspired. He worked as a crew of one. If there was music, I can't recall. But what transpired was more than a handshake. It was an embrace. I knew under his eye I was in good hands. I could walk away certain that I'd been taken care of.

Inside of these last couple of years I've observed this series he'd been putting together of couples. I wondered where it would live beyond the format of an online post. Every portrait is intimate and immediately inviting. Like a secret you've been given a back-door key to. Many appearing side by side gazing back at us, unflinching. Each allowing us, the room, to freeze time with them. As I flip through this collection I find myself longing. I find myself looking back. I was a person who was loved. I am a person who is loved. I love back. I remember being loved. Confidence springs from affection. Safety nets ease. To dream and wander and wonder. Imagine you're in a crowded room. Your gaze roving. Perhaps you feel a set of eyes on you. Maybe it's a hand at the small of your back or your waist. It's a whisper in your ear. A shoulder to your shoulder. A hand to your hand. To be held. To be seen. To be shared.

Curiosity

BRANDON KYLE GOODMAN

When I was twenty-four, one of my good friends and I were discussing something about science. Maybe about molecules or cells. The way my friend was speaking, I was enraptured by her delivery and trying to follow along. Key word, "trying." She, sensing my intrigue and internal struggle to keep up, lovingly offered, "If you're curious about something, always look it up. If there's something you don't know or understand, research it."

Growing up, directives to look something up were stressful, because it meant grabbing one of my grandmother's encyclopedias or dictionaries. Flipping through page after page of small font type and having to read all the things I didn't care about to find answers to my original questions made me stop wanting to ask. Not wanting to ask for fear of being told to "look it up" followed me into adulthood. Now let's be real, part of this we can attribute to laziness, because in the age of YouTube, social media, and Google, getting answers has never been easier or quicker. But part of it is ego. We put an incredible amount of value on having all the answers, and we go to the greatest lengths to protect our egos by believing that if we don't know the answer, it's because the question wasn't worth asking. In reality, the breadth of human existence and experience is vast, complex, and nuanced. There's no world in which any of us could know everything about anything—so what exactly are we protecting ourselves from?

They say, "curiosity killed the cat," so beneath our indignation and/or laziness, is there an unconscious fear that looking things up will kill us? Irrational, but perhaps. Certainly, we've also been conditioned to not question. It's a lesson we begin learning really young as a way to keep us in our place. As a Black person I know firsthand that some of that has to do with safety—making sure a Black child knows how to respect any authority that could view them as a threat. But a lot of it has to do with respecting power. The power of adults. The power of the cool kids. The power of a boss. How many of us questioned a command from our parents and were met with a threatening "Because I said so"? How many of us were made fun of in school for asking a "dumb question" about some new trend that seemingly everyone else knew about? Now let me ask a harder question. How many of us have become the parent, cool kid, or supervisor creating the same environment in which questions can lead to ridicule, mockery, or punishment? I've definitely had my moments.

In trying to understand why I have these moments, I reflected on the history of my relationship to curiosity and came to the realization that I hated being wrong. Societally, we hate being wrong. Our worth is so rooted in being correct, is steeped in what we feel like we know. Someone challenging that, or implying we might have misunderstood something, or explaining to us that something is no longer "true" challenges our sense of self. Triggers that inner child who was taught to respect power. Threatens our current hold on power. But when my friend said, "look it up," it was such a joy not to feel the piercing twinge of unspoken shame for not having the answer in the first place. She didn't judge me for not knowing something, and I wondered if I could extend that same graciousness to myself. Could I shift my relationship with curiosity from something that threatens power to something that lovingly empowers?

What I discovered is that curiosity is actually the gift of existence. Being curious about others and about ourselves continually unlocks the trapdoors within us and deepens our wells of empathy. It allows us to find healing in the chaos of humanity. It's not about everyone being seen as the same, but instead allows us to understand others and ourselves exactly as we are. That understanding can lead us across a bridge to appreciation for who we are. A bridge to love for what we are. It can allow us perspective on why we make the good or bad decisions we make. Why we perhaps got something wrong in an interaction and how we can do better. Curiosity is a non-judgmental North Star. The truth of who we are. The truth of the people around us. And at the feet of those truths is the opportunity to honor and hold sacred that which we've learned.

Race is hard. Understanding the nuances and intricacies of an ever-expanding lexicon of gender, sexuality, and identity is hard. Laying your ego down and saying, "I'm having trouble keeping up" is hard. But as my therapist reminded me, the root word of "curiosity" is "cure." If we want to see a world where racism, homophobia, transphobia, bigotry, bias, and hate no longer exist, we first have to be curious about where in ourselves these things exist. That's also hard. But in the spirit of asking questions, can you take a breath? Can you take your character off the witness stand? Can you hold yourself accountable when you mess up and know that it is not a reflection of your worth? Can you be tender, gentle, and gracious with yourself as you learn?

Ask the hard questions. The hardest questions. It's true that sometimes you may not always want to ask another person because they might not have the emotional capacity to share their experience and it's not their responsibility to educate you. But that's precisely what makes Ryan's book so special. He's fostered a space for thoughtful questions about relationships, queerness, race, love, and their intersections to thrive. He's made a bed where fear and hard truths can be reckoned with compassionately. He's woven curiosity into the fabric of his artistry, creating a project that reminds us that true power comes not from already knowing, but from being vulnerable enough to "look it up."

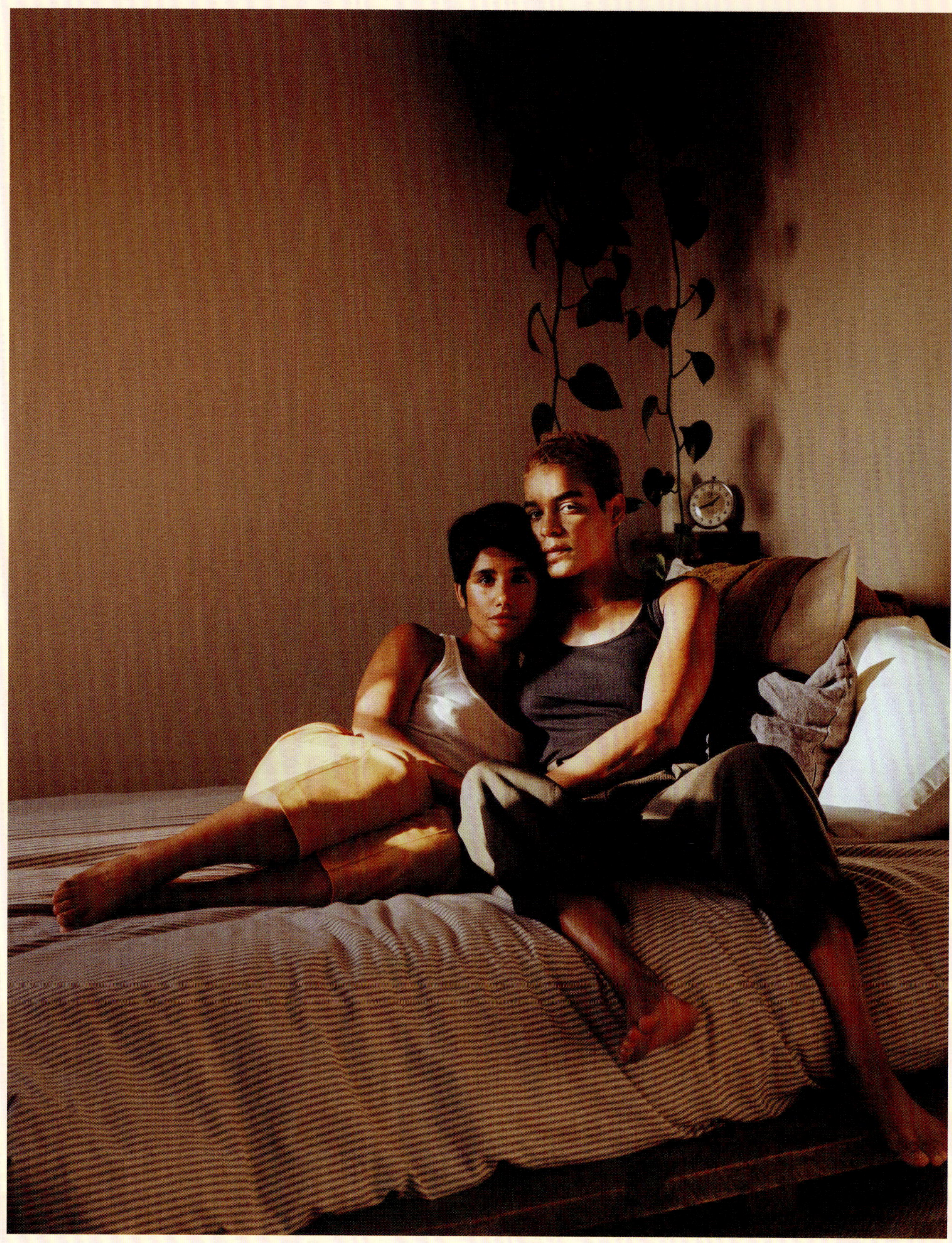

Introduction

RYAN PFLUGER

I exist at the intersection of marginalization and privilege. I am queer—I am nonbinary—but I'm also white. Grappling with how to handle that as an artist—for my work to investigate a nuanced and complicated space—has been a long journey. I have always seen myself as a storyteller. Until now my stories have been told exclusively through photographs. I've managed to weave intricate narratives in a single frame. Yet, no matter who or what the subject was, the perspective was one-sided. Control was inevitably in my hands.

Part of the reason I became a photographer was to gain some semblance of control over a life that always seemed to ebb and flow based exclusively on the decisions of others. My father a drug addict, mother an alcoholic. I was outed by my mother at thirteen—an age when I didn't even know what that meant for me. Control became an abstract concept that I was never privy to.

The driving force to be behind the lens, though, was my instinctual desire for people to feel seen, thoughtfully and lovingly. Being seen through the eyes of judgement, racism, homophobia, sexism, transphobia, and so on is indefinably damaging. Deep scars of trauma never fully leave us despite the healing work we do. But those scars fade into the deeper recesses of our mind the more work we do. The emotions become easier to manage. The walls fewer. It was the people who shared that space of healing in my life who were paramount to the hastening of that process. As creating photographs became less of a craft and more a part of my being, I discovered my gift to create art also held space for others—that relinquishing the control I had so desperately craved can be more powerful than possessing it. Photography became a vessel of healing.

The language we often use to describe photography can be violent and objectifying. The male gaze. The taking of someone's portrait or having a photo shoot. The directing of subjects. We intellectualize and celebrate the photographer's work and intentions, while maintaining assumptions and fetishizing those depicted in a singular frozen moment of time. There is rarely a "subject statement"; instead we get an artist's statement. When I started this body of work, I knew it couldn't exist under this framework. I needed a new set of parameters. The scholar Kimberlé Crenshaw coined the term *intersectionality* in 1989—a framework for understanding the advantages and disadvantages one experiences based on race, gender, sexuality, class, etc. Yet, there appeared to be little if any exploration of this within the photographic medium.

The community I exist in—the queer community—is one that is defined by intersectionality. It is vast and encompasses nuanced identities. It has taught me how to look at the world. I knew exploring intersectionality through interracial queer couples would give the scope I needed to show that. At the same time, I understood my inherent privilege as a white person behind the lens. To test the waters, I began by photographing couples I knew or who were in my extended social circle. Couples would pick where they wanted to be photographed and decide what they would wear or how undressed they were comfortable being. No expectations and no release forms. The only requirement—touching. If they decided down the line they no longer wanted to be a part of what I was creating, the choice was always in their hands.

After those first sessions, seeing the photographs I made, I knew there was no turning back. I no longer needed to exist at the intersection I had been navigating for so long in my work. A new path emerged—the one I had been desperately searching for.

To allow this body of work to grow organically, there couldn't be curation on my part. I turned to social media, announcing I was looking for interracial couples to collaborate with me. There were no requirements or restrictions outside of that, and I would photograph anyone who reached out. I was connecting with strangers again, as I have done through the Internet for the better part of two decades, but now during a pandemic where connection felt intangible.

The more couples I photographed and stories I heard, the more I realized how many misconceptions still existed for me. Which was humbling to say the least. I would often look at emails from couples in bed at night, much to my partner's dismay. One night he said, "I thought you were only photographing queer couples," and my immediate response was "that's why I'm doing this." It was a hetero-passing couple that had caught his eye. I didn't want assumptions or perceptions or stereotypes to exist in what I was creating. This work needed the couples' voices. So, I asked for just that, with general prompts, but everyone had the freedom to share what they wished.

Two cross-country trips, over a thousand rolls of film, and sixteen months later, I had photographed over a hundred and twenty couples. Some couples broke up and chose to not be a part of this project anymore. Others still wanted to be involved to share their stories of transition and loss. Couples dropped communication before and after I photographed them. Others became good friends and vocal supporters of what I'm doing. That is the beauty of relinquishing control. Allowing the space for things to evolve and change—for marginalized people to have control over their narratives regardless of my intentions. To listen and learn. That is why *Holding Space* exists.

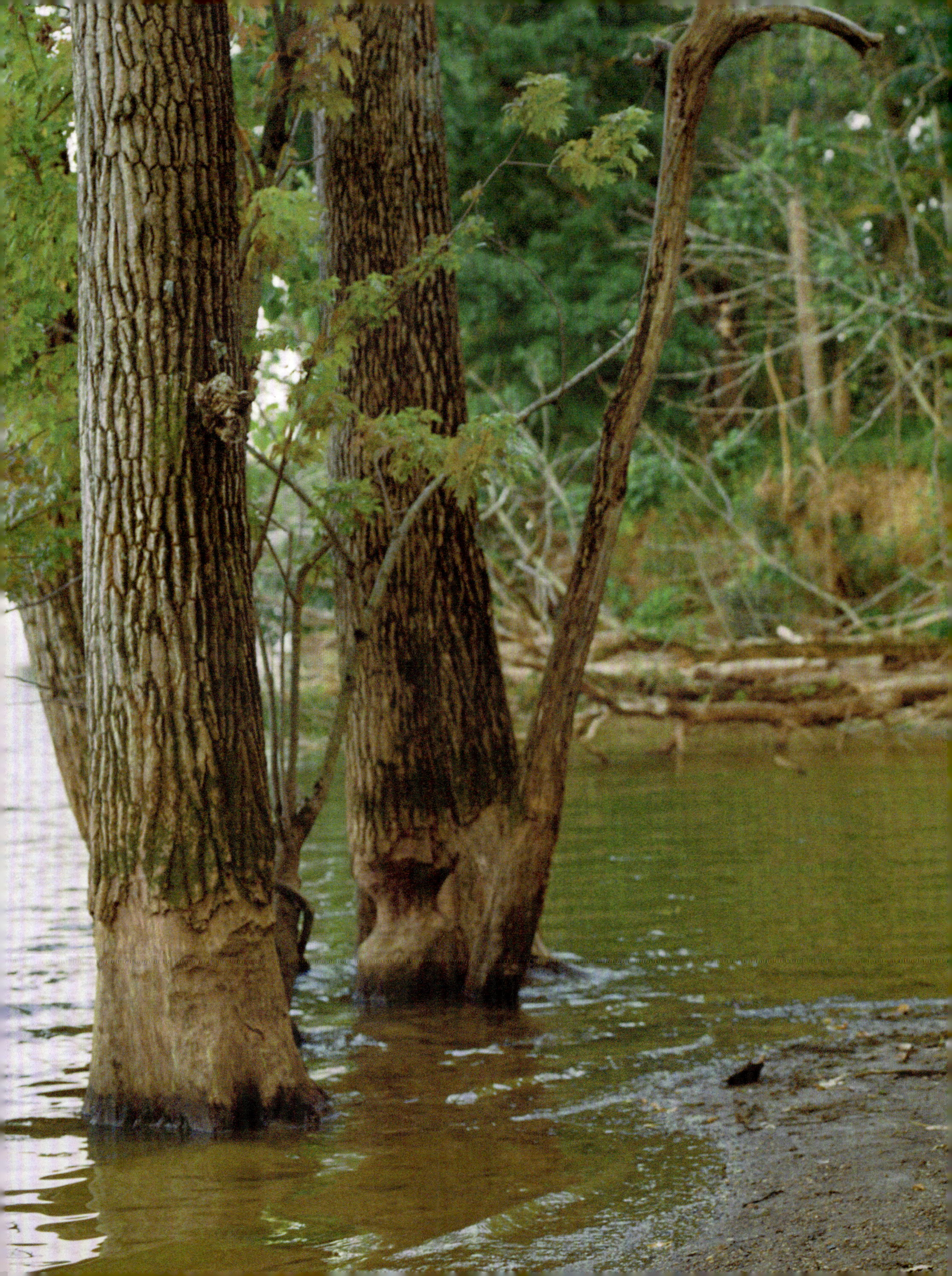

PORTRAITS

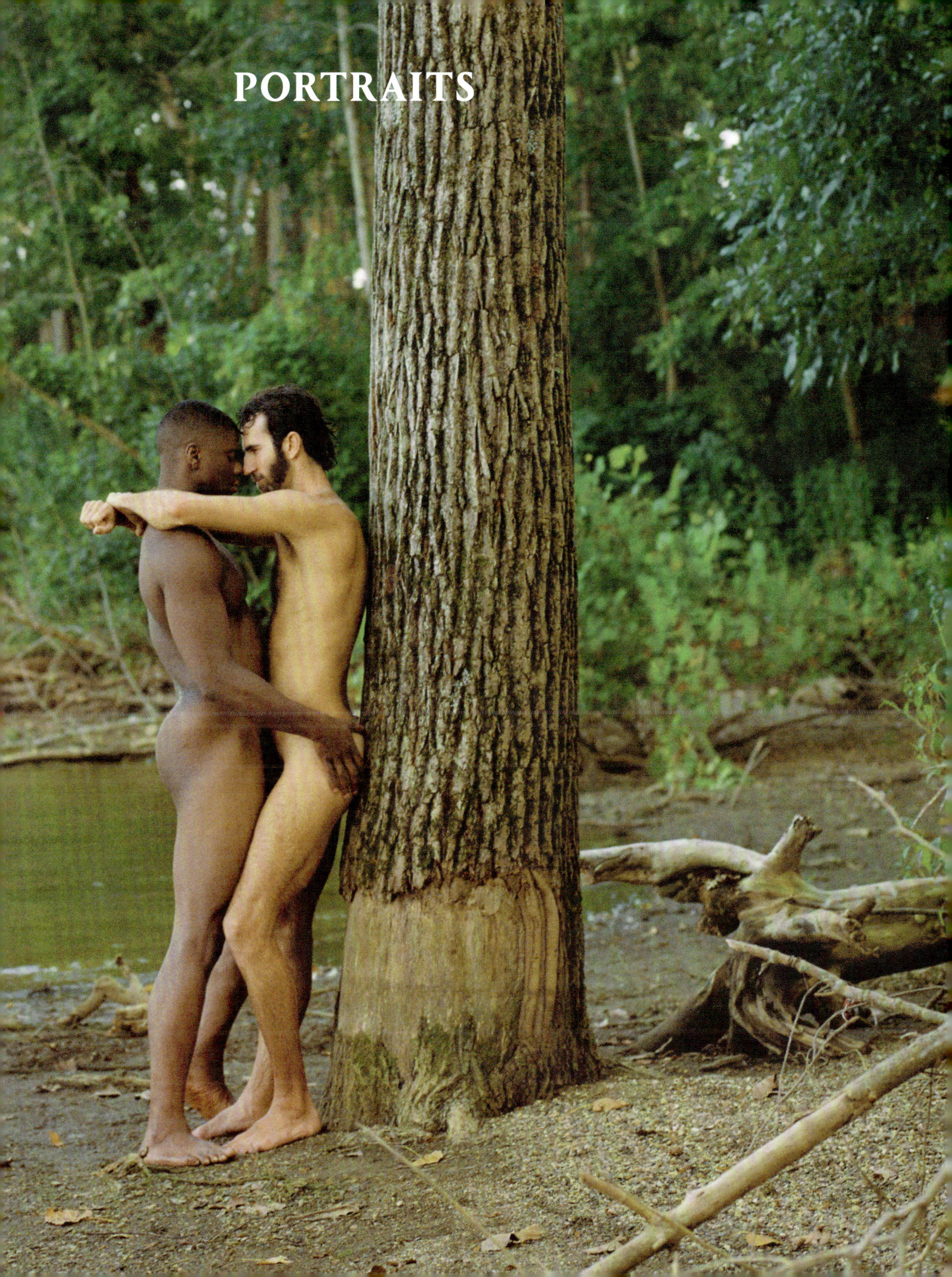

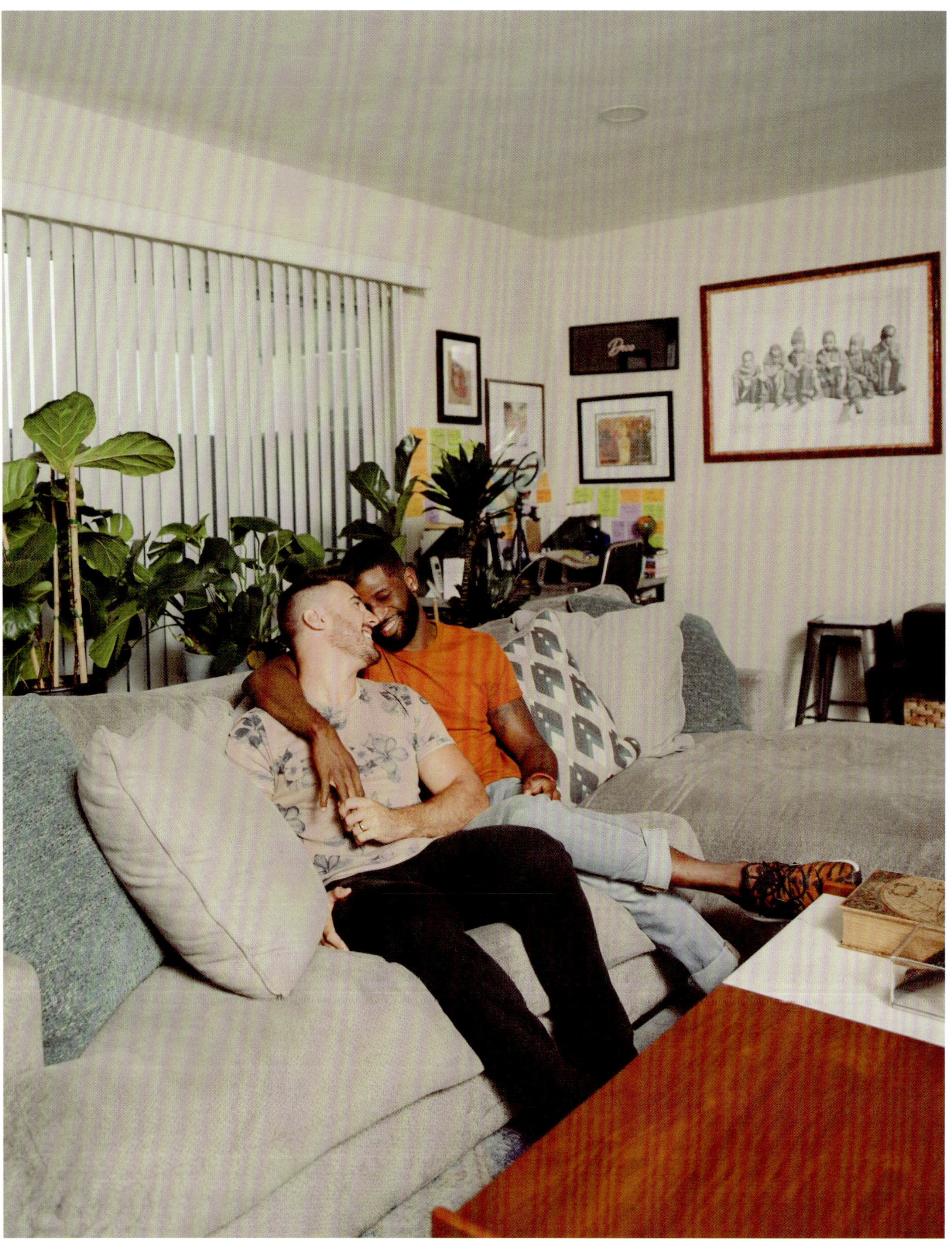

Brandon *(They/He)* & Matthew *(He/Him)*

LOS ANGELES, CA

BRANDON

I think one of the most concerning things is hearing a white person say, "I don't see race." Even more concerning is if that white person is in an interracial relationship. It tells me that the Black/POC person in that relationship isn't being seen in the totality of their identity. I'm a Black, gay, non-binary person, and I am all those things at the exact same time. If I had a white queer spouse who thought they understood my experience just because they're also queer, I'd be in some real trouble.

The reason my husband Matthew and I continue to have a blossoming relationship is not just because of the compatibility of our interests and communication styles, but because he actively does the work to understand his privileges and dismantle them or use them to serve others. Are there hiccups? Of course. But he takes responsibility, apologizes, learns (or unlearns), and commits to doing better the next time around. Seeing him so invested gives me hope in other white folx being able to be partners (not allies) in the fight for equality and equity of Black lives.

I truly say, "fuck allyship." An "ally" can dip in and leave when it gets hard. Can check out when it's no longer convenient. My Black queer life doesn't afford me the luxury to have "allies." And I certainly can't be married to one. A "partner" knows whatever happens to the other person, happens to you. That's true romantically, but that's the same energy needed in our friendships, families, professional relationships, even with strangers at the grocery store. Be a partner who says, "I won't tolerate racism or bigotry of any kind."

I love knowing I have a husband who is my partner in this fight for Black lives. Who, whether I'm present or not, remains conscious of his privilege and uses it to be a partner to anyone he's around in any space he occupies. I also know that he is not the norm, and so I feel incredibly lucky to know him, to love him, and to be loved by him so deeply. Our partnership and his heart continues to expand my existence.

MATTHEW

I truly cannot put into words the impact that my relationship with Brandon has had on my life. Being queer, I did not grow up seeing or believing in the kind of intimate, supportive, and committed love that we are building together. I didn't think it was possible for me, but I knew I had to try. Not only has our relationship totally expanded my vision for what's possible in love, it's also allowed me the space and safety to come to terms with my own identity and learn how to love myself more fully.

Being in an interracial queer partnership is easily the hardest thing I've ever done and it's also the most transformative. While I had already done a lot of work to unlearn and unpack my own racism before meeting Brandon, I hadn't come close to the depths of work that I would be doing once we were together. A pivotal piece in that is seeing firsthand how Brandon shows up in the world and how the world often does not show up in return.

In living together, I have had the privilege to see the raw impact living in a racist, homophobic, and heterosexist world has on my partner. As a white partner I often have two choices: ignore it and see it as something done by white people at large and/or institutions and systems. Or acknowledge that I have a part in it as well. This has been and continues to be a challenge. I was groomed by a white supremacist society to believe that my needs and my comfort always come first. They do not. I am constantly challenged to admit that my and my partner's lived experiences are vastly different, and the only way I can ensure that Brandon remains safe in this world is to do everything possible to not perpetuate racism and white privilege at home. I have learned so, so, so much about microaggressions and privilege because of Brandon's patience and willingness to support me in that growth. I also own it; it is my work and no one else's.

Once I figured out that racism is not Brandon's fight that I need to support but a fight that I need to get into myself, a lot of my anti-racism work started to shift. White partners of POC need to realize this is just as much for us and on us as it is for our partners. As much as racism has been internalized, we need the commitment to internalize anti-racism.

Christine *(She/Her)* & Hanna *(She/Her)*

SANTA FE, NM

CHRISTINE

We were always opposites in many ways. But from the perspective of loving life, we were best friends and soulmates. Our first date was five hours of conversation; our second, visiting the MoMA in New York and talking about sex dreams so loudly that security kicked us out; our third, wandering Rockaway Beach until the sun set and kissing in the dark. She was always the person I wanted to travel the world with, finding outrageous clubs and getting lost in coffee shops. I never felt more in the world, or of the world, than when I was with her.

It's maybe ironic then that it felt like the outer world pulled us apart. Or maybe it was the unkind part of the outer world that I had internalized and couldn't kick. As years passed and we grew closer and closer in friendship and love, moving across the country together and creating a home, everything also got harder. It seemed like the further we got into the relationship, the more people treated us differently, deferring to my whiteness in ways I didn't always see or prevent. At work, people asked if I owned the house. In social groups, they made eye contact with me alone. Roommates asked me, not her, about the rent. We could talk about it at home, we could fight or cry or laugh about it in private, but inevitably the next time we were in the world, it happened all over again and the wounds would rip back open. Eventually, it split us apart.

Sometimes I've wondered if we could have made it work had we lived in a different world. Navigating race and gender within our workplaces, friend groups, families, and within ourselves often felt like too much. But on the other hand, maybe it was always about my relationship to the silence whiteness taught me. Being able to stand up for your person consistently and proudly is an essential part of every loving relationship, and no one should have to wait for their partner to find their voice in that arena.

But the thing is, she and I remain family. I love her more than any human on the planet, and I am committed to fighting for her and her friendship for the rest of my life and using my voice when racism surfaces. Now that we are no longer in a romantic partnership, we talk about race, gender, love, life, and every other thing under the sun with more freedom than ever. She's still the one I want to get lost with in Berlin clubs and Paris coffee shops. I don't know the moral of all this. But I know that I am grateful.

HANNA

A poignant lesson throughout this relationship has been realizing the importance of public and private relationship dynamics, and how that interplay can impact the tone, tenor, and feel of a relationship. Privately, Christine and I have a beautiful, heart-centered connection based on creativity, imagination, mutual understanding, humor, and cat co-parenting. The private dynamic is rare and enriching. However, what is felt and practiced in the private space—the energy and dynamic of it—does not follow into our public energy.

In public or in interpersonal relationships between me, Christine, and others, the dynamic is usually exclusionary and extractive. I'm usually excluded from the dynamic and Christine and the other person are usually extractive—engaging in order to take or get something from each other. Interestingly, this dynamic does not occur when my friends engage with us. I have never witnessed or been involved in dynamics like this before this relationship (I think, because I don't have any close friends who are cis, WASP American women, beyond basic acquaintances or coworkers). So, through this relationship, I have seen a form of social engagement that I never want to find myself part of again. But more importantly, I learned that I need the private and public relationship spheres to be synchronized. A fun and loving home life needs to translate to feeling trust—stemming from love—in the public sphere. If, for instance, a couple with a loving home life encounters racism, classism, homophobia, or ignorance in public space and among friends, will both partners say and do something? Or will only one person say and do something and then be made to look crazy by the other partner and people external to the relationship? The courage to say or act, I realized through this relationship, is an extremely important expression of love, and it is a carrying over of love from the private into the public sphere.

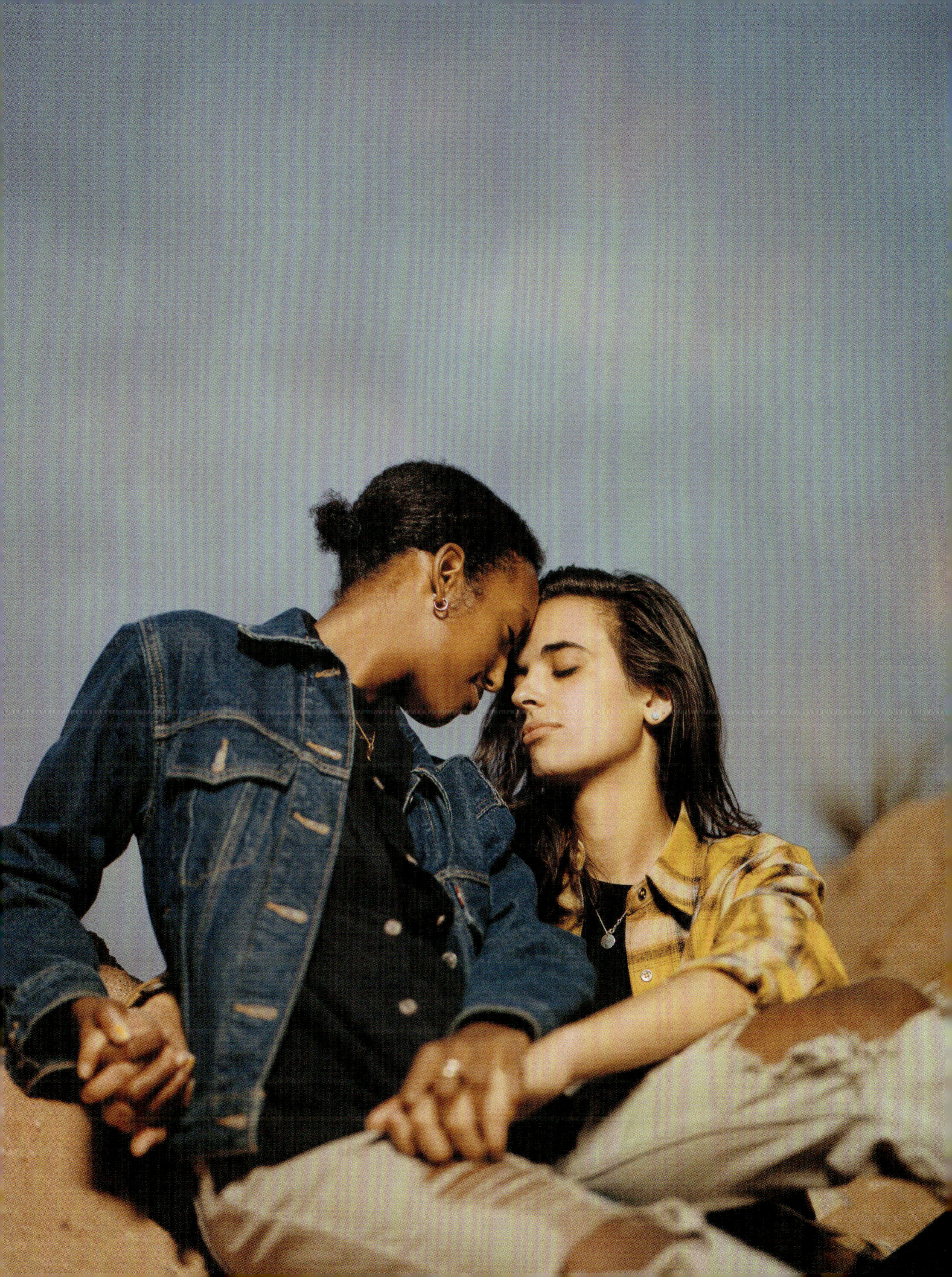

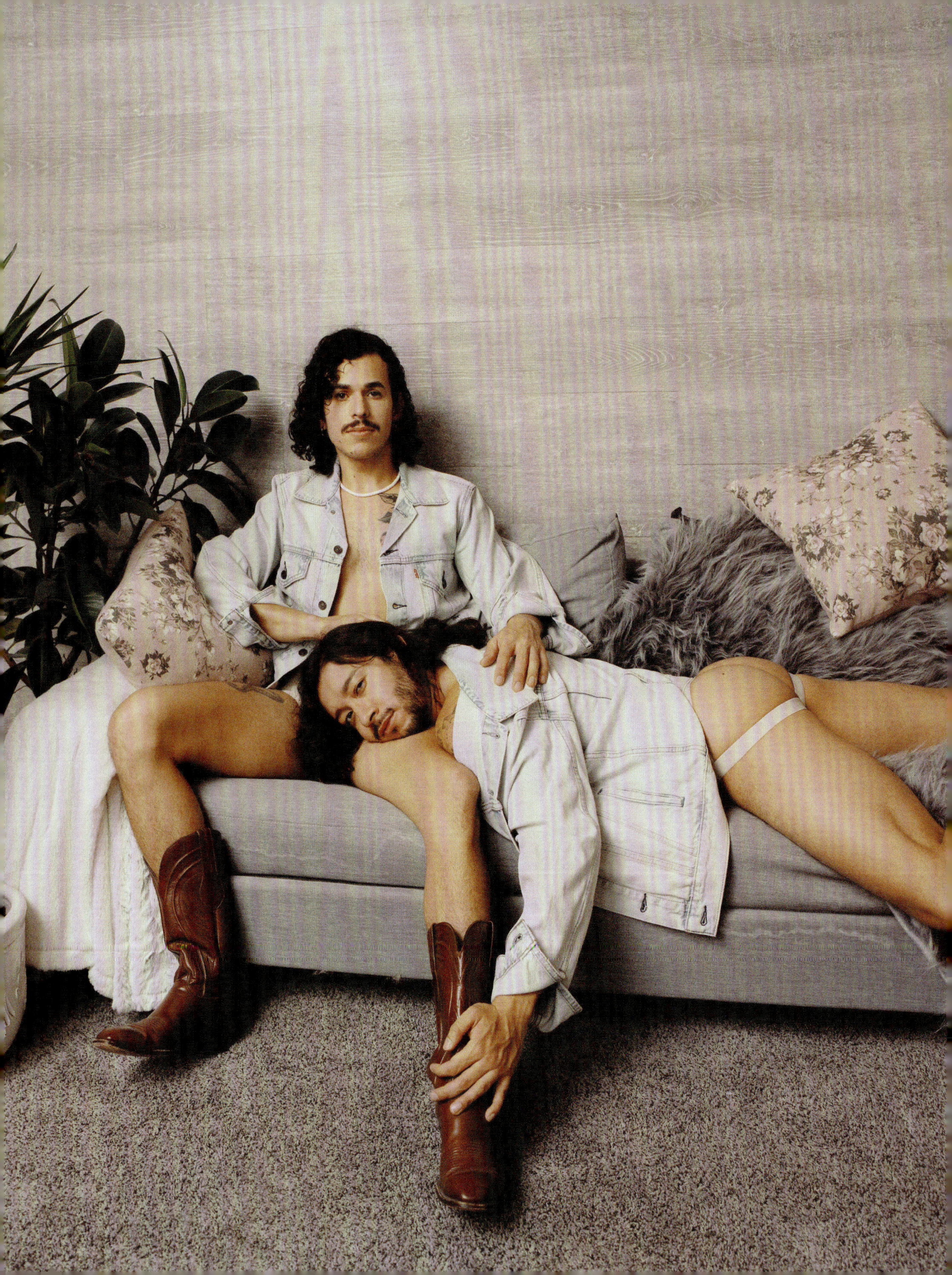

Aaron *(He/Him)* & Andy *(He/Him)*

EL PASO, TX

AARON & ANDY

At the time this photo was taken, we had been together for just over a year. Having recently celebrated our first anniversary, we realize that there is still a multitude of enriching experiences for us to have. As we exist within and outside of our identities, we've individually found ways to embrace the ways in which we express ourselves, either through our race or our gender, especially with the space and support we give one another. The energies that live within us found their balance and have made us a significantly tender pair with no need for external validation.

Growing up and choosing to remain in El Paso allows us to bridge shared experiences. While learning about each other through our similarities, we find a level of excitement with the parts of us that come from different backgrounds—Southeast Asian ancestry from the Philippines and traditional Mexican culture. We are curious and willing to embrace parts of each other that we have not experienced in the past. Although, sometimes withholding particular phrases and words in our own languages to maintain an air of mystery and seduction is just as exciting. The points in which our shared experiences begin to diverge are the ones we celebrate the most—a cultural gesture or a story from a particular upbringing and the joy that comes from allowing the other person to experience that for the first time. We look to the future with excitement as our identities continue to learn from each other throughout our relationship.

Adam *(He/Him)* & Mitchell *(He/Him)*

BROOKLYN, NY

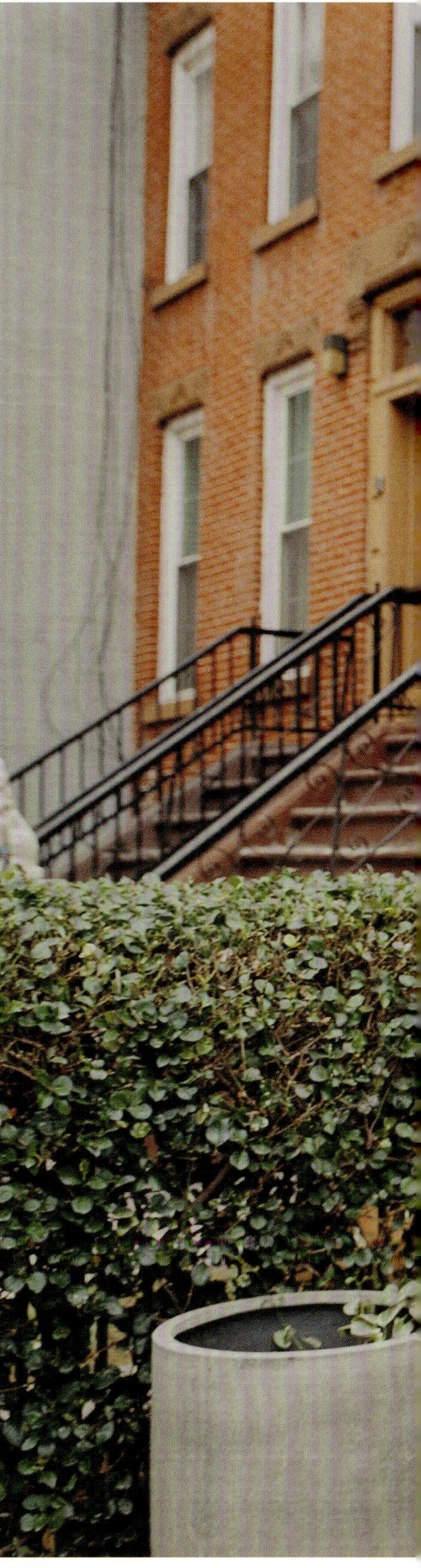

ADAM: What's nice about being from two different backgrounds is intentionally deciding which cultural traditions from each we want to observe and celebrate together.

MITCHELL: That's true. It's nice that neither of us were super regimented around our cultural identities, but I'm also struck by how different we are, especially when it comes to communication styles, because it so closely tracks with cultural stereotypes: the quiet Japanese and the loud Jew. Like *ugh*, why are we so obvious?

ADAM: But we are also really specific versions, like I'm a very specific type of Jewish person who grew up Orthodox in Canada and you are a very specific type of Japanese-Okinawan-American person from Hawai'i. I guess I am just wary of any conversation that seeks to flatten people.

MITCHELL: Me too. Those nuances matter, but I think when it comes to communication styles, we kind of conform to type [laughter]. I also feel like you're more culturally Jewish than you are letting on.

ADAM: Yes, I am extremely Jewish actually. I share Jewish things with you because I feel like I'm gaining all this stuff from you, and I want to offer you something, like *Thank you for introducing me to ten foods. Here's matzo balls.*

MITCHELL: Does it feel transactional?

ADAM: No, it's an exchange. When you are in a state of receiving all this stuff that helps you understand the person that you love more, you want to give them more pieces. It's a beautiful gift.

MITCHELL: Do you remember that period early in our relationship when you were obsessed with the parallels between "Shalom" and "Aloha"?

ADAM: I just thought it was cute that culturally we each have a word for hello and goodbye and peace. I thought that was such a romantic idea. Sometimes I think about it and I'm like, I can't believe I married a Japanese man. Not because I thought I would end up with a Jewish person, or a white person, but I guess because I didn't know that I could ever marry a guy, do you know what I mean?

MITCHELL: When you were young, even that first step was hard to imagine.

ADAM: Yeah, so now when I'm frying Spam to make musubi I think *This is the least kosher thing I could ever do for my gay husband*. It's so far from the reality I knew was possible, and that makes it extra special because it's like, this is so good that you couldn't even imagine it. You couldn't even guess.

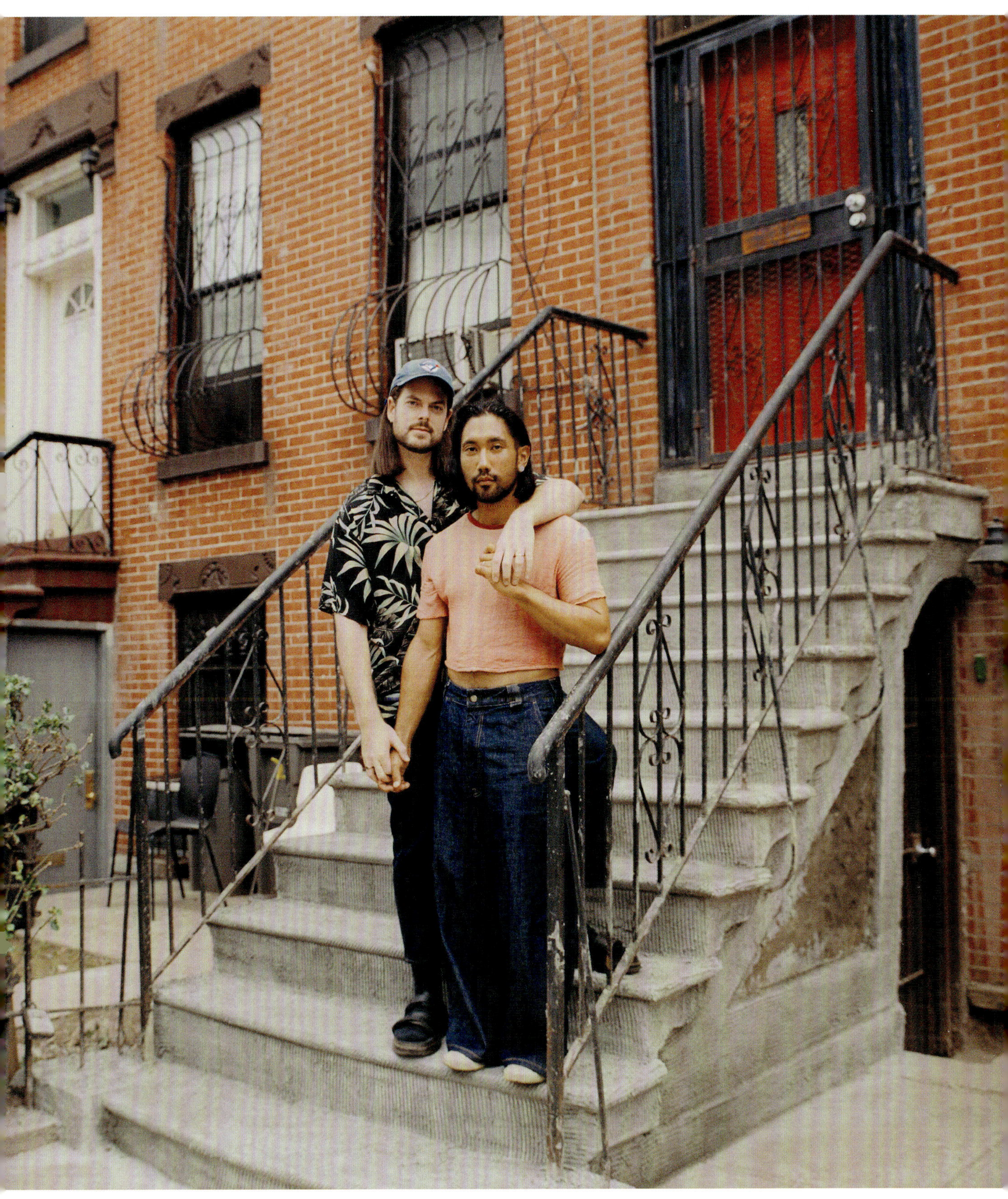

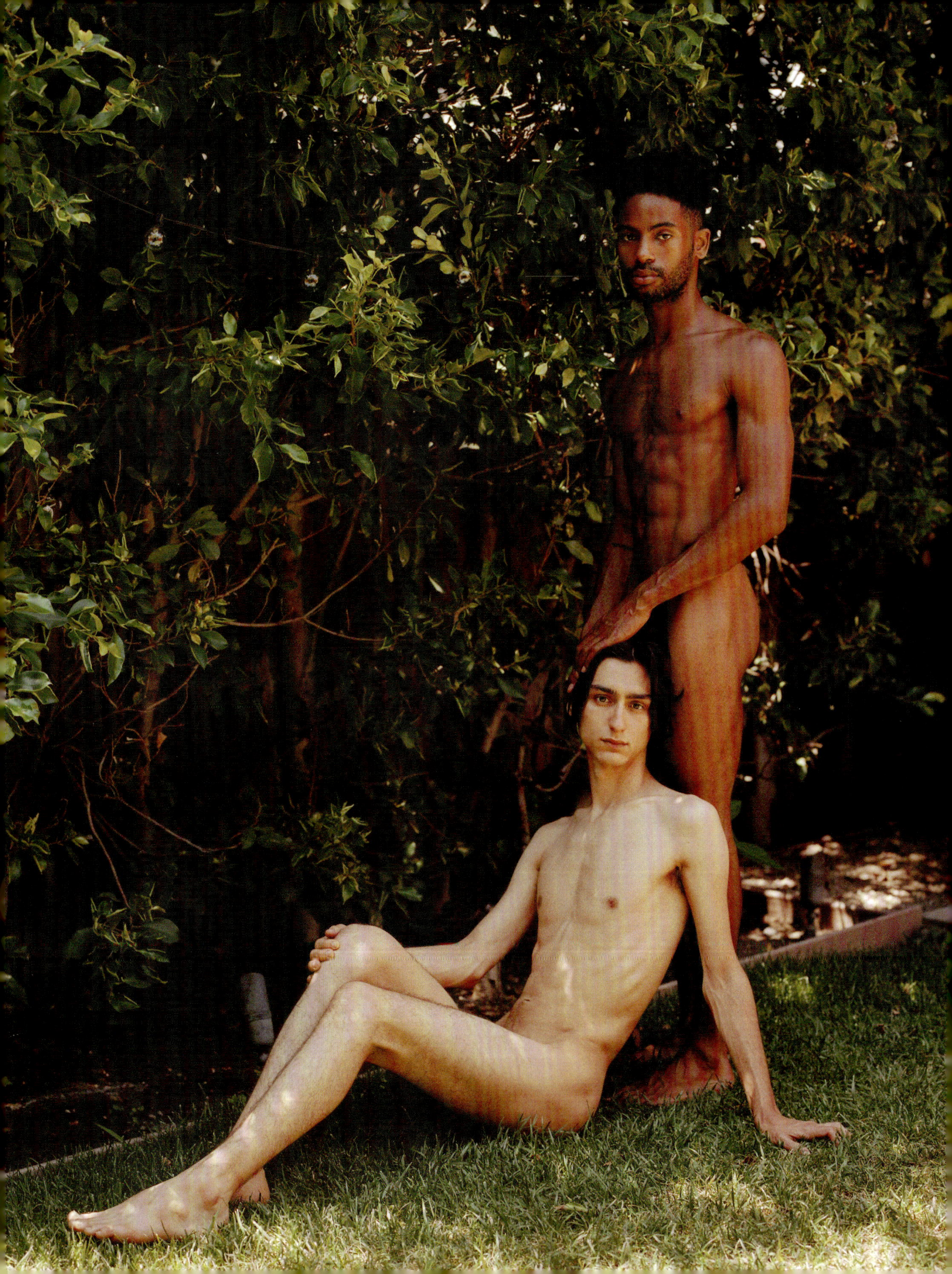

Akeem *(He/Him)* & Samuel *(He/Him)*

LOS ANGELES, CA

AKEEM

Since we first met on Grindr, our relationship brought together two unique backgrounds: water (me) and fire (Samuel). I am of African American heritage and originally from southern Mississippi. Samuel is from Barcelona and is of Jewish-American descent. Despite our different desires, truths, and fears, there was a unique familiarity that made space for us to better understand each other. These realities came into play when we decided to move in together early in 2020. Back then, everyone's collective naivete was not prepared to process a pandemic and global uprisings and their impact on every couple's romantic life—especially interracial ones. During the BLM marches, we had numerous passionate conversations about how different yet how incredibly similar our heritages were.

On one hand, I kept a lid on my experience as a queer, Black man. I felt that my experience was often misconstrued and stereotyped; the pen was in society's hand to detail what I could and should be as a Black man in the country. On the other hand, Samuel grew up having to process the impact of his hearing loss and neurodiverse background. His Jewish and Catalan identity is deeply rooted in his family's intergenerational struggles. I have a similar relationship with my family.

SAMUEL

Addressing racial inequities, finding common ground, and understanding our own intersectionality was a process for both of us. Eventually, these challenging conversations resulted in more empathy between us and equipped both with tools to apply with others as well.

Despite no longer being in a romantic relationship, our shared love still holds us together (we're still trying to figure out what this means). Ironically, this new life chapter offers us another chance to fight against the norm by continuing to love one another in ways that society does not expect or promote. We challenged the system when we decided to be together, and we're challenging it again by staying in each other's lives and preserving the bridges we've built. But it wasn't easy for us to get here, and it certainly required putting our egos aside.

This transition has been a painful recovery that showed us how to set ourselves free from toxic insecurities and all the hard feelings imposed on us by society's random constructs. We want to carry on this journey by understanding more about how to nourish ourselves individually and collectively.

Alyss *(He/They)* & Angelica *(She/Her)*

LOS ANGELES, CA

ALYSS

Note: I don't capitalize "christianity," "bible," and "church" as an intentional sign of disrespect.

At eighteen, I left Texas with the hopes of leaving conservative christianity behind me—I could never find myself among the pages of the bible as a trans, nonbinary person. I headed to California and attended Bethel Conservatory of the Arts (BCA) in Redding to get my BA in performing arts, where I quickly realized I had actually enlisted myself in a conversion therapy program.

At BCA I endured three years of exorcisms (grueling "therapy" sessions meant to convince me that "god" didn't make me gay or transgender), as well as verbal, physical, and sexual abuse. I stayed in this place far too long, even after trying to commit suicide, which, according to christians, I deserved for being queer.

During quarantine in 2020, I realized that I didn't hate myself or my queerness. I had just been acting under the influence of people who think it is an abomination for me to exist. So I left BCA and ran as fast as I could to Los Angeles, where I met Angelica.

If I saved my life by leaving christianity, Angelica made my life worth living. Since being with her I am the happiest that I have ever been. I have grown and gained so much love and empathy by being at her side. It baffles me to think I had ever believed the church when it told me something this beautiful was a sin.

ANGELICA

I came to terms with the fact that I wasn't straight when I was nineteen. This realization surfaced without much friction—emerging much like a seed finally breaking soil to become a seedling—when I dared to dream of the possibility of love without limits.

But as a first-generation Filipina American whose parents wagered everything for a better life in foreign lands, I was given a clear sense of my path in life. Being gay wasn't—couldn't possibly be—part of the plan. While I did come out to my friends, I didn't dare move beyond that liminal space for the next eight years.

Plants meet their eventual demise when they've become root-bound in their pots. In this manner, I came to understand that I could never fully love myself if I stayed duty bound to what I believed my path should be. So, at the ripe age of twenty-seven, I finally came out to my parents and my family.

Expectedly, it wasn't the Jennifer-Garner-in-*Love, Simon*-type of acceptance I sorely coveted. A pregnant pause gave birth to an awkward understanding. But at long last, I had finally given myself the chance to live authentically as me, which opened up the possibility of one day blooming alongside Alyss.

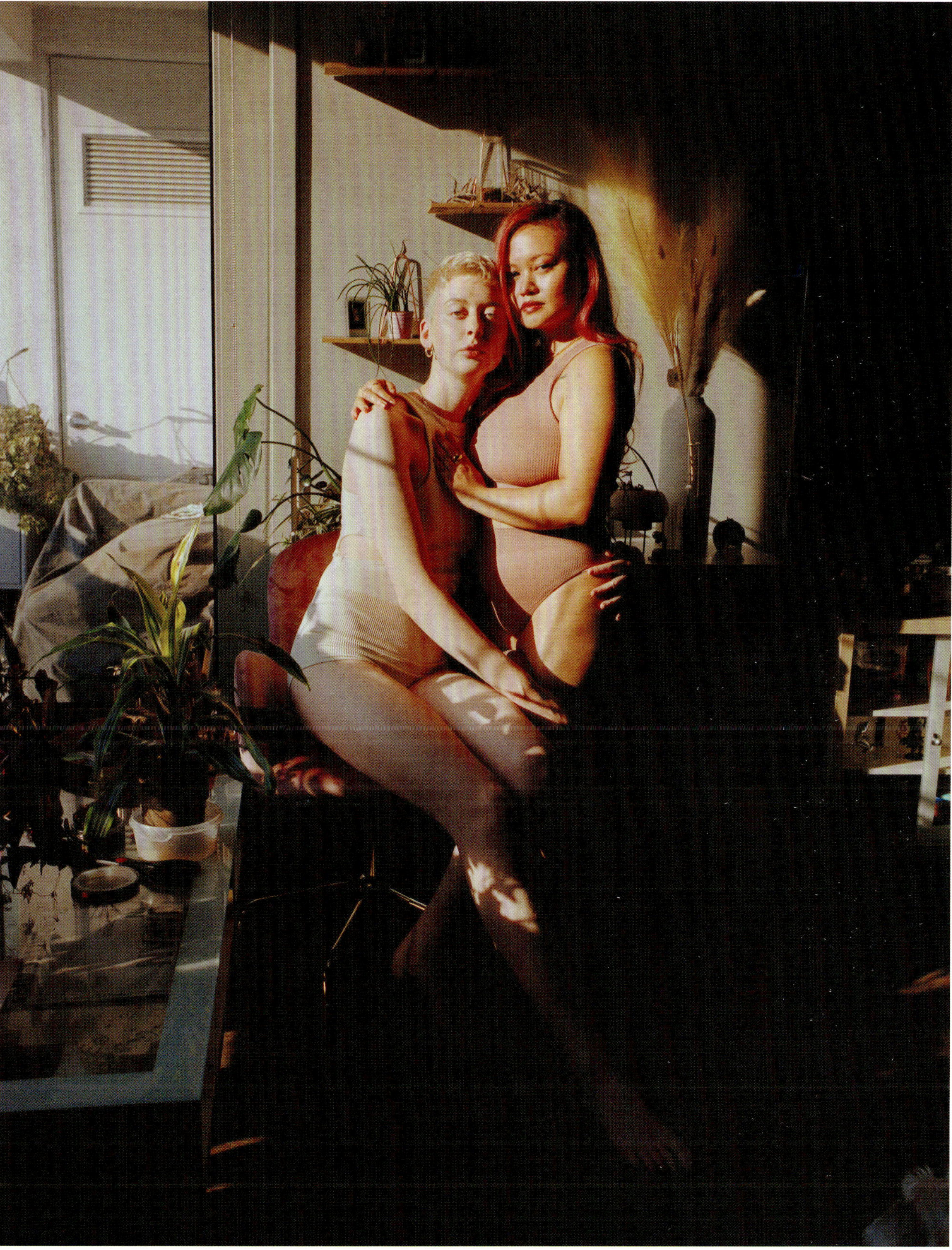

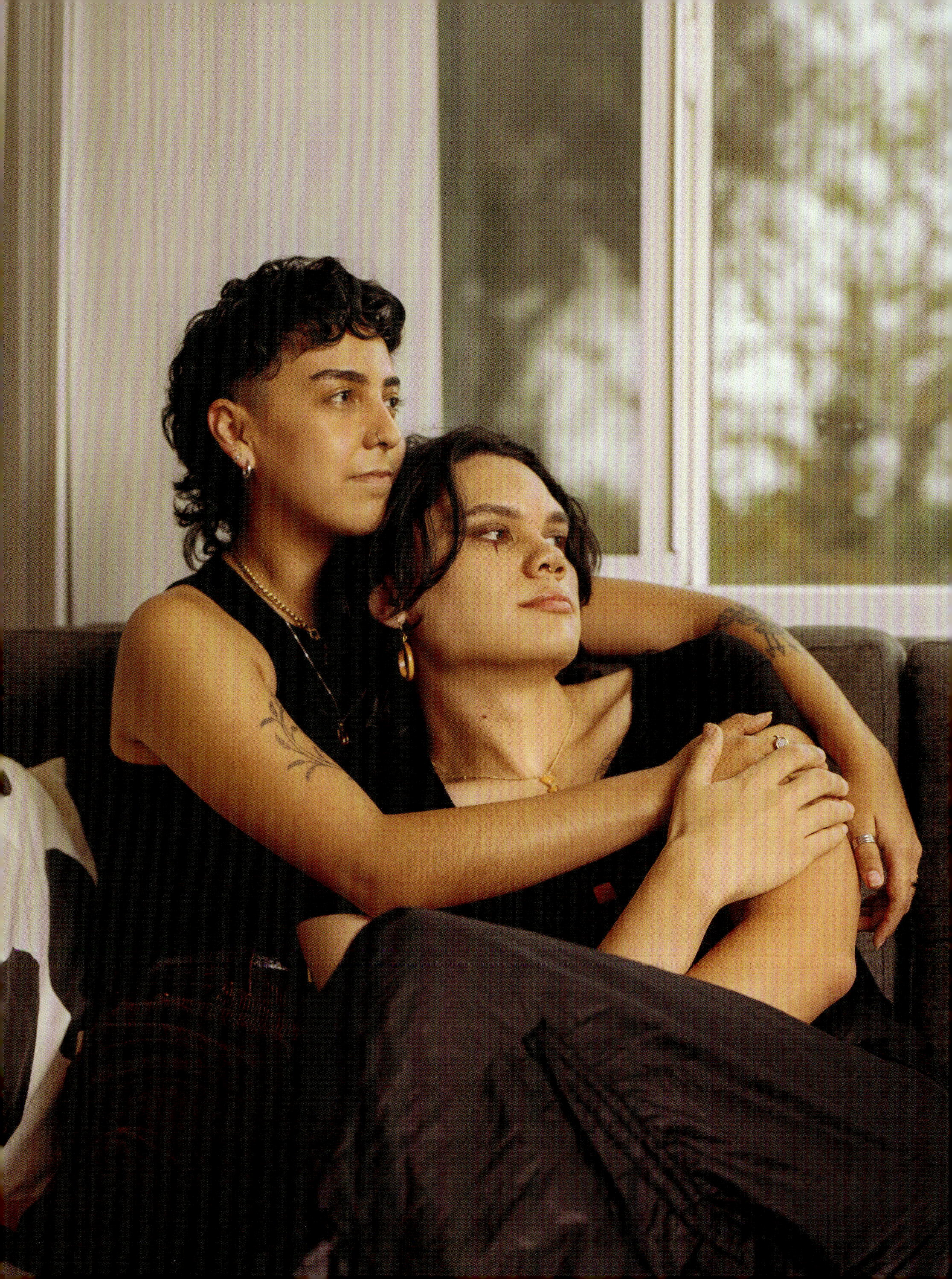

Andi *(They/Them)* & Connor *(He/Him)*

LOS ANGELES, CA

ANDI

We're the type of couple that's always together. We're known for answering FaceTime calls cuddled up on the couch and taking too long to get ready together. This is the first queer relationship for both of us. We started off pretty timid in our queer identities, but self-discovery has been a big part of our closeness.

Being brown, I'd always felt left out of Western narratives. I was raised to be color-blind and to ignore how race affects the world, which was really damaging to my self-worth. It wasn't until I surrounded myself with other brown queer people that I started to accept myself rather than assimilate. When we first met, I saw a lot of myself in Connor. I could tell he had never thought to question his ethnicity, gender, or sexuality. At this point in my life, I had started to question any and all things I was raised with. My queer family provided me all the love and support I needed to find myself, and I was honored to provide that space for Connor.

CONNOR

We love how ambiguous the word *queer* is. It feels less like a specific label and more like a way to tell people what we're not. Not straight and not cisgender. How we present means a lot to us. We combat our dysphoria together by playing a lot of dress up. My femininity complements Andi's masculinity on some days, or we're both androgynous on others. On most days we're matching.

Being mixed, I felt guilty identifying as Filipino. Even though I'm first-gen on my dad's side, I felt far removed from my culture. I grew up in a predominantly white suburb, and my Filipino family also aspired to achieve traditional American values. It wasn't until I met Andi that I began to come into my identity, both in terms of gender and ethnicity. They were quick to point out how often I doubted myself. I'm still working on overcoming the feeling of not being queer enough or Filipino enough. My parents naming me Connor didn't help. I'm probably gonna change that soon.

Andre *(He/Him)* & Jordan *(He/Him)*

LOS ANGELES, CA

ANDRE

Familiarity can be as conflicting as it is comforting. We've come to learn that truth time and time again in our relationship. When we first met, things fell right into place. The levity with which we approach life and our aptitude for conversation made our first date feel like our thirtieth. Jordan grew up in Oklahoma in a religious household. He's lived in various cities; in each one, he was a minority. He learned Spanish and Portuguese while abroad and works in healthcare as a physical therapist. He had and continues to have a remarkable ability to compartmentalize his feelings—a product of trauma and a mark of grit. I am a first generation Brazilian immigrant who speaks Portuguese natively and Spanish, well, conversantly. I similarly grew up in a very religious household and work in healthcare as a surgical resident. And while I tend to spend more time with my emotions, we both share a resilience to life's pains and social inequalities.

We acknowledged our commonalities right away. Our shared hardships and minority status helped us feel seen by each other. We understood each other's dark days and knew when and how to bring the other person comfort. As our time together went on, however, the disparate nuances of our minority identities became clearer. Jordan wears his minority status on his skin. I, on the other hand, can hide in plain sight. This difference has forced us to rethink how we see ourselves, how we make sense of our pasts, and how our experiences are ultimately individual. As quickly as our familiarity pulled us closer, it also smacked us in the face.

But here is what we both know for sure: We know the hurt of rejection. We know the pain of feeling alone. We know how to swallow our pride and when it's time to speak up. We know how to tuck away our emotions and let our rational minds tide us over. We know the power of unconditional love.

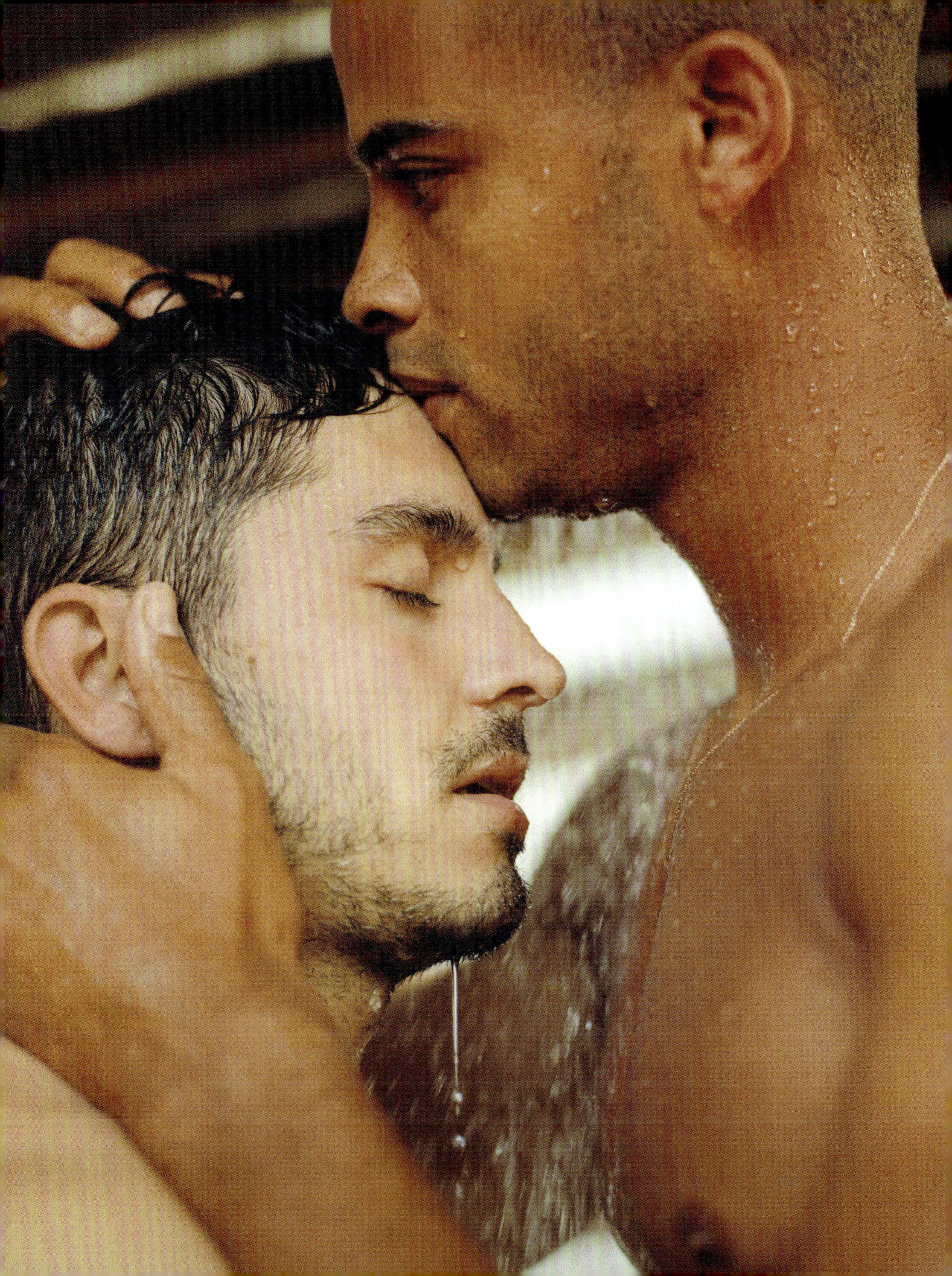

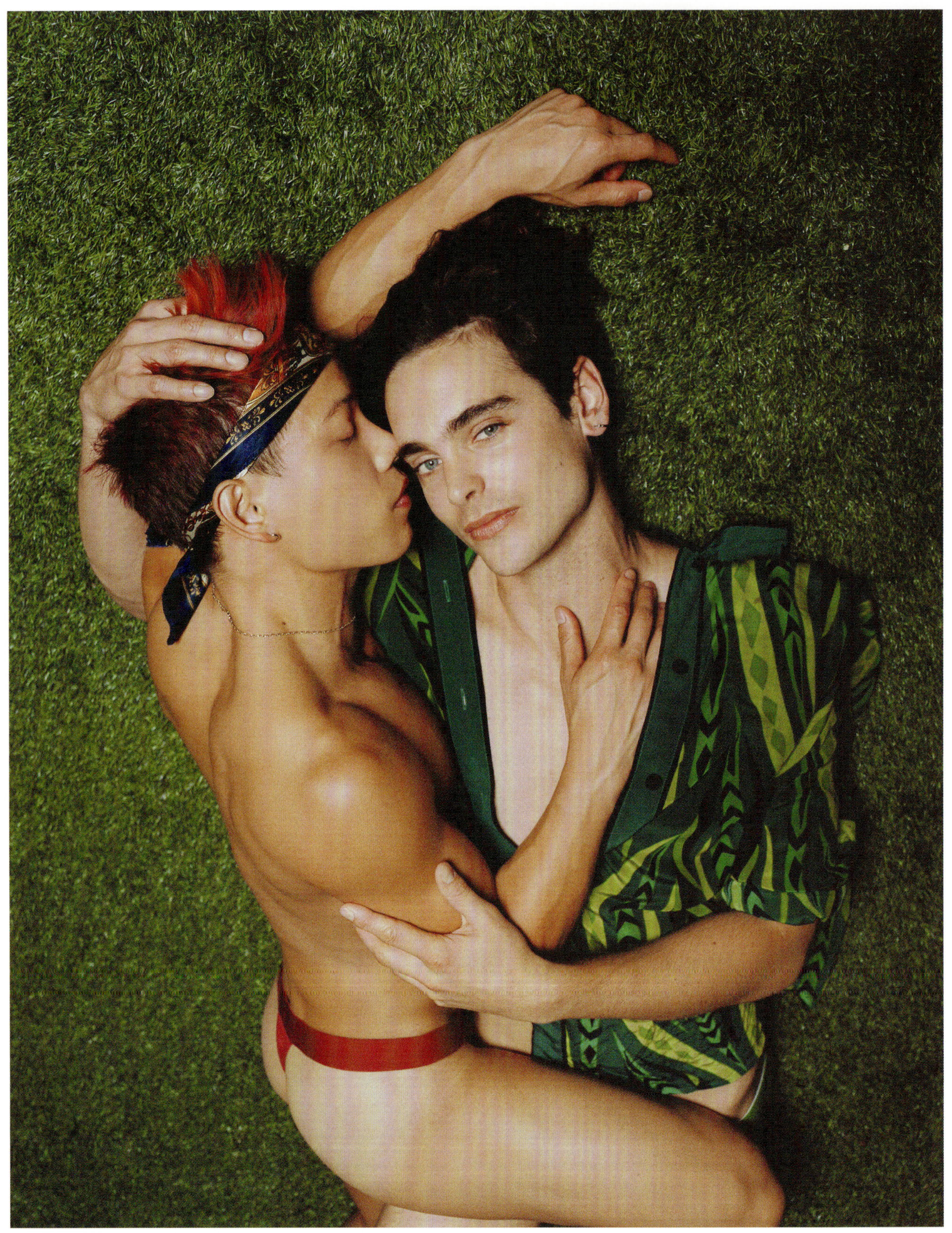

Ashton *(He/Him)* & Mitch *(He/Him)*

BROOKLYN, NY

ASHTON

The secret to our relationship is laughter. I knew Mitch was different from anyone I had ever dated because I felt I could let my guard down and truly laugh from the belly with him. We joke that we're both like cats—even when the claws occasionally come out, you'll find us completely wrapped up and smitten with each other by night's end. We also have our little rituals—for instance, we have coffee together every day, no matter what's on our crazy schedules. We brew the coffee at home, fix it how we both like, and sip while in our bathrobes, taking in the stillness of the morning in each other's company. Every relationship has its challenges, but the bottom line is we genuinely enjoy spending all these little moments with each other. I'm happy that when it comes to race, Mitch is full of empathy and curiosity—I have never felt like I had to change myself to be palatable to him.

MITCH

I remember going to Ashton's family's place in Colorado one Christmas. It was the first time meeting his immediate family, along with a bunch of his aunts, uncles, and cousins. That is when I learned that in Vietnamese culture aunts and uncles go by number. First born, second, and so forth. I also needed a crash course in learning each of their Vietnamese and English names. It was like discovering a completely new side to Ashton's identity.

I'm a cis, white, gay male from Edmonton, Alberta. I grew up in a conservative family (went to many rodeos growing up if that helps paint a picture). That said, no matter how difficult things were at times, my family always instilled in me a sense of self-pride no matter the circumstances—and surprise, I'm proud ;)

I think having different backgrounds has created an incredible balance where Ashton and I can communicate freely, without judgment, even during difficult circumstances or conversations. There have been countless moments where I have overheard people talking about us in public. "Oh, he's into Asians" or "Why is he with an Asian?" or "He is obviously a potato queen." This was many years ago, so I'm not sure how bold those people (gay men) would feel saying that now. I'm not with Ashton because he is Asian. I'm with him because he's Ashton.

Our relationship has evolved and continues to evolve. I never thought Ashton would be a morning person, but after many mornings of me waking him up with my annoying cheerfulness, he has slowly caved and started to enjoy those morning coffees, haha.

Bex *(They/Them)* & Alicia *(She/Her)*

LOS ANGELES, CA

BEX

First off, we're both actors. We met on a job that both of us were advised against taking because it was "a short film that doesn't pay." The script made us both cry, and we told our representation (separately) that we needed to be a part of this project. From the first day of rehearsals, we were drawn to one another. We talked for hours every day, connecting over art, magic, and food allergies. On about the second day, I came out to the entire production as trans nonbinary. It was my first time coming out in a public setting. I think Alicia was blown away by the confidence I had in that moment. Since that day I don't think I've ever seen Alicia shrink away from a conversation about gender or sexuality. Her first kiss was with a girl, but at thirty she still hadn't come out. My openness of self in an industry that told us to hide who we are made her reflect on the places where she hadn't been her truest self. Ever since, we've been growing together, side by side. Like sunflowers. When the sun hides, we grow with the light from one another.

ALICIA

We both come from marginalized backgrounds, Bex being a southern Jewish person and myself being brown-skinned American. We empathized deeply from the start with each other's struggles and families.

I think the biggest surprise and eye-opening moment for Bex was finding out that I would choose "white" as my race on documents when I clearly don't look "white." "What's your ethnicity?" It's an overwhelmingly common question on documents that sends me into an identity crisis every time. Dentist offices, gym memberships, job applications, cable subscriptions, etc. Why do they need to know? What do they plan to do with this information? And why is "are you Latino/Hispanic" its own question off to the side? Just the way in which the question is presented makes me very uncomfortable. From my lived experience, if I say I'm Latine, more likely than not I'm gonna be othered and/or discriminated against. My father is dark-skinned Mexican American, and my mom is fourth-generation Portuguese American, aka yt. Call me difficult but I don't think it's anyone's business other than maybe a state census to have that information, but if I must answer before I can proceed, I'm going to use that white privilege.

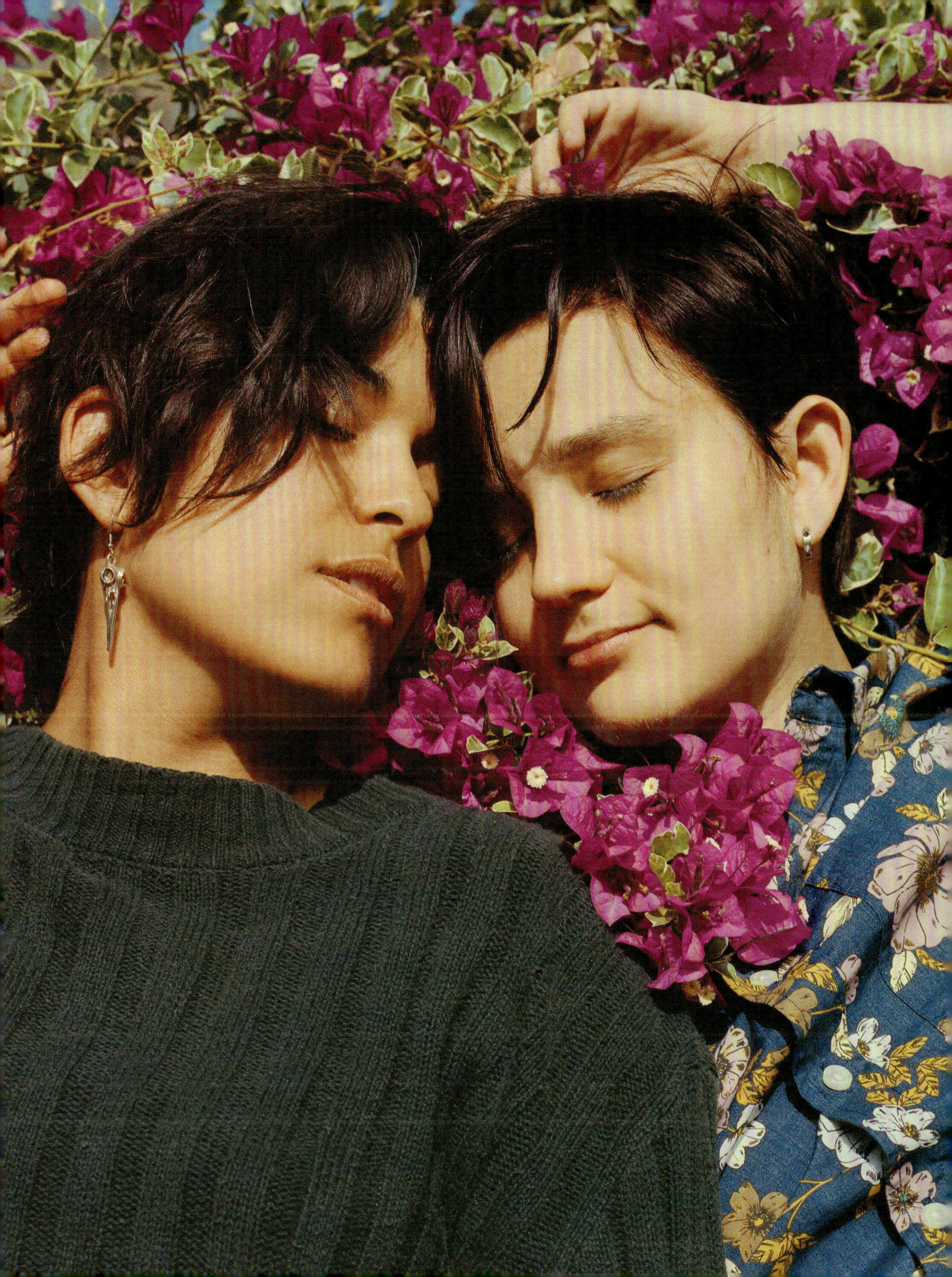

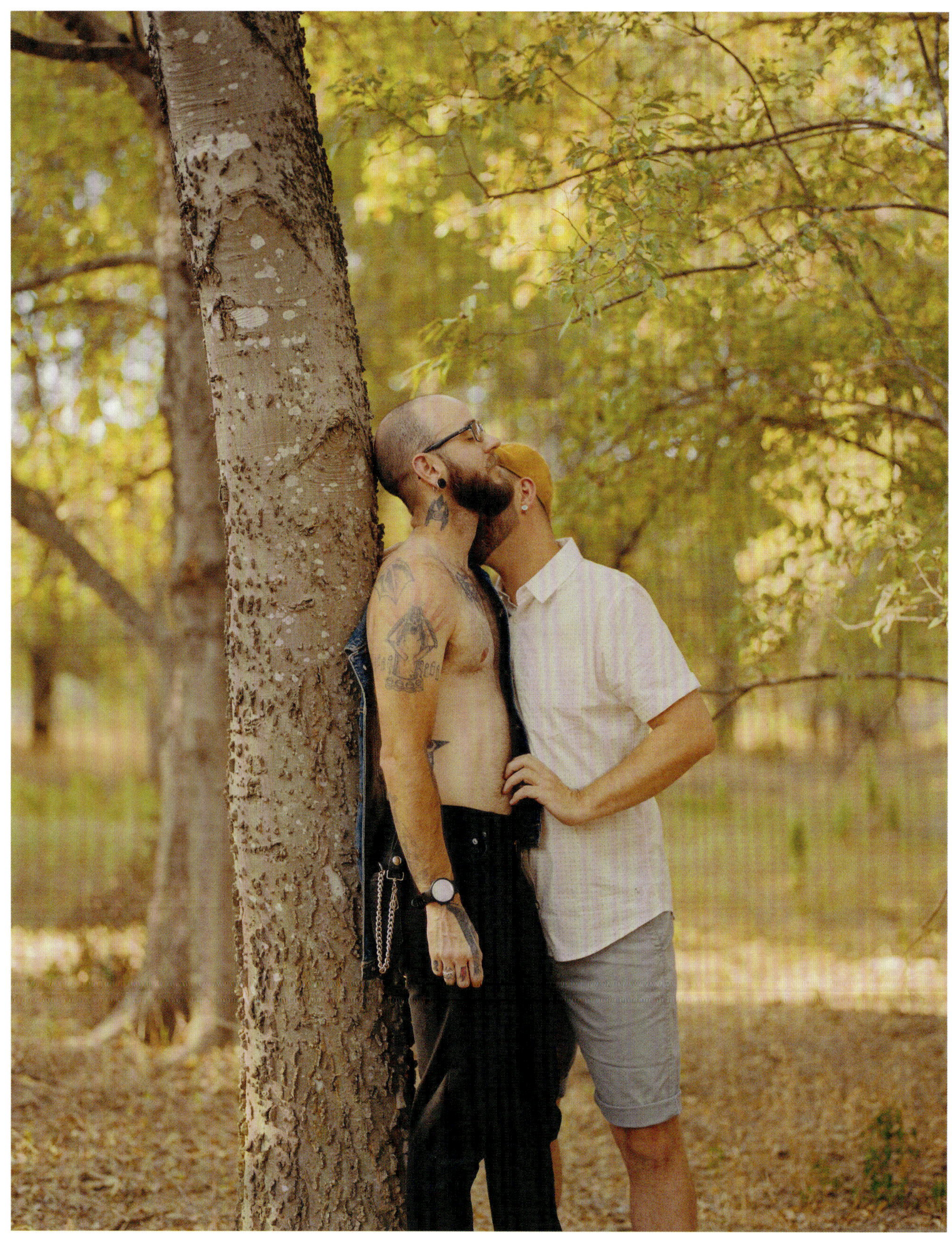

Bobby *(He/Him)* & Kaedyn *(He/Him)*

AUSTIN, TX

BOBBY

Kaedyn tells a lot of stories about being involved in sports as a kid. I think very visually, and so I always imagined this rough little boy running around raising hell. One day, one of these stories involved changing from a dress into a soccer uniform in the car. I had this moment then where I realized that as a trans man, the reality of his childhood was vastly different than the one in my mind's eye. It gave me a whole unfamiliar perspective of what growing up trans looked like for him. It also gave me insight into my own mind in an interesting way, in that I only see him as the man he has become, and the mischievous little boy that he is when it's just the two of us. I honestly can't say which one I love more—one gives me the freedom to be the visible queer couple I never saw as a child, and the other gives me the freedom to be the silly little boy that I never felt safe to be.

KAEDYN

When I first met Bobby, I didn't know anything about his background, or that he was of mixed race, as he presents fairly white when you are just looking at him. Once I got to know his family, and how they had to change their names to assimilate for fear of deportation as undocumented immigrants, it offered a lot of insight about growing up biracial in America, where racism still runs rampant. I thought families changed their names during immigration to celebrate a new culture. I never thought about families doing that out of necessity, or safety. I've watched Bobby grow into embracing his culture more and more, especially from the safety of the stage through his drag and male burlesque personas, and then letting that bleed into our home and the way he moves through the world. In turn, it has caused my love for him to grow, as he accepts all parts of himself.

Bradford *(He/Him)* & Jackson *(He/They)*

LOS ANGELES, CA

BRADFORD

The night before we became official, Jackson and I were rear-ended on an LA highway. As the driver, I was distraught and without direction. The other driver and I are both Black men, so I dismissed the idea of calling the cops. The thought of the police joining us on the side of the nighttime highway made my heart beat faster. I handled it with the other driver then drove off. We pulled over again to recoup, and once I parked, Jackson hugged me with a tightness that I didn't know I needed. When I explained why I didn't call the police, he just hugged me tighter. It was our first crisis, and we weren't even a couple yet, but Jackson knew to listen to me and console me, which was invaluable.

JACKSON

When I first told Bradford I thought I might be nonbinary, I was worried that not fully identifying as a man would turn him away. I had a fear that my deviation from an entirely male identity would change things in our dynamic, the bedroom, and how he talked to me. However, his support and understanding of my confusion proved the contrary. Although I still haven't discovered my gender identity, we make light of it by using "he/they" as a noun instead of "man" when referring to me. This helped me appreciate that our love goes beyond a "one or the other" contingency, and that we truly connect with each other instead of our labels.

BRADFORD & JACKSON

Our journey began with three college hookups, a Snapchat streak, and a few FaceTimes. Neither of us had tried long distance before. With Jackson living in Columbus, Ohio, and Bradford living in LA, we were nervous, but we knew that what we had was worth exploring. On the morning of July 5, 2021, we became determined to make light work of the 2,000 miles between our homes.

We run on a constantly ticking clock. Whenever we visit, we make the most of our time together to learn each other's boundaries, identities, and desires. We joke that departure day is "the day that doesn't exist" because it's always the hardest. By the time we round the corner on the airport terminal, the countdown resets until the next time. When we're together, we're inseparable, and when we're apart, we're counting. We love each other and persevere through the distance one day at a time.

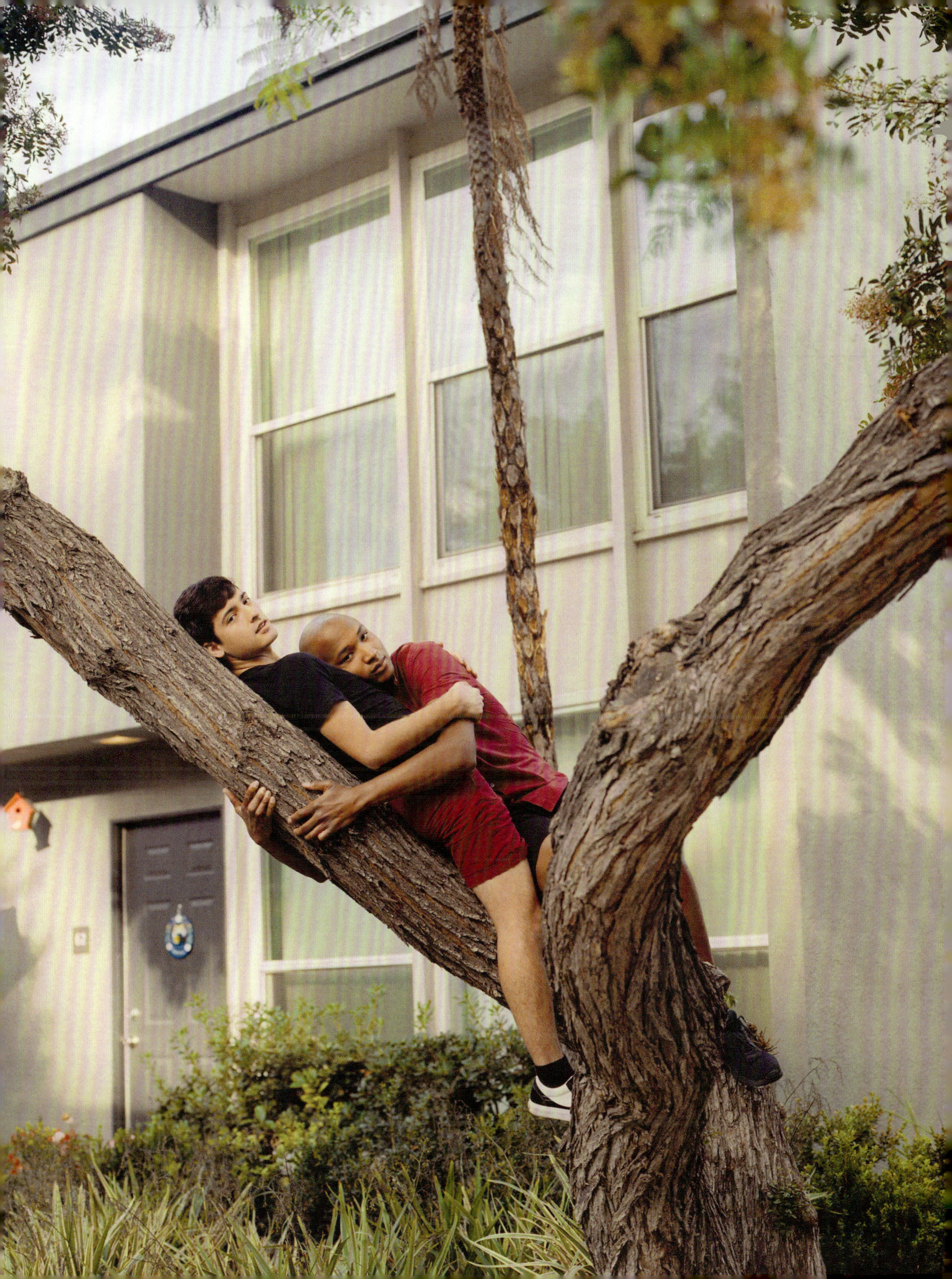

Bronson *(He/Him)* & Sam *(He/Him)*

PALM SPRINGS, CA

BRONSON

We had our first date in March 2015 at a queer bar in Manhattan. I remember immediately being attracted to the way Sam's chuckles transformed into joyful cackles as we laughed at each other's first-date banter. We held hands that night as we walked to the subway and my heart was set on fire. We became inseparable.

Sam is British and was working in the States on short-term contracts as an art director. He'd have to return home for a few days in between contracts—you know, normal convoluted visa stuff, or so we thought. On one routine trip back to the US, Sam was mistakenly denied entry to the country and forced to fly back to England permanently.

Twelve hours later, I arrived in England to figure out what to do about our relationship. We felt overwhelmed, but in love, so we did what would be the best Google search of our lives. "Gay lawyers USA." The lawyer let us know that the fastest way for us to be together was to get married. Sam was twenty-one and I was twenty-seven and we had been dating for six months, but we looked at each other and instantly decided that if we need to get married in order to keep dating, then that's what we'd do. And that's what we did, six years ago.

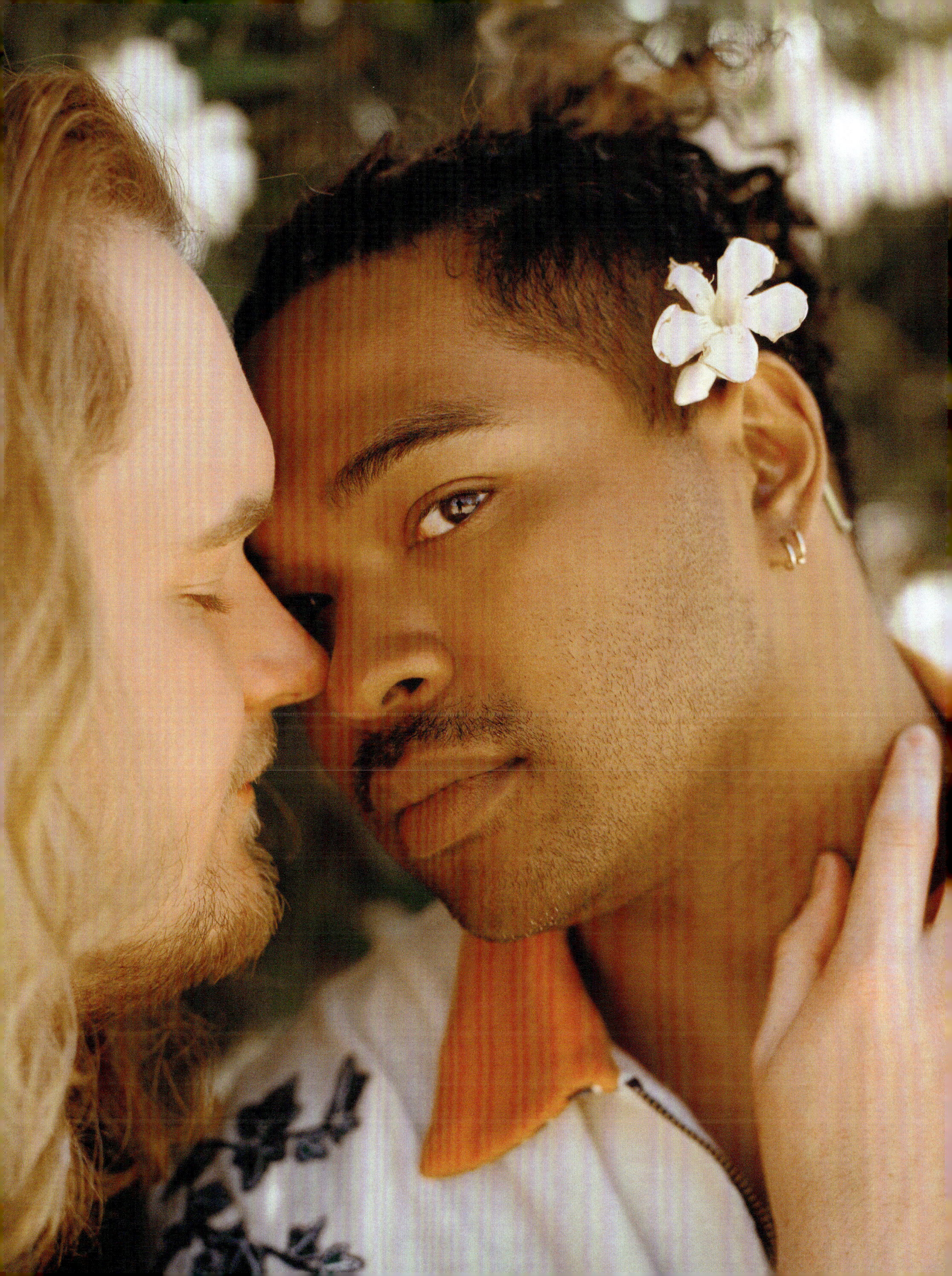

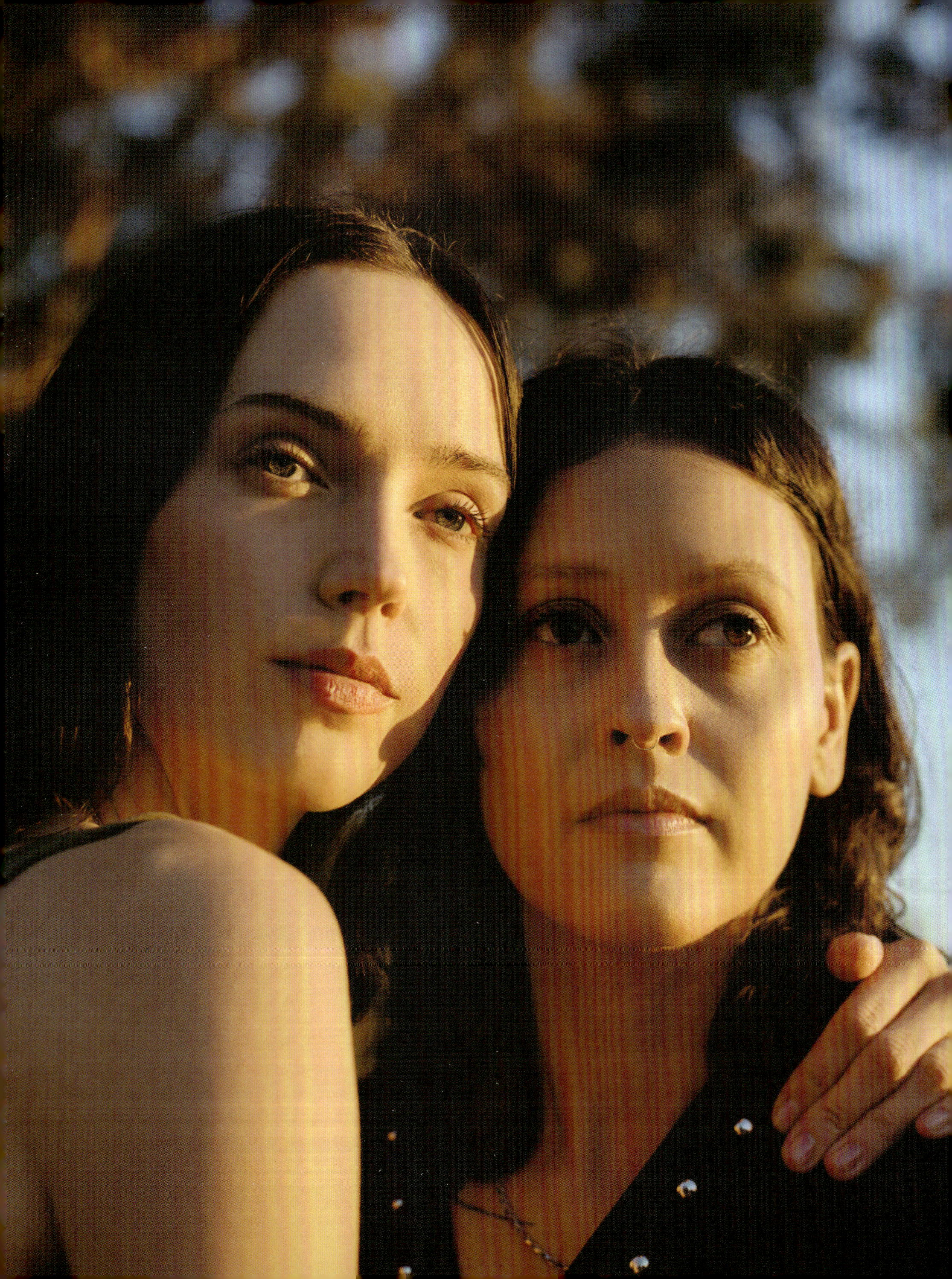

Camilla *(She/They)* & Linnea *(She/They)*

LOS ANGELES, CA

CAMILLA

There is healing and growth when one is heard. There is exponential growth to be had when still and hearing each other's truths—a superpower for our continuum connection. A necessary yet magical glue that binds together our individual worlds of experiences and emotions, the stories and skin we were born as.

To listen is to nourish the magical glue with strength and malleability. It safely holds the abundance of love and admiration Linnea and I have for each other.

LINNEA

Our love teaches us, more than ever, that true listening is essential to love. I learn that all your experiences are facts and I believe in your memories alongside you, alongside my own.

There is so much to know about Camilla. A literacy grown by participation and conversation, recognition, the ever flowing and most important getting-to-know-you of my lifetime so far.

Chris *(He/Him)* & Alex *(He/Him)*

LOS ANGELES, CA

CHRIS

Alex has always felt like a sunset to me. The first time I saw Alex smile, I knew it was my mission to love him. To protect him. Make him feel free and safe.

Life has switched us back and forth from positions of being healed and healing. Because that's what love is in part, I think. You realize it sooner or later. But for me, it's not draining, not at the root of it at least. In fact, loving Alex completes me. Feeling Alex's walls collapse around my love for the first time felt like coming home.

My love poured into his scars, wounds that had never been treated or even seen. He laid his head on my chest, and as his tears fell, they became my tears falling down. I knew in that instance I had no choice but to love him with all of who I am. Loving this man fills me with life, and it is within this force I know that there is nothing that can keep us down.

I find myself falling every day. But not just in the good moments. The bad ones too. The scary ones. The moments that prove how strong our love is. The moments I want to run away, but I don't because I'm anchored to his side. We have been through nightmares together, but we have been through just as many dreams. Dreams I could have never even imagined. I know I wouldn't be truly alive without him by my side.

I have never felt safer around anyone. He's so warm and kind. His protection is powerful. I constantly have watched him do so much to take care of others. I watched him with this shield up, protecting everyone, and I wondered who was shielding him? How could anyone forget to make sure he was protected? I'm honored to catch his tears. To make him laugh. To support his dreams. To hold him in my arms.

When he finally felt safe enough to put that shield down and let me in, I put my own shield up over him. Ever since, I still cannot fathom how lucky I am to have the love of such a beautiful guy.

ALEX

When I first saw Chris walk past me down the street, I knew he was special. His soft eyes and strong jawline caught my eye and had me chasing him; but after we met it was his heart that made me fall wholly and completely. When he holds me, I know why I exist. When he's in my arms, I feel so strong. Our combined energies are one and his love teaches me. It teaches me it's okay to be who I am. To feel the things I feel and dare to dream for more. Loving him I feel power. Loving him I feel energy. Loving him can be easier than breathing.

His patience gave me the time I needed to let my guard down. His understanding let me make mistakes. My trust in him let me know he will always be there to catch me when I fall, and I, him.

The love and care he has shown me helped reduce a front I had kept up for too long. For a lengthy period of time I didn't cry. In fact, I didn't feel a lot at all for years. When I met Chris, his love gave me the space and trust I needed to learn that my feelings are valid, real, and important. Being close to him, I was able to let go of so much bullshit I was holding on to. Lying in his arms one night, I was finally able to let go. I cried hard and long, feeling so much at once. His protection and love did that for me.

I initially didn't consider us within the context of our races, because my love for him is so much deeper than that. The light in his eyes, that's him. The way he smiles, that's Chris. He's unique and I've always looked at him that way. But he's also Mexican American, while I am white. I was privileged that I didn't have to consider how people in certain places may act toward me on a day-to-day basis, but I had to learn about this based on the way I've seen some people treat him. I want to protect him from this even though he shouldn't be going through it.

When the world was cruel to him and took & took from him, I saw him hurt so much. I didn't know what to do other than love him. To do my best to heal him with love the way his love continues to heal me. For this I am so grateful.

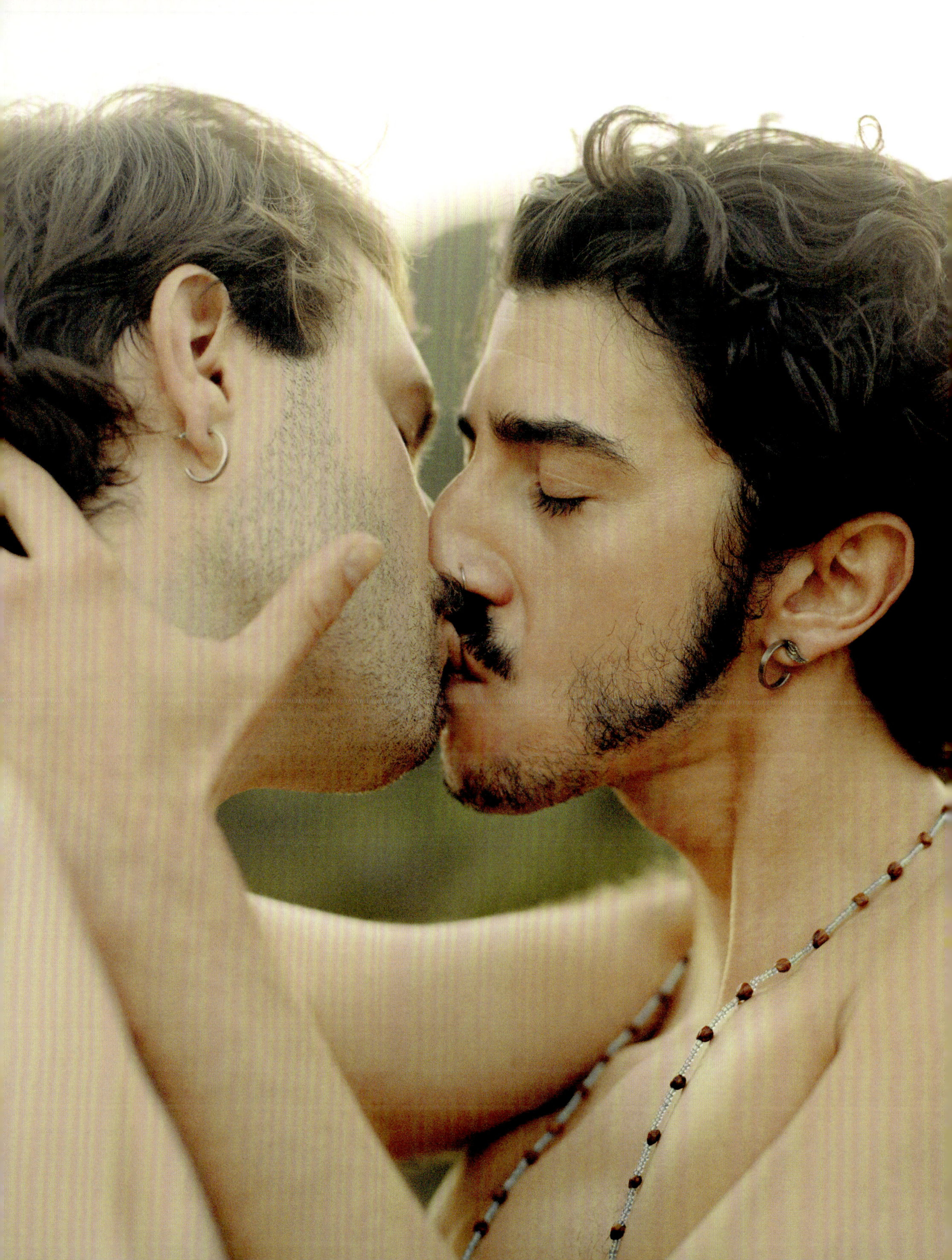

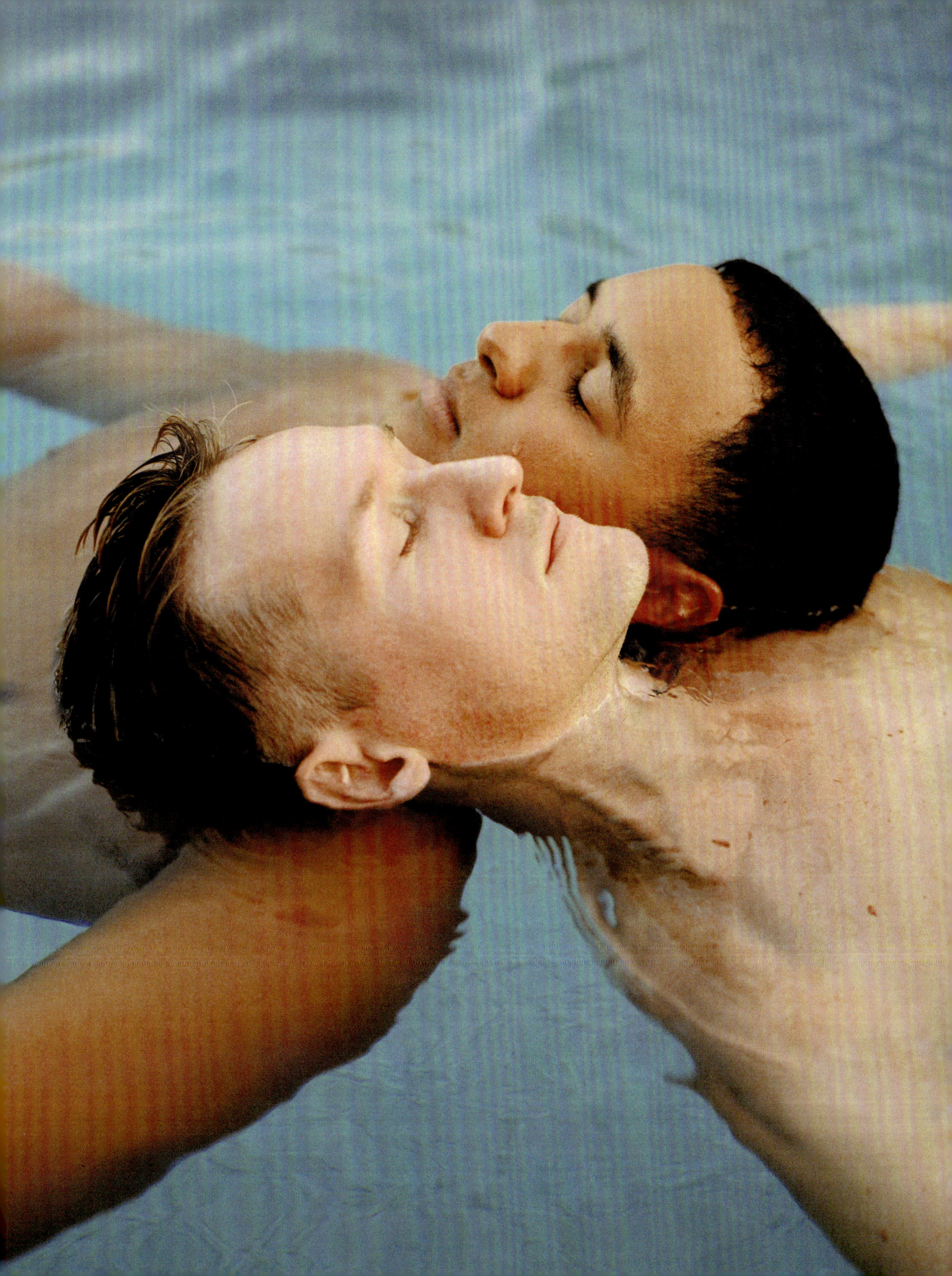

Chris *(He/Him)* & Joe *(He/Him)*

LOS ANGELES, CA

CHRIS: I'm from Loganville, Georgia—located in Walton County, the location of the last mass lynching in the United States—about thirty-five minutes southeast of Atlanta, where you could count the number of Black people on your fingers and toes. It was shocking to move to that community around age seven, as I had come from a community that was remarkably diverse. But because I grew up in an interracial family with parents from the South, I was consistently taught how to embrace what made me different.

JOE: I grew up in rural southeast Ohio where diversity was something generally talked about positively in the public sphere but hardly ever seen in the community around me. It was not until college and moving to Chicago that I was exposed to other people and ideas that pushed me to think independently. Chris and I met in Summer 2014 in Chicago. Although we were both dating and meeting other gay men at the time, we became aware of each other through a mutual friend's Snapchat (shout-out to you, Zak!). We connected over the fact that we grew up in small towns with a lot of similarities, but we still had very different experiences about race and sexuality which shaped our understanding of each other.

CHRIS: Early in our relationship before we were officially a couple, I joined Joe's family at home for Christmas. They welcomed me with open arms and love as much as anyone could possibly hope for from a new partner's family, especially as a gay couple. Following some drinks with his brothers and sister-in-law after Christmas Eve dinner, we talked through plans to go to a local dive bar to continue the fun. As we were deciding on one of the only two options within a twenty-minute drive, Joe's brothers and parents suddenly paused and said we had to go to the further of the two, the other bar was not an option. In simple terms, due to things they had seen in the past they were concerned that we would attract unwanted attention as a gay couple, particularly because of my race. This certainly wasn't the first time I had experienced something like this, but for Joe it was eye opening, particularly being in the place he was raised.

At times we have struggled, as we're sure most interracial couples have, to find common understanding through our completely different lived experiences. Particularly for Joe, there were different gay experiences that he wasn't familiar with as a white male within our community. Being willing to listen and absorb, while understanding that he will never have a similar experience, allowed us to grow closer through these struggles.

JOE: We've been fortunate to have Chris's parents be an easily accessible example of a positive and healthy interracial couple who we could always look to for their history and perspective. We've worked independently and together to try and understand each other on all levels. We both tend to lean into conversations about difficult and taboo topics, which made it easier to discuss race early on in our relationship. As the nation began to reckon with race in 2020, we found ourselves become an axis for our diverse group of friends and acquaintances as they reflected on their personal journey with race. We are proud to be one of the few queer interracial couples within our immediate or extended family/friend circles, which has encouraged us to speak to our experiences and help others learn alongside us. As they say, the journey is never over. As we continue to grow, we look forward to bringing back our understandings to the communities we grew up with, as well as the communities and chosen families we continue to nurture.

Christopher *(He/They)* & Jon *(He/Him)*

LOS ANGELES, CA

JON

We matched on Tinder, a couple days after Chris moved to Boston for a new job while I was visiting my parents. We had a twenty-four-hour first date and have been together ever since. Our families are perfectly fine with us dating—it turns out that Caribbean Americans and Italian Americans have a lot in common. My ninety-something-year-old grandmother was more concerned that Chris's hair was purple (it was blue) the first time they met than that her grandson was in a gay interracial relationship. That is not to say that hair doesn't matter. One of the first things I learned is that I could only have one opinion about Chris's varying Black hairstyles. Whether afro, braids, twists, or faux locs, I would be sure to like it. This wasn't a joke. Little moments like this have led to many conversations about race and ethnicity, but they have only brought us closer together.

CHRISTOPHER

We look at it like this: if you want to be a good partner to someone, you must be comfortable with making sense of differences in perspective and context. Where we grew up, how people gender us, the things our parents and aunts and uncles said, the experiences we've had at school and at work, all these things are shaped by our different racial identities. So, we talk about them. Funny enough, the hardest part about being in an interracial relationship, especially a queer one, is that people of all backgrounds project a lot of weird baggage onto us. For example, the constant assumption that we either have a particular racial fetish (we both like and enjoy playing with a wide spectrum of men!), or that we would be interested in being cast in someone else's racial fetish fantasy hookup (no thanks random white man that hit on us at a gay bar!). Having different racial backgrounds matters for us, but not in the ways that people tend to think it does.

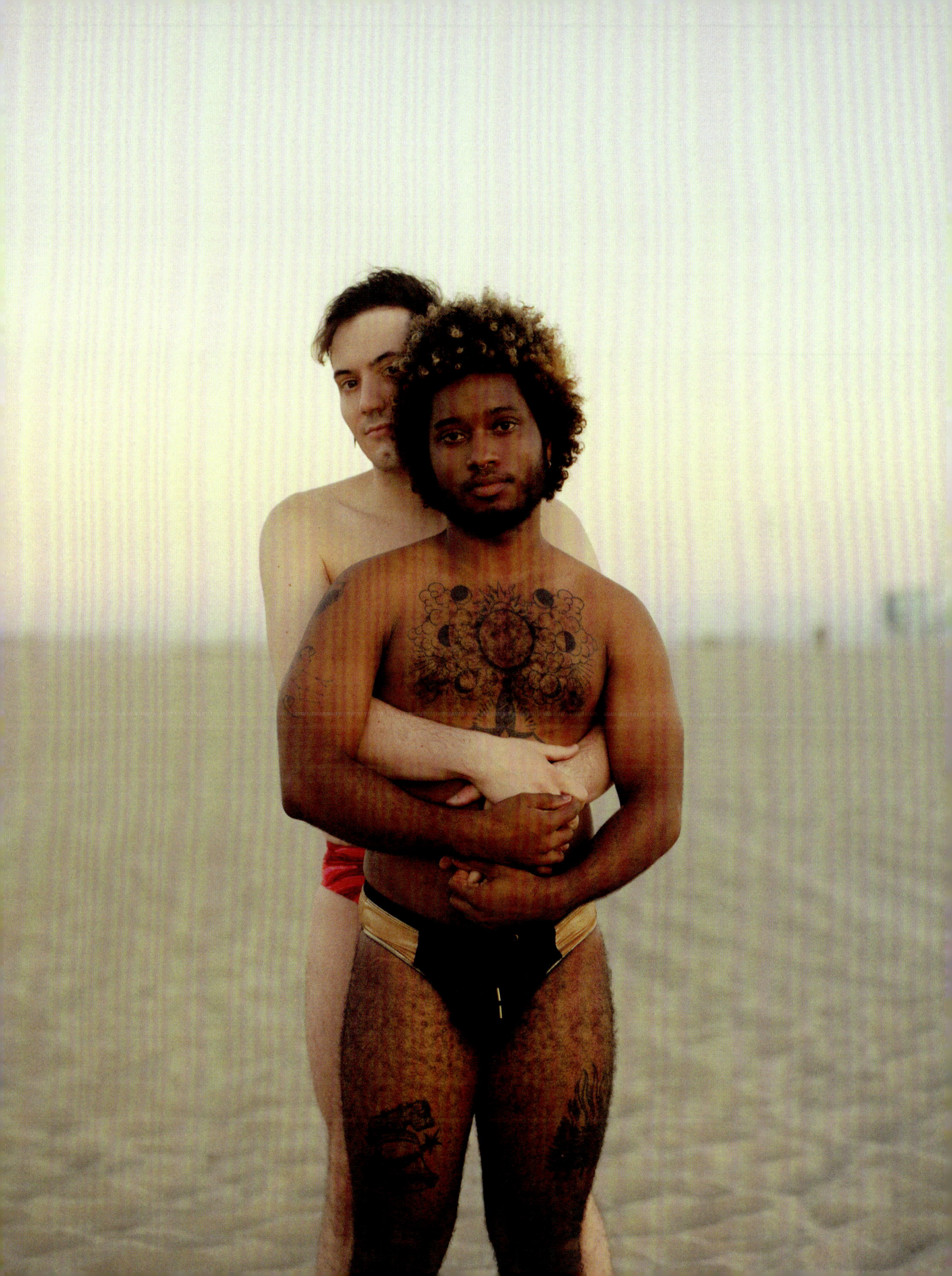

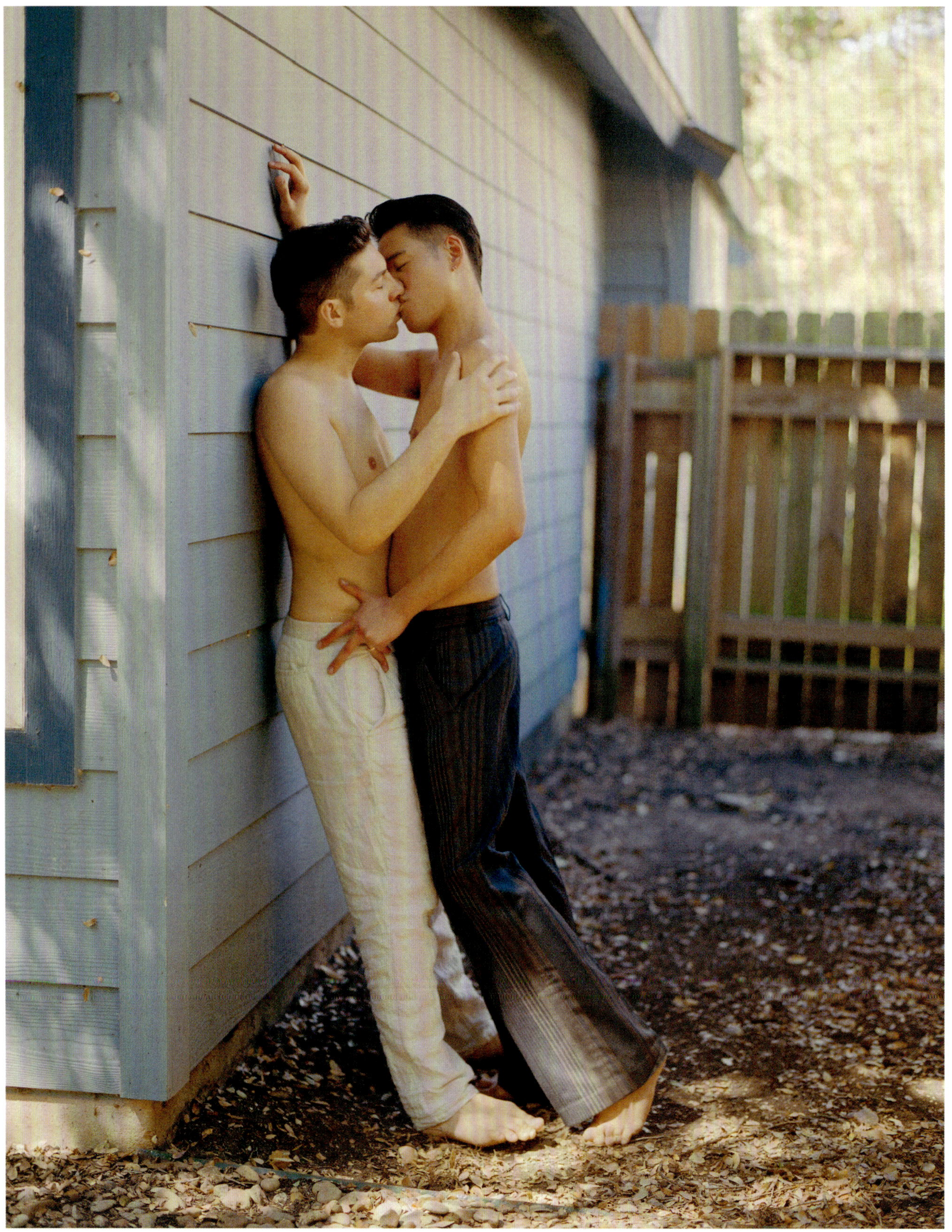

CJ *(He/Him)* & Xian *(He/Him)*

AUSTIN, TX

CJ & XIAN

On our wedding night, we decided to splurge on an expensive dinner for ourselves. (We had eschewed a typical wedding for a lunch hour "I do" at the local courthouse.) We were seated next to a more mature couple and when they learned it was our wedding night, they secretly paid for our dinner and offered an ounce of marital wisdom: "Always make time to enjoy nice meals together."

Coming together from very different parts of the world, food was (and remains) both historian and matchmaker for us. Our shared love of food has been a unifying element in our lives, often explaining our very different experiences growing up in vastly different worlds better than words could ever express. Through laksa and lasagna, we came to understand each other's geographical and emotional topographies. Food melded space, time, and memory, providing excitement and comfort.

We hold a special space for food in our story. A space where we share our lives with friends and family, with room for all to partake in. A space where Kuala Lumpur and Pennsylvania can be the same.

Colby *(He/Him)* & Michael *(He/Him)*

LOS ANGELES, CA

COLBY & MICHAEL

After spending a few years as friends in New York (OK, maybe a little more than friends sometimes) and slowly growing closer, we decided to take a leap together and move to Los Angeles. We had both been considering it for a while, and the timing seemed right in our individual lives. We weren't completely unaware of our feelings for each other. There was one talk in particular where we discussed our friendship and the move as roommates, and how we didn't want to get into a relationship. We were going to keep it platonic and explore all that Los Angeles and the scene had to offer! Well…that didn't last long. After about two months of living together as "roommates," we felt a synchronicity between us that we both wanted to go deeper into. We don't have an official anniversary because it feels like the transition from friends to roommates to partners in life happened organically over time, but fall in LA always reminds us of those months when we realized we wanted to be more than friends and roommates. A lot of hurdles came our way in the following year: grappling with our age difference, our different career paths, our styles of communication, but after any hard talk or argument we always decided we were worth it to each other. Loving each other unconditionally has taught us just as much about ourselves as about our partner, and that growth individually has helped us grow together even more.

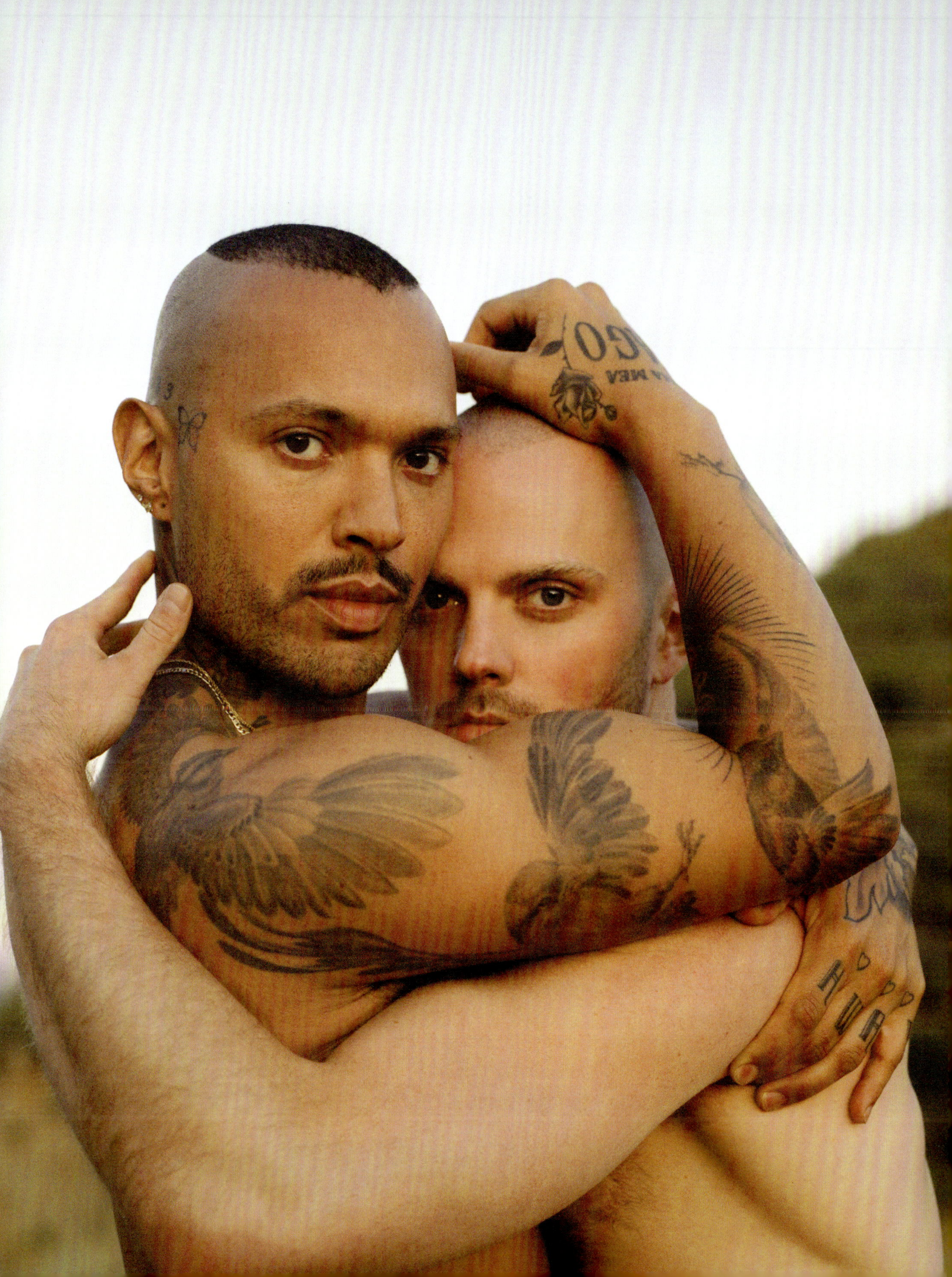

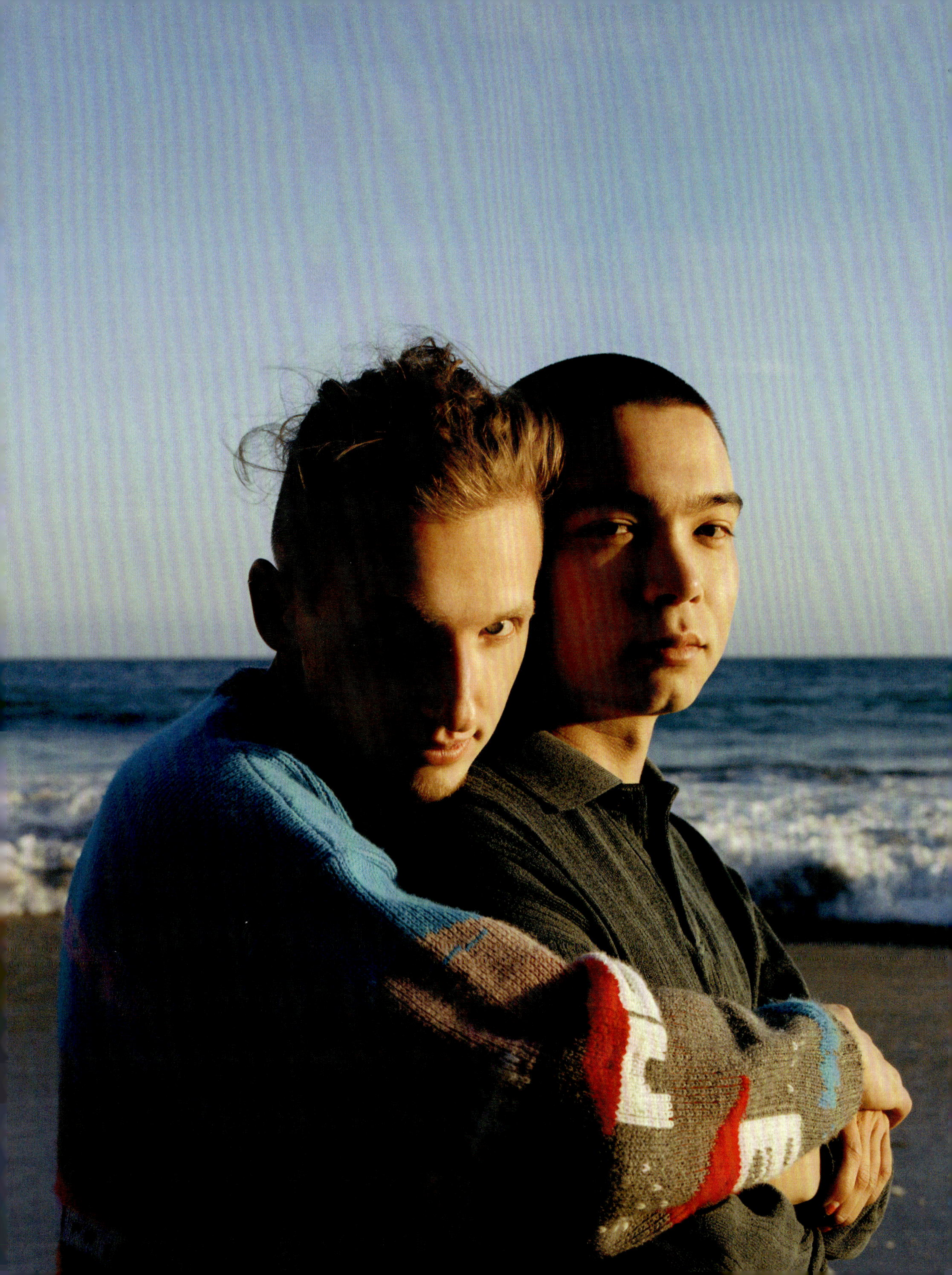

Cooper *(He/Him)* & Trent *(He/Him)*

SANTA BARBARA, CA

COOPER

Our relationship has been a trial by fire, sheltering together through various stages of the pandemic, living long distance for months, and moving in together. The period when I got to know Trent in the most profound way was when his father passed a year into our relationship. Though incomparable with grief itself, helping a partner deal with grief is a painful and revealing experience. Trent is one of the strongest people I know. While his patience can be tested, I continually see the depth of his generosity, in giving food to strangers, in being a steady shoulder to lean on for his friends, and in dealing with difficult and sometimes abusive family members. As we've grown together, my perceptions of him have expanded as well. Not just a cute boy living in the next college town over, he is a man I can laugh with, who I can cry with, and who I can trust.

TRENT

Cooper is the first person I've been in a real relationship with. He has shown me how fulfilling it is to be in an honest and trusting partnership where anything can be discussed with open understanding. We got together just before the pandemic began, three months before I planned on moving back to California from Oregon. Consequently, we were immediately tasked with deciding whether we would quarantine together. When we first made the decision, there was not a doubt in my mind that we would have to break up when I moved home—long distance just didn't seem like something I would be able to handle. Ultimately, we stuck it out and we dealt with the distance. He has been everything and more than I could wish for in a partner, and he came into my life at the most perfect time. While my personal life was crumbling at its foundation, he was a loving source of consistency, his steadfastness keeping me calm. Cooper is proof to my younger self that there is someone out there who will constructively help me grow as a person while still loving me through my toughest moments.

Cory *(He/Him)* & Andrew *(He/Him)*

LOS ANGELES, CA

CORY & ANDREW

We met in a tiny bar in Hong Kong, where Andrew hit on one of Cory's best friends. It's a cute story to tell, but Cory being unfairly overlooked is a pattern we've seen far too often as we've navigated the world together. Despite being fortunate enough to spend much of our time in queer spaces, we still see first-hand the implicit bias that exists even within our own community. One time, at a bar in San Francisco, we were sharing a drink and holding hands. A white guy came up to Andrew and began aggressively complimenting and hitting on him. He didn't even acknowledge that Cory was there.

As an interracial and intergenerational queer couple, we've learned a lot about seeing the world through each other's eyes. From day one, our life experiences could not have been more different. Andrew grew up with endless possibilities, in a supportive and open-minded family in the San Francisco Bay Area. Cory was born in Vietnam and moved to Texas as a refugee at age two. On one of our first dates in Hong Kong, Andrew told Cory about wanting to move to Los Angeles to pursue a career in screenwriting. Cory very honestly expressed that he has always resented Hollywood for its historically stereotyped, at best, portrayal of the Asian American experience.

Andrew especially appreciates how Cory has challenged him to see the world through a new lens. Andrew has grown to better understand and acknowledge his own privilege and has learned that part of being an ally is actively making space for those voices that are overlooked. Sometimes, making space isn't enough; you have to actively give up some of your own.

As our relationship has grown, we have had many conversations about the importance of equity. Equity is not about everyone getting the same thing; equity is about everyone getting what they need to feel like they belong.

We are now married, live between Los Angeles and Tucson, and share the most magnificent ginger cat, Velcro. We are proud to have created a life where we both feel a sense of ownership and belonging. Still, we know that even within our own community, there's a long way to go to break down barriers and challenge biases.

We are committed to the process, *togayther*.

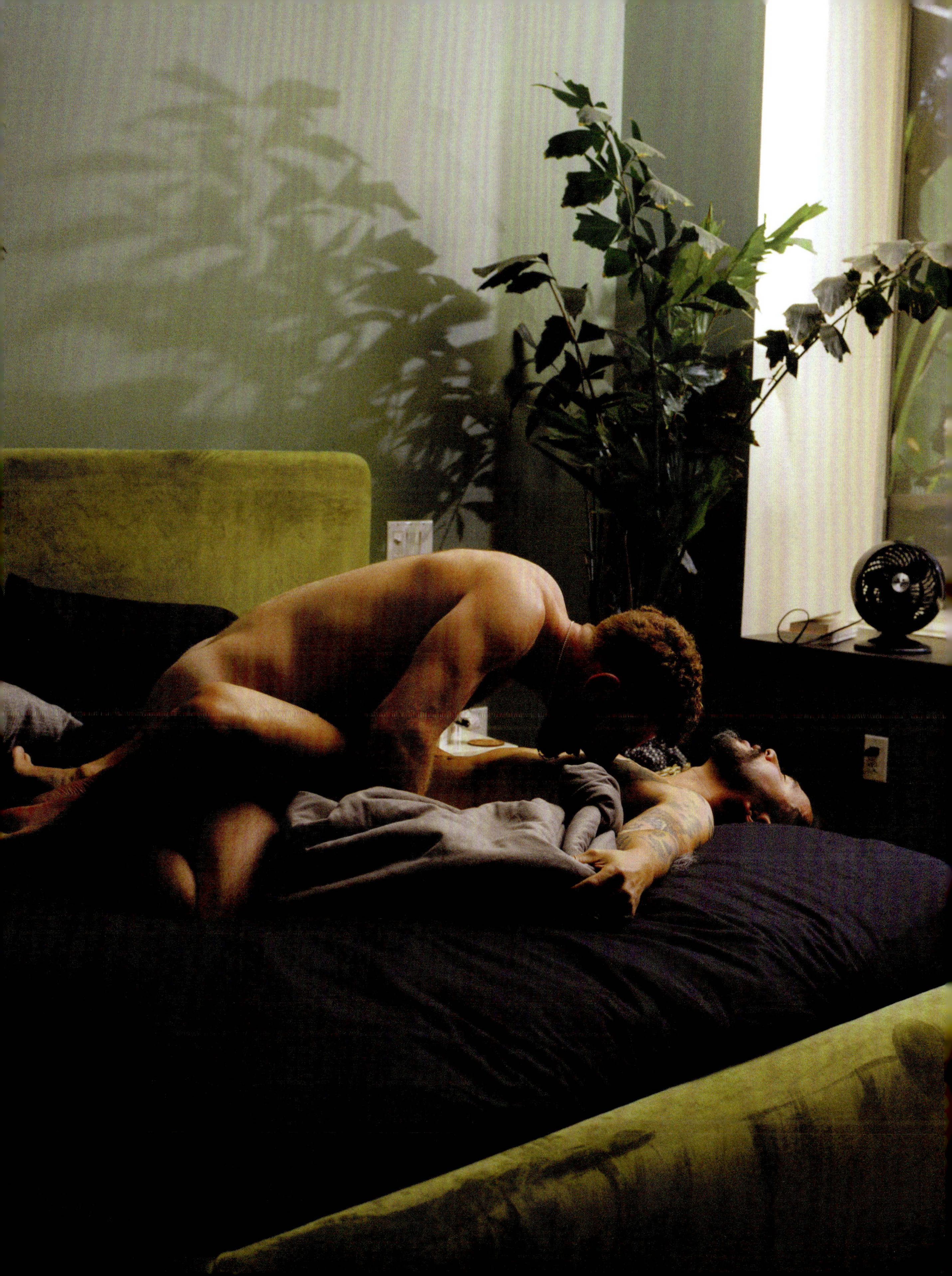

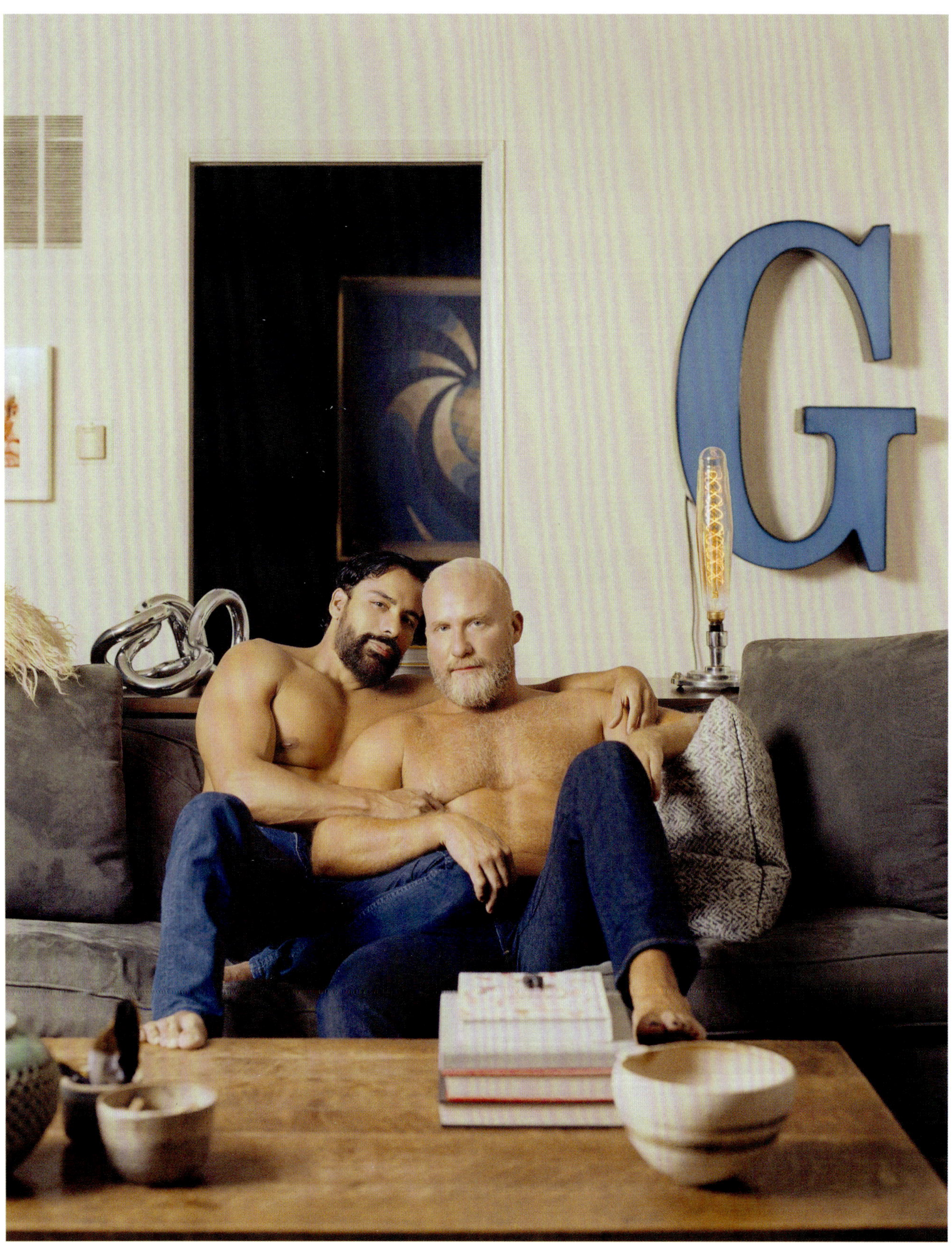

Court *(He/Him)* & Adaris *(He/Him)*

LOS ANGELES, CA

COURT

We met on Scruff and chatted for a few months before we met in person. Adaris told me he was shy! If you saw his photos, you would never think he's shy, but he is. I thought he was the most beautiful man I'd ever seen. I wasn't sure what he saw in me. He has the most beautiful, soft, caramel brown skin, curly, jet-black hair, big, soulful, brown eyes, and a little gap between his front teeth that makes me melt every time he smiles. When we finally met, we had really incredible sex and I invited him to have dinner with me after. We were fuck buddies for a few months with no intention of getting into a relationship, and then it just sort of happened. I was away in Italy and just had that sense of, "I want him to be my person." When I came home, I asked him to be my boyfriend and he said yes.

ADARIS

If you haven't learned anything from your partner after a period of time, what are you doing? I have learned so many enduring and beautiful things because of all the pivotal moments I have shared with Court. One important thing, out of many, is that I deserve to have a good man next to me. I have endured bad relationships, relationships that have made me realize I deserve better. My relationship with Court is magical. All the unforgettable experiences, the constant caring, and the love that he has given me throughout our journey have transformed me into who I am. Court has brought so much happiness into my life. He has treated me like I deserve to be treated, like no one else has ever treated me before, and has made me realize I'm worthy.

COURT

A moment that I will never forget is the day we celebrated Adaris's US citizenship, something for which he had been waiting over twenty years. At that point we had been together a little over a year and it was the first time he told me how he came to the US. It was a long, arduous journey that started when he was only twelve years old. Throughout his many attempts, he lived experiences that I can't fathom, especially being so young. What strikes me most is how Adaris never let these hardships alter the caring, loving, and strong man that he is, but rather made him appreciate life and live it more fully.

My love and admiration for Adaris has grown exponentially as he has allowed me to know these parts of him. His experiences have also shed a light on my privilege as a white gay man born on US soil. When we have a misunderstanding related to language and culture, I take a deep breath and think, "If I'm having a hard time expressing myself, how is this for him?" I can collect my thoughts and approach them in a softer way. There are many barriers in our relationship—language, culture, religion—that are also areas that have offered growth, awareness, and, yes, humor.

ADARIS

I honestly can say that it has felt easier for me to go around the world with my partner because of his race. I have seen and experienced the world in a much different way than if I were by myself. I think that there is still so much racism from ignorant people. Having a six-foot-four white man as my partner has definitely prevented many bad experiences. I love Court's connection to his sexuality, and I love to see people's faces when they see this beautiful, gorgeous man next to me. People love seeing us together. Their looks say everything, and I love it. So, our sexuality and identity have absolutely been an advantage for us. We are so blessed to feel this sense of welcoming and support.

COURT

When I became a sex and intimacy coach full time, my own sexual personal identity started to shift. Through my own explorations, I have really found more freedom in identifying as queer and pansexual. This transition was challenging at first for Adaris, and is potentially still challenging, but my work has also become a source of pride for him, something he celebrates, which feels like a victory. It was a bit of a bait and switch on my part. He fell in love with an executive who had a stable, respectable job, and suddenly, he has to tell his traditional Latino family that his boyfriend is a sex coach! I understand all the baggage that comes with that, and, in the process, what I have witnessed in him is how relentlessly he defends and protects me against harm. I know if push came to shove, he'd have my back in any fight.

Grayson *(He/They)* & Grey *(She/He/They)*

LOS ANGELES, CA

GREY

The winter of 2019 was brutal and exciting for me. I had relapsed, been harassed at my job, and was making all my money as a full-time club kid. Then in the blink of an eye everything changed. Even before a state of emergency was declared I knew I wasn't going to be a New Yorker for much longer. I fled the city after the first two months of the pandemic. I had not seen my family in years, my body was failing me as my blood disorder got increasingly worse, and my heart was longing to connect with someone. As much as I loved the community I had in New York City, I knew that there was someone out west waiting for me to return.

Not to be that spooky indigenous queer, but I knew he was coming. The most amazing start of this partnership was knowing. I hate surprises, and the universe must know that because I was born with the gift of seeing. I've had dreams since I was a kid about my partner, all the way down to the face, identity, zip code. I waited twenty-three years until I came across them—I never dated anyone, never slept with anyone, I just patiently (most of the time) waited. We've known each other before in many different lives—he's a part of me.

The day we met was a cluster of cosmic connectivity. I overdosed the same night he messaged me for the first time, which I didn't see until days later. I thought the timing was hilarious and cruel, that the universe must be fucking with me. Although I wasn't well and obviously had a lot of things to work out, I let go of my need to be "deserving" of love. I wasn't in the place I wanted to be in my body or my spirit, but my heart was the same heart that chose to keep beating and keep believing in some sort of divine intervention.

A few days after my overdose, and after talking to Grayson a bit, I had an early morning visitation from my ancestors where I was shown an alternate path. They were not pleased with my behavior and asked me if I wanted to go home with them or stay and open the rest of these doors. I chose to keep living. Later that morning Grayson spontaneously showed up at my house with flowers. I was dying and the moment I decided to live, he arrived.

I don't think anyone could've imagined me with an ex-Mormon, white, trans, masc angel from Idaho, but it makes perfect sense. Although our life together hasn't been and won't be easy, it does exist. And it exists for a reason. Being in this partnership I've seen and experienced more racism, bigotry, transphobia, colonized constructs, and policing than ever before in my entire life as an Afro-Indigenous, gender-queer gay. It's not an easy partnership in the outside world, but inside of our loving home and arms it's like butter. We work on decolonizing our brains every day and leaning more into my culture and our natural ways of being. I love life with Grayson. I'm more like the person I always aspired to be with him—I'm my child self and my elder self all in one; I'm safe and I don't run. I never had a safe place before, I never owned furniture or invested in my time here on earth. And now the idea of leaving this planet keeps me up at night because oh my fucking gawd all I wanna do is stay with my lover. I know we will always find each other, but man am I grateful for this particular time.

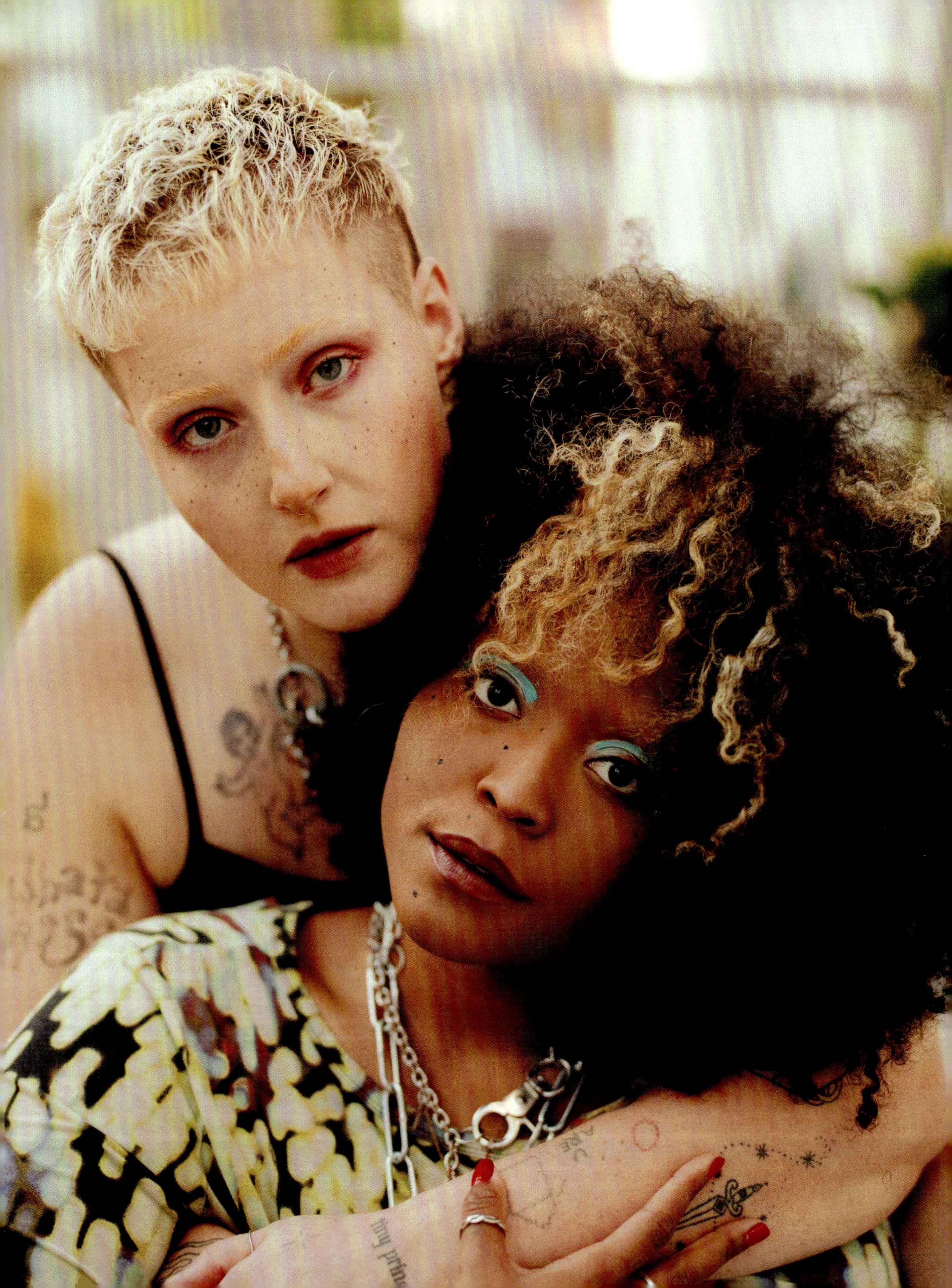

GRAYSON

Talking about the past few years, or the past few months even, can be hard for me. I left home at fourteen, so really the past ten years can be difficult to revisit and summarize. I grew up a devout Mormon. I never questioned the church. I was told my whole life "Doubt your doubts before you doubt your faith." A great way to fill children with self-doubt and a fear of asking questions. Some people see Mormonism as a religion, but for me it is an organized cult, and a prison. It took me a great deal of time to consciously register my queerness, and it took me some time after that to realize my extreme discomfort with body/gender. So it's safe to say I had to spend some time decolonizing my mind before meeting my darling. Still, when we met I was in rough shape, but I think she related to that herself. Really, I think we both needed to care and be cared for. A perfect match.

I never would have thought I'd be so lucky. Be so noticed, so seen. I wasn't a quiet child, but that didn't matter because no one heard me. I was a loud ghost. I danced and screamed and did everything I could to get love or attention. To witness and be that child now, loved so tenderly, fed so well, and so very noticed, is a healing I never thought was coming. I thought I would always feel what I felt before meeting Grey. Like I was melting. My darling is a chef and soothes my eating disorder with patience and food made of pure love. My baby is a free thinker and a soul of the earth and the sky. She knows how to thank the trees and hates bugs but cries when they die. She knows how to set a spiritual boundary and a physical one. Before her I told people my inner child was dead. Didn't know the kid, didn't want to. Now my kid and her kid are best friends, who tell each other everything. All the bad, scary, spooky, magic, abundant, delicious things. We make art together, we make plans together, we take care of other kids together. We come from very different families and mostly different places, but no other match could be for me. I feel like I am made up of her and she of me.

Coyote *(He/They)* & Tee *(She/They)*

LOS ANGELES, CA

TEE: It's so easy for me to love you. From the first time we ever talked over DM, I knew that our time together would be fluid. It doesn't matter how much time we spend apart from each other, or how many nights we spend together, I can always melt into your arms like it's the first time you ever held me. I can talk to you so naturally; our thoughts and words mingle without hesitation. Loving you feels instinctual, like a habit I was born with. It feels like I was born to love you.

COYOTE: I tell you all the time how I don't think I can get tired of you. I am already an excitable person, but you make me feel like every day is a holiday. I come home with the biggest smile and wake up feeling gratitude for a life with you. You never make me question if I am lovable as a two-spirit person. I know I always tease about whether you desire me more when I am hyper masculine or feminine (my traditional standards of presentation). I can feel you loving something deeper than the surface of me and it makes me feel so alive. That is why I always plan these dates and adventures for us—I want you to be an old grandma with so many fond memories to look back on. And I'll be there reminding you of every single one of them.

TEE: We always tell each other how we want to retire in a farm somewhere when we're old, raising baby goats. Considering how lazy we both are, we'd likely do a horrible job raising those goats. But it'll probably be a lot of fun. I don't think I really prioritized fun until I met you. It's such a basic, fundamental idea, to have fun. I was caught up in so much sadness and isolation. I didn't know that I could enter every day with so much excitement, looking forward to all the fun things ahead of me. You make the most mundane things fun, like taking a bath or going on a long drive. I used to stay up every night because of anxiety. Now I sleep like a baby, thinking about all the fun we're going to have together the next day.

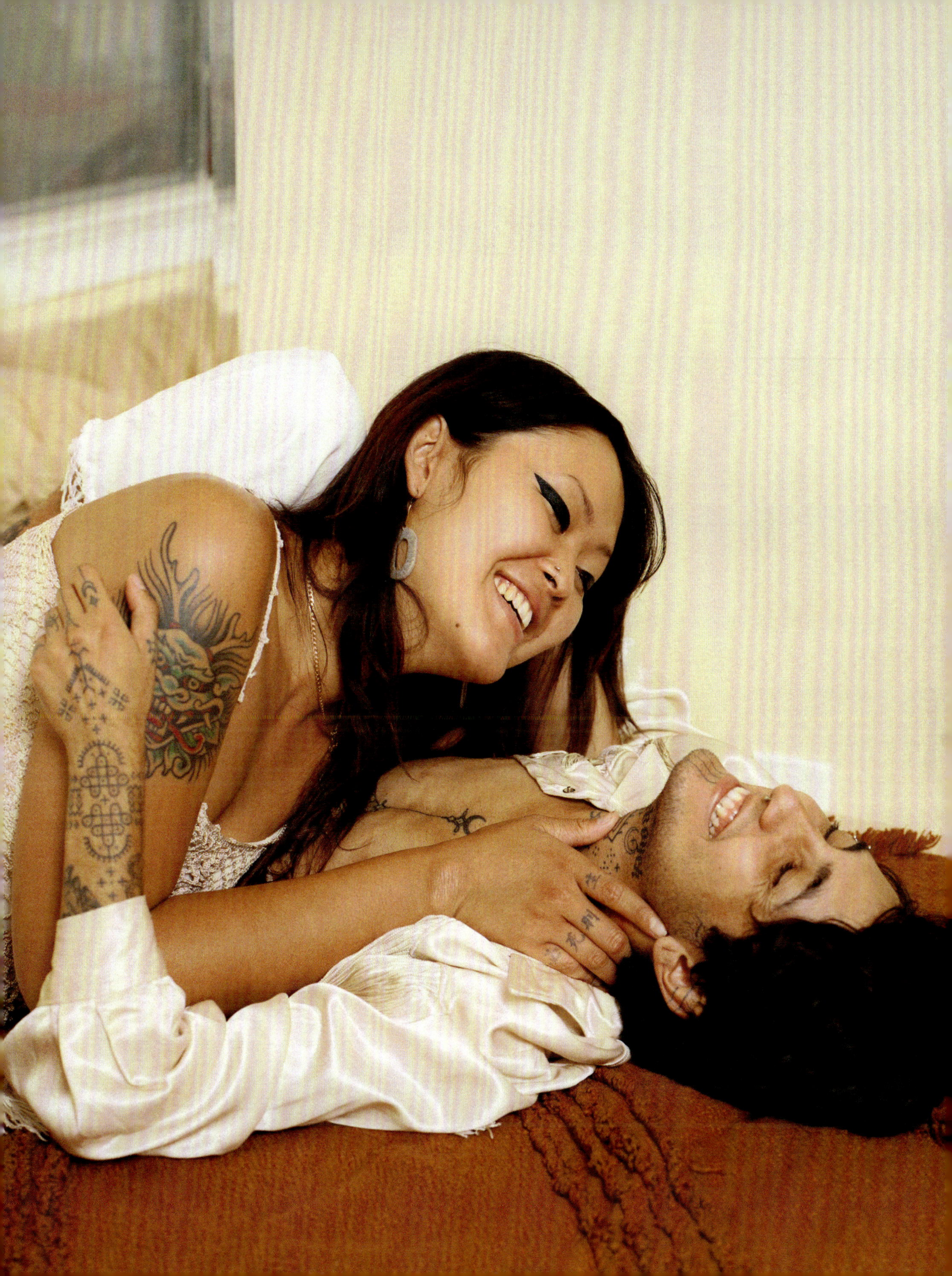

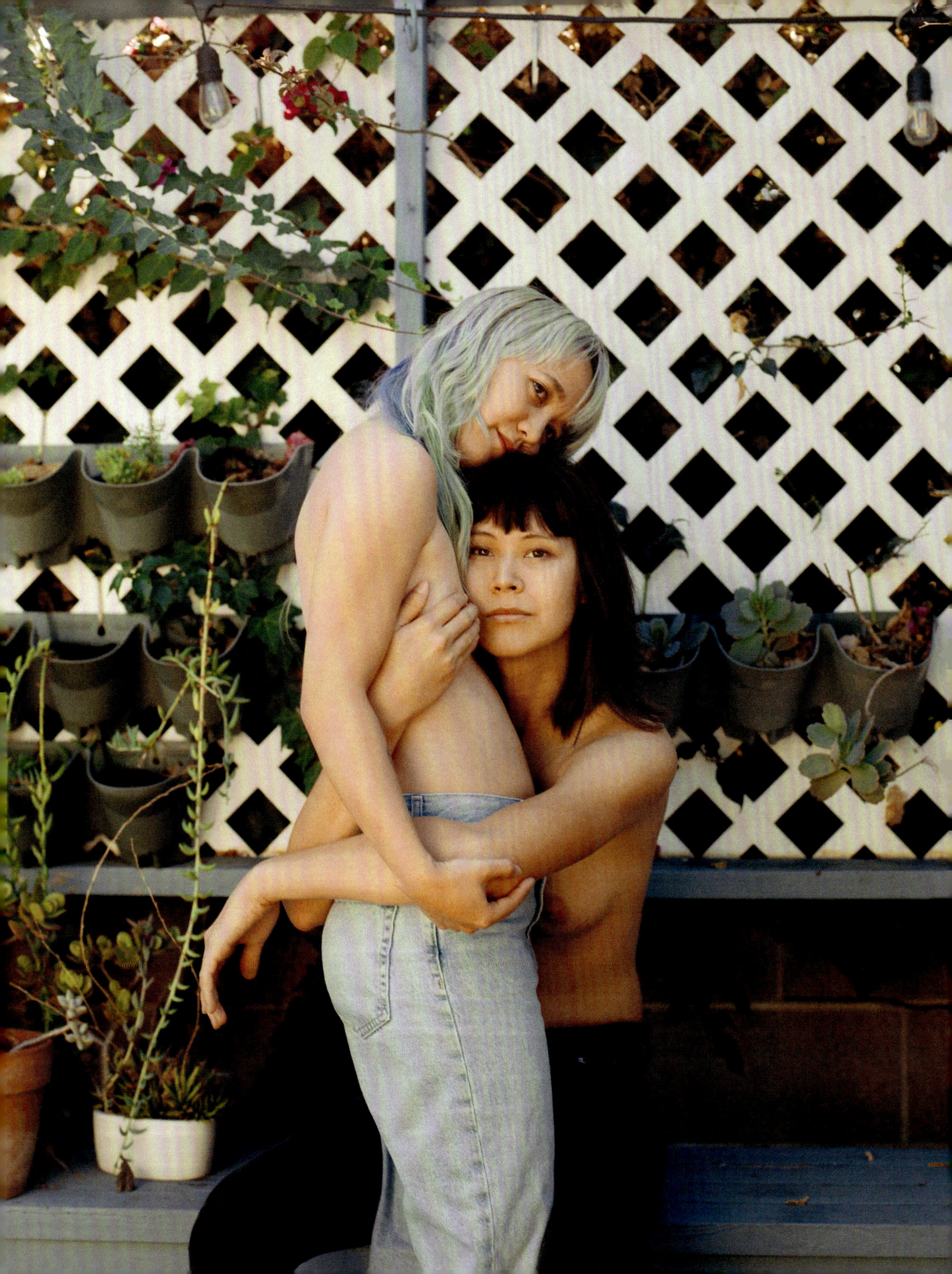

Cynthia *(She/Her)* & Ren *(She/Her)*

LOS ANGELES, CA

REN

We were both coming into this with negative experiences from past relationships. There was initially a lot of hesitancy and timidness. We were extremely shy toward one another on our initial dates because of our hapa (half-Asian) backgrounds. We were having a great time but were also too apprehensive to make the first move. One of my fondest memories of Cynthia is from our third date. After an amazing night, to put it mildly, both of us were still too chickenshit and scared to do anything. She mentioned how growing up in a Japanese household, it was sort of ingrained the mentality of being afraid to be rude or burdening others by doing something as simple as asking for a fork or something extra at a restaurant. After that date she messaged me: "A girl should ask for extra forks!" She had finally broken out of her racial stereotype to make the first move. It was incredibly cute.

CYNTHIA

We've been inseparable since then. When I look at Ren, I'm home. I feel so completely comfortable to just exist as I am with her. I love her for exactly who she is and wouldn't change anything about her. I've never felt so much peace with someone. Because I didn't have good examples growing up and have had not-so-great previous relationships, I had zero expectations for love and accepted that it would always be difficult. But forget what you've heard. Love can be easy with the right person. It should be.

Daniel *(He/Him)* & Nick *(He/Him)*

BROOKLYN, NY

NICK

I grew up in Honolulu, in a predominately Asian and Pacific Islander neighborhood, and Dan grew up in a mostly white suburb of Connecticut. Although very different we experienced these places similarly, as spaces of heteronormative conformity. In the pre-Internet 90s we both lacked access to a diversity of queer role models, and it seemed that the only way for us to find our chosen families was to leave the places where we grew up. We both ended up in New York City, where so many people don't fit in and nonconformity can be celebrated. We met and built a life here together.

As an Asian person and as a white person, we know we will always experience the world differently. As a couple we are always aware of being perceived in different ways. We are constantly recalibrating and assessing each other's state of being in unspoken ways everywhere we go. When we go back together to the places where we grew up, these shifts in perception, both of each other and ourselves, become even more tangible. These shifts feel destabilizing, though they continue to bring us closer and strengthen our bond.

We've had our most difficult conversations in our apartment and backyard in Brooklyn. These are the spaces where we realized that constant communication and brutal honesty are the best tools to explore our relationship. After all these years we are learning that the home we have always been looking for is not tied to a physical space. Home is being together in whatever part of the world we happen to be in.

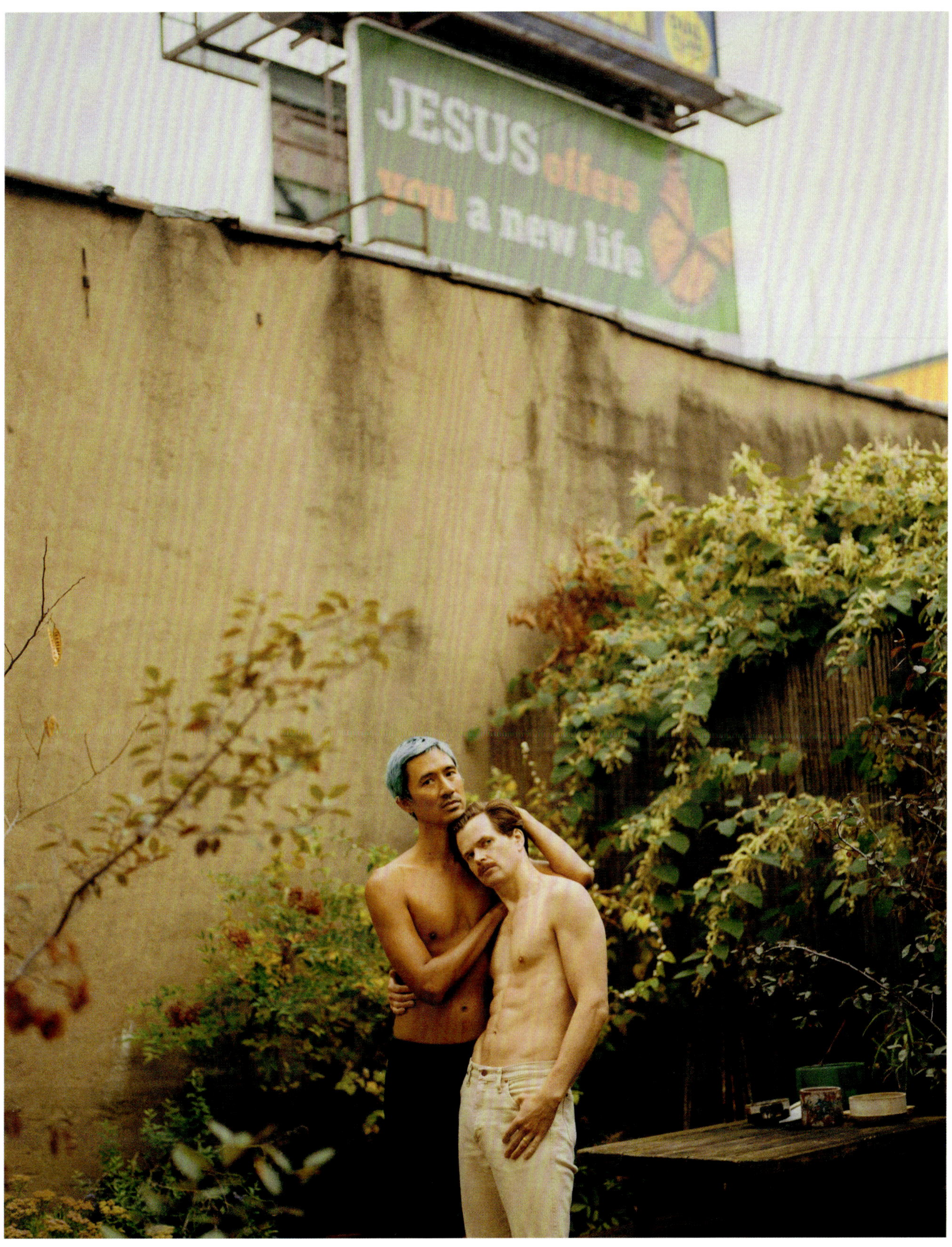
JESUS offers
you a new life

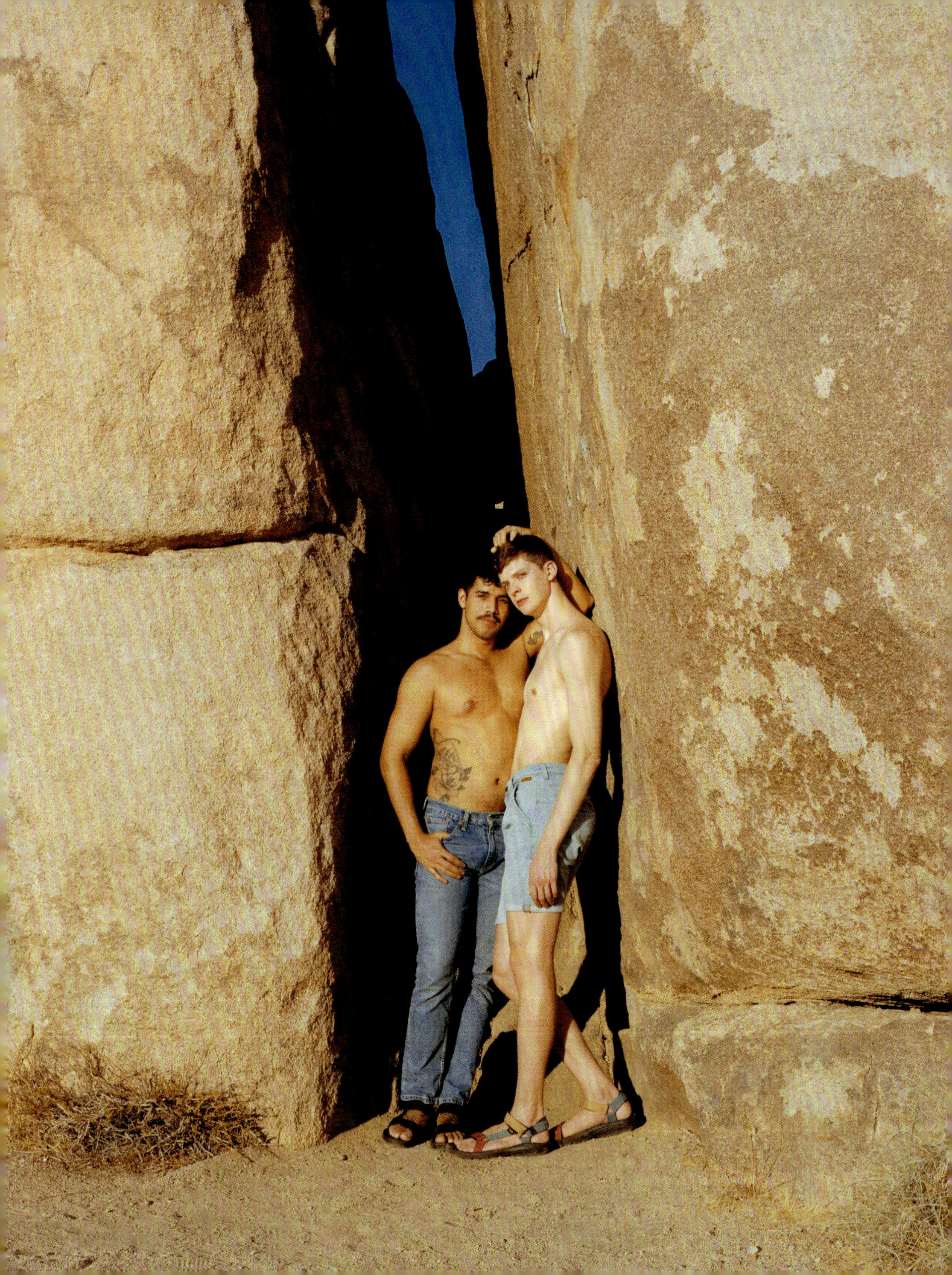

David *(He/Him)* **& Marcus** *(He/She/They)*

LOS ANGELES, CA

Our queerness has taught us not to fear the vastness of our emotions. We've spent so much time hiding parts of ourselves that I think we carry that into our romantic relationships. Once you allow yourself to let go of those fears of rejection, life flows more easily.

David *(He/Him)* & Michael *(He/Him)*

LOS ANGELES, CA

DAVID

I think it's amazing how love finds you when you least expect it. We're still learning so much and growing so much, but I love that we're doing it together. We started our relationship at the height of the pandemic, and it was amazing to be able to run to Michael and feel safe in his arms. I always voice my opinion on the climate of today's society and what it means to be a young Black man in America, where it's impossible for me to feel safe just walking to the store. So it was eye-opening for me to have my partner hold me close and tearfully look me deep in the eyes, and tell me to be safe when leaving his house. He told me that he found himself finally realizing how scary it is to be in a world where something so simple as the way you look could cost you everything. I feel like these are the small moments that have brought us closer together. His understanding and providing a safe space for me is everything I could've possibly asked for. Here we are a whole year and a half later and I couldn't be more satisfied and content with what we have created and continue to create together.

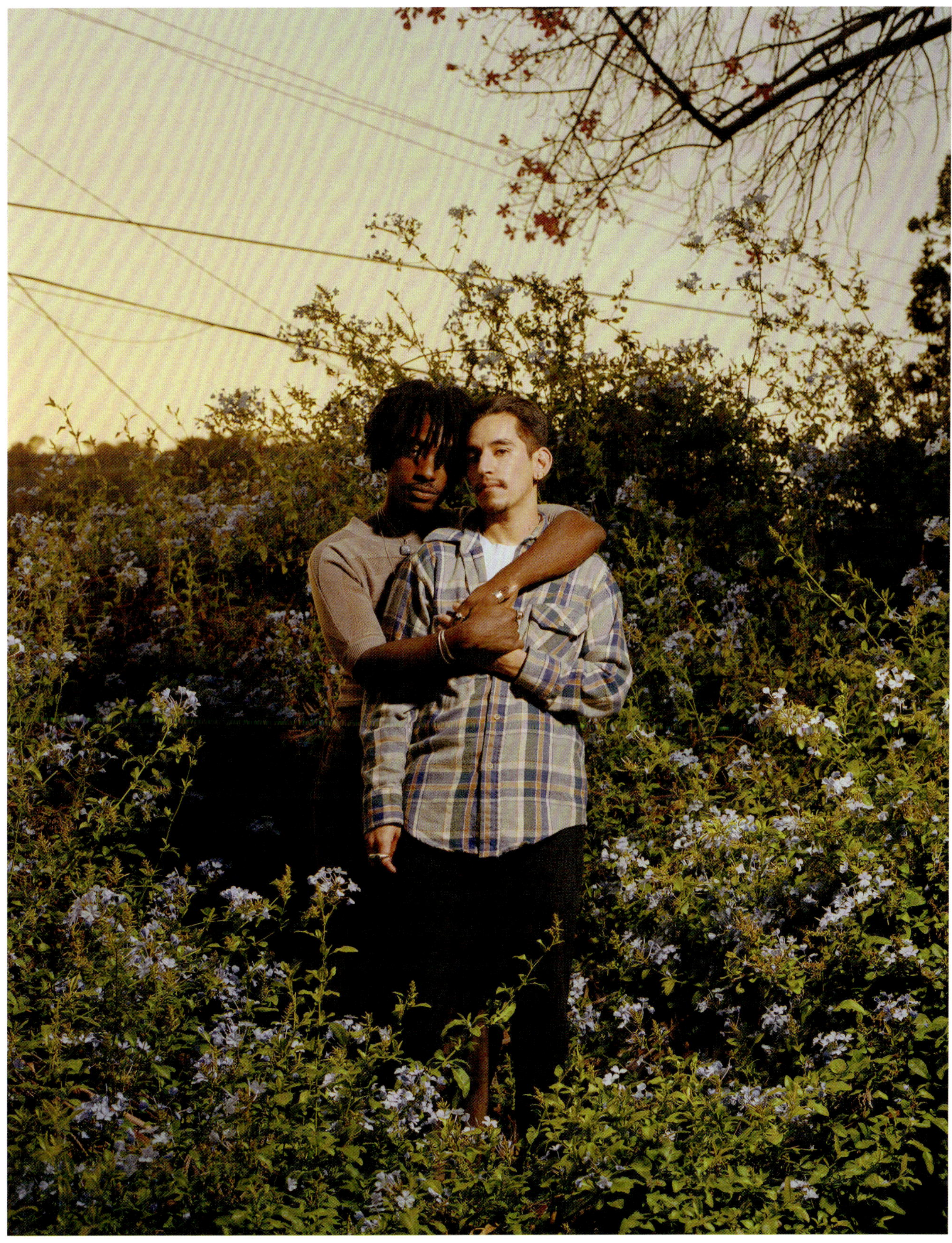

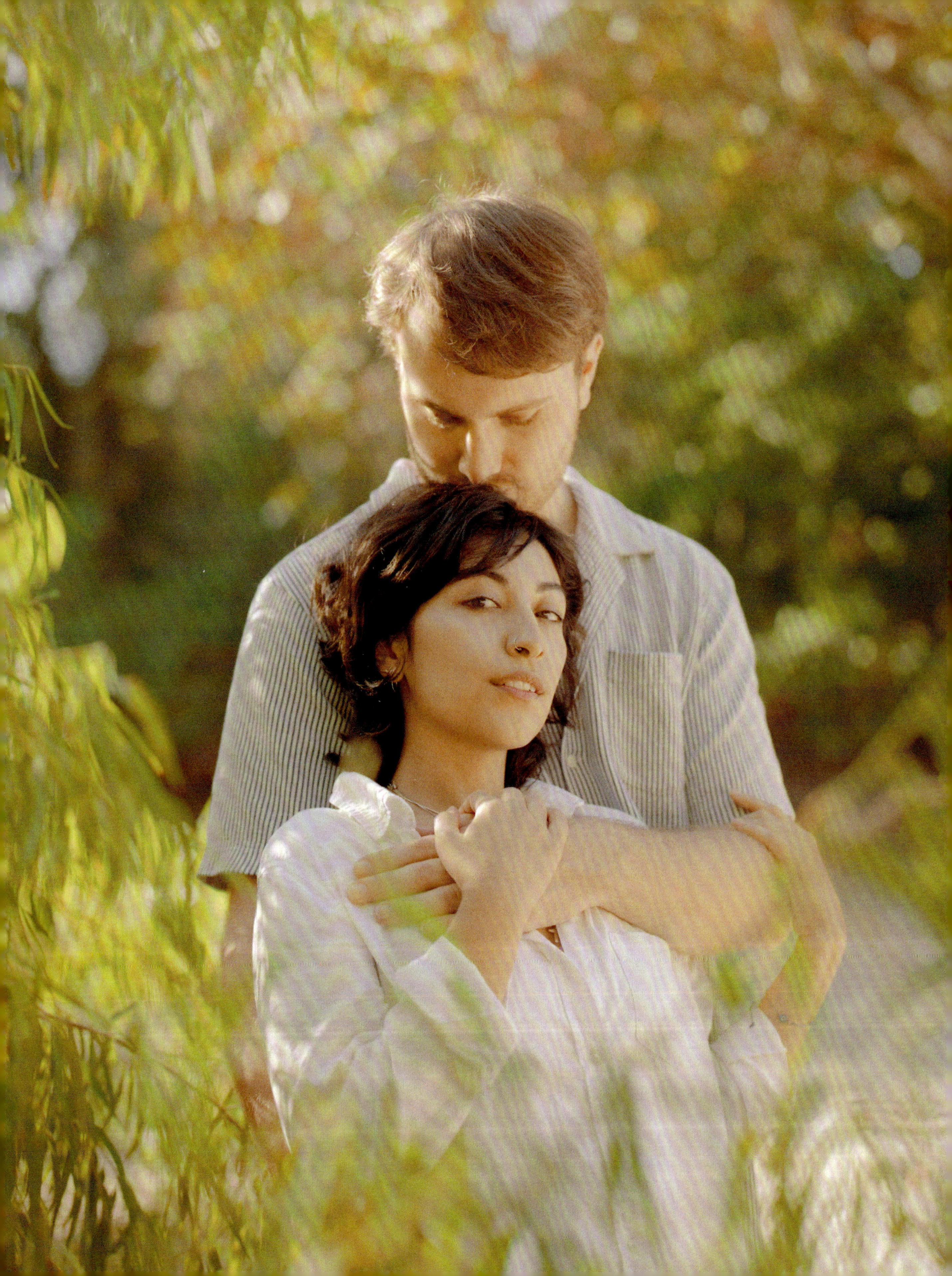

Devynn *(They/Them)* & Rob *(He/Him)*

AUSTIN, TX

DEVYNN

Coming out to each other happened during radically different chapters in our lives. Each time it caught us a little by surprise, but we found a certain comfort in each other. After discovering the term *nonbinary*, I finally felt like something made sense—something about me, the way I think and feel. It was several years until I was finally able to come out to myself fully and then to my partner, Robert. Even now, I don't fully understand what the future might look like, but that doesn't matter; he still loves me and accepts me with open arms for who I am and who I will become as we both grow. We kiss away scars through love and acceptance.

ROB

Early in our relationship, Devynn came out to me as bisexual. I later came out to them as queer, and they later came out to me as nonbinary. Thanks to this tradition, neither of us really knows if we have finished coming out to each other. However, we've always felt complete in each other's presence. We allow ourselves to perceive and be perceived in ways that we would have felt shame and guilt about in the past. Even when we're met with uncertainty in our lives and identities, we're enduring it together. Negative feelings will be defeated by love and patience, and knowing that despite everything, we're still eager to get to know and love the people we strive to become.

Dominique *(He/Him)* & Devon *(He/Him)*

SAN DIEGO, CA

DOMINIQUE

I am a Black, queer gay man. Although I am white and Black, I choose to identify as Black in most spaces because that most aligns with how the world views and interacts with me, and how I move though the spaces I choose to occupy. As a graduate student and therapist, my Blackness is most evident in these academic and professional spaces, as well as in spaces that are LGBTQ+. I choose to identify as both queer and gay because those identities best encapsulate me. Queerness is expansive and captures my feminine, masculine, and Black identities, while gay highlights my attraction to men. Devon makes me feel comfortable and empowered in all my identities in a way that no one else has. I did not expect that someone who is lighter in skin tone than me would be able to. He makes me wonder if Eartha Kitt was right when she said, "A man has always wanted to lay me down, but he never wanted to pick me up." Devon consistently encourages and uplifts me.

DEVON

Since I first came out, how I define myself has continued to shift as I grow through my experiences in the world. I am a mixed (white and Latino) queer man. I grew up very detached from the culture and experiences of my Mexican background, and learning to decenter my whiteness and reconnect with that part of myself has been an important piece of my journey. It has also been important for me to understand the ways in which I, as a partner, can celebrate and center Dominique's Blackness in the spaces we occupy together. In describing my sexuality and gender, I use the term *queer* because—inspired by the late queer theorist José Esteban Muñoz's interpretation of queerness—it creates a space in which I can play with identity and redefine norms and expectations for who I can be, away from cis-hetero/homonormativity. Being in a partnership with Dominique and acknowledging his own connection to queerness is a beautiful experience, simply because his ability to make me feel comforted and supported in all my identities encourages me to show up for him in my fullest and most honest form.

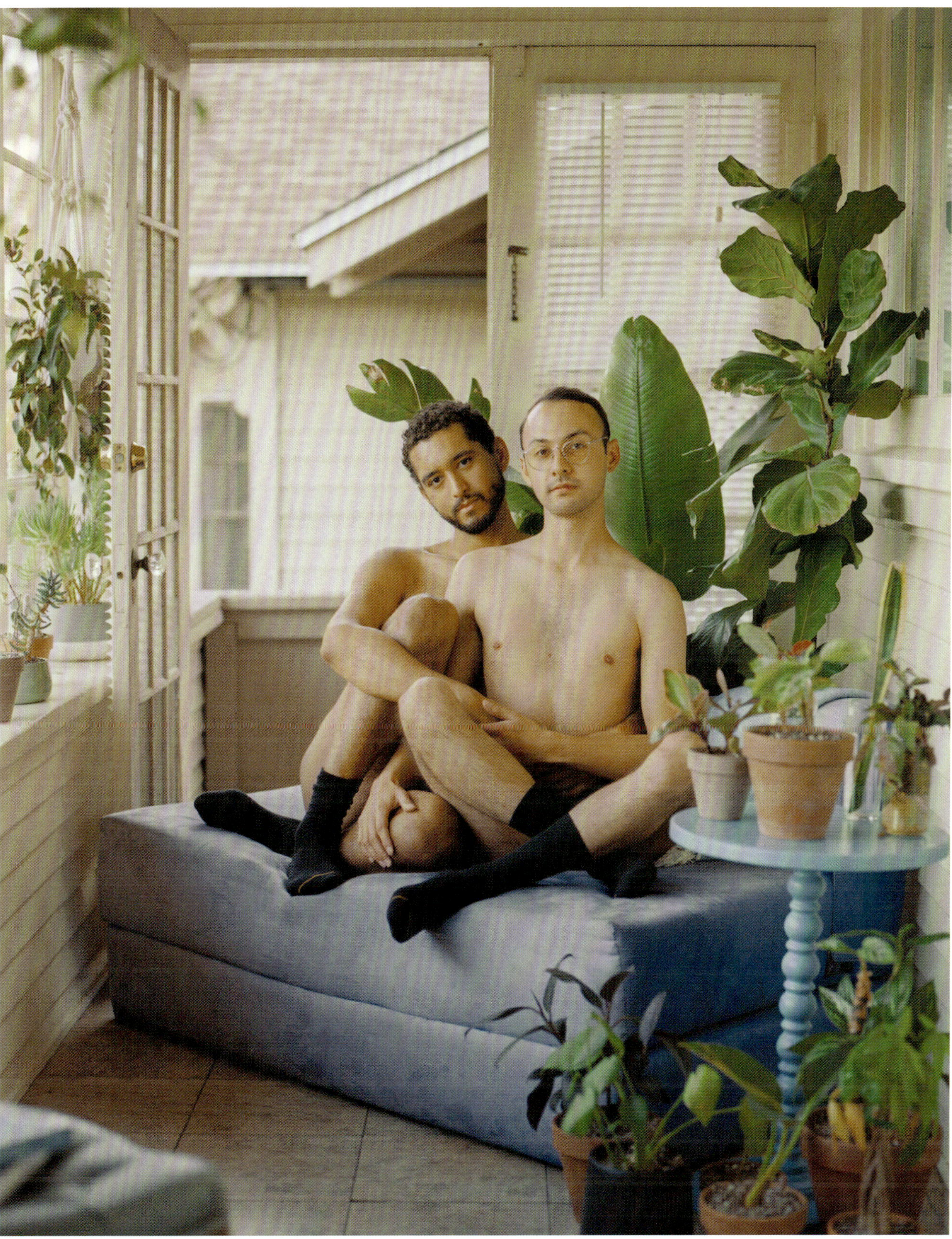

Doug *(He/Him)* & Andrew *(He/Him)*

LOS ANGELES, CA

ANDREW

One of the most satisfying but equally challenging things about being in a partnership like ours is truly being witnessed, being seen. And not just in the big, shiny moments, but also in the moments of sorrow, loss, and disappointment, in the mundane moments of everyday life.

We both experience periods of feeling low or anxious, and we've grown as a couple to be able to share those feelings with each other without the fear of judgment. For the first few months of 2021 I felt consistently flat, as I attempted to process everything that had happened during 2020. I was able to be vulnerable with Doug, and he was always there, listening deeply, allowing me to feel what I needed to feel without trying to fix anything. It is still difficult for me to be seen in this way, but the trust that we have developed and continue to grow makes sharing my inner world a little bit easier each time.

Ultimately, we both feel that we are here to help each other heal from past trauma, feel truly loved, and thrive in the world.

DOUG

Coming from different countries and cultures, open communication has been essential. We have had to learn to trust that we can have challenging conversations, express our truths and perspectives, and know that we have a solid foundation of love to hold us up.

2020 was a landmark year. Throughout all the challenges one of the things I'm most grateful for is the growth that occurred in our relationship as a result of radical honesty. In 2020 race came to the forefront of our relationship in a way it never had before. We charted new territory together and learned so much about how to support each other even when our lived experiences were not the same. How to emotionally hold each other up and how to feel free to fall apart with each other.

We are a very private couple and one of the choices we made early on was to keep our relationship offline. We wanted to protect it. It was something special, sacred even, not for the consumption of prying eyes and opinions. I firmly believe this choice gave us a real chance. A chance to truly know each other and what our relationship could become, dictated only by us. In this age where everything happens online, it felt rebellious and almost illegal to have something that was just ours.

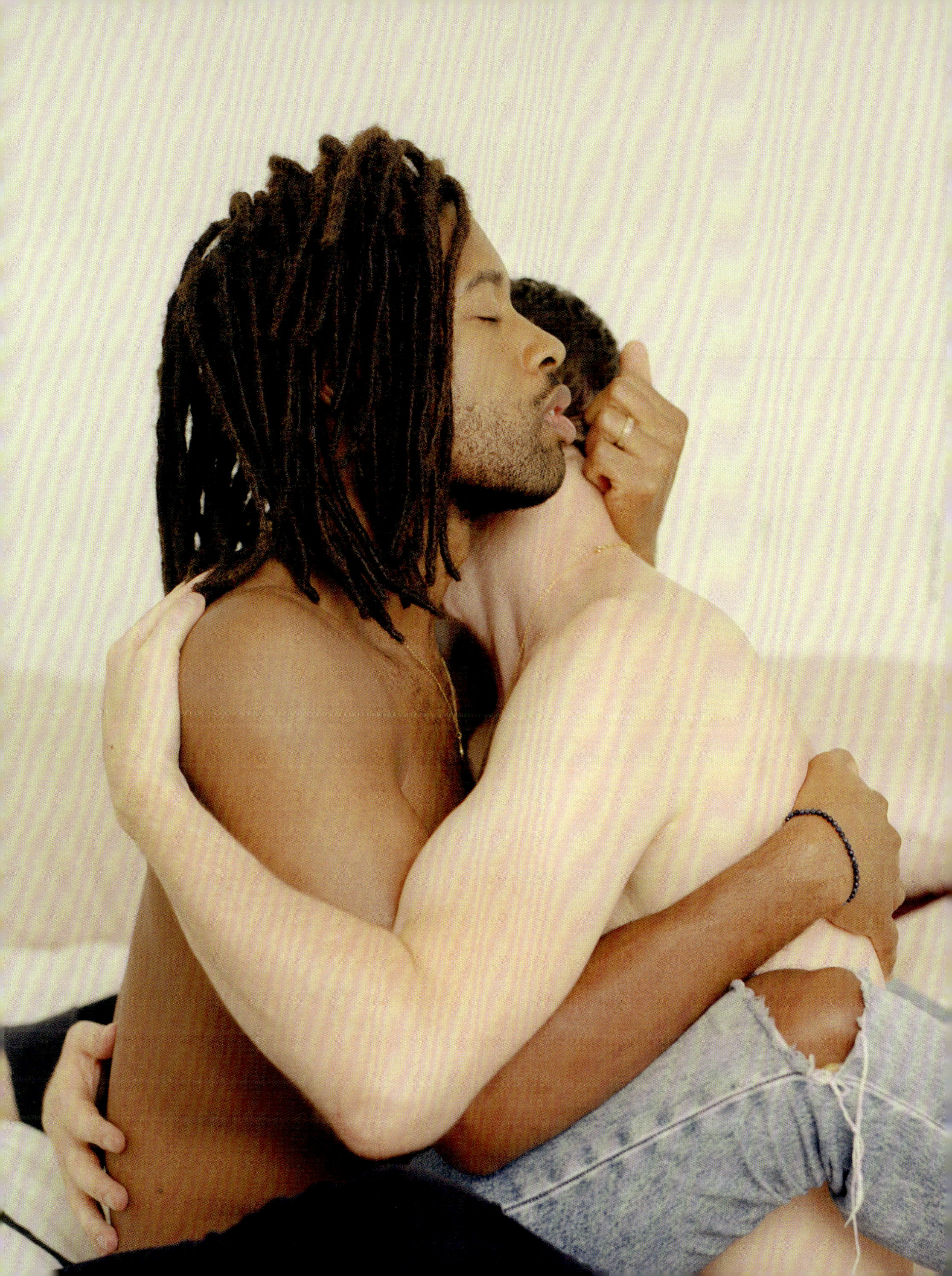

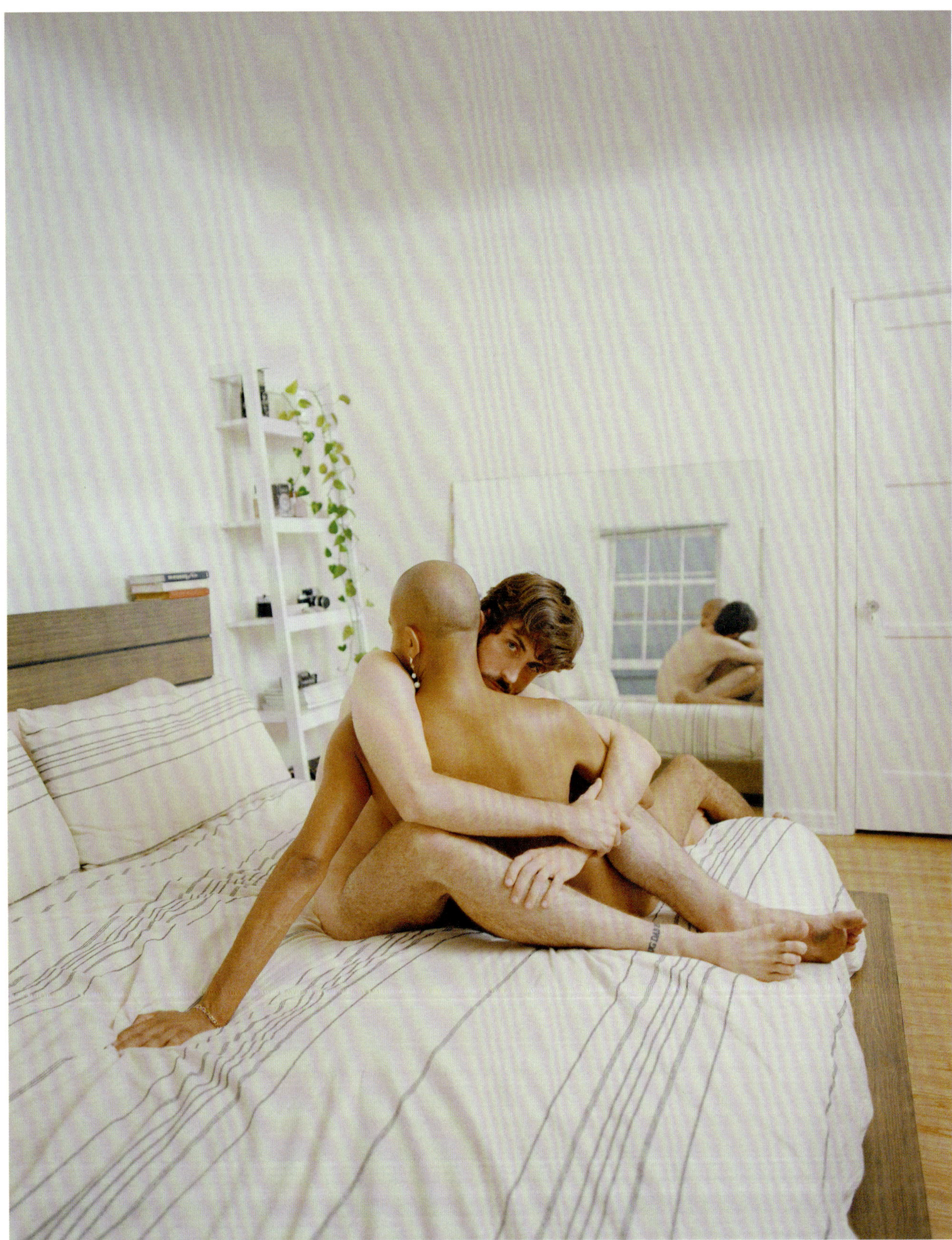

Drew *(He/Him)* & Jerrold *(He/Him)*

LOS ANGELES, CA

JERROLD

Being in an interracial relationship for over fourteen years in America has been no small feat. We had the luxury of finding each other at the age of twenty-one in the progressive city of Los Angeles, yet we've still shared many moments of discrimination. The slurs of white men shouting from their car windows as we wait for an Uber. The hate crime in broad daylight when three Black men assaulted and robbed us in the street, kicking and punching us to the ground because we were walking hand in hand. The feeling that there isn't a group that we particularly belong to in the gay community. In these dark, infuriating, and confusing moments is where we've realized that the only choice available to us is to embrace each other. Holding on tightly while also allowing ourselves to give each other space. We've made mistakes along the way in how we give each other that space, but it's the gray areas in our unique relationship that empower us to write our own narrative and make our own rules. Even when we see headlines about police brutality and the relentless efforts of others to restrict and invalidate queer lives, or a glare from a stranger because of a public display of affection, we still find our relationship flourishing. However dark the world around us can be, we're aware of the fact that together we're brighter than all of it. Strengthening the foundation and support we have for each other is our number one priority as best friends and husbands. It gives us the courage to be vulnerable with each other and with others. We can channel that fury and disappointment in our country and focus it on what always matters the most—the two of us.

Elizabeth (Liz) *(She/Her)* & Carlena *(She/Her)*

LOS ANGELES, CA

CARLENA

Elizabeth and I quite literally collided into one another's lives on a street corner in West Hollywood one night during Pride. Confetti littered the empty streets as the Ferris wheel flashed multicolored lights in the distance, and like any cheesy Hollywood film, time really did stand still.

Our love has been one of my greatest teachers. Through collaboration and partnership, my compassion for Elizabeth and her story has only deepened my compassion for myself; it is here where I have learned how to hold space for all we have experienced individually and heal through our union together.

My historical trauma taught me my fierce independence: I built a rigid structure in order to survive, and yet sometimes that rigid structure caused more pain than relief. It is with Elizabeth where I have learned to soften that structure, to lean into relational vulnerability and watch how our stories can expand in new directions when we do it together.

Each and every day I am humbled by the intersectionality of our love. By the way our individual ethnicities, races, upbringings, and queer identities guide us toward an even deeper understanding of self and other. I trust that it is in every difficult moment and tough conversation that surrounds these topics where our love lights our blind spots.

It is here where I have learned how to truly and deeply love and be loved. And under love's umbrella, be a partner, an ally, a voice, and most importantly, a best friend.

LIZ

Love has always been one of my greatest inspirations because it defies constructs of race, gender, and sexuality. I've witnessed it firsthand with my own parents and within my own life. When my father and mother fell in love, it was illegal for them to be together. Living under apartheid in South Africa, my white father and Black mother had to flee the country to be in a relationship. Their story, very much like my own, is a testament to the fact that love knows no bounds. Yet, despite a span of over fifty years between my parents' story and my own, the struggles we face remain very much the same.

We are constantly being faced with criticisms and hostilities from those who may not understand or approve of what our love looks like. We continue to have to get out in the streets to protest and advocate for our rights as women, people of color, and members of the LGBTQ community.

Being a queer, biracial woman in a relationship with another queer, biracial woman presents its own set of challenges. Having to face a lot of the same challenges continues to bring Carlena and me closer together and strengthens our connection and understanding of each other. It allows us to hold a space for one another that is unlike anything I've ever experienced before. It continues to be one of the things I cherish most about our relationship. My hope is that by continuing to love one another openly and fearlessly, future generations will be inspired to also love without any bounds.

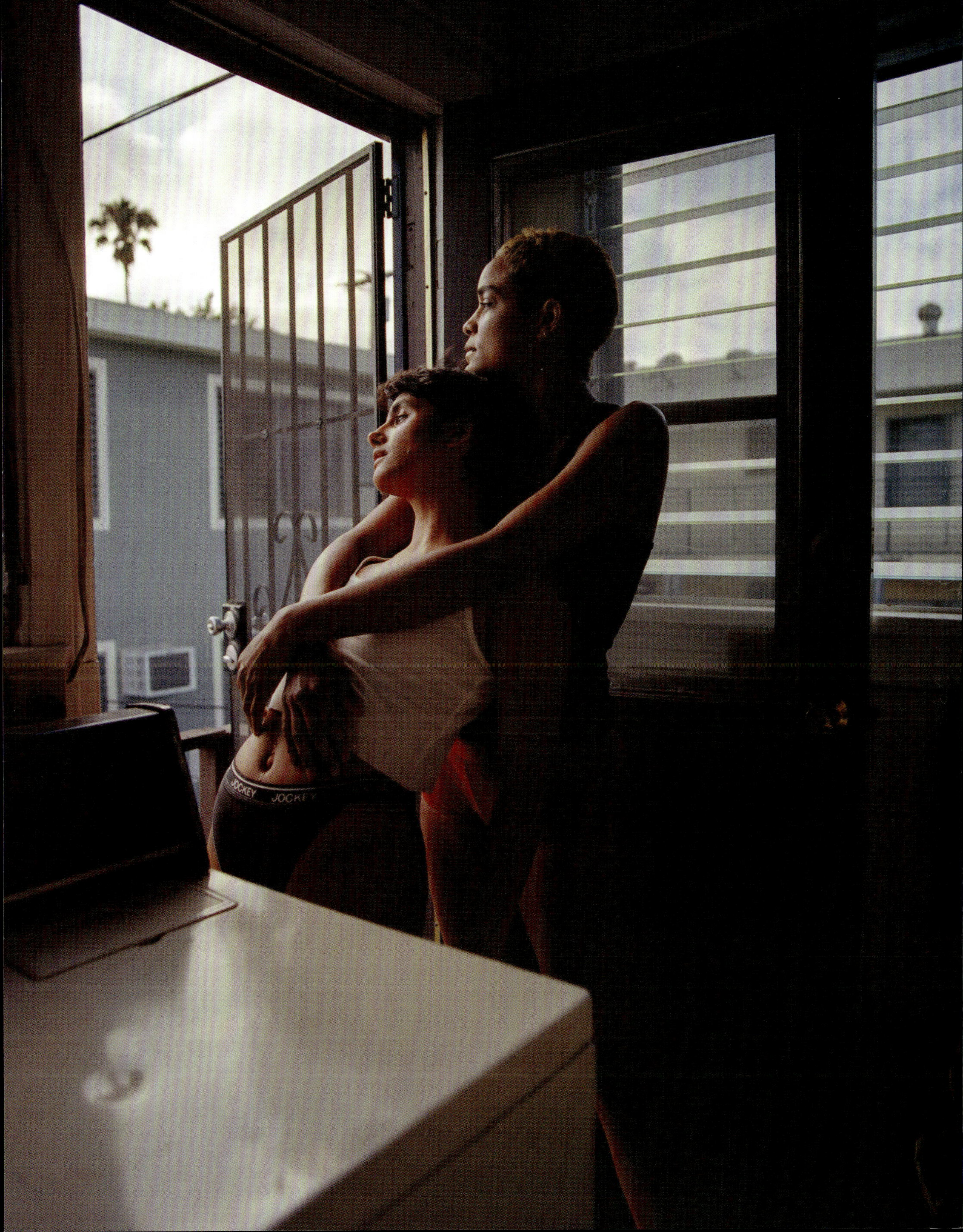
JOCKEY

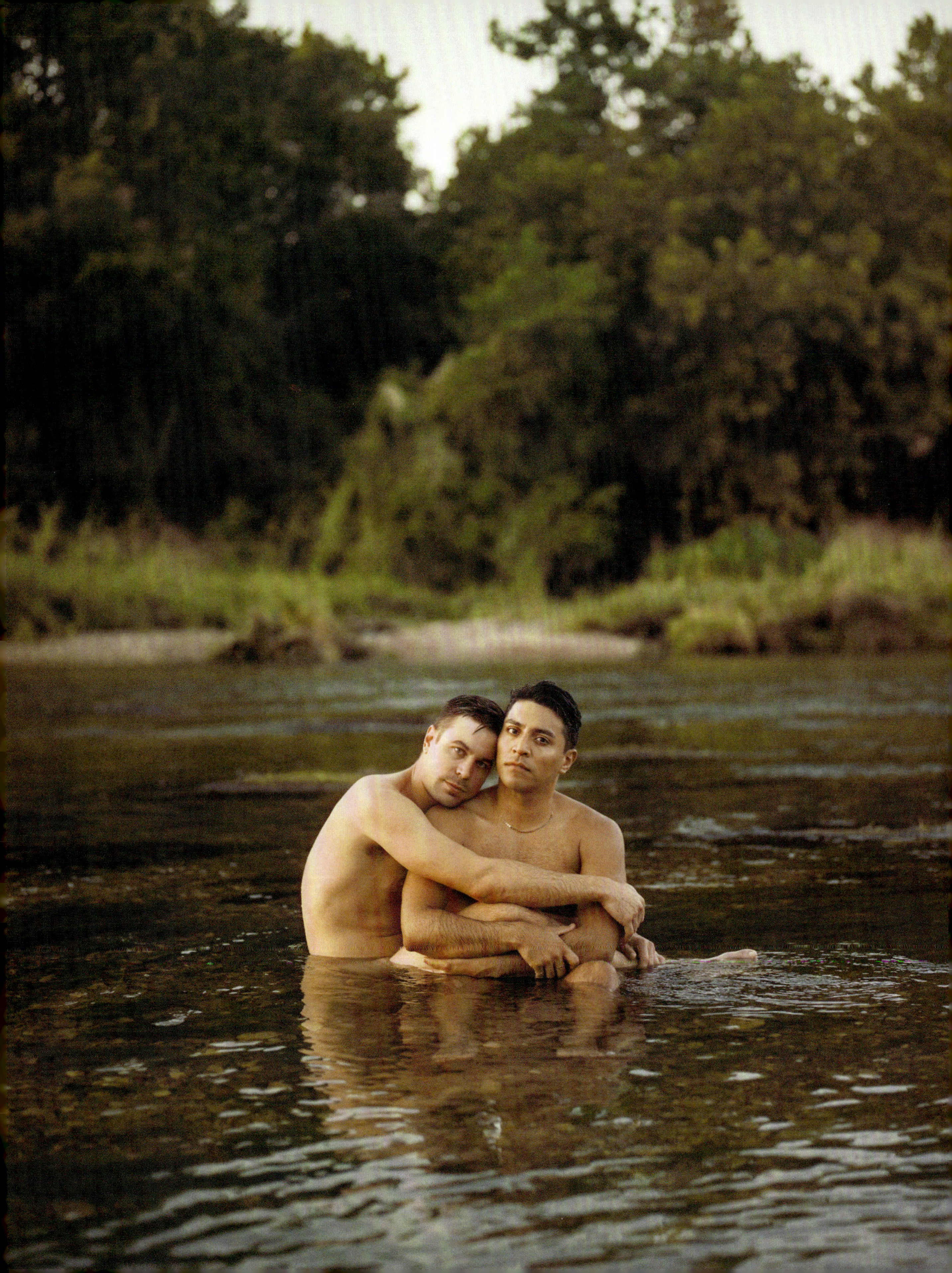

Ezequiel *(He/Him)* & Chris *(He/Him)*

AUSTIN, TX

EZEQUIEL

When we first met, I was struck by his gilded sensibility, porn mustache, and cheeky humor. I had dated white guys before. I had even asked one guy if he had a fetish for Latino men on our first date. I didn't do that with Duke (Chris). I wanted to look past race and believe if just for a moment that we were simply two humans attracted and interested in one another.

CHRIS

When I met Ezequiel, I was not new to the different lives we had led. I was intrigued to meet someone so endearingly charismatic, with a smile as wide and mouthy as my own. From day one he offered me his honest truth, and I, in turn, gave him mine.

My parents always said they regretted the lack of diversity I experienced in the white community I grew up in. I never understood how undervalued someone can feel in the world until I dated a man who told me he used to bleach his skin to be lighter. It was a heartbreaking reality to face. I guess I had failed to see why someone I saw as so beautiful could be seen as anything less than. It began a dialogue about race and identity that traveled with me from person to person, relationship to relationship.

EZEQUIEL

Subconsciously, I held prejudices against Chris and the expected stereotypes of him: pretty boy attitude, superficial dialogue, and general white fragility. Instead, what I got challenged my own judgments, gave me the space to be my own individual, and the best sex I've had in way too damn long. When I walk into mostly white spaces, the melanin of my darker skin tone is not lost on me. I've grown to love my skin, yet I still battle with imposter syndrome, racial prejudices against me, etc. To be in an interracial relationship is to have daily reminders of the differences in our experiences—daily opportunities to become frustrated over injustices and/or dig deep and build empathy for one another.

CHRIS

My privilege is that I never had to go through life thinking about race, and I may never understand what being in an interracial relationship really means, but every day I strive to support and learn more about Ezequiel.

Fabian *(He/Him)* **& Ryan** *(He/Him)*

LOS ANGELES, CA

We're both very independent, we're both artists (architect and actor), and we're both Aries. So from the beginning of our relationship, freedom to be ourselves while supporting each other's pursuits has been one of our most important values.

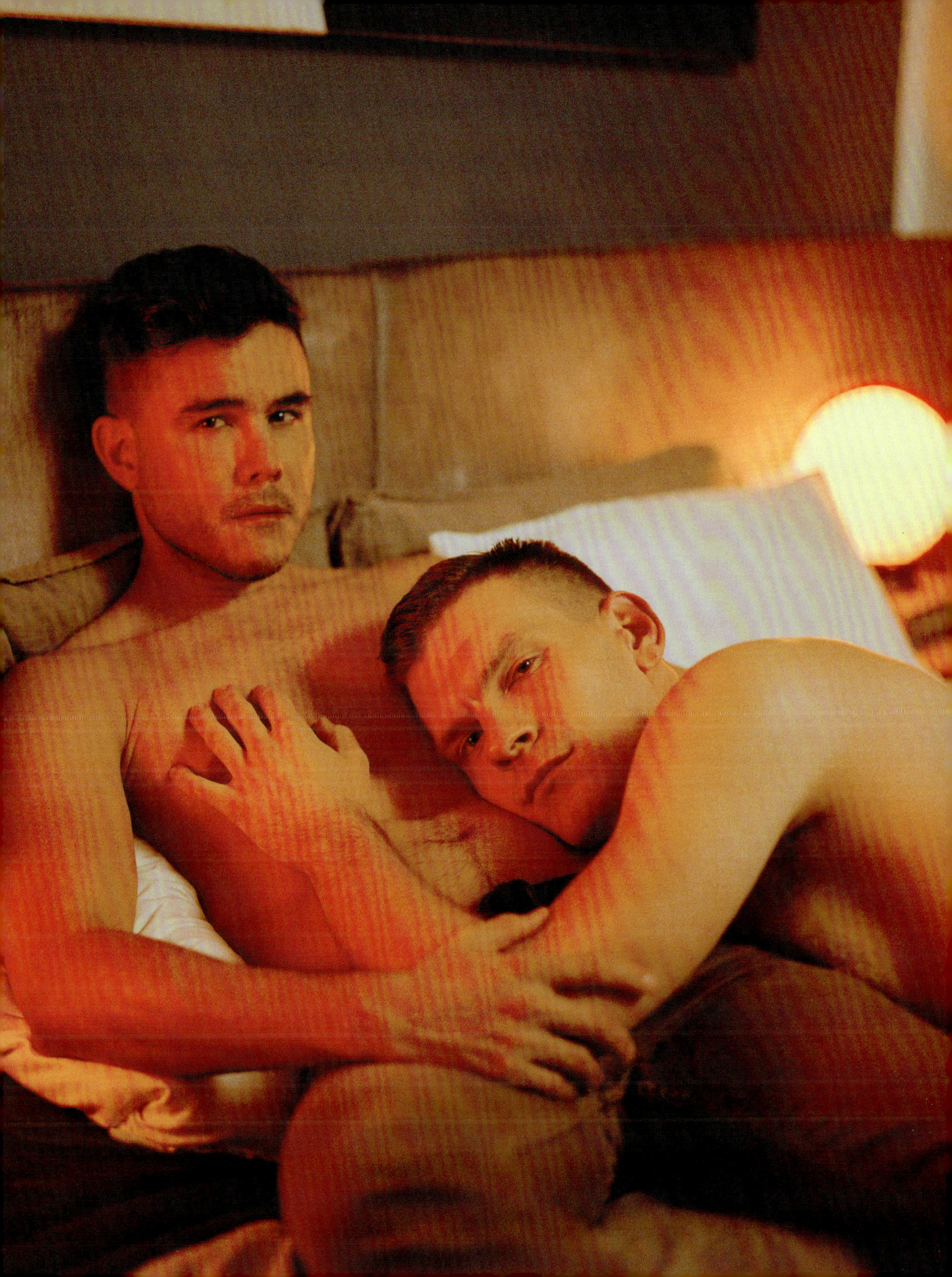

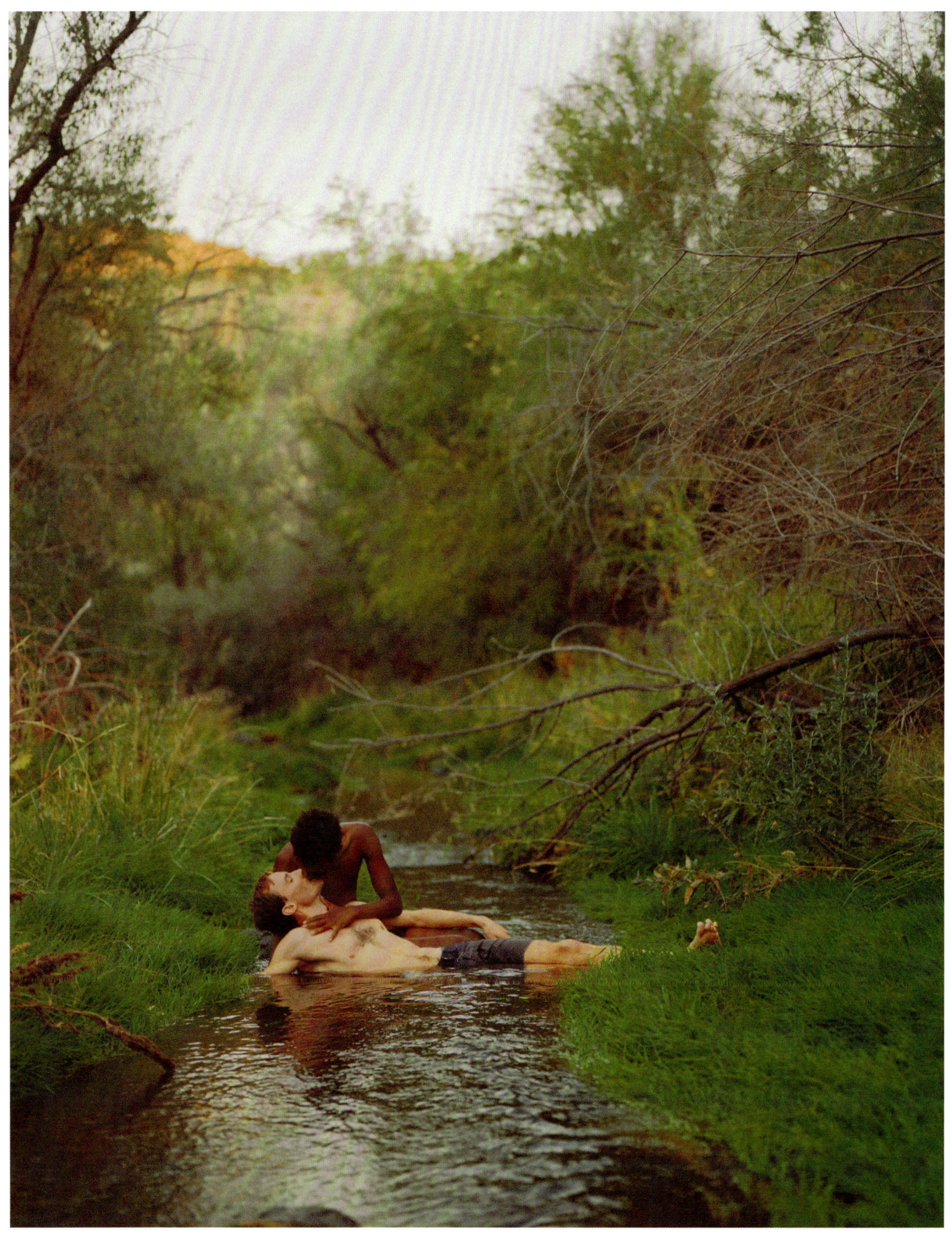

Garrett *(He/Him)* & Jay *(He/Him)*

SANTA FE, NM

JAY

I came out because of Garrett. He was the first man I ever loved, and in order to keep him in my life, I thought I should do what he wanted and come out before I was ready. There was a lack of balance in the early stages of our relationship. Garrett was unafraid, bodacious, and controlling. I believed my role was to shrink, allow, and accept whatever he wanted. It even got to the point where I only felt comfortable around him when I was drunk. Hiding had always been a habit of mine, and the fear of losing him did nothing but build my walls higher. So, thankfully, we broke up. On the week of our birthdays.

GARRETT

I never wanted to change for Jayson. Back in college, where we met, I knew Jay's feelings for me were greater than mine for him. I thought he was very lucky to have me—ushering him into queerdom, teaching him about life, entertaining him with ceaseless bits. I took advantage of his softness. He moved through life at a slower, gentler pace, and honestly, I thought I was doing him a favor by cranking up his speed. His secret calls for compromise, for compassion went completely unnoticed by me as I barreled through him with the unfailing knowledge that I was making his life better. Then, after one final disastrous trip to Six Flags, I ended it.

After a year, we both found ourselves in Santa Fe, New Mexico, working together as artistic collaborators. Although we may sound like a flaming dumpster fire of a pairing, time, the Enneagram, and God allowed for a miraculous fresh start. We're not perfect, we have more questions than answers, and Jayson is still trying to expand my woefully white palate (mustard grits??). But above all, we acknowledge that our love cannot survive on feelings alone. Love requires the radical courage needed to tell the truth and genuine gratitude for the myriad of ways in which we are different.

Griffin *(He/Him)* & Matt *(He/Him)*

LOS ANGELES, CA

MATT

"I hate how I look in this picture!" That's what I told my husband when he showed it to me. I'm the red-headed Jewish daddy on the left holding the toddler above my head. Once upon a time, I was a competitive yogi with a six-pack and all the accoutrements that I thought gay men are "supposed" to have to be attractive/desirable/valid. Now, I have a dad bod.

Let me be clear: I don't have a problem with dad bods in principle. I just don't like being the one to have it.

The African American eternally skinny supermodel on the right is my husband. When I tell him I don't like how I look in this picture, he scolds me: "Stop saying that! You told me that your mother used to say that shit about herself and that it made you insecure about your own body. We don't need to repeat that cycle!"

Indeed. We don't. In fact, our little family is the poster child for "breaking cycles."

Our children—who are not yet legally our children though we've been the only parents they've known since birth—so, our foster kids (three and eighteen months) are Armenian and Cambodian, respectively. From my loins there will spring forth no other little white Jews. From my husband's, no Black Christians. Our family bond is not biological.

And yet. Here we are—descendants of slavery and genocide all—eating overly salted edamame and sipping miso soup through a straw from the sushi delivery that arrived minutes earlier, trying to figure out how to break the nefarious cycles of pain that have plagued us; how to create the various cycles of love that might remake us.

Each of us in this picture—whether by choice or by circumstance—was brought together to be new: to escape broken families or to envision how we can improve what we came from.

We are a mess. We sometimes fall back into old habits. We often fail to hold space for the traumas and tears that brought each of us to this moment.

But. We're getting better at loving the strangers among us who are closest to our hearts. And...slowly...we are learning to love ourselves—dad bods and all.

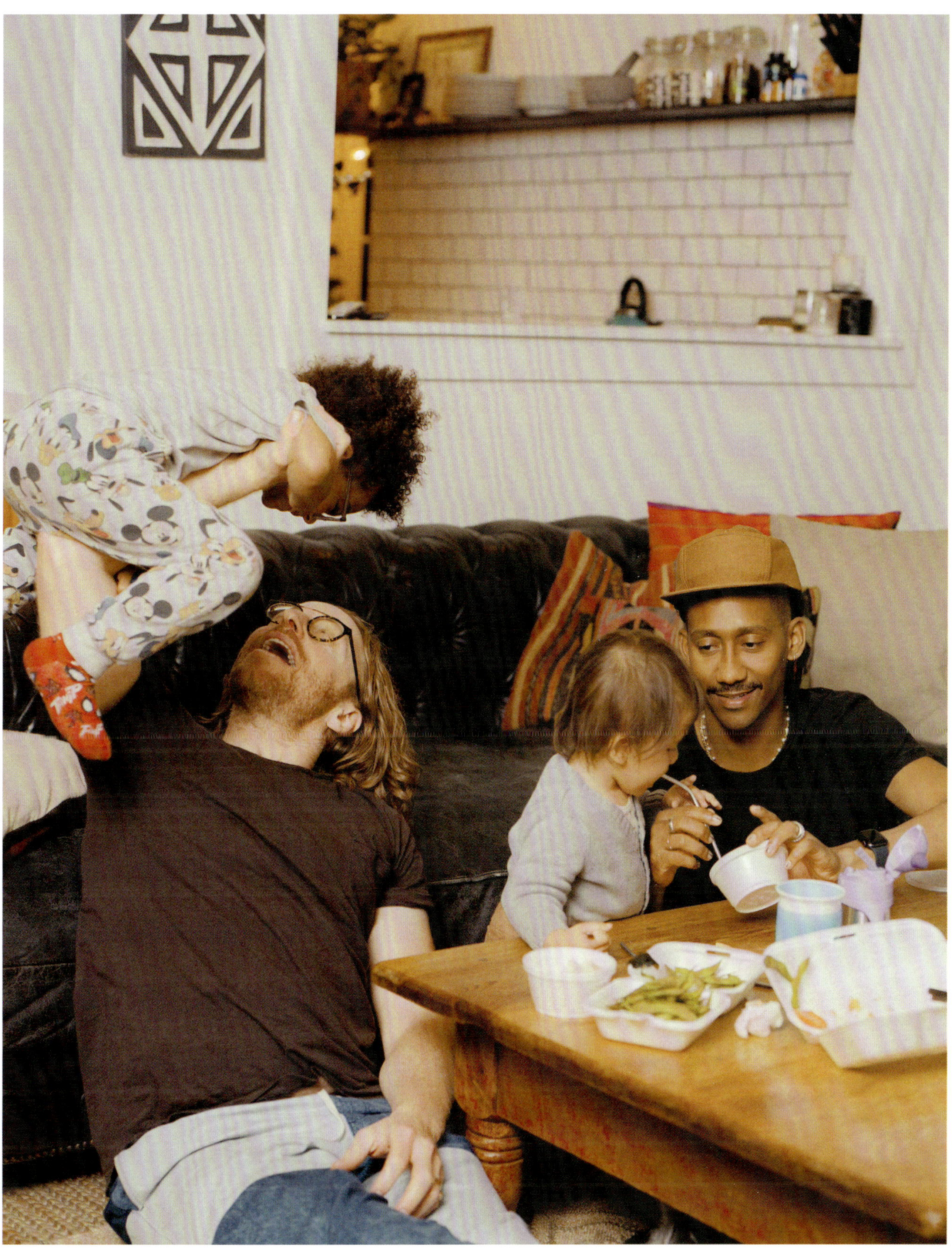

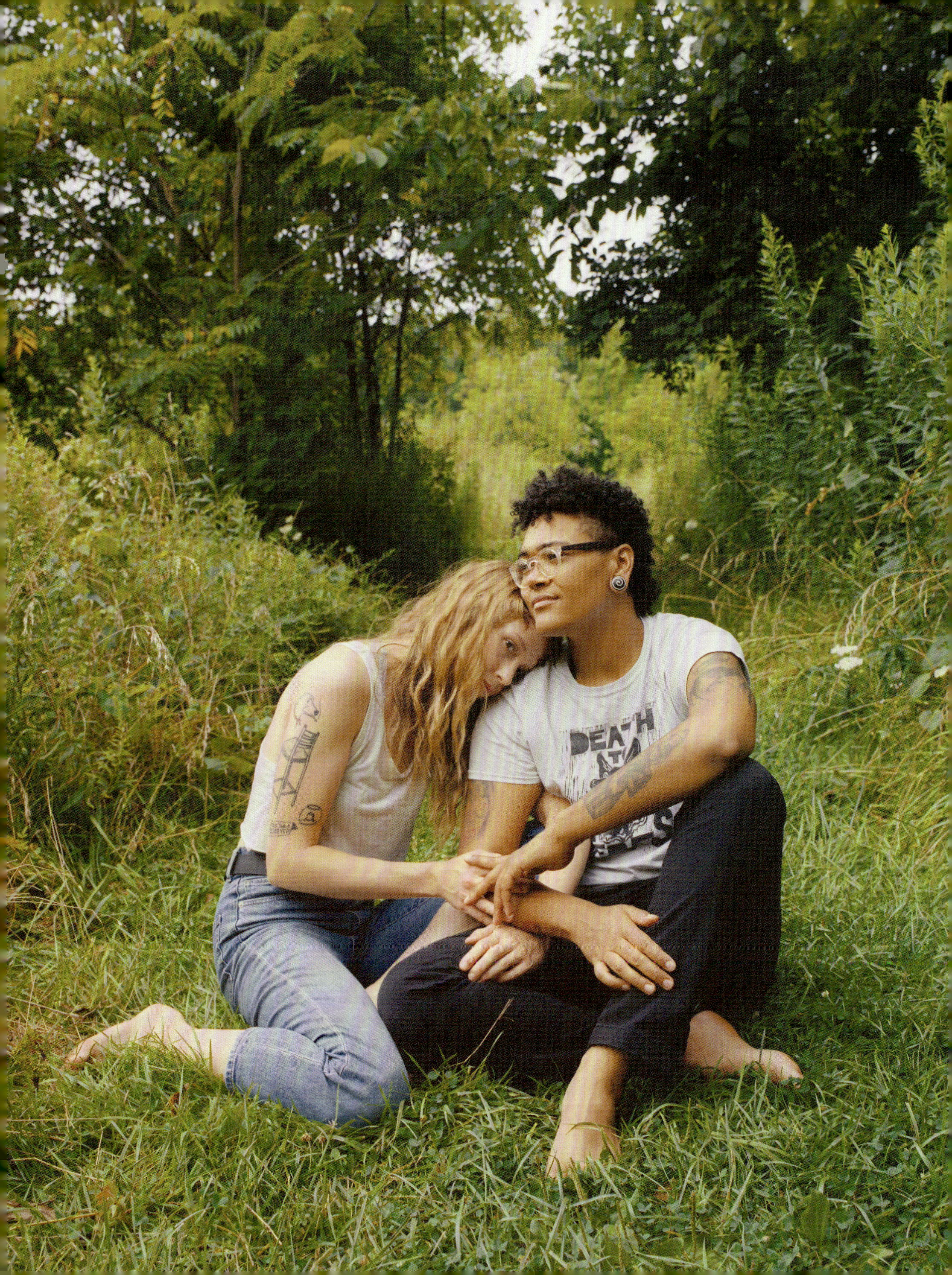
DEATH

Hannah *(She/Her)* & Jess *(She/Her)*

DAYTON, OH

JESS

Hannah is the kitchen crew chief at a downtown, contemporary Italian-inspired restaurant. She has dreams of opening her own space, bringing an experimental perspective to the concept of comfort food.

I'm a student at the University of Dayton with a focus in ceramics and figurative painting. I have a pottery business known as Muddstud. The name is symbolic, as I consider my utilitarian vessels sculptural forms representing the complexities of androgyny. I balance gentle curves with crisp, geometric lines that force the viewer to question what they're looking at. I have a big goal in this community to bring to Dayton the visibility I never had. I want to show other queer, Black, and certainly biracial individuals that we have our own cultural perspectives, and that we have a right to participate in the arena. Growing up, I was inspired by the works in museums but noticed nothing looked like me. The African Art wing was always in the basement. I want this community to know that we are here and we are relevant.

We got together through the restaurant she works for. I bartended there and she came in alone. For no reason really, I wanted her to like me. I really wanted her to leave her number because she was lovely, but she didn't "look" gay, so I was too nervous to ask.

She came in with a man and two children the following week, so I assumed she was married and forgot about it, but I guess she was swooning over me every time she came in. One night I saw her downtown at a bar, and I abandoned my friends to talk to her. When I learned she knew how to throw pottery, my heart swelled.

My mother didn't tell my grandparents she was getting married until the day it happened; and when she told them he was Black, my grandmother bawled. In the late 80s, my parents were turned down by several renters for being an interracial couple. I remember the way people would stare when we would visit the small Indiana town where my grandparents resided, and I could hear them call us things. As a teenager, other Black kids on the bus would tease and mimic me for wearing ties with T-shirts and listening to Nirvana. Growing up biracial allows you to create your own cultural perspective because it doesn't cleanly land anywhere.

I grew up very religious, so my attraction to women was at first an inconvenience. When I was seventeen, my church poured anointing oil over my head and "prayed my gay away." My childhood was filled with shame and the disappointment of my parents and the church for being an awkward, androgynous queer artist. After a while, it becomes easier to hate yourself.

Sometimes I still have to remind myself that I am not less but more of a being for the way we love.

J *(She/They)* & Rob *(He/Him)*

LOS ANGELES, CA

My dearest J,

I thought you'd just be another bout of exchanging pleasantries that never materialized into more. I thought you'd just be another hookup. I thought you'd be done with me once we put our clothes back on. I thought you'd be another name I'd forget as the days went on. I never thought you would be the name I could never forget. J. "Hi, I'm J" were your first words to me and I swear your voice was the sweetest sound. It told me, "You're safe here." Warm eyes that looked into mine and made me not want to break our stare. I held on to your every word that night. They pierced my soul and filled me with a euphoria like I'd never felt before. Every detail. It was intoxicating. It is intoxicating.

My sweet girl.
Your touch gives me peace.
I'm secure when you see me.
Your embrace makes me feel at home.
Your affection gives me life.

You look to the moon and the sun and the stars for signs and fortunes and answers. That makes you smile. You tell me I overanalyze every decision I make, but I would give that up to follow your lead because nothing makes me happier than your joy.

My heart will always be yours to keep.

You make it so easy to love you.

Love,
Rob

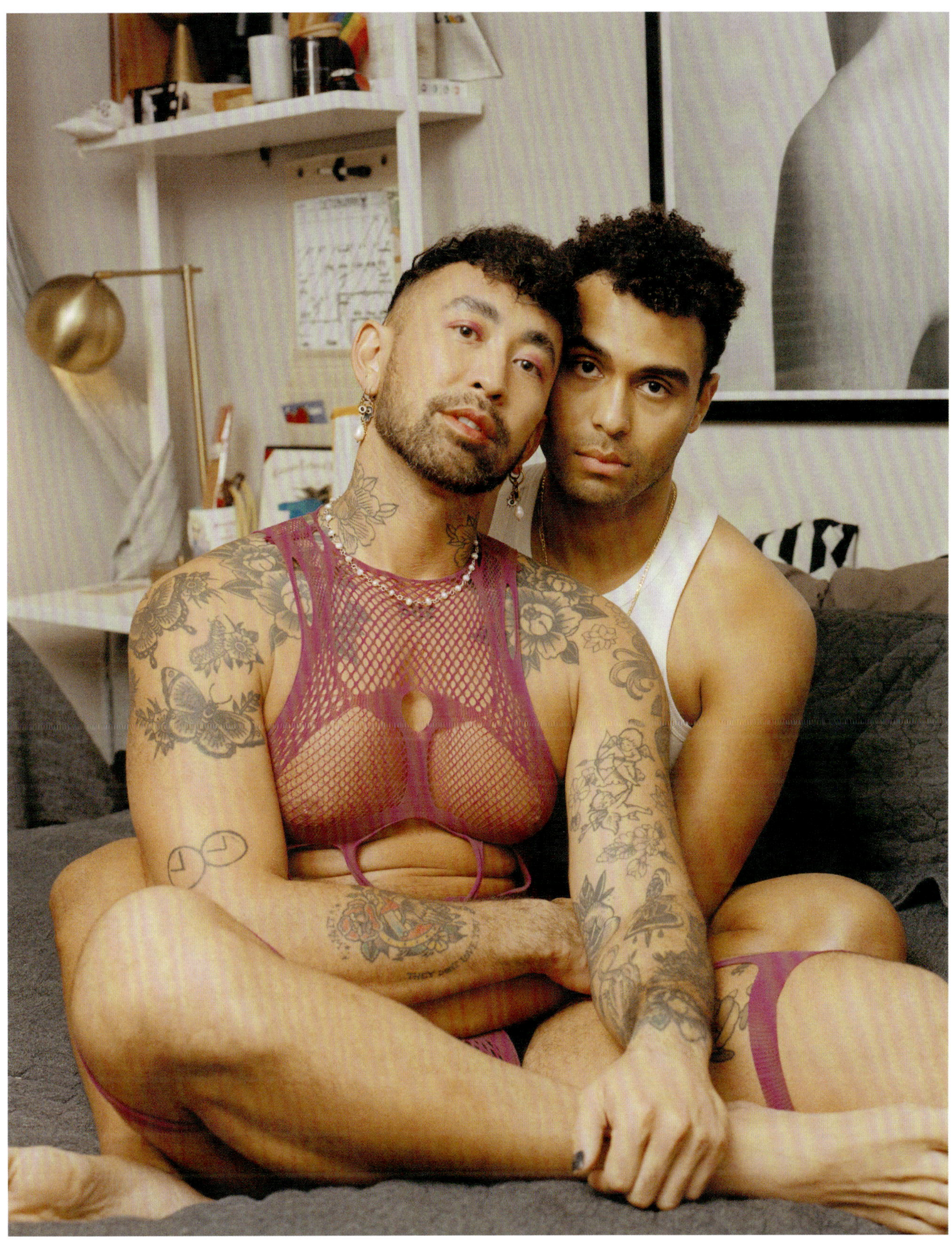

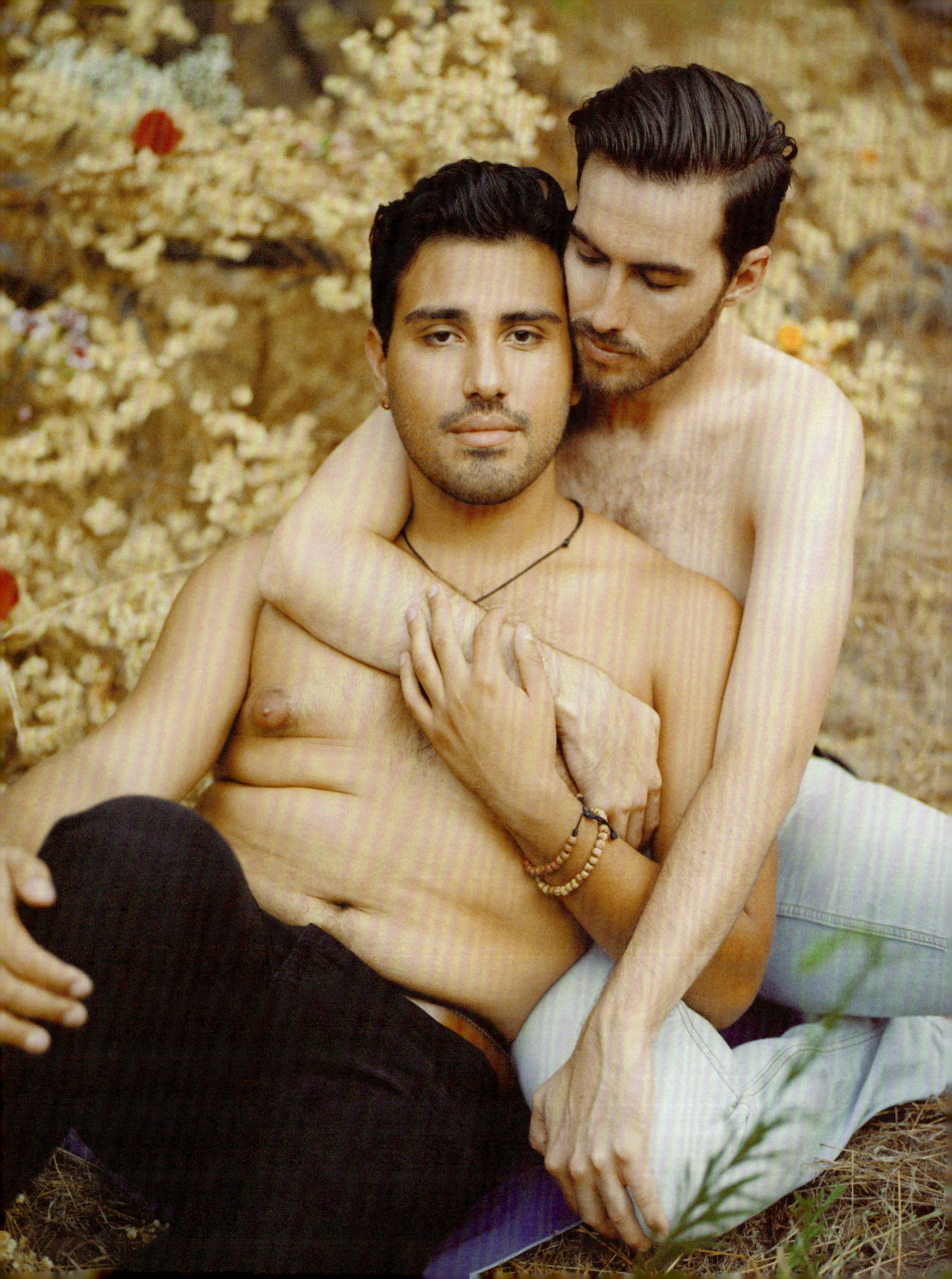

Jacob *(He/Him)* & Leo *(He/Him)*

ORANGE COUNTY, CA

To be honest, it can sometimes feel scary to be open about our relationship in everyday life. Often, just holding hands on the street feels like we're putting ourselves in real danger—but we push ourselves to do it because we owe it to ourselves to live.

Jari *(She/Her)* & Deniz *(They/Them)*

BROOKLYN, NY

JARI

There is a unique comfort being in a relationship with another trans person. It is one that many trans folks, because of societal oppression, don't get to experience. There are assumptions that suggest our transition is invalid if we are not in a relationship with cis people. For Deniz and I, I think it's been quite the opposite. The comfort in knowing that my body and how I choose to express my gender are never up for question. That I am never stunted in my process of exploring, and my whole self is welcomed with loving arms. We make conscious effort and space to make sure that this is in the thread of our relationship, that both of us have room to expand ourselves, have room to combust, while also having the confidence that there will be someone to pick up our pieces if possible.

I am a Fat Black Trans Woman. It doesn't get much harder than that. I've had to really look out for my own well-being, both physically and mentally. I wasn't often offered help or supported—it has always been assumed that I'm strong enough to do it myself, which in most cases is true, but not always. Within this relationship, I find myself prioritized in ways I thought weren't possible—that have allowed me to unpack a sense of unworthiness that has been projected onto me and women like me. This isn't my first time being in an interracial relationship, but it is the first time that people have assumed a whole lot and have navigated according to what society has indoctrinated us with. I often watch people create and assume our story in their heads, about what our lives are like, what gender roles we take, or what our sex must look like. Sometimes Deniz and I cackle to one another as we share an inside joke of sorts: "They have no FUCKING idea."

And then there are the times that I am silent, the times in which I realize that white people will speak to Deniz first and then me, or not at all to me. Or the times where conventionally attractive people see no value in our relationship and unnecessarily challenge me because how can someone so fit and white and beautiful be in love with someone who society has deemed the bottom of desirability. Deniz never lets those moments go unchecked. I admire the way they navigate protecting me and sticking up for me, but never speaking for me or taking away my autonomy. Deniz goes through unique obstacles as well while being in a relationship with me. Assumptions that my partner is a man, which invalidate them as a nonbinary person; that my partner shares the disgustingly competitive mindset of patriarchy, which values the idea of ownership; that because Deniz is in a relationship with me, someone who they consider a low standard, their body is up for grabs as well as a "better" alternative.

Being publicly in love with Deniz has come with its challenges, yes, things we can't control, but it could never measure up to the genuine and deep-souled beauty that has come out of this relationship. Not once have I been put in situations where I have had to dim my love for my body, quiet my Blackness, or humble my pride as I succeed as a trans woman. If anything, it has been the opposite. The joy in loving someone who loves and celebrates you as much as you do, and who willingly will pick up that slack of love and celebration when you may not be feeling that for yourself, is an experience I wish for so many queer people. We have expected nothing and in return have felt everything beautiful.

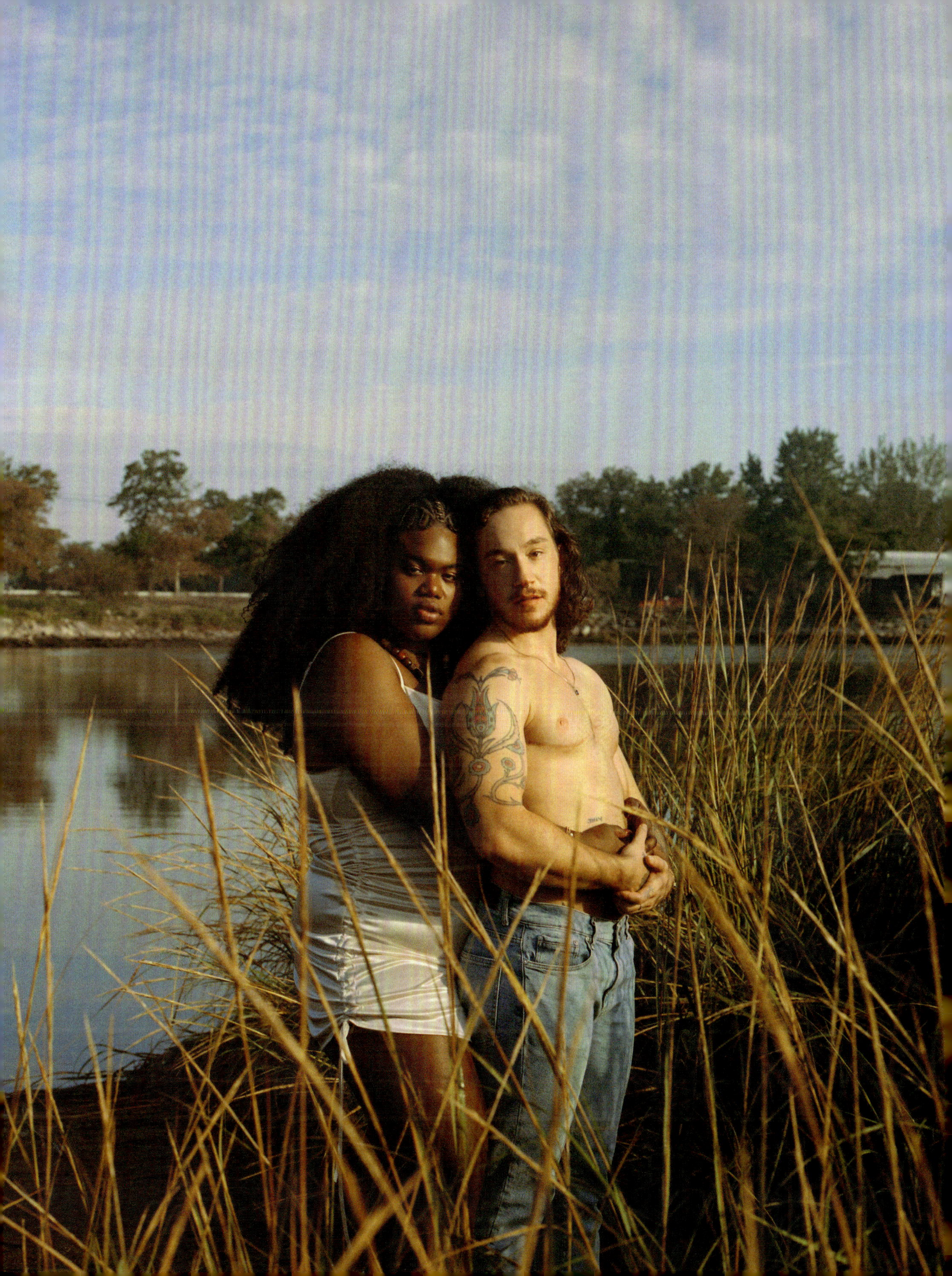

DENIZ

Living in a white supremacist–informed society, we're force-fed that Blackness is unlovable. That fatness is unlovable. That transness is unlovable. That femininity is supposed to be small, quiet, conventionally attractive and white, and if it isn't, it too is unlovable. This only inspires me to love these parts of my partner louder. To hold her hand tighter. To acknowledge and call out looks from strangers that hypersexualize her but are respectful of me. Jari's Blackness, fatness, and transness are not all that she is, but they are what most people will see and use as a way to question our relationship and to validate their confusion as to why we are together. In many "interracial" relationships, especially those that include a white partner, I've noticed some erasure of our partner's otherness. White partners are quick to make colorblind statements or only start to have conversations regarding race post-summer 2020, as though race hasn't always been a part of the relationship. The intent of this may come from a place of not wanting to limit our partner to how they are perceived by the world outside our relationship, but this actively ignores the power dynamics within our relationship. This is not something that Jari and I shy away from, but something we are careful to acknowledge and bring into every conversation. Something I tell Jari I will never do is threaten abandonment or threaten to break up. It breaks trust, it can be manipulative, but most importantly it may leave her feeling disposable, something that the world already tells Black trans women they are, and something she will never be to me. I think that white partners especially, and any partner who holds a majority of the power in the relationship, need to recognize our positionality and the unique opportunities we have to advocate for our partners. We need to be advocating for our partners out of compassion, love, and support, not white saviorism. My love for my partner is unconditional, so is my want to see her thrive within and outside of this relationship.

Jenn *(She/Her)* & Larisse *(She/Her)*

GLENDALE, CA

LARISSE: Six years and we're still here…together. Holy moly balls! So, how'd we meet?

JENN: We met online. You had one profile photo up and it was your back.

LARISSE: Ha! Yup. I got a fresh haircut and wanted to put myself out there…but didn't want to put myself out there. Why did you reach out to me?

JENN: What prompted me to write you was your line: "Try not to fall in love with me when you meet me! Seeking friends." Oh please! So cocky, yet you can't post your own face. Why are you here on a dating site if you're just looking for friends? I did think you were clever, had beautiful hair, and were well put together (from your backside), so why not? And the rest is history!

LARISSE: Okay, lookit, I had just gotten out of a long-term relationship. It was more of a disclaimer than arrogance, thank you.

JENN: We both had no business getting into a serious relationship to be honest, but we did it.

LARISSE: Mm-hmm. I was still pretty damaged from my previous one.

JENN: And I was dealing with my mental health. Only two months into our relationship, you bailed me out of jail. I was on the 710 South offramp of Long Beach Boulevard when a man hit my car and drove away. Instead of calling 911, I went after him. He ended up calling the cops on me and the next thing I knew, I was in handcuffs.

LARISSE: That was the worst! You called telling me you got into a little fender bender and would call me back. Hours passed and you never called me. I was so worried. My best friend Amy instructed me to check the hospitals and jails. I was like, jails??? I looked it up anyways, and there you were. "Assault with a deadly weapon." I was in utter shock! The director of operations of a laboratory at that time, calling off from work to bail my partner out of jail. Like, wow! Who am I with? You explained the whole situation. I understood where you were coming from but did not understand your decision making.

JENN: You didn't understand nor were you sympathetic for a long time.

LARISSE: Absolutely. I was also upset you showed no appreciation for me bailing you out. You were keeping to yourself and closed off. Why is it so hard to say thank you, I thought?

JENN: I was drowning in my own depression, embarrassed that happened, and didn't know how to say thank you. I internalized my emotions and have spent much of my life self-medicating with prescription pills to avoid my feelings. As simple as it may sound, to say thank you, it would have been fake at the time. I showed my appreciation to you weeks later in an in-depth letter.

LARISSE: Coming from a background where I had to put depression to the side and push through, I could not empathize at the time. I was the "Let's go, what's the issue, get over it, c'mon, surface" type of person. I was raised in Los Angeles by my hero, a single mom with three kids. I am the first-generation Filipina American–born in my family, where there was no time for bullshit. There was no way I was letting my mom down from the struggles she went through for my older brothers and me.

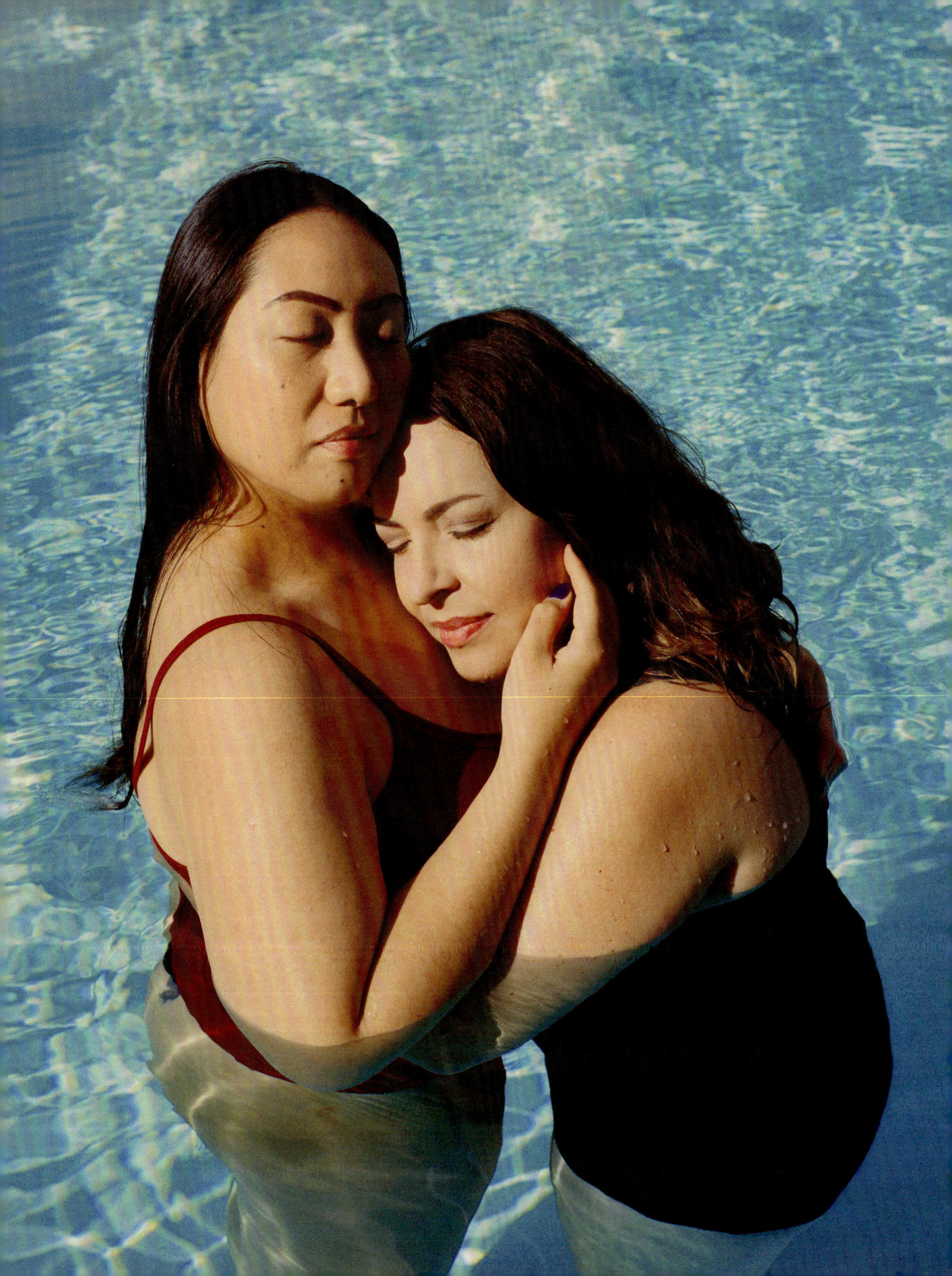

JENN: I was raised in rural Texas with both parents until they divorced when I was fifteen. My mom was emotionally absent during her struggles with alcoholism. My father overcompensated by being severely strict. It was an environment where you didn't talk back and you did what you are told. It wasn't a warm and cozy home.

LARISSE: We both dealt with our adversities differently. Knowing what I know now and what I've learned, I surely didn't help with your progress. It took me years to comprehend that. Putting a lot of my own emotions to the side and not dealing with them fucked me up too. I am now a big advocate for therapy.

JENN: There's such a stigma to getting help. Our relationship and I would not be where it is today without the assistance of therapy. (Thanks, Jeff!) It also took me years to understand that you don't mean to be offensive. It's the way you jest, like when you called me "Slutter-McSlutterson" as a joke and I secretly cried to my old therapist about it. I found that out from being around your family. They are all genuinely kindhearted and inclusive, yet curt.

LARISSE: Oh yeah, sorry. I wouldn't have called you that if I had known it would hurt you that way. Right?! They're crazy, but I love them to death! I love love your family too! We've learned from each other and our families, which has helped us grow as individuals and as a couple. Nothing is easy. We couldn't be more opposite.

JENN: But we've worked together thus far to build this life with our rad cat Lil' G, and will do so forever and ever. You're a badass hustler, facilitator, provider, and organizer who cares so much about spreading love and helping others.

LARISSE: You're my favorite everything... Boss carpenter, creative artist, anything fixer-upper, animal saver, mom-in-law whisperer, and the most thoughtful person in the universe.

JENN: I think we're done? Let's go buy weed?

LARISSE: For sure!

Jason *(They/Them)* & Matt *(He/Him)*

SAN FRANCISCO, CA

MATT

There's this white, heteronormative script about romantic partnerships that tells us our partner should be part of every aspect of our life, especially our family and social circles. But this isn't always safe, realistic, or even desirable for everyone, particularly when there are racial, cultural, class, or other differences. And to us, acknowledging those contexts and being attentive to them is a queer way of loving one another.

About six months into our relationship, I insisted that Jason come with me to a party of mostly older and white family friends. They resisted but finally relented, and when we arrived at the party, the first interaction was with an older white woman who told Jason they looked exactly like a different Asian person named Jason, going so far as to pull up a photo of this stranger. I was mortified, Jason was anxious to get out of that space, and the evening was ruined. But this became a powerful lesson, making me more aware of the toll on Jason in navigating majority white spaces. It taught me to think carefully about the social circles and relationships in my life Jason should be connected to. Rather than following that normative script that they should be a part of all of them because we are together. This has allowed us to have more conversations about family and social events, with check-ins about whether they want to take part or asking them to join if it's important to me.

JASON

Sometimes I choose to opt out for my own well-being, but other times, I do want to go along and be in those spaces with Matt. For both of us, these practices are informed on one level by our love for each other as queer people, but also by our political commitments to abolition. It's not always as black and white as cutting someone out from your life. Choosing to struggle through our differences as opposed to disposing of people is a principle I try to practice.

Sometimes, though, it's not always possible, and certain spaces are simply unavailable to partners, such as my family, who does not know about my gender or sexuality for reasons out of both love and fear. I am in this middle space where they are in one way cut off from one aspect of my life but are still connected in other ways. I exist in parts to them, and I struggle to understand what familial love can look like when you can't show up as your whole self. This is an area we are still navigating, as Matt yearns to know this part of my life while I maintain boundaries for my own safety. Yet none of this feels like a hindrance to our partnership; instead, in rejecting the scripts embedded in us by whiteness and heteronormativity, we can be better, more loving partners in the world as it actually is.

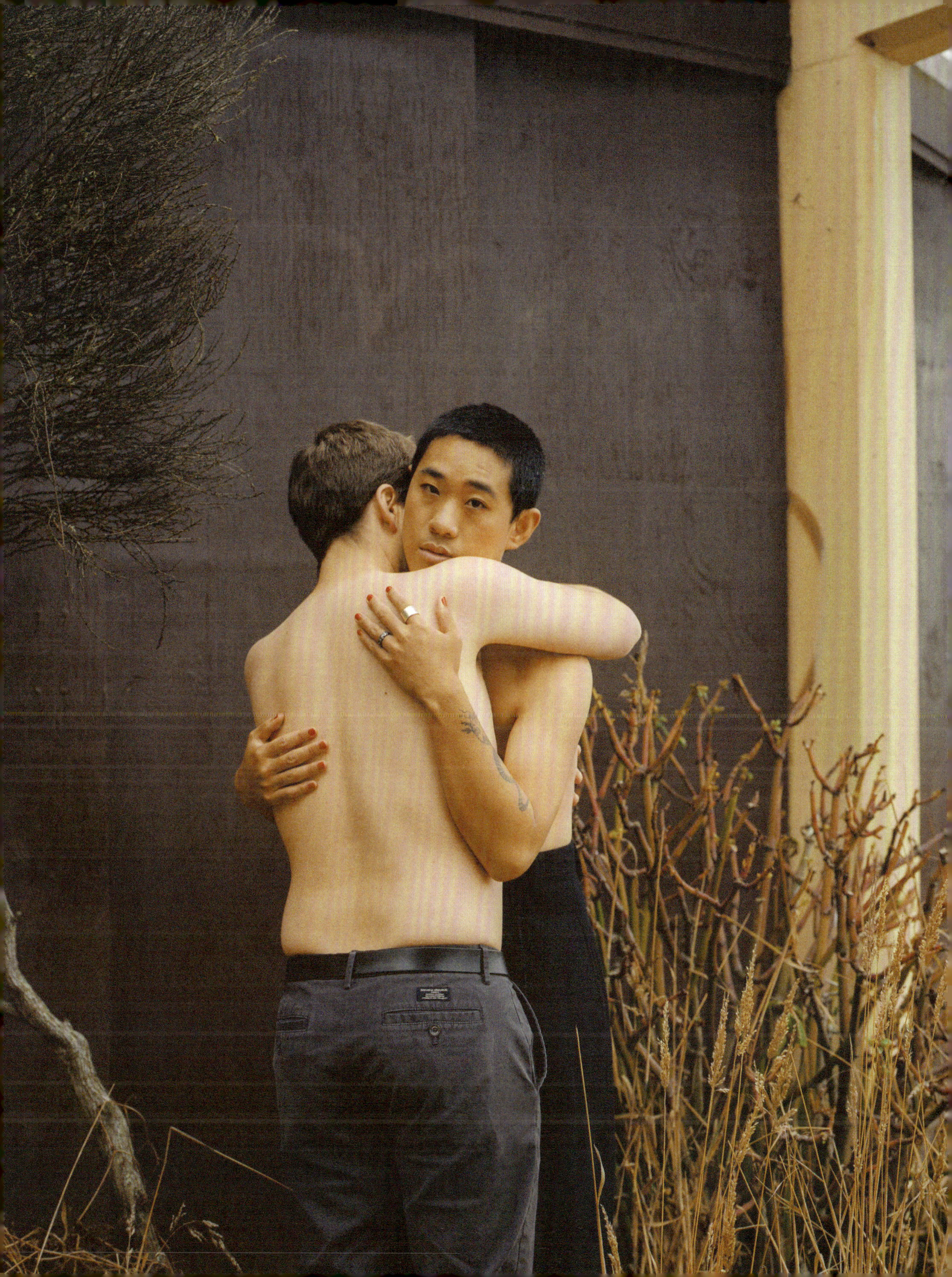

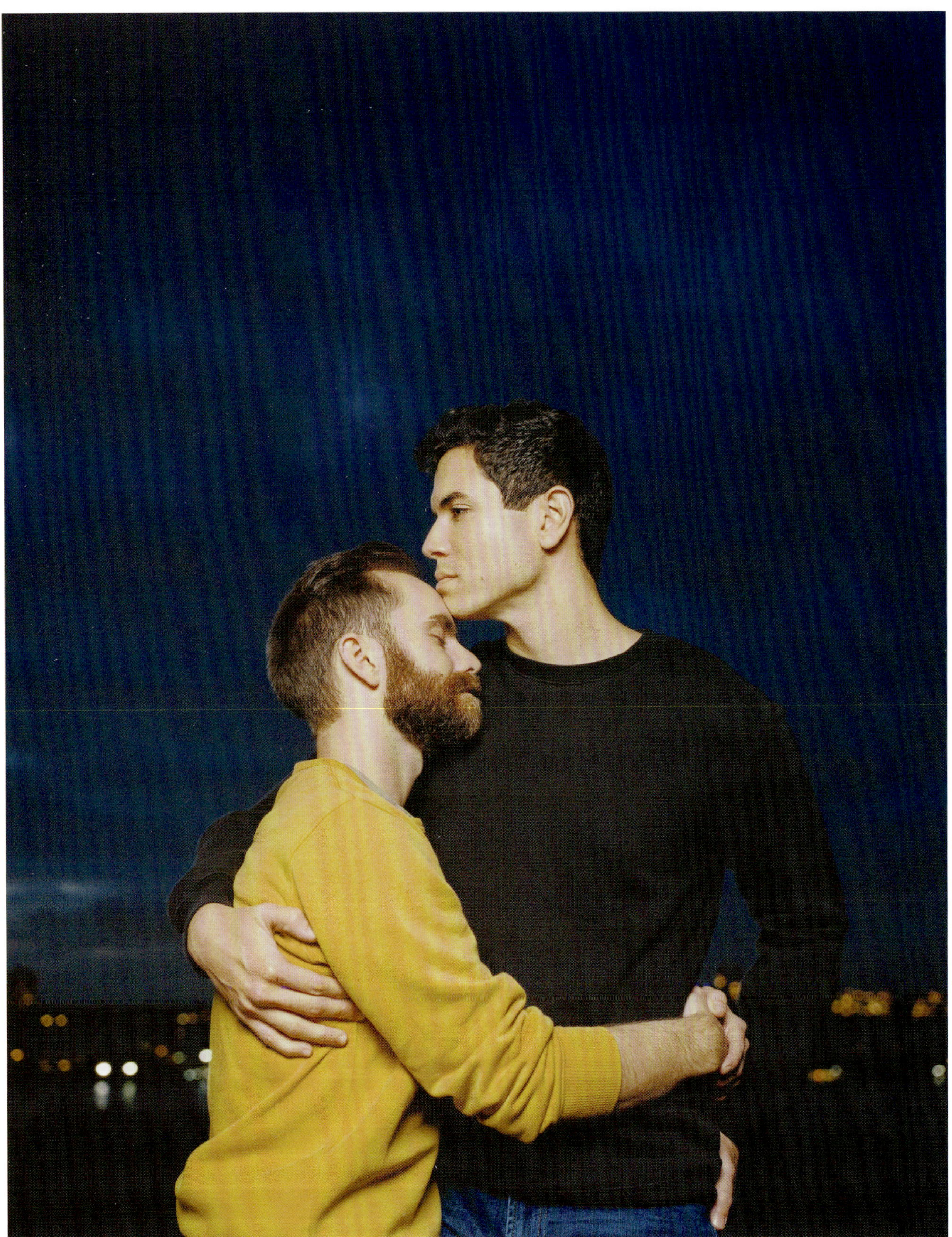

Jason *(He/Him)* & Michael *(He/Him)*

NEW YORK, NY

MICHAEL

This photo was taken five days before our wedding. Preoccupied and anxious, we were amid one of the most hectic weeks of our lives. But despite the never-ending list of things to do, we took this opportunity to slow down and hold each other, letting ourselves be captured in the intimate days leading up to making the biggest commitment we would ever make—marriage to another human being.

As cisgendered gay men in our thirties, we were born and raised in a time when marriage was not yet an option for same-sex couples. Nonetheless, Jason had always dreamt of making that commitment to someone. Michael, on the other hand, was less certain... not of the commitment itself, but of the institution of marriage that is treated as the end goal for all "serious" couples. Time and time again, we've been told that marriage is the logical next step for two people who want to spend the rest of their lives together. But instead of blindly following the heteronormative path that had already been laid out for us, Michael wanted to examine why. What, exactly, would marriage bring us that we didn't already have?

Okay... marriage has some legal perks, to be sure. But when it came to throwing a wedding, we still had some thinking to do. Ultimately, we decided that our wedding would be a celebration of our community, the people who helped us get here. The support of our families and chosen families has been the bedrock of our foundation. Without them, there is no us. Our wedding would pay homage to our loved ones while also giving us the opportunity to promise a steadfast commitment to one another.

As we cycled through all the words and phrases that would come together to create our wedding vows, the word we kept coming back to was *growth*. Vastly different from when we first met, the promise to grow alongside and through one another was perhaps the most important promise we would make in a few days. Marriage wouldn't serve as some sort of security blanket, but as an oath to move through life together honoring the ways in which we would inevitably change.

Defining marriage on our own terms was something that we took enormous pride in as part of the queer community. Our rules, our way. And in case you were wondering, the wedding was perfect.

Jay *(He/Him)* & Zach *(He/Him)*

COLUMBUS, OH

We are vastly different people. But if anything, our differences made our connection stronger because they broadened our perspectives and challenged our own views. After a while, though, we realized that "together" wasn't going to work for us, and we decided to go our separate ways. We could take what we learned together and grow from it. Our journey together was part of our understanding of how we could be better, more compassionate lovers. The passion we shared together doesn't have to leave but can add to the burning fuel that ignites our spirits.

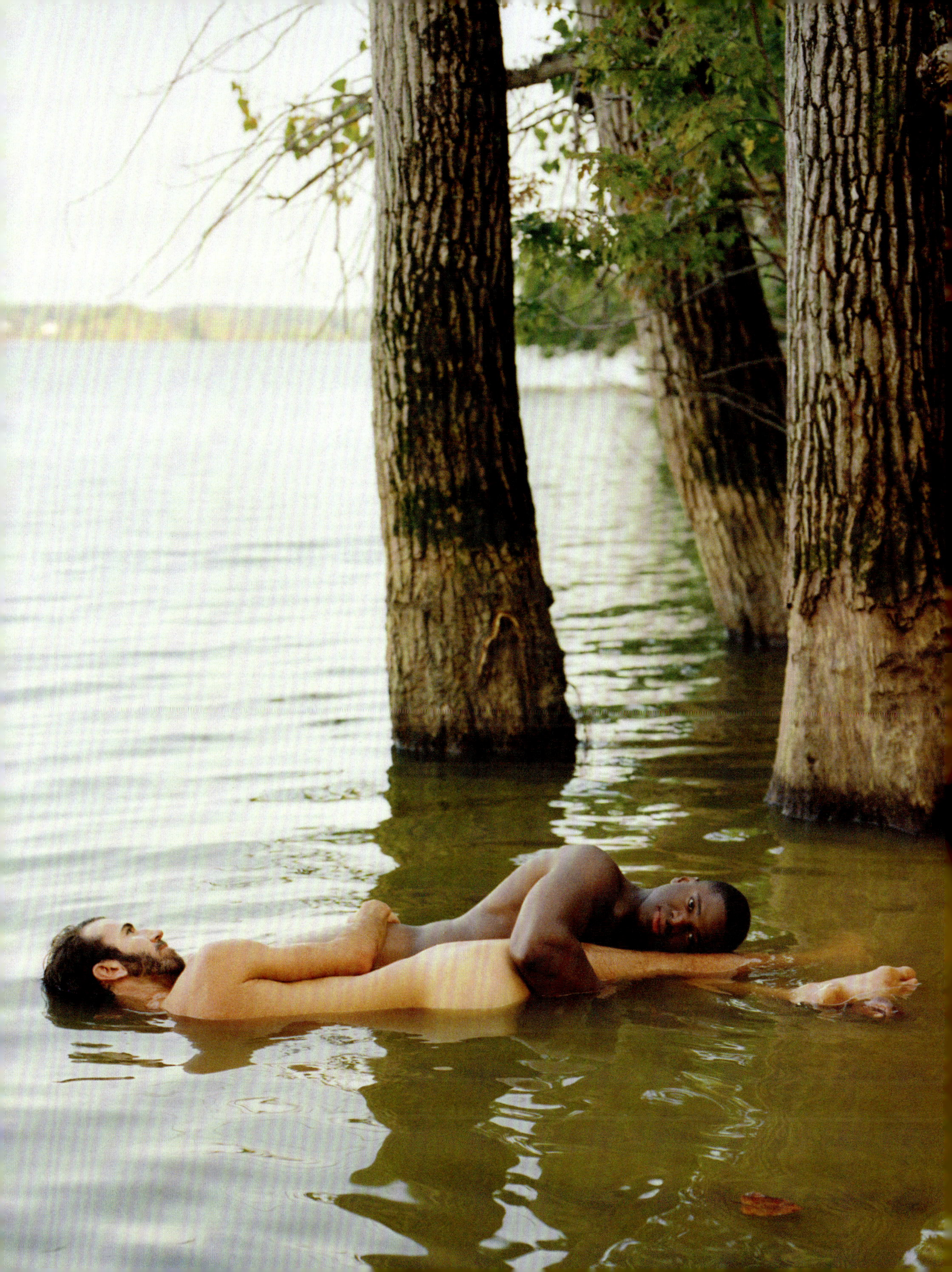

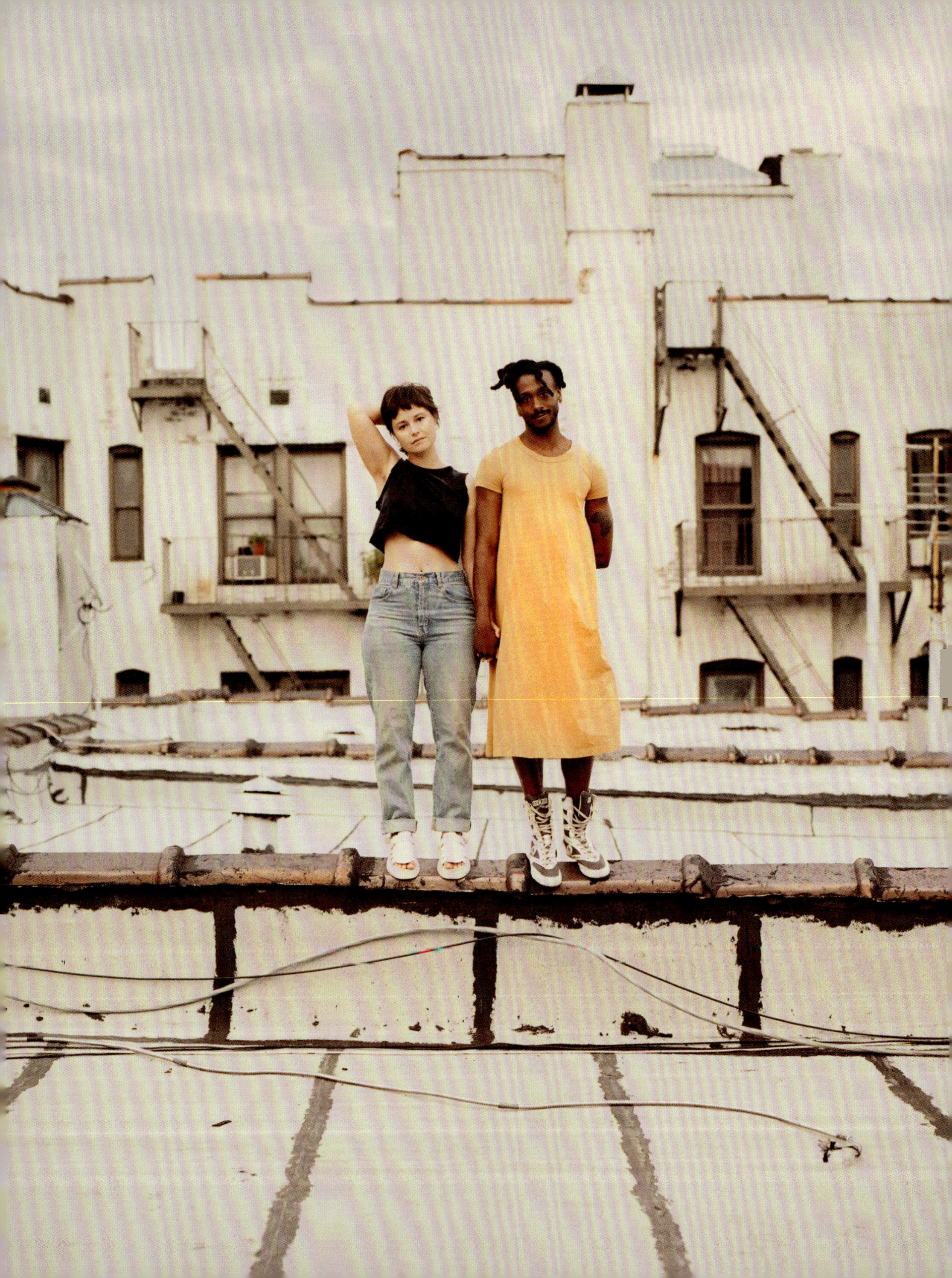

Jo *(They/Them)* & Zac *(They/Them)*

BROOKLYN, NY

JO

We fell in love over the phone. Covid hit shortly after we met, and Zac got stuck in North Carolina, while I was in New York. They would ask me on these phone dates, and I found it cute how formal they were about it. By the time they moved back to New York in July, we were in love, although it was a while before we said it. We are different in many ways—the obvious things like race and nationality, but also in our characters, our rhythms, our interests. Mostly it feels kind of miraculous to us how different we are, as in, how did we even find each other? We've both had some bad experiences in queer spaces, which has made us very careful about figuring out our own dynamic, what queerness is for us, trying not to be idealistic about it. We talk a lot about race, gender, and sexuality, but increasingly it feels like those things slip away, like we lose ourselves in the nuance of being together, which is its own creative thing that we are figuring out in real time.

ZAC

We keep, I think, moving further away from the performance of gender, even as others continue to read it into our bodies and relationship. At the level of intimacy we strive for, the very notion of discrete locality must be called into question, and the ideological matrix of gender is not only problematic but so obsolete as to be without any merit of consideration, at least between us. What can I say other than it is incredibly life-affirming when Jo and I are able to achieve the level of coordination needed to experience the sensation of "them," and that it helps when I say "I love them" or "I trust them."

Jobel *(He/Him)* & Joey *(He/They)*

LOS ANGELES, CA

JOBEL

On New Year's Day 2021, Joey and I sat at our kitchen table to discuss how we would have an open marriage. It was an awkward conversation at first, but in the end, we were both satisfied to admit our desires and confront our relationship. Growing up in Filipino and Mexican households, both Joey and I didn't have examples of unconventional marriages. We experienced marriages only from a traditional point of view, so deciding to challenge that was scary for us. We feared that we could potentially do this wrong and damage our relationship. But as we talked about rules and boundaries for this "new marriage," we realized how deeply we love each other. We remembered that two years earlier we had spent New Year's Day in the hospital, lying in bed together. We were reminded how vulnerable life is and how lucky we are to have each other. That was just an example of what we've been through as a couple. It encouraged us to view this step as progress in our relationship and not something to fear or feel ashamed of. The beauty that we are coming to experience in owning our sexuality is that we can define what it means for us and how we want to experience it. Joey and I dated for four years and have been married for almost three years. It feels right that we are evolving, growing independently, and yet somehow managing to support each other on our separate journeys.

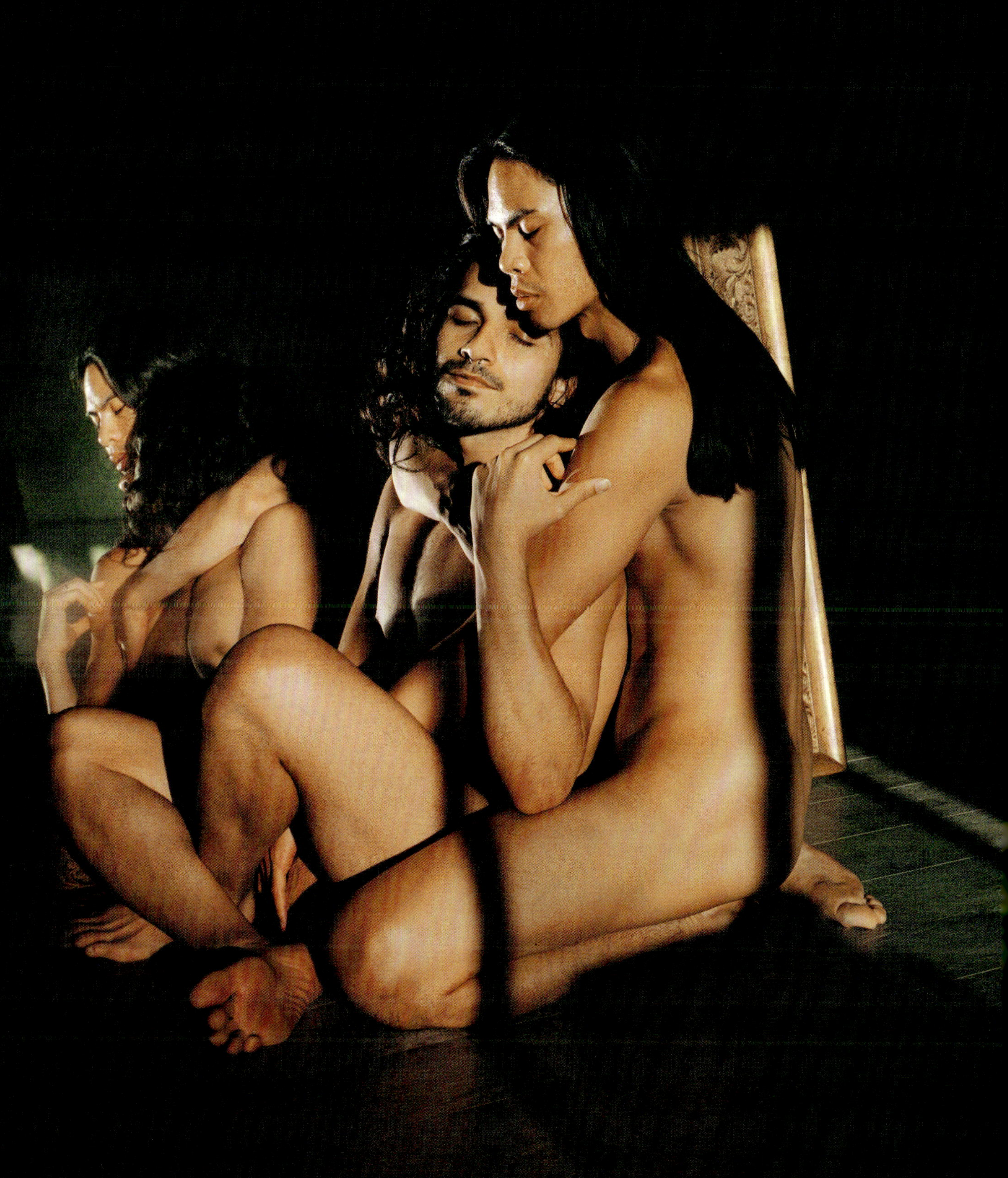

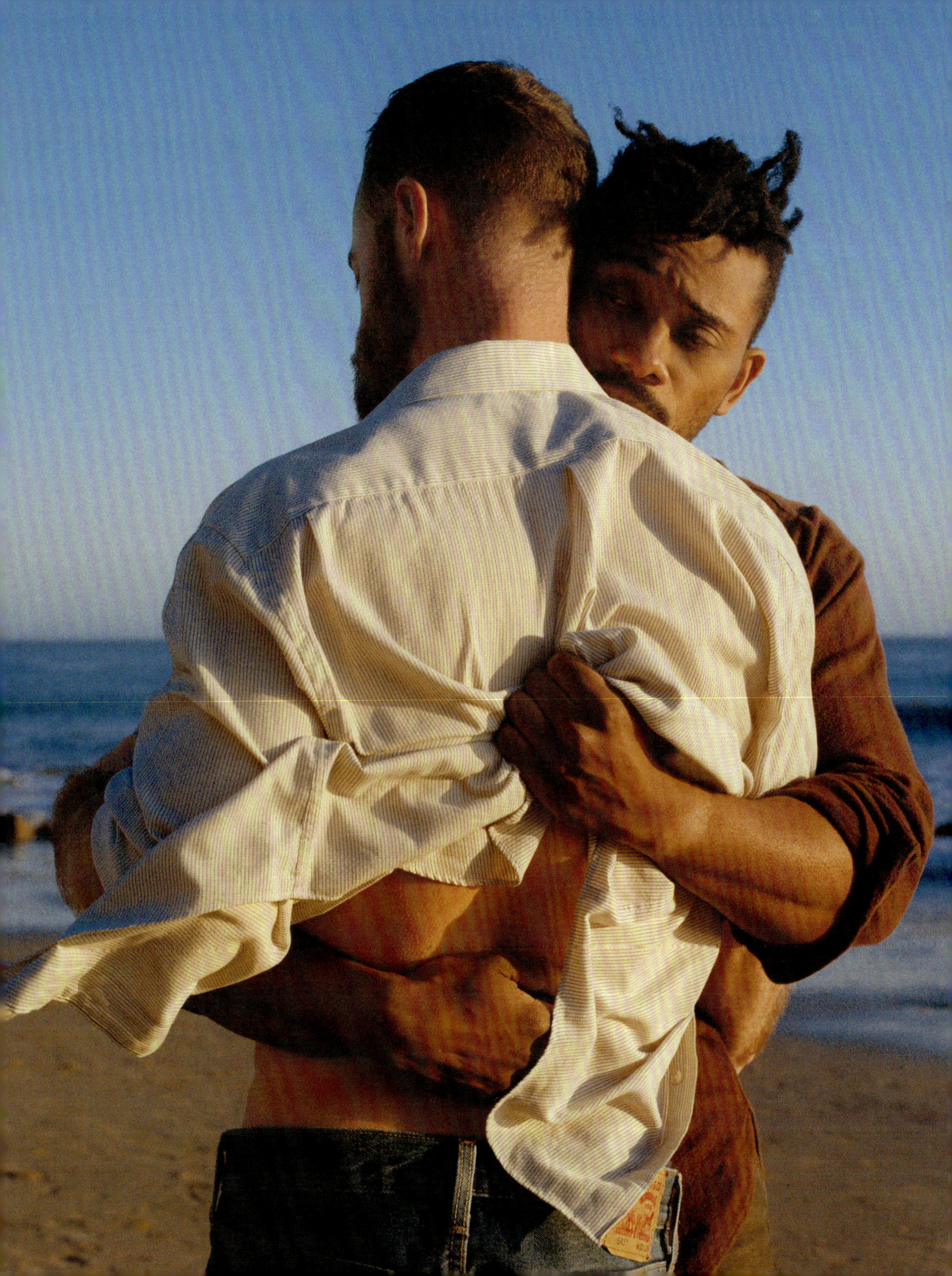

Joel *(He/Him)* & Justin *(He/Him)*

LOS ANGELES, CA

JOEL

We met through a now-defunct gay dating site. I messaged him because his profile auto-played a song by Xiu Xiu, an obscure-ish musician I liked. I thought, "Wow, he's cute and cool." He was in Los Angeles and I was in New York, and we were both so, so broke. We messaged all day every day, but could only afford to visit each other every few months. For Christmas I bought him a plane ticket that cost a couple months' disposable income.

After a year, he moved to New York and moved in with me. The first weekend after he moved here, he made cookies and we took the subway to the beach. The water was so warm and we were both so excited. It was one of the best beach days, one of the best weekends.

A few years ago, we invented the concept of a love ricochet: when you're having a great day, your happiness and excitement about the world radiates and bounces around and hits someone and you love them extra. And when you love someone, it radiates and bounces and hits the world and you're extra happy and excited about your day.

We became official ten years ago. Since then, there've been a lot of ricochets and weekends like that first one.

JUSTIN

When Joel and I met, I was jobless, fighting cancer, and living in my childhood home. I lacked anything anyone would call privilege. Maybe that made Joel feel safe to love me. And because I could glimpse the value he saw in me, I felt safe to love him back.

I was taught we're made whole only when we're with someone else. That lacking is necessary for love. That no one is enough on their own. This belief makes self-fulfillment a relationship hazard. When we think this way, we deny ourselves love's greatest power and virtue—that we love not because we need to, but because we choose to anyway.

At first our relationship felt easy, filling each other in, creating one whole. But we soon learned that those parts of each of us that felt empty were room for self-growth. And in the ten years we've been together, we have both grown so much—for each other, despite each other, with each other. And year after year we rise to the challenge of accepting our and each other's new shapes, choosing to love each other again, and again.

Johnny *(He/Him)* & Will *(He/Him)*

LOS ANGELES, CA

JOHNNY

I don't remember the specific moment that I noticed, but I remember talking about race/privilege etc. and just being taken aback by how much work and understanding Will already had. I had assumed there would be a lot of "teaching" because of our different identities and how we show up in the world, but it always felt like we were having these conversations with very few teachable moments. It opened my eyes to the idea that there are white folks and allies doing the work.

I identify as a cis queer man and Will does as well, so I think there are a lot of similarities, but because of the other layers with me being Latine etc., it offers more conversations about how we as queer men stand up for others unlike us. It was always such a bonding experience to be able to have these conversations. I still remember Will's mom asking me if there were any Thanksgiving family recipes my mom made that she could try so that I'd feel more at home when I went to their family's Thanksgiving celebration. It was so sweet and really showed where Will's care for others comes from.

When Will and I made the transition from partners to best friends it felt seamless and almost like a rebirth. I mean we absolutely shed tears and had moments, but the love was always there and has never left. The idea of a soul mate to me doesn't mean that it can only be one person. So often we shove people into boxes in our lives to fit some societal inventory, but Will surpasses all of them. While our relationship isn't currently romantic, I find not much has changed in his importance in my life. This transition and new definition for us feels exactly like our romantic partnership did: a relationship without judgment, full of support, love, and mutual understanding.

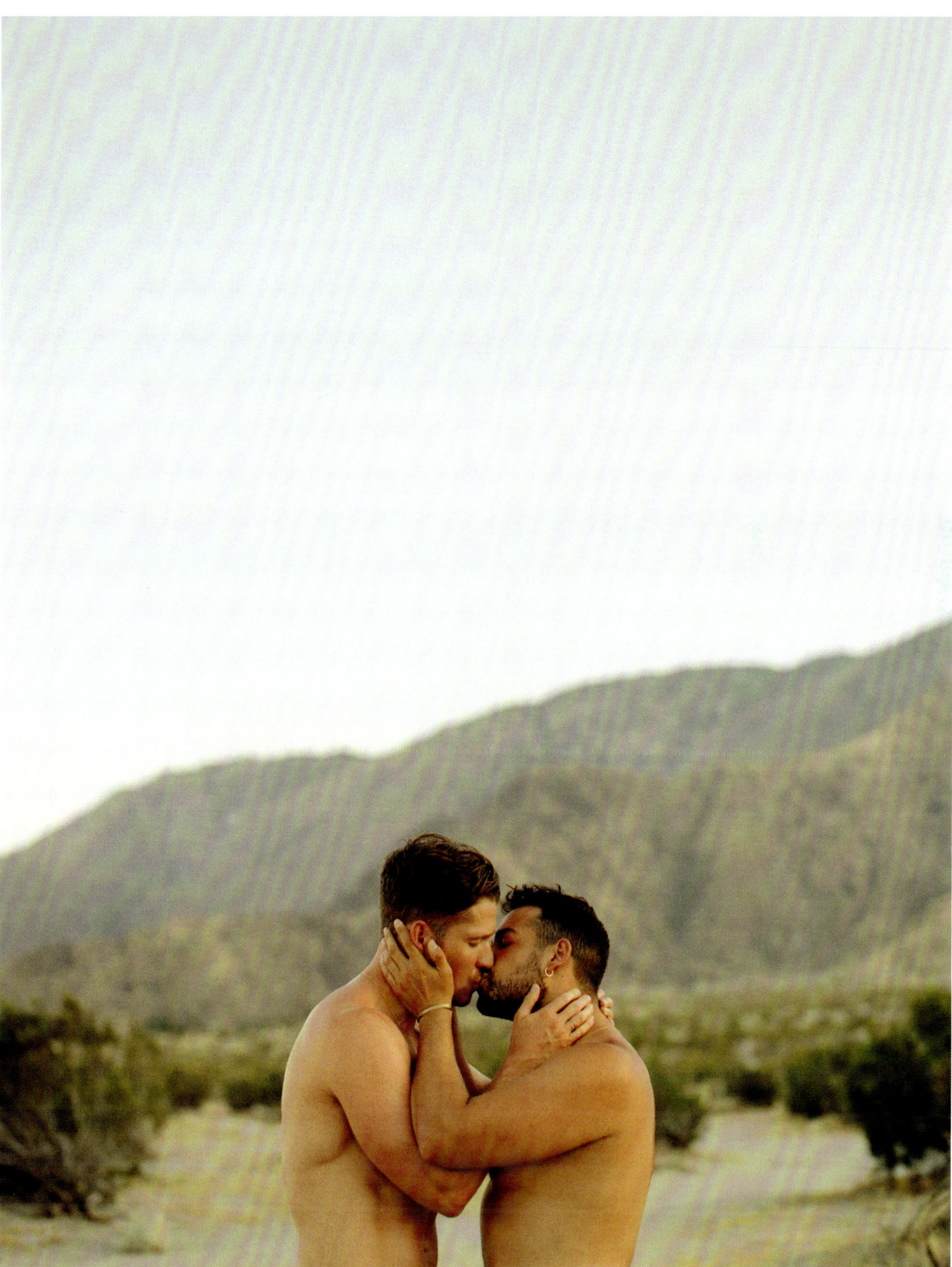

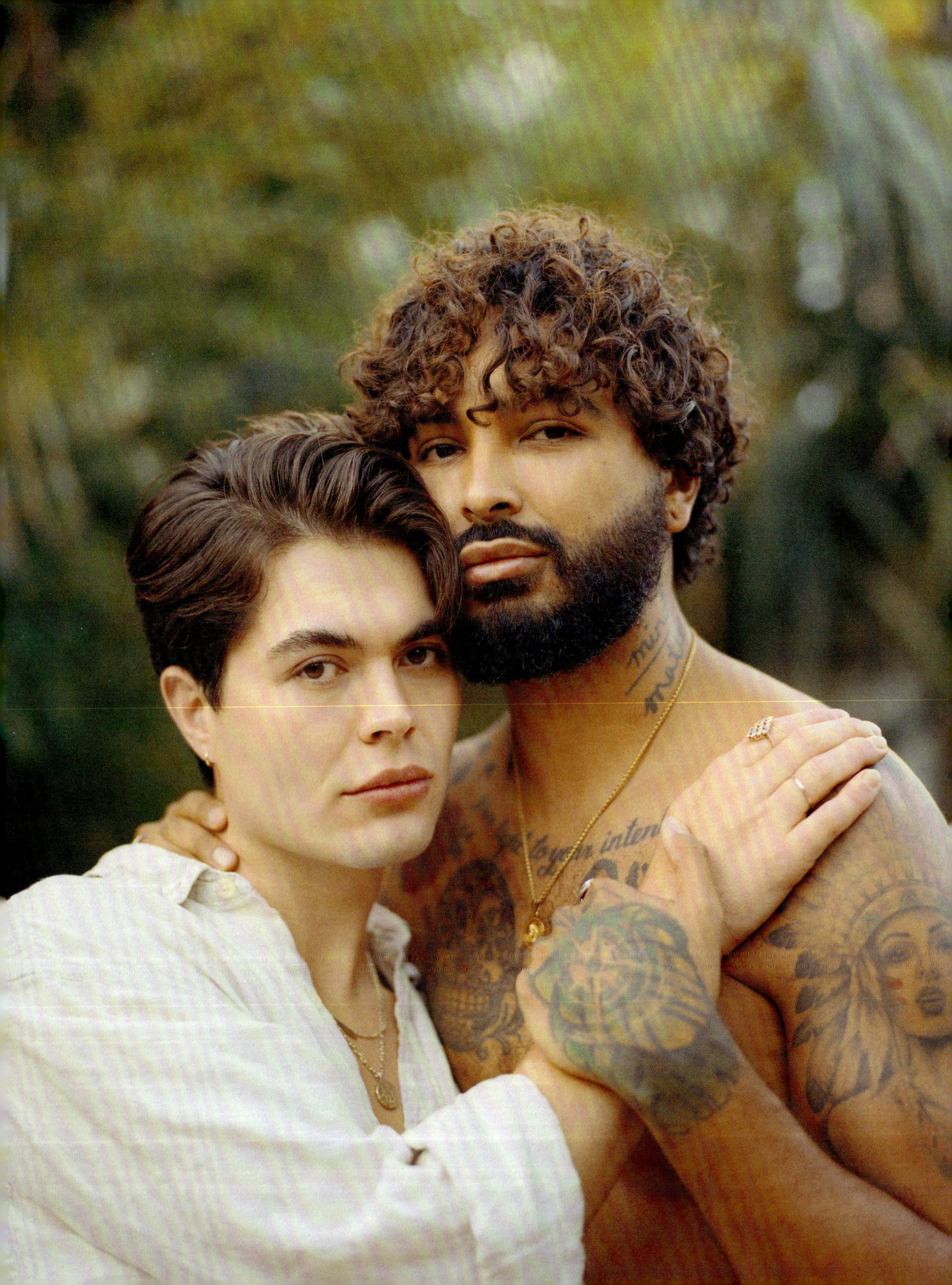

Jorden *(He/Him)* & Eamon *(He/Him)*

LOS ANGELES, CA

JORDEN

Privilege has been a very consistent discussion in the three and a half years that we've been together. We are six years apart in age but belong to different generations. So, it has been a patient practice of understanding and communication to make sure we feel supported. How we were raised directly correlates to how we perceive not only the world but each other, and as a result, it influences our dispositions as individuals as well.

Though Eamon is multiracial and feels connected to being Hispanic, he is generally perceived to be white. Whereas I, also multiracial, am ethnically ambiguous and have had a harder time identifying with a specific heritage. Both of us have had to face outrageous discrimination. Eamon, who is a drag performer, was asked by a member of our own community not to perform songs by artists of color because it offended Black and Brown people. When I have stood up for social injustice and prejudice, the validity of my "Blackness" has come into question (by Black and Brown people). Sometimes, the hard reality is that we are ostracized by the very communities we belong to, simply because we don't look the part.

Joseph *(He/Him)* & James *(He/Him)*

BROOKLYN, NY

JOSEPH

I first met James at a twelve-step meeting. I was broken, maybe on the way to being less broken. He was vibrant in a pink crop top. But he conspicuously avoided me. There was so much that I didn't know in those early days, about myself, about life, and James just sort of let me process. I think it is beautiful that we met in recovery, as part of an ongoing negotiation of spirituality, despair, joy, and potential. Eventually we managed to break down some of the pretense, even the fear, and—I don't know how else to say it—live a good life.

I'm Cherokee, and we have a notion of living in a good way that is core to our ethics. So, to do that I have to be honest with myself and with others. And James and I have been very honest with each other about what we each need and why we need it. Of course, we navigate the world in different ways. That much is unavoidable. But what makes sense about it to me is that there is something at the core of our relationship that has to do with having an honest humility and a drive for truth. This may sound abstract, but I'm talking about not letting the small things accumulate into big things; having the ability to admit when we are wrong, or when we have done wrong. The ability to admit when we don't know something. We're both still working on all of it! But part of the deal is that I have been able to become more rooted in myself and my own culture because of the space that such a relationship affords me. There is tremendous power in that, in knowing that the process of knowing love is part of the story we create in relation.

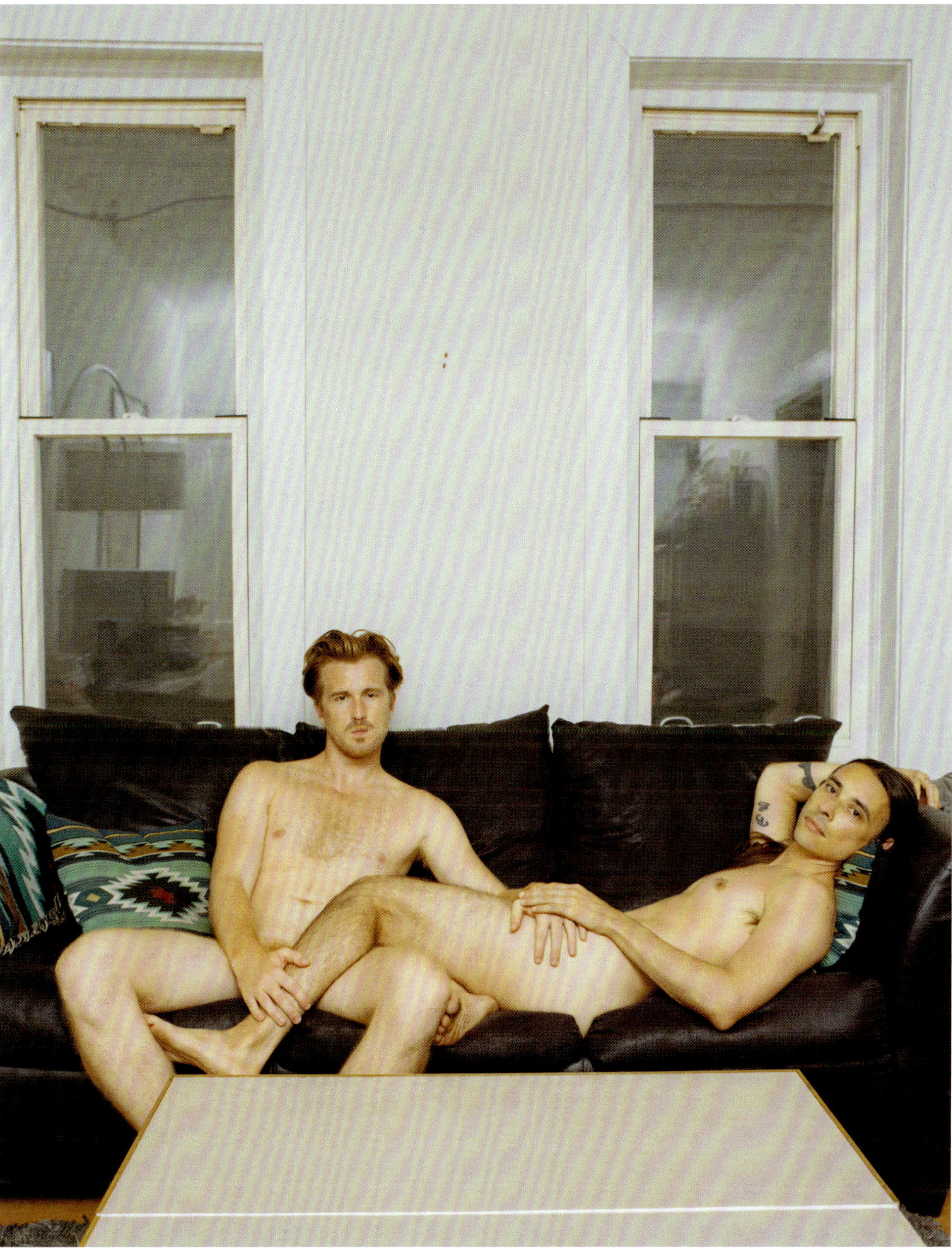

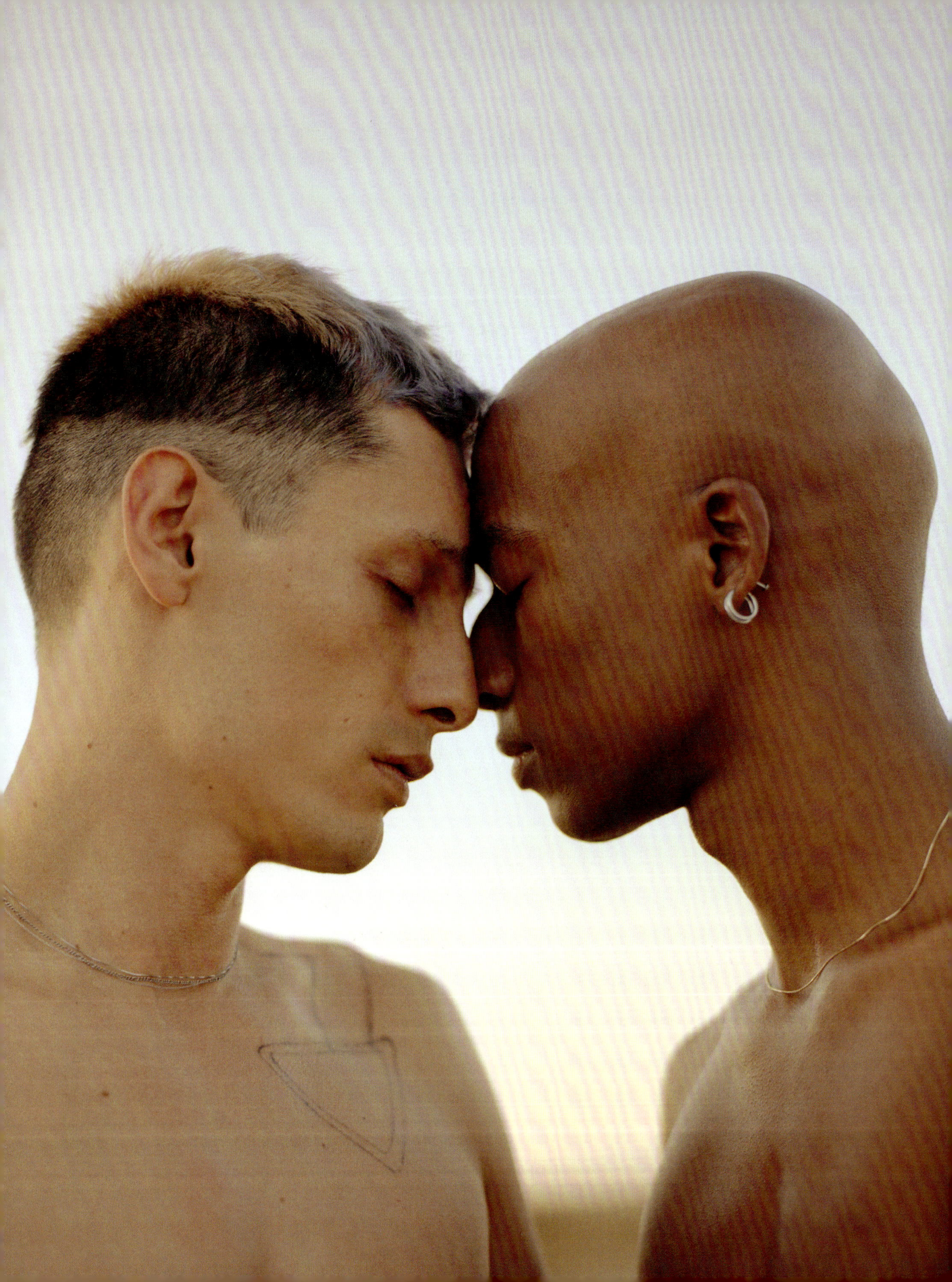

Juan *(He/Him)* & Tyler *(He/Him)*

JOSHUA TREE, CA

JUAN & TYLER

We met in a dark warehouse under a strobe light, drowned in hard techno. It was an angry time. A few days before the 45th's inauguration. We didn't speak to each other for the first hour, only a few taps and nudges with our feet and elbows before finally locking eyes. Since then, step by step, we've continued to walk forward by moving toward each other.

Over our five years together, we have slowly learned to let each other see the parts we had never shown anyone else. Letting go of unspoken expectation allows us to navigate our relationship with compassion and kindness.

We understand that we, like love, are imperfect—mostly beautiful, but sometimes ugly. Working through the ugly times has brought a level of deep trust within ourselves and each other that we had not experienced until now. It's magical, and we are forever grateful for the night we both slugged onto the dance floor and embraced each other.

Julius *(He/Him)* & Enzo *(He/Him)*

BROOKLYN, NY

JULIUS

The words "Once you have seen / You cannot unsee" are engraved across our wedding rings (which are made to fit perfectly together, like puzzle pieces). This is the truth that we have come to know about our union. We have the tacit understanding that committing to our love is a necessary act of faith.

When we first met, the electricity of our courtship was like a bolt of recognition that collapsed any distance between us. As I discovered more of Enzo's magic, I glimpsed reflections of the deepest parts of myself.

I am a child of the Jamaican diaspora and the promise of my ancestors' dreams. My roots are nourished by our culture of joy and my grandmother's lessons of worthiness, work, and generosity.

Enzo was raised in the south of France, and his cultural values, his passionate and open Mediterranean spirit, are things I hope to nurture in children of my own. It was this recognition that led to my realization that I want to start a family with Enzo, and I knew there was no going back.

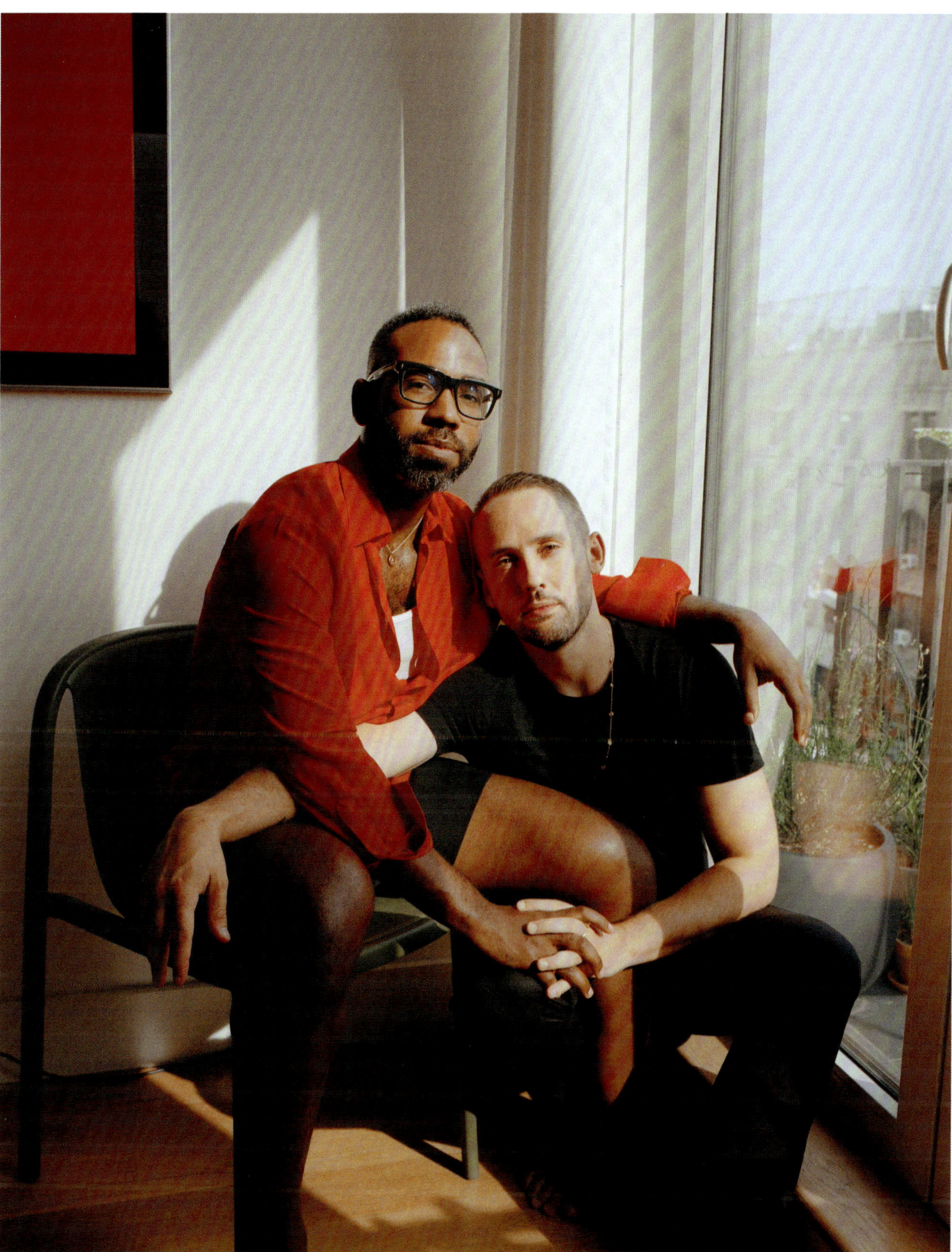

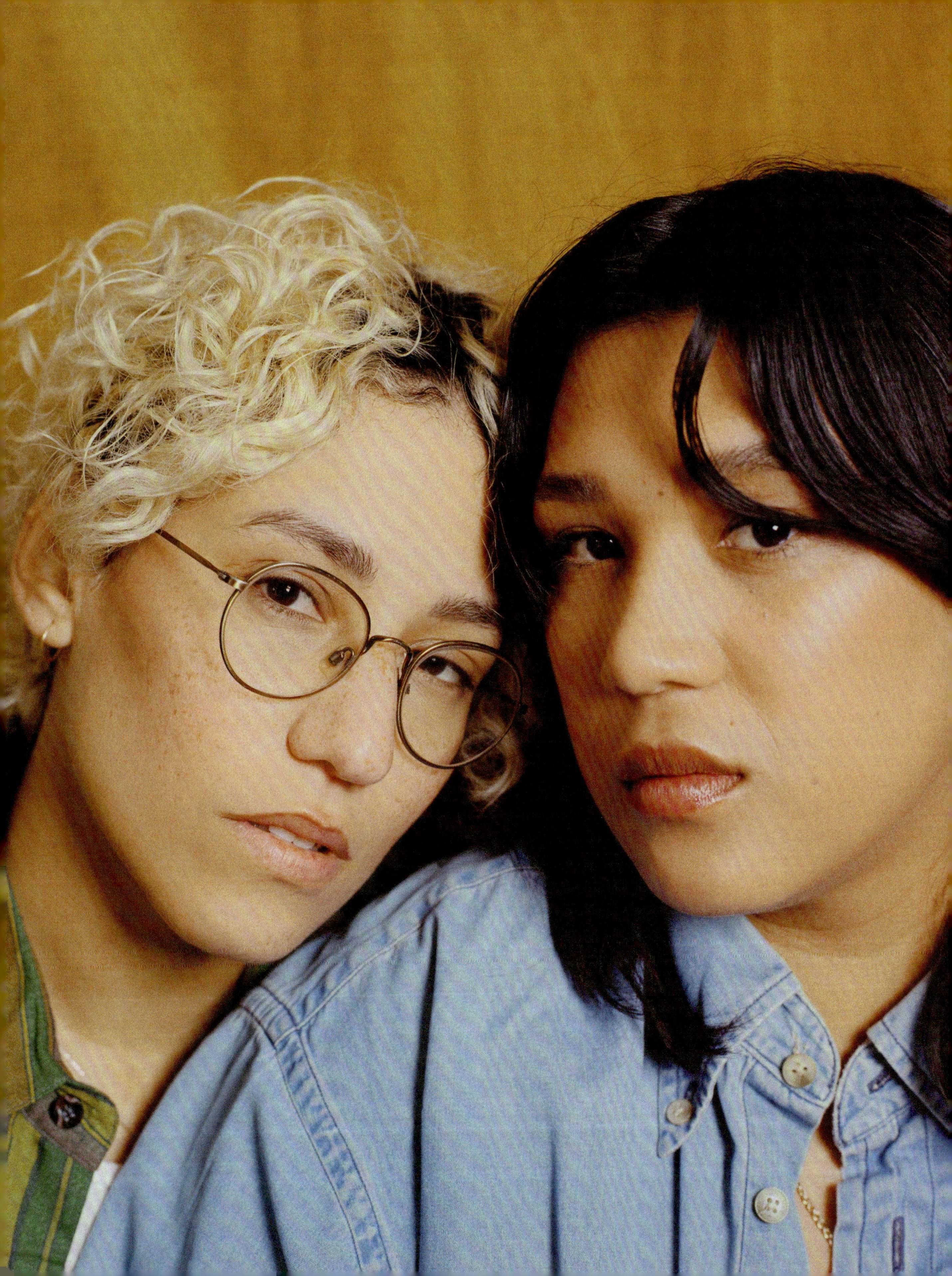

Keila *(They/Them)* & Jazz *(She/They)*

LOS ANGELES, CA

KEILA & JAZZ

We've been together for the better part of 4,000 days. Throughout our entire twenties. People often look at us in bewilderment that we've been together as long as we have. But at some point, we realized that there wasn't some unspoken secret to relationships. All it really takes is a choice. We were best friends, and the foundation of respect and transparency we had to build upon was firm. So was our desire to not mess up the very meaningful friendship we had built.

It hasn't been free from adversity. It isn't all romance and butterflies, though there is still plenty of that. It's seeing each other through the toughest shit. Saying the things that are painful to say because it means honesty. Being queer, we didn't necessarily have a clear-cut framework for what a partnership should look like. It's freeing and inspiring. It means designing a full life for ourselves that wasn't mapped out. It's standing at the precipice of a turning point and knowing that we are free to leave but want to stay. It's enduring through discomfort. Holding ourselves accountable. Making safe spaces where there never were any. It's deconstructing the idea of who we should be and empowering each other to become whoever we are.

We've managed to grow into many different iterations of the two humans we were when we started this journey eleven years ago, and we continue to make the choice to stay together. We grow out and in and sideways and apart and somehow we keep growing our way back to one another.

We've been told, "If you don't make it then love doesn't exist." But we feel the opposite. If we don't make it and we gave it all we had and loved each other enough to see that we need new soil to grow, then that is entirely proof that love exists. That the love we have for one another is not selfish. That love can exist for the sake of loving. And if the day ever comes that we can't continue to flourish hand in hand, then we know we will have been better for this journey. So, while we're here, we keep choosing to make a home in each other.

KT *(They/Them)* & Jax *(He/Him)*

BROOKLYN, NY

KT

The party was men-at-work themed. I dressed as a Trader Joe's manager and Jax was an overly cautious night runner, complete with short shorts and a reflective vest. In reality, I am a (newly out) genderqueer, agnostic Filipinx, and Jax is a gay, trans Jewish man. We were both single and looking for completely different things. Jax was only interested in dating men. My biggest rule was "no more white men." We would have never picked each other out from a lineup of potential romantic options.

Jax was one of three people to ask me out that day and the one that checked the fewest of my boxes. But something told me to give him a shot. On our first date, we went roller skating at a covered outdoor rink. While it rained outside the rink, we talked openly about our childhoods, our dreams, and what we wanted our families to look like. We even talked about Israel and Palestine, a conversation neither of us thought we would have on our first date, but it set a tone for us. One that's honest and transparent, where we are willing to have these hard discussions. It helped us relax and allowed us to feel comfortable discussing their identities and hardships with each other, trusting that we would fully hear each other. Our date lasted five hours. While we were eating ice cream, looking at the NYC skyline, I asked if I could kiss Jax. It was the first time I kissed someone on a first date.

Each of us went home with a list of things to learn so we could better understand each other. Jax spent hours listening to podcasts and reading about Filipino culture, food, history, and language. I watched videos posted by trans men about medical transitioning, current legislature, and societal issues that affect the trans community. We learned the vocabulary surrounding the other's struggles, building our cultural competencies so we could hear each other with more humility.

JAX

In a lot of ways, our relationship feels cosmic—we even have the same birthday. It feels like we were meant to meet at this time in our lives as these versions of ourselves. We have very different upbringings and identities, but we also share experiences and traits we thought no one else would understand. Our strength lies in our desire to learn more about each other, even when conversations are hard. By doing so, we have been able to explore ourselves and our identities, as well as deepen our relationship in ways neither of us has ever done before. In the past few months, KT realized that they are non-binary and has spent emotional energy learning about themselves and sharing this news with their loved ones. I resumed my journey toward the transition goals that I had put on hold during a time when I felt more alone. The unconditional love and support that we provide for each other—both when experiencing situations that the other understands and situations that the other can never imagine themselves in—is what keeps us going. Our relationship requires the work that neither of us ever expected another person to do for each other. Yet, it doesn't feel hard. Together we are constantly listening, learning, and adapting. We might not have checked each other's boxes, but maybe the boxes were wrong.

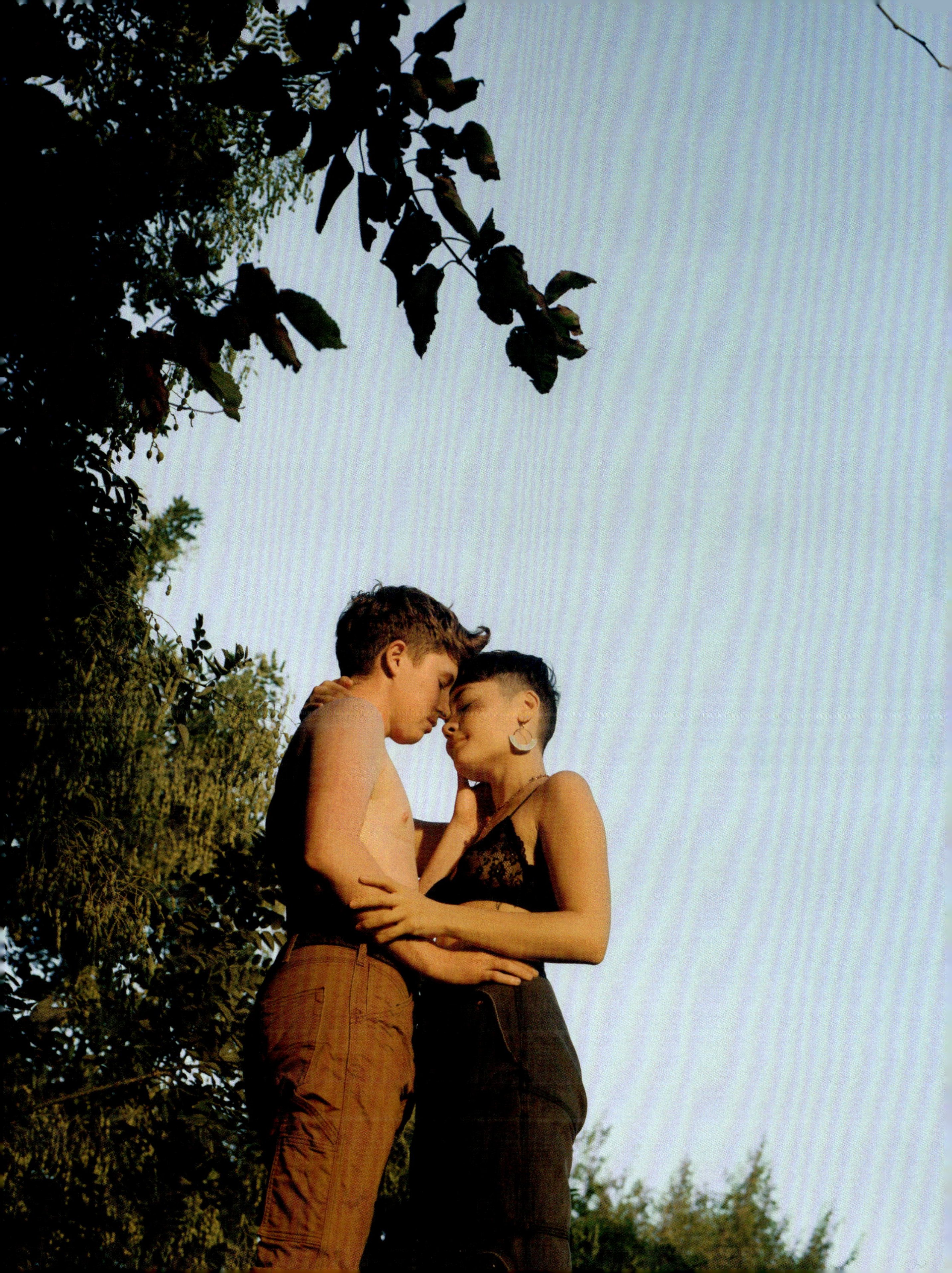

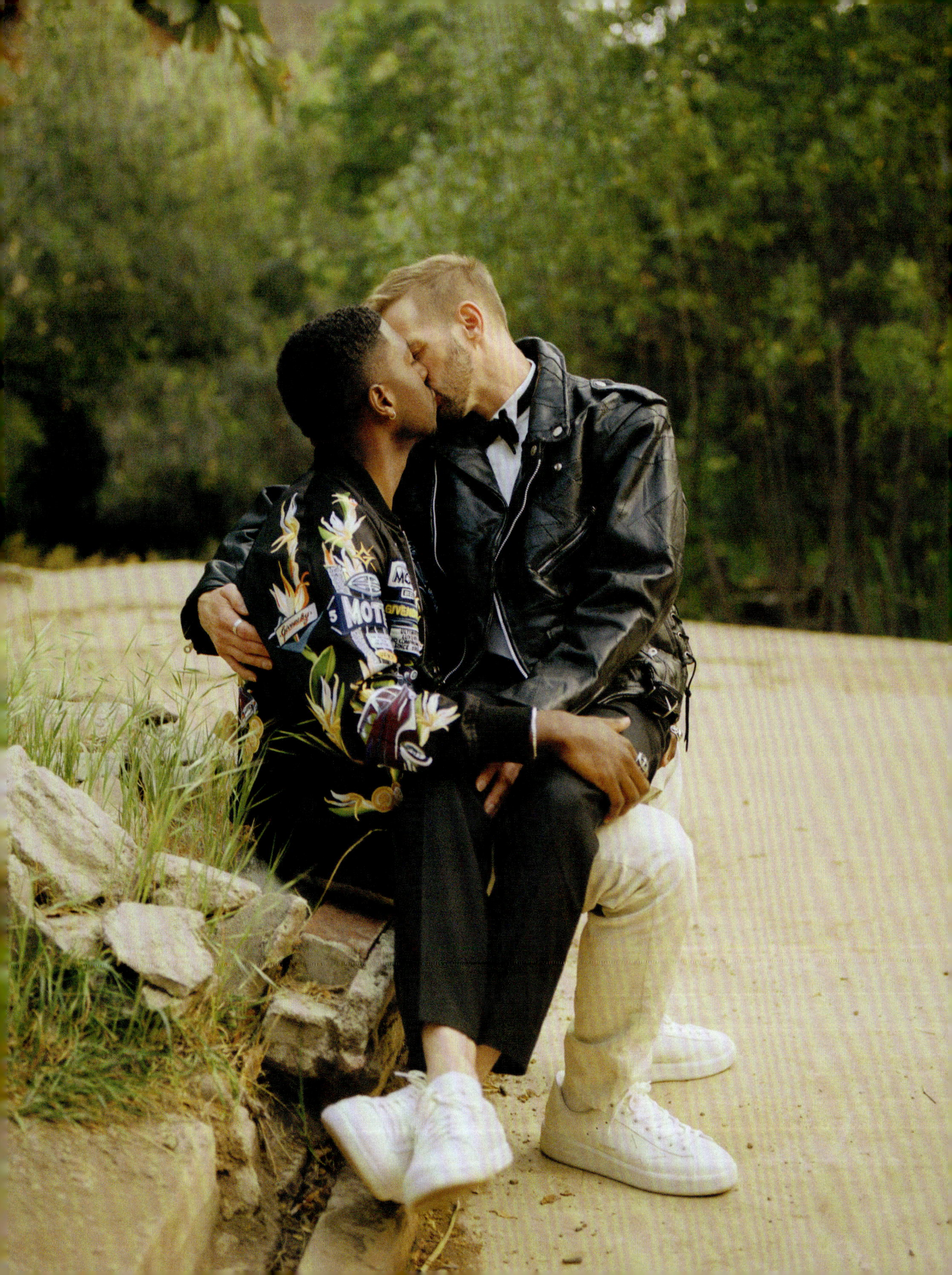

Kwaku *(He/Him)* & Peter *(He/Him)*

LOS ANGELES, CA

KWAKU

When we look at this photo, it is impossible for us not to feel the connection. We are different races, ages, and nationalities, and yet our differences have added tremendous perspective and helped us grow. We have challenged each other's thoughts, emotions, beliefs, and values. Unlike us, love is not black and white.

When I met Peter, I was not a complete individual. I still had a lot of learning and growing to do. I was always an open-minded person, but I was not out. This was a very difficult time in my life because the beliefs and experiences I had come to know as an adult conflicted with those I learned during my upbringing. I didn't possess the intellectual capacity to understand my sexuality, because I had never afforded myself the mental freedom to do so. This all becomes incredibly complicated when you choose self-hate then meet someone who "sees" you.

I ran a marathon from myself. Feeling judged and stripped by my own thoughts and projections. I felt naked in front of everyone I interacted with, constantly living with the fear and danger of being discovered by anyone who peered deep enough into a closet to find me. I never asked to be there after all, it's like society places you there. I eventually chose freedom from depression and confusion. I discovered my queerness wasn't a flaw but a profound strength. What could be stronger than accepting yourself?

PETER

When I met Kwaku, I was not spiritual. It was not until later that my spirituality emerged out of a willingness to be vulnerable. I had no comprehension of how important this was in order for us to be together. Our love for each other grew from our deep spiritual connection. When I reflect now, I realize it existed long before I recognized it. When I finally developed the understanding and the desire to be part of something bigger than myself, it showed up in every aspect of my life, including romantically, and that is a tremendous gift.

I had searched for love, and yet it had always eluded me. I "thought" I was in love, but how could it truly be? The people who professed it were not invested in my growth. Sure, they may have wanted me to change things about myself, but those changes were for them, not for me. I needed to open myself to greater connections, beyond the tangible. In doing so I found vulnerability, spirituality, and the possibility of someone who was so invested in my growth, they could choose not to be with me in order to help me grow. The greatest love of all is to sacrifice your desires to help someone become the person they need to be.

Acknowledging our differences gives us the courage to break out of our own emotional prisons. To shake off conventional thoughts about our races or sexualities. Only then are we able to sincerely learn what it means to love ourselves first. To us this love has and will always remain in our hearts as a miracle love. One that, despite all the odds, lived and breathed and changed our lives forever.

Laurel *(She/Her)* & Peyton *(She/Her)*

LOS ANGELES, CA

LAUREL

Our relationship has evolved so much since we first met. Each year has felt so different—long, short, like we've known each other forever, but also like we're still learning and changing daily.

The last two years have forced us to confront things that otherwise would have taken longer to find. It's also brought us closer in so many ways, brought us to new levels of understanding each other—how we exist in the world, how we process, and the things we each need to feel present, happy, grounded with ourselves and each other.

We started couples therapy this year, something we'd talked about for a while. I've never done that with a partner. It's been good and hard and different than I was expecting. I think it's given us more patience with each other, more flexibility, more willingness to let the other person call us on our shit.

In the past, confronting hard things in relationships felt difficult and scary; I was avoidant in a lot of ways. With Peyton, it's hard at times, but it's also become a lot less scary, which feels like a gift she's given me—the room to build the trust to know that we can get into some hard shit and it'll still be OK, she'll still be there after, and we'll go through it together. Now it feels more like it's just the work that needs to be done, so we can be happy, be better, be good partners to each other.

PEYTON

We talk about race all the time. But there was one night something racist happened to me at work (unfortunately not the first or last time), and while I could feel Laurel being so on my side and so hurt for me, it felt like her allyship was louder than my pain. That was the first time we talked about the way we discuss race with each other, and though I knew her anger was in protection of me, we had to have a conversation about how sometimes I just need to be heard and not necessarily "helped."

We grow together every single day. Sometimes that feels further apart. Sometimes that feels closer than ever. Older. Younger. I like to think wiser, more compassionate, more in love. We've seen so many iterations of one another. I was twenty-four when we met. I look at that girl and she's such a baby version of who I am now. I think I was still trying to find my bearings then, figuring out life and New York and simultaneously falling in love. Laurel was thirty-three, which feels like the last year she stopped considering herself young. Her hair was long. Her walls were up. After three to four years I'd say we're both much softer than we seem. We are both more stubborn than we initially realized and are just so incredibly resilient.

We're currently in relationship therapy, a new frontier for us both, and I worry about where we would be or the things we would have said if we weren't. We communicate in opposition and have such vastly different family dynamics. We needed someone to almost act as a translator for us. We're learning to really listen. We're learning we can't solve everything. We're learning so much more about each other. I think this is the hardest I've ever worked at a relationship and the hardest I've loved as well.

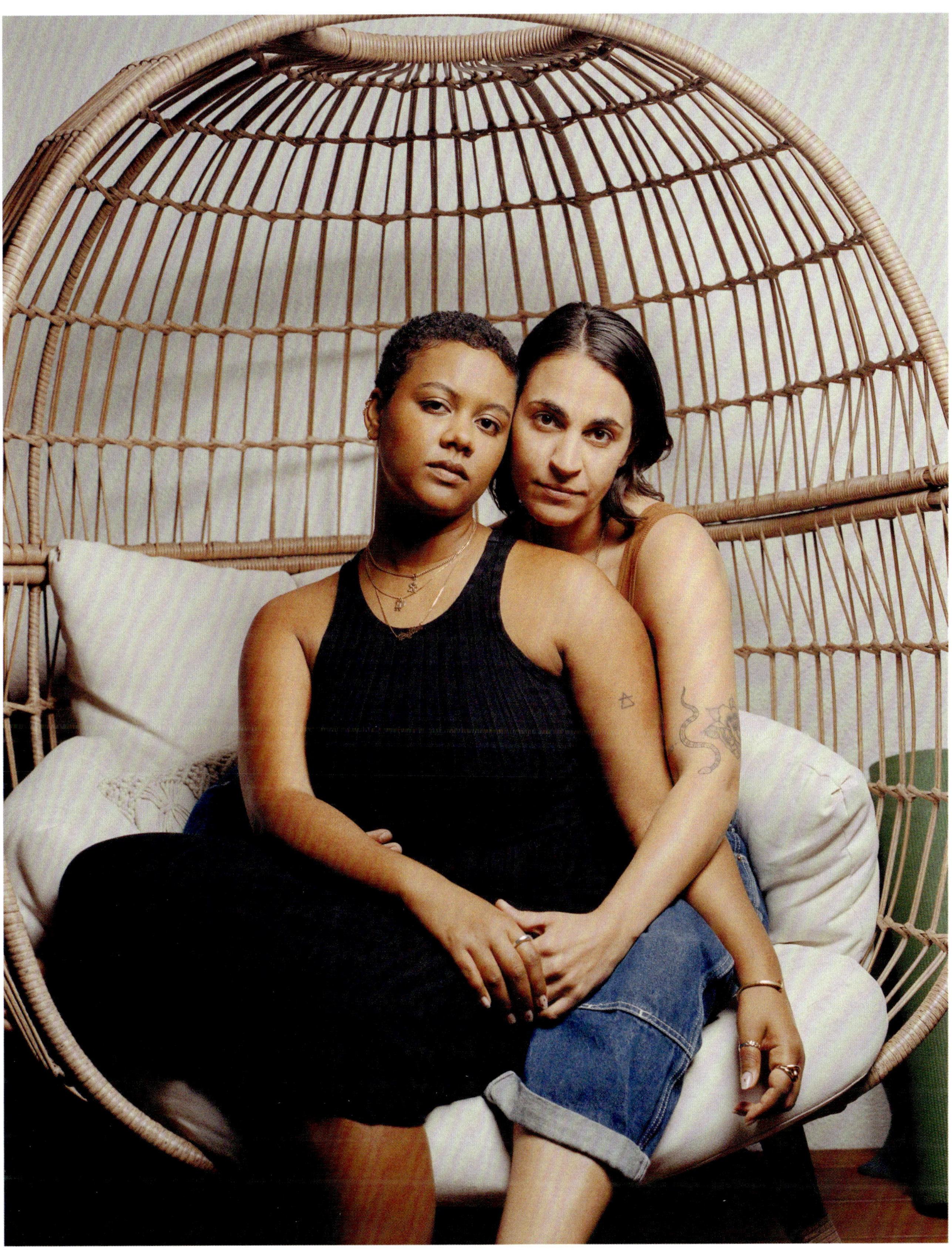

Lee *(They/Them)* **& Victoria** *(She/Her)*

LOS ANGELES, CA

LEE: When we first met, I wasn't looking for anything serious. My friends called me a player. I even used the term *hoetation,* adopted from the HBO series *Insecure*. When I asked Victoria to hang out, I had the same intentions, to be honest. It wasn't until I really got to know her that I was like, "Shit, I really like this person." Some people say it always happens when you're not looking for it or least expect it. And that's truly what happened here. That was spring of 2016 and now we're in 2022. In those six years we've lived in three different places together and even recently just got engaged! We've gone through so much growth individually and together, having met at twenty-three and twenty-four. It's actually been really beautiful to support each other through it all and have someone to lean on when times get tough, and do it in a city that we met in and was all so new to us.

VICTORIA: Lee was definitely in hoetation, and I was told to steer clear by mutual friends. I kept a wall up for a while because, from my own experiences, I generally don't like giving people a chance. I'm usually a long-term relationship person and let very few people into my heart—whether that be a cultural thing or maybe how I was raised. I remember specifically getting to know Lee and thinking this is not my usual route, but who was I to let go of this person actively trying to get to know who I was beyond surface-level knowledge. I'm glad I listened to that voice at the time.

LEE: I identify as a transmasc, nonbinary person. Before I transitioned, I never considered myself a lesbian. I never felt like I really aligned with that term. But I was a "girl" who liked girls, so that had to be it, right? But deep down I knew I never felt like a cisgender female, which is why I struggled with identifying with the term *lesbian*, even though I hadn't yet come to terms with being nonbinary. I knew I felt different but never fully felt male, and at the time I didn't realize you could be somewhere in between, and that gender was a whole wide spectrum! I also identify with queer as an umbrella term when it comes to community. When it comes to my relationship and relationships in general, I know I am sexually attracted to women and in love with Victoria, but I never rule anything out. We are committed to each other, and I love her as a person and a being. But as I've learned, gender is expansive, and people can evolve and tap into something later, and find that they may be attracted to someone whom they never would have imagined. That's the beauty of being queer. It allows you to ebb and flow within gender, orientation, and self-expression.

VICTORIA: I identify as gay/lesbian/queer. It's funny because I always liked and dated femme girls until I met Lee. Maybe it's like what Lee said above with evolving into something you didn't expect of yourself. When we met, Lee was always more masculine but also had that balance of feminine energy in beautiful subtleties. When they told me they felt more nonbinary and wanted to have top surgery, I'll be honest, it was an adjustment for me. I have a hard time with change, even though this made sense to me. You always want your partner to be happy, and I wanted them to do whatever that meant for them.

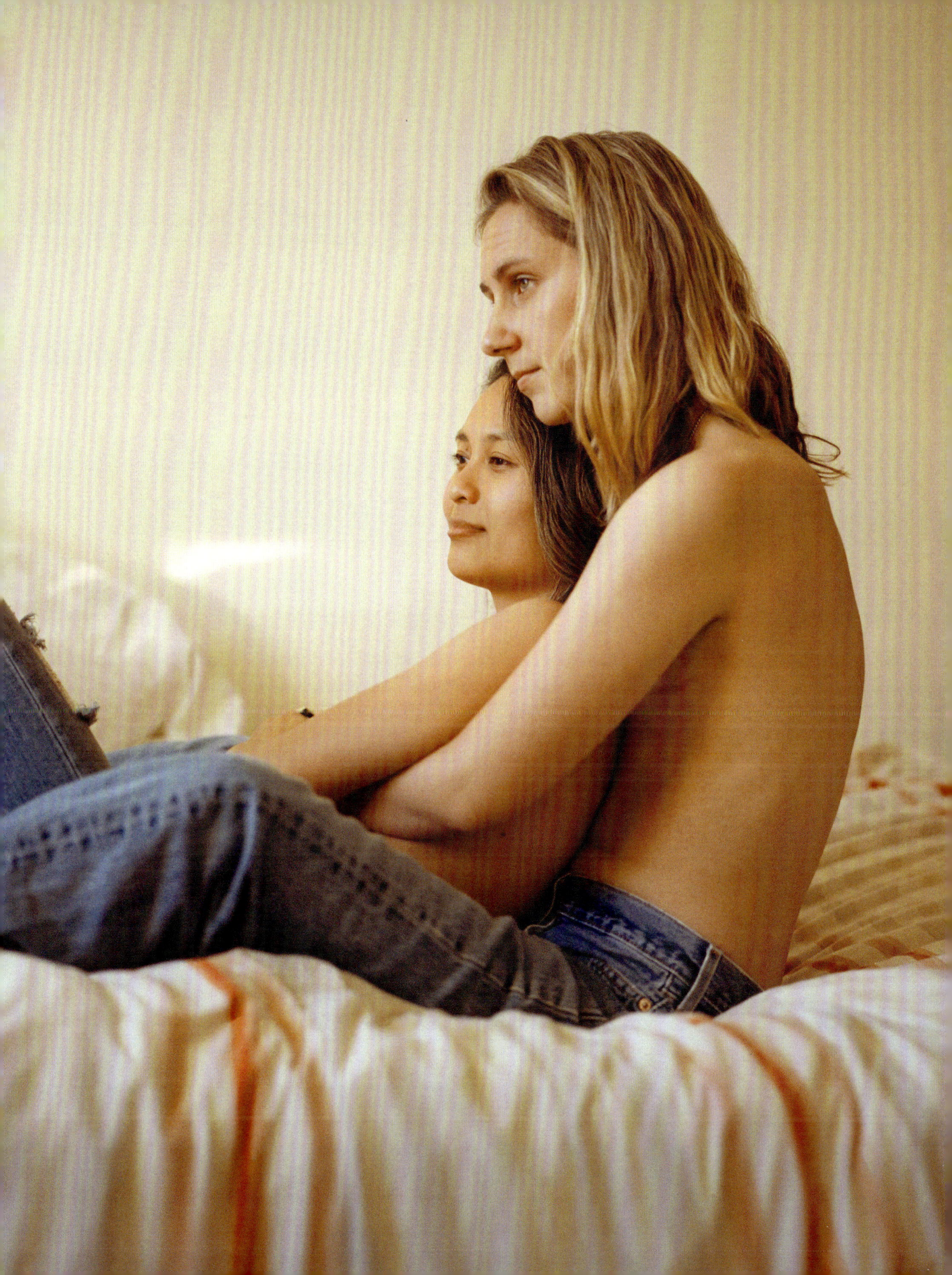

LEE: When Victoria came out to her parents, her mom said some awful things to her that made me hurt terribly for her. I learned that being queer or gay was not accepted in Vietnamese culture. I didn't have the greatest coming-out experiences either, but there is something about seeing your partner in pain that makes you want to take on that pain for them.

One time we were in Anaheim and stopped to eat at Portillo's. An older lady approached us to ask us if we knew where she could refill her soda. We both had our mouths full of food. I couldn't answer, Victoria answered loud and clear. But the woman turned to me and asked if Vicky spoke English. The lady left our table and Vicky immediately started crying. I didn't know how to react to this older lady and protect Victoria at the same time. Do I confront her? Yell at her? I had so many emotions piercing through my veins. Later, when Asian hate crimes were on the rise, I saw how affected Vicky was by the numerous stories coming to light. It was heartbreaking watching her live in fear just to run a simple errand. I wasn't sure I could help her. Even more recently, we had a neighbor's friend cough on our fence and yell, "Covid!" The incident sent Vicky into another spiral and she called me crying. I rushed home to comfort her. I will never know what it is to experience this as a white person, but all I can do is listen to her needs and do my best to help her in these situations.

But I'd be lying if I didn't say I feared it would change my perception and love for them. Not that I was only attracted to the physical parts of them, but I was simply afraid it would change the emotional parts I was connected to. At the end of the day, they were still them and it's been amazing to watch them grow and uncover layers I never even saw before now that they are feeling 100% authentically in their skin.

When starting my own queer journey, I went through so much hurt and anger. When I finally had the confidence to claim myself as gay/queer/lesbian, there was relief because I knew who I was. Watching Lee go through that process of finding themselves again, after initially coming out as gay, and now as nonbinary—going through the hurt and the anger AGAIN with family, especially—made me feel so helpless. I learned the pain experienced from a trans person is so raw and sometimes so heartbreaking, but once that person finds their footing, it is the most beautiful thing to witness and be a part of.

VICTORIA: This one time we were in DTLA at a jazz club and Lee went to the bathroom. Lee is very androgynous looking, so upon entering the women's bathroom (they use the women's as a default when there isn't a gender-neutral bathroom available because they feel safer), they were aggressively followed by the security guard. Lee had lights shone on them while they were in the stall, not realizing why they were being yelled at to come out. They were kicked out of the bathroom for not looking like a "female" in the bouncer's eyes. I've never been followed that way because of my appearance. Nor do I do confrontation. But seeing Lee shrink and visibly shaking because of society's perception of gender makes me livid and prepared to take any and all names.

Leo *(They/Them)* & Sofia-Noor *(She/Her)*

BROOKLYN, NY

SOFIA-NOOR

Being a first-generation immigrant of Swedish and Iranian parents, I was taught very early on that I had to act and speak a certain way to essentially become my parents' archetype of an ideal child in a heteronormative world. Sadly, I have experienced a lot of self-neglect to perform for others, leading me to deprive myself of authenticity in order to please my family and community. But finally realizing that it is OK to be the black sheep, that I have the ability to be something different, I notice that I feel more seen and secure in my identity and now consider it to be a superpower I hold.

As mixed, queer POC individuals breaking free from the traditional mindset of our childhood, my partner and I share a great deal of comfort in existing together in our world today.

When I look back on how Leo and I met, and who we were when we finally knew of the other's existence, it almost feels foreign. We were younger and ultimately different people, and I understand now how it was the beginning of a big transitional period for us within our relationship. I'd like to think that we were destined to meet each other exactly when we did. I immediately knew that Leo was my person, and I am forever grateful for them. I had never felt so seen or heard until I met Leo. Very early on, with understanding and softness, we voiced who we were and what our fears were. It was so natural; it was so raw and real from the start. Before we knew it, the beautiful creation of a magical safe space had unfolded where we could be ourselves and continue to evolve individually and collectively.

For two years we were long distance. Now we live with one another in New York. It's vulnerable; there is no hiding, and that can be terrifying. It fluctuates every day, the level of confidence, of comfort, of self, but there is always an abundance of love, and I would not trade it for anything in the world. I'm endlessly inspired by Leo and our journey with how far we have come.

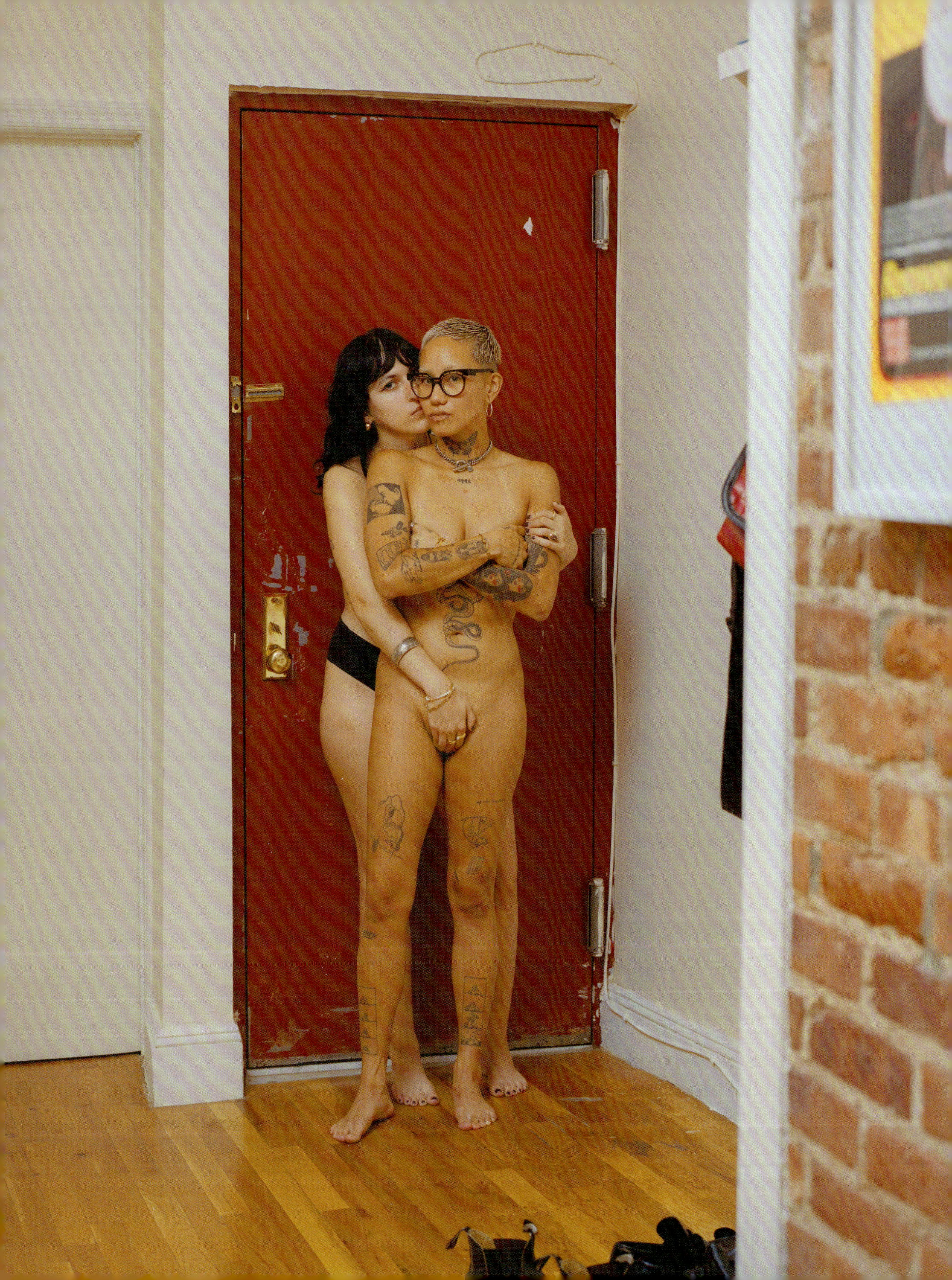

LEO

Being a child of a toxic arranged marriage between two individuals with differing morals, beliefs, and sexuality, I feel as if I took on an incredible weight to discover my own independence at a young age. While this survival technique can bring immense strength from the experience of heavy trauma, it can also be detrimental as one transitions into adulthood. There weren't many truthful opportunities to view the basis of life—relationships, trust, love, self—other than what I taught myself as I was broken. Using escapism to fill a void, I fantasized heavily, creating an unreachable place filled with unrealistic expectations that I deemed "healthy."

At every turn, being so complicated yet so simplistic, the experience of life is a thrilling and fearful journey. There's a constant game of tug-of-war, involving unlearning and relearning, falling short and triumphing, but regardless, throughout time, everything will evolve. Life, love, existence, my partner—sometimes with me, and sometimes without me.

No matter the hardships, I think unconditionally caring for someone—not peering at them as an extension of myself but individually in all their unbiased entirety—helps me understand the meaning of what it is to love. Over time, I have discovered that love in every form is the altruistic and uncomfortable act of surrendering. It's the messy, slow process of being transparent as I deal with confrontation and accountability, both personally and outwardly. I find that as I feed myself this concept into my deliverance of love to her, I find more resilience and solitude as an individual and as a partner. Instead of running away from her, I can run to her. Sofia-Noor provides me with the truest sense of security and safety that I have ever felt in this lifetime.

Liz *(She/Her)* & Lloren *(She/Her)*

LOS ANGELES, CA

LIZ

Lloren and I grew up differently yet with somewhat parallel lives. We were both raised in predominantly white neighborhoods (Lloren a pastor's daughter in Calabasas, California, me in Mormon country in Salt Lake City) where being gay was not accepted publicly. We grew up dealing with identity issues as a result. Lloren is a Black queer woman who grew up with more money than me, in a two-parent home where college was a given, along with other movie-style perks. I grew up in a single-parent home with a mother who struggled financially. I'm a queer woman of color and ethnically ambiguous. I went to college in my thirties when I could afford it and paid and paved my way for most of life's journeys. Yet I realized despite all the privileges of Lloren's youth and upbringing, when we are in public people treat her differently than me. In the summer of 2020, we were arrested during the downtown LA protests. She was taken first. After being handcuffed and held on a bus for eight hours, Lloren fought to get us off, yet they only let me out. I realized then that my ambiguity granted more privileges.

LLOREN

Race and sexual identity are a huge part of our daily conversations. We communicate when we feel someone has mistreated us because perhaps one of us missed it due to our respective lenses. Sometimes Liz feels dismissed from the Black community because of her racial ambiguity. I make sure she is seen. Liz has told me that because of me, people in our community see her as a Black woman which is something she doesn't experience by herself. Sexuality is also transparent. What we are feeling from day to day needs to be at the forefront of our dialogue. Being a gold star queer myself, and Liz being fluid, we have to discuss the honesty of our sexual attractions and energy exchanges. Liz recently proposed and we said yes to forever. In order to continue to see each other through the rest of our lives, we have to be honest with ourselves and live that truth. Although we are not polyamorous, we do believe it's natural to feel things, and it's the conversation that is most important. Many times it doesn't come to fruition, but the opportunity to express these natural feelings is why we choose each other every day.

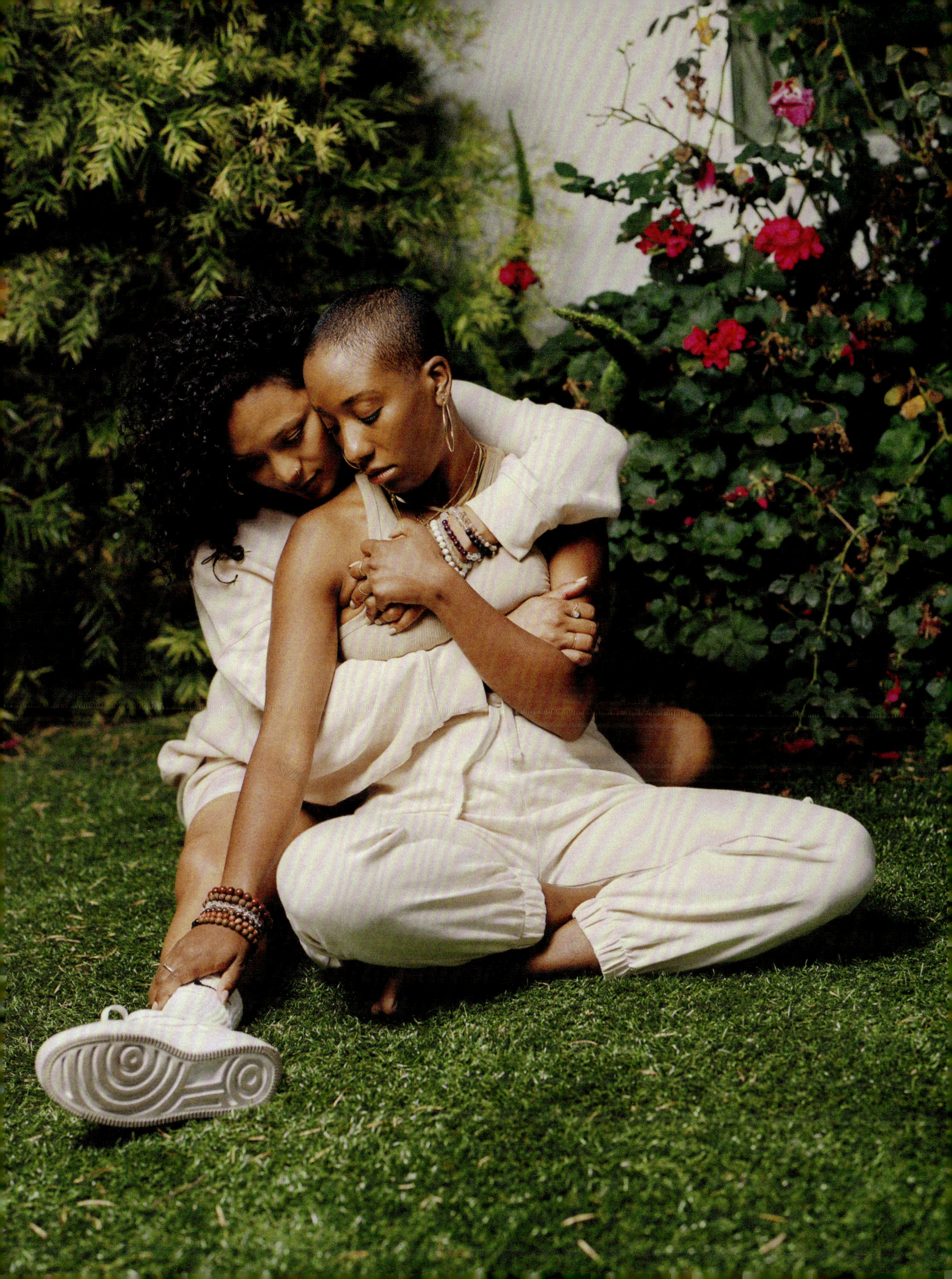

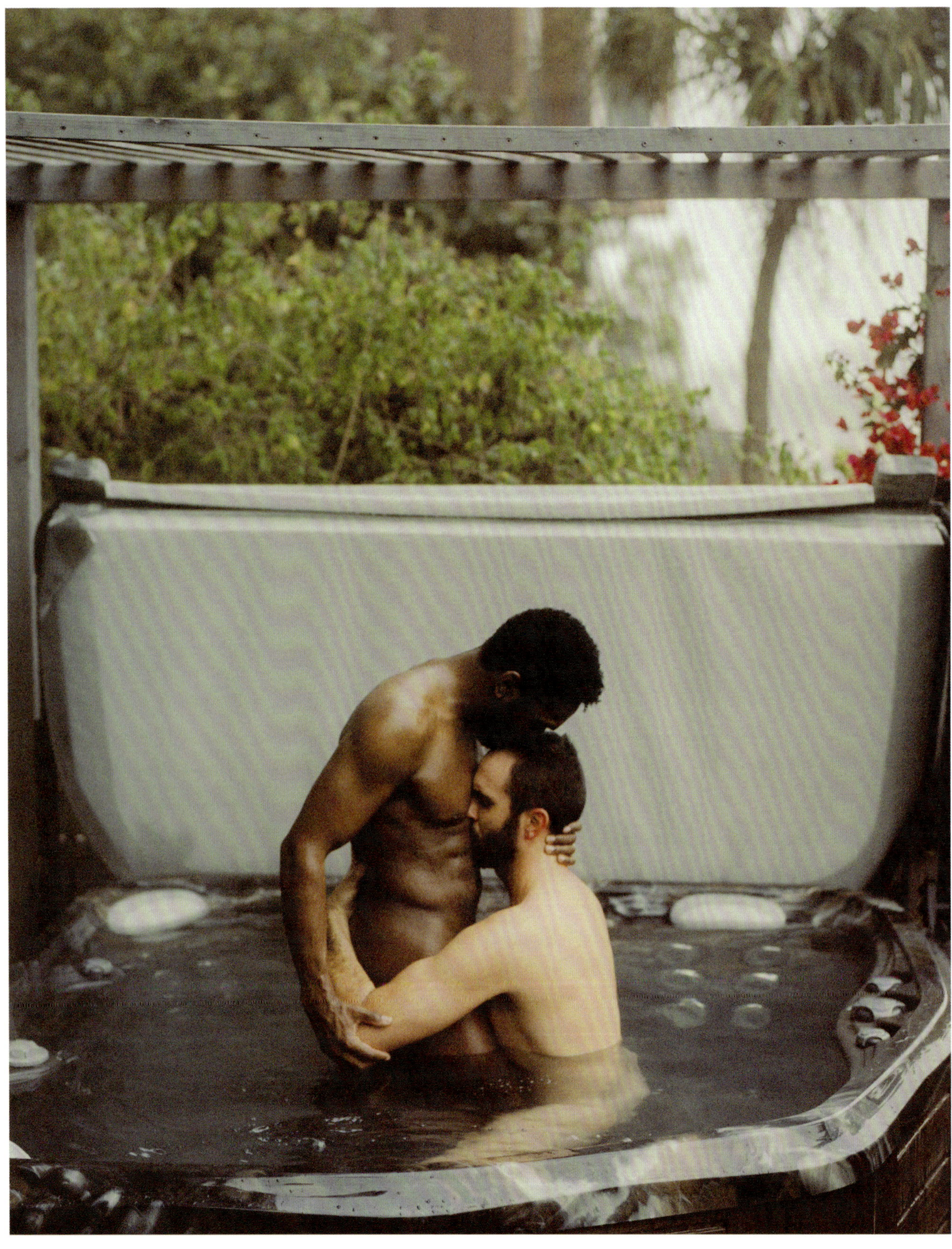

Lowell *(He/Him)* & Adam *(He/Him)*

SAN FRANCISCO, CA

The most intimate moments of our relationship have been ones where we've taken steps forward together, like getting engaged and married. The act of privately and later publicly committing to each other was dizzying and sobering. On the eve of our wedding, we wrote a letter to our future children.

October 2017

Child,

Your fathers met eight years ago at a college dinner party, playing footsie under the table while bonding over the bad food. We came from different worlds, but quickly discovered we shared the same mind. We fell in love and made sacrifices to be together. We moved across the country twice, we broke up twice, we made up twice, we fell in love again and again. We've broken and rewritten the rules of our relationship, and along the way, we've discovered how honesty and empathy are the essence of a true partnership.

This weekend, we are getting married. It's a major step in our journey together, and we couldn't be prouder of the story we've written. This week we'll bring together our closest friends and family to celebrate the beginning of our lives as a family. One day, you'll feel the love that surrounds us.

We're most proud of the joy that we have created in our relationship. For us, this joy comes from feeling both a sense of freedom from and responsibility to one another. It's our dream that you will feel the love and joy that exists between us and that you find that joy for yourself in this world.

We can't tell you how to love or what love will feel like for you, but we can tell you a little bit more about what it felt like for us. Our recipe for love looks something like this:

> **New Love Stew**
> Combine laughter, a sense of adventure,
> and mutual attraction. Whisk. Salt to taste.
> Heat over medium flame.
> Taste for honesty, self-awareness, and those
> butterflies in your stomach.
> Don't overthink it. Enjoy with friends.

It's our hope that you are healthy and that you have a sense of humor. If we can teach you to laugh and smile, you'll have most of what it takes to go out into the world and write your own beautiful story.

Know that we love you without conditions and that we are so blessed to have you in our lives.

Love, Dads

Luke *(He/Him)* & Brandon *(He/Him)*

LOS ANGELES, CA

You speak the language of my spirit

As open to me, am I to him
I would fall into his arms at any given whim.

Our love knows no bounds, only stars
and infinite skies
Not our first meeting, but the time sure does fly
when souls depart, circle back and press restart;
I've known you for many lifetimes.

You speak the language of my spirit, as I do yours.
A fluent conversation we find ourselves in, yet again.
Our differences are a plenty,
but this love does not bend.
Picked up, right where we left off eons ago
Taking things slow, was never in our nature.

Fast forward, I'm caressing your skin as it soaks
up the sun that peers through our windows
Our home is foreign to labels, adversity does not
live here, only our hearts are allowed to dwell
in this sacred atmosphere.

You me, and me you.
Together forever, our love is true.
Difficult, sure. But difficult is a fire I would walk
through, to find you and only you, once more.

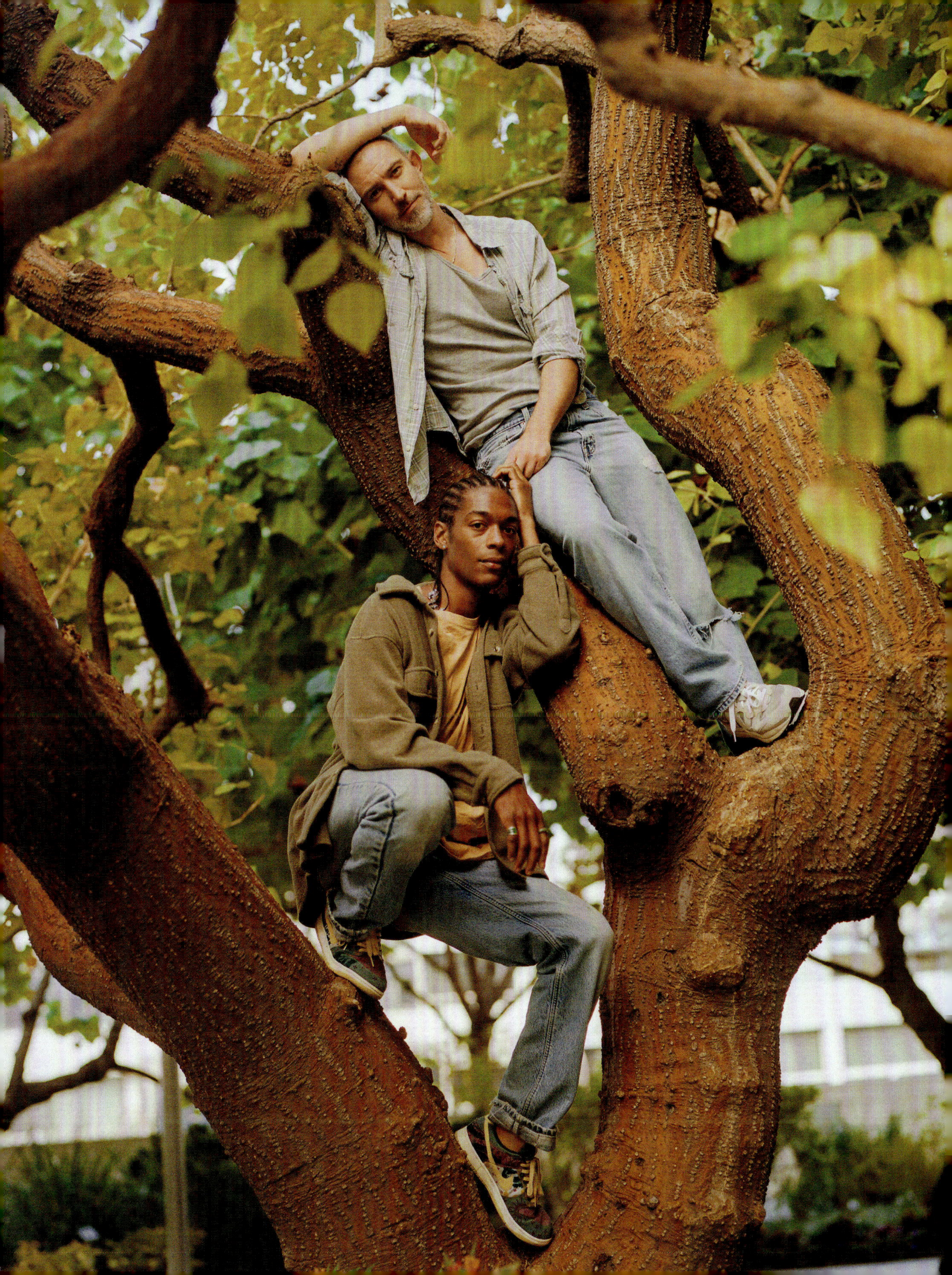

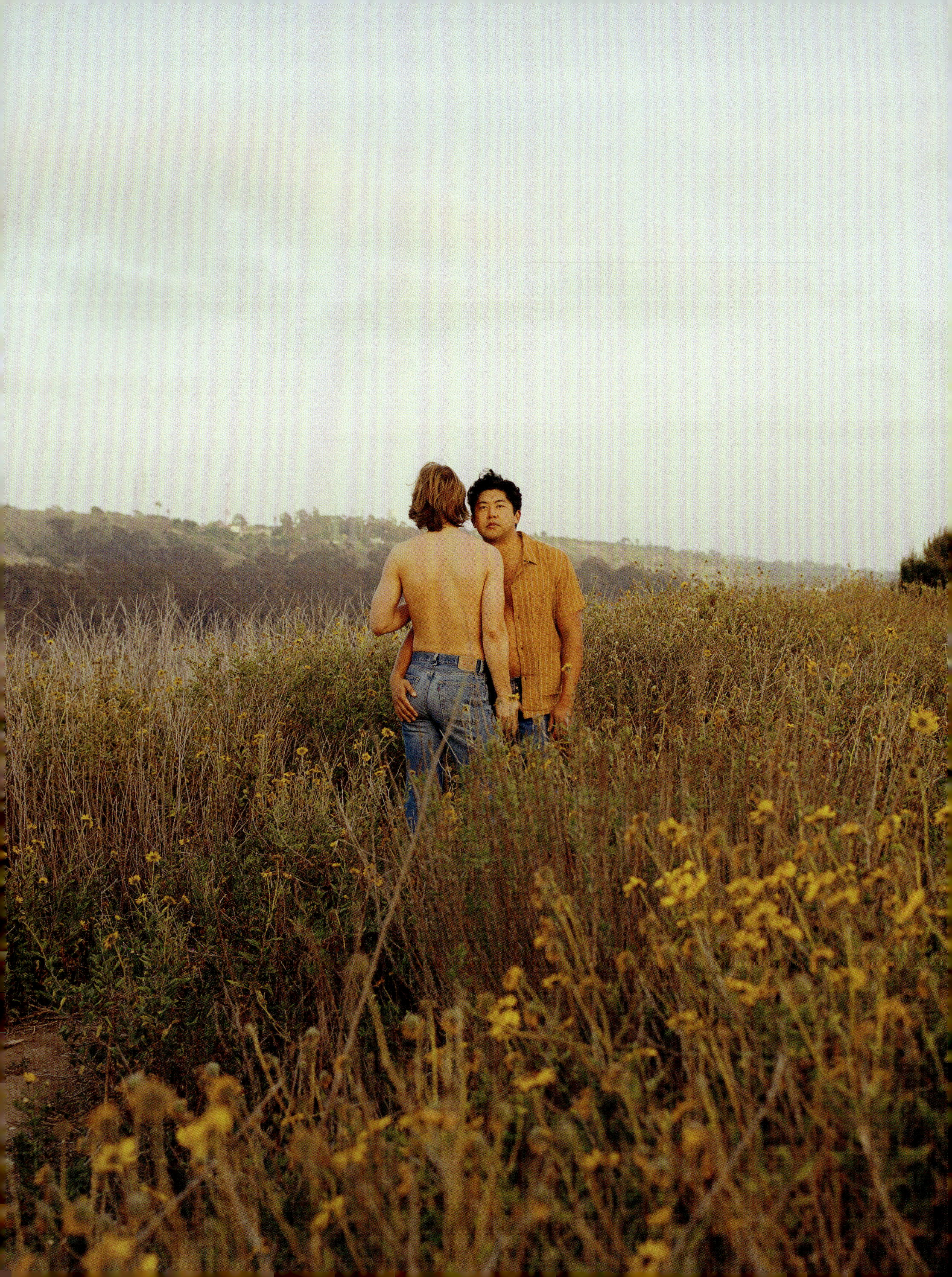

Martin *(He/Him)* & Ryan *(He/Him)*

LOS ANGELES, CA

MARTIN

At the time of this photo, we were visiting my mom in LA, staying in my childhood home and enjoying the West Coast after a cramped winter in New York. It was Ryan's first time meeting my mom, and it was my first time returning home since the start of the pandemic. It would also be the last time I ever saw my mom.

After the trip home, we began looking for an apartment together in New York, both of us sensing a new confidence in our relationship. I had watched my mom and Ryan bond over stories of her growing up in the Philippines, escaping an abusive relationship, bringing my sister and me to America, and navigating an interracial relationship herself. Through her, Ryan learned more about me in that week than I could have told him myself in an entire month. So, several months later, on a sunny July afternoon, we signed a lease for a one-bedroom in Brooklyn. Afterward, during a celebratory lunch, I received a phone call that my mother had taken her own life.

Ryan watched me crumble at the news of my mother's death. I reached out to old family friends and relatives, trying to piece together why this had happened. I learned stories my mother never shared about the hardships she faced not just in the Philippines but in the United States: her own mental health struggles and abuse from my biological dad in the Philippines; how she tried so hard to assimilate in the US; and the extent to which she was struggling with the dissolution of another marriage, this time with the man she had moved to the US for. In these stories I saw myself, someone struggling to live in America who isn't straight, white, Christian, or "from here." I'm a direct result of the places, countries, families, and traumas my mother left behind when forging a new life.

Since this photo, Ryan and I have talked about our different experiences regarding race and sexuality in ways we never had before. While I'm still unpacking my mother's legacy and the grief I'm left with, what I've learned about my mom and myself has strengthened my resolve in this relationship. Hopefully as I continue to uncover and face the traumas my mom carried through her incredible life, Ryan and I will foster the kind of life together she always dreamed of for herself.

Martin *(He/Him)* & Zack *(He/Him)*

SAN FRANCISCO, CA

We met over five years ago at a rooftop party in Brooklyn. A few months later we started dating, and a year and a half after that we moved in together—both of our first times living with a partner. Not only do we come from different cultural backgrounds (Z is from America & M is from Denmark), there's also an eleven-year age difference between us. Navigating change has been a major theme for our relationship. The change that comes with moving to a new country, coming out to friends and family, understanding what kind of relationship you actually want to share versus the kinds that have been modeled for you, and ultimately the never-ending change that comes with growing more and more every day. We've experienced a lot, things both good and challenging, but we continue to learn and grow together.

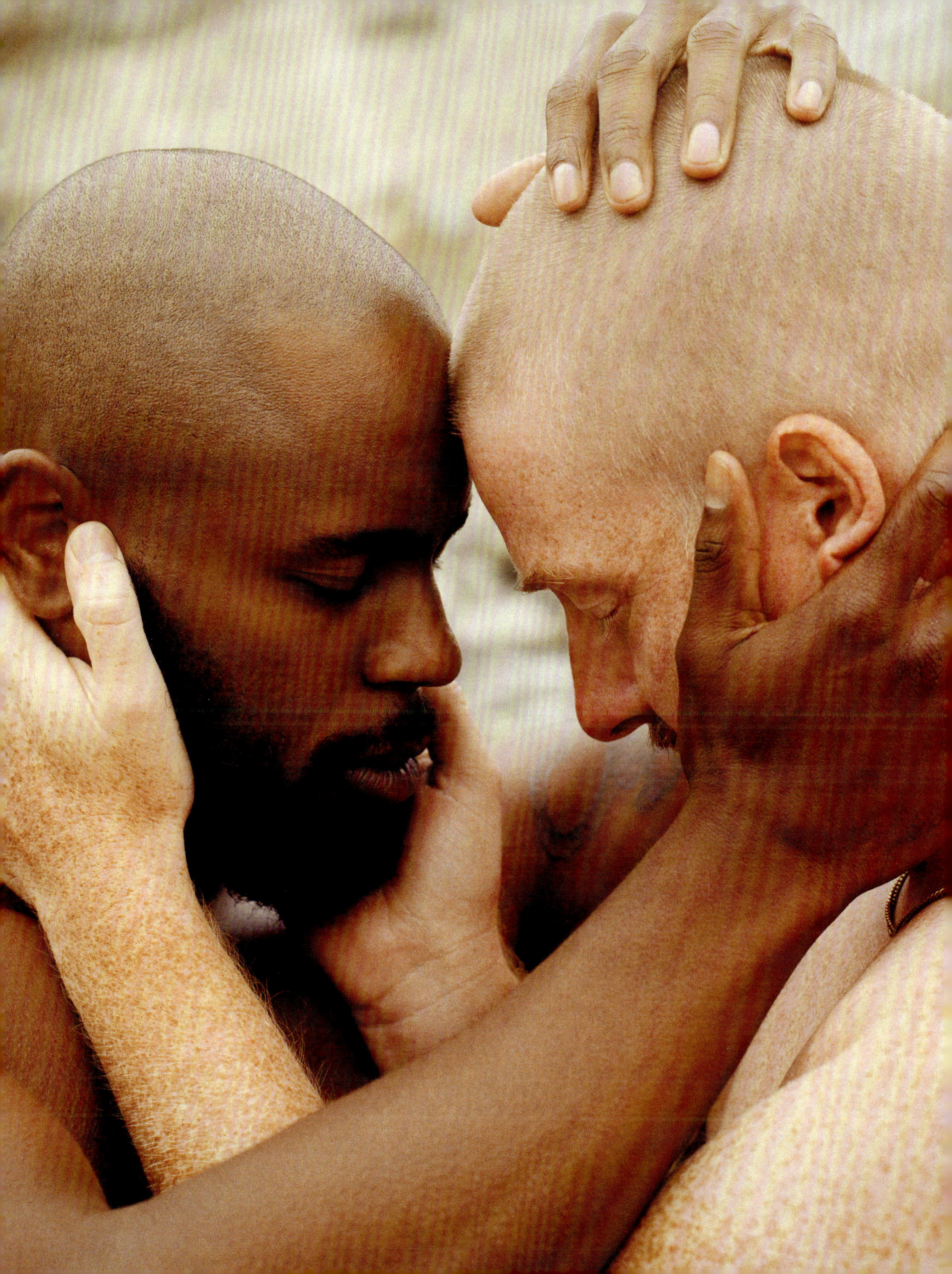

Matt *(He/Him)* & Matt *(He/Him)*

JOSHUA TREE, CA

MATT & MATT

While there is a lot that we share within our identities and relationship (we're gay men, we're photographers, and we even share the same first name), honoring our differences has been vital to the success of our partnership. We started dating just barely into our twenties, now twelve years ago, at a time when so much in our lives was in flux. We were just beginning to find ourselves and move into adulthood, and we chose to walk that journey together. That sometimes meant being acutely aware of being in an interracial relationship—how we moved through life individually was different but informed how we needed to move through life together. With that basic understanding and respect, and by allowing each other the room to flourish as individuals, we grew together as partners. We discovered how to navigate our relationship in a way that works for us: we could be in a loving and committed relationship without having to subscribe to heteronormative standards. Letting go of judgments and striving toward true authenticity within ourselves makes us solid and reliable partners for each other, so that we can nurture a life of joy, camaraderie, passion, integrity, and curiosity.

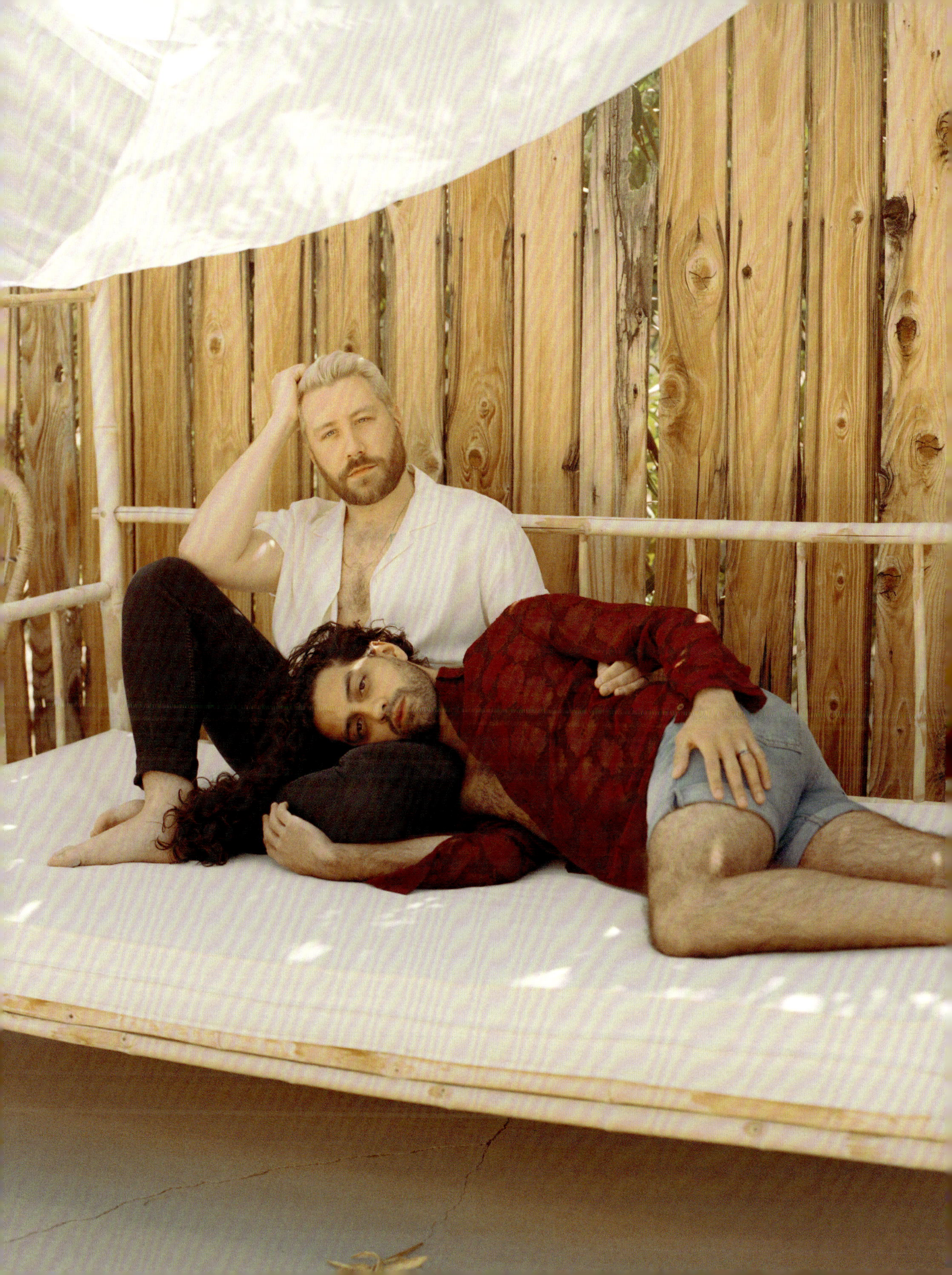

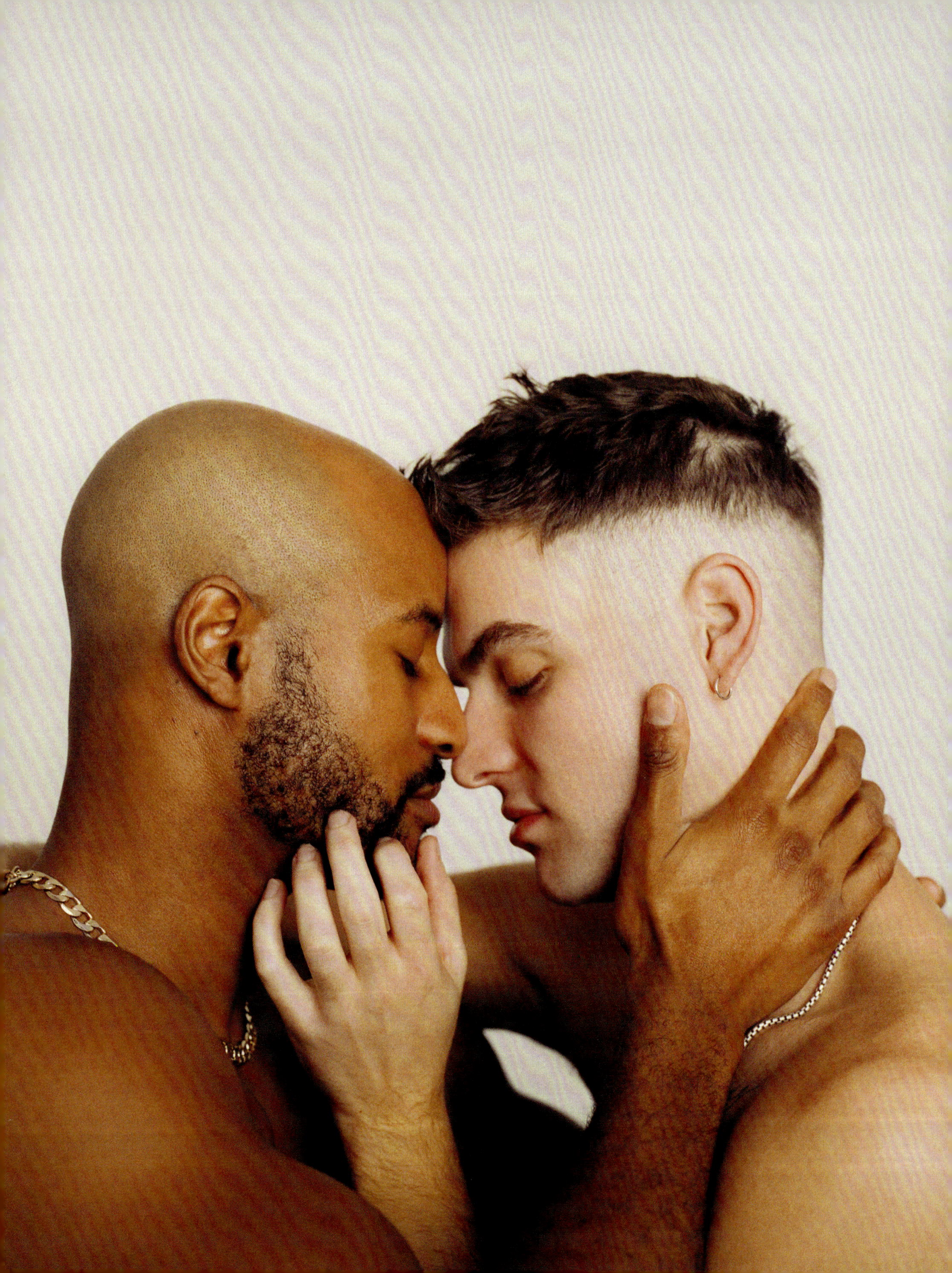

Max *(He/Him)* & Nick *(He/Him)*

LOS ANGELES, CA

MAX

Interracial relationships are hard, and being gay adds another layer of complexity. After watching the George Floyd protests occur in my hometown, both remote and in person, I didn't know if I could date a white person. I didn't know if I had the energy to explain so many of the learned experiences of four-hundred-plus years of oppression that Black Americans have faced, information that is critical to understanding and loving me, and yet I swiped right when I saw Nick on Tinder. The photo showed a handsome, tall, dark-haired man with chiseled abs and an intense model stare. Something about the combination of his bluntly worded profile and seminude body on full display told me that he would be more direct and honest than the people I had dated prior. I was impressed at his entrepreneurial nature and the makeup skills he developed through years of self-training. Fast forward to over a year later, dating Nick has taught me the importance of finding a partner with whom I can communicate about (individual and joint) hopes and dreams, but also about the difficult and awkward topics that can complicate any relationship. We have (and will continue to) discuss our thoughts on racism, sexual expectations and boundaries, and also what we each define as requirements for a supportive and successful relationship. Every day of our relationship is work, and each one is not butterflies and roses, but we are both invested in continuing to develop and grow together.

NICK

I have never had a relationship longer than six months, until now. I thought that because I share every aspect of my life with the Internet, and wear women's clothing and makeup, it would be a while until I found a relationship. I needed to find someone who could see past the layers of foundation, glitter, and social media followers. Then one day I was swiped right on Tinder after seeing Max's beaming smile. I thought it was too good to be true, but we clicked from the start. We skipped the small talk and on the first date discussed our political and societal beliefs. One thing I know for sure is that Max has everything I want in a partner. He believes in me more than I even believe in myself most days and lifts me to heights I never thought were possible. He inspires me each day to be the very best version of myself. He has shown me that the true meaning of a "partner" is so much more than cute pics, boyfriend tags on YouTube, and hot sex. Having someone that has your back and is there for you is the most magical feeling I've ever had.

Michael *(He/Him)* & Tavi *(He/Him)*

LOS ANGELES, CA

TAVI: It wasn't the easiest road when it came to how I identified growing up. Being a Black, Christian Baptist in a small town in Georgia, I faced many adversities throughout my childhood and young adult years. I didn't officially identify as gay until my early twenties. Prior to that, because of my own internal struggles, I stayed away from anything that remotely appeared to be gay. That time became a period of acceptance and finding my identity within my orientation. This made it difficult to establish relationships with other guys throughout this time, because though I had accepted that I was gay, I was still very uncomfortable within my own skin. It has taken years for me to love on myself the way I do now.

MICHAEL: I am a biracial individual. My mom is African American, and my father is white. I got the heat from both sides. I know what it felt like to be called a white boy, a Black boy, and let's just add being gay as the cherry on top. I remember being teased for my ethnicity. Feeling like I'm not accepted in the white crowd because of my hair having a different texture than the other white kids. While feeling disconnected from my Black community because my skin is a bit lighter. I had to live with the stigma of being perceived "better than" my Black peers. If I wasn't being teased for my race, then I had a target on my back because of being gay. I used to feel sad and would cry because I wanted to be accepted by what I identified as, yet both communities looked at me as a different breed. I went through that for a reason I believe—so I can understand the difficulties I had growing up, so I can be a light for someone else in a younger generation. I know there is someone that is going through what I did and needs guidance and a friend. Growing up, I tried to hide certain things about myself because they weren't seen as masculine. Even though deep down I knew what I was. In my early twenties, I explored and got exposed to gay culture. I felt like I found my tribe, who are just as cool and different as me. As time went on, I started being OK with my masculine and feminine energy. My aunt helped me embrace my true self—someone who enjoys all aspects of life, with no limitations based on what people say is wrong and right. Tavi and I had similar upbringings. Both of us were misunderstood for the decisions that really made us glow and light up. I could have so seen us being friends growing up.

TAVI: I would have to say these past two years, with all the police brutality that was heavily displayed in mainstream media, caused me to start viewing the world around me differently. Though I grew up in the South, I thought I had never experienced racism. It wasn't until these past couple of years where my eyes started to see differently. I began to see how hard it is not only being a Black man in America, but a gay Black man in America. It felt as if the odds were ten times not in my favor. I'm grateful that I went through that moment because it helped me mold even more into my true self. This is my first long-term relationship, and boy has it been a challenge. We've embraced some very hard and ugly truths about ourselves and each other. In the beginning, we didn't communicate so well. And though we're still working on it, our communication has evolved immensely. Since we've both been actively working on ourselves, we've become aware of how many of our behaviors derive from unhealthy and traumatic childhood experiences. Michael is my best friend, and that's one thing that I find to be so important in our relationship. I say this all the time (because it's true), he stalked me, and he put a spell on me!

MICHAEL: We have grown so much throughout our relationship. We have both understood, over time, that neither of us is wrong for feeling how we feel. We've created a bond that is full of life. I love that we have grown to know who we are and be what we are. Two Black, queer men, creating our journey and living life true to us.

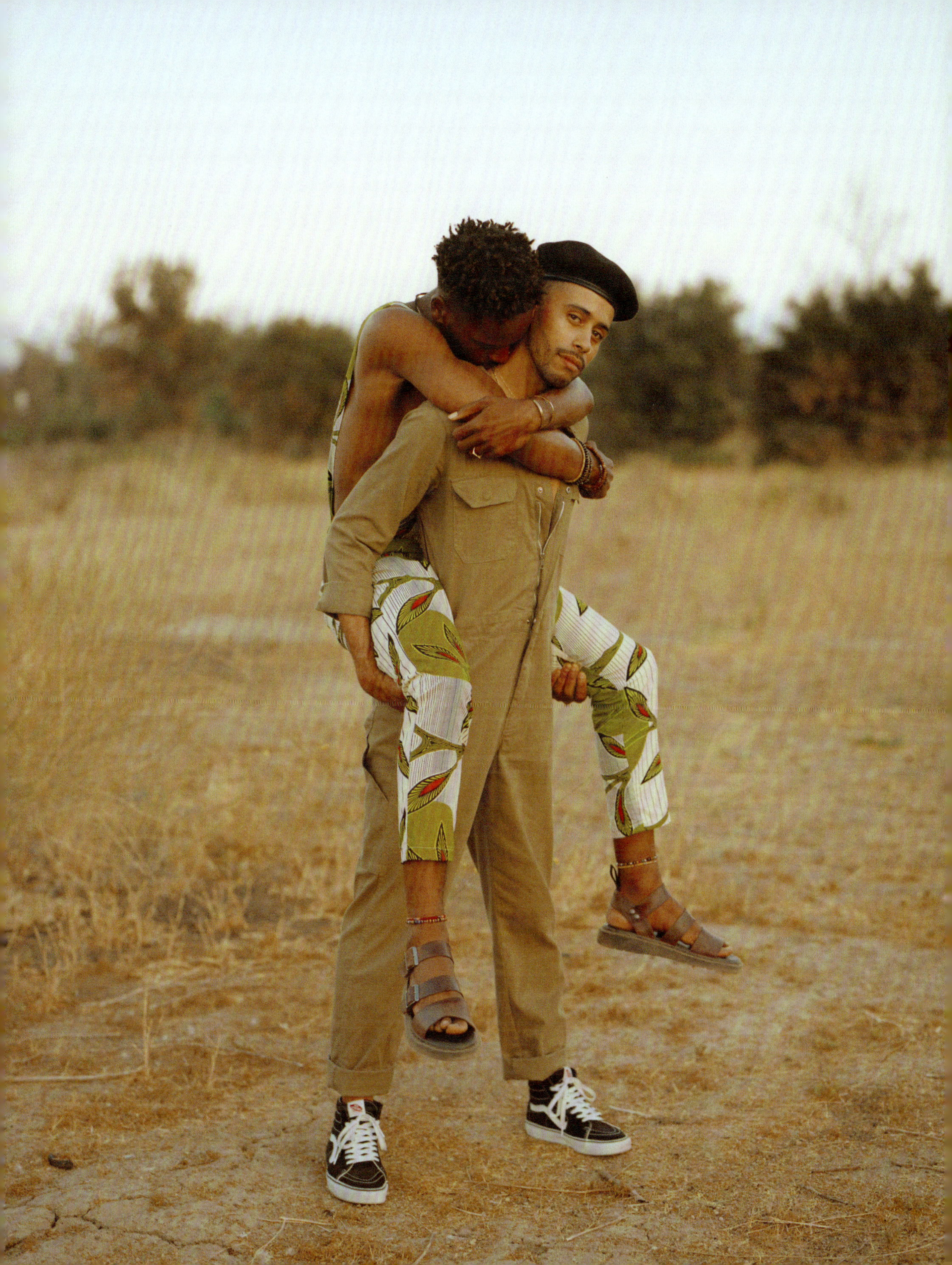

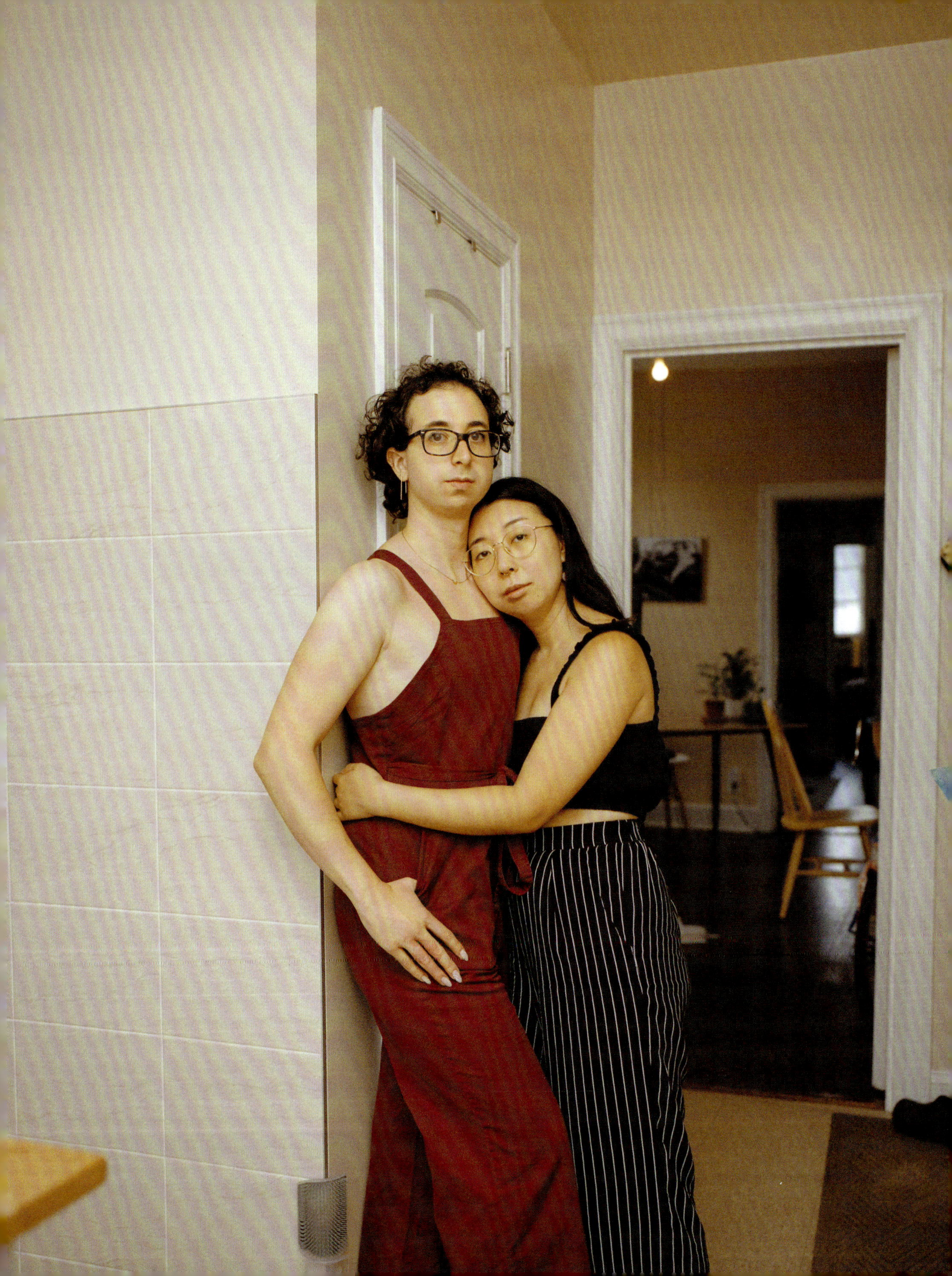

Michelle *(She/Her)* & Marcy *(She/Her)*

BROOKLYN, NY

MICHELLE

Before I met Marcy, I never really understood what people meant when they said their significant other was their best friend. My deepest, most fulfilling friendships—my best friends—had been almost exclusively with women. I had only ever dated men in the past, and while I can look back on those relationships fondly, I can't really say they fulfilled me emotionally or romantically. I had the thought that, Oh, maybe I'm not really clicking with men. Maybe I connect better with women. Then I met Marcy, and as she went through her own gender journey, the questions I had about my sexuality came to the forefront of our relationship. I've given myself a lot more space to think more deeply about gender and my own queerness. I'm still trying to understand what these words mean to me, but I'm happy I can say I have someone who is both my best friend and partner to be here with me as I explore questions about my identity.

MARCY

I haven't always been proud to say, "I am a woman." Instead, I'd opt to blend in as best as I could. I wanted to hide myself, be quiet, and take up as little space as possible. I was born the first male in a very large, extended Jewish family—and that visibility always made me uncomfortable. Everything I was, and all expectation of me, was related to my assigned gender.

When I met Michelle, I'd only just started digging into the parts of myself I'd kept buried. No matter how hard the talks, she always offered more of herself to me. She's given me love where I expected pain. She's healed me where I felt shame. I always gave myself the excuse that I wasn't feminine enough, not queer enough—never enough that I could be trans. She makes me feel like I'm enough.

Miles *(He/Him)* & Tim *(He/Him)*

NEW YORK, NY

MILES

If you want to quickly understand how different we are, all you have to do is visit us in the morning. If it's after 6 a.m., Tim has undoubtedly emptied the dishwasher, poured himself a cold brew, and wrapped himself in a blanket to update his daily to-do list. And if it's before 7:30 a.m., Miles is absolutely still in bed, either asleep or giving an Oscar-worthy performance of mummified-under-the-covers-pretending-to-be-asleep to match Tim's level of chattiness and insistence that he greet the day.

But mornings are also the time when you'll see what holds us together. Because all Miles's performance usually yields is Tim launching himself flying squirrel style onto the bed and ripping off the covers for a high-volume kiss attack. And for all Tim's careful planning, come afternoon, it's not uncommon for Miles to have graced his to-do list with such helpful additions as "Get a clue—now is my moment!" and "Celebrate Miles (a little more each day)." In short, we try not to take ourselves, or our differences, too seriously. And when we do butt heads, it's always laughter that brings us back together.

As a Black guy from the Bay Area and a white guy from suburban Atlanta, we didn't grow up with a model of what being together could look like. Could we allow ourselves to love another man, especially one of a different race, openly and fully? Could we love ourselves because of, not despite, that choice?

Because there is no instruction manual for us, it's given us the freedom to create our own. And what we keep coming back to is that at our core, we're just two people who enjoy brightening each other's days.

Seven years of mornings together haven't made Miles any more likely to join Tim in starting the day with a bang, or Tim to respect Miles's desire to roll into things with a little quiet, cozy reflection. But they do serve as a daily reminder of how a good laugh together can be all it takes to make a relationship feel like home.

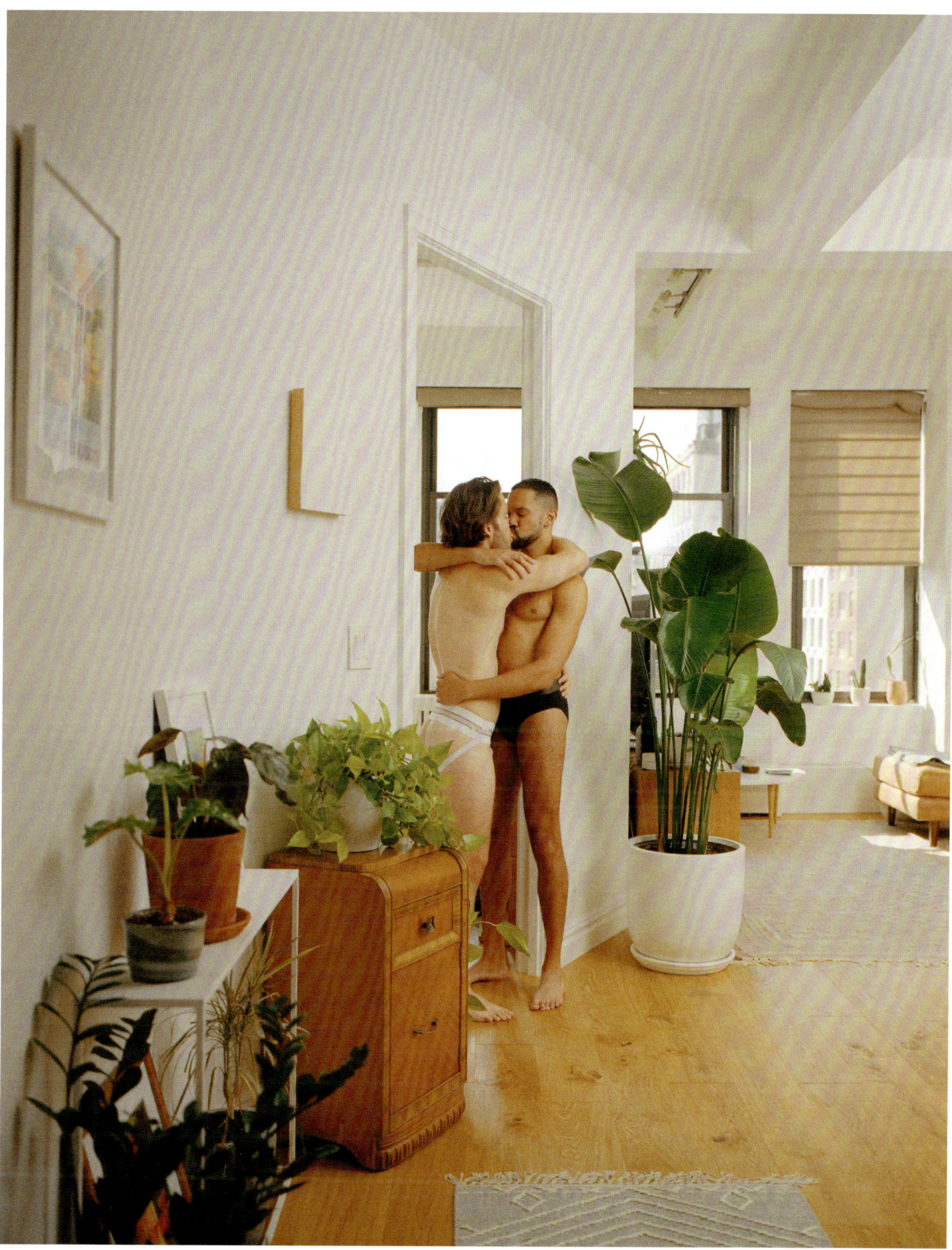

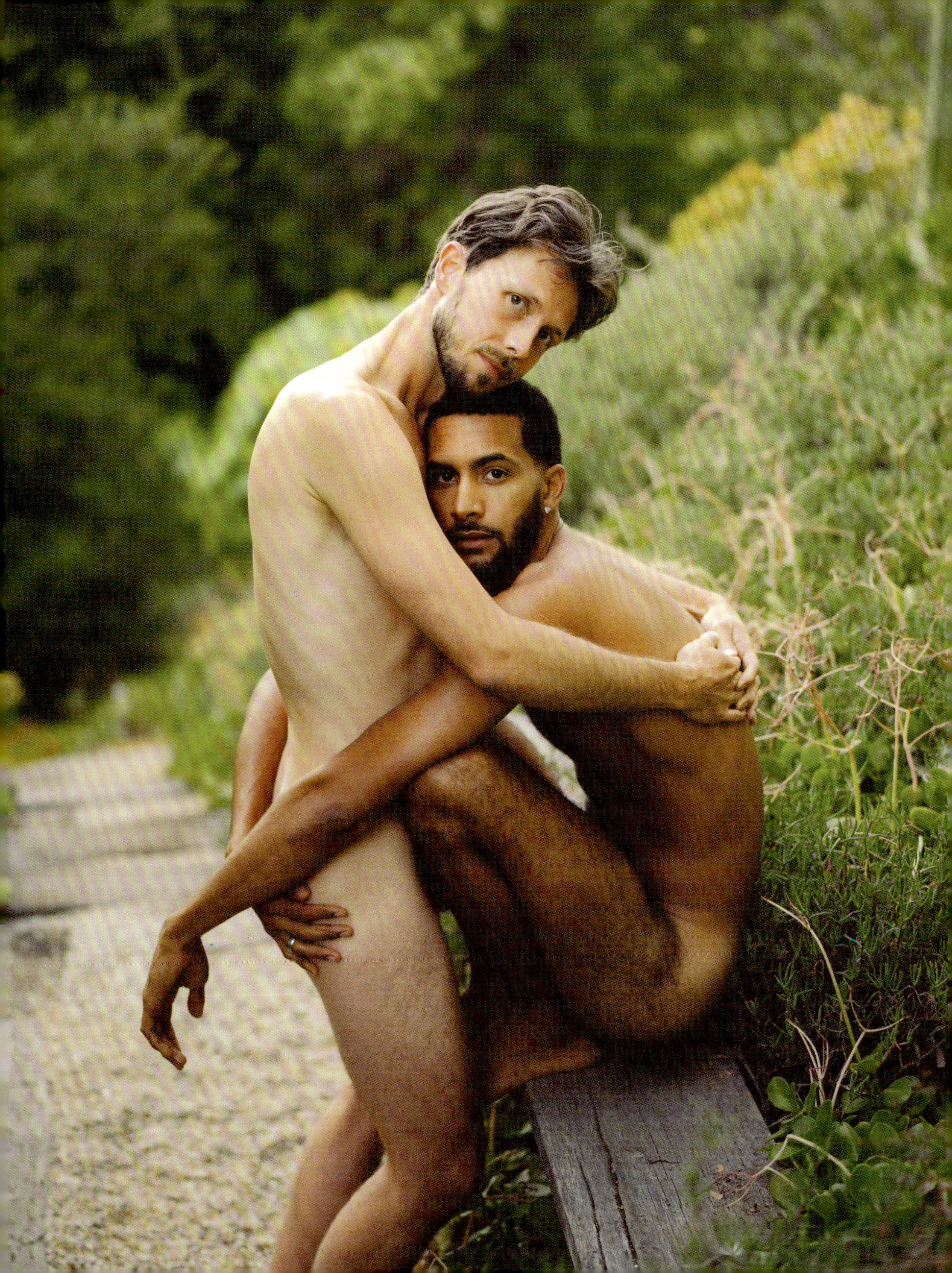

Milo *(He/Him)* & Legacy *(He/They)*

LOS ANGELES, CA

MILO

There has always been an ease and gentleness in our relationship. Legacy has such a big heart—his spirit has a beautiful, calm quality to it. It was easy to develop a deep love for him. His compassion for the planet, for animals, and for other people is ever present. Legacy is always teaching me how to show up better in the world—loving everyone, suspending judgment, and flying above negativity.

There is, of course, a deep physical and sexual attraction, too. A magnetic pull toward holding hands, a poetry to how our bodies intertwine. I've always felt safe in his arms and presence.

And even with this deep love and attraction, we decided to uncouple but remain in each other's lives. There was simply too much good to part ways with. The journey from couple to friends has been a winding road. In some ways it would be easier to close the door on each other, to avoid the messiness of dealing with jealousy and confusion. But forging this new path—one rooted in unconditional love—has also been deeply healing and rewarding.

Queer relationships aren't tied to the limited, binary expectations that typically define heterosexual relationships. Moving through different iterations of intimacy, connection, and commitment has felt authentic and necessary. Wanting the best for each other, while always focusing on honesty, allows things to flow.

LEGACY

I'm extremely grateful for Milo and our journey together. We have a lot in common, which made everything natural with our bond. Our relationship never felt boring. Always ready for an adventure! He's highly motivated, which is a gift I needed to be around at times. He's an encyclopedia of information and facts. A true storyteller. I've always felt abundant and nurtured by his warm heart engulfing my aura.

For myself, I tend to feel that I'm open and multifaceted. A unique blend of being an introvert and extrovert. Making me easy flowing. Life is always moving. I was fortunate to be with Milo because we would constantly experience new ideas and paths to improve ourselves. I think that the key to a relationship is experiencing new things on your own and with your partner.

As for now, I don't usually talk to an ex. It's easy to just ghost, but I feel it can be unhealthy for you and them. Our minds tend to make up things that aren't real. You learn to observe and let go, so I'm growing in that space. I love Milo for being Milo and for being a loyal friend. He has an enormous heart and soul. Creating more healthy space in our friendship has been peaceful for us. I feel we are embracing a new form of love.

Nathan *(He/Him)* & Dorian *(He/Him)*

LOS ANGELES, CA

NATHAN

I feel like a lot of people who know me have grown to think of me as a funny and positive person, and this is likely because I have done a pretty good job at masking my depression. Early on in my life, I found that making others laugh became my strategy for being accepted. Humor made up for the lack of unconditional acceptance from my religious family and the surrounding conservative neighborhood. If they weren't going to like that I was gay, I thought they may at least like me because I was funny?

Unfortunately, this early feeling of thinking I needed to be funny in order to receive love affected my adult relationships in ways I wasn't aware of until I met Dorian. Although I'd been doing work on myself before we met, there is definitely a specific quality of his that highlighted a lingering discomfort in me: Dorian is very quiet, probably the quietest person I have ever dated. At first this made me very anxious because I felt like I needed to entertain him during any quiet, empty spaces to keep him interested.

But after the many dates where silence prevailed, I slowly felt my anxiety diminish as I realized our silence was not due to an awkwardness but to an admiration of who we were without the pressure of trying to be interesting. For the first time in my life, I felt I could be in the company of another and just simply be. And despite my early fears of feeling like I wouldn't be enough without the performance, Dorian wanted to stay. I feel lucky to know him and I'm so grateful for our time together loving one another just as we are.

DORIAN

My whole life I've felt alone, with no one to tell my insecurities, aspirations, fears, or dreams to. I recall being the type of person who didn't feel connected to anyone around me, despite the relationships I had with my friends and family. When I first started dating Nathan, I knew I was holding back and acting in a way that didn't feel like my true authentic self. I'd ask myself why I felt this way and would feel frustrated for not finding an answer. Nathan appeared to be the complete opposite, he seemed in tune with his feelings, emotions, and self-healing. As he shared his healing process with me, I learned that somewhere along the way I had also built a wall to protect the inner child in me. Nathan has helped me reflect on my feelings of disconnection and how they relate to my people-pleasing tendencies.

I quickly realized once I met Nathan that I'd never felt a genuine connection with anyone the way I had with him. Opening up to him was, and at times continues to be, a challenge for me. But now that we have both opened up to one another, I can see that we both shared the same early fears of being our authentic selves.

Love is a new feeling for me, it has been both beautiful and scary, but I couldn't imagine myself being with anyone other than him. Right from the beginning I knew Nathan had something special about him. His personality is always uplifting, and he wears his heart on his sleeve. Being with him has made me a stronger person. Loving him feels effortless and I couldn't have asked for anything more from him.

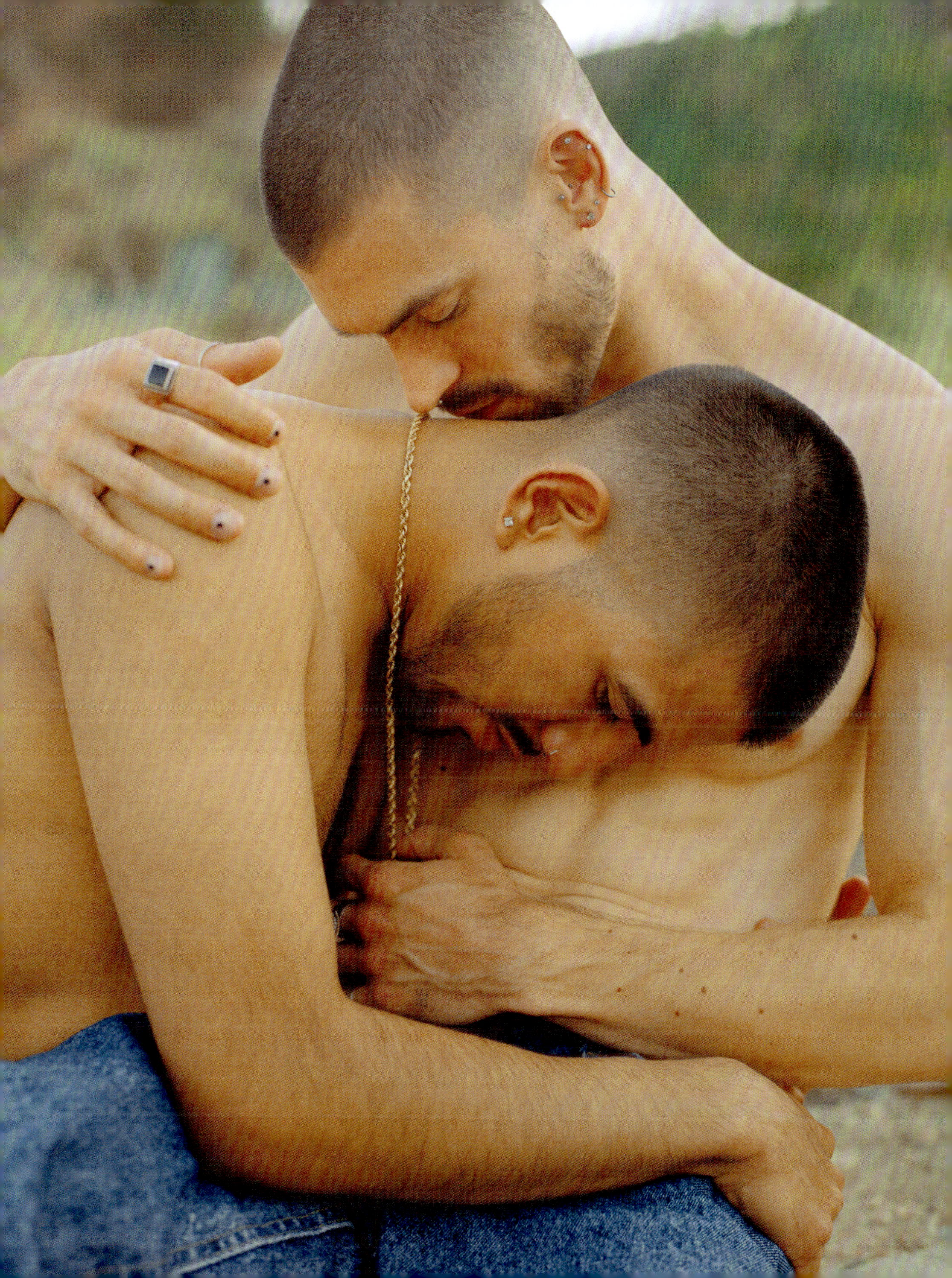

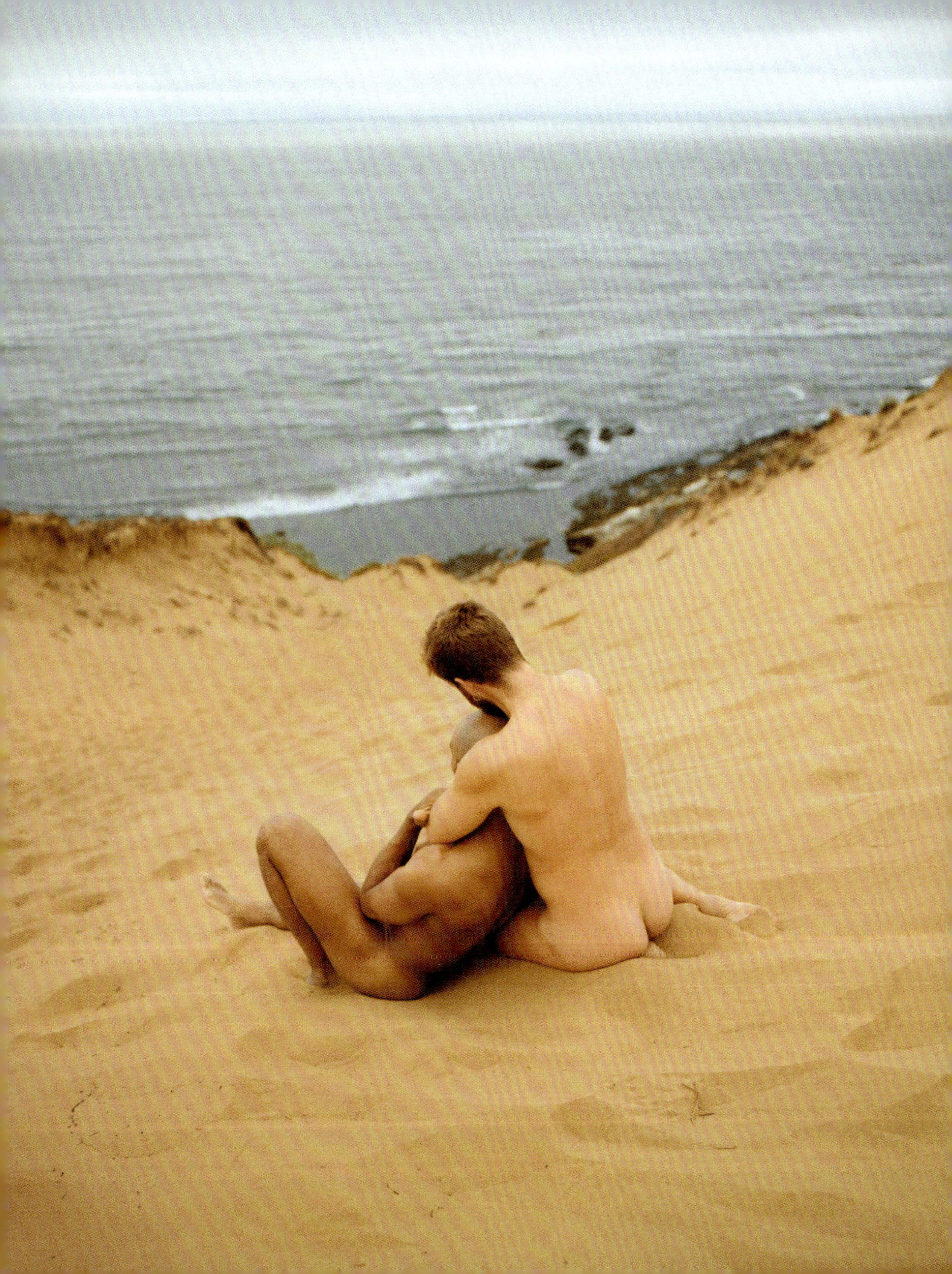

Nicholas *(He/Him)* & Jevon *(He/Him)*

SAN LUIS OBISPO, CA

NICHOLAS

When we were long-distance, Jevon asked me to write about where I saw myself in one year's time. My defensive little identity said, "Fuck is this?! How bout we just unfold and see, huh?" What I did instead was ask for help (to read his version), so I could understand what he was really asking. When I saw his words, my shoulders fell and my heart rose.

A profoundly simple thing I've been able to learn and practice from Jevon is that where I find rigidity or even threat, there is instead opportunity for softness and ease.

JEVON

Knowing Nicholas and the flow he's created for himself has helped me see more colors on the spectrum. I always loved schedules. I filled my time with things that I knew as "valuable." No "maybes" or "I don't knows." Just yes or no. Black or white. Don't make it complicated. Nicholas loves his body's (variable) alarm clock, resting, garden time, play time, porch time, etc. He is an artist and so are many of his friends. He and his friends helped open my eyes to a land of no rules. A land of having process time and space to think and be. Time to create and express. I get to do a type of work in our relationship that I will always be grateful for. I know more about myself and the world around me. Or at least, I know more about what I don't know in ways that fuel curiosity and compassion. I'm held in new ways as I lean further into loving my own body, process, and expression. It's not so black and white for me anymore. Now I grab the jumbo pack of crayons, the one with that lil sharpener in the back.

Nick *(He/They)* & Dez *(He/They)*

LOS ANGELES, CA

DEZ

From the beginning, our relationship has suffered under a quiet, lavender miasma that seems to whisper at first. Then it clears, starkly, swept away by a scream of divinely technicolored intervention. At the time Ryan contacted us, we were trying to figure out how to spend the sixth anniversary of the day we met. Meanwhile, surrounded by raging California forest fires, shifts in our financial and emotional dynamics were igniting rare and explosive arguments between us. Scheduling our portrait that day, by convenience and chance, was a reset that neither of us could have manifested alone.

Despite, or because of, our various identity differences, there's been a shared heaviness that we've been slowly lifting together since the day we met. My grandmother Delores and a very special friend David Milan had stopped living in their human forms; that same year, Nick's father David also escaped the limits of spacetime. When I met Nick, I hadn't fully processed these losses for myself, and they were in unequivocal physical pain and emotional turmoil. From the jump, we've known that we can hold each other in the hardest of times despite outside forces, i.e., isms, 45 (president), protests, Covid, Lulu pooping on the floor, in-laws, etc.

Artists in the thick of grief glued to the other's way of being, we quite naturally began to trade creative insights, meeting as two grieving individuals trying to ground ourselves and resurface renewed. The first three years went by unbelievably fast; we were so completely absorbed in each other's medium and presence and sensitivity. I watched Nick dance with both ease and vigor, running in circles, fall, get back up and teach. Nick watched me refocus as I frantically moved away from painting into writing and performance, while around us the world seemed to sour even further. In retrospect, what brought us together and keeps us entangled still is healing through creativity.

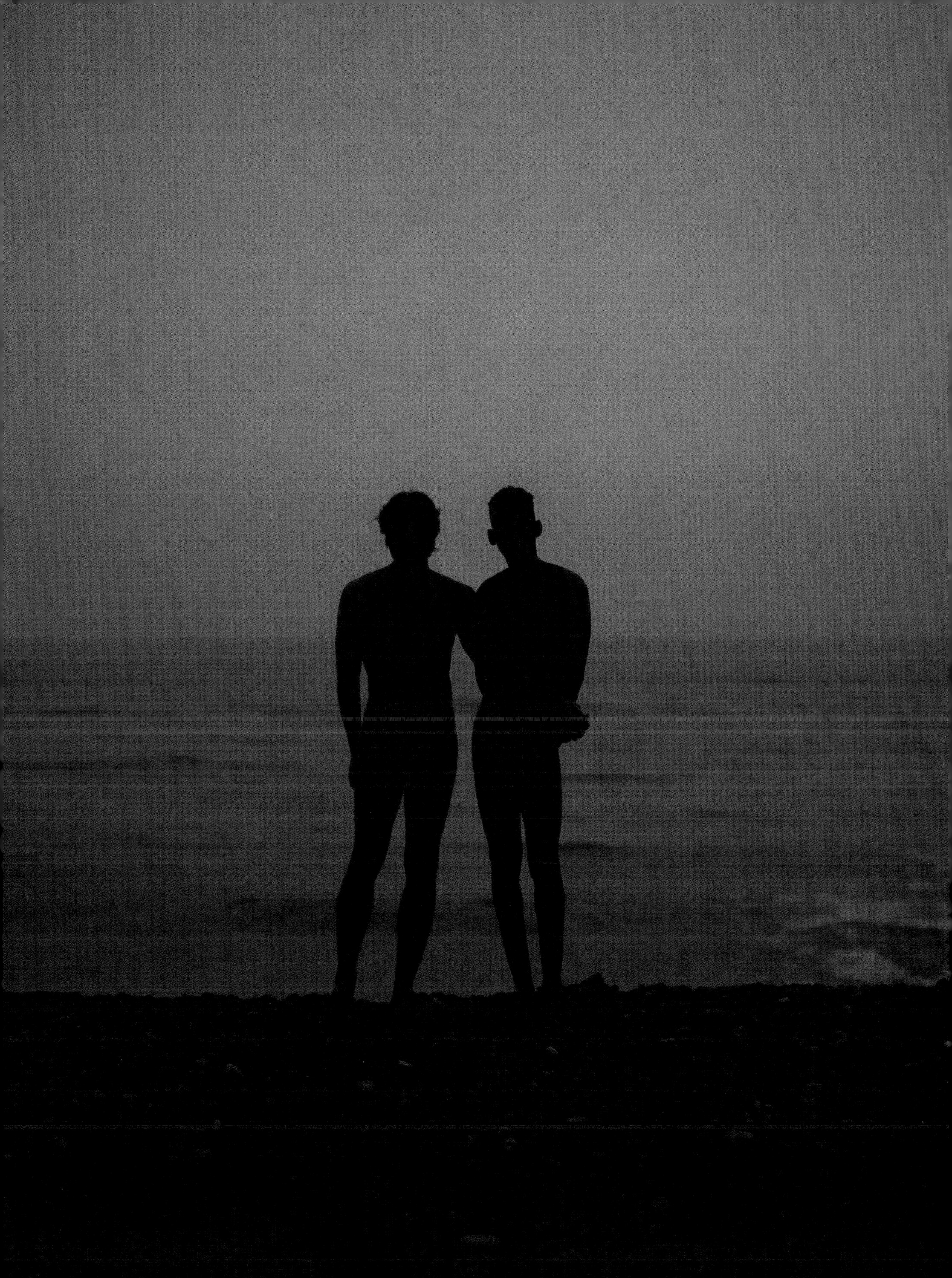

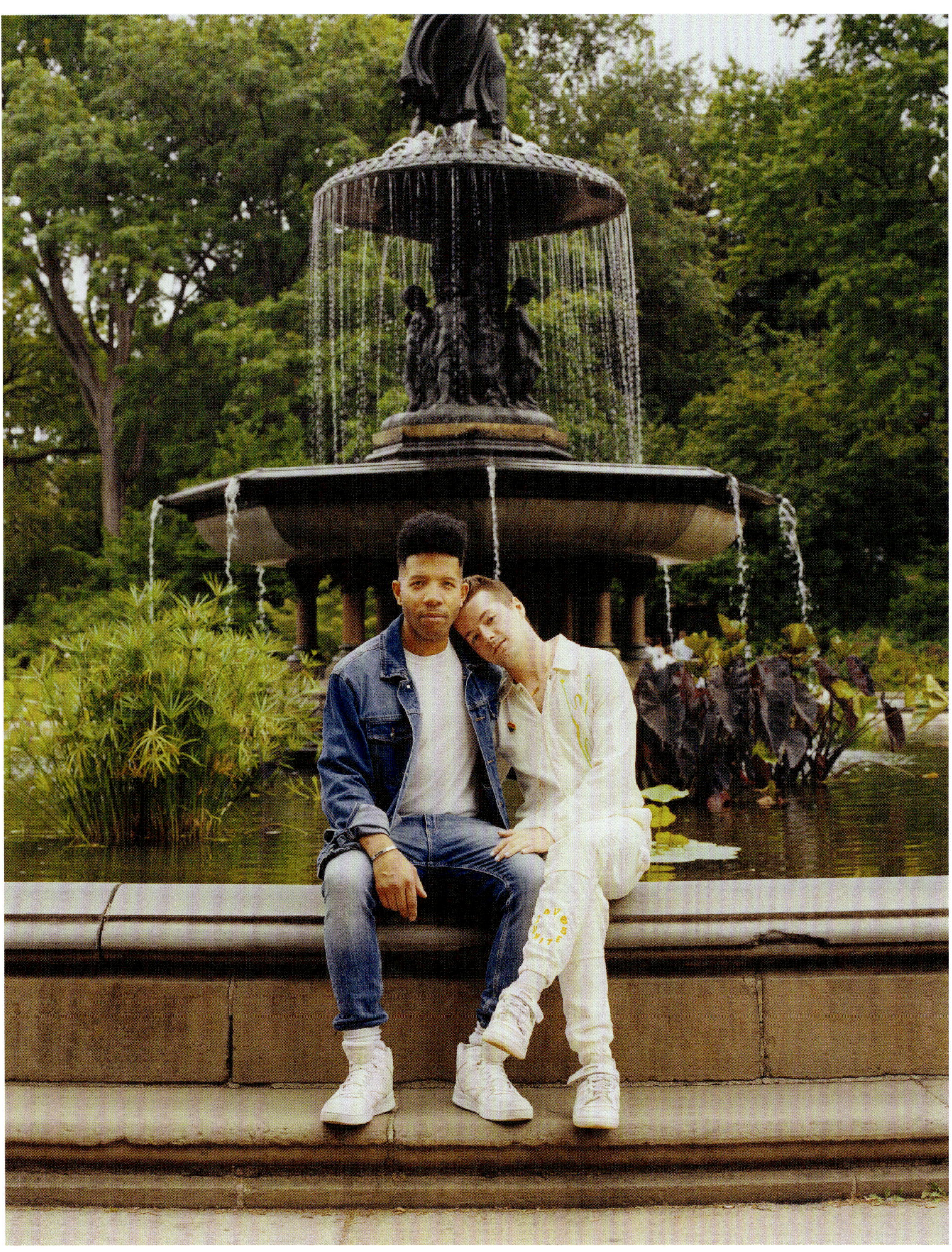

Nick *(He/They)* & Jay *(He/Him)*

NEW YORK, NY

JAY

One of the most pivotal learning moments of our relationship was in the first year, when Nick shared that in high school he had been sexually taken advantage of by a dance teacher. I was shocked and my heart absolutely broke for him. I can't imagine what it must have been like, being so young and vulnerable, entrusting someone he valued as a mentor, just to be taken advantage of. It had to leave scars that only time could heal. When we met, he was in college, so it hadn't been very long since it had happened.

The first two years of our relationship was riddled with problems, mostly having to do with Nick's lying and infidelity. I always got the feeling he was hiding something or maybe he didn't think he could fully open up about certain things. I tried to be as patient as possible, knowing that previous trauma, especially something as painful as what Nick had gone through, can change our ability to trust or communicate effectively with our partner. Thankfully, over time his walls slowly came down and we were able to work through a lot of the issues we struggled with at the start. Now some of our biggest challenges are deciding what to do for dinner at one in the afternoon, and whether I can sit through a two-and-a-half-hour Marvel movie he's excited about.

NICK

Jay and I have been through many hardships together, often because of my own doing. The first two years of our relationship was a lot of me learning about what it takes to be in a relationship. Prior to Jay, the only relationships I had were high school "infatuation-ships," and so I didn't know what it was like to compromise and value someone else's needs just as much as your own, especially if they are completely different. I was leading a double life when I met Jay—wanting to be this loving, ideal boyfriend, but stuck in these old bad habits of mindlessly pursuing sex regardless of my relationship status or what it did to my body. It wasn't until this past year when I started therapy for the first time since my assault that I was able to confront the demons that made me not prioritize the relationship and person who made me feel safer and more loved than I've ever felt. I was able to make sense of how the shame I carried around that experience and how it hurt my family impacted my ability to trust a partner or feel like I deserved all the love I was receiving from Jay.

Nico *(They/Them)* & Christani *(They/Them)*

LOS ANGELES, CA

CHRISTANI

From the beginning, we've talked openly about what it means for us to be partners with different ethnicities, gender experiences, and class backgrounds. While we are both trans and nonbinary, I am Black and South Asian, and Nico is Chinese. In public spaces and even in our families of origin, we often feel like we have to perform gender in very binary ways in order to be believed or loved or safe. Together, we created a healing space where we uplift and protect all the versions of ourselves that exist beyond the binary and white imagination. For us, being together means celebrating our identities and seeing each other fully in a world that doesn't acknowledge us. It also means being conscious of how power dynamics show up in our relationship.

NICO

We are learning more and more about how we can better care for each other. We're both working through what it's like to be out to our immigrant families and how our boundaries often separate us from our cultures and communities. Recreating rituals, sharing languages, and passing on stories with someone willing to discover all that you are has deepened the connection we have with our identities. We teach each other phrases in Jamaican Patois and Cantonese. We cook dishes that remind us of home, and we wear jade necklaces for good luck and protection.

As we nurture each other, what's most exciting is imagining and dreaming together. How do we adorn our altar? How can we transform what our family looks like? How will we continue to grow into ourselves and our communities?

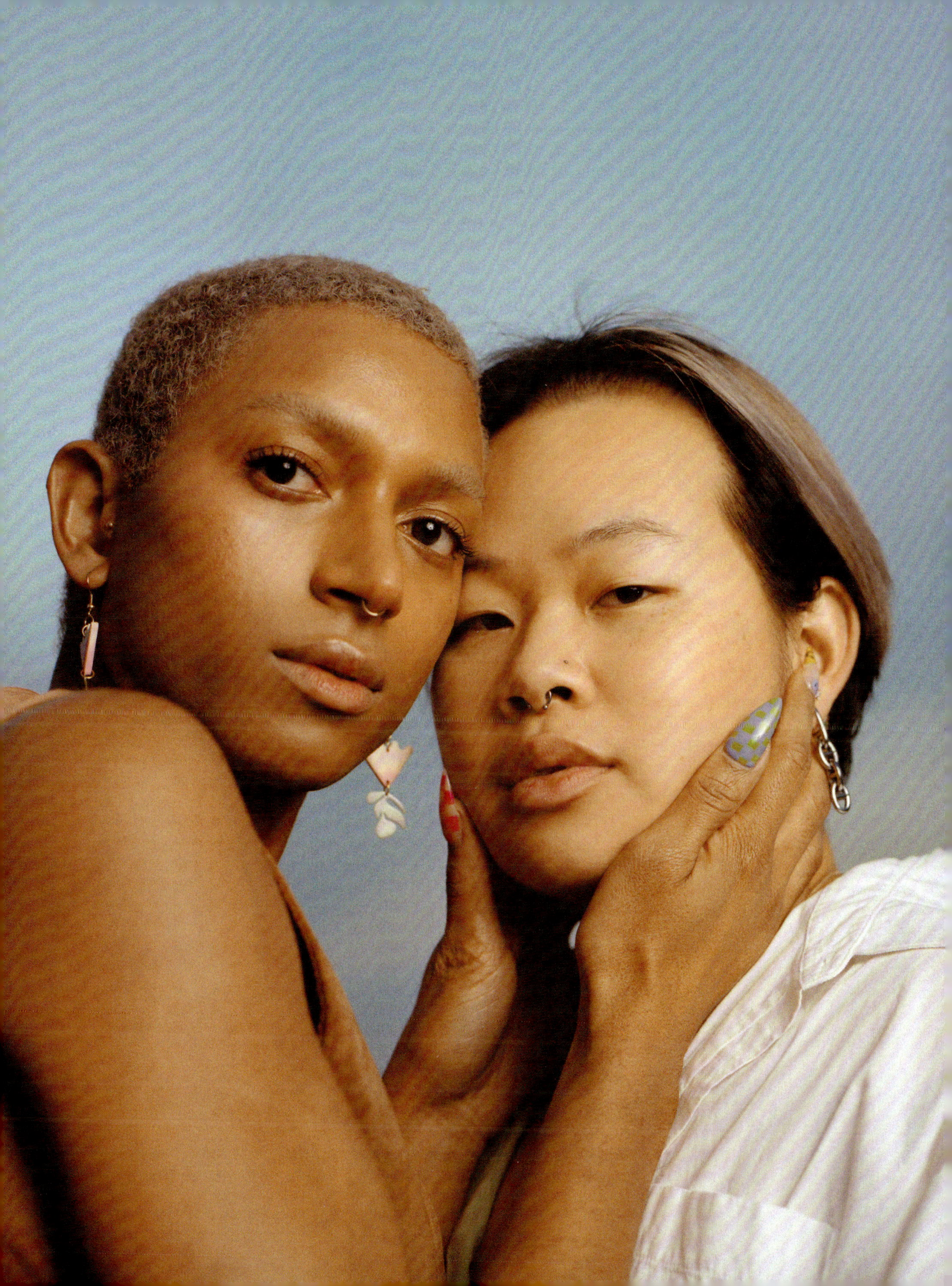

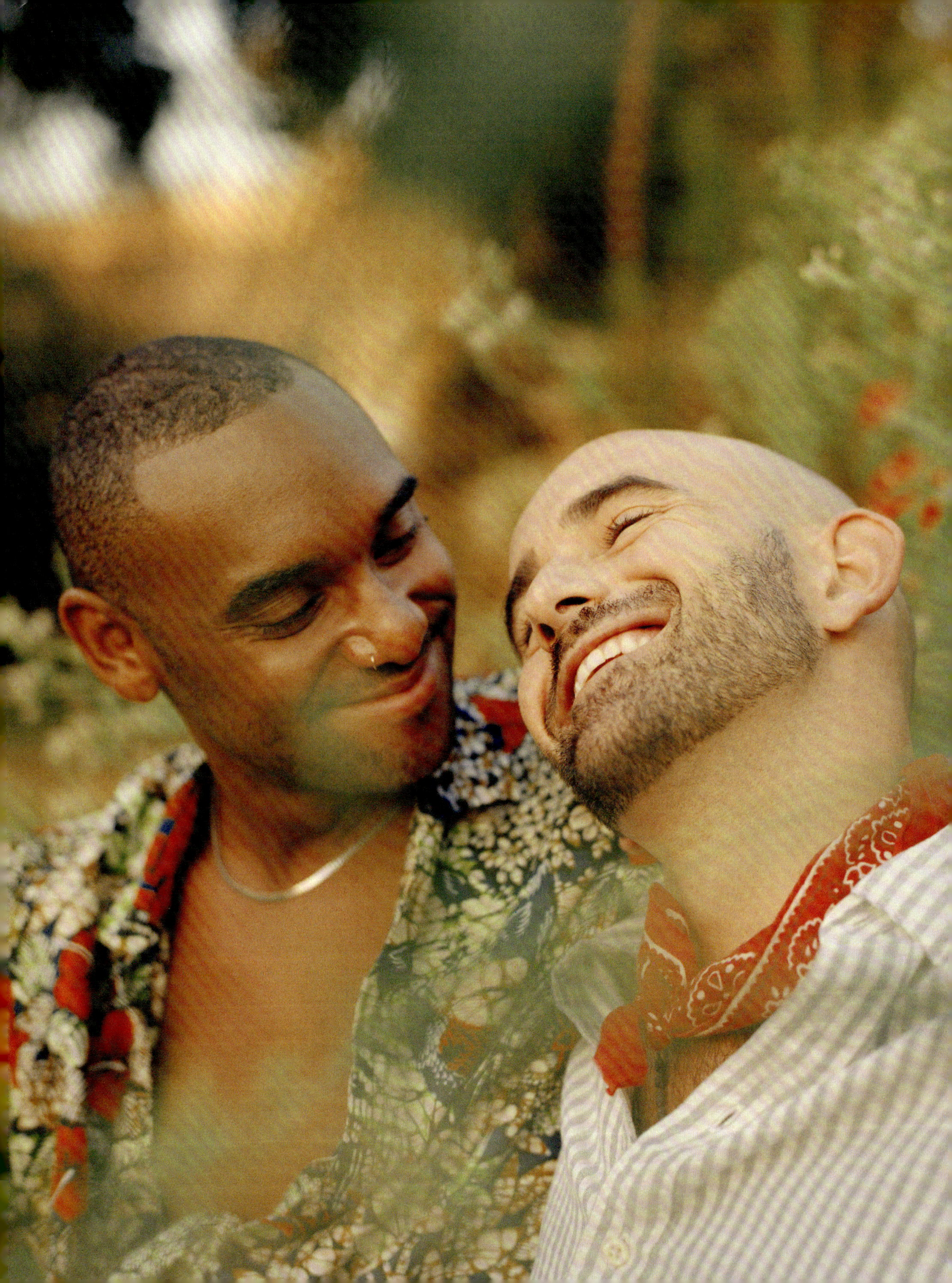

Nico *(He/Him)* & Jeremy *(He/Him)*

LOS ANGELES, CA

Note: Nico and I just broke up, and we decided it made sense to use the note that I shared with him as our text here.

JEREMY

I love you. You've helped me by creating a safe space for me to explore and work through the dark shit in my past. I will forever be grateful for that. In the same breath, you've also become a security blanket for me, a crutch through crippling anxiety. Which is why I relish the safety you provide for me in the outside world, despite the needs I've identified inside my own world. You are supportive, warm, caring—truly an incredible boyfriend. And I don't want you to change.

But I need someone who can relate to the pain I've been through. To the challenges I face as a Black, queer man trying to build a new world. Someone who knows what to say when I'm depressed, who can give me the right look when another Black person is gunned down. Someone who can challenge me when I'm thinking too inside the box. Someone who can be a co-conspirator.

I've felt this way for a while but have pushed it aside because you are an incredible boyfriend, and I felt dumb and ungrateful for wanting something else. I thought that with time—with different friends, a different job, or living in a new city—things would settle out between us. But it's not fair to you or to me to wait for what-ifs.

I can't imagine you not in my life—and breaking up terrifies me—but I think that's what's best.

Nicolette *(She/Her)* & Nina *(They/She)*

BROOKLYN, NY

NINA

Our backgrounds are worlds apart, not only between one another, but also within our own families. But for that, we've found a closeness with one another.

Nicolette's parents are Persian-Jewish and English immigrants, and she was born and raised in Los Angeles. Nina's parents are Filipino by way of Hawai'i and Eastern European Jewish by way of Long Island. Nina was born in Brooklyn but raised in suburban Ohio.

We both grew up in nuclear family units that looked different from the rest of our blood relatives, for better or worse. Both our parents found each other through whatever mysterious circumstances bring people of such different backgrounds together and have been together for decades. We found that each of our mothers (both Virgos) would speak in Farsi or Tagalog respectively with their close family, while our fathers have barely picked up a word in decades. We found our own experiences with Mizrahi and Ashkenazi Judaism. We found a shared love of rice, crispy rice, things served with rice, and generally sharing foods from our cultures with friends.

When we found each other, we found a shared experience of being an "other." But really what we found in each other was a natural state of curiosity and openness for others. As the children of parents of entirely different backgrounds, we came to be the center of our family's Venn diagrams—always picking up bits and pieces from each parent of what they chose to take or leave of their own cultures; what they've learned and shared (or not) with one another; what they extended to either of us. We've inherently understood that we would never know everything about one or the other background. We've each had our own experiences of others assuming untrue homogeneous experiences of us or getting the full "what are you?" questioning, but we live in the "both/and" experience. Living in that shared experience of the "both/and" has been one of the most special things we share as a couple, and one of the things that has brought us together.

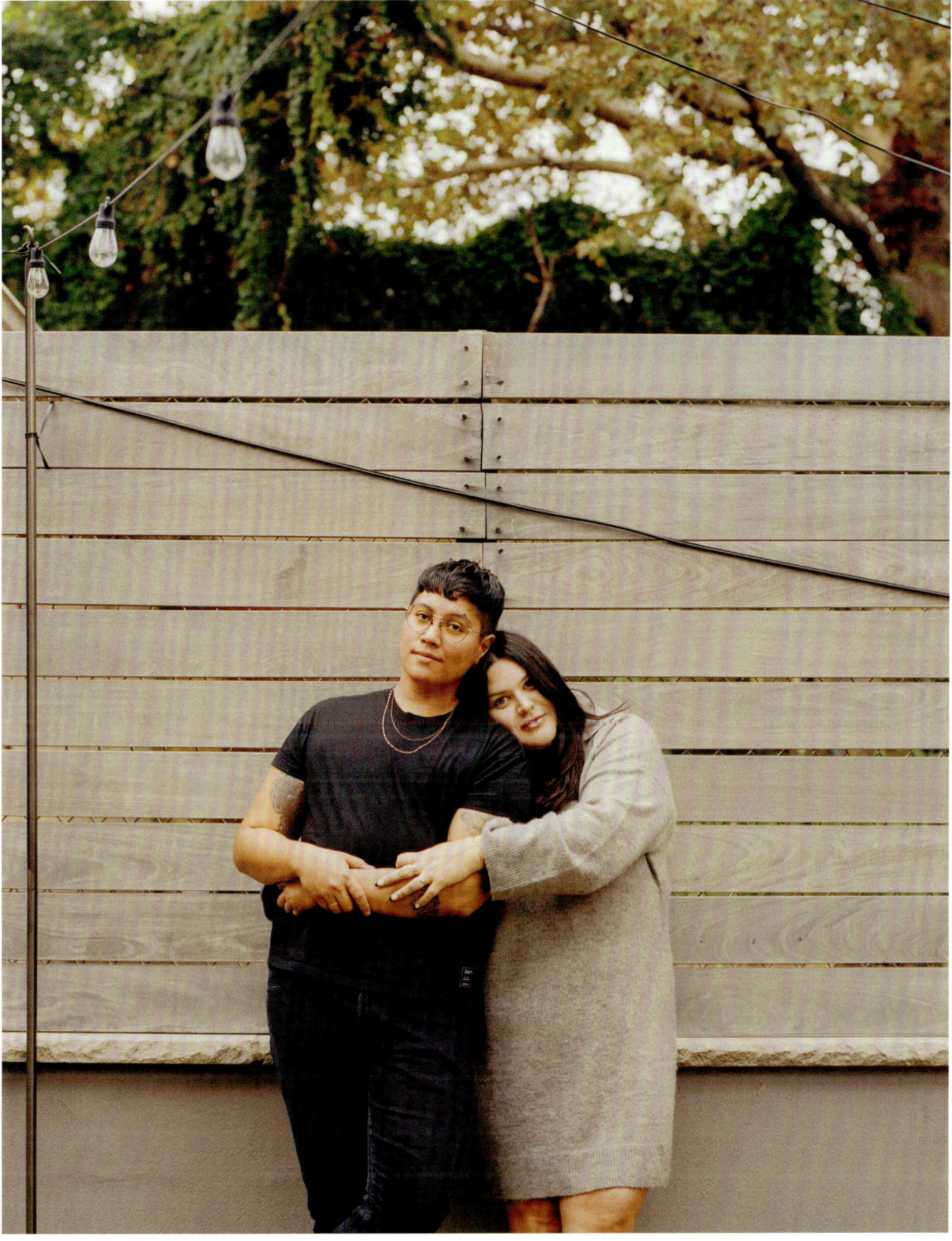

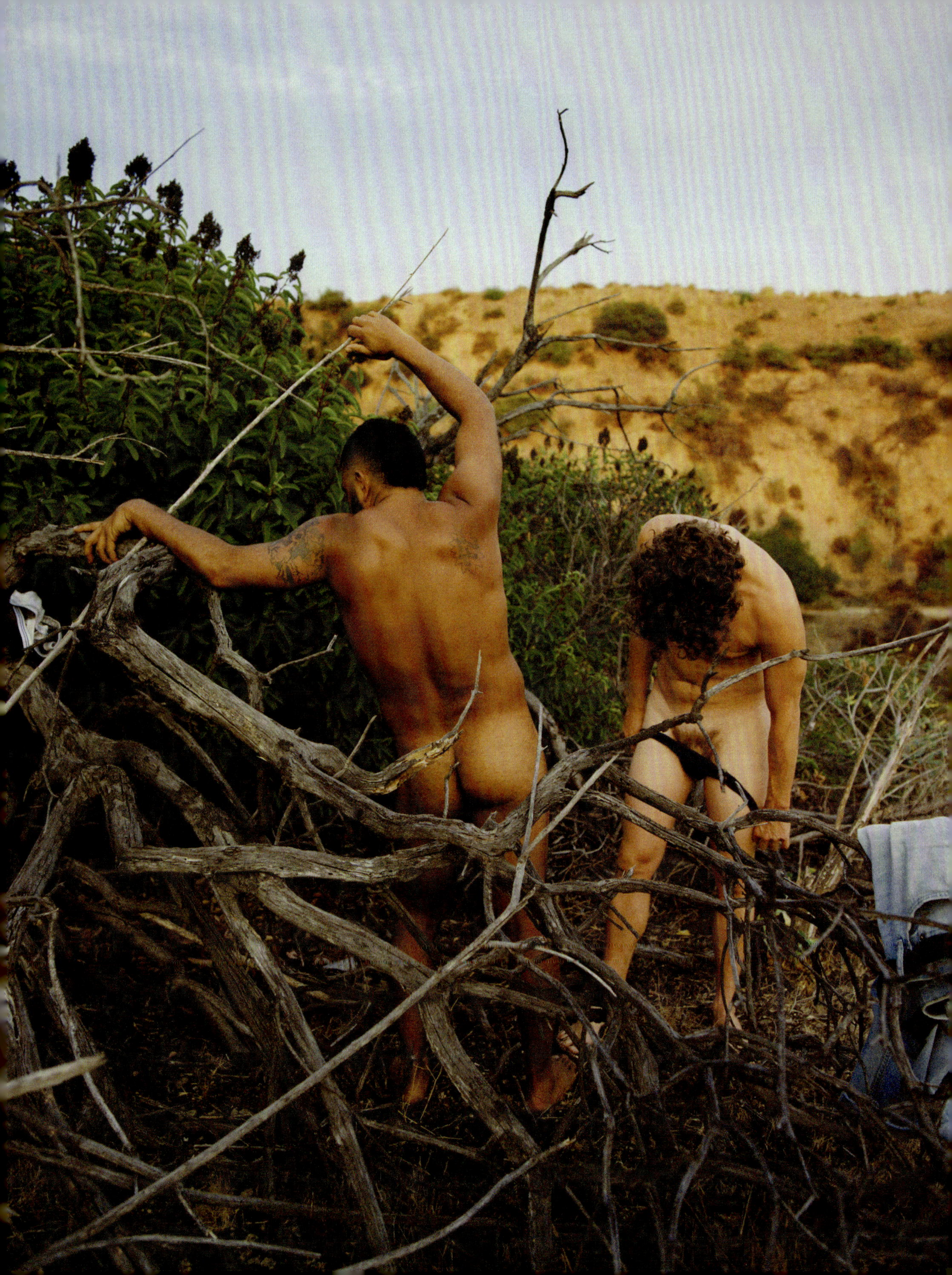

Owen *(He/Him)* & Zaid *(He/Him)*

LOS ANGELES, CA

ZAID

We were born into different cultural backgrounds: I'm a Guatemalan altar boy and Owen is a New York Jew, both of us momma's boys. I moved to Los Angeles in 1990 from Guatemala City when I was sixteen years old. Less than a year later I ran away because I was gay. After a few tumbles I was graciously adopted by the parents of a classmate, reformed Jews in Los Feliz. We celebrated Shabbat every Friday well into my mid-twenties. Now, having Shabbat with Owen's family is such a beautiful way to end the week. And there are the many holidays and celebrations he spends with my own family here in LA. Owen studied Spanish in Cuba for some time, and he can speak with my visiting tias.

After five lovely years together, we began having honest conversations about our sexuality and needs. Being thirteen years apart has been the biggest challenge for us. Sexual fantasies (and the potential to fulfill them in seemingly every corner of Los Angeles) is an ever-present topic. So we agreed that we both want to be with each other and enjoy a respectful, safe, open relationship. There is still a lot of stigma about it. With open, honest communication, we feel more connected than ever and responsible and loving to each other. We continue to grow together and build a life with each other. We are best friends, still with passion and benefits.

Parker *(He/They)* **& Julian** *(He/Him)*

LOS ANGELES, CA

For two people with vibrant imaginations, our relationship wasn't one that either of us ever dreamed—an audacious Black boy from Phoenix paired with a shy white boy from St. Louis. Who'd have thought we would be building a life side by side in Los Angeles? Our differences challenge us in many ways, but these challenges also provide us unique opportunities for growth, connection, and joy. We will be the first to say it: we are not perfect. There are many times when exchanging, "I love you," we are really saying, "I forgive you." But it is this forgiveness and love that has helped us carve out a safe, creative, and warm space in one another—a home far from Phoenix and St. Louis.

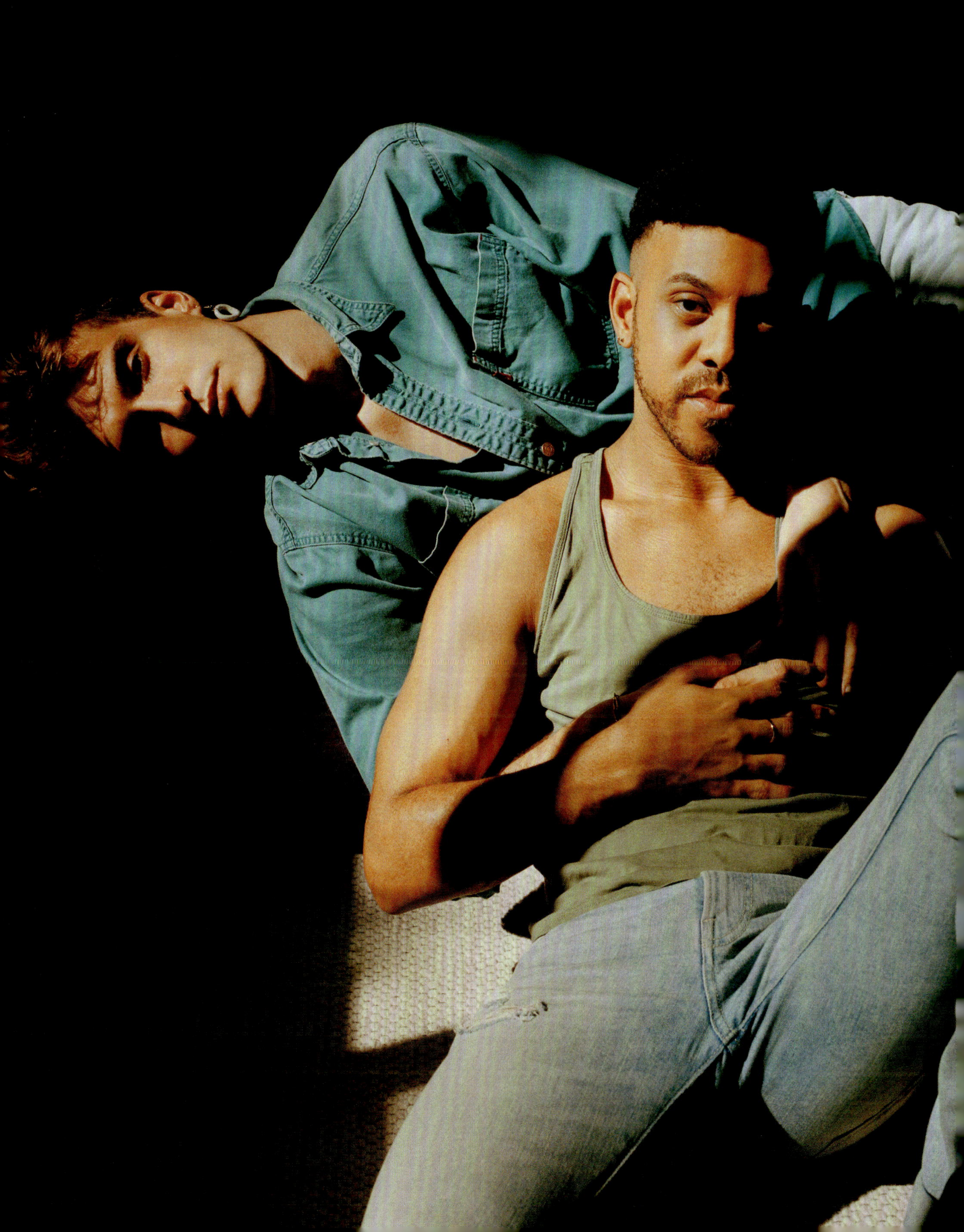

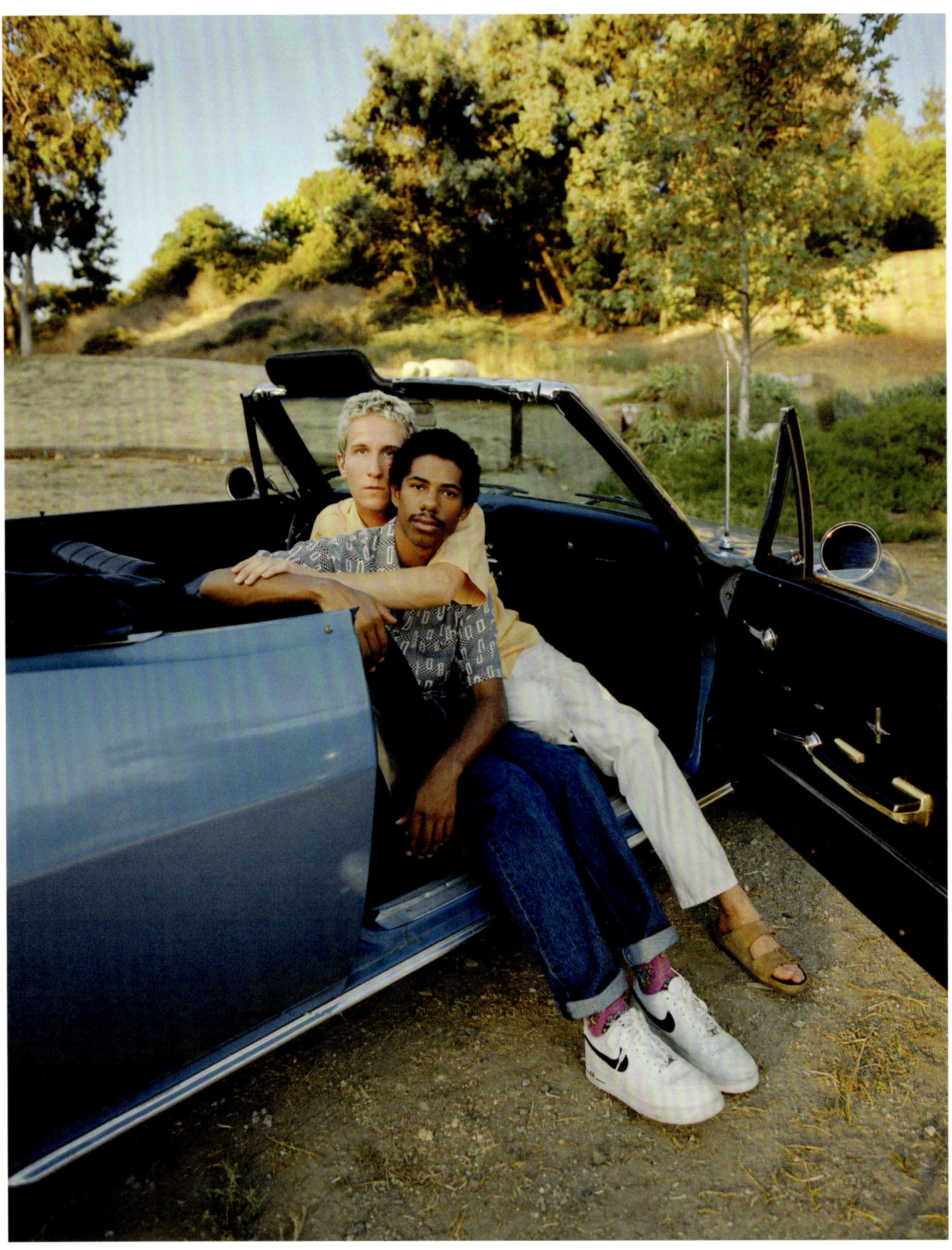

Patrick *(He/Him)* & Nathan *(He/Him)*

LOS ANGELES, CA

NATHAN

Around the time that Patrick and I met, I was nearing rock bottom. Staring my graduation from USC dead in the face, I was extremely depressed. I had crashed from my high after playing saxophone in two or three shows with Solange Knowles (minor roles, but enough to sway Patrick, clearly) the year before.

My love of music clashed with the actual act of going to classes, writing papers, and the toxicity of music school cliques. I stayed up all night and slept long into the day, unless the relentless anxiety of failing my classes eventually dragged me out of bed. I was unsure about my career, the people I surrounded myself with, and recent affirmation of my sexual identify.

Enter Patrick. He was seemingly everything that I had been looking for, and likely what I needed to keep me from falling off the edge. Creative, intensely attractive, and—almost above all else—has extensive knowledge about hip-hop and R&B music. So I did what any Internet-age kid does, sending a DM, exposing my dry, unfazed, and unamused flirting style to any number of online backdoor hackers who may have been prying.

If anyone had been watching, they would have seen it didn't take long for me and Patrick to realize we were into one another. One night, after a few missed connections, I pulled up to my apartment to see a tall, skinny, blond-haired, blue-eyed guy—grinning ear to ear, mind you—leaning against the hood of his 2006 eggshell-white Honda sedan. From there, we've been locked in.

We've had to navigate our own internal biases, the biases of our families, and the opinions of those around us. Patrick never ceases to amaze me in his willingness to learn and adapt or change his mindset after being equipped with new information. He's intensely curious and has always stayed on the forefront of arming himself with knowledge to better himself and his community. Patrick has taught me so much about love, genuineness of heart, and leaning into the robustness of feeling out every emotion, no matter how difficult.

He's been with me through extreme lows, has brought me immense joy, and always welcomes me home with open arms.

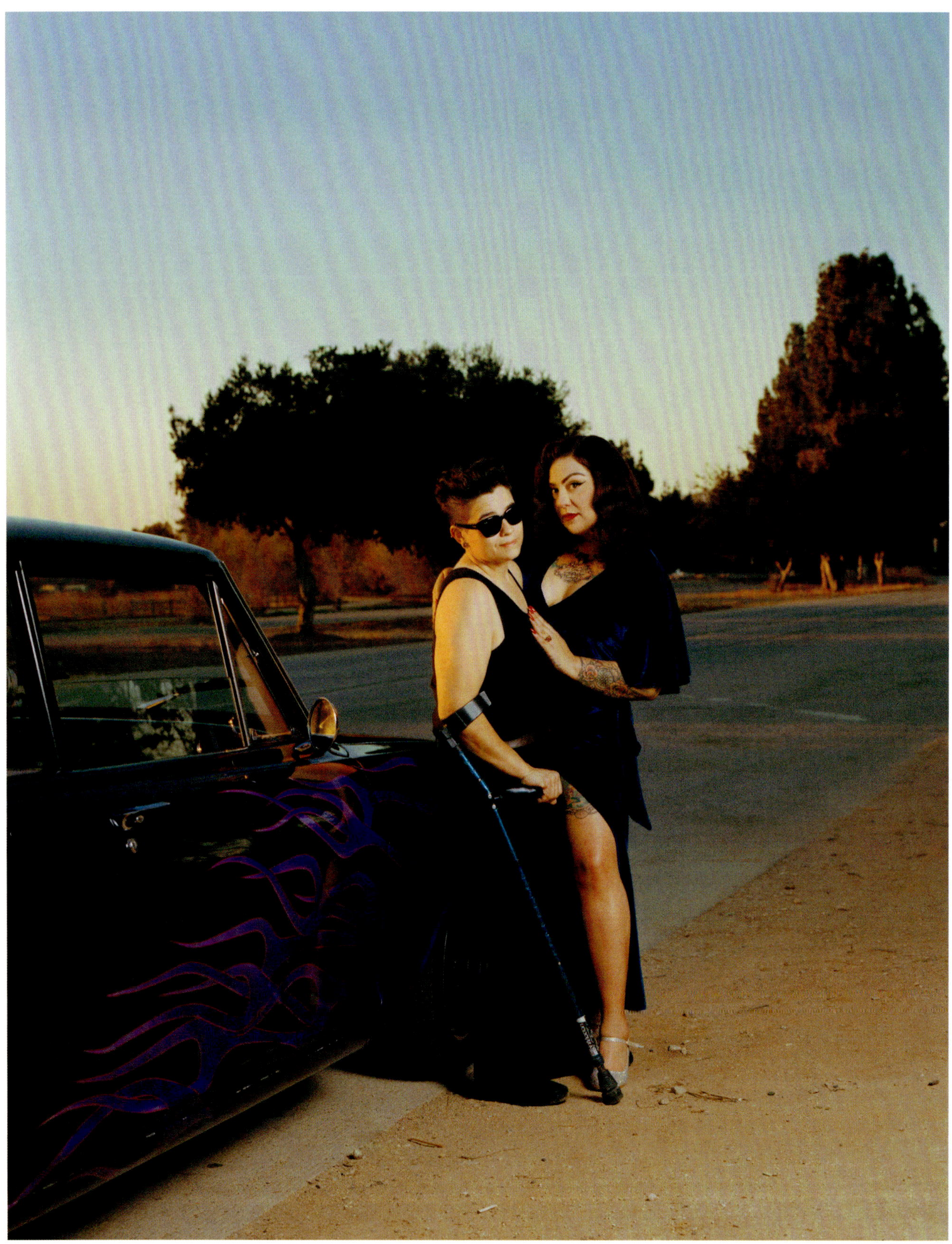

Patty *(She/Her)* & Jezel *(She/Her)*

LOS ANGELES, CA

PATTY

When we met, we had instantaneous electric chemistry. As we got to know one another we realized our disabilities intersected and we would have to continuously learn how to work through them. I grew up being in and out of the hospital for mental illnesses and chronic pain. Later I was diagnosed with borderline personality disorder, bipolar, PTSD, fibromyalgia, narcolepsy, a heart condition, and other chronic illnesses. Jezel had an open book pelvic fracture, lacerations to vital organs, fractures to her scapula and vertebrae, and also a below-the-knee amputation after an accident that left her with long-term nerve damage and persistent pain she must constantly manage.

While we both have disabilities we maneuver through, this world treats us differently. Jezel's disability is visible and mine isn't. Because of this, I realized I had internalized ableism that I continuously have to work on. I've also learned to accept help and if I'm being honest, not take for granted the privilege of having all my limbs. Jezel taught me not to let anything stop you from trying to live life to the absolute fullest.

I navigate physical spaces differently because of Jezel, and Jezel navigates relationships differently because of me. Jezel had to come up close and personal with the reality of invisible illnesses like mine, and because of that she's really tapped into her empathy toward others. She learned that you really never know what's going on with others simply by looking at them.

Navigating the world as queer, disabled women of color isn't always a walk in the park, but with one another by our side, we know that the walk won't be done alone. And who knows, maybe we can stop and smell those flowers from time to time. Or we can say fuck the walk, let's go on a Sunday cruise. Chasing those sunsets and singing to old tunes...that's always much more fun anyway.

Rachel *(She/Her)* & Hope *(She/Her)*

LOS ANGELES, CA

HOPE

I identify as a queer woman of color, more specifically mixed-race and Black, and Rachel is a queer, white, secular Jew. Adopted as a baby by a white gay couple, I've always somewhat existed in mixed-race families and relationships. While this experience has definitely had an impact on my desire to connect and build chosen family with other Black and Brown people, it has also made the idea of being in an interracial relationship seem not entirely implausible. That said, it does come with its challenges.

One moment early on in our relationship, I was with Rachel at a friend's home who had several of their white acquaintances over. The Breonna Taylor verdict had been decided that evening and it weighed heavy on my heart. As the evening progressed, it became too difficult for me to bear witness to white people carrying on their evening as normal. It struck me how disconnected they can be from Black pain, how they can opt in and out of joy much easier than those who know society wants us dead. I grew increasingly uncomfortable, and later that night at Rachel's house I brought this up. It was one of our first conversations like this, since we were only two weeks in. The dissonance of the evening had been frustrating, but our conversation had affirmed my care for her when she listened, agreed, and comforted me. This moment ultimately brought us closer together, while also shining a spotlight on the gulf between our two identities. Rachel continues to grow and is much more cognizant of the microaggressions that I face on a day-to-day basis living as a Black woman in America. In our time together we both acknowledge that constant check-ins and open conversations about race give us the best chance at being able to understand and support one another.

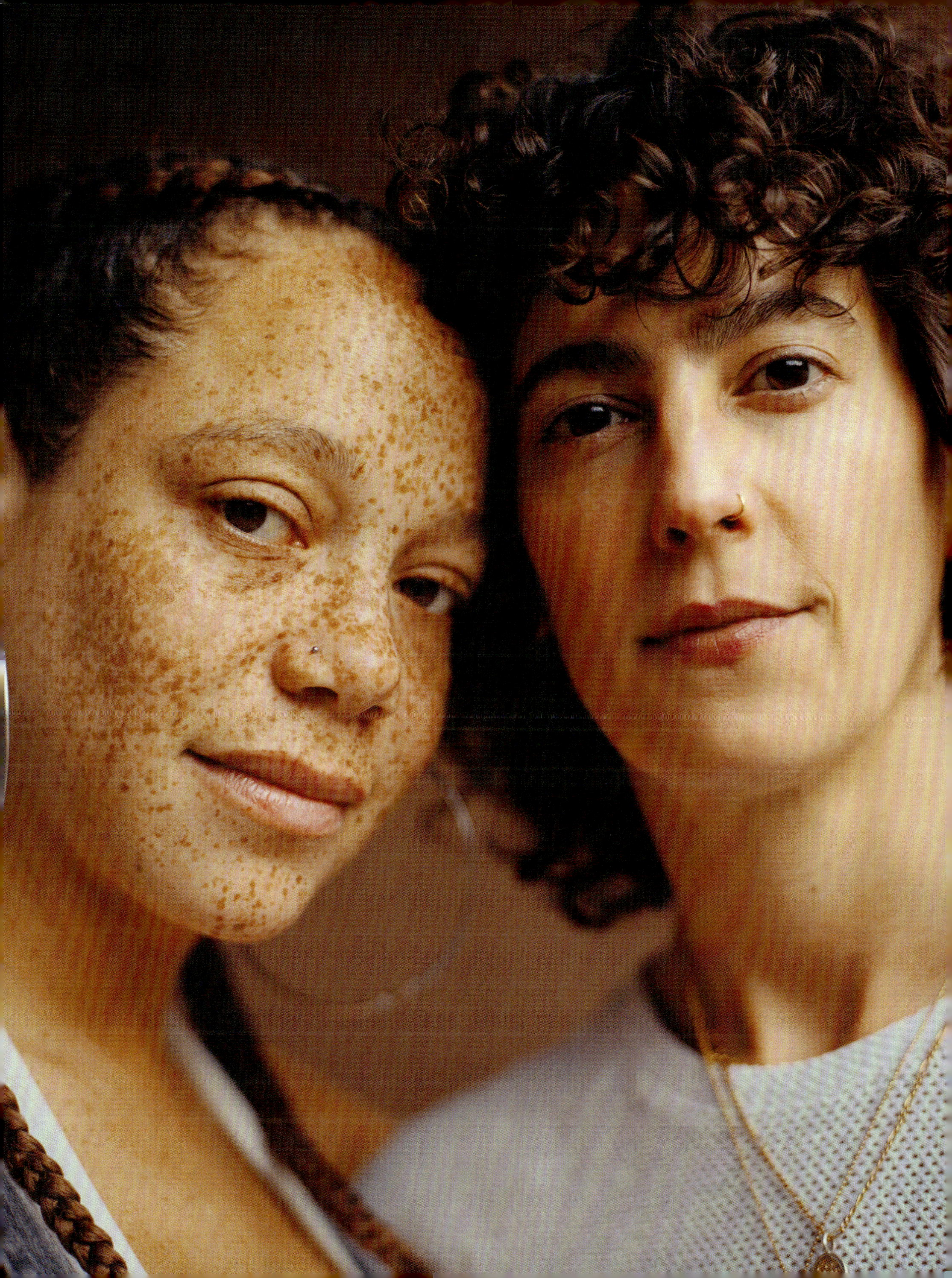

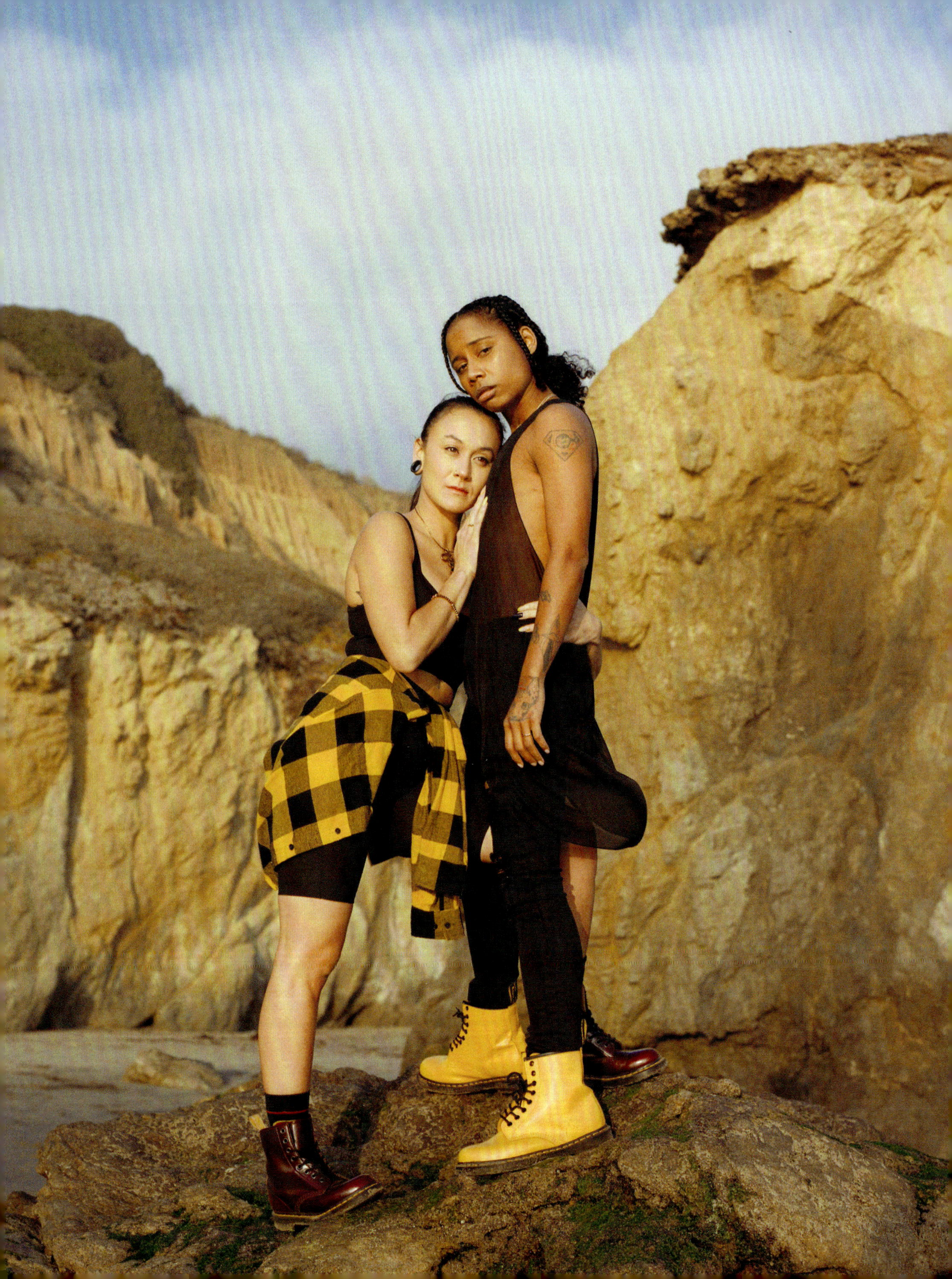

RAW *(She/They)* & ’issa *(She/Her)*

LOS ANGELES, CA

RAW

Pre-motherhood, my dating palette could be described as slut-ever, a colorful and promiscuous hodgepodge of pussy. I, an Afro-latinx, gender-fluid stegosaurus, found myself in cahoots mostly with other Black and Latinx women. It wasn’t until I met ’issa that I realized I had some internal prejudices against Asians. Firstly, I never dated or ran in any circles with any Pacific Islanders. I don’t know if this was intentional—there just weren’t many in Michigan where I grew up. And it wasn’t that my Protestant, pastor parents were anti-anyone, they just were pro-us. Us, meaning, Black folk. Add a lil systemic racism and white supremacy to the pot, and you have long-standing rifts between many marginalized communities.

So when ’issa slid into my DMs a couple years back, I really didn’t know how to respond. When this fine Filipina proceeded to tell me she listened to the likes of J Dilla, Madlib, and Nina Simone, my ignorant ass was baffled. What do you know about J Dilla? I could feel the disgust through the direct message. And she deservingly sonned me. Humbled. How ignorant of me. As if she were exempt from genres of music based on her ethnicity and culture. As if I knew what her culture even was, based on her looks. As if many marginalized communities don’t gravitate toward jazz, blues, and hip-hop…as well as contribute to it. Talk about an evolutionary level up for me! Dating outside of my norm is rad because it opens my world to new cultures and experiences. It has afforded me an experience of altruistic love while allowing life to flourish beyond the limiting constructs of race, gender, and sex. Both my partner and I are biracial human beings, but more importantly, we are so many other rad things. Our hunger for creating, for art, humanity, social activism, and hip-hop is what keeps our relationship full of life. The points we have little control over that make us different are probably the least exciting parts.

RJ *(He/Him)* & Braxton *(He/Him)*

LOS ANGELES, CA

RJ

This has to be the first relationship I've ever been in where I've never been made to feel like I'm "too much" or "too out there" or "too big of a personality." I won't say that this is solely because Braxton is the first queer person of color I've been with, since he is such a kind, compassionate, dynamic person in his own right. But at the same time, I don't think this is purely coincidental. Both of us have weathered so many horrific experiences, and we both know what it's like to live in a world that tries to devalue us based on who we are. So much of his strength that I admire comes from overcoming those obstacles. So much of his perspective that enraptures me comes from staying true to who he is. And so much of my own growth stems from the fact that I have a partner who's also a role model.

BRAXTON

Funny story: our first date lasted only an hour. I had this idea of exactly what I wanted in a partner. I had already drawn out my life plan before thinking of how things could be if I actually allowed another person to open my eyes to new and exciting things in life and not conform to the idea of the "perfect relationship."

I ran off and continued my journey for the ideal match only to find myself coming back to him. I figured, "Hey, I tried what I THOUGHT I wanted, now let's just have some fun and see where this goes."

Coming into this relationship, RJ and I both carried lots of trauma. Trauma from previous relationships, family connections, as well as demons of our own. Right from the beginning we found a very safe space where we could open up, communicate, and find a way to heal each of our wounds. RJ has been the rock that I never knew I needed. He has opened up windows into my soul that I had kept closed from the world for years. He has allowed me to be my creative self with no apologies. I knew that I had found someone special when we spent our first few nights together just cuddling and talking about our life journey. RJ has taught me one thing for sure: feelings don't have to be rational; they are your own feelings, and no one really has to understand them, but the key is to respect them.

The feelings I have for Ricardo are stronger than I can put into words. He has managed to find a cozy location deep in my heart, and I'll forever hold that space for him.

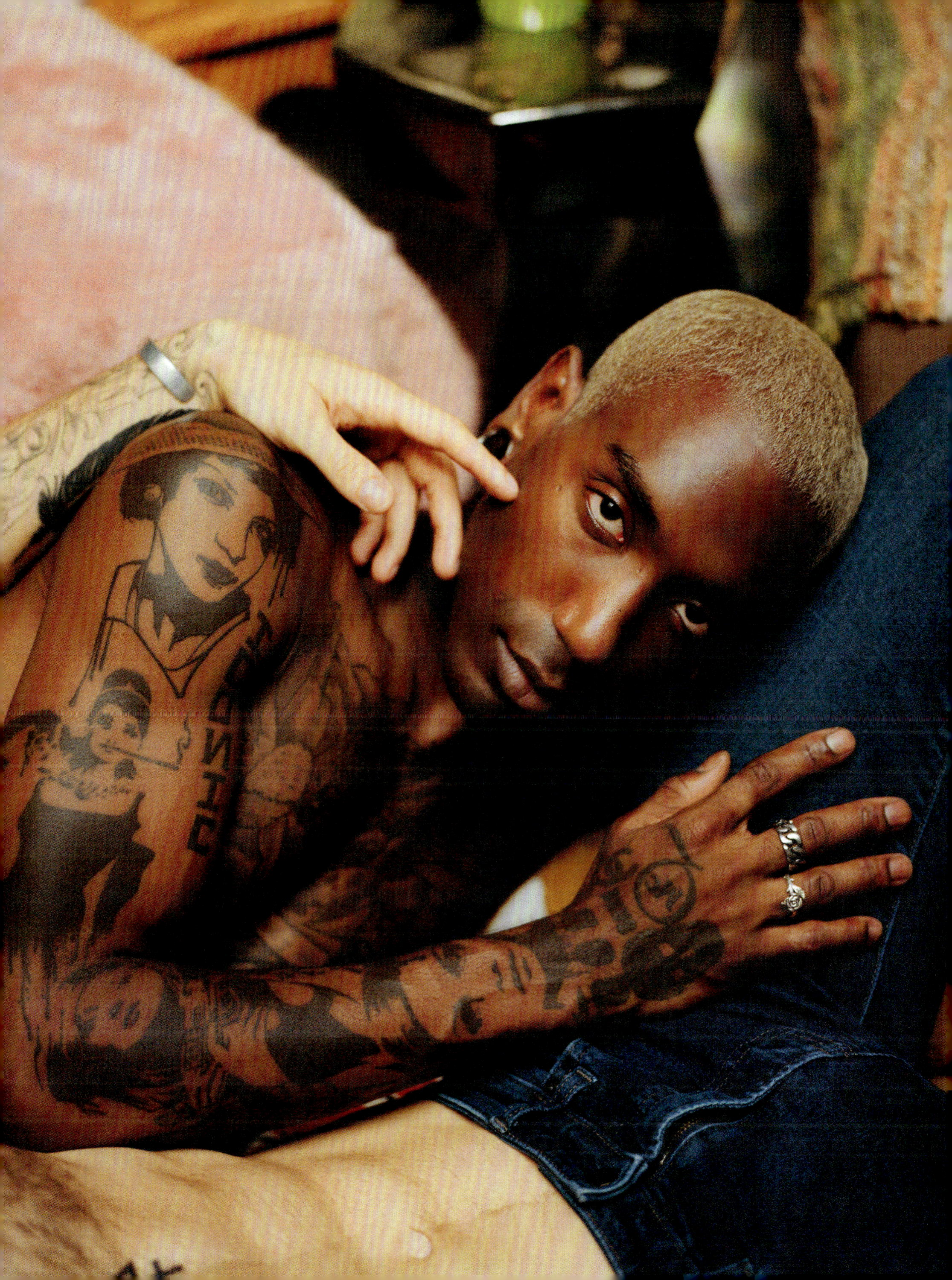

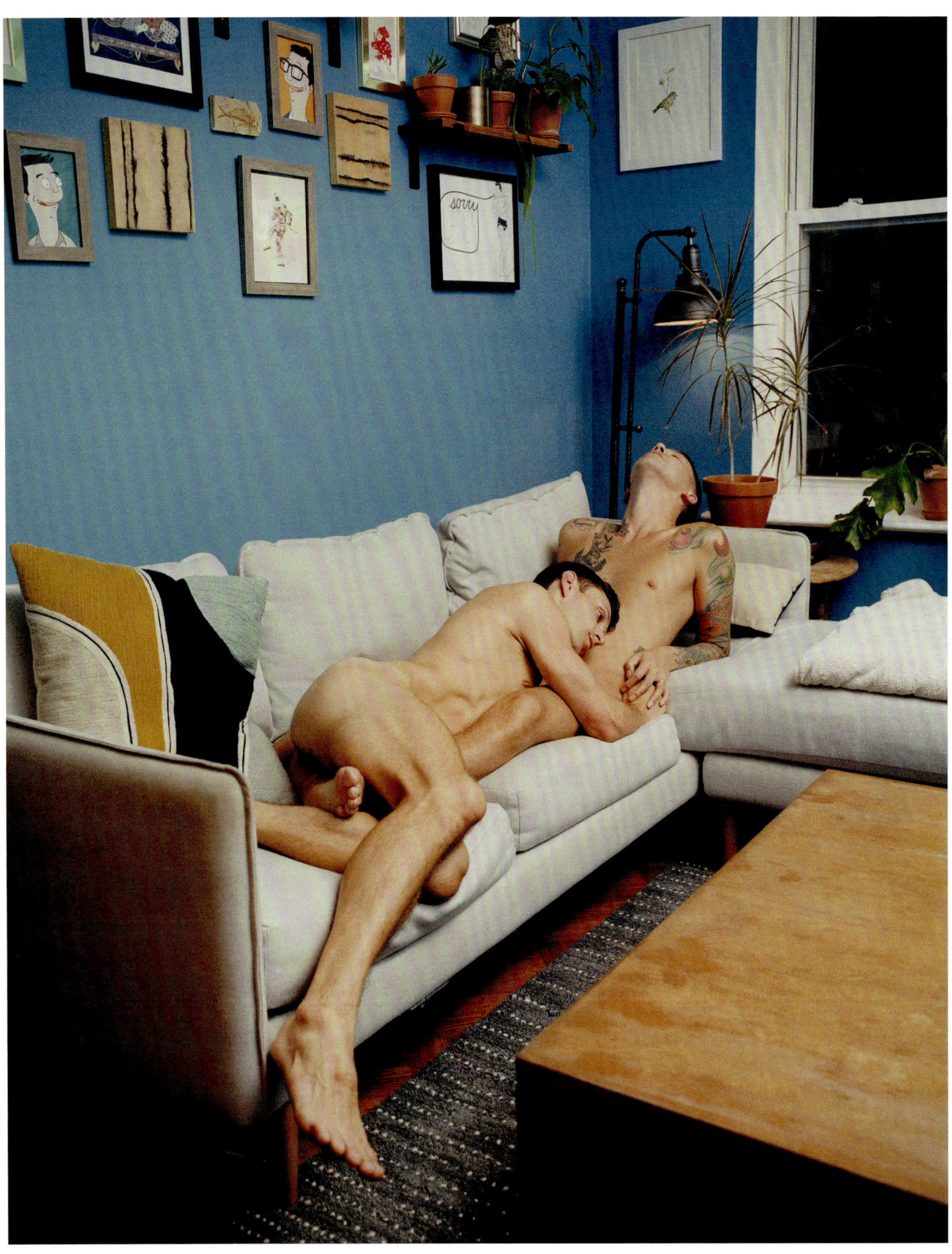
sorry

Robbie *(He/Him)* & John *(He/Him)*

QUEENS, NY

JOHN

I'll never forget how quickly you caught my eye. Bleached hair, covered in tattoos, and an irrepressible charisma. We exchanged a few words, and an impression was made, though apparently only on one side. Meeting you the second and third times, I still found you charming even as I became increasingly annoyed that you retained no recollection of me. On the fourth introduction I was determined to have nothing to do with you. Nevertheless, you persisted, and I gave you my number figuring you wouldn't remember me. But then you did.

Things started playfully, but as time went on, I realized that beyond all you did to make me happy, the most important things you brought me were comfort and security. You became a grounding force in my life, and six years later I remain in awe of all you do to be the best partner you can be. My only hope is that I'm able to return the favor. I hope I can be there for you through all the good times and the bad, and that I'm able to make your life better for it. I love you, babe. And I can't wait to be married to you.

ROBBIE

I found the happiness I was looking for in a partner. Admittedly, it wasn't love at first sight, because, well, I was intoxicated every time I introduced myself to you—four times to be exact. But that last time it stuck and I'm so happy it did. At least I was persistent, right?

When I found you, everything was easy. Talking to you was easy. Laughing with you was easy. Listening to you was easy. And kissing you—kissing you was especially easy. You gave me the opportunity to love you. I took it and ran with it and never looked back. You never gave me a reason to look back. You've always been my North Star.

I vow to put our relationship first. I vow to honor and respect you, to laugh with you and to make you smile, to not take any moment I have with you for granted, and to be by your side when times are tough. I vow to think about you every morning after I wake up and every night before I go to sleep. I vow to grow old with you and to accept every part of you. I vow to support you. I vow to love you. Forever and always.

Robert *(He/Him)* & Paul *(He/Him)*

NEW YORK, NY

PAUL

Our first date was in 2013, and all we really remember is that it was winter when we met. Robert was two hours late because of Mies (now *our* dog), who was getting his shots at a free drive. We ended up in the lobby of the Ace Hotel sharing fries. We were twenty and twenty-three at the time. A few dates and months later I told Robert I loved him, and Robert tripped on his words. But later he handed me a notebook with "I love You" inscribed on the first page. I used that notebook during my first year in undergrad and still have it today.

ROBERT

Together we're working toward our future, Paul as an artist and me as a financial planner. When we first met, instead of enjoying our youth with friends and partying, we both had to hustle just to make sure we could afford a life of independence in New York. Where the biggest goal we could possibly imagine was living beyond a five-by-seven-foot bedroom and providing for ourselves and our dog.

We have both worked very hard, at our relationship as well as our passions. We want to create the best world to live in. As our relationship developed, we learned that the most important thing we could do is to communicate. Communicate in every sense of the word, truthfully expressing what drives our motives in our arguments, how the other person is presenting themselves, understanding the other's perspective, and most importantly, using that information to better our relationship. Over several years we've grown into a partnership of support and one that breaks down problems, from how to assemble furniture to how to navigate starting a new career. Today we're continuing to grow with each other, focusing on turning individual goals into joint priorities.

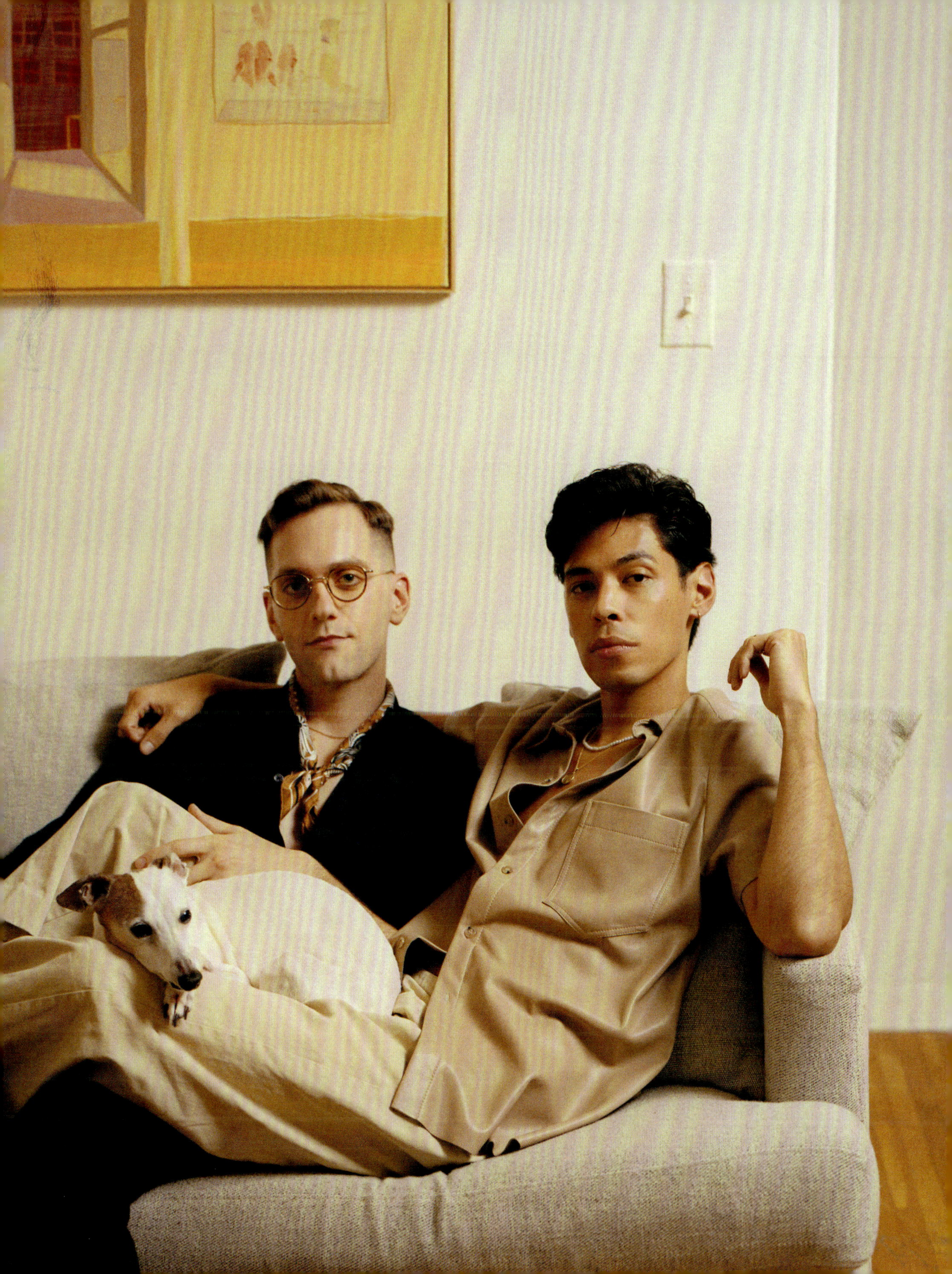

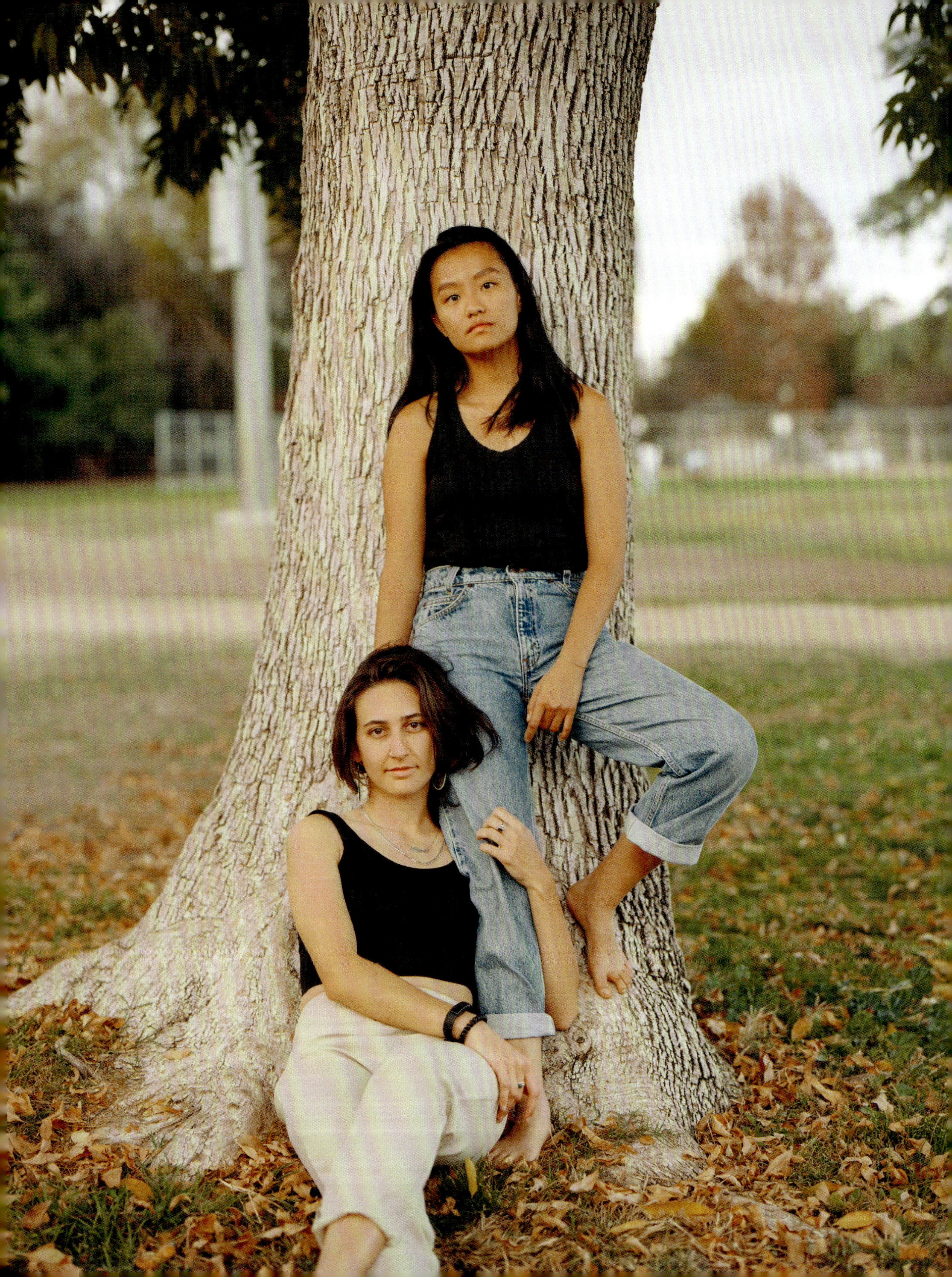

Ruby *(She/Her)* & Romi *(She/Her)*

LOS ANGELES, CA

RUBY

I explain my last name every few days. "I'm adopted," I decode. The cashiers, Uber drivers, and other non-invited inquisitors nod in satisfaction as I resolve their curiosity. At the age of one, I was adopted from China into a Puerto Rican family. With that, I adopted their food, their culture, their language, and their name. Twenty-four years later, I have only just begun to understand the Chinese body I occupy, my Puerto Rican upbringing, and the incongruence between the two. Like a rumor out of control, my physical identity exists often uncontextualized. While shrouded by notions and biases associated with Chineseness, moving through the world in this body is also a privilege. A few months ago, I confided in Romi that I was nervous about being too loud or abrasive in certain social situations. Humorously, she assured me that Asian women aren't generally perceived that way, in fact quite the opposite. Upon reflection, Romi's comment re-illuminated a reality of my identity that is usually eclipsed by doubt. This is one of many conversations we have had about self-image and self-perception. In conversations like these, we paint and repaint complex portraits of our identities in pursuit of a more adequate encapsulation of the people we are.

ROMI

I have never been one to wear my identity on my sleeve. That isn't to say that I am not proud of my identities—I am. But my hesitancy around being loud and proud is driven by fear. In 1942, my grandfather escaped from a Jewish roundup in Paris, and with his stories I inherited a fear of being persecuted (along with other third-gen survivor traits like stocking up on enough dry food to feed a shtetl!). And now, when I hold Ruby's hand in public, a similar feeling creeps in—the fear of being identified as "other" and what violence might accompany that. But when I walk down the street, I am a white woman in America. With Ruby, conversations about identity are common. We encourage each other to speak openly and without judgment while challenging the nuances of our complex identities. As I continue to examine why I tend to conceal my more vulnerable identities from the world, I must also recognize that my ability to choose how much Jewishness or queerness I share is my biggest privilege of all.

Ryan *(He/Him)* & Zach *(He/Him)*

PHOENIX, AZ

RYAN

Growing up, I played baseball my whole life. High school, college, and professionally overseas. In the hypermasculine environment that was and still significantly is the current world of sports, I always felt like I had to portray myself in a more masculine way. For me, this was something I had to actively work at because I naturally have what most of society would consider "feminine" tendencies. Everyday I was extremely conscious about what I was wearing, how I talked, and my mannerisms, so I could be one of the guys and not give any indications that I was gay.

When I came out after college while playing baseball overseas, it took me a while to figure out the gay scene and where I fit into it. One thing I quickly realized was that the majority of gays that I met were more attracted to masculine men. Guys that were athletic, had muscles, and all these stereotypical qualities of what a man was supposed to be were just as idolized in the gay world as they were in the sports world. So again, I found myself acting more masculine than I naturally am.

But when I met my now-husband Zach, that all changed for me. With him, I felt I could be more myself than I had ever thought possible. I even got comfortable enough to perform in drag publicly! I felt this weight lifted off my shoulders because I was no longer trying to impress guys. I already had one who loved and accepted all of me so I could just be myself. Now, I can wear things seen as a bit more feminine, I can speak and say things exactly how I'm thinking of them, and I can use whatever mannerisms I want without overthinking if that's what a man should do—gay, athlete, or otherwise.

I am a Hispanic gay male athlete who can be as masculine and feminine as I want to be. It's because of Zach I feel like I can fully be myself. I love him with all of my heart for allowing me to find and accept my true self.

ZACH

It took me a while on my journey to accept my sexuality as a gay man. I had my first gay sexual encounter while living abroad in Jordan when I was nineteen. I wasn't aware or even prepared at the time to understand that I was gay. If anything, I felt asexual with little to no interest in women and didn't even consider men. My roommate at the time saw something different, assumed I was gay, and made a move that I wasn't ready for.

I didn't come out for another six years. I questioned throughout that time if I was gay. Maybe it was a one-off thing? Maybe I was bisexual. I knew it wasn't either of those things, but I didn't want to be gay. Leading up to my twenty-fifth birthday, I remember telling myself, "You are about to be a quarter of a century old. You've had enough time to figure it out. Accept it and move on." I began coming out to my friends and loved ones, slowly but surely.

It took me almost a year and a half to come out to my family. It wasn't until I met Ryan that I got the confidence to come out to most of my siblings and my parents. Having that person who could comfort me if things went wrong, who I knew I could count on to accept me whether the family member I had opened up to did or not. He was just the assurance I needed, and I am so thankful to have had him for my journey.

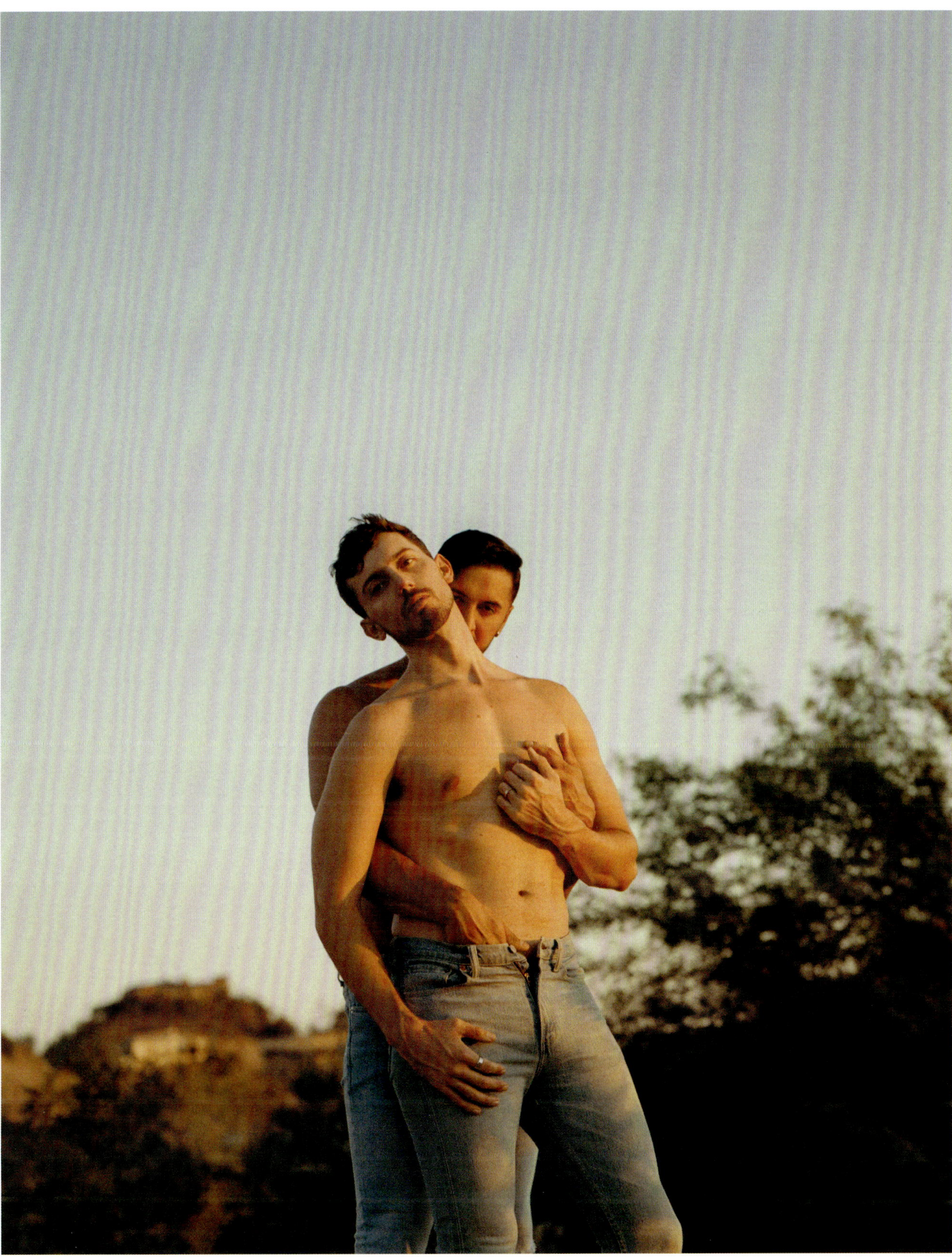

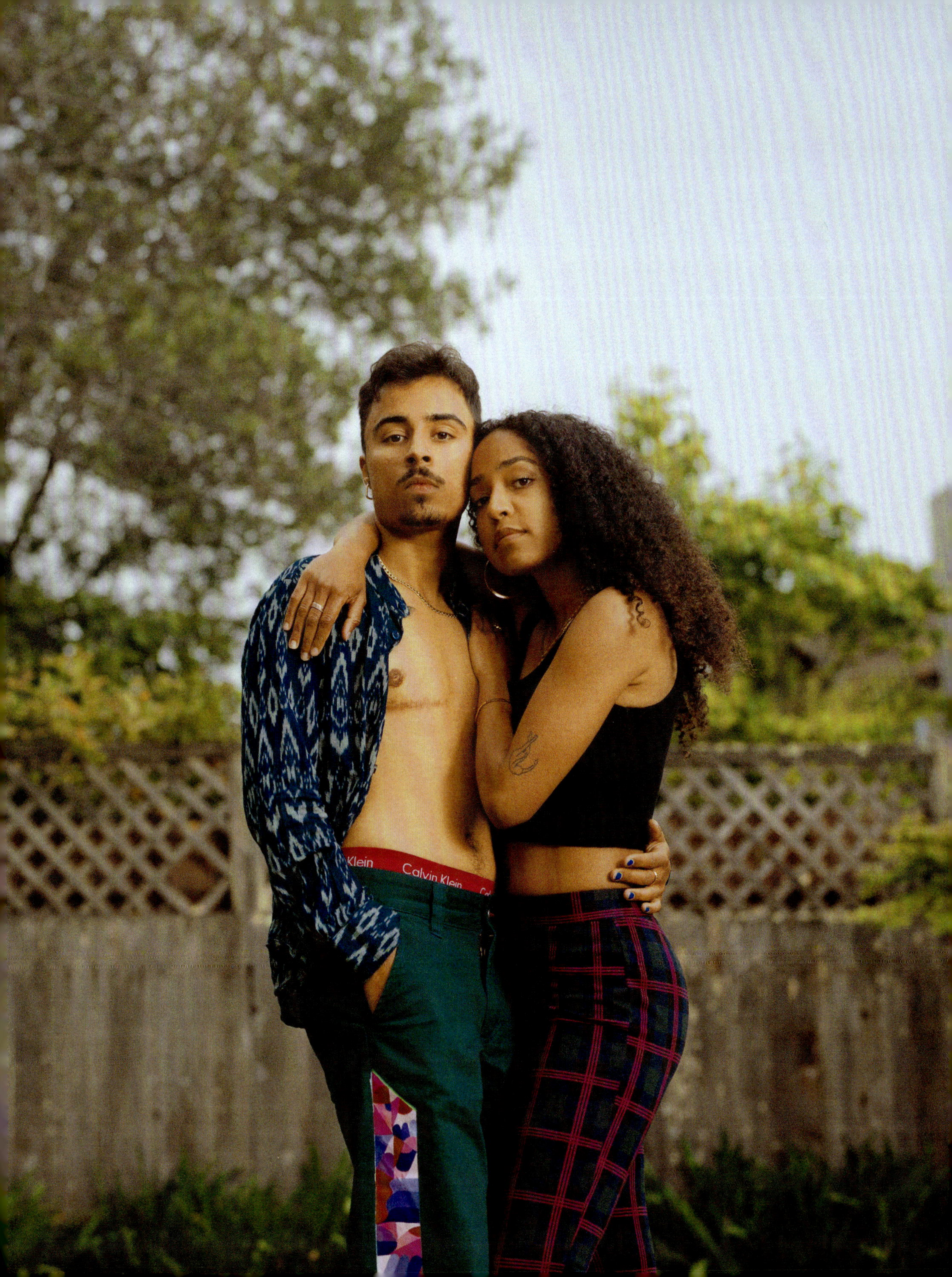
Calvin Klein

Sabrina *(She/Her)* & Mila *(He/Him)*

SAN FRANCISCO, CA

SABRINA

When I first got to know Mila, I was really drawn to the ways he was confident and so unapologetically himself. It really shows not only in the ways he carries himself as a trans man, but how he shows up as an artist as well. It's something I'm constantly learning from Mila. He teaches me how to be less scared, how to be my most authentic self, and how to think more creatively.

From the beginning of our relationship to now, we've learned how to be better communicators and listeners, and most importantly, I feel like we champion growth in one another. I really love that we've been on different journeys together through college and now through art, and I feel like Mila is an important collaborator, friend, and love in this part of my life.

MILA

Sabrina and I are both half Indian. She is mixed with Black, and I am mixed with white. Both of us are usually mistaken for the wrong half; people don't necessarily see our Indian half. This has created interesting points of cultural references for which we have different experiences but similar understandings. We met in the Sociology Club in college and became friends, then slowly more. Our relationship has evolved into a very domestic and creative relationship since the pandemic. We have gotten to know each other's practices, passions, and perspectives, creating love, opportunity, and support along the way.

I identify as a mixed-race trans man from the Bay Area. For me, this means I grew up in one of the best places to be mixed and queer. This identity has meant many different things to me throughout my life, but at the moment it feels very special and sacred to me. It's not always at the forefront of my mind, but it's always dictating my perceptions of people and ideas of community.

Going to UC Berkeley and living in a POC-cooperative housing unit changed everything for me. My eyes were opened to all the nuances of experience that were put under the POC label, and I learned how to love and adore myself as well. It changed everything about the possibilities I saw for myself and the confidence I had in myself as a person in the queer community.

Sabrina *(She/They)* & Shauna *(She/Her)*

LOS ANGELES, CA

SHAUNA

We got married September 1, 2012, in the enchanted northern woods of Vermont. Our guests were all chosen family (aside from parents and siblings). The dress code was white, the vibe was bliss, and we danced our forever into the full blue moon night.

Both sets of parents had grown to love our love but were still struggling with how to communicate it to their respective families (I'm Irish American and Sabrina's half Pakistani, half Swiss).

The morning after our ceremony, my dad clenched back tears while telling us he'd called each of his siblings to tell them the good news directly: his first daughter is married to an amazing woman "and we're thrilled about it." They all congratulated him. The joy of his release was palpable.

We had built such a bubble of queer, open love and community that I'd almost forgotten about certain circumstances. Specifically, I didn't know much about what to expect with Sabrina's extended family.

SABRINA

Ever since I came out in my teens, my dad's slogan was, "OK, that's fine…but let's keep it a secret from the family." I remember thinking to myself, What's the long-term plan with this secret? I show up to family things with my "best friend"? Eventually we have a "little kid best friend"? We're just a wacky group of friends!

I grew up surrounded by my big, beautiful Muslim extended family. After we were married, I felt the jig was up: I had to tell them. I wrote an email basically saying, "I'm gay, I'm married, I'm happy," and sent it to twenty-seven email addresses. I received a total of zero responses. When we finally did get reactions, it felt like a dramatic Bollywood plot. They could not tolerate "my choice" and spoke about me in the past tense. It was the first time my parents had been exposed to this specific kind of pain, and it hurt so deeply to see them hurt.

Coming out can feel like jumping off a cliff. You brace yourself to spit the words out and hope that on the other side the water's deep enough to catch you. Initially, it felt like I'd hit the rocks with my extended family, but looking back I've realized that in the relationships that really matter, the water is always there. It may take a while to shore up—proclaiming the "choice" to live this beautiful, free, and gay life can be shocking juxtaposed to the "choice" to adhere to one's own beautiful religious path. But over the years, the aunts and uncles and cousins who filled my upbringing with love have folded back in my life and my inbox asking, "How is Shauna? Send me pictures of that cutie Wolfie," and to admit the undeniable: "Wow, that family of yours is beautiful."

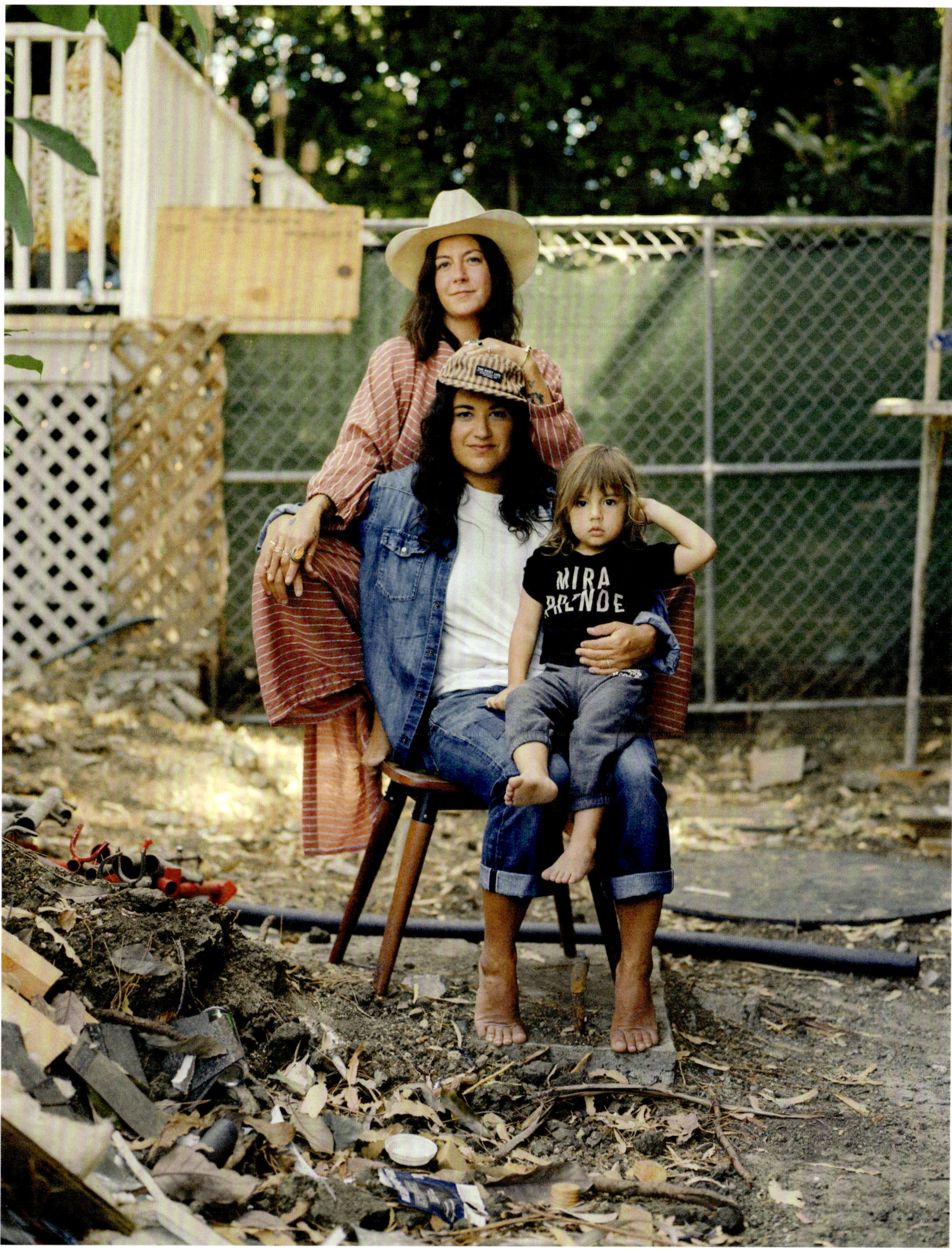
MIRA

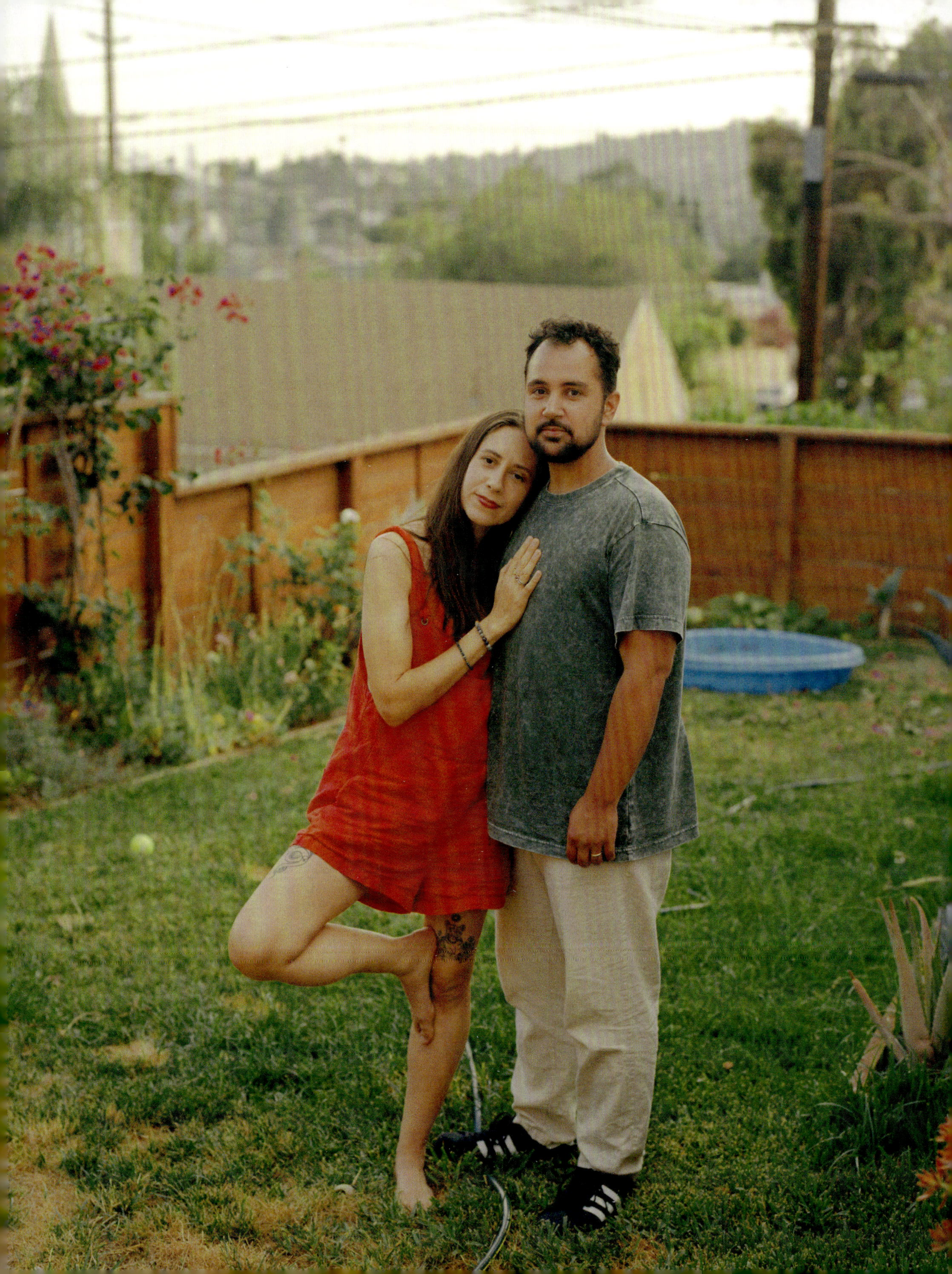

Sarah *(She/Her)* & Oliver *(He/Him)*

LOS ANGELES, CA

OLIVER: Sarah is a lesbian, and I am a queer trans man. I realized at some point that my identity often trumps Sarah's. People will smile and nod when she says she's a lesbian but not identify her as "really queer," as if my being a man erases her chosen identity. In the beginning we occasionally bought into other's opinions and wondered what it meant for us. As time went on, it became clear we were not the problem. We're just two people in love. Of course, labels are useful, and identity is the root of human expression, but as Ru Paul said, "What other people think about me is none of my business." There is space for all kinds of queerness and expressions, and Sarah's identity does not take away from mine, nor should mine take away from hers. Being queer is complicated in the best ways.

SARAH: It's been a strange, and at times, alienating experience to go through life passing as a straight couple. We are almost never read as who we truly are.

I've spent so much of my life coming out and building community around dyke culture. As a femme, my identity often felt invisible in queer community, and as someone married to a trans man, it can feel erased. Queer community is really important to me, and in Portland, where we met, everyone knew our identities, and in general, I felt welcomed in the queer community.

Once we moved to LA, it felt lonely. A lot of queer people we met weren't interested in being our friends because they thought we were straight. It made me realize how important my queerness was to me, and how, of course, I also misread people. What connections do we miss when we assume things about people based on a first glance?

Seeing people's reactions to Oliver has made me protective of him. As a brown person, he's been pulled over by cops way more than I have, and when we were signing our mortgage papers, the white mortgage broker who had met us three times and had seen his name on all the papers called him Javier. It's things like this that constantly remind me to check myself and my own unconscious white bias and entitlement. I'm also hyper aware of how Oliver works hard to dispel any fears that people might have of him by being gregarious, accommodating, and charming. It's interesting to think about how much of our personalities and behaviors are shaped by coping mechanisms, race, gender, and survival.

As a cis person, being with Oliver has opened my perspective greatly. I can take my confidence in being out for granted, and it's been hard for me to understand why he wouldn't be out in more areas of his life, which of course is transphobic. I remember once when he explained to me that trying to have dialogues about gender, feminism, and trans issues would be more impactful with his cis, straight male coworkers if they assumed he was cis as well. It reminded me of how thoughtful and logical he is, and how he is always thinking of the best ways to serve the collective.

OLIVER: Sarah is the most interesting person I've ever met. We have been together for ten years, and to this day, I can ask her questions having no clue how she will answer, or how she came to that conclusion. I know one of Sarah's core wounds is not being understood or being underestimated, so we are well matched in that I am deeply intrigued by her. How will she combine the dog sneezing with her impromptu song about how we have to eat the brussels sprouts before they go bad? Every day I stay tuned in to find out.

SARAH: Oliver and I have made it work because we both respect one another deeply. We are still learning about one another, and we can apologize quickly after we do or say regrettable things. A sense of humor is a must. We are both spiritual in our own ways, and that allows us to see the bigger picture. We love to talk about philosophy, history, biology, and the meaning of life. He's the smartest person I know. He's an ICU nurse, and I find it hot to be married to someone who saves lives for a vocation.

Satya *(He/Him)* & Carter *(He/Him)*

LOS ANGELES, CA

It's in the in-between moments that we need each other most.

SATYA & CARTER

For a queer person, the concept of home is not to be taken for granted. We both had the privilege of growing up in families that allowed us to be ourselves, so escaping was never a necessity for us as it has been—and continues to be—for so many other queer folks. However, we have both known the loss of home—parents dying too young, families uprooted across countries and continents…

Our relationship continues to be the exciting adventure it was when we first met, but also functions as a stable constant, a source of comfort and familiarity. So much of that came from moving into our first house together. At the time of this photograph, that home was all in boxes and our new one had no walls or windows. We launched into a month of couch-surfing and suitcase-living that very day—a period that challenged us in many ways. But it also reinforced the fact that at the core of our relationship we were becoming something new to each other—each other's home.

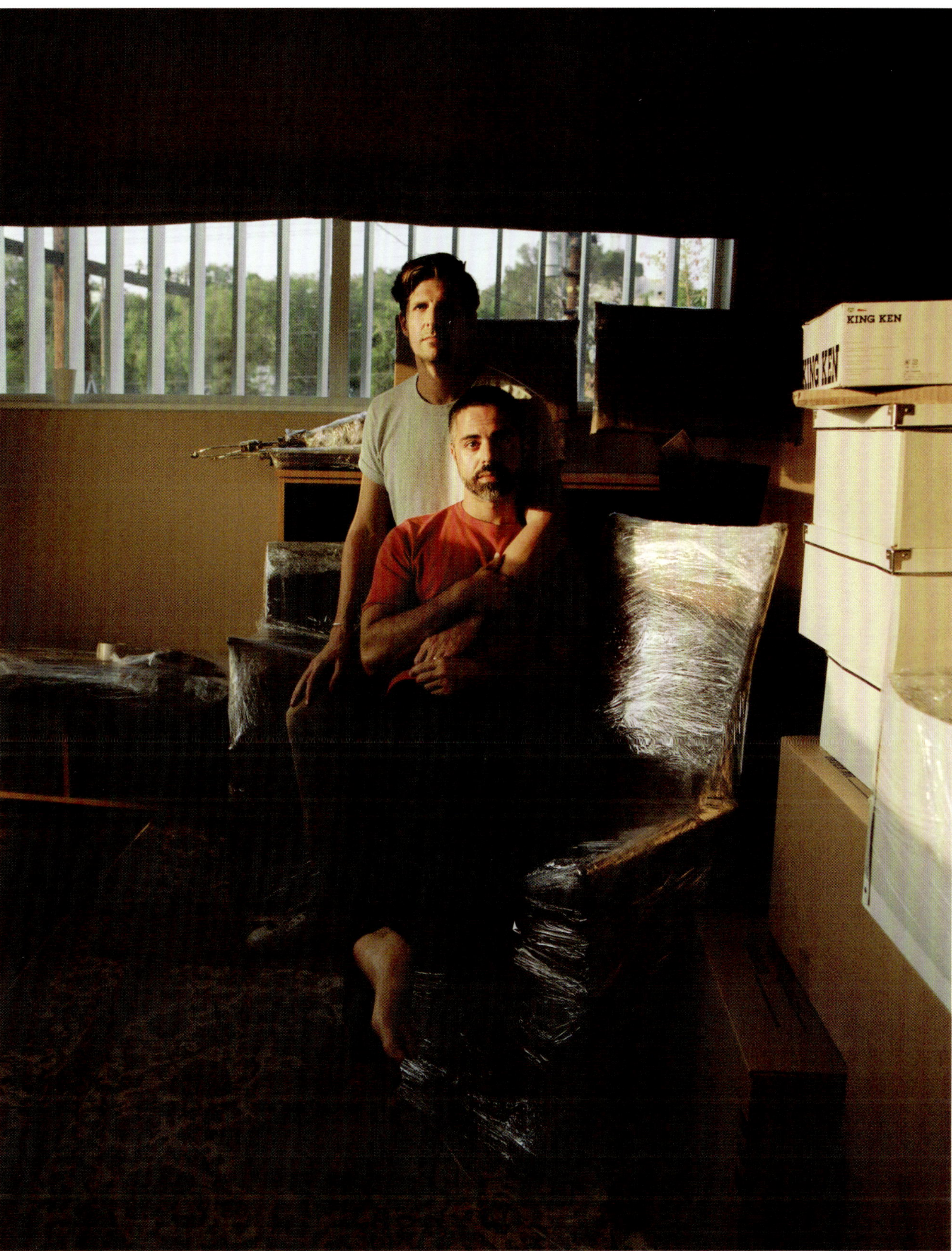
KING KEN
KING KEN

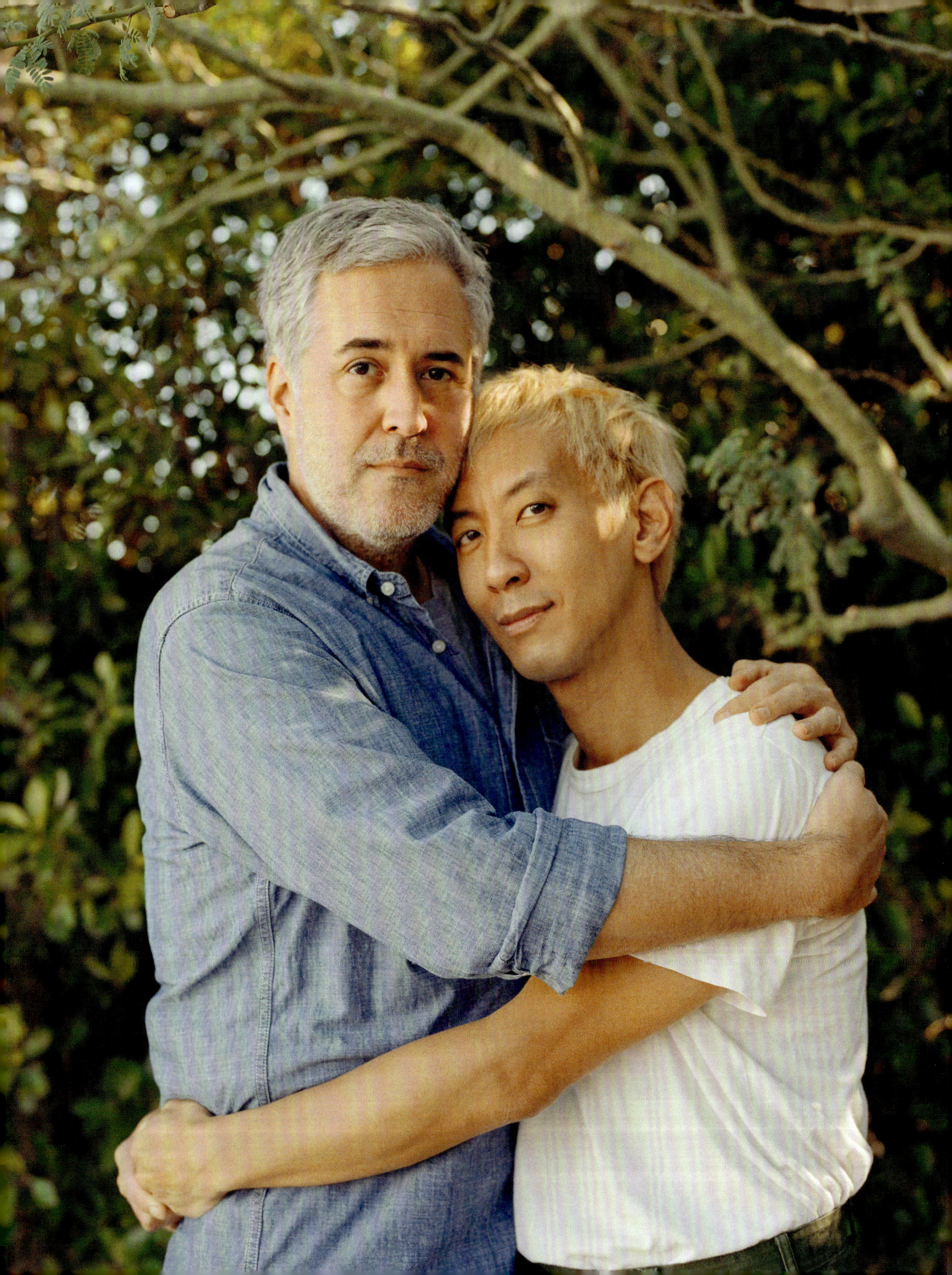

Sidney *(He/Him)* & Sean *(He/Him)*

PALM SPRINGS, CA

As they say, "If you can't love yourself, how in the hell are you gonna love somebody else?" So very true.

SEAN

In 2002, I came out to my friends and coworkers. It wasn't until 2010, five years into my relationship with Sidney, that I came out to my family. I attributed my hesitancy to my religious upbringing by conservative parents, the stigma attached to gays (AIDS), and being interracial (Irish/Mexican) in a predominantly white neighborhood in a conservative county (Orange Country, CA). What it all came down to was self-loathing—not feeling comfortable in my own skin, not fully accepting my sexuality. I wasn't being fair to myself and, most importantly, to Sidney.

SIDNEY

Unlike Sean, I was fully out since birth, but that didn't make things any easier. If anything, I was a target for bullies and sexual predators. As a result, I was extremely cautious to not show any signs of weakness. I developed a defense mechanism—a front, pretending all is well all the time by suppressing my feelings, emotions, self. Eventually, I started breaking. Worst of all, I was lying to myself and Sean.

We met in an elevator, so it's no surprise we've had our share of ups and downs. The ups were amazing, and, in retrospect, the downs were as well—no matter how fucked-up they may seem at the time, they're learning experiences. Without them and the willingness to work on them, we doubt we would have evolved much as a couple, or, more importantly, as individuals. Also, therapy helps.

Theo *(He/Him)* & Sean *(He/Him)*

AUSTIN, TX

THEO

Sean is the first man that I've been with who made me feel like I needed to step my pussy up. Somehow this Hawaiian, mixed white man is calling me out. Seeing through all my bullshit. I wasn't even offended. I felt seen.

SEAN

Theo thought he had to do all this shit to impress me. I already liked *him*. I didn't need anything extra. I liked him. I felt like a kid again. I started falling in love then. It's beautiful! And the sex...is lit!

Creating is a huge part of how we process our emotions. We've spent our lives performing, and even before dating our connection to our creative endeavors drew us together. We both put ourselves out there, unapologetically. Our creative energy has always made us stand out on our own. We get to share that space together now. No matter what people might say about us. We enjoy learning from each other and exploring the feminine and masculine, the carnal and sacred.

Society has way more things to say about us than we do. The conversations we have around race aren't always our choice. But we learn a lot from each other's experiences and do our best to protect one another. Theo is always ready for a fight. Sean prefers to avoid conflict. Safety is a question sometimes. We intimidate people. It's weird, but we kinda like it.

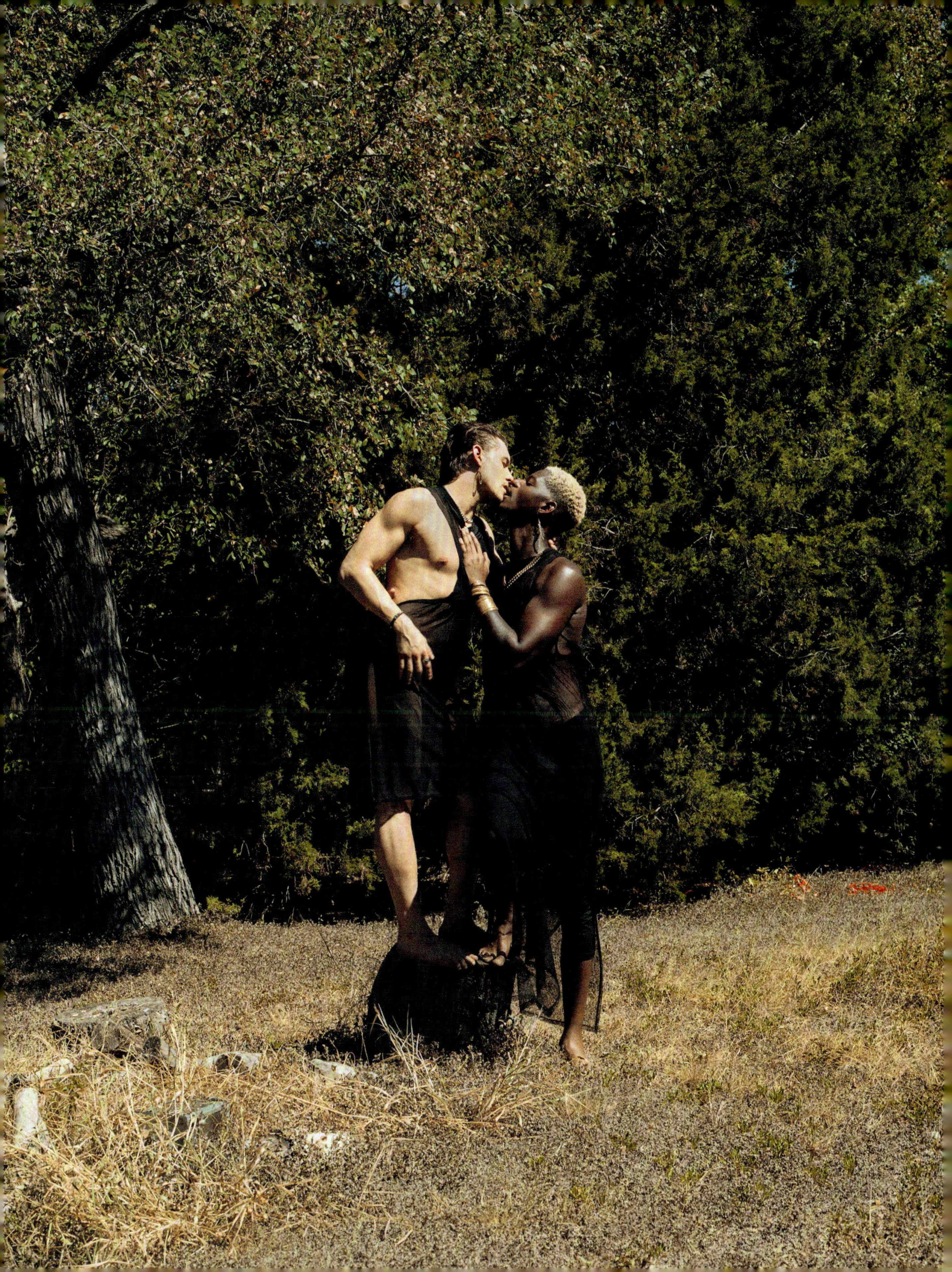

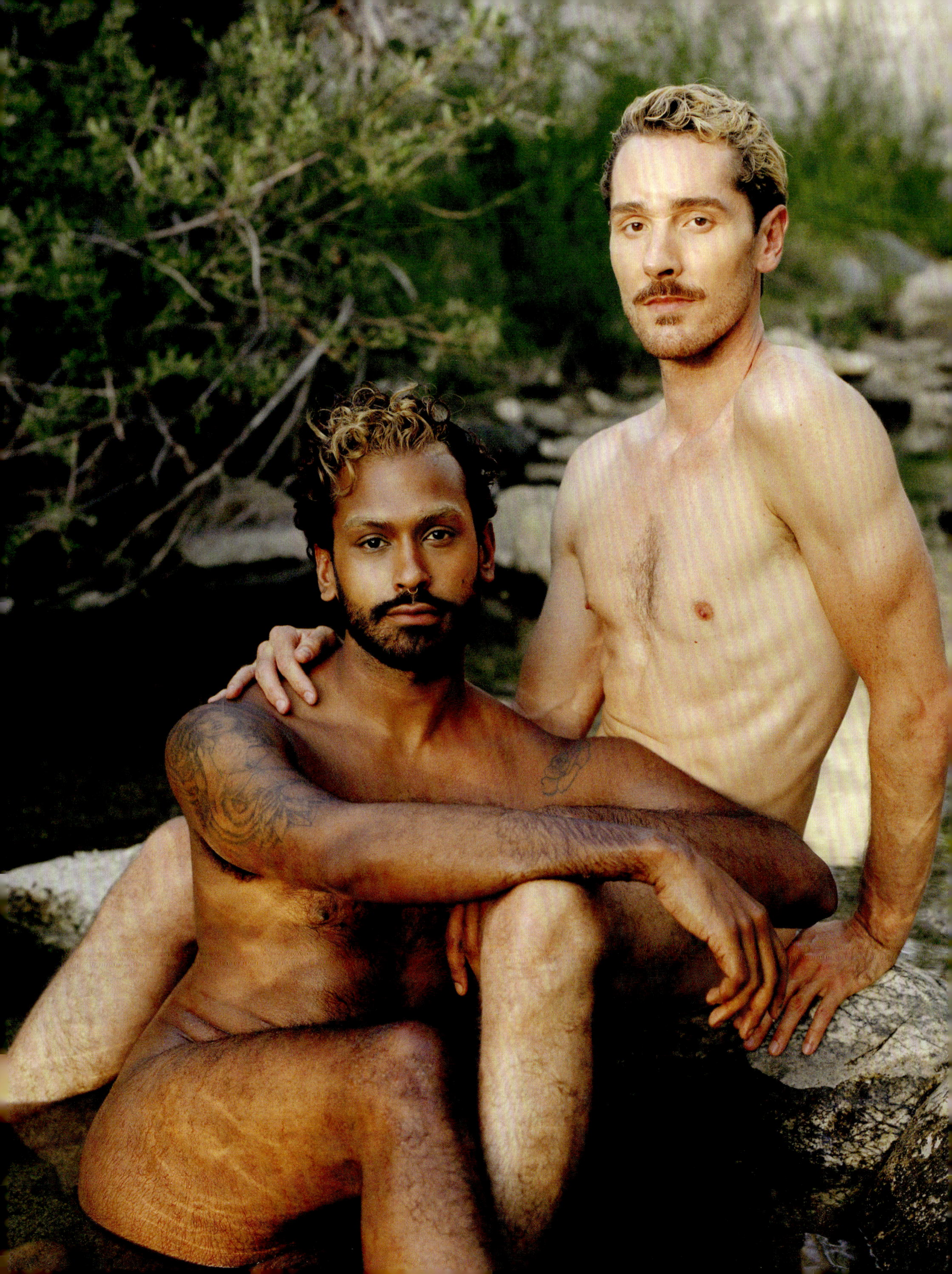

T.J. *(He/Him)* & Brandyn *(They/Them)*

LOS ANGELES, CA

T.J.

During the pandemic, without the usual distractions and preoccupations, Brandyn went on a journey to explore their gender identity. More specifically, they interrogated the cultural and societal pressures to conform to the binary. At first, I had a hard time with this new expression of being nonbinary. I was uncomfortable with the ambiguity, even though I considered myself to be open and accepting. Identifying as gay and liking men was hard enough to come to terms with, and now it felt like I was starting over again. I defiantly and selfishly made choices that put distance between us. For months our interactions were filled with tension that we had not previously known. I even started sleeping in our guest bedroom. We came to a breaking point and decided to find a therapist who helped me focus on my own insecurities and explore why my partner's newfound expression was a source of pain. It was hard to acknowledge that I wasn't giving my partner the care and love I would afford to others in a similar situation. Imagining my life without Brandyn's presence was a bleak picture—less colorful, less fun, less joyful. I'm grateful for the patience and discussions that helped shine light on dark areas around my knowledge of gender and love. Realizing that isolation doesn't foster understanding has been crucial to getting out of my state of despair with the larger world. I'm grateful for our willingness to help each other on our individual journeys.

BRANDYN

When you get into a relationship in your early twenties, you think you know what's going on. But you have no idea. Some of us figure "it" out earlier than others, and some never do. Growing up as a second-generation Caribbean and youngest of three, my insecurities started very early. When I was ready to move to the United States, I thought I knew what I wanted—simply put, to feel free. To feel like I could be myself and have people love me for it.

That was not my gay New York experience. Instead, I felt a sense of isolation, always feeling too femme, too fat, too hairy, too poor, too different. When I met T.J. I felt lucky. Not necessarily because I met someone, but because I should be grateful anyone even wanted to choose me. His love made me feel special and was the catalyst for my self-liberation. Somewhere along the line, my refusal to adhere to conventional gender standards sent him down a spiral. Rolled eyes turned to bickering, which led to fighting, followed by ignoring each other and then sleeping apart.

I loved him, faults and all, and yet the source of my power seemed to scare him. I thought I saw our end in sight—why should I stay with someone who would choose to take out his hurt on me? I suggested we talk, take time and space, and see if when alone, we still craved each other's company. I had never seen him cry this way; the kind of cry that made me see he realized all he had to fight for. And all he had to lose.

Therapy was our saving grace—hearing our thoughts and inner feelings brought to light what was important and what was not. Now we have direction, a multiyear plan and dreams for "our" future. Sometimes you can believe in someone far more than they believe in themselves. I always knew I deserved love, and I finally have it.

Trinica *(She/Her)* & Melissa *(She/Her)*

AUSTIN, TX

TRINICA

We met in college—me, a young queer woman fresh off the heels of coming out to my high school friends; her, a staunchly conservative Christian Chicana. I loved her right away. She reminded me of home, of the largely Latinx population that surrounded me as I grew up. But there were times I didn't know if our friendship would work. I remember asking her to go see a presentation by a trans guy, and she said, "I can't be seen supporting something like that in public." It broke my heart. I felt like she was unknowingly saying she wouldn't support me. I was so scared to come out and lose her in my life. Then I was even more terrified when I realized I loved her and thought it would ruin our friendship.

MELISSA

We're now engaged, and I can't imagine life without her. I think what we've learned in the past nine years of knowing each other is how to communicate. We both came from families that sucked at talking about the hard things, and it's taken a lot of work, adaptability, and practice to teach ourselves healthy relationship skills. There are definite similarities between my conservative, Christian/Chicanx background and her Caribbean background, but there are things neither of us will ever be able to fully understand about each other, which is a painful realization. She couldn't empathize with what I went through when my parents disowned me for being queer and told me I would go to hell. I couldn't empathize with her devastation at being called a racial slur when we lived in San Francisco, or the trauma she's internalized after every police killing of another Black person. All we can do is try to empathize, try to comfort each other, and try to listen instead of coming up with solutions. Sometimes there isn't a solution—loving someone with a different life experience means acknowledging that.

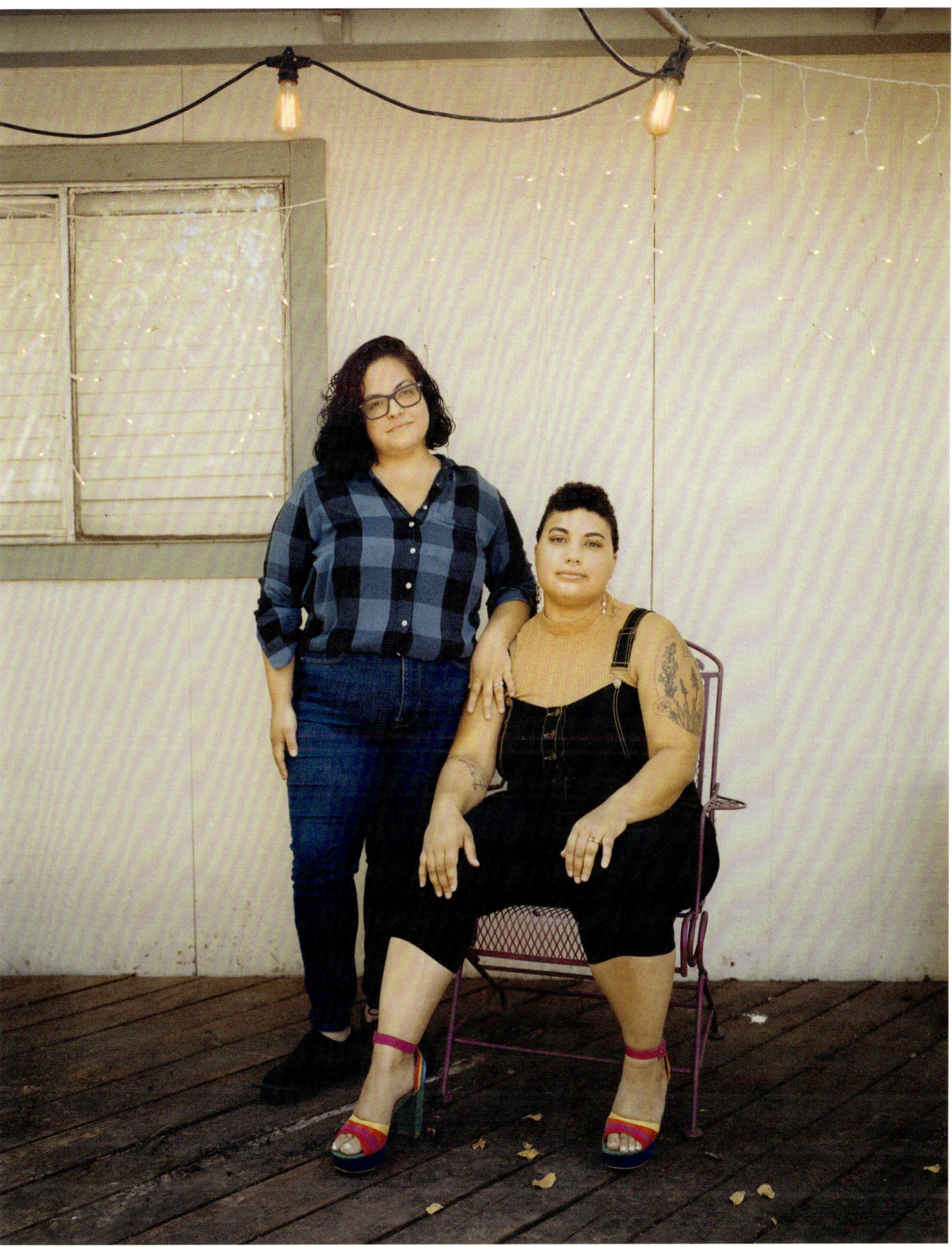

Tyler *(He/Him)* & Justin *(He/Him)*

AUSTIN, TX

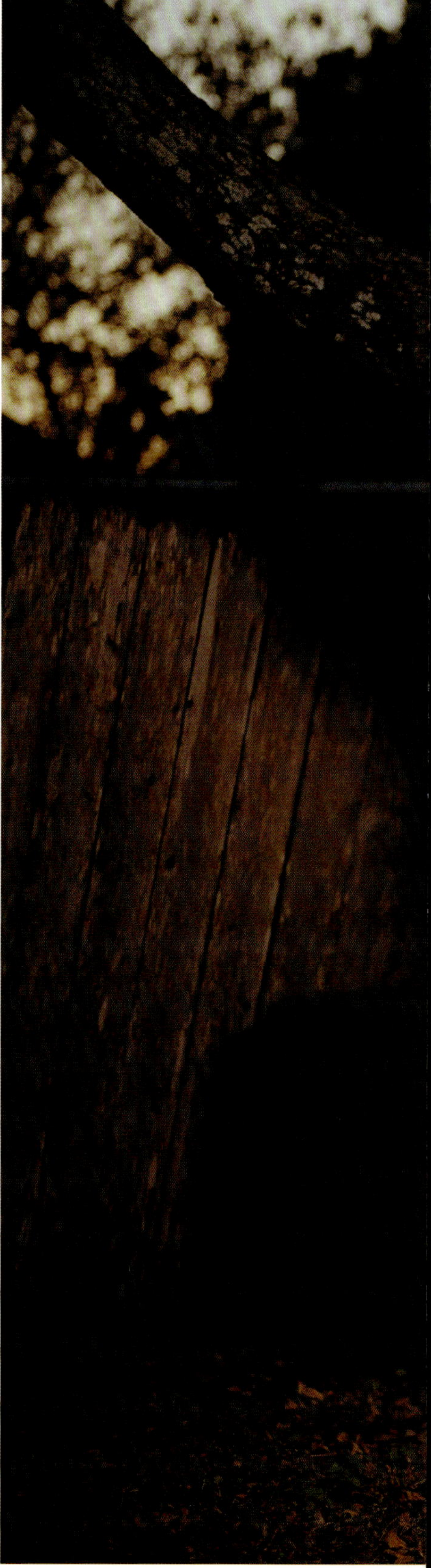

TYLER & JUSTIN

Timing is both a friend and a foe, depending on how you look at it. We met on Tinder during the height of the pandemic, only to realize we had met eleven years earlier while both of us were in other relationships. Somehow fate chose to bring us together in what most people would consider an impossible time for romance, let alone love. To see how we would feel spending one-on-one time together, we took a chance and set up an at-home date. Both anxious and excited, we clicked instantly.

While all these amazing things were blossoming, another hurdle was approaching. One of us was recently diagnosed as HIV positive—after the pandemic started, and after losing a long-held, beloved job. Both of us being new to a positive and negative relationship was incredibly challenging in different ways. We stood by one another through the fear of what it meant as a couple and as individuals.

When we first met, we had both been out of the dating scene for five years. We were and are trying to heal from past relationship trauma and grow together at the same time. But we have found so much joy in just getting to build a foundation based on trust and honesty. Before we knew it, half a year had flown by—we were feeling fulfilled, and we hadn't even had sex. Neither one of us had ever experienced a long courting, but it's a beautiful and cherished part of our beginnings.

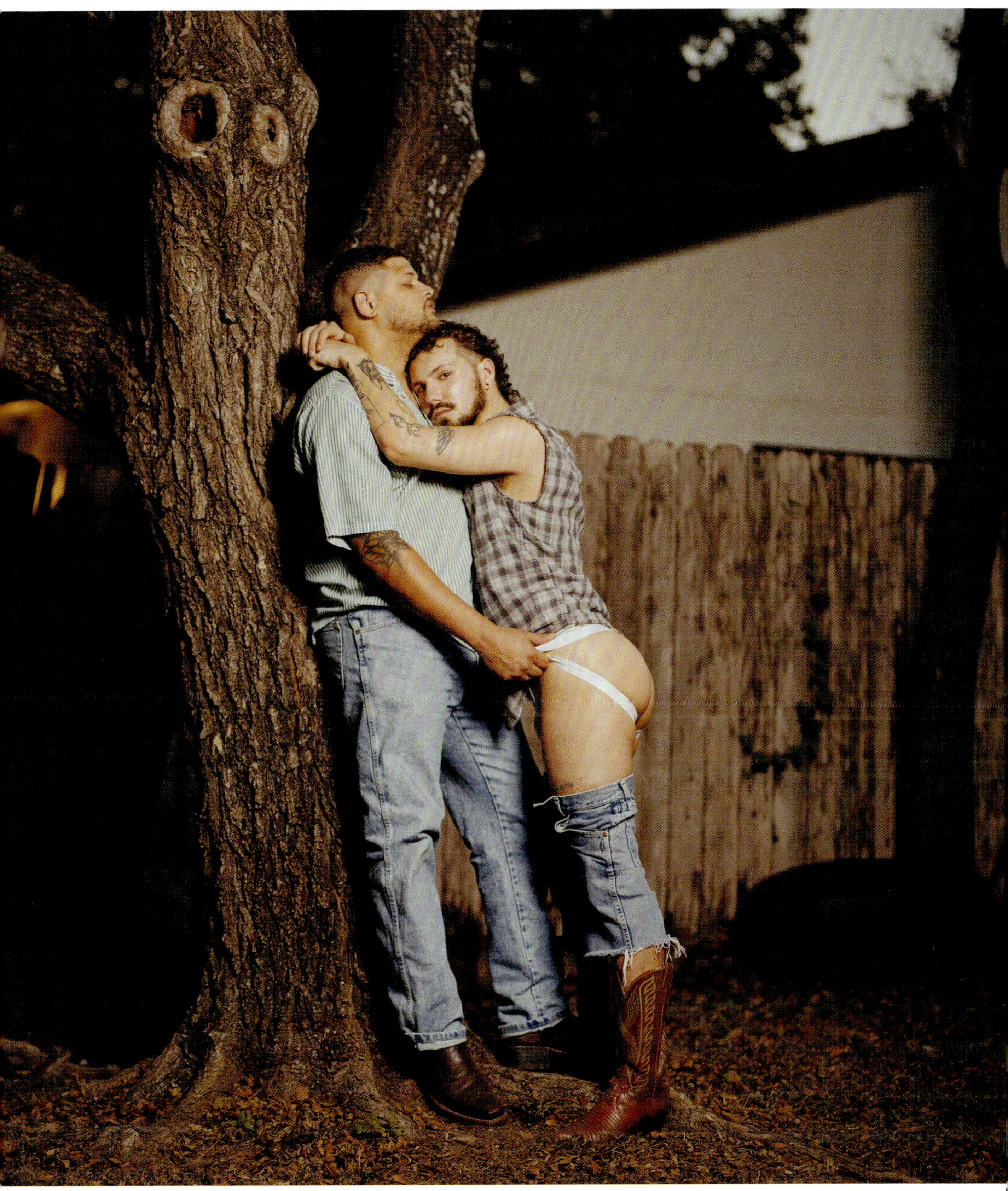

Wilson *(He/Him)* & Ricky *(He/Him)*

SAN FRANCISCO, CA

WILSON

On the front porch, you listen attentively as I pour out familial frustrations. No one's listened to me in years. You nod along as your delicate fingers roll premium-grade Gorilla Glue into a crinkled RAW paper. I'm telling you about my time at the rehabilitation center in backwoods Arkansas, my battles with depression and disordered eating. You share about your father's death and struggles you've experienced as a Black dancer in the white-dominated ballet profession. We don't know whether to touch each other yet, but our eyes are open, and maybe more importantly, we see each other. And I can't get enough.

I'm playing video games, do you want to come over?

I'm crying in the shower, do you want to come over?

You tell me you love me the week after we meet. Why do I believe you? Is it that you give me so much reassurance that I can't help but trust every word you say? I can't get enough.

People mistake your kindness for weakness, your introspection for hesitance. But I see someone hyperaware, completely in tune with every emotion you feel. Quiet, only when considering the perfect words to relay. It's in your patience with me that I learn to truly be patient and present with myself. So, when you say you love me, I believe you. And I can't get enough.

You trust me with your culture, teaching me how to make traditional garnachas and taking me home to Miami for the holidays to introduce me to the family—where you tell me you haven't felt complete since your dad passed. You say my love for you makes you feel purposeful. And I hold you as you cry on Christmas Eve. You don't know that without me you'd still be radiant and filled with divine intention. I would give my life to preserve your gifts, your beauty, and shield you from any pain the world projects upon you. For you to be upheld forever. Forever goes on, and I still can't get enough.

RICKY

You make me feel safe. You make me feel seen. You make me feel heard.

From the first time we kissed, I knew there was a future ahead of us. It was a feeling that was so unfamiliar yet so fulfilling. I don't believe we crossed paths by mistake. We were always supposed to meet, and that day was finally here. We dated for a week before I said, "I love you." I will happily admit that I said it first. Intuitively, I knew that was the first of many times to come.

You aren't afraid to be vulnerable with me and that's something I cherish so deeply. You have further opened my eyes to the injustice in this world. You have given me the courage to speak up when I know somethin' ain't right! Your unabashedly persistent activism toward making sure that my community and me are well respected and never mistreated is remarkable and should never go unnoticed. You are so bright. We share our past traumas with each other only to find out we share a similar past. It's comforting. Although there are some things I can't relate to. It hurts. You've done exceptionally well with the hand you were dealt.

I'm here for you forever and always. I love you.

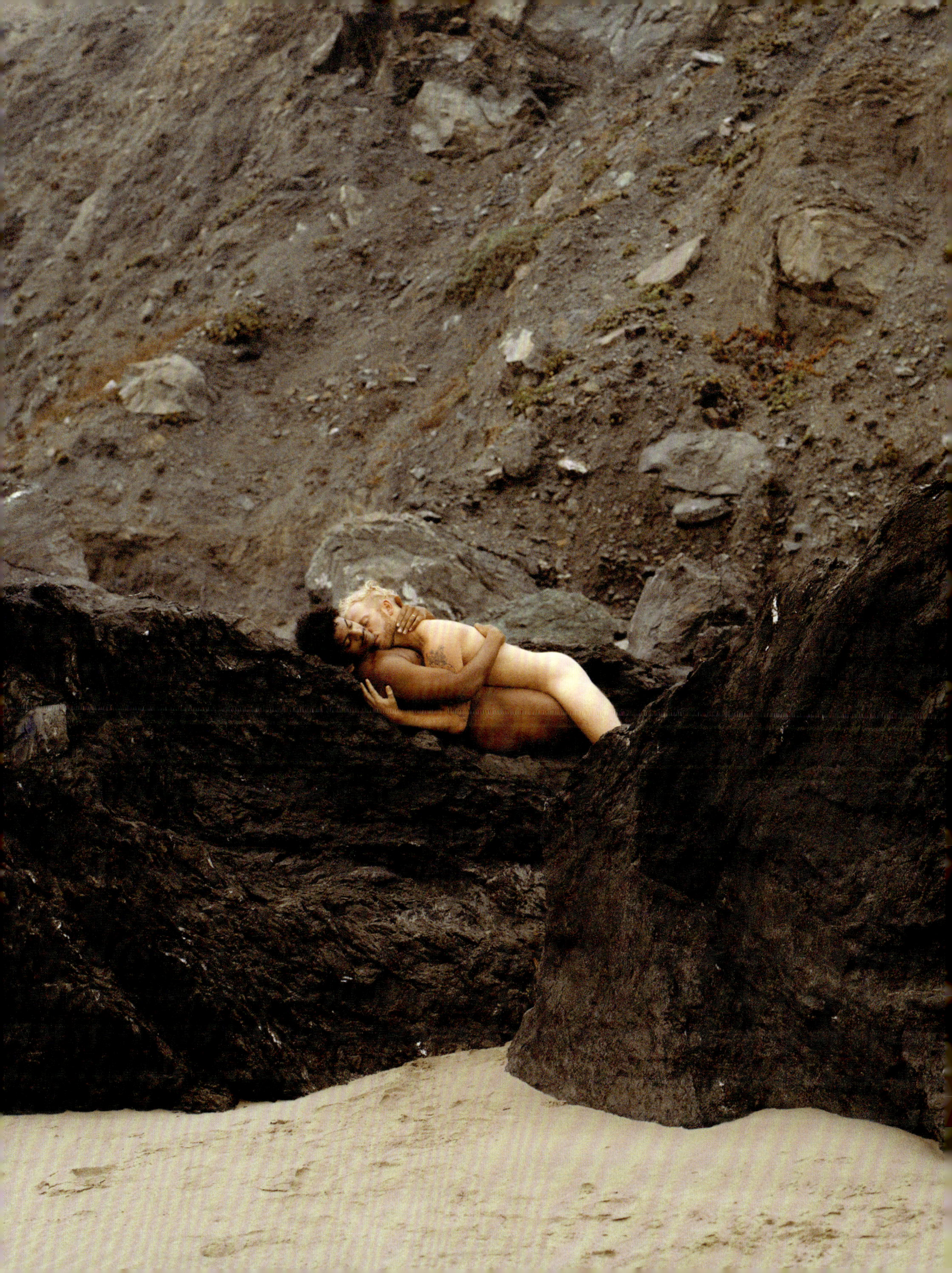

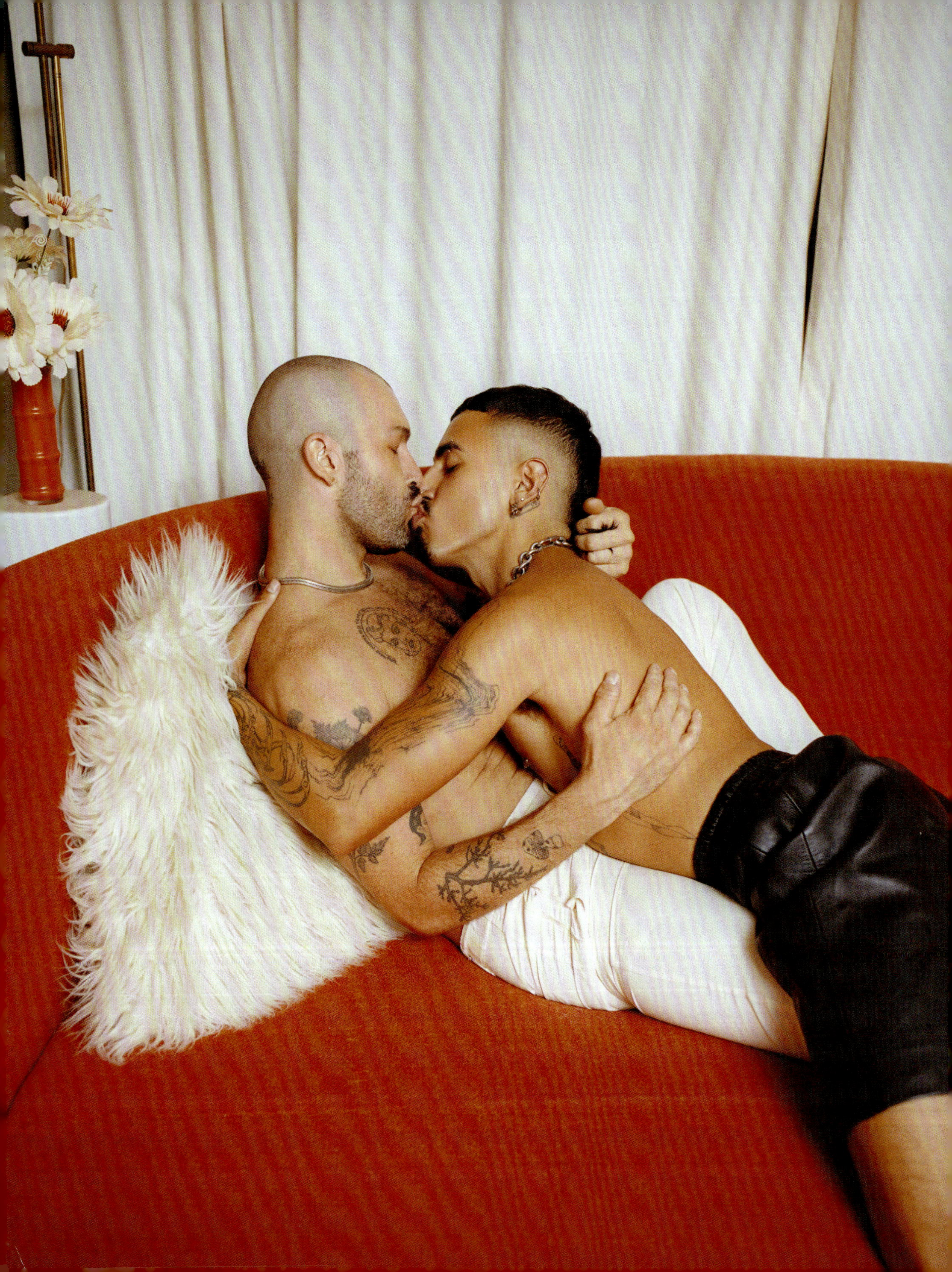

Zach *(He/Him)* & Luis *(He/Him)*

BROOKLYN, NY

ZACH

It's hard not to love someone who loves me as fiercely as you do.

I live for being in direct competition with you to take better care of one another. You are truly a gift sent to heal my heart. I didn't anticipate the amount of love I could hold inside of me when I thought so many holes had been left behind.

I am proud of you. Your dedication, your constant growth, and how we help each other on that journey. You are fearlessly yourself, and I'll make sure as long as I'm here you'll be safe to do so.

To my baby, I love you with all my heart.

LUIS

I am so thankful to have found a person like you, someone who has loved me and taken me as I am in a world where that can be so hard to find. You have eased me of so many worries, I don't have to have any guards up with you, and that's such a beautiful feeling. You have such a bright and radiating soul, you make me look forward to gloomy rainy days with you because you even make the darkest days bright. You continue to teach me new things every single day, from the way you navigate your own life to the way you treat me and your loved ones. Most importantly, thank you for giving me the love that I did not even know I was looking for or needed. In a world that is so lonely and scary, I have found love that has given me a genuine feeling of home, comfort, and acceptance. A love that shines so bright. I love you so so much, baby. You are the greatest gift I could ever receive, and I cherish our love with every inch of my body.

ACKNOWLEDGMENTS

This work would not exist without the incredible support and word of mouth from the Queer community. To the fags, queens, femmes, daddies, dykes, studs, enbys, twinks, and everything in between, this is my love letter to y'all.

Cory, my love, who supported me the entire way through. From creating spreadsheets and giving back rubs to help ease the stress. You gave me the space when I needed it and the comfort when I didn't know I needed it. My pooch, Sarah Connor, who gave me levity all the times I was overwhelmed.

Nicol and Erik, thank you for continually being cheerleaders and believing in me and my work even when I didn't. Even though neither of you are in this book, your spirit and influence can be seen on every page.

Jeff, my ex-husband, who proves that relationships may change and evolve but that love knows no bounds. You have given me the tremendous gift of a lifelong friendship.

Rebecca and Erin at my agency for championing this work and accommodating my constantly changing schedule.

Kyle and Luis, who showed me how to love when I was still learning how to love myself.

Holly, my editor, for taking the risk on me and providing the knowledge and advice I needed for my first book.

And to all the colleagues, friends, and editors who have supported what I do and how I see the world—thank you for making me feel seen.

Published by
Princeton Architectural Press
70 West 36th Street
New York, NY 10018
www.papress.com

Printed and bound in China
25 24 23 22 4 3 2 1 First edition

ISBN 978-1-64896-157-1

Editor: Holly La Due
Designer: Natalie Snodgrass

Library of Congress Cataloging-in-Publication Data
available upon request.

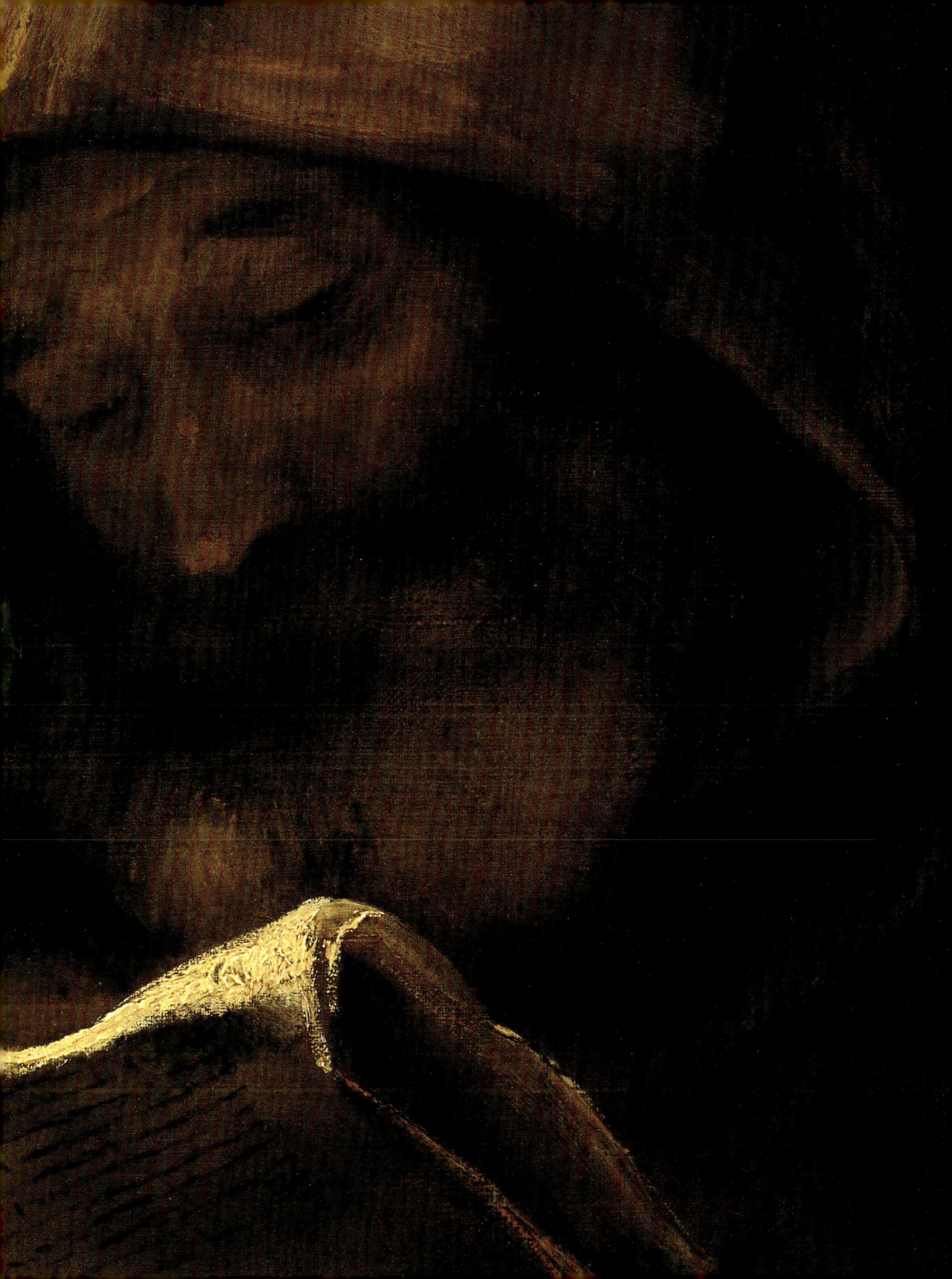

The exhibition was organized by the National Gallery of Art, Washington, in association with the J. Paul Getty Museum, Los Angeles.

Generous support for this exhibition at the National Gallery of Art was provided by Mr. and Mrs. Thomas A. Saunders, III.

Exhibition Dates

National Gallery of Art, Washington
30 January–1 May 2005

The J. Paul Getty Museum, Los Angeles
7 June–28 August 2005

Produced by the Publishing Office, National Gallery of Art, Washington
www.nga.gov

Judy Metro *Editor in Chief*
Ulrike Mills *Editor*
Margaret Bauer *Design Manager*
Chris Vogel *Production Manager*

This book was designed by side view/ Hannah Smotrich, Ann Arbor, Michigan. It was typeset in Poliphilus, Blado, and Caecilia and printed on Garda Matt by Conti Tipocolor, Florence, Italy.

Notes to the Reader

Dimensions of works of art in this catalogue are given in centimeters followed by inches. Height precedes width.

The following references are cited throughout the catalogue:

B. Adam Bartsch, *Catalogue raisonné de toutes les estampes qui forment l'oeuvre de Rembrandt...*, 2 vols. (Vienna, 1797)

Ben. Otto Benesch, *The Drawings of Rembrandt: A Critical and Chronological Catalogue*, 6 vols. (London, 1954–1957); enlarged ed. Eva Benesch, ed., 6 vols. (London, 1973)

Br. Abraham Bredius, *Rembrandt, Schilderijen* (Vienna, 1935) (also English ed., Oxford, 1942)

front cover: Rembrandt van Rijn
Self-Portrait as the Apostle Paul
(detail, cat. 11)

back cover: Rembrandt van Rijn
The Virgin of Sorrows (detail, cat. 14)

title page: Rembrandt van Rijn
Monk (Saint Francis?) Reading
(detail, cat. 16)

page 12–13: Rembrandt van Rijn
The Apostle Simon (detail, cat. 10)

page 38–39: Rembrandt van Rijn
The Apostle Paul (detail, cat. 2)

page 56–57: Rembrandt van Rijn
An Elderly Man as the Apostle Paul
(detail, cat. 4)

page 68–69: Rembrandt van Rijn
The Resurrected Christ (detail, cat. 6)

page 140–141: Rembrandt van Rijn
The Virgin of Sorrows (detail, cat. 14)

Library of Congress Cataloging-in-Publication Data

Wheelock, Arthur K.
Rembrandt's late religious portraits / Arthur K. Wheelock Jr. ; with
Volker Manuth, Peter C. Sutton, and Anne T. Woollett.
p. cm.

Catalog of an exhibition to be held at the National Gallery of Art, Washington, D.C., Jan. 30, 2005–May 1, 2005, and at the J. Paul Getty Museum, Los Angeles, June 7–Aug. 28, 2005.
Includes bibliographical references and index.

ISBN 0-226-89443-6 (hardcover : alk. paper)

1. Rembrandt Harmenszoon van Rijn, 1606–1669—Exhibitions.
2. Religious leaders—Netherlands—Portraits—Exhibitions. I. Rembrandt Harmenszoon van Rijn, 1606–1669.
II. National Gallery of Art (U.S.)
III. J. Paul Getty Museum. IV. Title.

ND653.R4A4 2004
759.9492—dc22 2004020869

Copublished by
The University of Chicago Press
1427 East 60th Street
Chicago, IL 60637-2954
www.press.uchicago.edu

10 9 8 7 6 5 4 3 2

∞ The paper used in this publication meets the minimum requirements of the American National Standard for Information Sciences — Permanence of Paper for Printed Library Materials, ANSI Z39.48-1992.

Contents

Director's Foreword

This exhibition explores one of the most fascinating aspects of Rembrandt's oeuvre, a remarkable group of half-length depictions of religious figures that he created in the late 1650s and early 1660s. It includes not only images of Christ, the Virgin Mary, and the apostles, but also portrayals of hermits and a number of the evangelists. Many questions surround these religious portraits, which are among the most powerfully expressive paintings Rembrandt ever created. What religious beliefs underlie these humanistic representations of religious figures? Did Rembrandt paint these works because of some inner need, or did he execute them on commission or as a speculative venture? Who were the models that served as his points of inspiration? Finally, did he paint these works in relationship to each other, perhaps as a series, formal or informal? By bringing together these paintings in this small focus exhibition, we hope to enhance our understanding of such compelling questions.

The exhibition and catalogue were coordinated by Arthur K. Wheelock Jr., curator of northern baroque painting at the National Gallery of Art. He wrote the introductory essay and a number of the entries. In organizing the show, he worked closely with other scholars of Dutch art, including Peter C. Sutton, director of the Bruce Museum, Greenwich, Connecticut, who suggested to Arthur several years ago that such an exhibition would present not only an intriguing topic for scholars but also a moving experience for the museum visitor. Peter contributed entries to the catalogue and an essay about Rembrandt's *portraits historiés,* a genre of portraiture in which an individual assumes the guise of a historical figure. The third essay, on the religious context for depictions of apostles and evangelists, was authored by Volker Manuth, a Rembrandt scholar and professor of art history at the University of Nijmegen, The Netherlands. Finally, Anne T. Woollett, curator at the J. Paul Getty Museum, contributed entries on the two depictions of the Apostle Bartholomew in the exhibition.

We are delighted that the exhibition will be seen at the J. Paul Getty Museum following its debut at the National Gallery of Art, and we are grateful to its former director, Deborah Gribbon, and to William Griswold, acting director and chief curator, for their enthusiastic interest in bringing the exhibition to the West Coast.

Rembrandt's Late Religious Portraits is made possible here at the Gallery by a generous gift from Mr. and Mrs. Thomas A. Saunders, III. As always, exhibitions of this nature can only be realized with the support and generosity of the lenders. We are most grateful to those private collectors and museums in the United States and Europe who have been willing to part with their precious Rembrandt paintings, in order that the curators might have an opportunity to explore new scholarship and the museum visitor might be able to view these extraordinary works by a beloved master.

Earl A. Powell III, *Director, National Gallery of Art*

Preface and Acknowledgments

Rembrandt van Rijn's evocative depictions of religious figures from the late 1650s and early 1660s are among this great master's most remarkable paintings. Executed shortly after the artist experienced financial crises in the mid-1650s, at a time when his expressive style of painting was no longer in demand by Amsterdam's elite, these half-length portrayals of Christ, the Virgin Mary, apostles, evangelists, monks, and other saints reflect Rembrandt's profound understanding of both the iconic and the human aspects of their beings. These paintings are in part historical portraits, in which the artist captures the figures' psychological state as well as their physical features. Rembrandt's identification with these figures was so complete that he actually portrayed himself as Saint Paul and occasionally represented other individuals in the guise of one of these biblical personages.

For more than eighty years scholars have postulated that these religious portraits formed part of a series, whether formal or informal. The hypothesis has never been tested because the relevant paintings, numbering around fifteen or sixteen, were distributed in collections around the world. The character of Rembrandt's purported series of apostles and evangelists was, in fact, a subject that captivated me as a graduate student in the late 1960s; I wrote a seminar paper on this topic while studying with Seymour Slive at Harvard University. It is thus with great pleasure that I dedicate this exhibition to my former professor, in appreciation of the inspiration that he has provided me all these years.

The widespread fascination with Rembrandt's late religious portraits and the questions surrounding their relationships to one another is evident in the generosity of loans to the exhibition from institutions in the United States and Europe. The sense of expectation is great: placing these paintings side by side provides a context in which they can "speak" to each other, where their shared characteristics can be fully appreciated. One can anticipate that seeing these overridingly forceful images together will be a unique visual and emotional experience. The exhibition will afford the opportunity to probe questions about Rembrandt's intentions for possible serial relationships among the various works, about smaller groupings that may also have existed, or pairs of paintings conceived as pendants, and about Rembrandt's painting techniques, particularly about the myriad ways he applied his medium and modeled his forms to create these imposing images. Almost certainly, the exhibition will raise broader issues surrounding the nature of Rembrandt's workshop, including the possible participation of other hands in the creation of some of these pictures.

I would like to thank my fellow authors for their support and excellent contributions to the catalogue, in particular Peter C. Sutton, who came to me with the idea of organizing this show and whose insights have been instrumental in determining its character. His contributions to the catalogue, as well as those of Volker Manuth and Anne T. Woollett, have added important dimensions to our understanding of these works.

Each of the authors has benefited from the extensive research about Rembrandt undertaken by scholars over the years. The frequent references to earlier generations of Rembrandt specialists, among them Otto Benesch, Wilhelm von Bode, Jacob Rosenberg, Frederik Schmidt-Degener, and Wilhelm Valentiner, reflect the profound importance these scholars have had on contemporary studies. The catalogue also reflects the substantial contributions, both direct and indirect, of many other, more recent scholars, among them Cliff Ackley, Ronni Baer, Robert Baldwin, Albert Blankert, Christopher Brown, Perry Chapman, Alan Chong, Stephanie Dickey, Sebastian Dudok van Heel, Egbert Haverkamp-Begemann, Jeroen Giltaij, Walter Liedtke, John Michael Montias, Simon Schama, Gary Schwartz, Christian Tümpel, Ernst van de Wetering, Julia Lloyd Williams, and Michael Zell. A number of individuals have greatly facilitated the loans of paintings under their care. We would like to thank in particular Erin Coe, Marcus Dekiert, Taco Dibbits, Hal Fischer, Matthieu Gilles, Christian Klemm, Jan Piet Filedt Kok, Vincent Pomarède, Axel Rüger, and Scott Schaefer.

I would also like to thank the many individuals at the National Gallery whose contributions have enhanced the exhibition, in particular Lynn Russell, head of education, who shared with me her ideas about Rembrandt's paintings of apostles and evangelists. The extensive resources and personal expertise of the staff at the National Gallery's library, including executive librarian Neal Turtell, Lamia Doumato, and Yuri Long, enormously aided research on the artist and his times. In the conservation department, Susanna Griswold skillfully conserved the Gallery's Rembrandt painting, *The Apostle Paul,* and discussed with me on various occasions aspects of the artist's painting techniques. I would also like to thank Melanie Gifford for her many astute observations about Rembrandt's manner of painting.

Many in the publishing office contributed to the production of this handsome catalogue: Judy Metro, editor in chief, supervised the project, while Ulrike Mills, with great care and patience, worked with the various authors to prepare and edit the manuscripts. Chris Vogel oversaw production and Margaret Bauer the design. Sara Sanders-Buell, Ira Bartfield, and Mariah Shay procured illustrations. Hannah Smotrich created the catalogue's elegant design. Linda Parshall translated the essay by Volker Manuth. D. Dodge Thompson, Ann B. Robertson, and Jennifer Rich in the Gallery's department of exhibitions handled the organization of the exhibition, and Michelle Fondas and Sally Freitag in the registrar's office coordinated the transportation of the works of art. Mark Leithauser and his outstanding department of installation and design developed the handsome installation of the exhibition.

Finally, I am extremely grateful to the staff, interns, and volunteers in the Gallery's department of northern baroque painting who have been involved in this project over the past few years. Anna Tummers helped formulate the initial exhibition concept, which Jan Leja developed with her thoughtful observations. Further research, including the compilation of the bibliography and appendix, was undertaken by Sohee Kim, Anneke Wertheim, and Molli Kuenstner. Diligently and with good humor, Molli also handled the many administrative demands connected with this project. To all those who have helped bring the project to its successful conclusion, I extend my deepest gratitude.

Arthur K. Wheelock Jr.
Curator of Northern Baroque Painting, National Gallery of Art

Lenders to the Exhibition

Bayerische Staatsgemäldesammlungen,
Alte Pinakothek, Munich
Göteborgs Konstmuseum, Göteborg
The Hyde Collection, Glens Falls, New York
The J. Paul Getty Museum, Los Angeles
Kunsthaus Zürich
The Metropolitan Museum of Art, New York
Musée Départemental d'Art Ancien et
Contemporain, Épinal
Musée du Louvre, Paris
Museum Boijmans Van Beuningen, Rotterdam
National Gallery of Art, Washington
The National Gallery, London
Private collection
Rijksmuseum, Amsterdam
Sinebrychoff Art Museum, Helsinki
Timken Museum of Art, San Diego

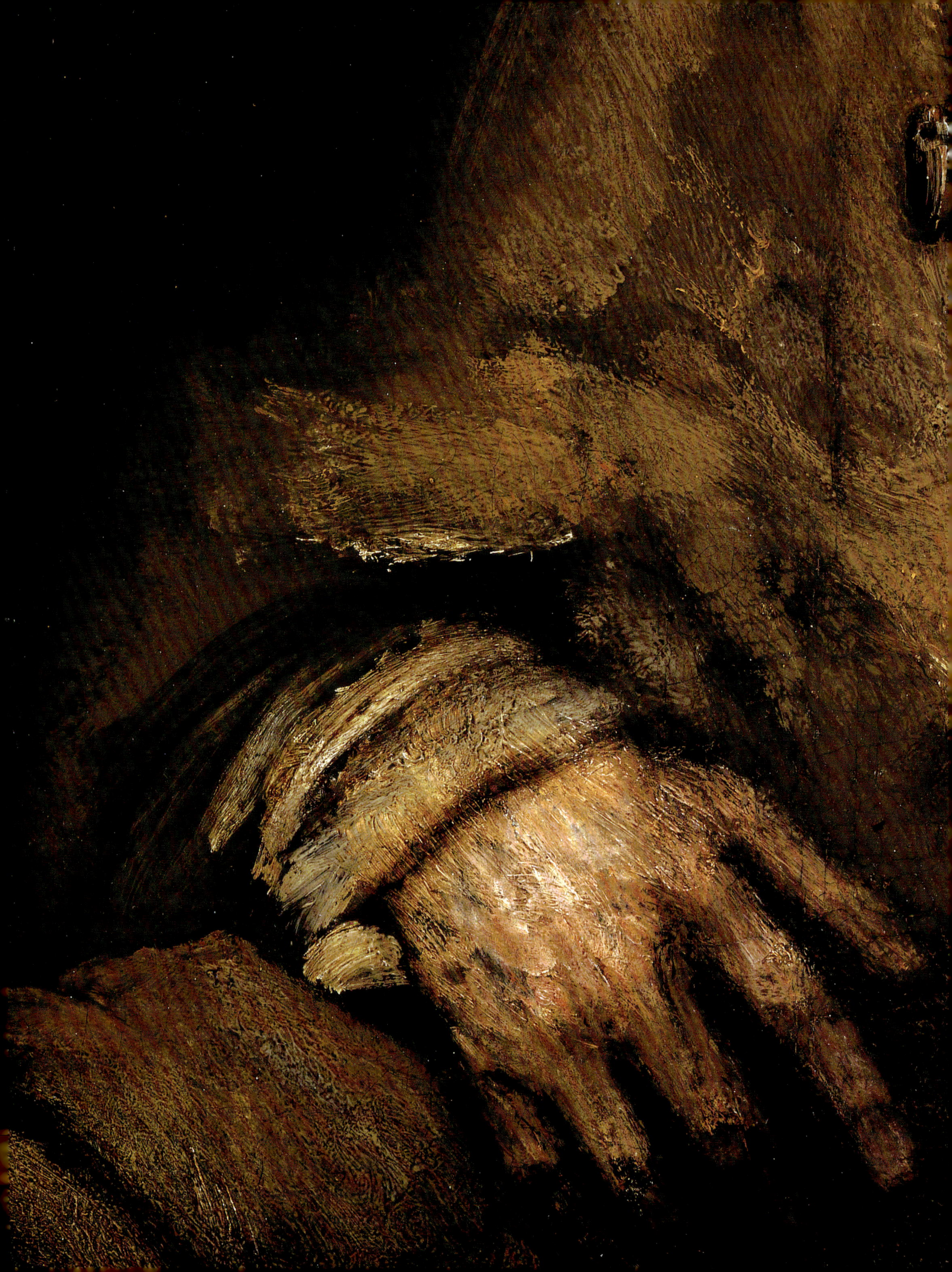

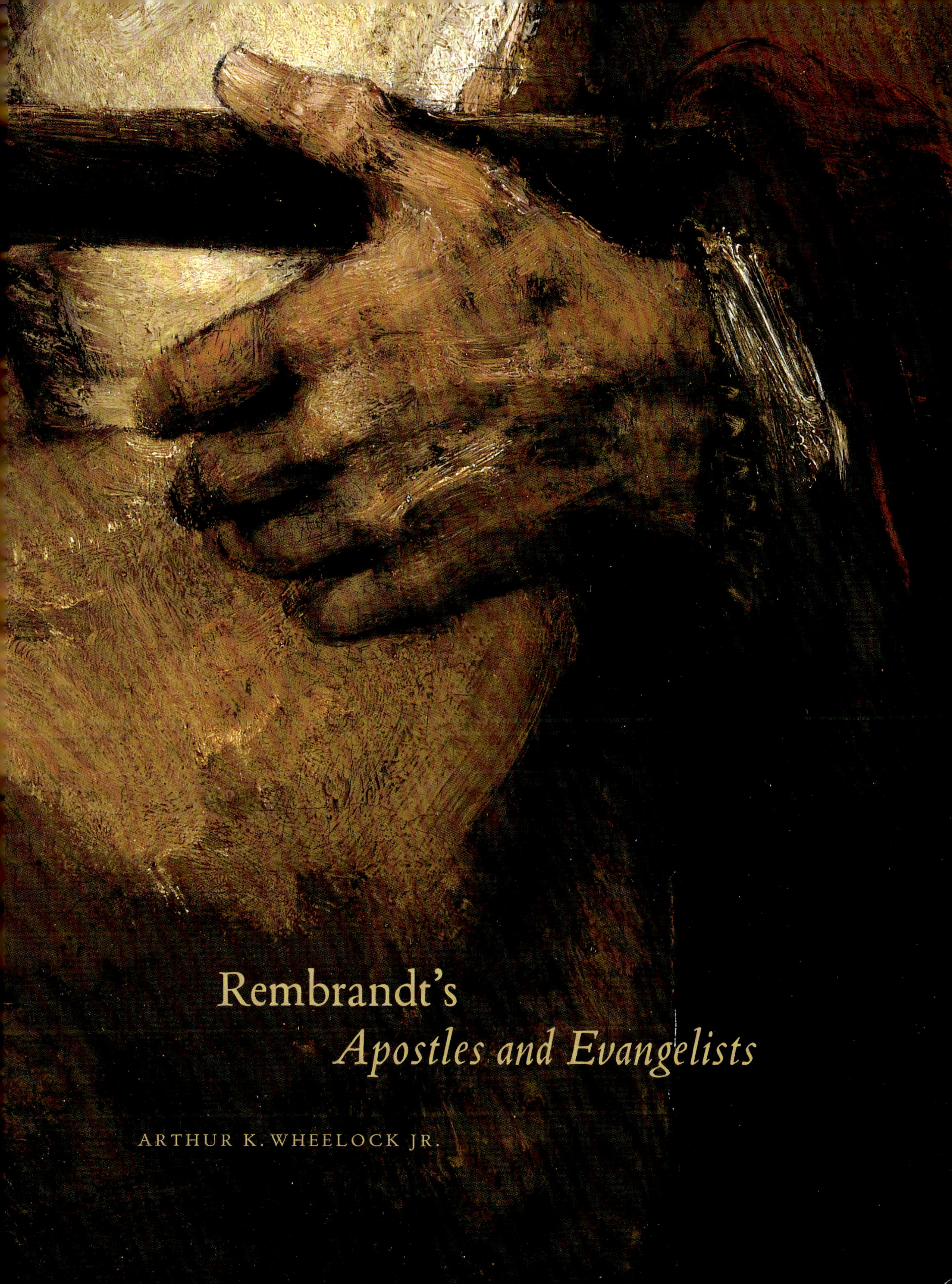
Rembrandt's
Apostles and Evangelists
ARTHUR K. WHEELOCK JR.

Rembrandt van Rijn (1606–1669) surely was one of the greatest interpreters of biblical stories.[1] Throughout his long and extraordinarily productive career in Leiden and Amsterdam, he turned repeatedly to the Bible as a source of inspiration for his paintings, drawings, and etchings, depicting not only scenes from the Old Testament and the Apocrypha but also stories found in the New Testament, particularly those centered on the life of Christ. Although his compositional and thematic choices as well as his pictorial style changed dramatically over the course of his career, he always demonstrated a remarkable empathy to the human dimension of these accounts, whatever their theological implications. Whether portraying Old Testament patriarchs such as Abraham or Jacob at moments of physical and spiritual crisis (fig. 1), or the Holy Family at rest in a simple dwelling (fig. 2), Rembrandt transformed the written word into vividly compelling pictorial language, replete with all the text's nuances of meaning.

Rembrandt's appreciation of the Bible is evident not only in his fascination with its narratives but also in his images of the great personages around whose lives the stories often revolve. He depicted these biblical figures as real people, not as idealized heroes but as men and women who walked the earth with passions and beliefs, with fears and anxieties similar to those felt by the rest of humanity. Particularly in the late 1650s and early 1660s he created an extraordinary group of "portraits" of religious figures. These images included Christ, the Virgin, and the apostles who devoted their lives to spreading the Gospel, among them Paul, Bartholomew, James, and Simon, as well as a number of the evangelists, monks, and later saints.[2] Although not all these figures can be specifically identified, in part because attributes are sometimes lacking, they all convey the deep spirituality of their inner being.[3]

Many questions surround these religious portraits. Nothing is known about Rembrandt's reasons for creating so many pictures of this type at this moment in his career. Did these works arise from the artist's inner needs? Were they painted for the market on speculation, or were they commissioned works? Were they created in relationship to each other, perhaps as a series, formal or informal? What is the reason for the differ-

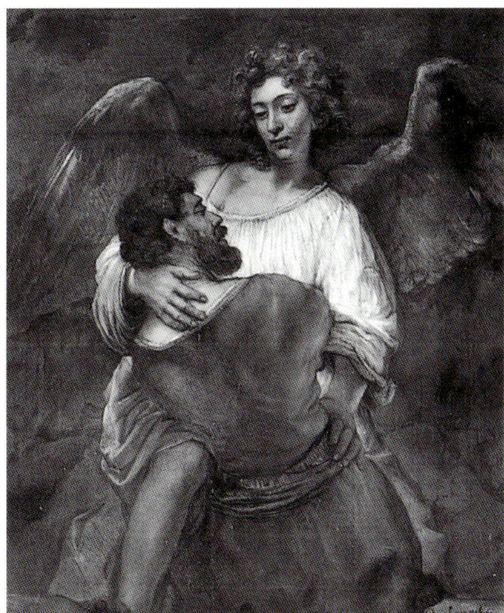

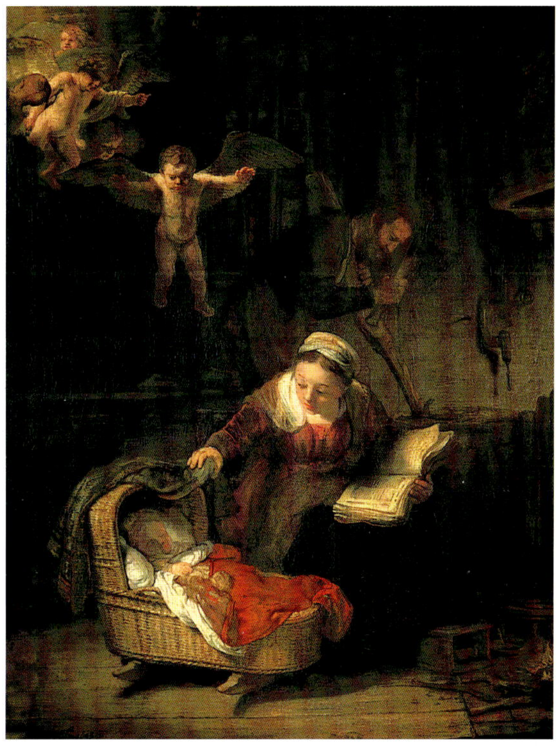

1
Rembrandt van Rijn
Jacob Wrestling with the Angel
c. 1659, oil on canvas,
Gemäldegalerie,
Staatliche Museen
zu Berlin

2
Rembrandt van Rijn
Holy Family
1645, oil on canvas,
The State Hermitage
Museum,
Saint Petersburg

ent styles and handling of paint evident in a number of these portrayals? Who were the models that served as Rembrandt's points of inspiration, and how did their individual characters and physiognomic types influence his images? Which iconographic sources lay behind these paintings? What religious beliefs underlie Rembrandt's powerfully humanistic representations of these religious figures? Last, but not least, what effects did the vicissitudes of Rembrandt's own life have on his decision to focus so much attention on figures whose lives were devoted to spiritual rather than material goals? By bringing together this group of paintings and a number of related works in this small focus exhibition, we hope to gain greater insight into these unresolved issues.

Rembrandt's Life

The biographical story of Rembrandt's later years is well known.[4] The late 1650s, the years in which Rembrandt began to focus on these portrayals of religious figures, were extremely difficult for the artist despite the enormous success and great renown he had achieved in the 1630s and 1640s. The most visible manifestation of that success had been the large house on the Sint-Anthonisbreestraat that he and his wife Saskia (1612-

1642) had purchased for a substantial sum from Christoffel Thijs in 1639. The house was situated on a fashionable street in a fine residential area where a number of artists and wealthy art lovers lived. Rembrandt's home also served as his studio, the place where he worked and trained apprentices and students. There, he displayed his enormous collection of paintings, drawings, prints, and decorative arts, which he quite publicly, and even ostentatiously, augmented with acquisitions at public auctions. Despite the appearance of financial well-being, Rembrandt's income seems to have declined in the 1640s, in part because he had fewer portrait commissions and in part because he lost money on various speculative investments; in fact, he had difficulties meeting the payments on his house.

When Saskia died in 1642, shortly after the birth of their son Titus, Rembrandt's domestic situation changed dramatically. Geertje Dircks (1600/1610-1656?), who had probably entered the household as a wet-nurse for Titus, seems to have lived with the artist as a common-law wife, a relationship that must have negatively affected his social standing. Rembrandt's relationship with Geertje became acrimonious when Hendrickje Stoffels (1626-1663) (see cat. 5, fig. 1) entered the household in 1647, probably to help care for Geertje, who was ill by this time. In the summer of 1654 it was discovered that Hendrickje was pregnant, a fact that led to her punishment by the Dutch Reformed Church, which accused her of "living in sin like a whore" with the artist. Rembrandt, who was not a member of the Reformed Church, escaped public condemnation, but the scandal further impaired his reputation in the community.[5]

Beyond the emotional turmoil that this event must have engendered in Rembrandt's and Hendrickje's lives, the artist had disputes with his neighbor, Daniel Pinto, about the costs necessary for shoring up a shared wall and the disruptions this construction project caused to the artist's work. Even more serious, however, were the large debts Rembrandt had accumulated. They prevented him from meeting final payments on the house when Christoffel Thijs demanded the full sum in 1653. As a consequence, in 1656 Rembrandt was forced to apply to the Supreme Court in The Hague for a *cessio bonorum,* a form of insolvency in which he surrendered his property to the Chamber of Insolvent Estates. A series of auctions resulted in 1657 and 1658 in which his extensive collection was sold to the highest bidder. In February 1658 his house on the Sint-Anthonisbreestraat, by now referred to as the Jodenbreestraat because of the large number of Jews who had moved into the neighborhood, was sold, and his household effects were auctioned as well.

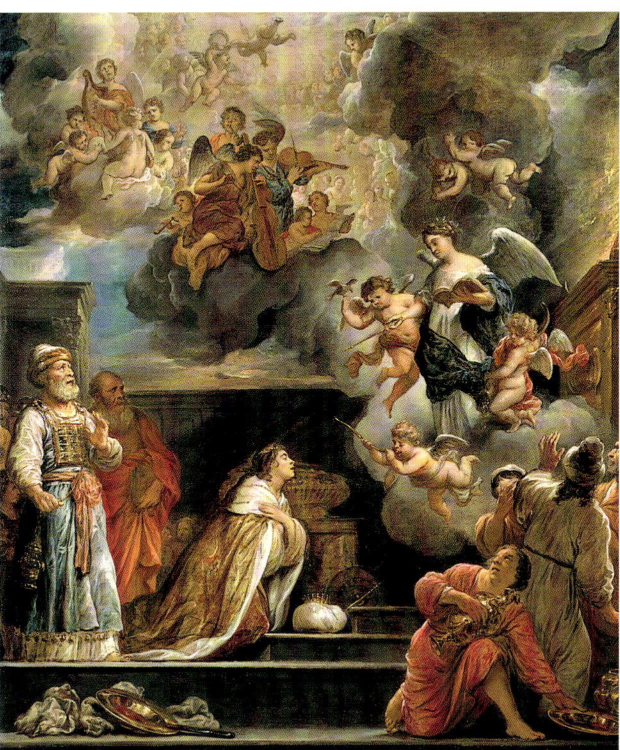

3
Govert Flinck
Solomon's Prayer for Wisdom
1659, oil on canvas, Bob Jones University Collection, Greenville, S.C.

Soon thereafter, probably early in 1658, Rembrandt, Hendrickje, and Titus moved to a small home on the Rozengracht, a canal situated in the Jordaan section of Amsterdam.[6] To protect himself from creditors, Rembrandt devised a scheme by which he would be in the employ of a company run by Hendrickje and Titus that was set up to sell paintings, prints, and drawings, as well as other artifacts. The document outlining this arrangement, giving Rembrandt free room and board and a stipend in exchange for his paintings, is dated 15 December 1660 but states that the arrangement had begun "more than two years ago."[7]

The Jordaan was also an area where other artists lived, including Rembrandt's former Leiden colleague Jan Lievens (1607–1674) and his former student Govert Flinck (1615–1660). By the mid-1650s both of these artists had abandoned Rembrandt's expressive style, with its thick impastos and pronounced chiaroscuro effects, in lieu of a more elegant manner of painting (fig. 3). They had also achieved great success in procuring important private and civic commissions. Just how they received Rembrandt into their community is unknown, but one can well imagine the reversal in Rembrandt's fortunes convinced them more than ever that the broad, rough style in which he worked was not conducive to success. This conviction must have become even stronger in 1659 when Flinck was granted the commission to paint twelve lunettes on the history of Claudius Civilis for the new town hall, and cemented in 1662 when, after Flinck's untimely death, Rembrandt's effort to paint one of the scenes, *The Conspiracy of Claudius Civilis,* was rejected by the town councillors. It may well be that other proposals by Rembrandt for the town hall were also rejected during these years, including a depiction of *Moses with the Tablets of the Law,* 1659 (fig. 4), which I believe he executed in anticipation of a commission for a chimney-piece in the aldermen's chamber.[8]

Younger Amsterdam artists largely deserted Rembrandt's manner of painting during the late 1650s and early 1660s. Indeed, no students are documented as being with Rembrandt from about 1655 until 1661, when the sixteen-year-old Arent de Gelder (1645-1727) arrived from Dordrecht to study with the artist for two years, from 1661 to 1663. While changing aesthetics may have played a role in this surprising transformation in Rembrandt's importance as a teacher, an even more determining feature may have been the turbulent state of his home and studio during the mid-1650s, not only as a result of the ongoing construction project, but also from the upheavals surrounding his bankruptcy and the resulting sale of his collection, home, and personal effects. Moreover, Rembrandt's smaller, less prestigious dwelling in the Jordaan almost certainly would not have had sufficient space for accommodating students and assistants, as had the house on the Sint-Anthonisbreestraat.

4
Rembrandt van Rijn
Moses with the Tablets of the Law
1659, oil on canvas, Gemäldegalerie, Staatliche Museen zu Berlin

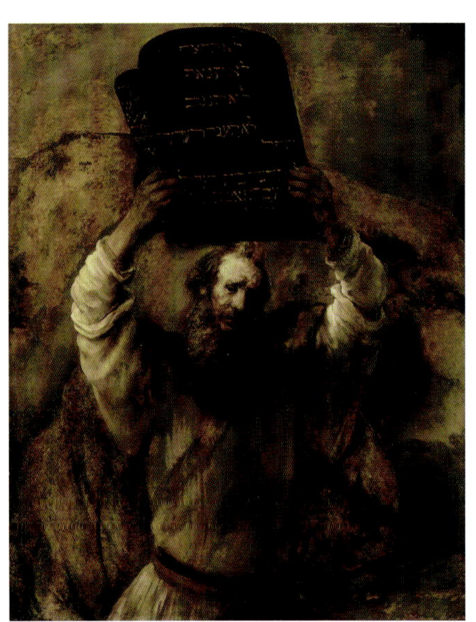

It should be emphasized, however, that little is known about Rembrandt's relationships with patrons or creditors during these difficult years in the late 1650s and early 1660s, and the extent of his financial hardships or the degree to which his work no longer appealed to contemporary taste should not be overstressed.[9] Because of the need to shelter income from local creditors it may be that Rembrandt, Hendrickje, and Titus found markets for the artist's paintings outside of Amsterdam. Also, the rejection of Rembrandt's efforts to procure commissions for the town hall may skew our perception of the artist's marketability. During these years, in fact, he executed a large number of self-portraits. They show the artist in a variety of manner, none of which suggests someone defeated by adversity (see cat. 4, fig. 1). We do not know for whom he painted these works, but it would seem that a ready market existed for images of this renowned master.

Rembrandt also retained a few important patrons who commissioned portraits, particularly those like Jacob Trip (fig. 5), who seem to have found little pleasure in the newest fashions. The commission Rembrandt

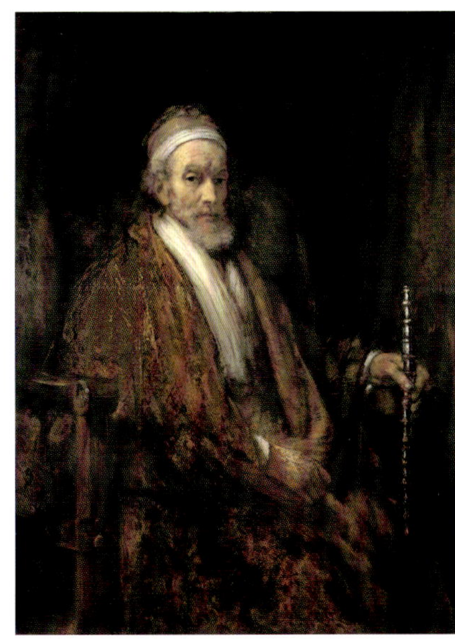

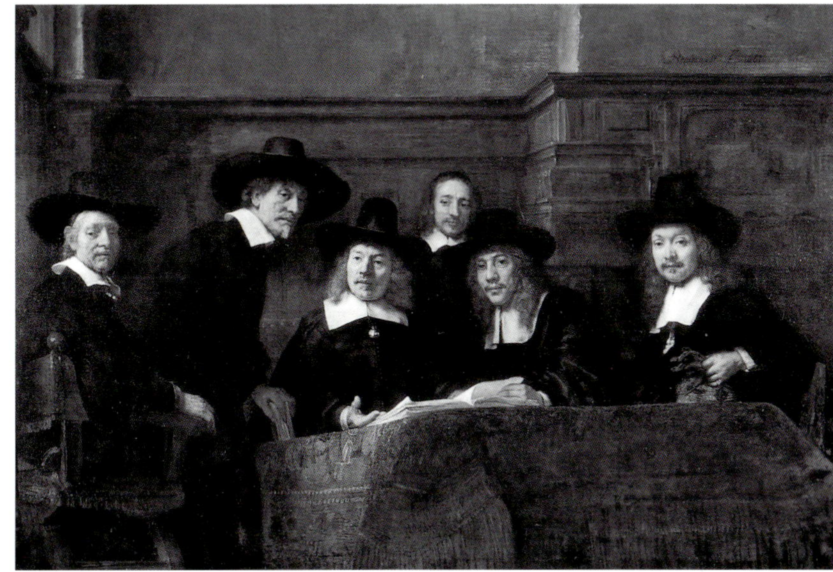

5
Rembrandt van Rijn
Jacob Trip
c. 1661, oil on canvas, The National Gallery, London

6
Rembrandt van Rijn
Syndics of the Cloth Draper's Guild
1661–1662, oil on canvas, Rijksmuseum, Amsterdam

received in 1661 to paint the large group portrait of the *Syndics of the Cloth Draper's Guild* (fig. 6) is further evidence that his mastery as a portraitist was valued and his work even deemed worthy of exhibiting in a public space. Rembrandt's artistic status at this stage of his life is evident in the heartfelt words of the poet Jeremias de Decker (1609–1666), who described Rembrandt as "the Apelles of our day" when he wrote about the portrait the artist had painted for him as a gift in 1666 (see fig. 20).[10]

Even with these successes in portraiture, Rembrandt continued to view himself as a history painter. Indeed, he executed biblical and mythological scenes, both large and small, until the last year of his life. Some of these he painted for private patrons and some for art dealers. One of these dealers was Hendrick Uylenburgh (c. 1587–1661). He lived near Rembrandt in the Jordaan, and it appears that Uylenburgh and his son Gerrit (c. 1625–after 1677) were actively involved in marketing Rembrandt's paintings at this period of his life.[11] Judging from the complex arrangements Rembrandt had with the art dealer Lodewijk van Ludick (1607–1669), however, in which he was obligated to repay loans with paintings, among them *The Circumcision* (fig. 7), it is entirely possible that the artist created a number of works during these years to repay debts.[12]

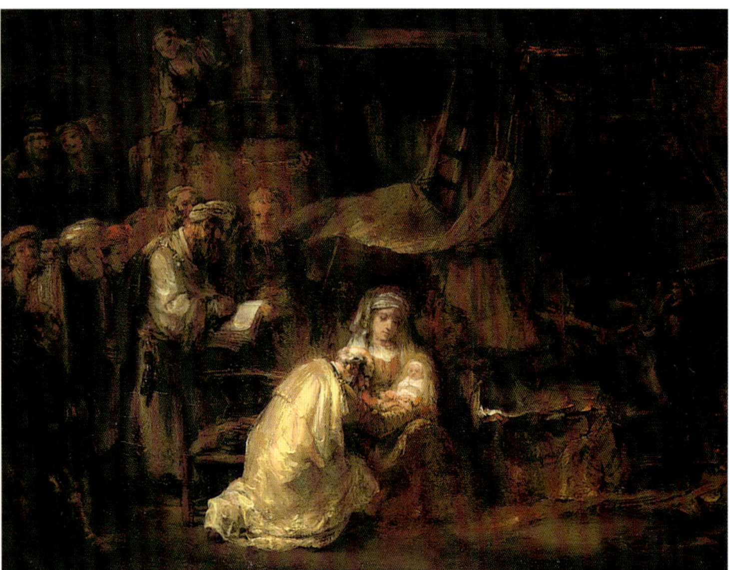

7
Rembrandt van Rijn
The Circumcision
1662, oil on canvas, National Gallery of Art, Washington, Widener Collection

Still, during the late 1650s Rembrandt was increasingly isolated from the artistic vortex of Amsterdam life. Moreover, his broadly consistent painting style seems to indicate that he was unwilling or unable to conform to the elegance generally preferred by contemporary taste. Even in these difficult years, it appears that Rembrandt single-mindedly pursued his own artistic vision, one that increasingly eschewed refinement and external beauty for images that sought to express spiritual beliefs and moral strength, not only in his religious and mythological paintings, but also in his portraits.

Theories about Rembrandt's Religious Portraits of the Late 1650s and Early 1660s

The religious portraits, primarily those depicting Christ, the Virgin, the apostles, and the evangelists that are the core of this exhibition, are among the most fascinating and provocative of these works, for they fall outside the subject range that concerned Rembrandt for most of his life. His focus on painting these images in the late 1650s and early 1660s seemingly lends credence to the belief that Rembrandt painted out of an inner conviction and without constraints foisted on him by the demands of the art market. No known commission exists for any of these works, and it is difficult to imagine a setting in Amsterdam or elsewhere in the Netherlands, either public or private, where a group of such paintings would have hung.[13] Wilhelm R. Valentiner, who initially argued that these works would have appealed to a Catholic patron and suggested that Rembrandt found markets for them outside the Netherlands, later hypothesized that the artist painted a series of apostles and evangelists for a "hidden" Mennonite church.[14] No evidence, however, supports either hypothesis.

The idea that Rembrandt conceived a number of these works as a series emerged in 1919, when Frederik Schmidt-Degener first proposed that the artist made a series of apostles and evangelists in 1661, which consisted of Saint Matthew (cat. 7), Saint Bartholomew (cat. 8), Saint Jacob, and his self-portrait as Saint Paul (cat. 11), as well as of Christ (cat. 15) and the Virgin Mary (cat. 14).[15] Although Schmidt-Degener acknowledged that he did not understand the full nature of their interrelationships, he saw these paintings as representing the fulfillment of Rembrandt's search to be a "universal artist." In the following year Valentiner identified more paintings, which he separated into two distinct groups, one of apostles, monks (cat. 16), and the resurrected Christ, and one of the four evangelists.[16] Valentiner's grouping of the evangelists, which he suggested Rembrandt might have painted for a commission from a Protestant church in England or Germany, consisted of two seated evangelists he identified as Saint Matthew (cat. 7) and Saint Mark (fig. 8, currently identified as Saint John), and two standing evangelists he identified as Saint Luke (cat. 13) and Saint John the Evangelist.[17] He added the latter three paintings by redating them to 1661 (they previously had been dated around 1663).[18] He believed at the center of this group would have hung images of Christ (cat. 15) and the Virgin Mary (cat. 14).

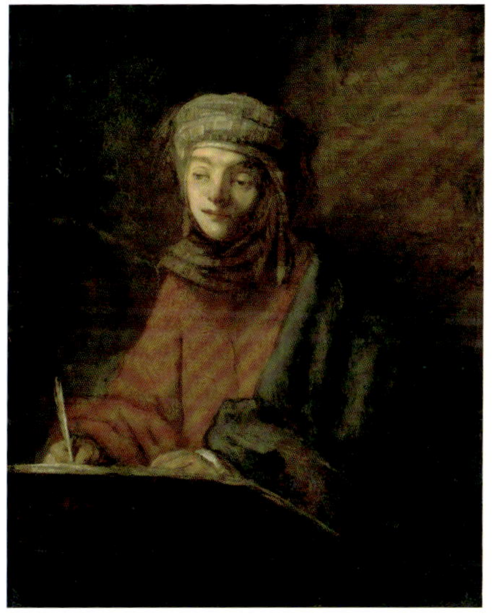

8
Rembrandt van Rijn
Saint John
1661, oil on canvas, Museum of Fine Arts, Boston, Francis Bartlett Donation

Interest in a presumed series of apostles and evangelists peaked in 1956 when a number of these paintings were included in a large Rembrandt exhibition held at the Rijksmuseum, Amsterdam. Simultaneously, Otto Benesch wrote an article in which he concluded that seven of Rembrandt's works from 1661 belonged to a loosely conceived and unfinished series of apostles and evangelists, a series that also included images of Christ and the Virgin Mary.[19] Benesch, unlike Valentiner, made no attempt to reconstruct the character of the so-called series, but he emphasized the parallels that existed between Rembrandt's late commissioned and religious portraits, where the expressive naturalism of the faces conveyed the figure's spiritual focus.

Although this exhibition centers on a number of the apostle and evangelist paintings discussed by these scholars, it also includes a few related works, among them some discussed by Benesch, that demonstrate the complex stylistic and thematic connections in Rembrandt's portraits

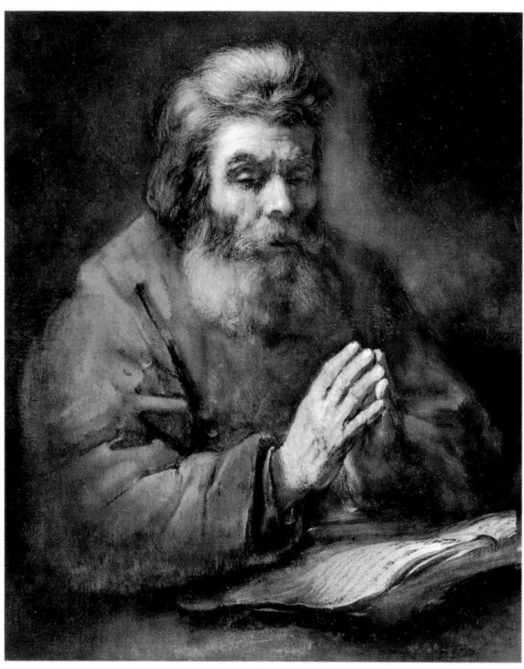

9
Follower of Rembrandt van Rijn, **Praying Apostle** c. 1661, oil on canvas, The Cleveland Museum of Art, Leonard C. Hanna, Jr., Fund

from this period of his career. Attribution issues, of course, must always be brought into consideration when dealing with Rembrandt, and while they are not the focus of this exhibition, they will be addressed in the individual catalogue entries. Schmidt-Degener, Valentiner, and Benesch, for example, all incorporated paintings into their proposed series that no longer are generally accepted as being by the master (fig. 9), and hence their conclusions about the relationships among the various works have to be modified. Nevertheless, the ideas they generated about these religious portraits have intrigued scholars ever since and serve as the point of departure for this essay.[20]

Rembrandt's Religious Beliefs

Any discussion of Rembrandt's depictions of apostles and evangelists raises questions about the artist's personal faith. Although scholars have studied the character of Rembrandt's interpretations of biblical stories and archivists have sought the evidence of contemporary documents, the specific nature of Rembrandt's religious beliefs remains largely unknown. Deductions have primarily been made on the basis of the types and aspects of the biblical stories he chose to depict. Interpreting the character of Rembrandt's beliefs and his personal identification with biblical stories and personages on the basis of the stylistic qualities of his work, including his treatment of light and the handling of paint, is also a complex matter. Without clearer documentation about the nature and purpose of his paintings, it has to be understood that interpretative assessments, however persuasively expressed, are based more on supposition than on factual analysis.

Rembrandt was raised as a Protestant, yet his family's sympathies lay not with the orthodox Calvinists but with the Remonstrants, who opposed the position of the Dutch Reformed Church on predestination.[21] Nevertheless, Rembrandt never joined a Remonstrant congregation, as had his brother Adriaen van Rijn (1597–1652), who lived in Warmond, just outside of Leiden.[22] At least through the early years of Rembrandt's career he managed to maintain close associations with both orthodox Calvinist and Remonstrant patrons. During the 1630s, for example, he received commissions not only from the orthodox preacher Johannes Elison (c. 1581–c. 1639) in 1634 (Br. 200), but also from the Remonstrant preacher Johannes Uytenbogaert (1557–1644) (fig. 10) in 1635.[23]

Rembrandt also had connections to members of other religious affiliations, including Roman Catholics. Pieter Lastman (1583–1633), with whom he studied in Amsterdam, was Catholic, and Rembrandt drew many compositional and thematic ideas from Lastman's example during the early years of his career.[24] Subsequently, Rembrandt was greatly inspired by other Catholic artists, including Peter Paul Rubens (1577–1640) and Titian (c. 1488–1576), whose expressive, painterly style strongly influenced his late work. Among the prints, drawings, and even paintings Rembrandt collected must have been Federico Barocci's etching *The Madonna in the Clouds,* which inspired one of the Dutch master's most remarkably "Catholic" images, his 1641 etching of the same subject (fig. 11).[25] Another, perhaps more personal image in the same vein is his 1652 etching *The Virgin with the Instruments of the Passion* (see cat. 14, fig. 2). Although it seems probable that these etchings, as well as his moving depiction of *The Virgin of Sorrows* (cat. 14), a painting intimately related to Rembrandt's series of apostles and evangelists, were intended primarily for Catholic patrons, nothing is known about markets for such works.

The most specific connection that can be made between Rembrandt and a religious sect comes from Filippo Baldinucci (1625–1696), who, on the basis of information provided to him by Berhardt Keil, a Rembrandt pupil in the early 1640s, reported in 1686 that Rembrandt "professed in those days the religion of the Menists [Mennonites], which, though false too, is yet opposed to that of Calvin, inasmuch as they do

10
Rembrandt van Rijn
Jan Uytenbogaert, the Preacher
1635, etching and burin, National Gallery of Art, Washington, Rosenwald Collection

11
Rembrandt van Rijn
Virgin and Child in the Clouds
(detail), 1641, etching, National Gallery of Art, Washington, Rosenwald Collection

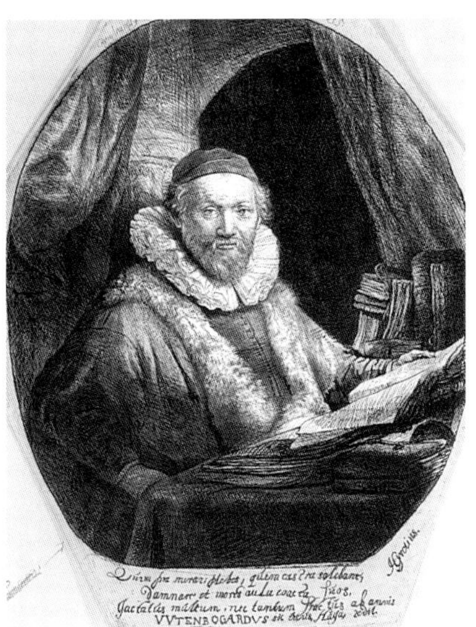

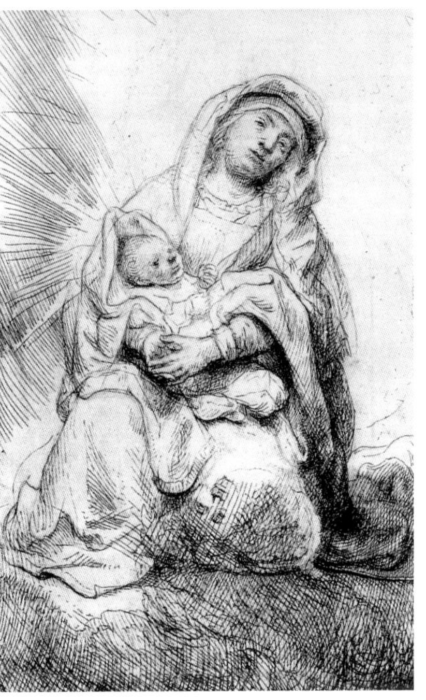

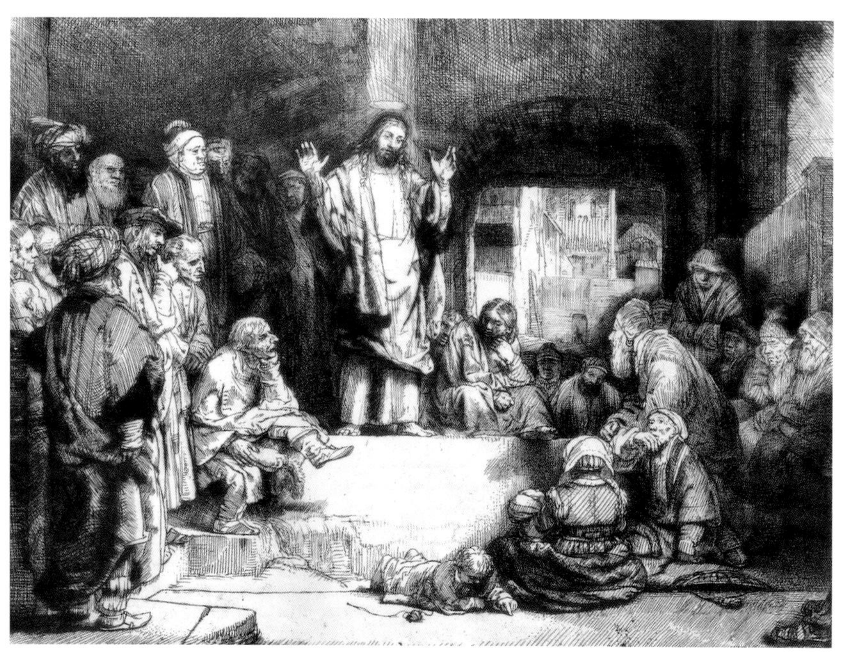

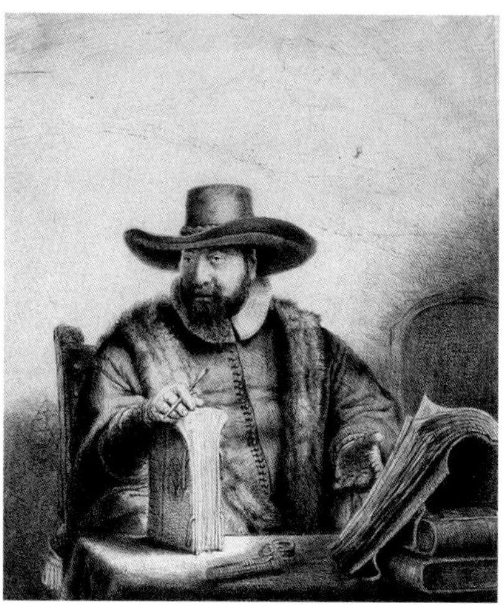

12 *right*
Rembrandt van Rijn
Cornelis Claesz Anslo
1641, etching and drypoint, National Gallery of Art, Washington, Rosenwald Collection

13 *left*
Rembrandt van Rijn
Christ Preaching
c. 1652, etching, drypoint, and burin, National Gallery of Art, Washington, Gift of W. G. Russell Allen

not practice the rite of baptism before the age of thirty."[26] Rembrandt had a number of extremely important associations with Mennonites throughout his career, including the Amsterdam art dealer Hendrick Uylenburgh, for whom he worked as a master-painter in the early 1630s, and his pupils Jacob Backer (1608-1651) and Govert Flinck.[27] Rembrandt's services as a portrait painter were sought after by the liberal faction of the Mennonites, called the Waterlanders, particularly during the later years of his career. Among his Mennonite sitters were the preacher Cornelis Claesz Anslo (1592-1646) in 1641 (fig. 12), Catrina Hooghsaet (1607-1685) in 1657, Lieven Willemsz van Coppenol (1599-after 1677) in 1658 (see cat. 7, fig. 3), and Volckert Jansz (1605/1610-1681), who appears in *Syndics of the Cloth Draper's Guild*, in 1661-1662 (see fig. 6).[28]

As Jakob Rosenberg has emphasized, it is not necessary to determine whether Rembrandt was actually a member of the Mennonite community in order to recognize his spiritual affinity to this community's basic beliefs, which centered on man's spiritual life in response to direct engagement with biblical texts.[29] Not only did Rembrandt depict a number of the biblical stories that Menno Simons had emphasized in his writings, such as those of Susanna, Esther, and Jacob and Esau, but the

Christ he portrayed was much the same as the one this founder of the Mennonites had envisioned: a teacher and healer of human suffering (fig. 13). Rembrandt, in his paintings, prints, and drawings, sought out biblical stories that revealed both man's fallibility and his humility in seeking God's mercy. The artist imbued many of his religious portraits with these qualities, and rather than forceful self-reliance, one senses in these figures internal doubt and the search for spiritual truth.

Relevant to the theme of this exhibition is the fact that the Mennonites felt strong associations with the first apostolic martyrs, not only because they themselves aspired to a simple and devout lifestyle, but also because of their own history of persecution.[30] Mennonites, who had been tortured and executed as heretics in the Netherlands during the sixteenth century, were still being prosecuted in Bern and Zurich.[31] Preachers constantly reminded congregations that their privileges were built on the martyrdoms of their forebears, which were recorded in Mennonite martyrologies, among them Thieleman J. van Braght's *Martyrs' Mirror,* published in Dordrecht in 1660.[32] In his tome, Van Braght exhorted his readers to follow the examples of the apostles and the Brethren, and to sacrifice the glories of this world to better enjoy those of the Kingdom of God.[33]

The concern for martyrdom in 1660 was not just theoretical. Van Braght records how a number of Mennonites, among them W. J. V. Coppenol, nephew of the calligrapher Lieven Willemsz Coppenol, "delegated...by the order of their churches," submitted a formal request to the burgomasters of Amsterdam asking them to write to the magistrates of Bern and Zurich "for the release of the [Mennonite] prisoners and the restoration of their goods." The letter, sent on 18 February 1660, had a favorable effect in Bern. Swiss Anabaptists were subsequently permitted to move from that city to Amsterdam in September of that year, and many settled in the rather poor neighborhood of Rozengracht where Rembrandt lived. Descriptions of these pilgrims have striking parallels with the types of individuals Rembrandt portrayed in the early 1660s, for their penitence and search for a deeper holiness in life became their distinguishing characteristics.[34] Thus, the Mennonites, through the publication of *Martyrs' Mirror* and the influx of Swiss pilgrims, may well have encouraged Rembrandt in depicting early Christian martyrs in the early 1660s. The Mennonites' explicit interest in the lives of the apostles may also offer clues about a possible market for such paintings.

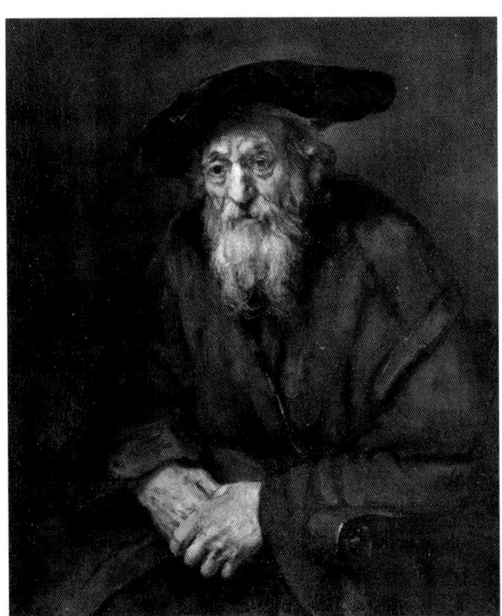

14
Rembrandt van Rijn
An Elderly Man
1654, oil on canvas,
The State Hermitage
Museum,
Saint Petersburg

Rembrandt and the Jews

While the spiritual beliefs of the Mennonites appealed to Rembrandt's concept of Christianity, he also had a notable sensitivity to Jewish traditions, which were reinforced by the broad allegorical connections the Dutch felt existed between the Republic and the ancient Israelites. Parallels between the Dutch experience, in which a small country fought successfully for its existence against a powerful oppressor, and the struggles of the Israelites lent legitimacy to the Dutch struggle against Spain. The Dutch, like the ancient Israelites, believed themselves to be a chosen people, favored and blessed by God's protection.[35]

Rembrandt had close contacts with Amsterdam Jews for much of his life. He seems to have found visual stimuli for many of his depictions of religious figures in the picturesque qualities of Ashkenazi Jews. These refugees from war-devastated central Europe started to emigrate from their homeland to Amsterdam in the 1640s, anticipating that they would find there a sense of freedom and security unmatched elsewhere in Western Europe.[36] Most of these Jews were poor and relatively uneducated, and they resorted to begging to support themselves in their new Dutch homeland. They wore their beards long and untrimmed, dressed in exotic long robes, and wore misshapen hats. In their physical appearance, religious fervor, and history of persecution, they harkened back to their biblical forebears, and Rembrandt sought to capture their character in a number of his paintings (fig. 14), prints, and drawings.[37] Some of these studies made from life served as inspiration for his religious paintings, both Old and New Testament scenes. One curious item is listed in the 1656 inventory of Rembrandt's possessions as "A head of Christ, a study from life."[38]

Rembrandt's relations with the Ashkenazi Jews seem to have been quite different from those he had with the Sephardic Jews, many of whom lived near him on the Sint-Anthonisbreestraat. Sephardic Jews were more interesting to him for their roles as artistic patrons than as sources of artistic inspiration. Having immigrated to Amsterdam from Spain and Portugal at the beginning of the seventeenth century, they had successfully assimilated themselves into Dutch society, and many of them became prosperous merchants and professionals. They generally adopted Dutch dress even as they built and maintained their own houses of worship, intent upon returning to their faith after the Spanish had forced them to convert to Catholicism in the late sixteenth century. Among the Sephardic Jews who commissioned works from the artist were his neighbor, the rabbi Manasseh Ben Israël, and the physician Ephraim Bueno, whose image he captured in an etching of 1647 (fig. 15). For Manasseh Ben Israël, Rembrandt created a series of etchings that illustrated the rabbi's messianic treatise, *Piedra gloriosa de la Estatua de Nebuchadnesar* (The Glorious Stone of the Statue of Nebuchadnezzar) (1655), a commission that demonstrates the artist's willing efforts to capture in pictorial form the ideas contained in this Jewish theological treatise.

Rembrandt's involvement with Manasseh Ben Israël's enterprise drew upon his earlier experiences in depicting the history of the Jewish people. Aside from the Bible, one of Rembrandt's most important textual sources for his Old Testament scenes was *Jewish Antiquities,* a copy of which is recorded in his 1656 inventory.[39] Written by the Jewish historian Flavius Josephus (c. 37–100), the book's intricate narrative, which embellished upon biblical stories, inspired a number of the artist's moving depictions of Old Testament stories, not only for the content they related but also for the ways in which they were told. As Christian Tümpel has noted, *Jewish Antiquities* often describes the psychological state of figures faced with painful choices, frequently as a result of God's commands.[40] Rembrandt's empathetic depictions of the inner struggles confronted by, among others, Abraham (fig. 16), David, Joseph, Esther, and Bathsheba reflect his awareness of the events of their lives as recounted in this remarkable text. A comparable sensitivity to human struggles faced by men of faith underlies Rembrandt's complex psychological characterizations of the apostles and evangelists.

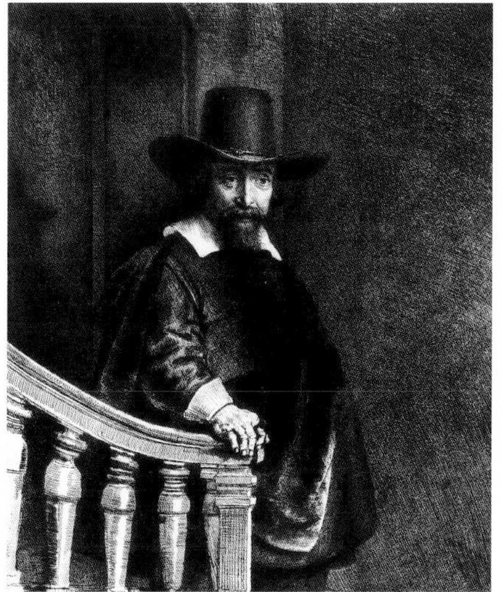

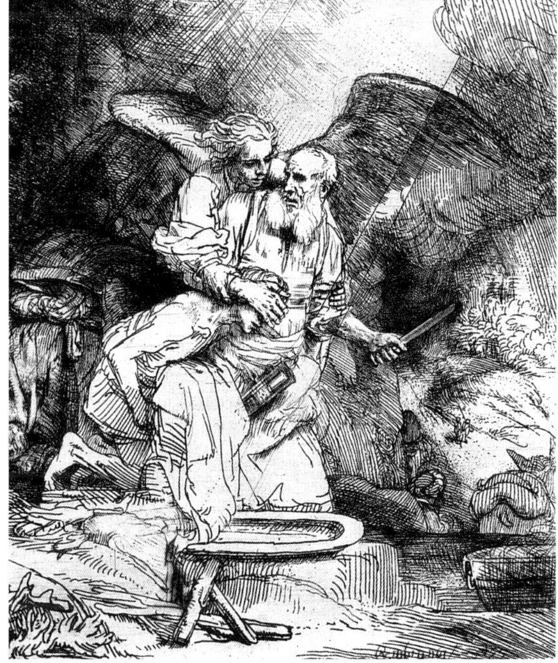

15
Rembrandt van Rijn
Ephraim Bueno
1647, drypoint and burin, The British Museum, London

16
Rembrandt van Rijn
Abraham's Sacrifice
1655, etching and drypoint, National Gallery of Art, Washington, Rosenwald Collection

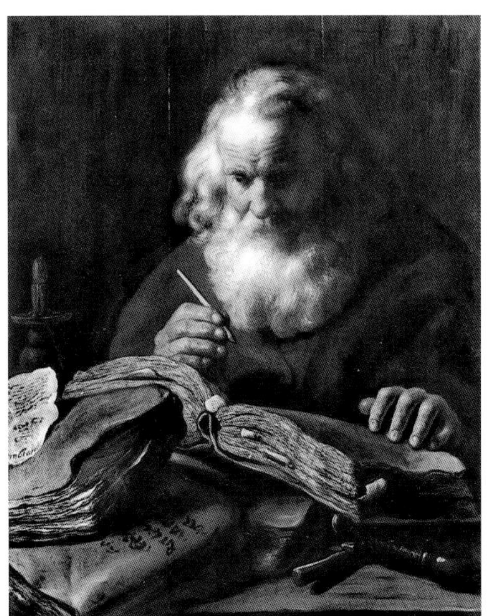

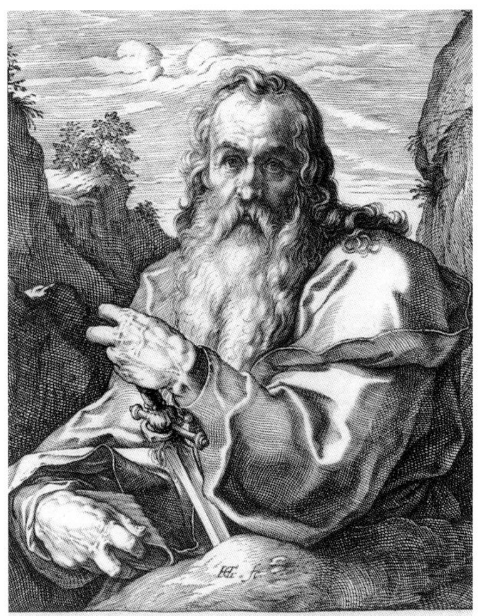

17
Jan Lievens
The Apostle Paul
c. 1626-1627,
oil on panel,
Collection of Isabel
and Alfred Bader

18
Hendrick Goltzius
Saint Paul
c. 1589, engraving,
National Gallery of
Art, Washington,
Rosenwald Collection

Rembrandt's Paintings within the Tradition of Apostle Series

Whatever the impact of his life story, religious beliefs, and personal encounters, the nature of Rembrandt's so-called series of apostles and evangelists was far different from traditional apostle series, such as the ones Peter Paul Rubens and Anthony van Dyck (1599-1641) executed in Antwerp in the second decade of the seventeenth century, or from evangelist series, such as that created by Jan Lievens in Leiden in 1626-1627.[41] Rubens and Van Dyck painted their images of Christ and the Twelve Apostles, each with their identifying attributes, on individual oak panels of identical size (see fig. 19).[42] As was characteristic for such series, Rubens' half-length apostles and Van Dyck's bust-length apostles not only represented idealized types, but they also were consistent in style, degree of finish, and artistic concept. Similar approaches are found in sixteenth- and seventeenth-century engraved apostle series, including those by Anton and Hieronymous Wierix (born c. 1555, and 1551-1619, respectively), by Johannes Sadeler I (1550-1600), and by Hendrick Goltzius (1558-1617) (fig. 18).[43]

Not all representations of apostles and evangelists, however, were fully idealized figures. For his series of Christ and the Apostles, Cornelis Ketel (1548-1616) used images of fellow artists and collectors.[44] As Urbach notes, apostle series were not normally destined for devotional purposes but for "galleries of apostles" in private homes, where they were exhibited as *viri illustri,* illustrious men of the Bible.[45] Hence, apostles were particularly appropriate subjects for a *portrait historié.* The figures in Lievens' evangelist series, which included *The Apostle Paul* (fig. 17), were also less than fully idealized. They were shown at a table deeply engaged in writing, much as Rembrandt would later depict them. Lievens included the saints' attributes when possible, as though they were a naturalistic element within the scene.[46]

Rembrandt conceived his group of religious figures from the late 1650s to the early 1660s in a far less systematic manner than is evident in these earlier series. His paintings are not precisely identical in size or consistent in style, degree of finish, or artistic concept. Some apostles are shown more than once, while others are not included at all. Some have attributes and some do not. Finally, both apostles and evangelists belong to this group. In all these respects Rembrandt's paintings differ from earlier prototypes, which makes it extremely difficult to determine whether he conceived any of these works as part of a series.

If one were to determine a "core group" of apostles and evangelists from those identified by earlier scholars, I would imagine them to be *The Evangelist Matthew and the Angel* (cat. 7), *The Apostle Bartholomew* (cat. 8), *The Apostle James the Major* (cat. 9), *The Apostle Simon* (cat. 10), *Self-Portrait as the Apostle Paul* (cat. 11), and *The Apostle James the Minor(?)* (cat. 12), even though attribution questions exist with this latter work. These paintings are dated in the same year, 1661, and they are similar enough in size that one could assume Rembrandt created them in a serial relationship.[47] *The Evangelist Matthew and the Angel, The Apostle Bartholomew, The Apostle Simon,* and *The Apostle James the Minor(?)* also share an intriguing pictorial characteristic: each image is surrounded by remnants of a black, painted border. *Self-Portrait as the Apostle Paul* has a border that is indicated by scratched lines. Yet the apostles and evangelists included in this group do not have the tight-knit iconographic integrity one would expect from a formal series. Other paintings generally associated with this group, such as *The Apostle Paul* (cat. 2), *Christ* (cat. 15), and *Monk (Saint Francis?) Reading* (cat. 16), are sufficiently different in scale or pictorial concept that they probably should be considered as related but separate entities. Moreover, among the paintings generally associated with this group are two depictions of Saint Bartholomew (cats. 3, 8) and two depictions of Saint Paul (cats. 2, 4), whereas none exists of other apostles, as, for example, Saint Peter.[48]

Even within the "core group," stylistic variations occur that suggest differences in artistic approach. *The Apostle Simon* (cat. 10), for example, is broadly executed with bold, slashing strokes of the brush and broad planes of color, with the figure's deep, brooding character conveyed through the heavy shadows crossing his face. Although Rembrandt adapted the head of the apostle from the same model, probably an Ashkenazi Jew who posed for *Moses with the Tablets of the Law,* 1659 (see fig. 4), the artist abstracted this man's features to create a powerful representation of a person weighed down by heavy burdens preying on his mind. *The Evangelist Matthew and the Angel* and *The Apostle Bartholomew* (cats. 7, 8), on the other hand, seem far less removed from a live model. Rembrandt's depiction of the faces of the evangelist and the apostle, while strikingly modeled with thick impastos, conveys the sitters' expressions by carefully recording their features, including eyes and eye sockets and lines on their foreheads.

The difference between Rembrandt's handling of paint in these images, particularly in *The Apostle Bartholomew* and one of his late portraits (see fig. 5), is minimal, which suggests that, unlike *The Apostle Simon,* the artist may have executed them directly from the model. If so, these works would have had a different point of departure than other paintings related to this group. For *The Apostle Bartholomew* one wonders whether Rembrandt used a friend or patron as his model, as had Cornelis Ketel in his series of apostles and evangelists. The painting could also have been commissioned as a *portrait historié* in which the sitter was depicted in the guise of Saint Bartholomew. Such a possibility raises numerous questions about the place of these images in the art market.

In the end, the varied appearances of these works and the seemingly unfinished character of this cycle of apostles and evangelists are reminiscent of the freely conceived series Rembrandt created at other stages of his career. The eight paintings belonging to the so-called Passion series he executed for Frederik Hendrik were not the result of a single, overarching commission, but were painted over a fifteen-year period, from the early 1630s to the mid-1640s. The works are similar but not identical in size; some are on panel and some on canvas, and their stylistic variations reflect the differing periods of execution. Two of the subjects, *The Birth of Christ* (Br. 574) and *The Circumcision,* are not generally included in Passion series.[49] A series of six etchings Rembrandt created in 1654 of the childhood of Christ is somewhat more consistent in character, although one of the etchings, *The Adoration of the Shepherds* (B. 45), is larger in size than the other scenes. A second series of etchings from around 1654 consists of four scenes from the life of Christ. These etchings are similar in size and stylistic character, but are quite varied in the subjects they depict. One scene is drawn from Christ's childhood, two are from the Passion, and one, *Christ at Emmaus* (B. 87) (see cat. 6, fig. 1), is from the period following Christ's Resurrection.[50]

Ernst van de Wetering suggests that Rembrandt's unstructured approach to creating works in series may result from his mercurial artistic temperament.[51] Arnold Houbraken (1660-1719) provided an insight into Rembrandt's character when he wrote: "But one thing is to be regretted and that is that he was so quick to change and move on to other things that many of his works were left only half-way finished."[52] An artist who was quick to "change and move on" may not have had the patience to carry through and complete a large series of works.

Houbraken's comments also raise the possibility that Rembrandt left some of his works unfinished, as, for example, *The Apostle Paul* (cat. 2), and that assistants may have completed them at a later date. This

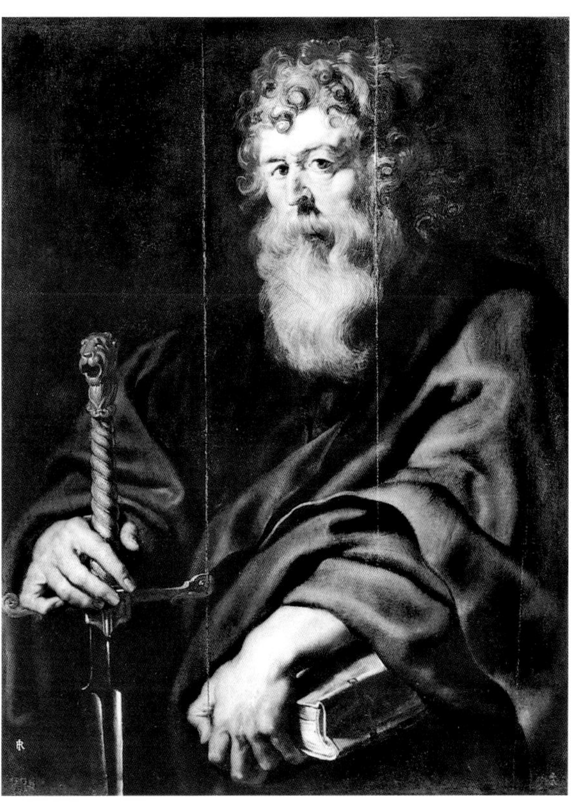

19
Sir Peter Paul Rubens
Apostle Paul
c. 1610, oil on panel,
Museo del Prado,
Madrid

prompts questions about the nature of Rembrandt's workshop during the late 1650s and early 1660s. As mentioned, the only documented student of Rembrandt's during this period was Arent de Gelder, who was with the master from 1661 to 1663. Yet, attribution issues exist for a number of works that were probably executed just prior to and just after De Gelder's tenure with Rembrandt, including several paintings depicting apostles and evangelists that have been traditionally associated with this group (see fig. 9). Who were these assistants, where did they work, and what was Rembrandt's relationship to them since he was officially employed by Titus and Hendrickje during these years?

The Theological Framework for Rembrandt's Images

While Rembrandt created memorable depictions of apostles and evangelists, enormous conceptual differences exist between them and those created by Peter Paul Rubens. Rubens, whose ideals coincided with those of the Counter-Reformation, was a Christian Humanist, a Catholic artist who sought to infuse his religious images with classical ideals drawn from antiquity and the Renaissance. He conceived of his apostles as heroic patriarchs, each a massive figure portrayed forcefully clutching his attribute. As seen in the *Apostle Paul* (fig. 19), Rubens' apostles are physically powerful men endowed with the wisdom of ancient philosophers.[53] This full-bearded patriarch seems all the more imposing because of the loosely draped, ocher-colored robe that covers his massive body. As Paul stands clasping the sword of his martyrdom in his right hand and a huge tome denoting his Epistles in the other, he stares directly out at the viewer, his deep-set eyes projecting the certainty of his faith and spiritual wisdom. Rubens' compelling portrayal of this apostle and others in this series visually expressed an important theological component of Counter-Reformation thought: the role of saints as intercessors for the faithful.

Rembrandt was less systematic than Rubens, and his apostles and evangelists project a very different character. As Benesch noted, they are "poor, rugged men" rather than heroic, and "skeptics" who have been turned into true believers through the "miraculous experiences of their lives" rather than figures whose "spiritual eminence is demonstrated by superior beauty and vigor of body."[54] Such a characterization is particularly true of Rembrandt's Saint Matthew, whose rough-hewn features, vigorously heightened with thick impastos, project the uncertainties of a mind struggling to comprehend the ideas being whispered into his ear. Attributes no longer play a dominant role in these presentations: Saint Matthew's source of inspiration is more boy than angel (cat. 7); the Apostle James the Major's identifying scallop shell inconspicuously serves to attach his cloak to his coat (cat. 9); and Saint Bartholomew's knife is innocuously held as though it were a familiar tool rather than the symbol of his martyrdom (cat. 3).[55]

Benesch wrote about the deep humanity of these works, noting they "have nothing to do with confessional distinctions." They are neither Protestant nor Catholic, "simply Christian, as simple, deep and human as Christian faith is."[56] The most profound image among them, for both Schmidt-Degener and Benesch, was Rembrandt's *Self-Portrait as the Apostle Paul* (cat. 11). The artist's questioning face, shrouded in half-light, seems to convey something of Paul's awareness of human limitations, even for those imbued with unbounded faith or, in Rembrandt's case, artistic genius. Appropriately, both scholars introduce into their discussions of Rembrandt's painting one of Saint Paul's most poignant commentaries: "And though I have the gift of prophecy, and understand all mysteries, and all knowledge; and though I have all faith, so that I could remove mountains, and have not charity, I am nothing" (1 Corinthians 13:3).

Such observations about the predominantly Christian character of Rembrandt's images need to be modified, for a marked difference exists between the idealized physicality and moral certainty of Rubens' apostles and those of Rembrandt, a difference grounded in the philosophical framework through which each artist viewed the world. Rubens fully embraced the notion — derived from antique writings on rhetoric and poetry — that strict rules of decorum applied to the creation of a work of art. Noble subjects required a dignified style, whereas humble subjects were best treated by lowly discourse.[57] This concept, espoused by Aristotle and reiterated by Cicero and Quintilian, was expanded upon in the sixteenth century by Neoplatonists such as Giovanni Paolo Lomazzo (1538-1600), who equated goodness with beauty and the bad with the vulgar.[58] As a Counter-Reformation artist, Rubens drew upon this powerful symbiosis of form and content to create moving images of heroic figures spiritually and physically committed to spreading the Gospel, even in anticipation of their own martyrdom.

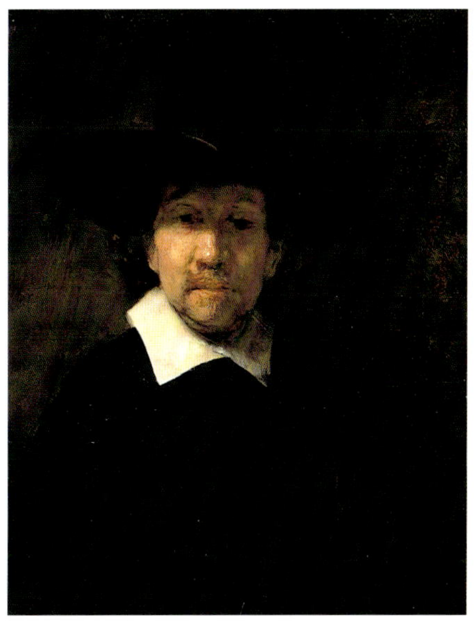

20
Rembrandt van Rijn
Jeremias de Decker
1666, oil on panel,
The State Hermitage Museum,
Saint Petersburg

Rembrandt, on the other hand, came from a Protestant heritage that viewed proper decorum in very different terms. This "Christian decorum" owed much to the preaching of Saint Paul, who wrote in his First Epistle to the Corinthians (1:27): "But the foolish things of the world had God chosen, that he may confound the wise; and the weak things of the world hath God chosen, that he may confound the strong." Saint Augustine expanded upon this sentiment when, in his *Confessions,* he wrote of the "lowliness" of Christianity when compared to the ostensible nobility of paganism, and the humble, even "unworthy," quality of the scriptures when compared to the dignified rhetoric of Cicero.[59] In the *City of God,* he reiterated that the "great mystery of incarnation" was the moment when "that true and benignant Redeemer brought low by his humility," manifested himself to humankind.[60]

John Calvin, who closely followed the writings of Augustine, emphasized these precepts about Christian simplicity. In his commentary on John 1:14 he wrote: "The majesty of God was not annihilated though it was surrounded by flesh; it was indeed concealed under the low condition of the flesh, so as to cause its splendor to be seen."[61] The seventeenth-century poet Jeremias de Decker, the proud possessor of Rembrandt's portrait gift (fig. 20), was sympathetic to Calvinist traditions and wrote in comparable terms.[62] In his poem, "Good Friday, or the Passion of Our Lord Jesus Christ," Decker compared the lowly manner of Christ's death to a veil that allows Christ's divinity to shine through for the eyes of the faithful.[63]

The impact of Saint Paul on both Martin Luther and Calvin was also crucial in developing the Reformation's concept of salvation. Paul believed that man is a sinner. He argued that the Judaic idea of winning God's approval by obedience to the law was a hopeless pursuit.[64] Instead, God's grace alone offers salvation. For the Protestants, Paul's life was a perfect example of God's grace and became the archetype of the essential Christian experience.[65] Not surprisingly, one of Rembrandt's most touching portraits of the late 1650s shows an elderly man in the guise of Saint Paul who, sitting before a roundel depicting the Sacrifice of Abraham, quietly reflects on the nature of faith (cat. 4).

With this background in mind, we can better understand the appeal of Saint Paul to Rembrandt. Although he had portrayed the apostle on numerous occasions in his paintings and prints, no other example has the gravity of his 1661 *Self-Portrait as the Apostle Paul,* in which he assumes the apostle's persona (cat. 11). This painting beautifully illustrates Rembrandt's approach to his depictions of the apostles and evangelists, not only his religious ideas and his complex personal history, but also his empathy with the subjects of his paintings. Rembrandt stares out at the viewer with a thoughtful yet quizzical expression, his associations with Paul indicated by the sword projecting from his doublet and the open manuscript in his hands. The Rembrandt/Saint Paul in this painting is the great but flawed man who, saved by God's grace, reveals the power of the Christian faith for others who struggle with their own human limitations.

Rembrandt's deeply brooding religious portraits from the late 1650s and early 1660s, which are dark in tonality yet luminous in light and color, convey both the determined faith and the uncertainties and anxieties of these humble individuals. As these religious figures, so vulnerable in their humanity, try to comprehend the mysteries of life and the Christian message, they also seem to struggle with an awareness of their own impending mortality. In Rembrandt's hands, their efforts to reconcile these conflicting forces are both heart-wrenching and profoundly human. Just how Rembrandt conceived these paintings in relation to each other is a question that may not ever be fully answered, but in their compelling cumulative power, his portrayals of those who devoted their lives to disseminating the message of the Gospel are one of the most poignant achievements of his memorable career.

Notes

1 I would like to thank Jan Leja, Lynn Russell, Anna Tummers, and Anneke Wertheim for their guidance and support in writing this essay.

2 In both their physical appearance and emotional characteristics, Rembrandt's religious images are so immediate and alive that the term "portrait" seems entirely appropriate when describing them.

3 Iconographic traditions of the appearance and attributes for saints were far from consistent. The identifications of religious figures therefore are frequently quite tenuous (see Appendix).

4 The biographical overview that follows depends heavily on the scholarly contributions of S.A.C. Dudok van Heel, in particular Dudok van Heel 1991 and Dudok van Heel 2001.

5 Rembrandt almost certainly did not marry Hendrickje because of a stipulation in Saskia's will stating that if he ever remarried, Titus would inherit Saskia's share of the property she had jointly held with Rembrandt.

6 Dudok van Heel 1991, 61, notes that rent for the home was a mere 225 guilders a year.

7 Strauss and Van der Meulen 1979, 462-465, doc. 1660/20.

8 Heppner 1935 proposed that Rembrandt's painting had been intended for this commission, which was later filled by Ferdinand Bol. Although Heppner's theory cannot be fully supported because the painting has not been cut down, as he suggested, one need not assume that the work ever actually hung as a chimneypiece in the aldermen's chamber. Rembrandt could well have painted this imposing image as a demonstration of how he would execute the larger canvas needed to fill the space in the town hall. He never received the commission, which was awarded to his former pupil, Ferdinand Bol (1616-1680).

9 Much intriguing information on Rembrandt's contacts with patrons is included in Schwartz 1985. For a recent commentary on Rembrandt's contacts during the late 1650s and early 1660s, see Crenshaw 2000.

10 As quoted in Schwartz 1985, 340. For this painting, see Bredius/Gerson 1969, 574-575, no. 320.

11 Schwartz 1985, 315, notes that in 1661 Rembrandt's transactions with Don Antonio Ruffo in Messina for a depiction of Alexander the Great were arranged with Isaac Just, who was a cousin of Gerrit Uylenburgh's wife-to-be. When Gerrit went bankrupt in 1675, he owned three paintings by Rembrandt.

12 For this transaction, see Wheelock 1995, 272-273, 275, note 12.

13 Only a few early inventories list works that may refer to paintings included in this group. The earliest is the 1667 inventory of the Delft preacher Gerrit van Heusden, who owned "a painting of Saint Paul by Rembrandt." See Strauss and Van der Meulen 1979, 568, doc. 1667/5. See also cat. 11, n. 1, for an item listed in the 1965 inventory of Everhard Jabach.

14 Valentiner 1920/1921, 222; Valentiner 1956, 400.

15 Schmidt-Degener 1919, 264-266. Schmidt-Degener believed Rembrandt used monks or pilgrims as models for these works. The present location of the painting Schmidt-Degener identified as *Saint Jacob* is unknown. It seems probable that this work was executed by a member of Rembrandt's workshop and not by the master.

16 Valentiner 1920/1921.

17 Valentiner 1920/1921, 222, suggested that the commission may have come from a German or English Protestant church, which were not as devoid of paintings as were Dutch Reformed churches, or from a private collector in a Catholic country.

18 Valentiner's proposal suffers from the fact that serious attribution issues surround the "Saint Mark" and the "Saint John" of his series. The Boston painting (fig. 8, which he believed to depict Saint Mark) may well be by Rembrandt; however, it has been extensively overpainted in the past and is in very poor condition. Because of these condition issues, it has not been included in this exhibition. The "Saint John," which was already doubted in Valentiner's day, is no longer attributed to Rembrandt. Its current location is unknown.

19 Benesch 1956; Benesch 1970.

20 Not all scholars have supported the notion that Rembrandt executed a "series" of apostles and evangelists in the late 1650s and early 1660s. Gerson in Bredius/Gerson 1969, 613, no. 614, and Giltaij and Jansen in Rotterdam 1988, 82, no. 26, rejected it as excessively hypothetical.

21 Rembrandt never joined the Reformed Church, and it seems unlikely, considering the social stigma placed upon Hendrickje in 1654 when she was denied Holy Communion by the church council, that Rembrandt drew closer to the Reformed Church during the period in which he was painting his half-length religious figures.

22 Dudok van Heel 2001, 20.

23 See John Michael Montias, "A Business Partner and a Pupil: Two Conjectural Essays on Rembrandt's Entourage," in *Rethinking Rembrandt,* ed. Alan Chong and Michael Zell (Zwolle, 2002), 129-158, esp. 143, 144.

24 Rembrandt's initial teacher in Leiden, Jacob Isaacsz van Swanenburg (1571-1638), was also Catholic.

25 Amsterdam and London 2000, 192, 193, no. 43.

26 As quoted in Rosenberg 1964, 180. For further discussion on Baldinucci's account in his publication, *Cominciamento, e progresso dell'arte dell'intagliare in rame, colle vite di molti de' più eccellenti Maestri della stessa professione* (Florence, 1686), including a transcription from his publication, see Slive 1953, 111, note 3.

27 For the relationship between Mennonite beliefs and some of Rembrandt's religious images from the 1630s, see Van de Wetering 2000, 52-55.

28 See Schwartz 1985, 219, 333, 336, 337. Schwartz suggests that Volckert Jansz was probably the man responsible for the commission to paint the *Syndics of the Cloth Draper's Guild;* see page 337.

29 Rosenberg 1964, 181.

30 See Stephanie S. Dickey, "Mennonite Martyrdom in Amsterdam and the Art of Rembrandt and His Contemporaries," in *Contemporary Explorations in the Culture of the Low Countries,* ed. William Z. Shetter and Inge Van der Cruysse (Lanham, Md., 1996), 81-103, esp. 84.

31 John Horsch, *Mennonites in Europe* (Scottsdale, Pa., 1950), 110.

32 *Martyrs' Mirror,* compiled by Thieleman Jansz van Braght and first published as *Bloedig toneel of martelaarspiegel der Doopsgesinde of weereloose Christenen* in Dordrecht, 1660, was translated into English by J. F. Solm as *The Bloody Theater, or Martyrs' Mirror of the Defenseless Christians,* 6th ed. (Scottsdale, Pa., 1951). See also A. Orley Swartzentruber, "The Piety and Theology of the Anabaptist Martyrs in Van Braght's *Martyrs' Mirror,*" *Mennonite Quarterly Review* 28 (1954), 5-27, 128-142.

33 *Martyrs' Mirror,* 7 (see note 32, above): "Those who had to abandon their secular business, and submit to despoilment of their money, goods and everything they had, so that outwardly they were very poor, possessed great riches within themselves through the grace of God."

34 John C. Wenger, *The Doctrines of the Mennonites* (Scottsdale, Pa., 1952), 67, writes that "the Swiss Brethren had a tremendous emphasis on what they called *Bussfertigkeit*...they were broken in heart, sincerely sorry for their imperfections and failure."

35 See, in particular, Simon Schama, *The Embarrassment of Riches* (New York, 1987), 93-125.

36 For an excellent discussion of the complicated nature of the reception of the Jews in Amsterdam in the seventeenth century, see Simon Schama, "A Different Jerusalem: The Jews in Rembrandt's Amsterdam," in Susan W. Morgenstein and Ruth E. Levine, *The Jews in the Age of Rembrandt* [exh. cat., The Judaic Museum of the Jewish Community Center of Greater Washington] (Rockville, Md., 1981), 3-18.

37 Although many of Rembrandt's images have been identified over the years as studies of Jews, Zell 2002, 40-57, has emphasized how difficult it is to determine whether unidentified sitters in Rembrandt's oeuvre are in fact Jewish. He has also noted the historical circumstances, particularly following World War II, under which ideas concerning Rembrandt's supposed sympathies with the Jews have entered art-historical literature.

38 Strauss and Van der Meulen 1979, 383, doc. 1656/12, no. 326: "Een Cristus tronie nae 't leven."

39 Strauss and Van der Meulen 1979, 379, doc. 1656/12, nos. 284 and 285.

40 Christian Tümpel, "Die Rezeption der Jüdischen Altertümer des Flavius Josephus in den holländischen Historiendarstellungen des 16. und 17. Jahrhunderts," in Herman Vekeman and Justus Müller Hofstede, eds., *Wort und Bild in der niederländischen Kunst und Literatur des 16. und 17. Jahrhunderts* (Erftstadt, 1984), 173-204.

41 By the 1610s a long-standing tradition already existed in Italy, Germany, and the Netherlands for depictions of apostles, not only singly but also as paired images and as complete series.

42 For Rubens' apostle series, which the master executed around 1610-1612 for the Duke of Lerma, see Vlieghe 1972, 34-48. Before Rubens shipped the series of Christ and the Twelve Apostles to Philip III's powerful minister in Spain, he had his workshop paint a number of identical and variant copies for subsequent sale. In a letter dated 28 April 1618, Rubens offered one of these series to Sir Dudley Carleton in The Hague. The apostles offered to Carleton may have belonged to a now-lost series recorded in prints made by Peter Isselburg of Cologne, probably between 1623 and 1626. For a discussion of Van Dyck's series, see Washington 1990, nos. 19-20. Around 1620 Hendrick Uylenburgh owned, and sold to the king of Poland, a series of the apostles made by Van Dyck or one of his assistants; see Lammertse 2002.

43 The series by Wierix was based on images by Maarten de Vos and Crispijn van den Broeck.

44 Van Mander 1604, 276r, as noted by Chapman 1990, 122.

45 Urbach 1983, 16-17.

46 For Lievens' series, see Sumowski 1983-1994, 3 (1983): 1792-1794, nos. 1229-1233.

47 See sizes given with catalogue entries.

48 In 1660, however, Rembrandt painted his monumental *The Denial of Saint Peter* (Rijksmuseum, Amsterdam) (Bredius/Gerson 1969, no. 594). This dramatic night scene similarly examines the apostle's internal struggle as he, under the questioning of the maid and in the glare of her candle, attempts to reconcile his faith with his own human doubt and incomprehension.

49 *The Circumcision* has been lost, but a reliable copy is in the Herzog Anton Ulrich-Museum in Braunschweig. See Van de Wetering 2000, 44.

50 This discussion is largely drawn from the insightful comments in Van de Wetering 2000, in particular 44-47.

51 Van de Wetering 2000, 44.

52 English translation taken from Van de Wetering 2000, 44. The source for the quote is Houbraken 1753, 1: 258: "Maar een ding is te beklagen dat hy zoo schigtig tot veranderingen, of tot wat anders gedreven, vele dingen maar ten halven op gemaakt heeft...."

53 As Urbach 1983, 5-6, notes, Molanus warned artists against painting "Apostles as old men, because as such they could not have been able to serve Christ actively." He recommended that artists take as their models heroes of antiquity, including Hercules.

54 Benesch 1970, 196.

55 This point is made by Schama 1999, 656.

56 Benesch 1970, 202. Benesch adapted this concept from Schmidt-Degener 1919, 266.

57 These observations are based on the excellent dissertation of Robert Baldwin. See Baldwin 1983.

58 Baldwin 1983, 4, for example, quotes from Aristotle's *Rhetoric*, book 3, chap. 7: "a weighty subject is not expressed in trivial language or a trivial subject in solemn language...."

59 See Baldwin 1983, 13.

60 Baldwin 1983, 14, quoted from Saint Augustine, *City of God*, 10, 24.

61 As noted by Baldwin 1983, 32.

62 Schwartz 1985, 340-342.

63 Baldwin 1983, 33-34.

64 Martin Luther wrote in the preface to his *Commentary on Romans* that Saint Paul did not consider the word "law" to refer to human laws, ones that were fulfilled by works. Instead, "God judges according to what is at the bottom of the heart, and for this reason, His law makes its demands on the inmost heart and cannot be satisfied with works...." (Martin Luther, *Commentary on Romans*, trans. J. Theodore Mueller [Grand Rapids, Mich., 1954], xiii.) I would like to thank Lynn Russell for bringing this reference to my attention.

65 I would like to thank Lynn Russell for emphasizing this point to me. For an excellent discussion of the impact of Saint Paul's life and preaching on Luther and Calvin, see Halewood 1982, 4-10.

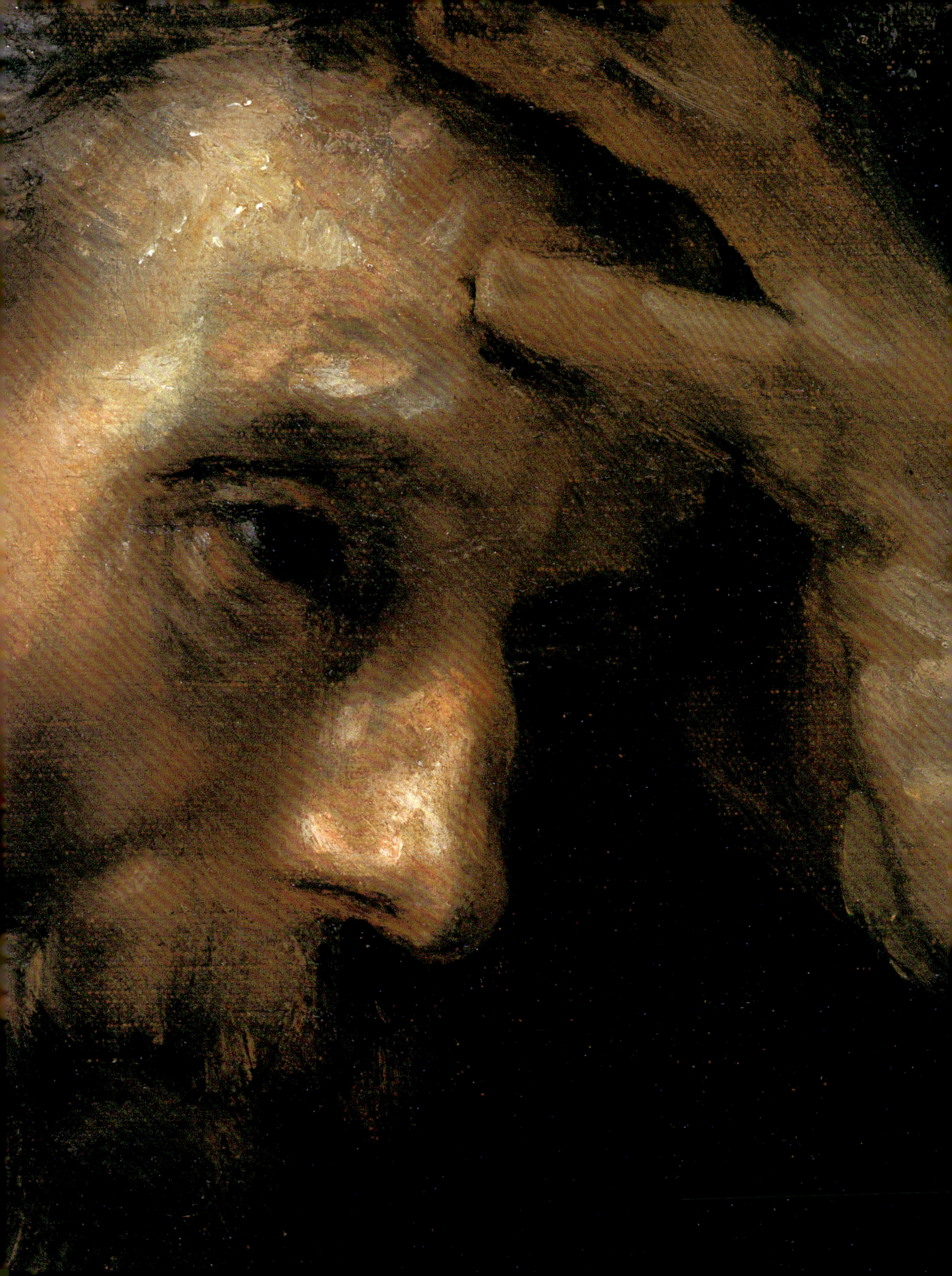

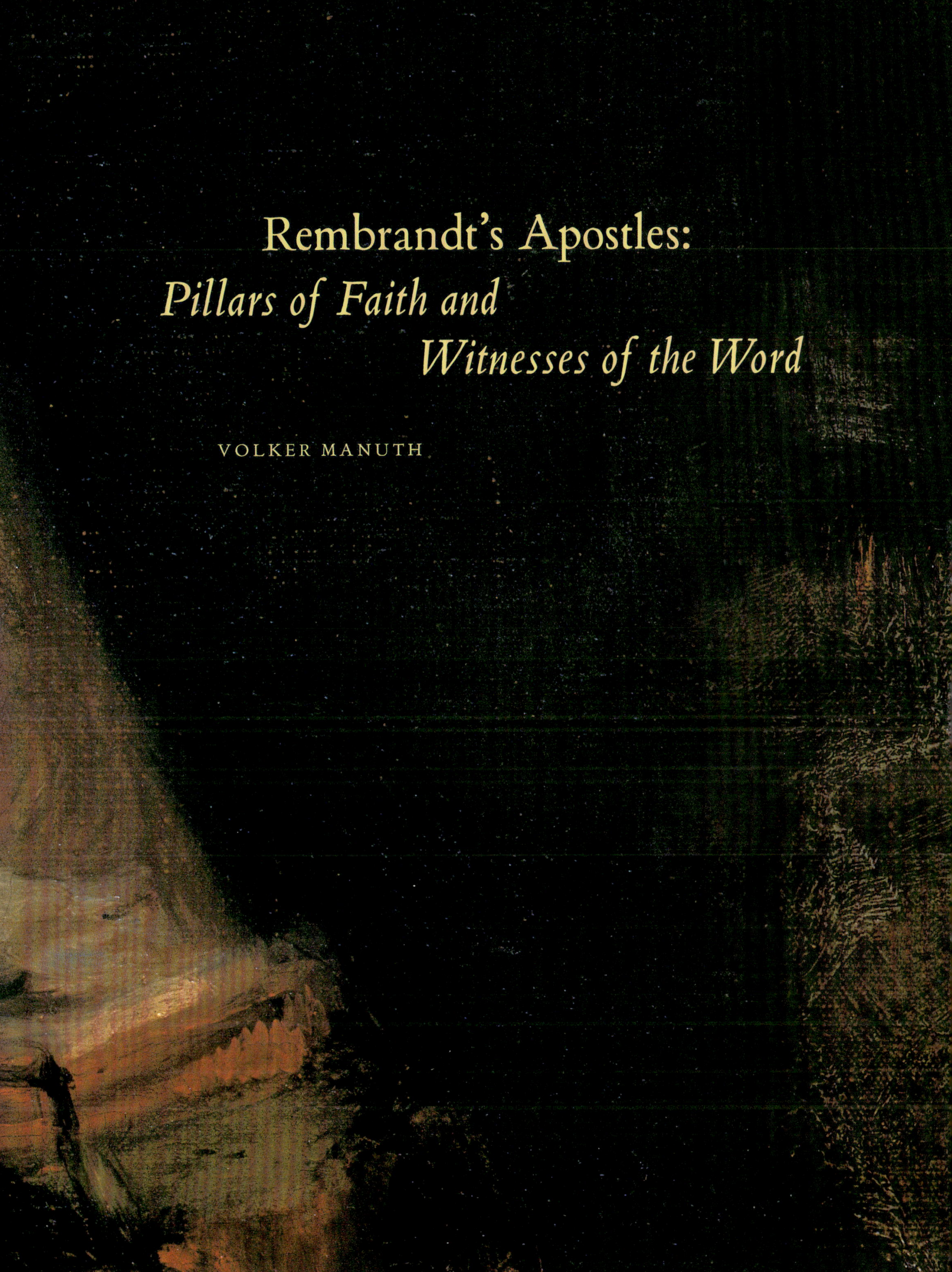

Rembrandt's Apostles: *Pillars of Faith and Witnesses of the Word*

VOLKER MANUTH

Rembrandt's depictions of apostles and evangelists are among the most imposing and also the most mysterious of his works. The half-length paintings of bearded men produced in the late 1650s and early 1660s, their attributes identifying them as both holy martyrs and members of the College of Apostles, seem at first glance incongruous with Rembrandt's oeuvre. Created in a predominantly Protestant environment in which traditional image-worship and the Catholic cult of saints had been renounced, Rembrandt's representations of apostles seem anachronistic remnants of a time when Catholicism dominated even the northern provinces of the Netherlands.

Neither the number nor the dimensions of the extant paintings offer conclusive evidence as to whether Rembrandt ever planned or executed a complete series of apostles, which would normally include twelve individual figures. Who would have been interested in separate representations of apostles or evangelists? What significance did these biblical figures have for Rembrandt's contemporaries? Were Rembrandt's representations of apostles intended to advocate a specific religious ideology? In order to address these questions, we must remind ourselves of the exceptional role traditionally accorded the apostles within the realm of Christian faith and imagery. Furthermore, in order to gain a better understanding of the meaning the apostles had for Rembrandt and his contemporaries, we must also consider the viewpoints of the various Protestant denominations in the United Provinces.

The role assigned to the apostles in the Gospels and in the Acts of the Apostles is that of Christ's chosen disciples and companions, and this is the starting point for their prominence and popularity in art from the early Christian period onward. The apostles knew Christ personally — they were eyewitnesses to his work and his suffering (Luke 24:48). Christ celebrated the Last Supper with them, and the words he uttered to consecrate the bread and wine on that occasion marked the institution of the Eucharist, the most important of the seven sacraments. After Christ's Ascension, on the day of the Jewish feast of Pentecost, the apostles came together to pray, and "there appeared unto them cloven tongues like as of fire, and it sat upon each of them. And they were all filled with the Holy Ghost..." (Acts 2:3-4). Inspired by the Holy Ghost and in the name of Christ, they traveled throughout the world to preach, perform miracles, and proclaim Christ's teachings.

The Gospels and the Acts sometimes contradict one another in naming the apostles (Matthew 10:2-4; Mark 3:16-19; Luke 6:13-16; and Acts 1:13), yet the number twelve, corresponding to the twelve tribes of Israel in the Old Testament, became firmly established early on. This number remained constant even after the removal of Judas Iscariot — following Christ's Ascension, he was replaced by Matthias, who was appointed by lot (Acts 1:26) — and the number still held after the title of apostle was later granted to Paul (Galatians 1:1). Even though variations in the scriptures regarding the composition of the College of Apostles are not unusual, artists generally represented the complete group as follows: Peter, Andrew, James the Major, John, Philip, Bartholomew, Thomas, Matthew, James the Minor, Thaddeus, Simon, and Paul or Matthias.

According to the Bible, Christ had conferred on the apostles his god-given power to advance his teachings and to forgive sins (John 20:21-23). He had instructed them to disseminate these teachings throughout the world and to baptize in the name of the Father, the Son, and the Holy Ghost (Matthew 28:19), thus making the apostles the foundation of his church. Their significance as "supports" of the church is especially apparent in the allegorical representation of the apostles as pillars. In his Epistle to the Galatians (2:9), the Apostle Paul speaks of "James, Cephas [that is, Peter], and John, who seemed to be pillars." In his Epistle to the Ephesians (2:20), Paul characterizes the church as "built upon the foundation of the apostles and prophets." The idea that the apostles also form the foundation of the heavenly Jerusalem is expressed repeatedly in the Bible, as, for instance, in Revelation 21:14: "And the wall of the city had twelve foundations, and in them the names of the twelve apostles of the Lamb."

Identified in the Bible as fundamental elements of Christianity, the apostles already occupied a distinctive position in early Christian art. Symbolic allusions to the Twelve Apostles as pillars are often found in the churches built by Constantine (c. 280-337), the first Roman emperor to accept the Christian faith.[1] He arranged for his own burial in the Church of the Holy Apostles in Constantinople, where he rests among twelve pedestals inscribed with the names of the apostles. A similar approach was used in Santa Costanza, the mausoleum of Constantine's daughter in Rome, whose tomb was surrounded by twelve pairs of columns while the drum of the dome had twelve windows. The Twelve Apostles, as primary witnesses to Christ's life, were also often depicted as his apprentices and companions in the decorations of the vaults and apses of early Christian churches and baptisteries, for instance in Santa Pudenziana in Rome and in the orthodox baptistery at Ravenna.

The concept of churches as earthly reflections of the kingdom of God, borne by the apostles and prophets, was widespread in the Middle Ages.[2] We find this idea in Abbot Suger's (1081–1151) description of the columns in the new early-Gothic choir, begun in 1140, of the Abbey Church of Saint Denis near Paris: "The inner ones, expressing the number of the twelve apostles, and the same number in the outer aisle, signifying the prophets, all rose up to support the lofty structure."[3] During the Second Coming of Christ, when, according to Christian belief, the resurrected and the living will be judged, the tribunal will consist of the apostles and other saints. The apostles are commonly depicted in this function on the "judgment portals" of medieval churches.[4] They frequently appear either as Christ's assessors at the Last Judgment, or as jamb figures who, in symbolic clarification of the biblical hierarchy, are often shown standing "on the shoulders" of prophets, the representatives of the Old Testament. Churches were also inseparably connected to the Twelve Apostles since, at the consecration of a new church, its structure was anointed at twelve different locations in the name of the apostles. These spots were often decorated with sculptures of the apostles or so-called apostle-sconces.

While various passages in the New Testament report on the lives and works of the apostles, there was so much interest in filling in the details of these accounts that they were embellished over time, and legends developed very early. The nonbiblical narratives, which included aspects of the lives and deaths of the apostles and other saints, influenced the representation of these figures in Christian art.[5] Jacobus de Voragine's *Golden Legend* (*Legenda Aurea*), compiled in the mid-thirteenth century and translated into almost all Western European languages, is perhaps the most popular compendium of these stories.[6] Special attention was given to the circumstances of the apostles' martyrdoms (fig. 1). They were among the first to have died for the Christian faith, and their stature as saints of the Church was correspondingly high; festivals of the apostles were celebrated in their honor. Special indulgences were granted for pilgrimages to the graves of individual apostles, for example to the grave of Peter in Rome or to that of James the Major in Santiago de Compostela in Spain.

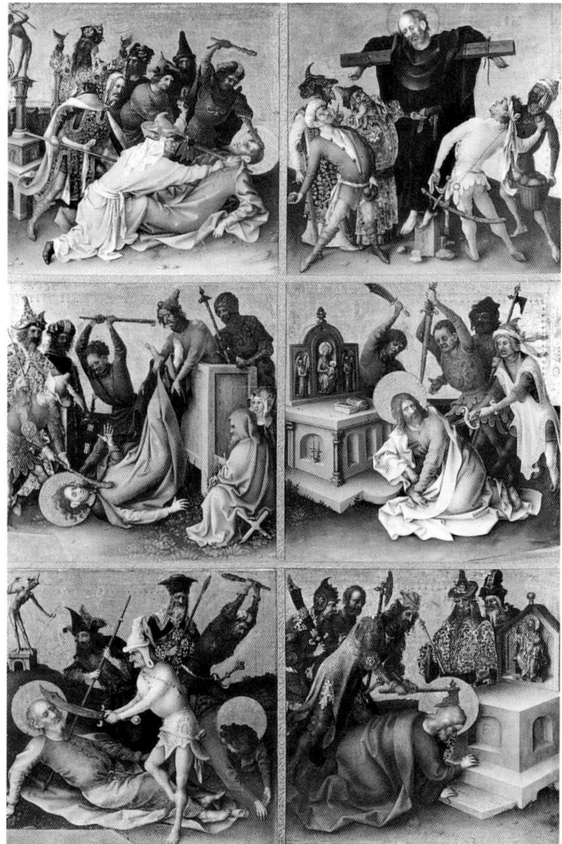
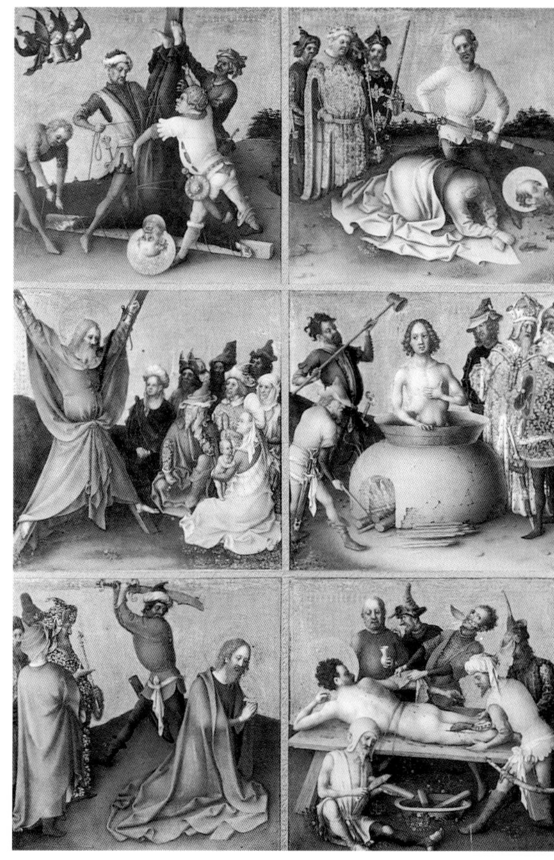

1
Stephan Lochner
Two Wings of an Altarpiece with the Martyrdom of the Apostles
c. 1435–1440, oil on panel, Städelsches Kunstinstitut, Frankfurt am Main

One of the most pertinent Christian texts is the Apostles' Creed (*symbolum apostolicum*), which contains in abbreviated form the fundamental tenets of the Christian faith. The name refers to a misconception that persisted well into the modern era, namely that the Creed was actually a joint effort by the Twelve Apostles.[7] The text retained its status even after the Reformation, when it was accepted by Protestant authorities as the work of the apostles and accordingly integrated into the catechisms and formal creeds used in Protestant instruction.[8]

While these examples demonstrate the prominent position of the apostles in pre-Reformation art, we will examine their importance in Protestantism, as well as whether, or in what ways, the artistic reception and representation of these figures changed. Because the Bible validated the apostles' role as eyewitnesses to Christ's life and works and in spreading the faith, they continued to be revered even after the Reformation. Artists were engaged by both the Catholic Church and by its opponents to depict the subject of the apostles, in order to help propagate controversial articles of faith. Complete series of all twelve figures were produced,

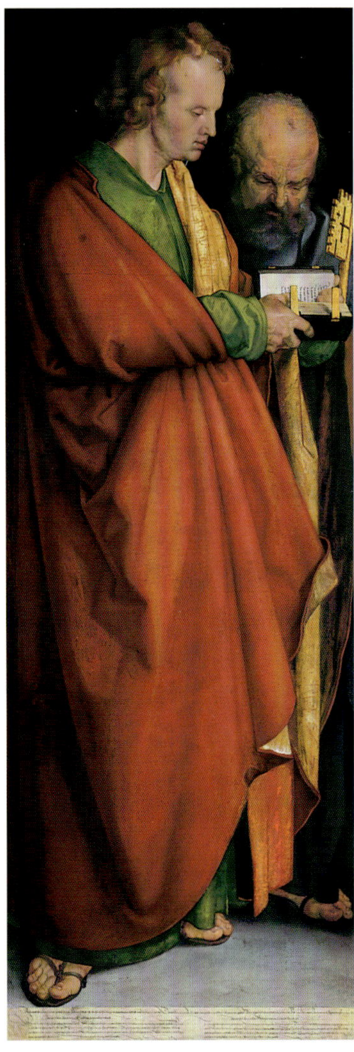

2
Albrecht Dürer
The Apostles John and Peter
1526, oil on panel, Bayerische Staatsgemälde-sammlungen, Alte Pinakothek, Munich

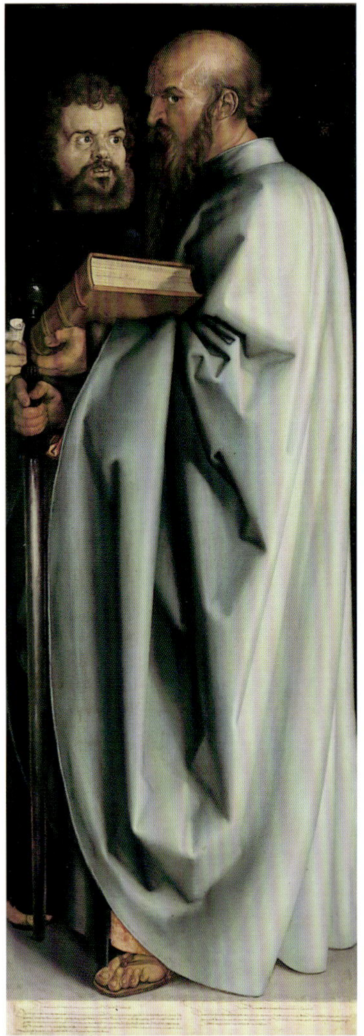

3
Albrecht Dürer
The Apostle Paul and Mark
1526, oil on panel, Bayerische Staatsgemälde-sammlungen, Alte Pinakothek, Munich

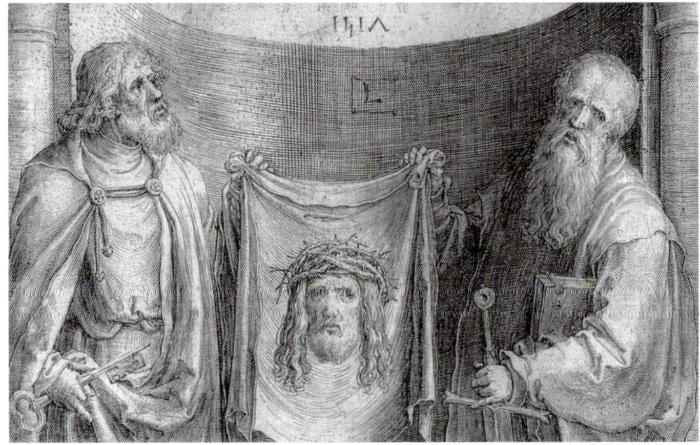

4
Lucas van Leyden
Saint Peter and Saint Paul with the Sudarium
1517, engraving, The British Museum, London

often connected with a portrayal of the Savior, but also representations of groups and individual apostles. Especially in the graphic arts, apostle series enjoyed great popularity among German and Netherlandish artists in the sixteenth century. Lucas Cranach the Elder (1472-1553), for example, completed a woodcut series around 1510/1515, just before the Reformation, and so did Maarten de Vos (1532-1603) (see cat. 3, fig. 2).[9]

A high point of Reformation-era painting is Albrecht Dürer's so-called Four Apostles of 1526 (figs. 2, 3).[10] One of the two panels represents the Apostles John and Peter, the other Paul and Mark the Evangelist. The artist donated both panels in his own memory to the town council of Nuremberg, his birthplace, and they remained on display in the town hall until 1627. Dürer arranged for inscriptions to be added at the feet of the life-size figures. The texts he chose are from Luther's 1522 translation of the Bible, warning, for example, of "false prophets and false teachers." In selecting these quotations from the Second Epistle of Peter (2:1-3), the First Epistle of John (4:1-3), and the Second Epistle of Paul to Timothy (3:1-7), among others, Dürer expressed his sympathy with Luther's teachings by acknowledging the authority of the apostles and their writings.

The placement of the figures, with Peter in the background and Paul in front, already illustrates a crucial difference that would develop between Catholic and Protestant representations of the apostles, namely the increasing Protestant emphasis on Paul at the expense of Peter. Before the Reformation, the two Princes of the Apostles had been represented side by side and had been granted more or less equal status, as seen, for example, in Lucas van Leyden's engraving of 1517 (fig. 4).[11] Subsequently, however, Paul's esteem increased among the Protestants. By delivering the keys to Peter, Christ had granted him the leading role among the apostles: "Thou art Peter, and upon this rock I will build my church.... And I will give unto thee the keys of the kingdom of heaven" (Matthew 16:18-19). This metaphor underlay the papal claim to the succession to and proprietorship of the See of Rome, a presumption that met with intense criticism among Protestant authorities. It was not Peter's position within the group of apostles that was questioned by the Protestants, but rather the papacy's claim to leadership through Peter.[12]

One proponent of this view was John Calvin (1509-1564), whose teachings provided the basis for the Reformed Church, which predominated in the northern Netherlands during Rembrandt's lifetime. As

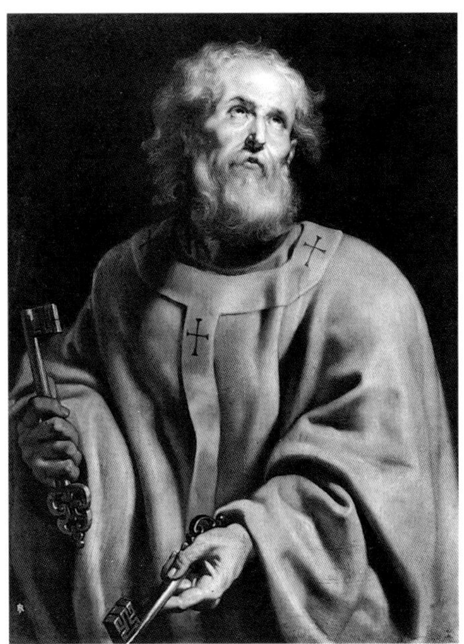

5
Peter Paul Rubens
The Apostle Peter
c. 1610, oil on panel,
Museo del Prado,
Madrid

part of a long discussion on the hierarchy of the apostles in his 1536 *Institutes of the Christian Religion,* Calvin wrote: "Peter was one of twelve, their equal and colleague, not their master," and "we ought to pay more regard to the apostleship of Paul than to that of Peter, since the Holy Spirit, in allotting them different provinces, destined Peter for the Jews and Paul for us."[13]

The divergent views among the confessions are reflected in depictions of the two apostles in seventeenth-century Netherlandish painting. In Rubens' so-called *Apostolado Lerma,* likely painted around 1610-1612 for the Spanish-Catholic Duke of Lerma and today in the Prado in Madrid, Peter is distinguished not just by his elegiacally upward-looking gaze, but also by his liturgical garment (fig. 5). The crosses that decorate it are a reference to his office, which, according to the Catholic faith, was bestowed by Christ. Yet it is extremely rare in northern Netherlandish painting of that time to find representations of Peter alone or as a pendant to Paul. Among the exceptions are two pictures by Jacob Gerritsz Cuyp (1594-1652?), dated 1627 (figs. 6, 7).[14] Notably, Cuyp shows Paul writing, whereas he portrays Peter as a repentant sinner. We see a similar approach to the apostle in one of Rembrandt's two extant paintings of Peter (fig. 8).[15] Rather than showing us the Prince of the Apostles filled with supreme energy and forceful conviction, Rembrandt paints a fragile-looking Peter alone at prayer, with his attribute, the keys to the kingdom of heaven, left on the ground beside him. Following this picture of 1631, Rembrandt seems to have painted Peter only once more as a single figure, a work dated 1632 that is now in the Nationalmuseum in Stockholm.[16] There are no indications that Rembrandt had plans to include Peter among his depictions of half-length apostle and evangelist portraits of the late 1650s and early 1660s.

Just as Catholics considered Peter primary among the apostles, his counterpart, Paul, became even more vital to the Protestants. Paul's significance was based on the doctrine of the justification by faith alone, which played a crucial role in his Epistles and became an extremely popular concept within the different Protestant denominations. Depictions of Paul are often found in Rembrandt's oeuvre, and the artist even made a self-portrait as the Apostle Paul in 1661 (see cat. 11), a work that may have been intended as part of a series of apostle portraits.[17]

Karel van Mander confirms that a number of artists used live models to render the heads in apostle portraits. In his biography of Cornelis Ketel he mentions a series of *tronijen*, head studies of the Twelve Apostles

6
Jacob Cuyp
Saint Paul at His Desk
1627, oil on canvas, Dordrechts Museum

7
Jacob Cuyp
Saint Peter Repentant
1627, oil on canvas, Dordrechts Museum

8 *bottom*
Rembrandt van Rijn
Saint Peter Repentant
1631, oil on canvas, The Israel Museum, Jerusalem, Gift of Judy and Michael Steinhardt, New York, to American Friends of the Israel Museum

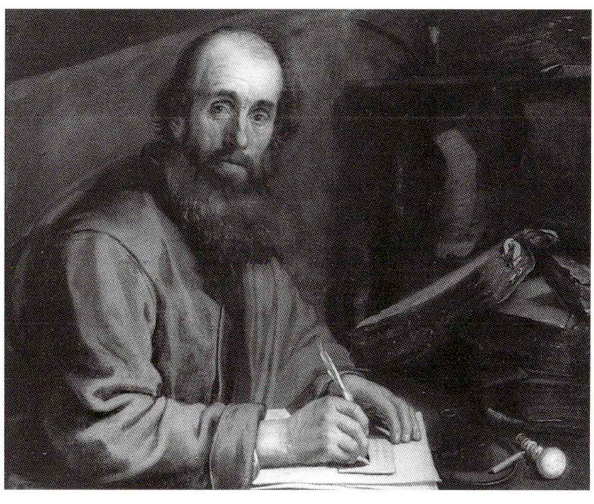

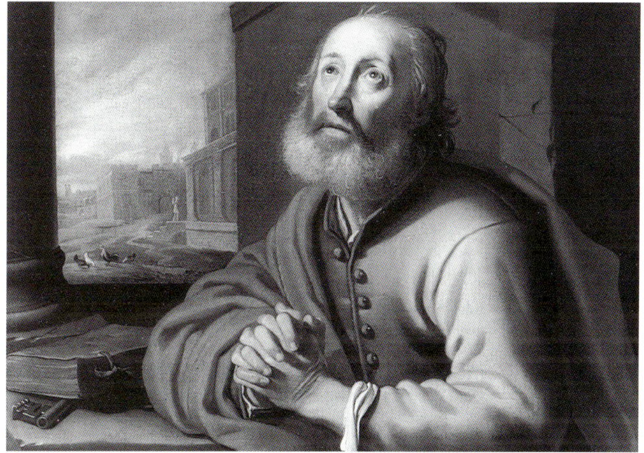

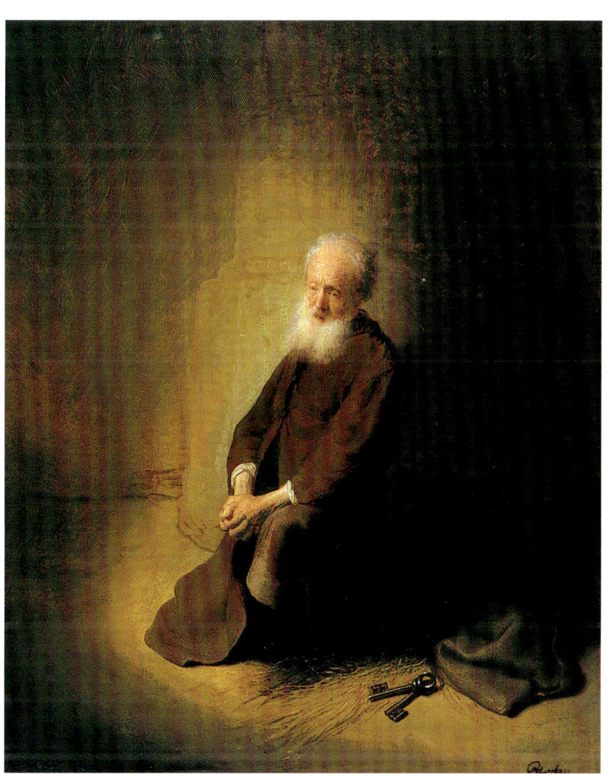

and Christ based on portraits of various painters and art lovers.[18] Anthony van Dyck seems to have given portraitlike features to at least one of the figures in an apostle series that he modeled on a Rubens prototype. According to his friend Jan Brueghel the Younger (1601–1678), one of Van Dyck's apostles represents Jan's uncle, the engraver Pieter de Jode (1570–1634). Brueghel recalled that when asked about this work, Van Dyck responded "that he would make it [the portrait] into a beautiful Apostle."[19]

Unlike the Catholics, members of the Reformed Church did not permit paintings or sculptures of apostles in their churches. Existing images were removed and often destroyed. A prominent example is the series of apostle sculptures made in 1620 for the choir piers in the Cathedral of Saint Jans in 's-Hertogenbosch, which were removed in 1634, some five years after Frederik Hendrik liberated the city from the Spanish in 1629. A drawing by Pieter Saenredam (fig. 9), dated 1632, shows the apostles beneath the baldachins on the choir piers.[20]

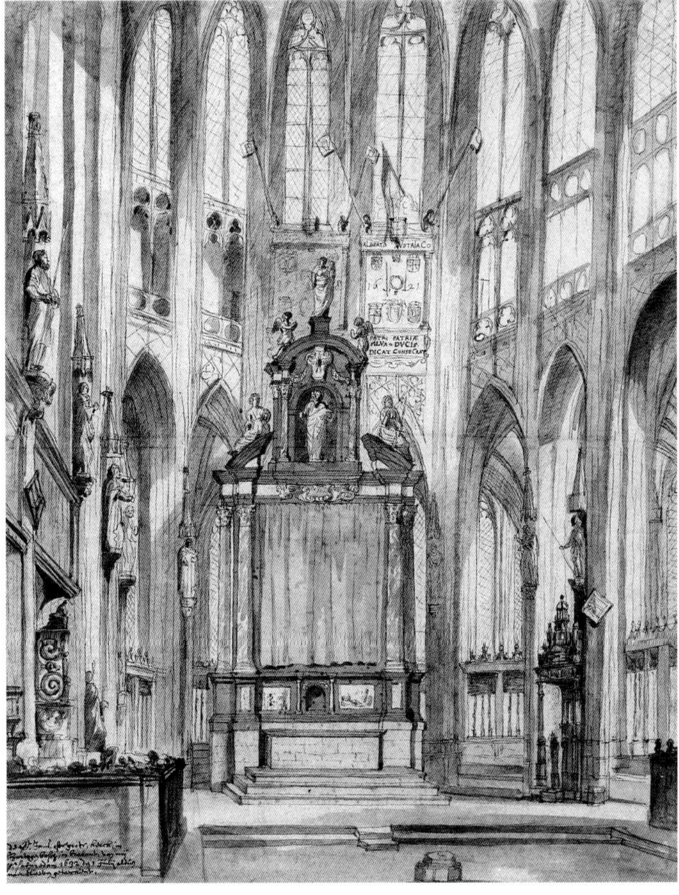

9
Pieter Saenredam
The Choir of the Saint Janskerk in 's-Hertogenbosch
1632, pen, watercolor and black chalk, The British Museum, London

The removal of these sculptures from the cathedral may not just have been prompted by the fact that they depicted apostles. It is well known that the Reformed Church feared certain paintings and sculptures in churches might tempt the faithful to idolatry. John Calvin was more severe in his condemnation of images than were most of the other Protestant reformers.[21] In his *Institutes of the Christian Religion* (1536), the fundamental text of the Reformed Church, he wrote:

> The only things, therefore, which ought to be painted or sculptured, are things which can be presented to the eye....Visible representations are of two classes — viz. historical, which give a representation of events, and pictorial, which merely exhibit bodily shapes and figures. The former are of some use for instruction or admonition. The latter, so far as I can see, are only fitted for amusement. And yet it is certain, that the latter are almost the only kind which have hitherto been exhibited in churches.[22]

Here Calvin makes it unmistakably clear that individual representations of the human figure — including depictions of apostles and evangelists — serve only to entertain and therefore warrant no place in a church. The fact that the apostles, as Christ's companions, play such a salient and respected role in the Bible made no difference in Calvin's view.

Yet the apostles assumed a seminal role within the doctrine of the Reformed Church. Calvin refers repeatedly to the authority of the apostles, who "are commended by many distinguished titles, as the Light of the world, and the Salt of the earth, to be heard in Christ's stead."[23] He presents them to the faithful as mediators and disseminators of Christian teachings. Christ himself had appointed them and instructed them: "Go ye therefore, and teach all nations, baptizing them in the name of the Father, and of the Son, and of the Holy Ghost" (Matthew 28:19). Calvin also emphasizes that the teachings communicated through the apostles are based exclusively on the authority of the word of Christ, who "in a manner dictated words to them."[24] According to Calvin, we share with them our faith and the directive to pray, hence, "if we lean to the word of God, we are in respect of this privilege their associates."[25]

These are but a few examples of the significance Calvin conferred on the apostles in his *Institutes of the Christian Religion.* They testify to the great popularity of these figures, still prevalent within the Reformed Church of Rembrandt's time. Prior to Calvin, Luther had already emphasized the special meaning of the apostles, not as saints to be worshipped but as men to be revered for their teachings, teachings that formed the foundation of the Christian Church. In Lutheran doctrine, these men occupied an important place particularly because they were considered examples of human weakness — Peter denied Christ; Thomas doubted; Paul had sinned before his conversion — yet each was, nonetheless, chosen by Christ to disseminate his teachings. The apostles' significance in many Protestant concerns is further evidenced by church festivals to commemorate them.[26]

Other Protestant groups, such as the Mennonites, named after their spiritual leader Menno Simons (1496–1561), also turned to the model of the apostles for the founding principles of their faith. Over the course of the seventeenth century the number of Mennonites increased, and they became influential in the northern provinces.[27] They were known for the purity and simplicity of their personal and communal life and their refusal to participate in the magistracy. Proponents of nonresistance, they did not carry or use weapons. *Doopsgezinden* (Mennonites), the name given to them in the Netherlands, signified their views on baptism: they rejected infant baptism because it is not mentioned in the New Testament; instead, they practiced baptism upon confession, and then only as the result of a conscious decision. This belief was based on the model of Christ and his apostles. A book published in Haarlem in 1632, which contains the foundations of the Mennonite faith, states "that [baptism] had been ordained and commanded by Christ exclusively on faith, repentance, and correction. Nor has this [baptism] been taught or used differently by his high apostles, who followed him in this."[28]

The Mennonites likewise followed the model of the apostles in striving for a modest way of life. Apostolic simplicity was observed in church doctrine and in the choice of the parish preachers, called teachers (*leraren*). At least in the early days of the movement, the *leraren* were not required to have any training in theology since their central duty was to tend to the biblical message. Here, too, they looked to the example of the apostles.

Some members of this group were among Rembrandt's patrons, such as Marten Looten, whose portrait Rembrandt completed in 1632.[29] Cornelis Claesz Anslo and his wife, Aeltje Gerritsdr Schouten,

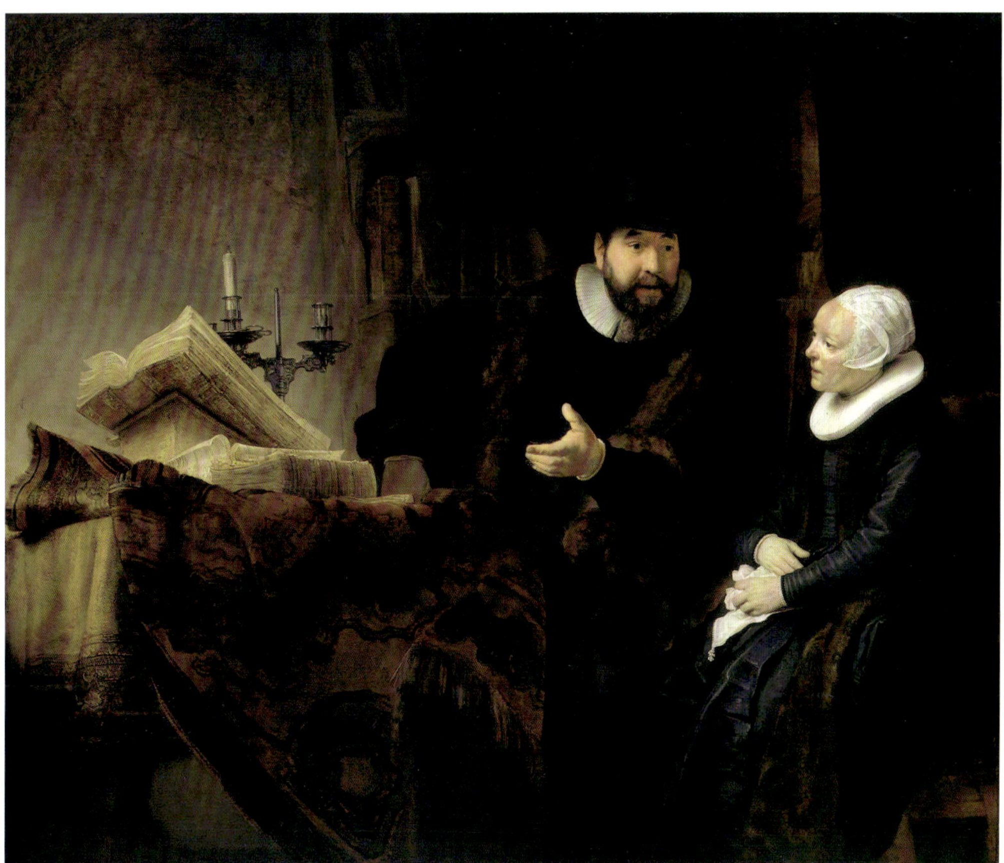

10
Rembrandt van Rijn
The Mennonite Preacher Anslo and His Wife
1641, oil on canvas, Gemäldegalerie, Staatliche Museen zu Berlin

whose portrait Rembrandt painted in 1641, were Mennonites (fig. 10).[30] Mennonite families produced many painters, such as Karel van Mander (1548–1606), Michiel Jansz van Mierevelt (1567–1641), Jacob Adriaensz Backer, Govert Flinck, and Lambert Jacobsz (c. 1598–1636).[31]

Lambert Jacobsz, the first teacher of both Backer and Flinck before the latter became Rembrandt's apprentice and workshop employee, was a painter, a *leraar* in the Mennonite community in Leeuwarden (Friesland), and an art dealer with connections in Amsterdam. His oeuvre consists of history paintings depicting scenes from the Old and New Testament, with rather small, sturdy figures in a landscape. He also painted compositions with biblical figures in three-quarter length, engaged in animated discussions. Toward the end of the 1620s Jacobsz painted a series of four evangelist portraits, now in the Musée des Beaux-Arts in Rouen.[32] More remarkable, however, is a series of the four fathers of the Western church, Ambrose, Augustine, Gregory, and Jerome, which is not only unusual in a Mennonite context but also extremely rare in northern Netherlandish painting of the seventeenth century.[33] Unfortunately, we

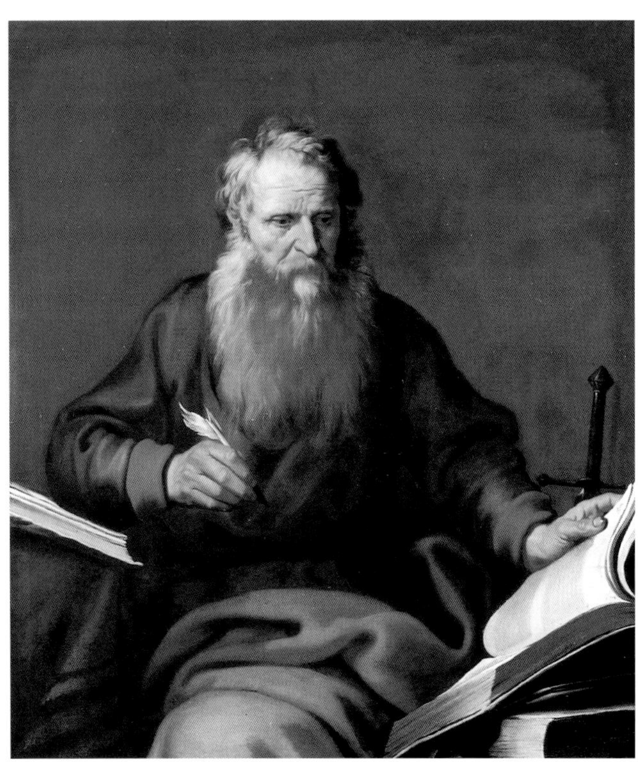

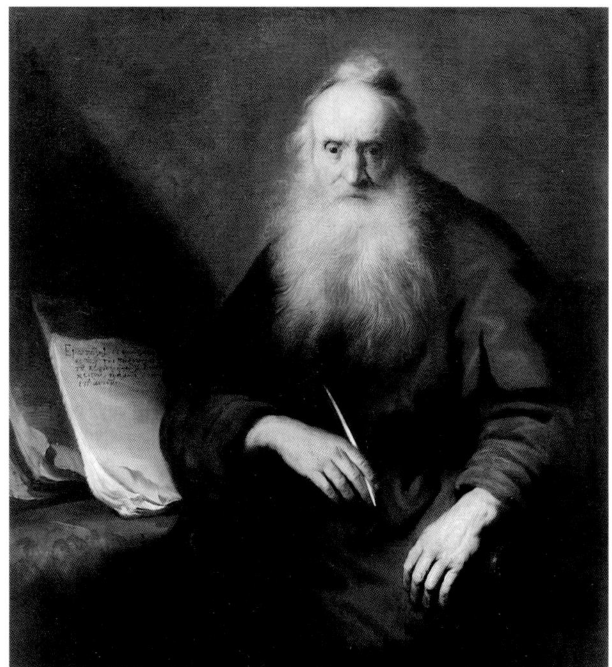

do not know who commissioned this series. Also unknown is the patron for Lambert Jacobsz's *The Apostle Paul* of 1629 (fig. 11), one of the earli-est large-format representations of the apostles in all of Dutch painting.[34] In its composition and in the strong contrasts between light and shadow in the figures' faces, this picture exhibits striking similarities to Jan Lievens' *The Apostle Paul Writing to the Thessalonians* (fig. 12) as well as to Govert Flinck's painting of the same subject (fig. 13).[35] Unfortunately, the exact genesis of these three paintings or their relationship to Rembrandt's red chalk drawing, probably also dating around 1629 (fig. 14), is unknown. It is notable that this group of artists around Rembrandt, all of whom knew each other, was almost simultaneously preoccupied with the apostle subject. The painting of the apostle Paul by the Mennonite Lambert Jacobsz makes it clear that the subject was of interest to this Protestant group as well.

In summary, the apostles remained a popular subject even after the Reformation. The enormous significance traditionally granted to Christ's twelve companions was questioned neither by the dominant authority of the Reformed Church nor by the various other Christian

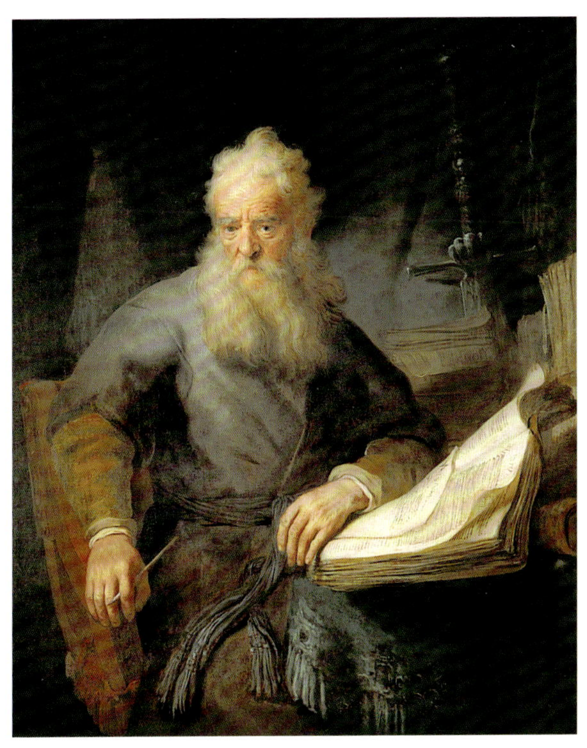

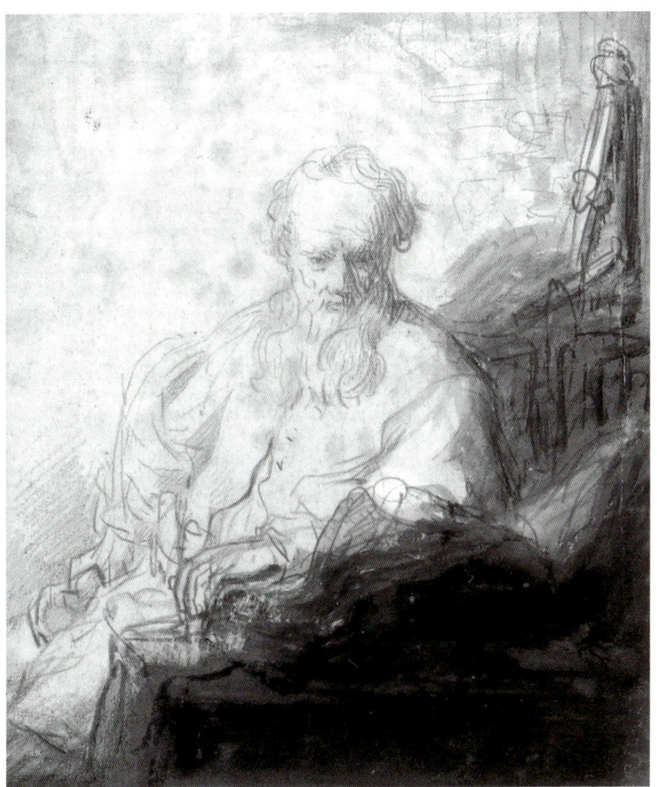

11
Lambert Jacobsz
The Apostle Paul
1629, oil on panel,
Fries Museum,
Leeuwarden

12
Jan Lievens
The Apostle Paul Writing to the Thessalonians
c. 1629, oil on canvas,
Kunsthalle Bremen

13
Govert Flinck
The Apostle Paul at His Writing Desk
c. 1630, oil on canvas,
Kunsthistorisches Museum, Vienna

14
Rembrandt van Rijn
The Apostle Paul
c. 1629, red chalk and wash in Indian ink,
Musée du Louvre,
Paris

denominations that made up the multiconfessional society of the northern provinces in the Netherlands during Rembrandt's time. As witnesses to Christ's works and disseminators of his teachings, the apostles' authority was widely recognized. The Reformed Church altered the rank and function of representations of the apostles and evangelists, but it did not change the conventions of representation or the pictorial tradition.

In order to ensure that viewers would be able to identify each apostle, Rembrandt and his fellow painters relied on the depiction of attributes, although these played only a secondary role. Nonetheless, the attributes preserved the concept of martyrdom associated with these holy men, a concept that held greater meaning for Catholics than for Protestants in the reception of the apostle images.[36] The apostles' role as witnesses to the biblical text was unquestioned. Their proximity to Christ and his teachings, authenticated through the Bible, meant that their representation was accepted throughout society and not seen as advocating a specific religious ideology.[37] This fact also increased the appeal of apostle portraits on the art market, something that Rembrandt would clearly have recognized in depicting these moving images from the late 1650s and early 1660s.

Notes

The author would like to thank Linda Parshall for the translation from the German.

1 On the allegorical interpretation of the apostles as "supports" of Christian churches, see John Onians, *Bearers of Meaning: The Classical Orders in Antiquity, the Middle Ages, and the Renaissance* (Princeton, 1988), 70–73.

2 Günter Bandmann, *Mittelalterliche Architektur als Bedeutungsträger* (Berlin, 1951), 45–112.

3 Abbot Suger, *Abbot Suger on the Abbey Church of St. Denis and Its Art Treasures,* ed. and trans. Erwin Panofsky, 2nd ed. (Princeton, 1979), 104.

4 On the iconography of the apostles, see Adolf Katzenellenbogen in *Reallexikon zur deutschen Kunstgeschichte* (Stuttgart, 1937), 811–829; Josef Myslivec in Kirschbaum 1968– (1968), 1:150–174; and Josef Engemann in *Lexikon des Mittelalters* (Munich, 2002), 1:786–789 (specifically on medieval iconography).

5 The most important collections of so-called apocryphal texts on the apostles and evangelists are assembled and discussed by David R. Cartlidge and J. Keith Elliott, *Art & the Christian Apocrypha* (London and New York, 2001), 172–235.

6 For a recent translation into English see De Voragine 1993.

7 O. Sydney Barr, *From the Apostles' Faith to the Apostles' Creed* (Oxford, 1964), 3–11. On the iconography of the Apostles' Creed and its connection to the apostles, see also Henk W. van Os in Kirschbaum 1968– (1968), 1:461–464.

8 For a discussion of the reception and function of the Apostles' Creed in Protestantism, see Hans-Martin Barth in *Theologische Realenzyklopädie* (Berlin and New York, 1978), 3:554–566.

9 For Cranach's woodcuts, see Dieter Koepplin and Tilman Falk, *Lukas Cranach: Gemälde, Zeichnungen, Druckgraphik,* 2 vols. [exh. cat., Kunstmuseum Basel] (Basel, 1974), 2:558, nos. 438–451.

10 For a detailed discussion of the "Four Apostles" and their theological implications, see Fedja Anzelewsky, *Albrecht Dürer: Das Malerische Werk,* 2 vols. (Berlin, 1991), 1:280–286, nos. 183, 184; and most recently Gisela Goldberg, Bruno Heimberg, and Martin Schawe, *Albrecht Dürer: Die Gemälde der Alten Pinakothek* (Munich, 1998), 479–559.

11 For this and the 1527 engraving of *Saints Peter and Paul Seated in a Landscape,* also by Lucas van Leyden, see Ellen S. Jacobowitz and Stephanie Loeb Stepanek, *The Prints of Lucas van Leyden & His Contemporaries* [exh. cat., National Gallery of Art] (Washington, 1983), 224, 225, no. 89.

12 For the discussion of the relationship between Peter and the other apostles and the theological implications of the so-called Petrine primacy, see Jaroslav Pelikan, *The Christian Tradition,* 4 vols. (Chicago and London, 1971–), "Reformation of Church and Dogma 1300–1700" (1984), 4:112–118. See also John Baptist Knipping, *De iconografie van de contra-reformatie in de Nederlanden,* 2 vols. (Hilversum, 1939/1940), 2:301.

13 Quotations from book 4, chap. 6, 7, and book 4, chap. 6, 15, Calvin 1989, 357, 363.

14 Alan Chong, "Peter and Paul by Jacob Cuyp: Rare Seventeenth-Century Dutch Pendants," *Mercury* 9 (1989): 10–19, and recently Sander Paarlberg, *Jacob Gerritsz. Cuyp* (1594–1652) [exh. cat., Dordrechts Museum] (Dordrecht, 2002), 88–91, nos. 3, 4. Although these depictions of Peter and Paul are not pendants (their dimensions and stylistic execution are different), they were almost certainly paired with other portrayals of the saints. For a set of pendants see Paul Dirkse, "Paulus en Petrus door Willem Bartsius," in Dirkse, *Begijnen, pastoors en predikanten. Religie en kunst in de Gouden Eeuw* (Leiden, 2001), 45–48.

15 *Corpus* 1982– (1982), 1:346–350, A36, and Albert Blankert in Melbourne and Canberra 1997, 102–104, no. 6.

16 *Corpus* 1982– (1986), 2:138–144, A46, and Melbourne and Canberra 1997, 105–107, no. 7.

17 Valentiner 1920/1921, 219–222. The idea of a series of apostles and evangelists was examined by Ludwig Münz in Münz 1948, 64–67, and by Otto Benesch in Benesch 1956, 335–354.

18 "Apart from the many other beautiful portraits made by him, he is presently working on the faces of the twelve apostles with Christ, larger or as large as life, being portraits of some painters and art lovers, very subtly handled and well drawn," in Van Mander/Miedema 1994, 1:362, fol. 276r. Compare also the essay by Peter Sutton in this catalogue.

19 For a recent discussion of Van Dyck's apostles series, see Lammertse 2002, esp. page 140. Christopher Brown has argued that Van Dyck's painting of the *Apostle James the Major* (Private collection, formerly Earl of Spencer, Althorp House) can be identified as the one mentioned by Jan Brueghel. See Christopher Brown and Hans Vlieghe, *Van Dyck 1599-1641* [exh. cat., Koninklijk Museum voor Schone Kunsten and Royal Academy] (Antwerp, London, and New York, 1999), 96, 97, no. 3.

20 For a discussion of the drawing see Adrianus M. Koldeweij, in *Buscoducis 1450-1629: Kunst uit de Bourgondische tijd te 's-Hertogenbosch de cultuur van late middeleeuwen en renaissance*, 2 vols. [exh. cat., Noordbrabants Museum] ('s-Hertogenbosch and Maarssen, 1990), 44, 45, no. 8. The drawing in the British Museum served in 1646 for Saenredam's painting of the same subject; see Gary Schwartz and Marten Jan Bok, *Pieter Saenredam: The Painter and His Time* (Maarssen, 1989), 268, 269, no. 94; and Wheelock 1995, 353-359, no. 1961.9.33. I thank Jos Koldeweij for drawing my attention to the series of sculptures and their removal in 1634. It should be noted that the existence of a complete apostles series does not necessarily imply that it was originally located in a church. We know, for example, that the above-mentioned apostles series by Van Dyck hung for a long time in the Antwerp residence of Guilliam Verhagen, the patron who commissioned it. Numerous artists saw and admired it there. See Lammertse 2002, 140.

21 For a detailed discussion of Protestantism's complex relationship to the visual arts, see Margarete Stirm, *Die Bilderfrage in der Reformation* (Gütersloh, 1977), 17-130 (on Luther), 161-223 (on Calvin). See also Carlos M.N. Eire, *War against the Idols: The Reformation of Worship from Erasmus to Calvin* (Cambridge, 1986), and David Freedberg, *Iconoclasm and Painting in the Revolt of the Netherlands, 1566-1609* (New York and London, 1988).

22 Quotation from book 1, chap. 11, 12, Calvin 1989, 100.

23 Quotation from book 4, chap. 8, 4, Calvin 1989, 391.

24 Quotation from book 4, chap. 8, 8, Calvin 1989, 394.

25 Quotation from book 3, chap. 20, 14, Calvin 1989, 160.

26 For Protestant ideas regarding the veneration of saints in general and the so-called *Aposteltage*, see Robert Lansemann, *Die Heiligentage besonders die Marien-, Apostel- und Engeltage in der Reformationszeit* (Göttingen, 1938), 135-156.

27 For important aspects of the history and theology of the Mennonites in the Netherlands see Simon Groenveld, J. P. Jacobszoon, and Simon L. Verheus, ed., *Wederdopers, menisten, doopsgezinden in Nederland 1530-1980* (Zutphen, 1993), and Alastair Hamilton, Sjouke Voolstra, and Piet Visser, *From Martyr to Muppy: A Historical Introduction to Cultural Assimilation Processes of a Religious Minority in the Netherlands: The Mennonites* (Amsterdam, 1994).

28 *Bekentenisse Des Gheloofs, na Godes Heylige Woordt, Alsoo de selvighe van vele Jaeren herwaerts/ende noch teghenwoordigh/by diemen Mennisten noemt/Ghelooft/Gheleert ende Beleeft word...* (Haarlem, 1632), 47, "datse van Christo alleen op gheloof/boete ende beteringhe gheordineert ende bevolen is/noch van zijn hooghe Apostelen achtervolgende desen/niet anders ghebruyckt noch gheleert en is" (author's translation).

29 Los Angeles County Museum of Art (Inv. no. M53-50-3). See *Corpus* 1982- (1986), 2:190-198, A52.

30 Gemäldegalerie, Staatliche Museen zu Berlin (no. 828L). See *Corpus* 1982- (1989), 3:403-415, A143.

31 See S.A.C. Dudok van Heel, "Doopsgezinden en schilderkunst in de 17de eeuw: leerlingen, opdrachtgevers en verzamelaars van Rembrandt," *Doopsgezinde Bijdragen* 6 (1980): 105-123; Piet Visser, "De artes als zinnebeeld: over doopsgezinden en hun relatie tot kunst en wetenschap," *De zeventiende eeuw* 5 (1989): 92-102; and Hessel Miedema, "Een schilderij van Karel van Mander de Oude (1548-1606); een doopsgezinde interpretatie," *Doopsgezinde Bijdragen* 16 (1990): 129-153.

32 See Sumowski 1983-1994, 6 (1994): 3719, nos. 2323-2326.

33 The four paintings are in "Het Princessehof," Stedelijk Museum, Leeuwarden. They measure 85 x 67 cm each and are dated 1629. See Sumowski 1983-1994, 6 (1994), 3719, nos. 2320, 2321.

34 For a discussion of this painting see Marijke van der Meij-Tolsma, "Lambert Jacobsz. (ca. 1598-1636). Kunstschilder en doopsgezind leraar te Leeuwarden," *Doopsgezinde Bijdragen* 15 (1989): 94-96, fig. 6.

35 For Lievens' painting, see *Jan Lievens: Ein Maler im Schatten Rembrandts* [exh. cat., Herzog Anton Ulrich-Museum] (Braunschweig, 1979), 78, 79, no. 22; Sumowski 1983-1994 (1986), 3:1796, no. 1240; and *Rembrandt & Lievens in Leiden* [exh. cat., Stedelijk Museum De Lakenhal] (Zwolle and Leiden, 1991), 103, no. 52. For the close similarities between the two paintings of the Apostle Paul by Lambert Jacobsz and Jan Lievens, see also Schwartz 1985, 103. For Flinck's painting, see Joachim W. von Moltke, *Govaert Flinck 1615-1660* (Amsterdam, 1965), 80, no. 71, and Sumowski 1983-1994 (1984), 2:1028, no. 643.

36 As biblical saints, however, they were still more acceptable to the Protestants than those not mentioned in the Bible.

37 On the relationship between the different denominations in the northern Netherlands and the iconography of biblical and other religious history paintings, see Volker Manuth, "Denomination and Iconography: The Choice of Subject Matter in the Biblical Painting of the Rembrandt Circle," *Simiolus* 22 (1993/1994), 235-252.

Rembrandt and the *Portrait Historié*

PETER C. SUTTON

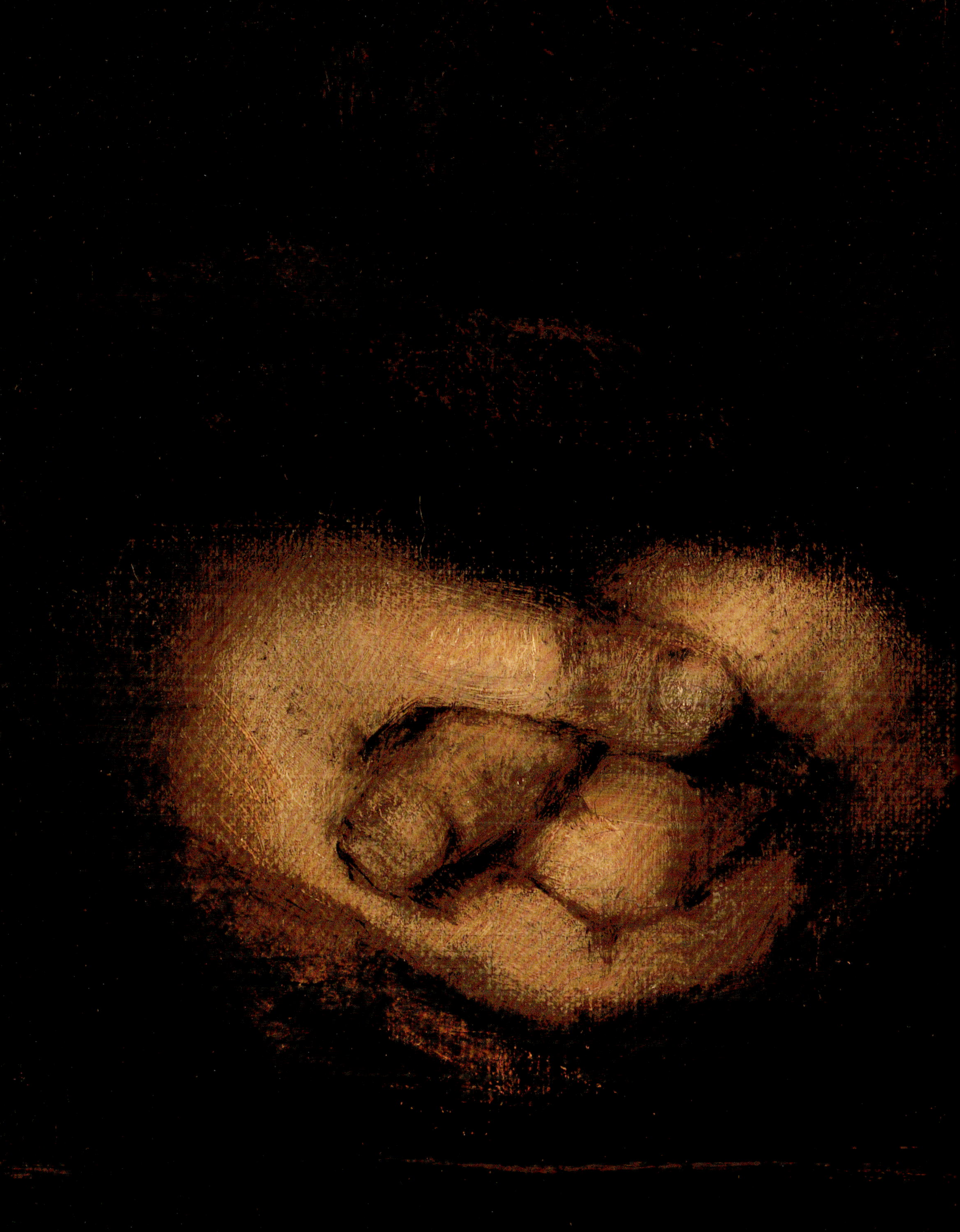

Rembrandt's *Self-Portrait as the Apostle Paul* (cat. 11) and one or two of his other self-portraits stand in the pictorial tradition of the *portrait historié*: the depiction of known individuals in the guise of biblical, mythological, or literary personages.[1] The tradition of painting historicized portraits was well-established by the mid-seventeenth century. Given the fact that Dutch and Flemish artists did more than artists anywhere else to advance this painting type, it is perhaps surprising that they had no word to refer collectively to this form of allegorical portrait. Rather, like the modern term "genre," which we employ today in the absence of a seventeenth-century Dutch equivalent to describe scenes of everyday life, a French term coined in the late eighteenth century applies to portraits of this type.[2] The painting of historicized portraits or *portraits historiés* includes single, double, group, and self-portraits, and is basically a synthesis of history painting and the portrait—a typological hybrid or *Mischform.* It traces its roots to antiquity, in the images of Alexander the Great as Hercules and the many portraits of Roman rulers in the role of gods. The painting type began to appear with regularity only after the Renaissance, first in the Netherlands in the later sixteenth century and blossoming in both the Dutch Republic and the southern Netherlands after about 1630.

The selection of subjects in *portraits historiés* probably was primarily dictated by the patron, since it was never an arbitrary but a highly personal choice. A historical subject was chosen for a specific iconographic meaning, which often was obvious but invariably apposite to the patron's personal values and ambitions. Dutch and Flemish artists depicted political leaders in the guise of King David or Perseus to promote their ambitions as liberators, or they might celebrate a wedding or marriage with an image of Old Testament couples, or with mythological figures such as Odysseus and Penelope. The proliferation of the *portrait historié* coincided with several cultural developments: the growth in the popularity of emblematic literature, which sought to codify allegorical associations; a taste for theatrical dramas and rhetoricians' performances featuring historical personages with contemporary implications; a fashion for poetry, especially epithalamiums, that featured allusions to biblical and mythological figures; and a passion for public spectacles, such as triumphal entries (*Blijde inkomsten*), that flattered the powerful with historical or literary precursors.

Among the earliest types of historicized portraits were images of artists as Saint Luke, their patron saint, painting the Virgin. According to Karel van Mander, Frans Floris (1519/1520–1570) portrayed the founder of the Antwerp Saint Luke's Guild, Ryckaert Aertsz, as Saint Luke in a painting for their guildhall.[3] Rogier van der Weyden (1399–1464), Maerten van Heemskerck (1498–1574), and many other artists depicted themselves as Saint Luke, painting or drawing the Virgin.[4] Van Mander also described several artists' depictions of known persons appearing in biblical scenes, for example, an *Ecce Homo* by Jan Mostaert (1475–1555/1556), and a *Christ and the Twelve Apostles* by Cornelis Ketel, which included "portraits of painters and collectors," specifically the talented sculptor and architect for the city of Amsterdam, Hendrick de Keyser (1565–1621).[5] It is uncertain whether the figures in these cases were meant to be recognizable as portraits or simply posed as models for history paintings. Yet according to Van Mander, in a painting of *Democritus and Heraclitus* that Ketel created for an Amsterdam collector, the patron, Hendrick van Os, specifically requested to be portrayed as Democritus.[6] Presumably a man who regarded himself as having an optimistic outlook and a bemused attitude toward human folly, Van Os evidently wanted to associate himself with the teachings of this Greek philosopher, whose views were traditionally contrasted with the dark and melancholic beliefs of Heraclitus, who wept for the world.[7] Still another biblical painting by Ketel mentioned by Van Mander offers precedents for Rembrandt's *The Apostle Paul* (cat. 2), since it, too, depicted the saint as an individual; in Van Mander's words, the painting was "naar t'leven van Rutger Jansz. gedaen" (done from life of Rutger Jansz). Here, again, one cannot be certain if it was intended to be a portrait of Rutger Jansz or if he simply posed for a history painting.[8]

The tradition of individuals assuming roles in religious pictures had its origins in donors' portraits in early Netherlandish altarpieces. The practice of adopting saintly guises in portraits also explains the many *portraits historiés* of highborn women in the role of the penitent Magdalene by Rogier van der Weyden (fig. 1), Joos van Cleve (?–1540/1541), Bernaert van Orley (1488–1541), the Master of the Female Half-Lengths, and others.[9] Jan van Scorel (1495–1562) also portrayed his beloved, Agatha van Schoonhoven, as Mary Magdalene.[10] In the many cases of Rembrandt's

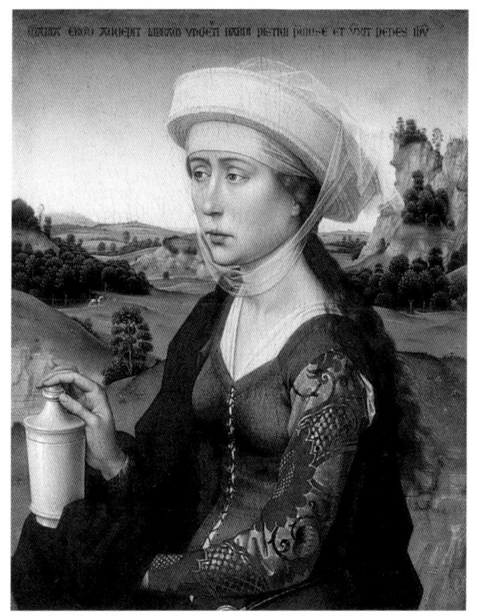

1
Rogier van der Weyden
Mary Magdalene
1450–1452,
oil on panel,
Musée du Louvre,
Paris

depictions of his loved ones in history paintings — namely Saskia as Flora, Bellona, and Minerva, or Hendrickje Stoffels as Flora, Juno, or Venus — it seems unlikely that they were posing for a *portrait historié,* with all the implicit associations of the sitter with the persona represented.[11] They seem simply to have served as models for an "anonymous" history painting.

While many artists painted *portraits historiés,* the painting type was especially popular among the Rembrandt school, begging the question of whether students were introduced to it in the master's studio. Religious subjects initially dominated the chosen themes for *portraits historiés* in Dutch art, but after about 1630 they began to give way to more mythological, literary, and historical subjects. Yet biblical themes persisted; for example, Jacob Gerritsz Cuyp (1594-1652?) honored Frederik Hendrik in 1630 in a political allegory for the town hall of 's-Hertogenbosch, in which the Prince of Orange was depicted as the Triumphant David returning from his victory over Samson.[12] Popular Old Testament themes for marriage portraits included Tobias and Sarah or Isaac and Rebecca.[13] Family groups were also often portrayed as members of the crowd in scenes of Saint John the Baptist preaching, for example in Werner van den Valckert's (1585-1627) painting, dated 1623, in the Catharijneconvent, Utrecht, or in depictions of portrait groups performing the Acts of Mercy, such as the Feeding the Hungry or Clothing the Naked.[14] Families were also depicted in the guise of another Old Testament subject: Elkana and Hanna Presenting Eli to Samuel.[15]

A special favorite of orphanages and foundling hospitals was the theme of Christ Blessing the Children, as in Werner van der Valckert's portrait of the family of Michiel Poppen of 1620 in the Catharijneconvent, Utrecht; Anthony van Dyck's family portrait (possibly of Rubens, Isabella Brant, and their children) in the National Gallery of Canada, Ottawa; and Jan de Bray's (1627-1697) painting of 1663 for the Saint Jacob's Hospital, Haarlem (now Frans Halsmuseum).[16] A less common subject, but one perfectly suited to the aspirations of the regents of Haarlem's Leprooshuis when they commissioned a *portrait historié,* was the Old Testament theme of Elisha Refusing the Gifts of Naaman. Naaman was the captain of the host of Syria whom Elisha cured of leprosy and who sought unsuccessfully to reward him.[17] Other biblical subjects treated by Rembrandt followers as *portraits historiés* included Abraham van Dijk's (1635/1636-1672) *Finding of Moses,* Gerrit W. Horst's (1612-1652) *Jacob and His Family before Meeting Esau,* and Pieter Verelst's (1644-1721?) *Moses and Raguel's Daughter,* 1643.[18] A painting listed in the estate inventory of the merchant Gabriel Leliencamp, which reportedly depicted him as the archangel Gabriel and his wife as the Virgin Mary, indicates the extent to which patrons' creative imagination could go when discovering biblical parallels between their own lives and Christian names.[19]

Many Dutch artists, including those from the Rembrandt school, also treated profane themes in *portraits historiés.*[20] Ferdinand Bol (1616–1680) portrayed himself and his wife and child as *Paris with Venus and Amor* in 1656 (Dordrechts Museum, Dordrecht), and also depicted a couple as *Bacchus and Ariadne on Naxos* in 1664 (The State Hermitage Museum, Saint Petersburg).[21] Jan de Bray, one of the greatest Dutch practitioners of the *portrait historié,* portrayed a married couple as *Odysseus and Penelope* (J. B. Speed Museum, Louisville), and Barent Graat (1628–1709) even depicted a couple as Bacchus and Venus.[22] Gerard (1592–1656) and William Honthorst (1594/1604–1666) popularized the story of Apollo and Diana as a *portrait historié* theme after Gerard depicted the king and queen of England in these roles in a monumental portrait painted in 1631 for Charles I (Buckingham Palace, London). The hunting theme of *Meleager and Atalante* from Ovid's *Metamorphoses* enjoyed special favor and was treated twice by Gerbrandt van den Eeckhout (1621–1674), in 1652 and 1666 (Gemäldegalerie, Berlin).[23] Just as Diana and Her Nymphs was the most popular subject of Dutch history painting, *portraits historiés* of ladies in the guise of Diana, as chaste goddess of the hunt, were also exceptionally popular.[24] Finally, Nicolaes Maes (1634–1693) made the theme of Ganymede a popular subject for portraits of children.

Roman history provided inspiring themes for family portraits as well. For example, the story of Coriolanus and his family was traditionally venerated as a theme underscoring the strength of family ties — the Roman general, who had joined forces with a neighboring people and returned to assault his own native city after he had been banished from Rome, was persuaded by his wife, mother, and two small sons to call off the attack. The subject was treated as a *portrait historié* by both Van den Eeckhout in 1662 and by Abraham van den Tempel (1622/1623–1672).[25] Van den Eeckhout also depicted a family in the *Continence of Scipio* (fig. 2), where the upright Roman general, refusing to be bribed, magnanimously returns a beautiful young maiden to her

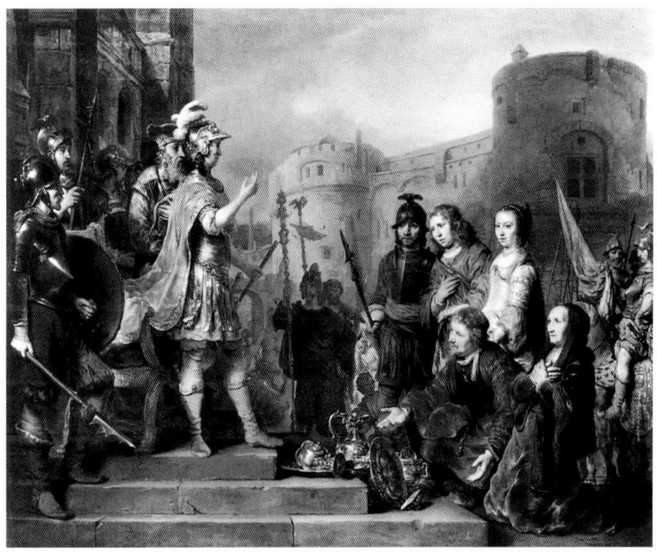

2
Gerbrandt van den Eeckhout
Continence of Scipio
165?, oil on canvas, Toledo Museum of Art

fiancé.[26] A painting of Scipio's daughter, Cornelia, by Jan van Bijlert (1597/1598?-1671) (Musée des Beaux-Arts, Orléans) advertised maternal values; Cornelia is shown responding to a Roman matron who boasted ostentatiously of her jewels, proudly proclaiming that her children were her own jewels.[27] Finally, in Jan de Bray's *Banquet of Cleopatra,* the artist, his wife, and his family crowd around the table, while his father, Salomon, and mother, Anna Westerbaen, play the roles of Anthony and Cleopatra.[28]

Dutch pastoral and arcadian literature, in particular P. C. Hooft's highly influential play, *Granida* (1605), also inspired numerous Dutch portraits.[29] Granida and Daifilo, as well as lesser-known shepherds and shepherdesses, became fashionable subjects for portraits, especially among the regent classes.[30] Govert Flinck's portraits of Rembrandt and Saskia are part of this historicized pastoral tradition.[31]

Rembrandt's *Self-Portrait as the Apostle Paul* (cat. 11) should be viewed within the tradition of the *portrait historié.*[32] It would seem, however, that seventeenth-century *portraits historiés* depicted fewer single-figure images than double or group portraits, perhaps because the highly individualized features of more than one figure alert the viewer to the fact that it is a historicized portrait rather than an anonymous history painting subject. Gonzales Coques' (1614-1684) *Portrait of a Woman as Saint Agnes* (The National Gallery, London) and Pieter de Grebber's (1600-1652/1654) *Paris with an Apple* of 1634 (fig. 3) are rare examples of a single-figure *portrait historié* in Dutch pictorial traditions. In taking up this tradition, Rembrandt seems to have revived earlier, fifteenth- and sixteenth-century practices that were precursors of the *portrait historié* of his day.

3
Pieter de Grebber
Paris with an Apple
1634, oil on panel,
Bayerische Staatsgemälde-sammlungen, Munich

In Protestant Holland, Saint Paul was regarded as the primary authority in the interpretation of the Gospel. He was the archetypal preacher of the faith, and his teachings, stressing divine grace and humility, had a pervasive influence. Over the course of his career, Rembrandt painted the saint several times using different models, and his choice of his own image in this case was undoubtedly inspired by more than mere convenience. It has been assumed by some that Rembrandt identified with Saint Paul's role as an explicator of the Bible and his mission as a teacher.[33] Others, however, have cautioned against speculating about Rembrandt's psychological motives for adopting this role, arguing that notions of self-awareness and self-analysis as we understand them today, following the advent of modern psychology, can be applied only anachronistically to Rembrandt.[34] Yet even if one assumes that the primary motivation of Rembrandt's self-portrait was to promote his renown by associating himself

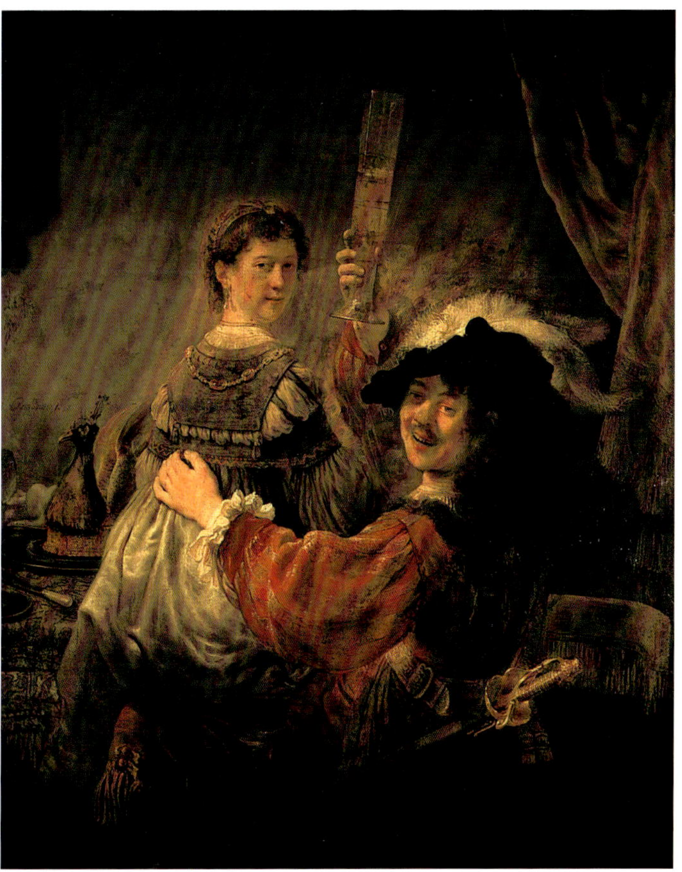

4
Rembrandt van Rijn
Rembrandt and Saskia or the Prodigal Son
1636, oil on canvas, Staatliche Kunstsammlungen, Gemäldegalerie Alte Meister, Dresden

with *uomo famoso,* the artist's identification with the saint's virtues and life as a teacher is consistent with the traditional functions of the *portrait historié.*

Rembrandt's painting of a tavern scene in Dresden (fig. 4) has also often been viewed as a self-portrait, with his young wife Saskia perched on his knee. The painting of this elegantly clad, carefree young couple seemed the very embodiment of *jeunesse dorée* until the scene was revealed to conform in many details to traditional depictions of the Prodigal Son Squandering His Inheritance.[35] The parable is a story of sin and redemption, as well as of divine grace, embodied in the father's forgiveness to his confessing son. If the picture is a *portrait historié,* are we to assume that Rembrandt was confessing to the prodigal's sins of the high life that he sought so ambitiously in his early years in Amsterdam? Artists' ostensible identification with the prodigal son can be traced back at least to Albrecht Dürer's engraving of 1498 of the prodigal at the swine trough, which Van Mander confirmed bears the great German artist's own features.[36] While Rembrandt's painting clearly departs from and even challenges the customary propriety of Dutch portraiture, we are undoubtedly reading too much into the work to assume that it is part of a psychobiography, or even an admission of "ambivalence" about his own social standing.[37] Instead, it seems likely that Rembrandt, like Jan Steen and Adriaen Brouwer, who regularly appear in comically compromised roles in their own tavern scenes, was simply adopting a pictorial persona to personally underscore the moral message of the story.

Rembrandt often depicted himself as a painter, but his last self-portrait as an artist is unusual in showing him laughing uproariously, with a figure or bust just visible in the shadows at the left (fig. 5). Long cited by romantic biographers as evidence of Rembrandt's indomitable spirit, laughing in the face of adversity, the picture is in fact a *portrait historié.* As Albert Blankert first demonstrated, Rembrandt has cast himself in the role of one of the famous artists of antiquity, the late fifth-century Greek painter, Zeuxis.[38] The most famous anecdotes about Zeuxis concerned his unrivaled illusionism and his achievement of ideal beauty in composing a picture of Helen of Troy by selecting the most beautiful parts of the most beautiful women in the world. The latter was often cited by later seventeenth-century classicists as support for their belief that art should represent only beautifully generalized things, not highly individualized and often ugly subjects like those depicted by Rembrandt. In this work Rembrandt showed a less well-known episode from Zeuxis' life, but one that Van Mander recounted.[39] The painter reportedly died from immoderate laughter while making a portrait of a "wrinkled droll old woman."[40] The subject evidently was well known in the Rembrandt circle; his student, Samuel van Hoogstraten, mentioned it in his *Inleyding tot de hooge schoole der schilderkonst,* and another pupil, Arent de Gelder, painted the same subject in a very similar manner in 1685 (fig. 6).[41] In both paintings the artist is seen at work, looking over his shoulder to laugh at the viewer.[42]

The reason for Rembrandt's choice of this subject for his last *portrait historié* has been debated. Blankert and others have argued that it is explained by art-theoretical discourse of the times: while the classicists rebuked Rembrandt with the example of Zeuxis' idealization of nature, Rembrandt rebutted their criticism by portraying Zeuxis painting an ugly subject.[43] Still others have emphasized another aspect of Zeuxis' fame, namely his gift for rendering emotions, which is the reason Hoogstraten twice refers in his book to Zeuxis laughing himself to death.[44] Rembrandt, particularly in his self-portraits, was also keenly interested in expressing emotions and may have depicted himself in the role of the ancient artist

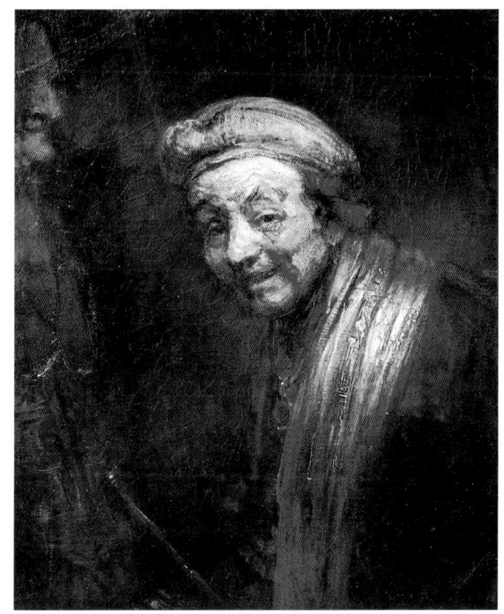

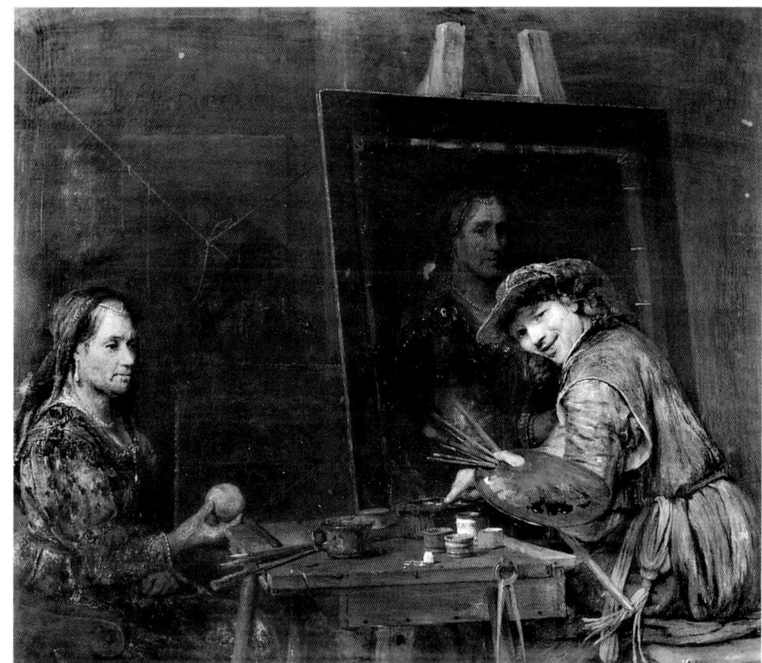

5
Rembrandt van Rijn
Self-Portrait as Zeuxis
1662, oil on canvas, Wallraf-Richartz-Museum, Cologne

6
Arent de Gelder
Self-Portrait as Zeuxis
1685, oil on canvas, Städelsches Kunstinstitut, Frankfurt am Main

to emphasize his own talent in this regard. Other authors have reminded us of still other qualities associated with Zeuxis: he was known for painting unusual subjects with an unexpected interpretive aspect, renowned for the high prices of his works, and said to have an inimitable style; he was also purportedly an eccentric, nonconforming sort.[45] While any of these qualities might touch a chord in Rembrandt, we should again avoid the temptation to probe the psychology of his choice of subject. The only thing of which we may be certain is that in representing himself as an artist who laughed himself to death, Rembrandt had not lost his sense of humor.

Within the group of saints and apostles exhibited here, several figures have highly individualized features, notably *The Apostle Bartholomew* (cat. 8), the *Bearded Man in a Cap* (cat. 1), and the *Saint Bavo* (cat. 17). While two depict a figure that recurs in other paintings by Rembrandt and therefore can be assumed to have been a regular model, the possibility must be considered that these works, too, are *portraits historiés.* Given the traditional importance of the client in the choice of this painting type's subject matter, we again regret not knowing more about the patrons for whom these works were painted.

Notes

1 The standard study of the *portrait historié* is still the dissertation by Rose Wishnevsky (see Wishnevsky 1967); however, it is far from comprehensive and excludes Rembrandt as an exceptional case. Rudi Ekkart and Volker Manuth are preparing an exhibition on this neglected topic for the Dordrechts Museum.

2 See "Zur Terminologie" in Wishnevsky 1967, 13-15.

3 Van Mander 1604, fol. 247b.

4 For Rogier van der Weyden, see his *Saint Luke Drawing the Virgin,* c. 1435-1440 (Museum of Fine Arts, Boston). For Maerten van Heemskerck, see his *Saint Luke Painting the Madonna,* 1532 (Frans Halsmuseum, Haarlem).

5 Van Mander 1604, fol. 229b and fol. 276a.

6 Van Mander 1604, fol. 278a.

7 See Albert Blankert, "Heraclitus en Democritus, in het bijzonder in de Nederlandse kunst van de 17e eeuw," *Nederlands Kunsthistorisch Jaarboek* 18 (1967): 31-124.

8 Van Mander 1604, fol. 275b.

9 See Decimal Index to the Art of the Lowlands (D.I.A.L.) 11 HH (Maria Magdalena VII 22). For the Van Cleve, see Friedlaender 1967-1976, 9, part 1 (1972): 59, no. 44; for the Master of the Female Half-Lengths, see Friedlaender 1967-1976, 12 (1975): 98-100, no. 81-104.

10 For Agatha van Schoonhoven as Mary Magdalene, see Friedlaender 1967-1976, 12 (1975): 124, no. 338.

11 For Saskia as Flora, see Bredius/Gerson 1969, 556, nos. 102, 103. For Saskia as Bellona and Minerva, see Bredius/Gerson 1969, 592, nos. 467 and 469, respectively. For Hendrickje Stoffels as Flora, Juno, and Venus, see Bredius/Gerson 1969, 557, no. 114; 617, no. 639; and 557, no. 117, respectively.

12 See Amsterdam and Jerusalem 1991, 244-245, no 27.

13 See Adriaen van Nieulandt's *Tobias and Sarah on the Road to Nineveh,* 1653 (Private collection, Edinburgh), and Ferdinand Bol's *Erasmus Sharlaken and Anna van Erckel as Isaac and Rebecca* (Dordrechts Museum, Dordrecht), in Amsterdam and Jerusalem 1991, 127, 128, figs. 85, 86.

14 For Van den Valckert, see Dijkstra et al. 2002, 265-266, no. RMCC S111. For other *portraits historiés* of John the Baptist, see Jacob Adriensz Backer in Sumowski 1983-1994, 1: 203, no. 73, and the lost painting by Nicolaes van der Heck mentioned in Houbracken 1753, 2: 8. For De Bray, see von Moltke 1938/1939, 468, no. 28, fig. 31. Gonzales Coques painted a similar subject. See sale Brussels (Fievez), 22 June 1922, no. 37.

15 On the subject, see Amsterdam and Jerusalem 1991, 129-130. See, for example, Lambert Doomer's (1624-1700) painting of this subject of 1668 in the Musée des Beaux-Arts, Orléans, and that by Gerbrandt van den Eeckhout in the Ashmolean Museum, Oxford, no. 433.

16 For Van der Valckert, see Dijkstra et al. 2002, 466, no. ABMS 127. For Van Dyck, see Washington 1990, 127-129, no. 18. For De Bray, see von Moltke 1938/1939, 466, no. 18, fig. 40.

17 See Peter de Grebber's painting of 1637, Frans Halsmuseum, Haarlem (no. 118), in Amsterdam and Jerusalem 1991, 250-251, no. 31.

18 See, respectively, Sumowski 1983-1994, 1: 670, no. 366; 2: 1391, no. 914; and 6: 3746, no. 2462.

19 Wilhelm Martin, *De Hollandsche Schilderkunst in de 17e eeuw,* 2 vols. (Amsterdam, 1942), 1: 39.

20 Wishnevsky 1967 suggests that Salomon de Bray's *Juno, Minerva, Venus, and Amor* of 1623, then in a South American private collection (see J. W. Moltke, "Salomon de Bray," *Marburger Jahrbuch für Kunstwissenschaft* 11/12 (1938/1939): 309-414; 383, no. 52, fig. 32), is the earliest dated *portrait historié* with a mythological theme. It is not clear, however, that the figures depicted are portraits.

21 See Albert Blankert, *Ferdinand Bol (1616-1680), Rembrandt's Pupil* (Doornspijk, 1982), 103, cat. 34, pls. 30, 151; cat. 167, pl. 178.

22 On De Bray, see von Moltke 1938/1939, 484, no. 178, fig. 24. On Graat, see sale Willem Six, Amsterdam, 12 May 1734, no. 147.

23 See Sumowski 1983-1994, 2: 729, no. 410, and 739, no. 461.

24 See Eric Jan Sluijter, "De 'Heydensche Fabulen' in de Noordnederlandse Schilderkunst circa 1590-1670," Ph.D. diss., Rijksuniversiteit te Leiden, 1986, 167-187. Also see, for example, Gerrit van Honthorst's painting of 1627 in Sanssoucci, Potsdam.

25 See Sumowski 1983-1994, 2: 734, no. 434, and 1: 311, no. 160.

26 See Washington, Detroit, and Amsterdam 1980, 174-175, no. 41.

27 See Paul Huys Janssen, *Jan Van Bijlert, 1597/98-1671: Catalogue Raisonné* (Amsterdam and Philadelphia, 1998), 172-173, cat. 196, pl. 163.

28 There are two versions, one of 1652/1656 in Hampton Court, and one of 1669 in the Currier Art Gallery, Manchester, New Hampshire. See von Moltke 1940/41, 484, no. 183, fig. 23, and no. 184.

29 Allison McNeil Kettering, *The Dutch Arcadia: Pastoral Art and Its Audience in the Golden Age* (Montclair, N.J., 1983).

30 See, for example, Jan Mijtens' (1614-1670) *Young Couple Portrayed as Granida and Daifilo* (Rijksmuseum, Amsterdam).

31 For the portraits, see Sumowski 1983-1994, 2: 1030-1031, nos. 655, 656.

32 See also Chapman 1990, 122, and Ernst van de Wetering in London and The Hague 1999, 22, 214.

33 Most recently Chapman 1990, 114-120.

34 See H.-J. Raupp, *Untersuchungen zu Künstlerbildnis und Künstlerdarstellung in den Niederlanden im 17. Jahrhundert* (Hildesheim, Zurich, and New York, 1984), 7, 8; Van de Wetering in London and The Hague 1999, 19.

35 See Ingvar Bergström, "Rembrandt's Double-Portrait of Himself and Saskia at the Dresden Gallery: A Tradition Transformed," *Nederlands Kunsthistorisch Jaarboek* 17 (1966): 143-169, and Chapman 1990, 114-120. Among the motifs related to this subject are the peacock pie, the raised *fluit* glass, the chalkboard for tallying drinks, and a second woman playing a lute, who was painted out and only appears in x-rays.

36 Van Mander 1604, fol. 209b.

37 Chapman 1990, 119.

38 See Blankert 1973.

39 Van Mander 1604, fol. 301a.

40 Van Mander's source was the Roman writer Marcus Verrius Flaccus; see Blankert 1973, 35.

41 See Van Hoogstraten 1678, 26, 78.

42 Rembrandt holds a maulstick, and x-rays reveal that he was originally holding up a brush. The prominence of the old woman in De Gelder's painting proves that the figure faintly seen at the left in the work by Rembrandt is not a classical bust, as was once believed, but an old woman; indeed, when the painting was sold in 1758 it was described as such.

43 See Blankert 1973, 35, and Blankert in Melbourne and Canberra 1997, 38-40; see also Chapman 1990, 103.

44 Van de Wetering in London and The Hague 1999, 219.

45 See Amy Golahny, *Rembrandt's Reading: The Artist's Bookshelf of Ancient Poetry and History* (Amsterdam, 2003), 204.

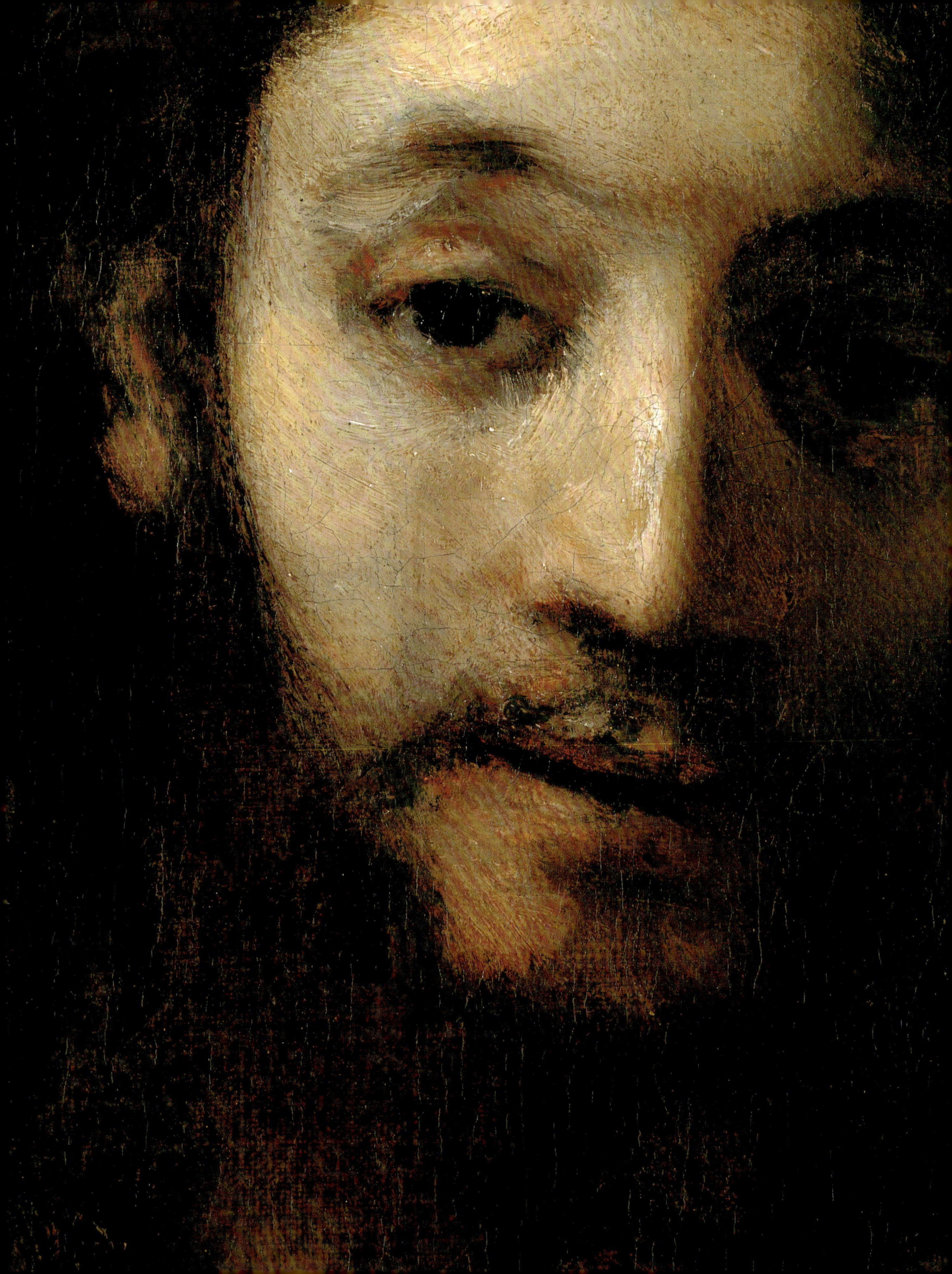

Catalogue

PCS Peter C. Sutton
AKW Arthur K. Wheelock Jr.
ATW Anne T. Woollett

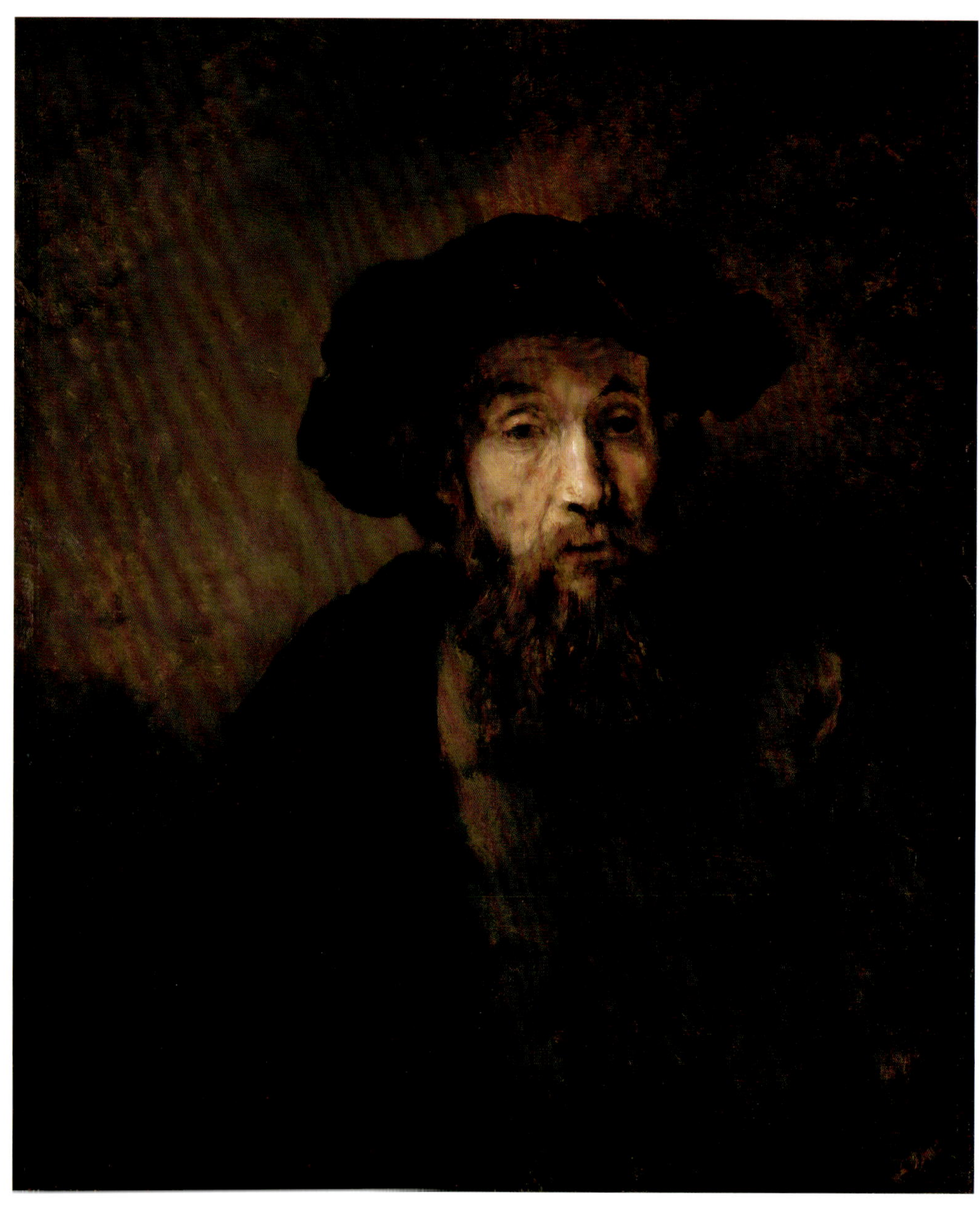

A Bearded Man in a Cap, 165(7?)
oil on canvas, 78 × 66.5 (30 11/16 × 26 3/16)
The National Gallery, London

I A Bearded Man in a Cap

Viewed frontally, in half-length and life-size, the man has a long, dark, graying beard, a reddish mustache, and dark hair. He wears a broad-brimmed black hat and a brown coat. Although he is seen almost full-face, his head and eyes are turned slightly to the viewer's right. His brow is furrowed and his gaze unfocused as he stares off meditatively into the distance behind the viewer. As so often in Rembrandt's later works, the fact that observers address the self-absorbed figure obliquely, from both a visual and a psychological viewpoint, encourages them to linger in appraising the subject's mood and state of mind.

Although the date marked on this painting has often been read as 1657, the last number is only barely legible. The remnants of the figure could be a "3" or a "7," the latter being more acceptable on stylistic grounds.[1] The subject was described simply as *An Old Man's Head* in the Duke of Argyll's sale in 1798, but in the sale of Jeremiah Harman's collection in 1844 it was called *A Jewish Rabbi.* The latter title has often been repeated but has no seventeenth-century basis. The man's features have been regarded as Levantine and, like many of the artist's later models, he may have been Jewish. There is nothing in his costume, however, to indicate that he is a rabbi. During the seventeenth century, the Netherlands was renowned for its religious tolerance and attracted many Jewish immigrants, notably the Marranos from Portugal, who counted a sizable number of prosperous merchants among their community, and poorer German Jews who sought refuge in Amsterdam following the outbreak of the Thirty Years War (1610-1648). Another wave of largely impoverished Polish Jews arrived after 1654. All three groups settled in Amsterdam in the vicinity of the Sint-Anthonisbreestraat, later known as the Jodenbreestraat, where Rembrandt lived from 1639 to 1659.

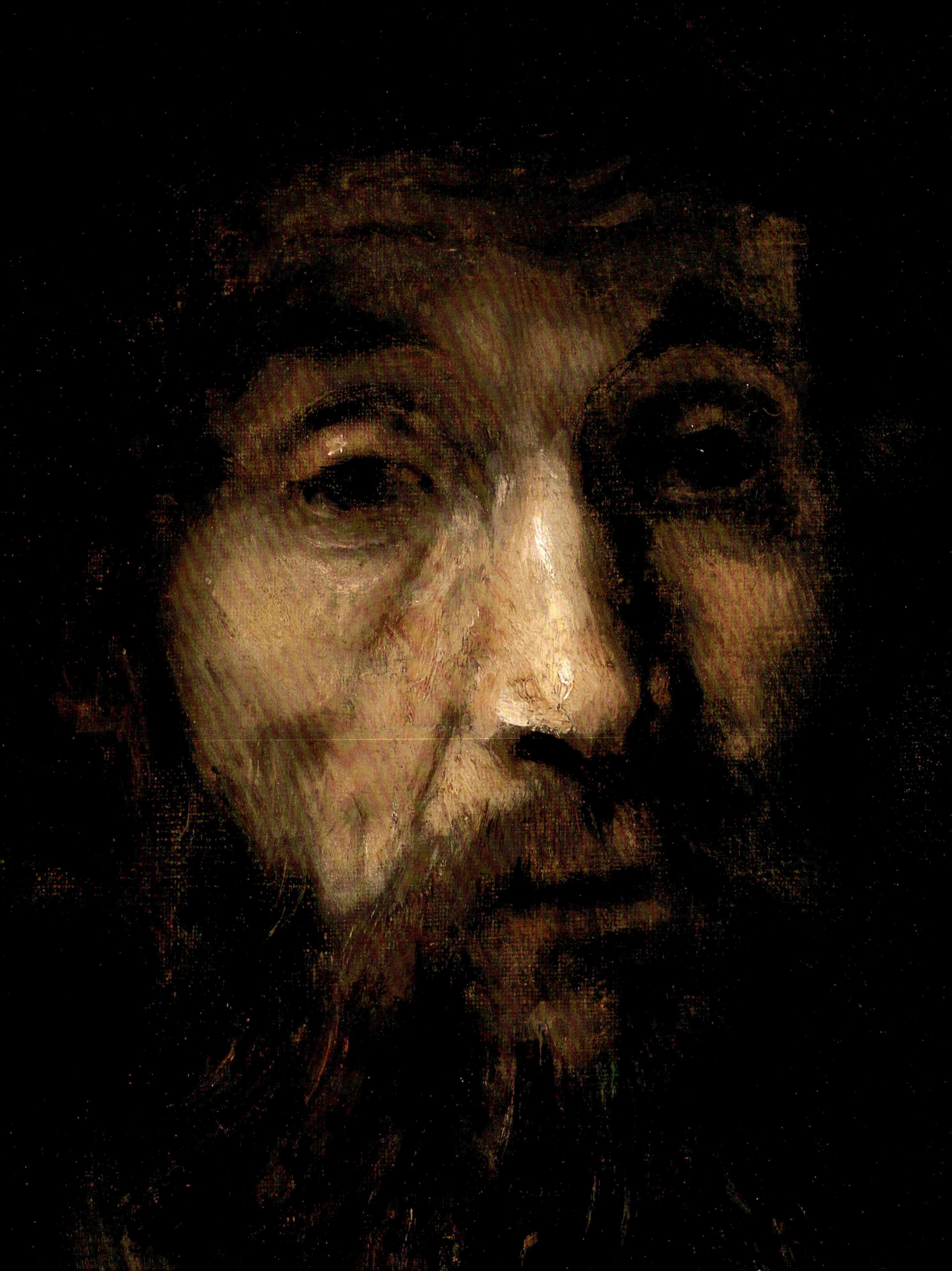

Rembrandt clearly had ties to the Jewish community. He provided illustrations for a book published by the renowned Portuguese rabbi Manasseh Ben Israël, who lived near the artist and has been assumed to be the subject of one of his portrait etchings (B. 269). He also portrayed the Portuguese Jewish physician, Ephraim Bonus (Wheelock essay, fig. 15). The synagogues of both the Portuguese and the German communities were in the neighborhood, and Rembrandt etched a Jewish house of worship. Notwithstanding Gary Schwartz's claim that Rembrandt's relationships with the Jews have been the subject of "much sentimental conjecture," the recent book by Michael Zell again affirms the closeness of those relations and Rembrandt's attraction to Jewish models.[2]

Although the identity of this model remains unknown, it would appear that Rembrandt painted his image from life. The artist executed the work quite directly, laying his paint in a restrained manner onto an ocher-colored upper ground layer. No significant pentimenti exist, only slight adjustments in the contour of the figure.[3] Nevertheless, since the last digit of the date is obscured by the model's right arm, it appears that Rembrandt returned to the painting after he had signed and dated it to make this adjustment.

The same model appears in *Aristotle Contemplating a Bust of Homer,* 1653 (cat. 2, fig. 3); *A Bearded Man in a Beret,* 1661 (fig. 1); *Saint Bavo* (cat. 17); and the so-called *Portrait of a Rabbi,* 1657, assigned to Rembrandt although sometimes doubted (Fine Arts Museums of San Francisco).[4] The model also served as the inspiration for *The Apostle Paul* (cat. 2). PCS

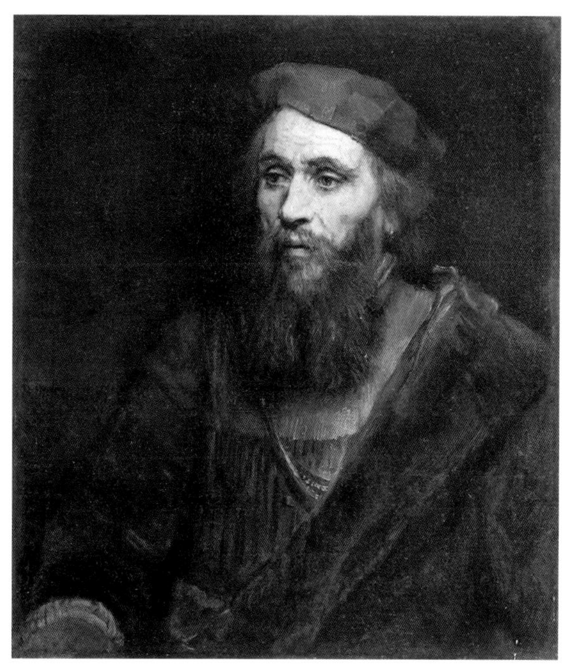

1
Rembrandt van Rijn
A Bearded Man in a Beret
1661, oil on canvas,
The State Hermitage Museum,
Saint Petersburg

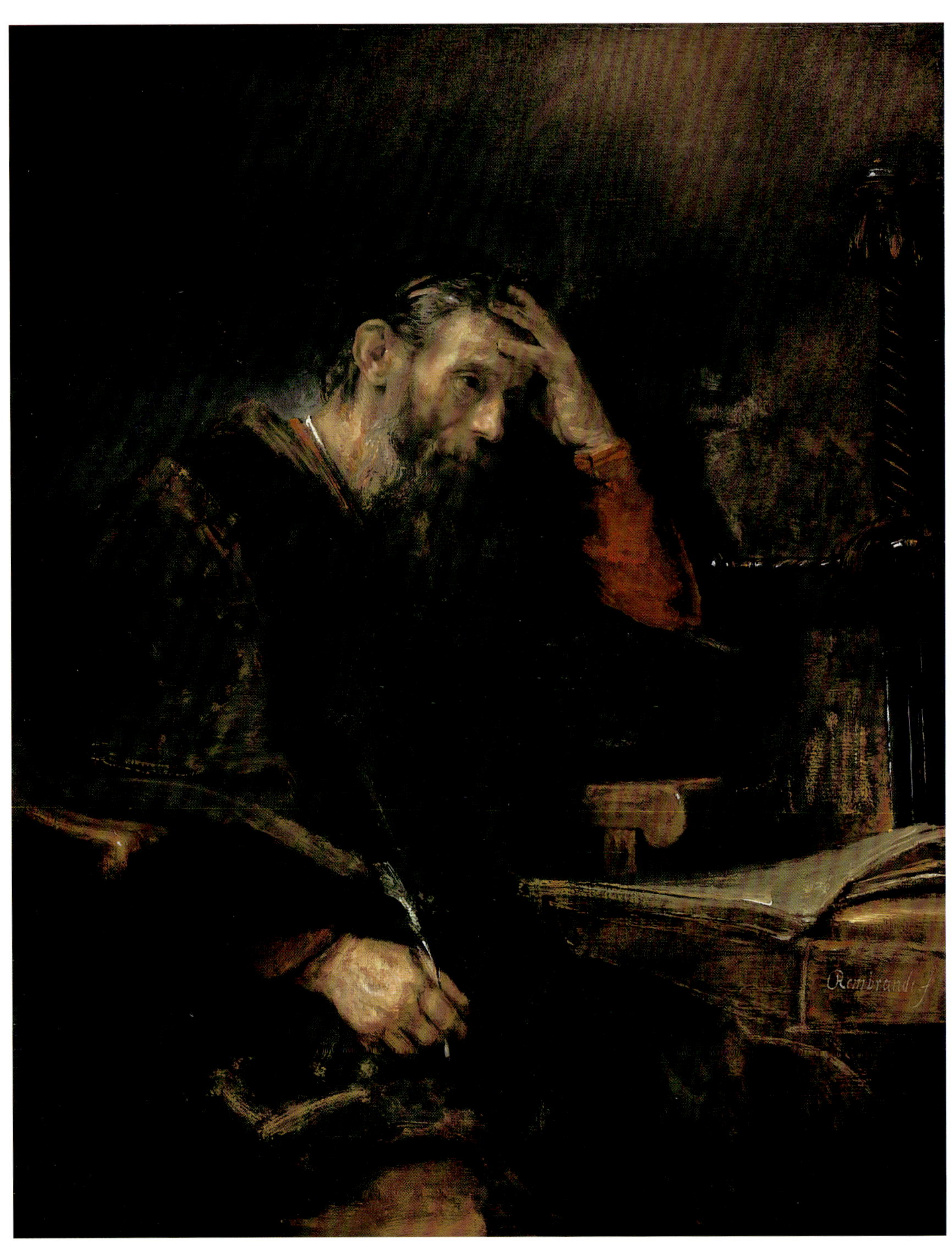

The Apostle Paul, c. 1657
oil on canvas, 131.5 × 104.4 (51 3/4 × 41 1/8)
National Gallery of Art, Washington,
Widener Collection 1942.9.59

2 The Apostle Paul

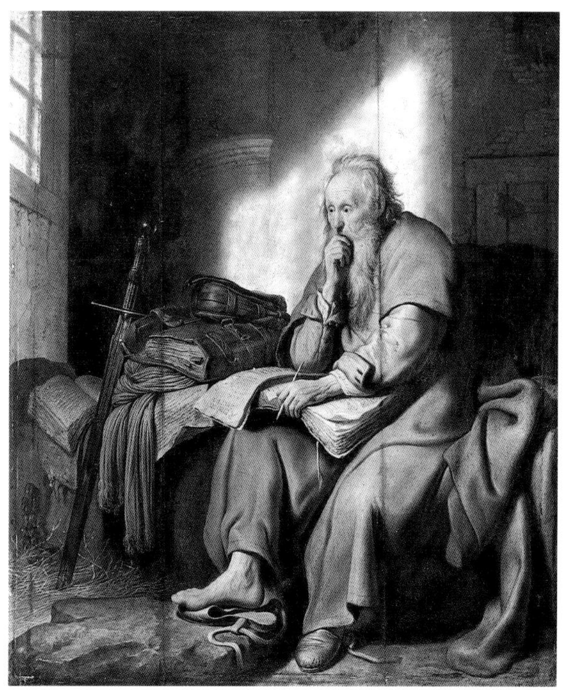

1
Rembrandt van Rijn
Saint Paul in Prison
1627, oil on panel,
Staatsgalerie, Stuttgart

Sitting before a table in the recesses of his prison cell, the Apostle Paul has brought his hand to his head as he ponders the words he is about to write in the Epistle that lies before him.[1] The weighty expression of his strong features underscores the depth of his belief and the purposefulness of his mission to spread Christianity to the heathen. The sword visible above the book is as much the "sword of the Spirit," the term he used to describe the word of God in his letter to the Ephesians (6:17), as it is the symbol of his military might before his conversion or the foreboding of his eventual martyrdom.

This large and imposing painting from the late 1650s depicts a figure that preoccupied Rembrandt throughout his life, from his 1627 *Saint Paul in Prison* (fig. 1), to his moving 1661 representation of himself in the guise of Saint Paul (cat. 11). As is evident from these three paintings, Rembrandt's concern with Paul, or Saul, was not the dramatic moment in the apostle's life when he was converted to Christianity on the road to Damascus. Rembrandt apparently never depicted, as did so many before him, Saul felled from his horse by a blinding light from heaven, or the companions of Saul accompanying their leader to Damascus, where, after his sight was restored, he was baptized and had his name changed to Paul.

Paul the apostle, however, captivated Rembrandt, perhaps because his writings were the most important source for Reformation theology or because he personified the Christian belief of grace received independently of merit. As Rembrandt grew older and experienced the anguish and shame of his unfortunate relationship with Geertje Dircks and his financial crises of the 1650s, the latter associations must have been strongly felt. Certainly, by the mid-1650s, Rembrandt began to focus even more intensely on the frailty and the strength of biblical figures, whether in his moving depiction of *Saul*

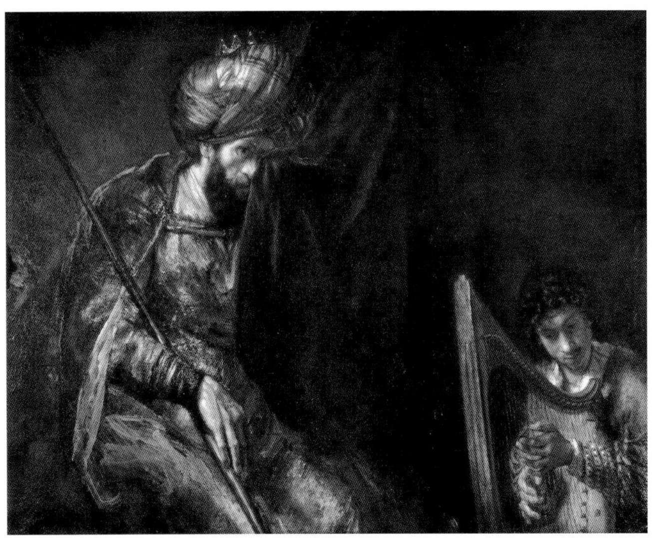

and David in the Mauritshuis, The Hague (fig. 2),[2] or in such reflective paintings as his portrait *An Elderly Man as the Apostle Paul,* of 1659 (cat. 4).

The 1627 representation of *Saint Paul in Prison* offers a fascinating point of comparison with the Washington painting, for it demonstrates differences in attitude characteristic of Rembrandt's stylistic and iconographic evolution. Whereas the Rembrandt of 1627 placed Paul in an identifiable environment, where bricks and mortar, wood and straw have been carefully delineated and where the light source can be specifically identified, the Rembrandt of the late 1650s suppressed such references to time and place. In his later representation he created the sense of the prison cell rather than its specific character. The gentle light that illuminates Paul's head, hand, and Epistle, for example, has no defined point of origin. Here, Rembrandt has also brought the viewer closer to the figure of the saint. He depicts Paul at half-length rather than full-length to allow the viewer to experience more fully the intensity of the apostle's expression.

Paul's expression is also markedly different in the two works. Whereas in the Stuttgart painting Paul brings his hand to his mouth and gazes into the distance, seemingly uncertain of the meanings of the words inscribed in the tomes surrounding him, in the Washington painting Paul rests his head in his hand as though he is pondering the significance of Christ's life. As he stares past his sword, his demeanor is pensive rather than bewildered. The differences are in part due to the broadness of Rembrandt's mature painting technique, which emphasizes the structure of form without focusing on the specifics of veins, wrinkles, and hair, and in part to the way light strikes Paul's head, which leaves his eyes obscured in shadow.

Paul's distinctive facial features, his flowing beard, long nose, and deep-set, slightly sad eyes, are those of a model that Rembrandt occasionally depicted in the 1650s and early 1660s (see cat. 1).[3] The artist had also adapted his features in 1653 for another contemplative, historicizing painting, *Aristotle Contemplating a Bust of Homer* (fig. 3). In *The Apostle Paul,* Rembrandt slightly generalized the model's facial characteristics, both to suggest the historical nature of the subject and to enhance the contemplative mood of the scene. Rembrandt would also have adapted his painting techniques for modeling the face so that they would better relate to the broad handling evident in the rest of the composition. The painting's large scale almost certainly suggests that it was designed to be seen from a distance, and probably from below, perhaps because it was planned for a specific location.[4]

These factors may have affected Rembrandt's manner of execution, for the paints are applied in a somewhat dryer, thinner manner than are those in *A Bearded Man in a Cap* (cat. 1). Nevertheless, the general painting techniques are comparable.[5] In each instance Rembrandt drew his brush across the canvas with economical strokes that suggest but do not define form. He applied flesh tones in a single layer over a warm primary layer and indicated features such as the eyes and nose with planes of color instead of accentuating them with sharp contour lines. He suggested the beard and hair, in which a few lightly colored strands stand out against the surrounding darker forms, with long, flowing strokes.

An extensive conservation treatment of the painting in 2000-2001 confirmed that *The Apostle Paul* had a complicated paint structure in many areas. As had been suspected previously through analyses of the x-radiographs, numerous compositional changes have occurred, particularly in the placement of the apostle's book, which was once propped so that his left elbow rested upon it.[6] With this alteration the nature of the gesture changed, from one in which the arm supported the head to one that suggests that the apostle's hand touches his forehead during a moment of inspiration. The x-radiographs also suggest that the painting underwent structural changes and that it was initially conceived as an oval composition.[7] With this original configuration (in conjunction with the raised position on the book), it seems unlikely that space existed for the sword, which raises questions as to whether Rembrandt originally planned his painting as a depiction of Saint Paul or as a more general representation of a biblical patriarch.

With the removal of the darkened varnish layers and later overpainting, it also became evident that at least two layers of paint are to be found in other areas of the painting, in particular the broad, dark strokes on the cloak covering Paul's right shoulder and some of the highlights in the face. The relatively murky paint applied with extremely free brushstrokes in this area lacks the clarity of the master's hand, which raises questions about when, why, and by whom these subsequent interventions were made. While it seems probable that they were carried out in Rembrandt's studio under the master's supervision, no conclusive technical information confirming that hypothesis has been discovered.[8]

In terms of scale and iconography, *The Apostle Paul* relates closely to *The Apostle Bartholomew,* which is signed and dated 1657 (cat. 3). Saint Bartholomew, who leans forward and almost aggressively stares out of the picture with an alert, inquisitive expression enlivening his rugged features, holds before him a knife signifying his martyrdom. His active, dynamic personality contrasts with Paul's more contemplative one, perhaps indicating that the adjustments to Paul's image were made in relationship to this work.[9] **AKW**

2 *opposite*
Rembrandt van Rijn
Saul and David
c. 1655 and c. 1660–1665, oil on canvas, Mauritshuis, The Hague

3
Rembrandt van Rijn
Aristotle Contemplating a Bust of Homer
1653, oil on canvas, The Metropolitan Museum of Art, New York

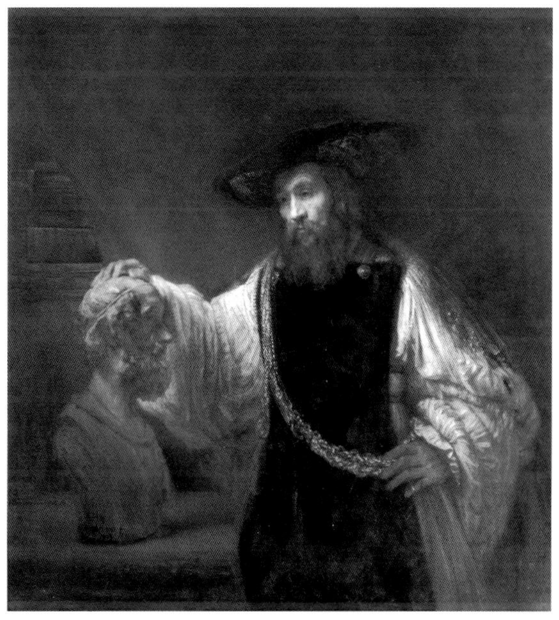

3 The Apostle Bartholomew

The saint leans forward in a low-backed chair, his gaze averted to the left, eyebrow cocked, and mouth slightly open, as if listening intently. Strong light brilliantly illuminates the right side of his face, revealing its hollow cheek and furrowed brow, and highlighting the curling texture of his short hair and beard. He is dressed in a plain brown robe over a white shirt, the cuff of which shows radiantly at the wrist; a heavier, buff-colored cloak covers the chair. In this proscribed composition, the glittering blade of the knife he holds with quiet equanimity has the effect of a more ostentatious gesture.

Little is known about the life of Bartholomew, who is mentioned only briefly in the New Testament as one of the Twelve Apostles.[1] The name Bartholomaios is Hebrew, meaning son of Talmai, which suggests that the apostle may have been of Hebrew descent. According to later medieval accounts, he traveled extensively through Asia, preaching the Gospel and converting the heathen in India and Armenia, where he is said to have been flayed alive and then beheaded.

While Rembrandt painted very few narrative scenes of martyrdom, he was preoccupied with the dramatic possibilities offered by the singularly horrific manner of Saint Bartholomew's death. In a small number of images of the saint, the artist explored the way in which an evocative attribute, the knife, served to amplify his characterization of Bartholomew, the emotional manifestations of the apostle's faith and anticipation of his corporeal fate. Rembrandt's depictions of the saint are all half-length in format, and together they show the powerful shift from the artist's early interest in conveying intense expression to later descriptions of psychological density. In *The Apostle Bartholomew*, c. 1633 (fig. 1), now attributed to Rembrandt and almost certainly produced in his studio, Bartholomew ostentatiously holds his traditional attribute almost under his chin, where the curved blade resonates with the troubled intensity of his stare. In later depictions, however, the knife decreases in prominence while Bartholomew's gaze becomes more powerful and enigmatic. In two paintings executed only four years apart, this large and arresting image and *The Apostle Bartholomew* (cat. 8), Rembrandt posits two opposing emotional states for the apostle: the active proselytizer, and the sage burdened by the implications of commitment to the Christian faith.

In the San Diego canvas, Rembrandt portrays the apostle as a fierce Christian protagonist. While the dynamic, tensile position of the figure, three-quarter

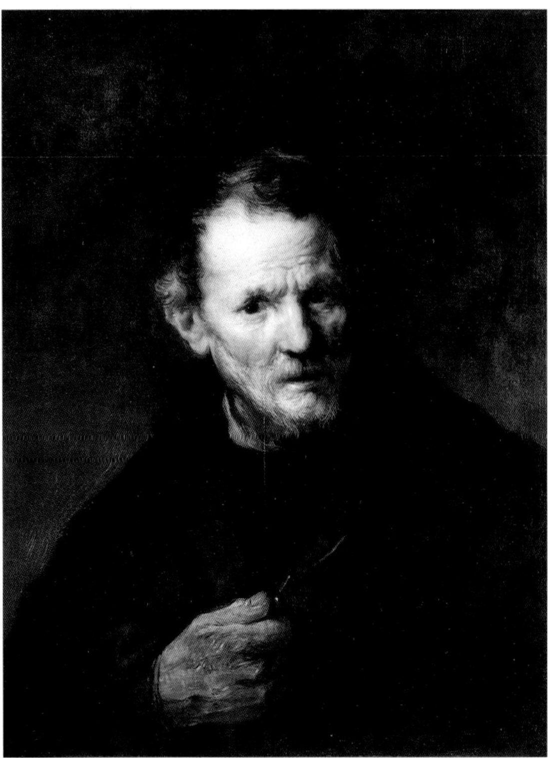

1
Attributed to Rembrandt van Rijn,
The Apostle Bartholomew
c. 1633, oil on panel, Worcester Art Museum, Charlotte E. Buffington Fund

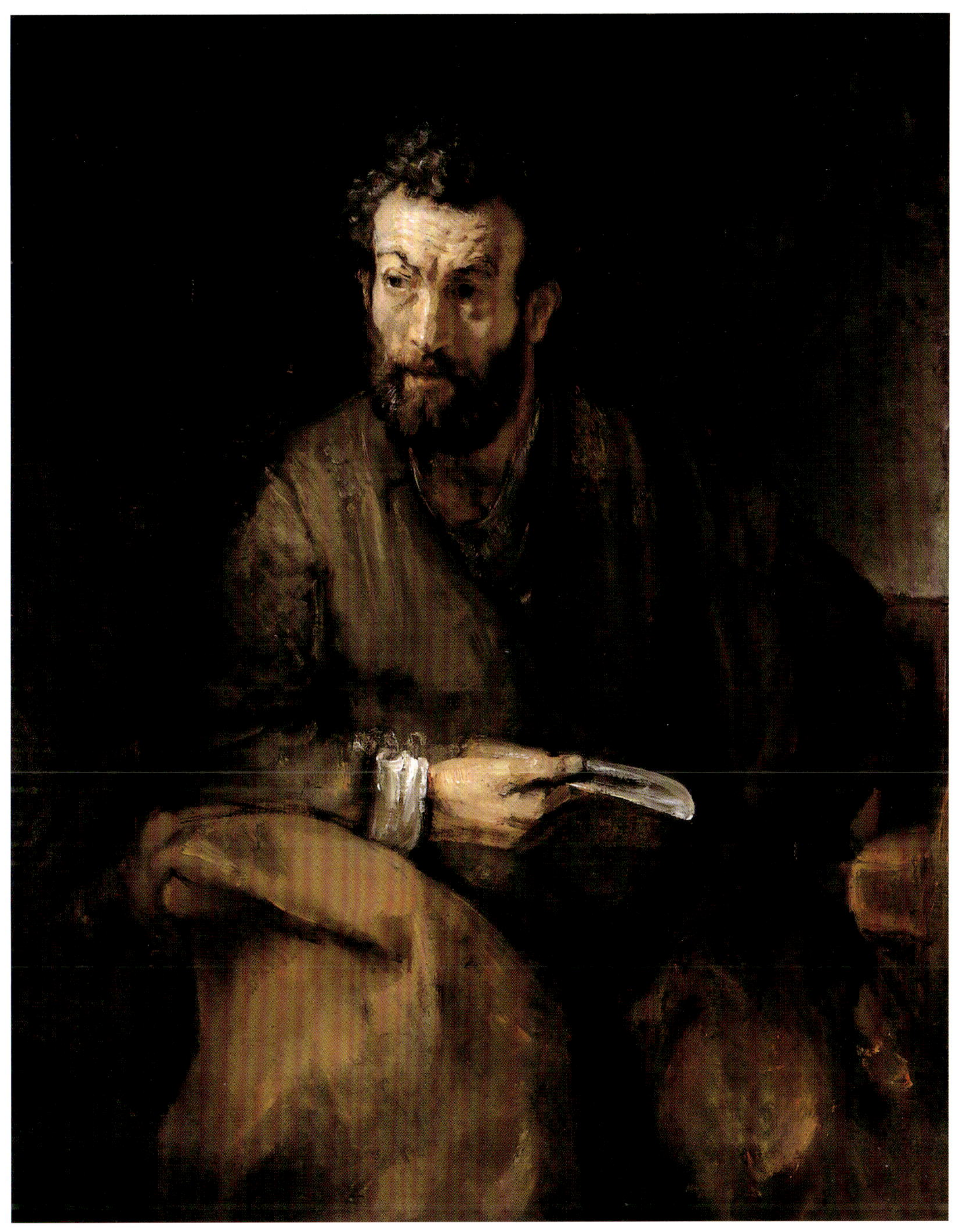

The Apostle Bartholomew, 1657
oil on canvas, 122.7 × 99.7 (48 3/8 × 39 1/4)
The Putnam Foundation,
Timken Museum of Art, San Diego

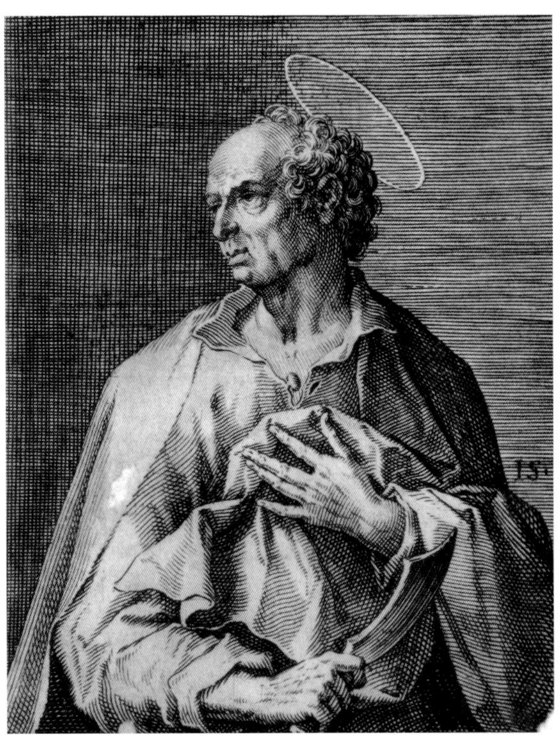

2
Johannes Sadeler I
after Maarten de Vos,
The Apostle Bartholomew (VI)
1585–1590, engraving,
The Metropolitan Museum of Art,
Harris Brisbane Dick Fund

length with his head averted, is formally analogous to Counter-Reformation examples (fig. 2), Rembrandt's portrayal of a relatively youthful man with rugged features reflects his own vision of biblical figures as unidealized, real people. Otto Benesch noted that the same model was used for *A Bearded Man* (Gemäldegalerie, Berlin), though the correspondence between the two is not particularly close.[2]

The effect of animation in *The Apostle Bartholomew* is all the more remarkable for the particularly limited range of Rembrandt's palette. The combination of vigorous, sculpting brushwork in the face contrasts with the broader, planar application in the cuff and hand, while the roughly indicated bulk of the figure serves as a rich foil for these two descriptive elements. At one time *The Apostle Paul* (cat. 2), which shares a similarly large format, was thought to have been a complementary pendant to the San Diego canvas, offering a contrast of the active and contemplative states, but evidence that *The Apostle Paul* may have originally had an oval format calls this hypothesis into question (see cat. 2).[3]

Both the Timken (cat. 3) and the Getty (cat. 8) paintings were in London during the second half of the eighteenth century, owned by members of the Society of Dilettanti, who were enthusiastic collectors of Rembrandt's work. William Fauquier, a governor of the Bank of England and secretary and treasurer of the Society from 1771 to 1774, purchased *The Apostle Bartholomew* (as *Man with a Knife*) from the artist and collector Jonathan Richardson. Sir Joshua Reynolds, who possessed a highly significant group of works by Rembrandt, provided the earliest identification of the subject as *The Apostle Bartholomew.*[4] The Getty painting eventually passed from the collection of the collector and dealer John Blackwood to the famous antiquarian collector Richard Payne Knight, who joined the Society in 1781. There is some evidence that the paintings of Saint Bartholomew were thought to be distasteful. The Timken painting reverted to its early descriptive title, *Man with a Knife,* while the Getty's *Apostle Bartholomew* was known by various fanciful titles. Dislike of the subject may account for the overpainting, presumably carried out during the nineteenth century, of the knife with a book, which was subsequently removed about 1912.[5] ATW

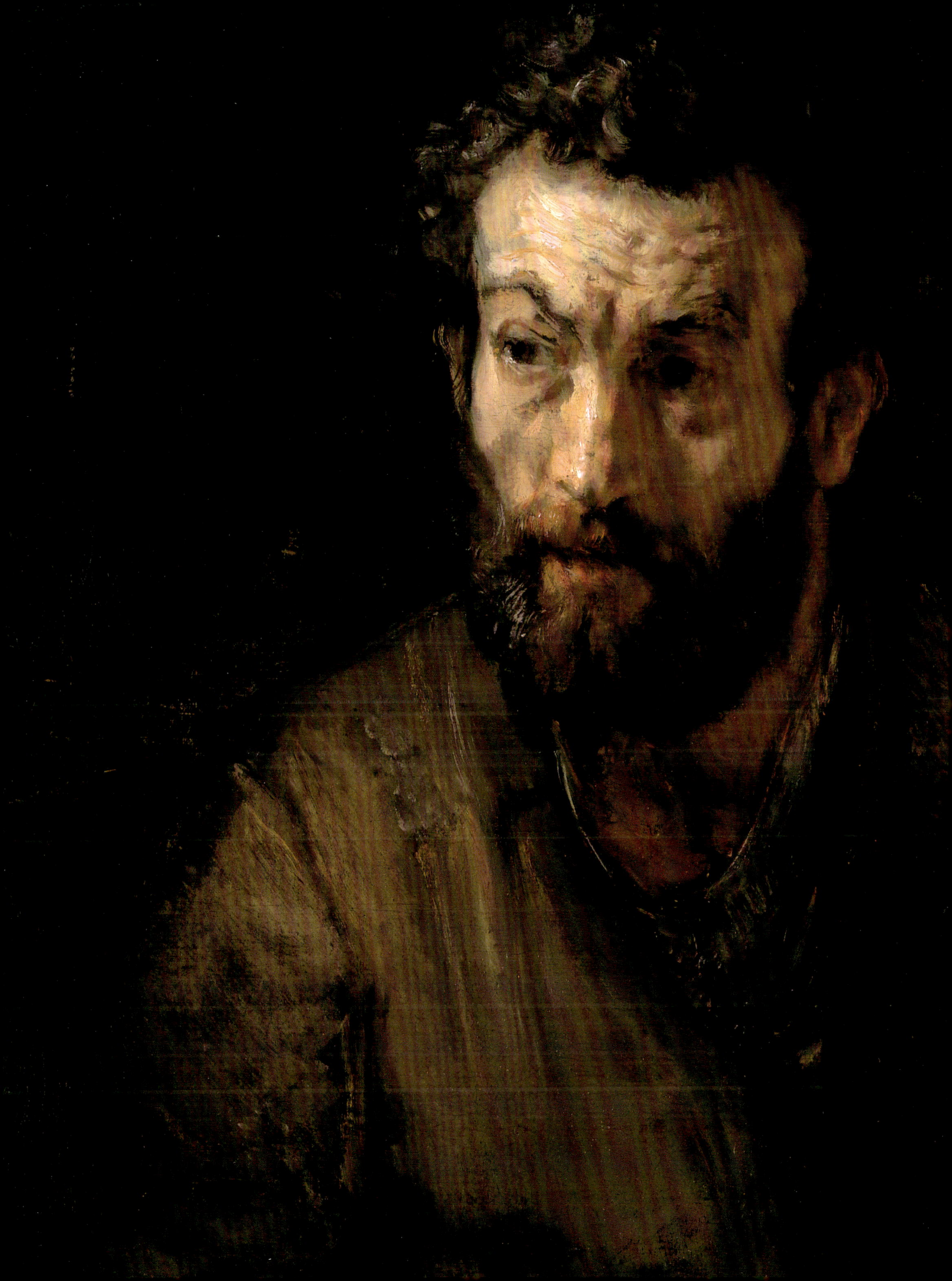

4 An Elderly Man as the Apostle Paul

Rembrandt's depictions of apostles and evangelists, particularly those from 1659 to 1661, demonstrate a consistency in approach that gives validity to the notion he conceived them in relationship to each other. Not only are these paintings similar in scale, but they are also executed with comparable color tonalities, largely in browns and ochers, with occasional touches of red adding visual accents. Posed with their attributes, these half-length apostles and evangelists tend to be thoughtful individuals, their faces softly illuminated by an unseen light source and their hands relegated to semidarkness. Here, Saint Paul, identifiable through the sword of his martyrdom leaning against the wall and the large tome open before him, gently clasps his hands as he stares off into the distance in quiet reflection. As in other paintings in this presumed series, the saint is situated in a darkened interior with little definition given to his surroundings.

Considering the stylistic and conceptual similarities among these representations of apostles and evangelists, Rembrandt's manner of modeling facial expressions nevertheless varies from work to work. Within this loosely defined group, no countenance is rendered as attentively as that of the figure in this painting. Using delicate strokes of the brush, the artist carefully modeled the man's features, beard, and mustache with great sensitivity and surety. Even though Rembrandt applied his paint thickly and rapidly, he was so certain of his intent that he made virtually no modifications to his original concept.[1] With an eye for observing those qualities that distinguish one human from another, he indicated not only the man's drooped left eyelid but also the puffiness under his eyes. He captured the reddish glow of the skin over the apostle's cheekbone and the smooth curve of his gray locks as they pass over his ear. Finally, Rembrandt saw within this model the gentle, reflective state of mind of a man who, like Saint Paul, thought deeply and at length about faith and matters of the spirit.

The care with which Rembrandt painted this image, and the immediacy of his rendering of the figure's features and expression, is comparable to that of his known portraits around 1659, as, for example, his *Self-Portrait,* which he executed that very year (fig. 1).[2] The portraitlike quality of this image, in fact, strongly suggests that the painting shows one of the artist's contemporaries in the guise of Saint Paul rather than an imaginative portrayal of the saint. The artist would assume the same role in the memorable self-portrait he painted two years later (cat. 11).[3]

Nothing is known of the early provenance of this painting, but if it was conceived as a *portrait historié,* it would almost certainly have been commissioned by the individual depicted. In that case, it is unlikely that the painting would have formed an integral part of an apostle series.[4] Even as a separate entity, this work could well have inspired Rembrandt to begin thinking about creating a series of paintings of apostles and evangelists.

Dimly visible behind the figure is an arched niche flanked by two roundels. The one on the left contains a depiction of Abraham's Sacrifice, a composition

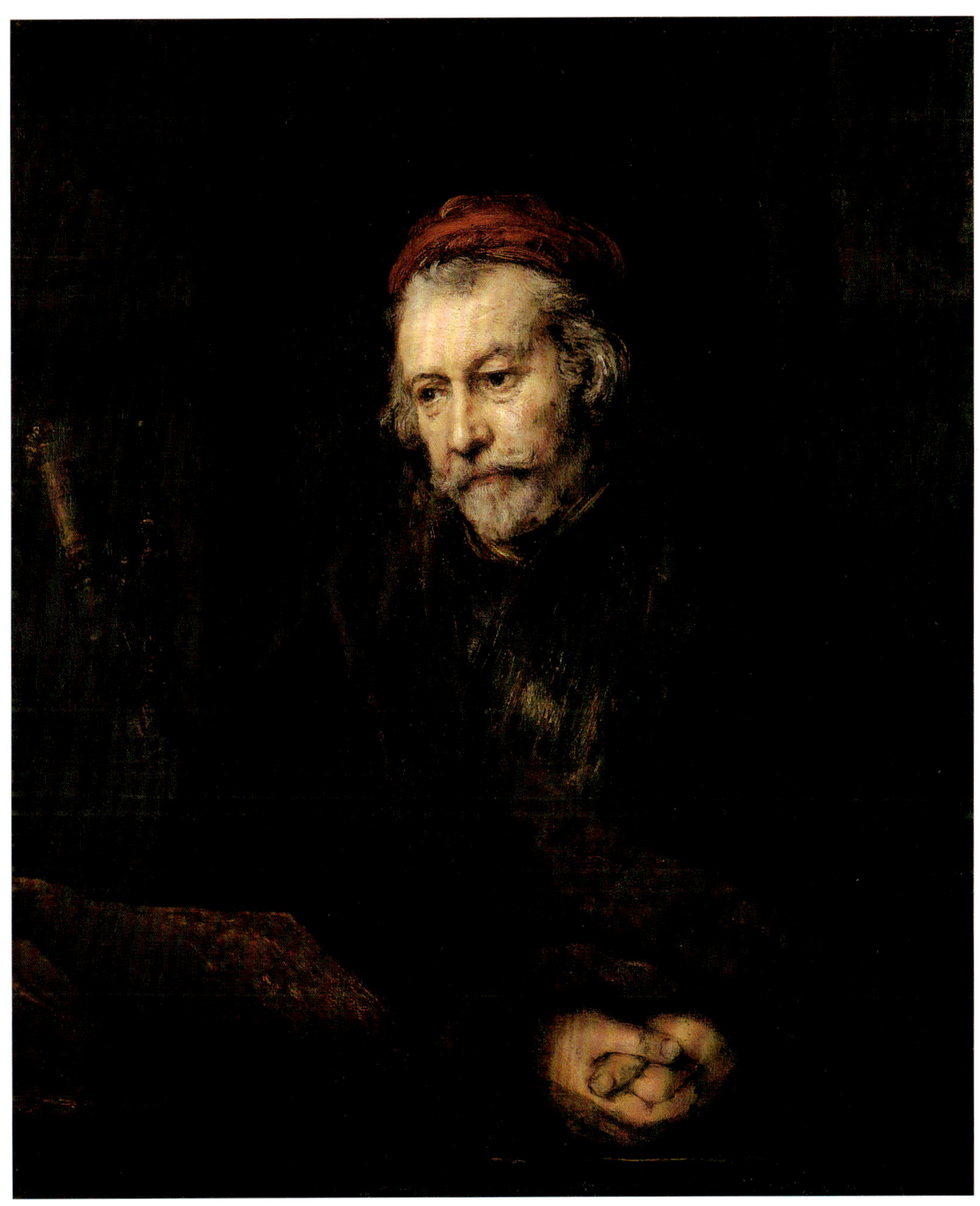

An Elderly Man as the Apostle Paul, 165(9?)
oil on canvas, 102 × 85.5 (40 1/8 × 33 5/8)
The National Gallery, London

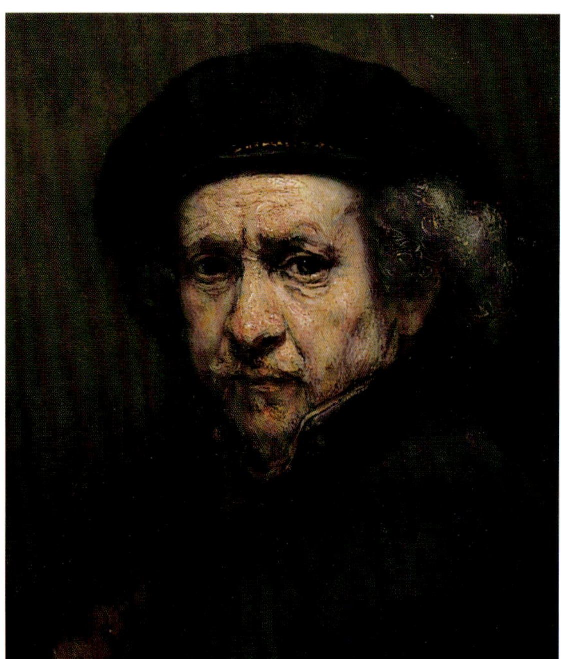

1
Rembrandt van Rijn
Self-Portrait
(detail), 1659, oil on canvas, National Gallery of Art, Washington, Andrew W. Mellon Collection

that resembles, in many respects, Rembrandt's etching of 1655.[5] The subject in the roundel is particularly appropriate in this context, for, in his Epistle to the Hebrews (11:17), Saint Paul cites Abraham as an exemplar of faith: "By faith Abraham, when he was tested, offered up Isaac, and he who had received the promises was ready to offer up his only son."[6] Nevertheless, the small biblical vignette in the painting's background is one additional element that distinguishes this work conceptually from related half-length representations of religious figures from this period in Rembrandt's career. The visual reminder of one of the essential elements of Saint Paul's teaching, the precedence of faith over good works, makes this a painting as much about Saint Paul as it is of Saint Paul, an essential characteristic of a *portrait historié.* AKW

5 Hendrickje Stoffels (as the Sorrowing Virgin?)

Hendrickje, with her hand at her chest, inclines slightly forward as she gazes to her right. Her quiet countenance and heavy body language convey a tinge of sadness and melancholy, as though she is trying to contain within herself deep-seated emotions that have affected the very core of her being. Rembrandt emphasized her expressive character through the thick impastos modeling her face and the strong light illuminating her features, in particular her liquid eyes and partially opened mouth. He covered her body with a dark, fur-lined cloak, subdued in tonality and soft of form, revealing only a delicate white chemise across her open bodice. An equally muted, although gold-flecked, robe draped over her right shoulder helps give visual emphasis to the direction of her gaze.

This painting, signed and dated 1660, is Rembrandt's last known portrayal of his companion Hendrickje Stoffels, who died, probably of the plague, in Amsterdam in July 1663.[1] Comparisons with earlier depictions of Hendrickje, shown here at age thirty-four, clearly demonstrate how she had changed over the years, her face having grown softer and puffier, and her neck thicker and less supple (fig. 1).[2] Even in this quiet, reflective painting, Rembrandt conveys the inner warmth and physical sensuality that characterize each and every image he painted of her. These very qualities may have inspired the artist to depict her occasionally in poses drawn from Venetian art.[3]

In the past this work was thought to be a pendant to a Rembrandt self-portrait, also dated 1660, in the Metropolitan Museum of Art.[4] Yet as Walter Liedtke has emphasized, this opinion cannot be substantiated.[5] As he notes, this painting should not be considered a conventional portrait but one in which Hendrickje assumes the guise of a biblical figure. Liedtke suggested that compositional relationships exist between this

1
Rembrandt van Rijn
Woman at an Open Door (Hendrickje Stoffels?)
late 1650s, oil on canvas, Gemäldegalerie, Staatliche Museen zu Berlin

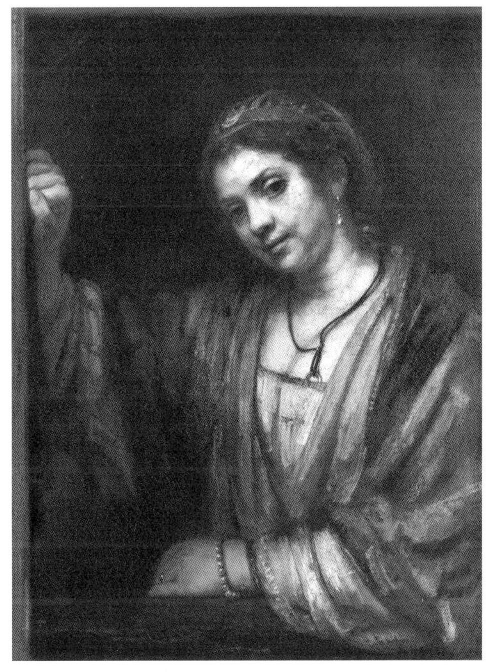

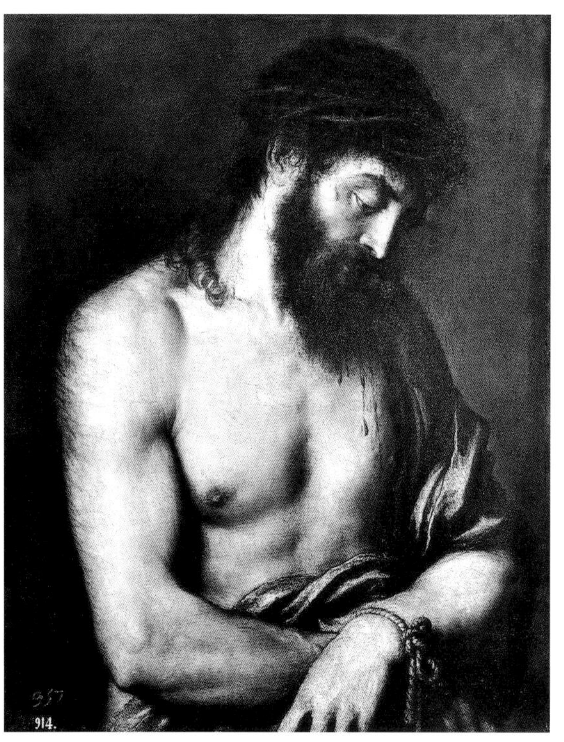

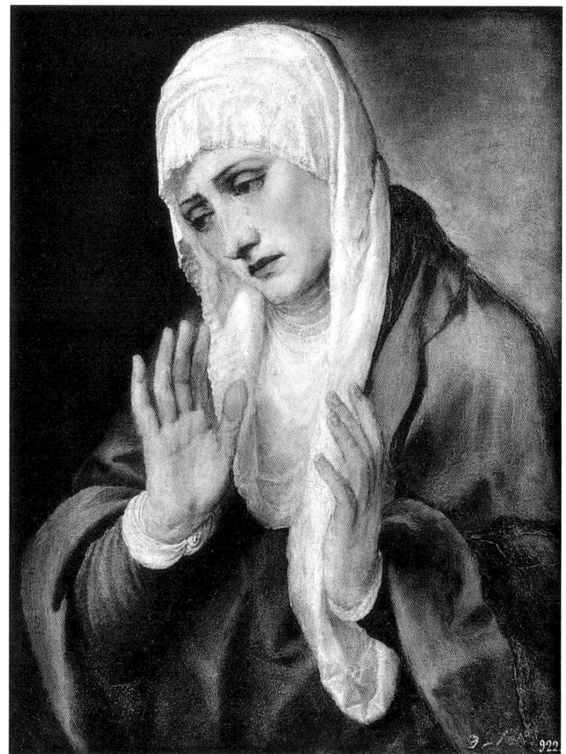

2
Titian
Ecce Homo
1547, oil on canvas,
Museo del Prado,
Madrid

3
Titian
Mater Dolorosa with Raised Hands
1554, oil on canvas,
Museo del Prado,
Madrid

work and Titian's *Repentant Magdalene,* a painting Rembrandt probably would have known through an engraving by Cornelis Cort of 1566.[6] Titian's composition does have certain parallels to Rembrandt's painting, particularly in the way the saint brings her hand to her breast, although it presents the saint looking upward rather than downward and to the side. While Liedtke does not conclude that Rembrandt intended for Hendrickje to assume the role of the Repentant Magdalene, he leaves open that possibility.

Rembrandt may have considered a Titian prototype when conceiving this work, but the matronly character of the sitter seems to belie identification with the Magdalene. A more probable interpretation is that Rembrandt conceived his image as a Sorrowing Virgin (*Mater Dolorosa*), a subject that Titian painted a number of times, generally as a pendant to an image of Christ as the *Ecce Homo* (fig. 2), in which he is shown with his hands bound and wearing a crown of thorns.[7] One of Titian's images of the *Mater Dolorosa* (fig. 3), in which the Virgin is seen with bent head and raised hands, was widely known through an engraving by Luca Bertelli, but Rembrandt also could

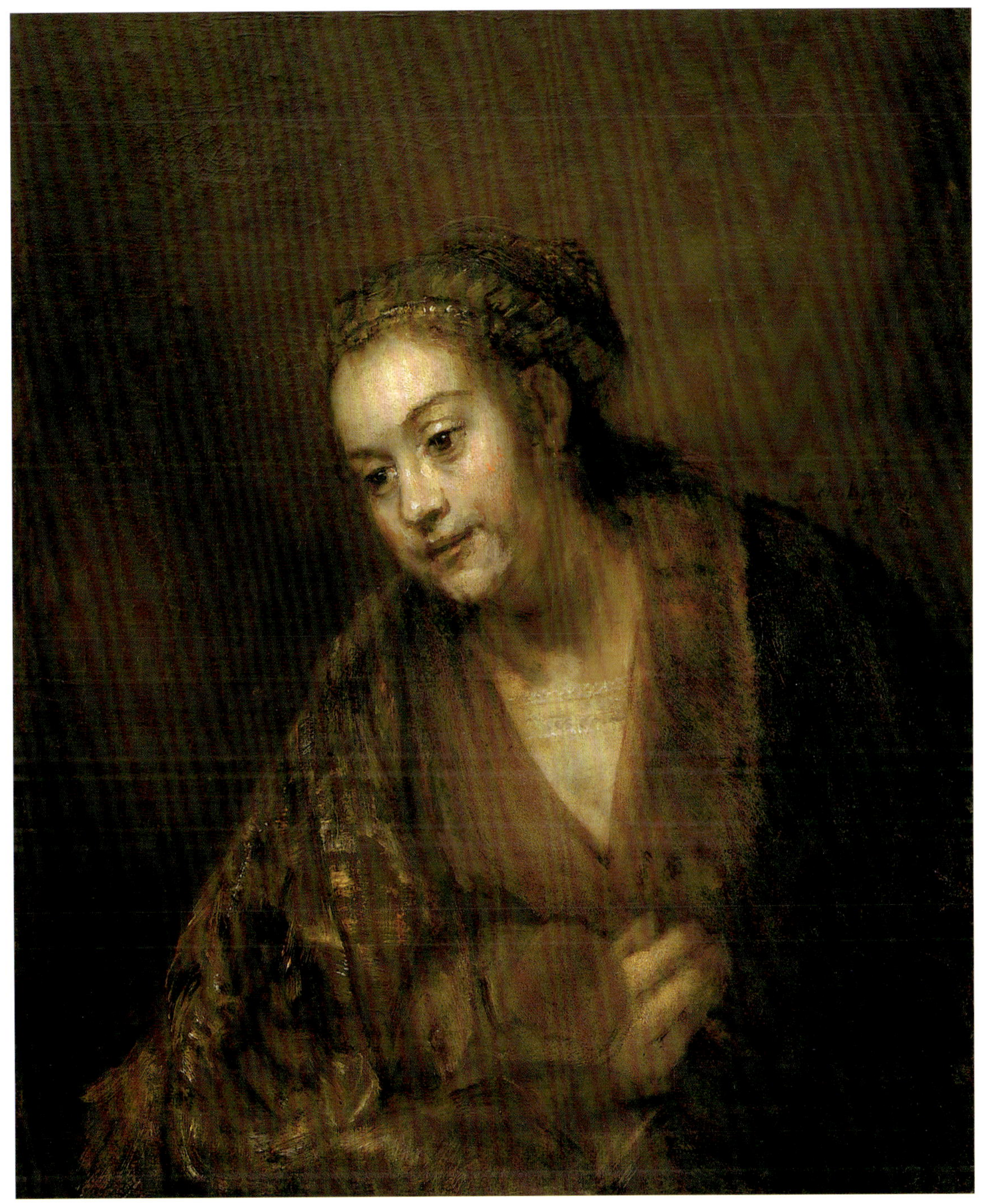

Hendrickje Stoffels (as the Sorrowing Virgin?), 1660
oil on canvas, 78.4 × 68.9 (30 7/8 × 27 1/8)
Lent by The Metropolitan Museum of Art,
Gift of Archer M. Huntington, in memory of his father,
Collis Potter Huntington, 1926

have known the image through one of the many copies of the painting. An even more probable visual source for this figure, given the context of Rembrandt's interest in a series of images of apostles and evangelists, is the engraving by Johannes Sadeler I after Maarten de Vos of the *Sorrowing Virgin* (fig. 4), an image that formed part of this Flemish master's engraved series of Christ, the Virgin, and the Twelve Apostles.

The tradition for including the Sorrowing Virgin in a series of the apostles almost certainly stems from the writings of the Pseudo-Bonaventura (c. 1300). The author, in his *The Meditations of the Life of Christ*, states that after his Resurrection Christ appeared to the tearful Virgin in her home, where she had been waiting in prayer. After embracing his mother, Christ, clothed in white, stood before her and displayed his wounds to prove that it was he.[8] Whatever the nature of Rembrandt's presumed series of apostles and evangelists, one could well imagine that Rembrandt conceived this emotionally charged image of Hendrickje/The Virgin in conjunction with *The Resurrected Christ* (cat. 6), perhaps even as pendants. Although the original format of both works has been altered, it appears that the paintings were originally comparable in size. They also have striking similarities in style and technique, and share in their quiet spirituality.[9] AKW

4
Johannes Sadeler I
after Maarten de Vos
Sorrowing Virgin
from the series Christ, the Virgin and the Twelve Apostles, c. 1585, engraving, The Metropolitan Museum of Art, Harris Brisbane Dick Fund

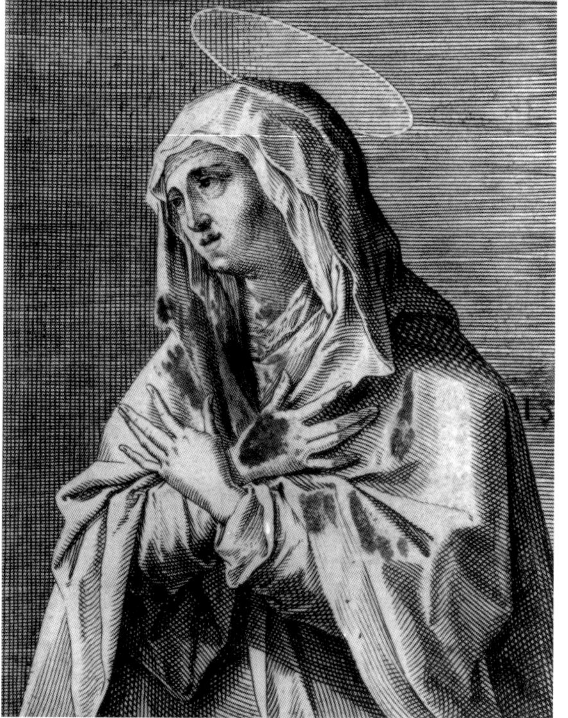

6 The Resurrected Christ

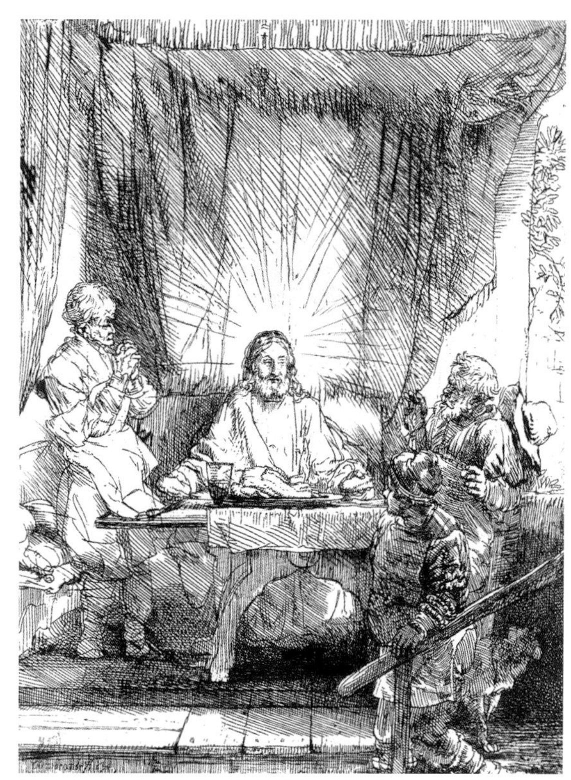

I
Rembrandt van Rijn
Christ at Emmaus
1654, etching, burin, and drypoint, National Gallery of Art, Washington, Rosenwald Collection

In this haunting image, Rembrandt presents the resurrected Christ as an austere yet vulnerable and deeply human savior. Christ's stark body and white robe and cloak, brilliantly lit from the upper left, glow out of the surrounding darkness, while a pale nimbus, in the shape of a golden crown, hovers above his head. Posed frontally as though he were a medieval icon, Christ looks directly at rather than down to the viewer, the wound at his side only barely visible below his outstretched cloak. His wide-eyed expression and parted lips suggest warmth and understanding, as though he has learned to appreciate human suffering and anguish through his own pain.

Throughout his career Rembrandt sought to express both the humanity and the mysteries contained in the life of Christ. Particularly fascinating to him were those episodes in which Christ returned after his death and resurrection to encounter Mary Magdalene, the Apostle Thomas, or his disciples at Emmaus, subjects that the artist explored in a number of his most memorable paintings, drawings, and prints. As he matured, Rembrandt's interpretations of such miraculous events also evolved. By the mid-1650s he had shifted his narrative focus away from the dramatic reactions of Christ's followers to his unexpected appearance in their midst, to the spiritual qualities emanating from Christ at the moment of revelation. For example, in his etchings of *Christ at Emmaus* (fig. 1) and *Christ Appearing to the Apostles,* 1656, Rembrandt focuses the viewer's attention on a quietly posed, central image of Christ, whose form is about to dissolve in radiant light as his presence is made known to his disciples.[1]

If Rembrandt utilized the visual force and power of iconic images to give such narrative scenes a sense of lasting human significance, he did so with equal, if not greater effect in *The Resurrected Christ.* Here, instead of

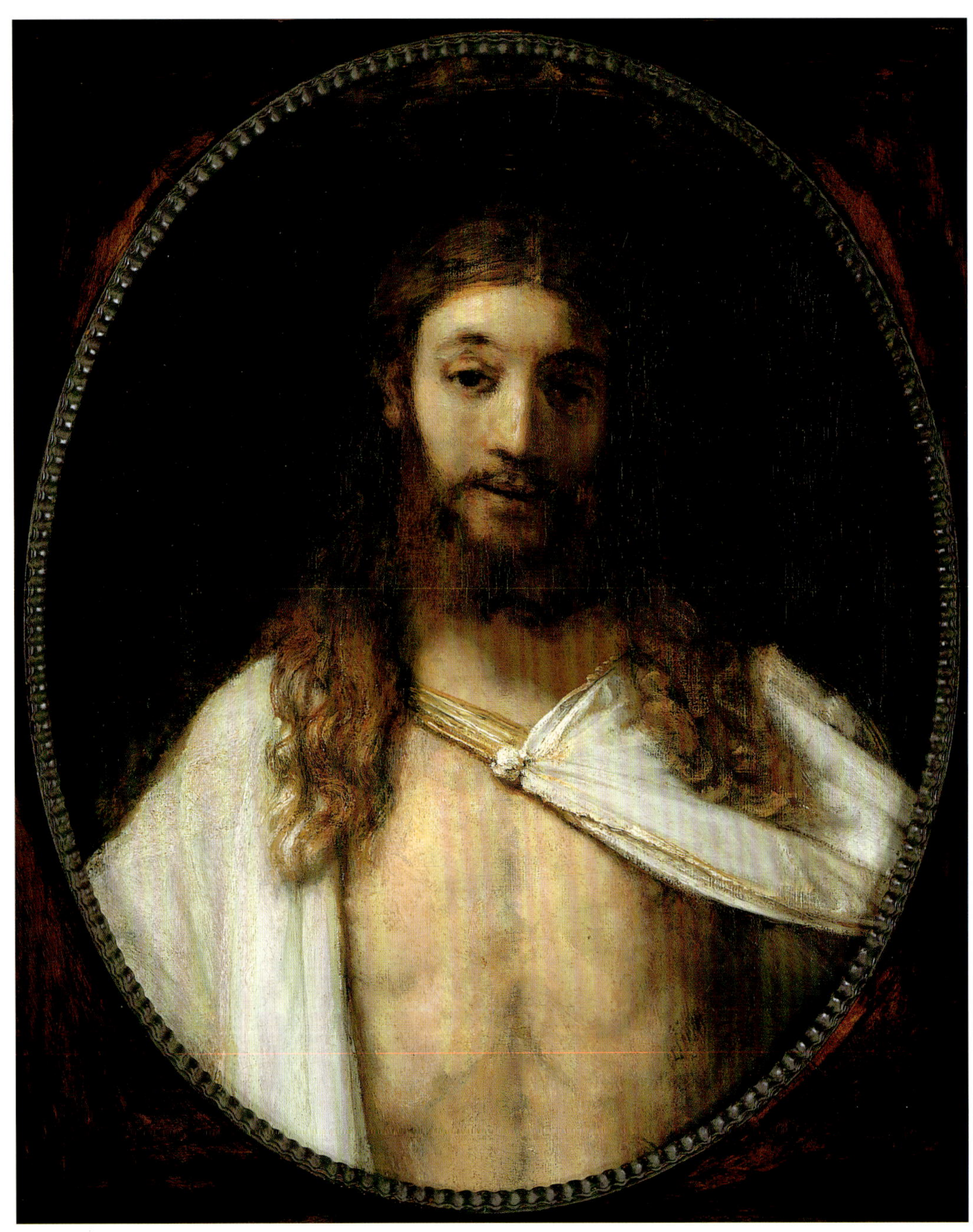

The Resurrected Christ, 1661
oil on canvas, 78.5 × 63 (31 × 24¾)
Bayerische Staatsgemäldesammlungen,
Alte Pinakothek, Munich

a powerful, idealized image of the Son of God in the manner of Peter Paul Rubens, Rembrandt transformed this iconic image into a compassionate figure. Christ is spiritual in his gaze, yet human and even vulnerable in his worldly experiences, and we empathize with him rather than worship him. Thus, although the painting has underlying connections to Catholic traditions born out of the Counter-Reformation, Rembrandt completely transformed the character and function of the work.

Rembrandt based this figure on a young Jew who seemed to embody those humble and caring qualities that the artist attributed to Jesus (fig. 2). But, in transforming the model into a Resurrected Christ, he idealized the figure by generalizing the model's features with broad brushstrokes that suggest rather than define form. He accented the steady radiance of Christ's gaze through the strong light that strikes the left side of his face. Finally, the severe patterns in the white robes that drape the body, the verticality of the white cloth falling from the right shoulder, and the sharp diagonal of the cloak stretching across the chest enhance the sense of lasting permanence that pervades this image.

The resulting portrayal, however imbued with Rembrandt's spirit, conforms to traditional concepts of Christ. Samuel van Hoogstraten, a pupil of Rembrandt in the mid-1640s who published a treatise on painting in 1678, quoted a description of Christ by the ancient writer Publius Lentulus that closely parallels Rembrandt's painting: "His hair is the color of a ripe hazelnut, parted on top in the manner of the Nazirites, and falling straight to the ears but curling below, with blonde highlights and fanning off his shoulders. He has a fair forehead and no wrinkles or marks on his face, his cheeks are tinged with pink…his beard is large and full but not long, and parted in the middle. His glance shows simplicity adorned with maturity, his eyes are clear and commanding, never apt to laugh but sooner inclined to cry."[2]

The image, although striking in its oval format, has probably been cut down from a rectangular shape. It has been suggested that Christ's extended left arm may have held a staff or a cross with a banner attached, the traditional iconography for the resurrected Christ.[3] This hypothesis seems unlikely, however, since thread distortions along the painting's sides indicate that the

2
Rembrandt van Rijn
Christ
c. 1656, oil on panel, Gemäldegalerie, Staatliche Museen zu Berlin

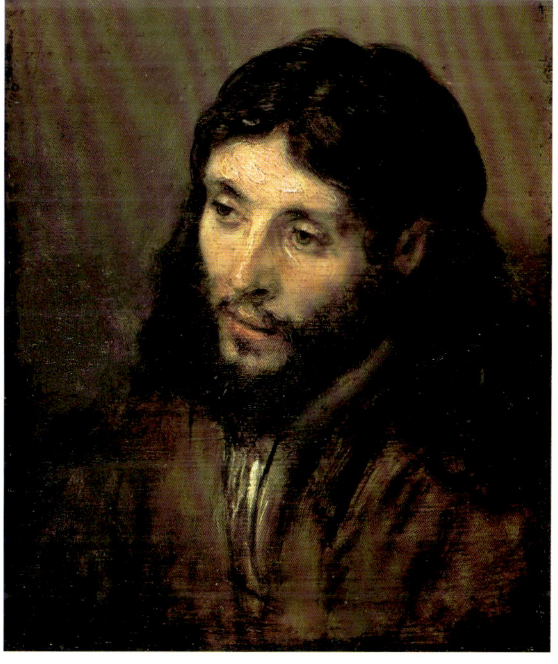

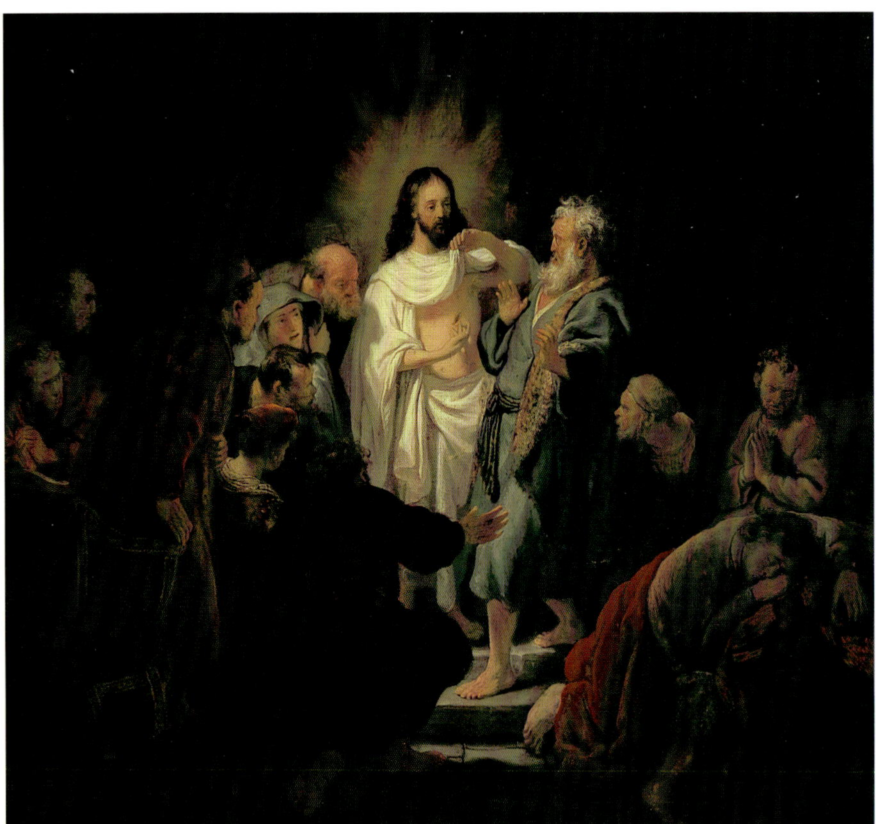

3
Rembrandt van Rijn
The Risen Christ Showing His Wound to the Apostle Thomas
(detail), 1634, oil on panel, Pushkin Museum of Fine Arts, Moscow

original dimensions would not have been sufficient to accommodate such a motif.[4] The gesture more likely was made to reveal the wound in Christ's side, as in Rembrandt's painting *The Risen Christ Showing His Wound to the Apostle Thomas,* 1634 (fig. 3), or in the master's etching *Christ Appearing to the Apostles,* 1650.[5]

In its original shape, the painting would have related much more closely than it does now to the powerfully evocative half-length apostles Rembrandt executed in the late 1650s and early 1660s. Indeed, without realizing that the painting had been cut down, Wilhelm R. Valentiner proposed that this work would have been the central image in a series of apostles and monks painted by Rembrandt in 1661.[6] Although it seems improbable that Rembrandt conceived of a series of these works in such a manner, one does wonder if the paintings were intended to form smaller groups. One intriguing possibility is that this painting could have been paired with an image of the Virgin, who met Christ briefly after his death and resurrection. For a further discussion of this possibility, see cat. 5. AKW

7 The Evangelist Matthew and the Angel

With his left hand gently fingering his full beard and his right hand poised to write, Matthew gazes into the distance as he tries to comprehend the words being softly whispered into his ear by the angel leaning over his shoulder. Rembrandt's painting conveys in real and tangible ways the spiritual inspiration that guided Matthew as he wrote his Gospel, as well as the character of the evangelist himself. From Matthew's rough features and sinewy hands, Rembrandt makes it clear that the former tax collector, whom Christ called to serve with him as an apostle, stemmed from a coarse background. His mind was not attuned to flights of fancy, nor was he a smooth practitioner of elegant prose. Rather, Matthew saw the world in physical terms and wrote with a direct clarity as he recorded the lessons of Jesus' ministry and the mysteries of his life in language that humanized Christ's divinity.

Rembrandt frequently turned to the Gospel of Saint Matthew when he sought to record episodes in Christ's life, perhaps because of Matthew's down-to-earth prose, but perhaps also because of the evangelist's emphasis on Christ's role as a healer and teacher. The importance of the Gospel in helping form Rembrandt's conception of Christ is particularly apparent in *Christ Healing the Sick (The Hundred Guilder Print)*, c. 1648 (fig. 1), where he incorporated various episodes described in chapter 19 into his depiction of Christ preaching to the multitudes.[1] The gentle Christ in this etching, the one who stands amidst the poor and the sick and who welcomes little children unto him, is at essence the Christ found in all the artist's subsequent images, whether prints or paintings (see cat. 15). Thus, it is not surprising that in 1661, when Rembrandt was so

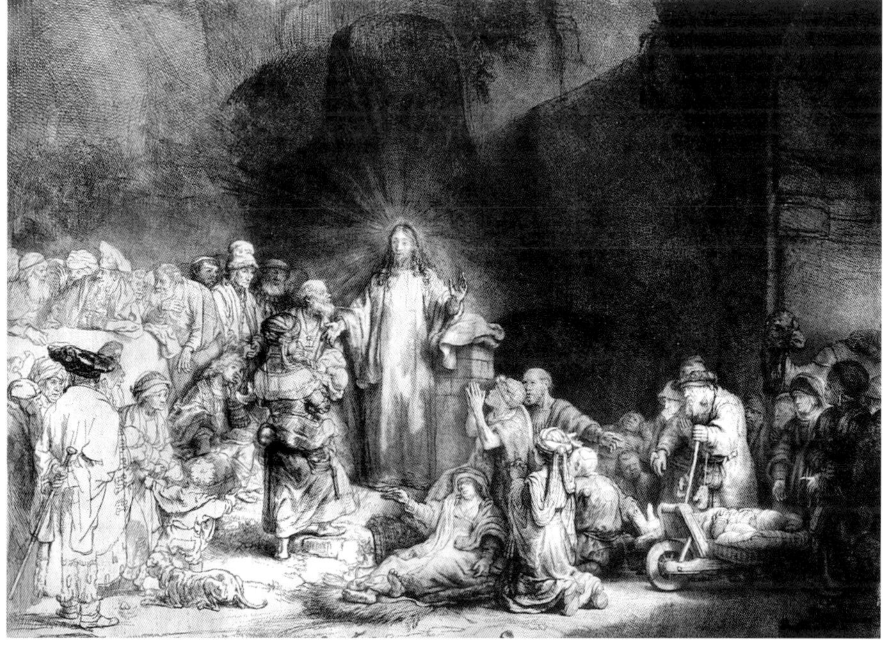

1
Rembrandt van Rijn
Christ Healing the Sick (The Hundred Guilder Print)
c. 1648, etching, drypoint, and burin, National Gallery of Art, Washington, Gift of R. Horace Gallatin

The Evangelist Matthew and the Angel, 1661
oil on canvas, 96 × 81 (37 13/16 × 31 7/8)
Musée du Louvre, Paris

intimately engaged in depicting half-length images of Christ and the apostles, he would devote such care to portraying this particular evangelist.

Matthew's traditional identifying attribute, other than a pen or a book, is the angel who brought him divine inspiration. Rembrandt has humanized the encounter by depicting the fair-haired angel as a young boy, without wings, tenderly touching Matthew's broad shoulder as he whispers in his ear. While light catches the angel's fingers and a portion of his face, it falls most strongly on the rich impastos that model Matthew's expressive head as he concentrates on the message so calmly being conveyed to him. Matthew is unaware of the angel and stares forward pensively, in response to his inspiration rather than to the angel's physical presence.

Rembrandt, who studied the human face for its poignant qualities throughout his life, had a remarkable ability to suggest the power of words as they pass from one individual to another. It was a challenge that he seems to have relished both in portraits, as when he captured the effects of a preacher's words in his wife's countenance in *The Mennonite Preacher Anslo and His Wife,* 1641 (see Manuth essay, fig. 10), and in history paintings, as in the greeting between Mary and Elizabeth in *The Visitation,* 1641 (Detroit Institute of Arts), or in the confrontation between the maid and Peter in the *Denial of Saint Peter,* 1660 (Rijksmuseum, Amsterdam).[2] Here, in this depiction of Saint Matthew, Rembrandt essentially merged the two genres — portraiture and history painting — as he carefully rendered the impact of the very intimate and personal nature of the young angel's message on the evangelist's expressive visage.

Rembrandt based *The Evangelist Matthew and the Angel* on a study of live models. The model for the angel is recognizable as the artist's son, Titus (cat. 8, fig. 1), and that for Saint Matthew is a bearded man whose distinctive features were recorded by various members of Rembrandt's studio in a number of small bust studies.[3] Rembrandt's forceful characterization of the figures, particularly through the thick impastos he used to model the saint's eloquent face and hands, indicate

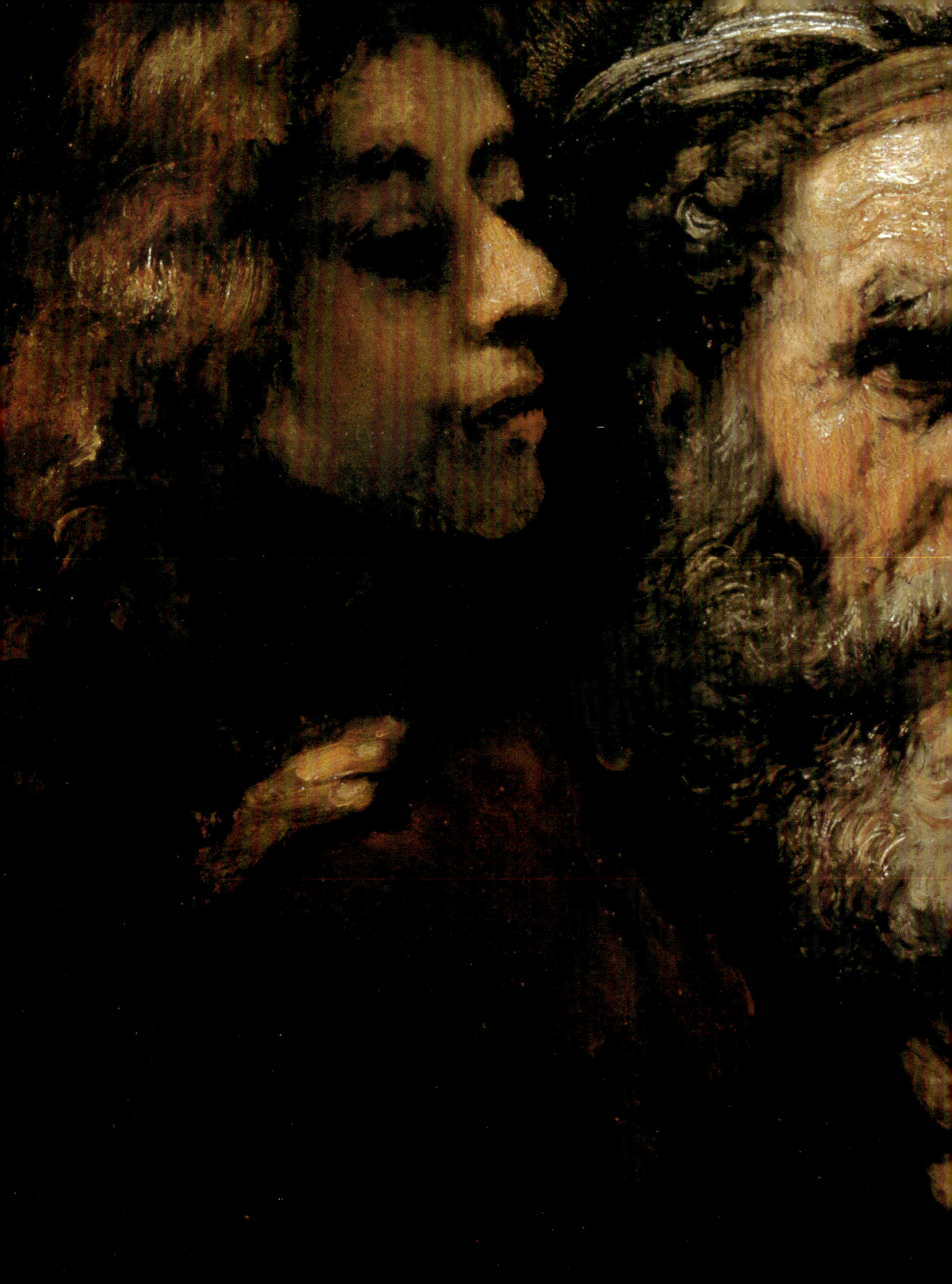

that he sought to convey their physical reality as well as the spiritual character of their encounter.

While the emotional power of the exchange is unique to Rembrandt, the idea of depicting the angel whispering inspiration into the evangelist's ear was probably not the master's invention. In 1656 Barent Fabritius (1624–1673), an artist who often painted under the sway of Rembrandt, similarly portrayed *The Evangelist Matthew* poised to write as he received guidance from an angel (fig. 2).[4] The most direct compositional prototype for *The Evangelist Matthew and the Angel* is found in Rembrandt's own work, in his etching of the Mennonite calligrapher Lieven Willemsz van Coppenol and his grandson, which the master executed c. 1658–1660 (fig. 3).[5] In this print Rembrandt depicted the master calligrapher's grandson looking over the elder man's shoulder in a manner not unlike that of the angel in the Louvre painting: just as Matthew

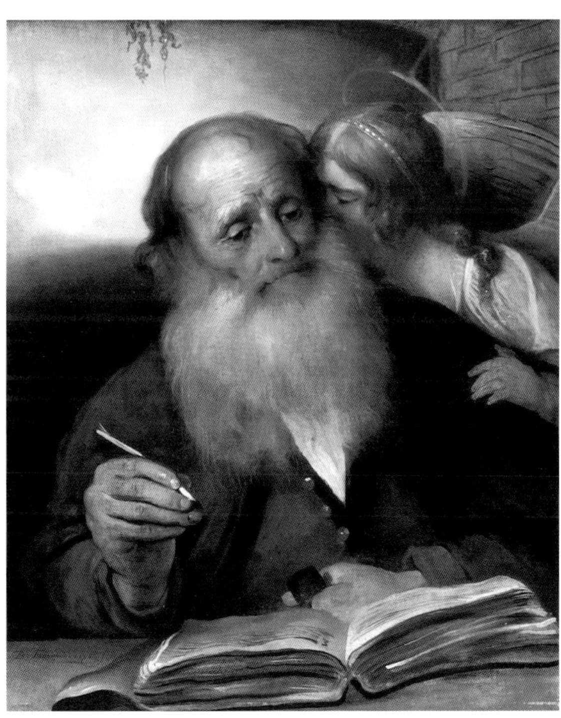

2
Barent Fabritius
The Evangelist Matthew
1656, oil on canvas, The Montreal Museum of Fine Arts, Gift of Mr. and Mrs. Michal Hornstein in honor of Frederik J. Duparc

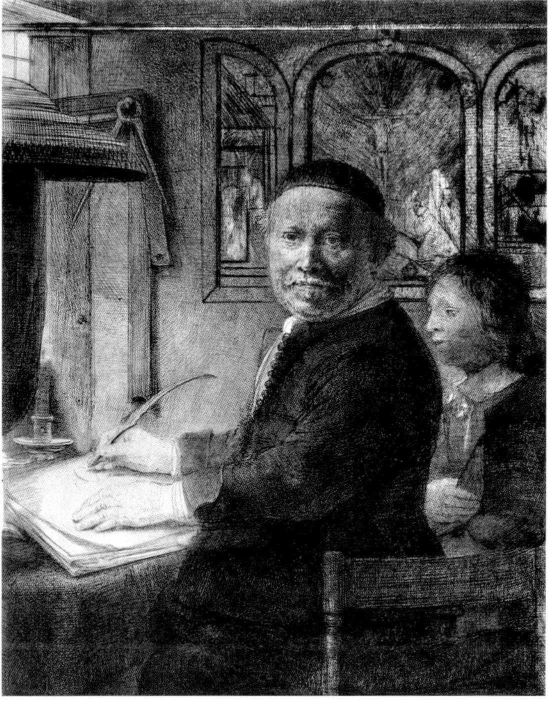

3
Rembrandt van Rijn
Lieven van Coppenol with His Grandson
c. 1658, etching, burin, and drypoint (4th state), The British Museum, London

is not cognizant of the source of his divine inspiration, Van Coppenol seems unaware of his grandson's presence. In the second state of the print, Rembrandt introduced a T-square on the back wall, an object not only appropriate to the calligrapher's needs but also the attribute generally given to Saint Matthew because of the factual, objective character of his Gospel.[6] By the fourth state of the etching Rembrandt made the religious associations of the image of Coppenol and his grandson quite explicit, for he introduced a triptych on the back wall containing scenes of the Annunciation, Crucifixion, and Resurrection.[7] Whether the fact that Coppenol was a Mennonite played a role in the religious associations Rembrandt incorporated into his print is not known, but the possibility should not be entirely discounted.[8]

Although there is no way to be certain of the exact chronology of the paintings of apostles and evangelists executed by Rembrandt in 1661, the very personal nature of this image, including the use of Titus as a model for the angel, indicates it is likely that the master began his series with this work. One could even postulate that this image served as the springboard for his depiction of *The Apostle Bartholomew* (cat. 8), where the saint, similarly executed in thick impastos, contemplatively faces the viewer frontally with his hand to his chin, in a pose remarkably akin to that of Matthew. It may also be that Rembrandt knew the tradition that Bartholomew carried Saint Matthew's Gospel to the East, in and around present-day India, or that the two were even thought to have traveled together.[9] **AKW**

8 The Apostle Bartholomew

A seated man with craggy features, depicted half-length and facing forward, contemplates profound matters with grave, mournful solemnity. He rests his elbow on a stone table and firmly grasps his chin with his left hand. In his right, he grips a short knife, which provides the clue to his identity. Strong light falls across his body, throwing the deep creases of his brow, cavernous eye sockets, and wrinkled hand into relief. His smooth, dark hair, cut short above the ears, contrasts with his wiry mustache. He is dressed in a gray-brown high-collared tunic laced at the midriff and a shirred white shirt; a russet cloak rests on his shoulders and falls over the front of the table. On the wall behind him, a cupboard or window has been roughly indicated.

Saint Bartholomew, like Saint Paul, was one of the few subjects in the late group of saints repeated by Rembrandt, revealing his interest in the apostle who suffered his martyrdom by being skinned alive. The San Diego *Apostle Bartholomew* (cat. 3), painted four years earlier, is larger and depicts the saint in a more agitated mode. While the Getty *Apostle Bartholomew* appears contained and reserved by comparison, it is one of Rembrandt's most arresting treatments of the late apostles, in which the portrait and historical subject lie in uneasy resolution. The saint was painted directly from a model without translation into a type, as in the San Diego canvas. His distinctive features have been retained, from the slightly round, dark eyes, to the expressively raised brow and protruding ears. The vividness with which Rembrandt has portrayed Bartholomew's lined forehead and slightly sagging features conveys a remarkable immediacy that forges a connection with the viewer.

Rembrandt had used similar frontal placements of the figure increasingly throughout the 1650s, utilizing the structural effect of broad brushwork and a muted palette to underscore the monumental solidity of his subjects. The apostle's strict frontal position may result from Rembrandt's work on several canvases during 1661 and the desire for a variety of poses among related compositions. Bartholomew's short hair, for example, though not unusual, appears particularly severe from this vantage. The pose in the Getty canvas, however, seems intended to present Bartholomew the man without impediment, and in particular to offer his face and hand for scrutiny. The chin-in-hand gesture, with its connotations of contemplation and even melancholy, had long been employed by the artist, beginning with the early *Saint Paul in Prison,* 1627 (see cat. 2, fig. 1), where the saint's uncertain ruminations are supported by the thorough description of an intellectual's paraphernalia. A number of drawings from the 1630s, for example *Portrait of a Young Man in a Flat Cap* (Ben. 435), appear to be rendered from life, and the gesture recurs in later compositions, such as the *Portrait of a Young Man Resting His Chin on His Hand (Titus, the Artist's Son),* 1660 (The Baltimore Museum of Art), but received its most sensitive treatment in *Titus at His Writing Desk* (fig. 1).[1]

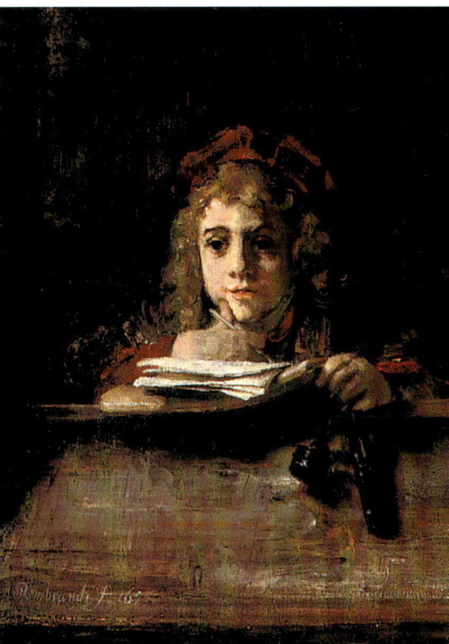

1
Rembrandt van Rijn
Titus at His Writing Desk
1655, oil on canvas,
Museum Boijmans Van Beuningen, Rotterdam

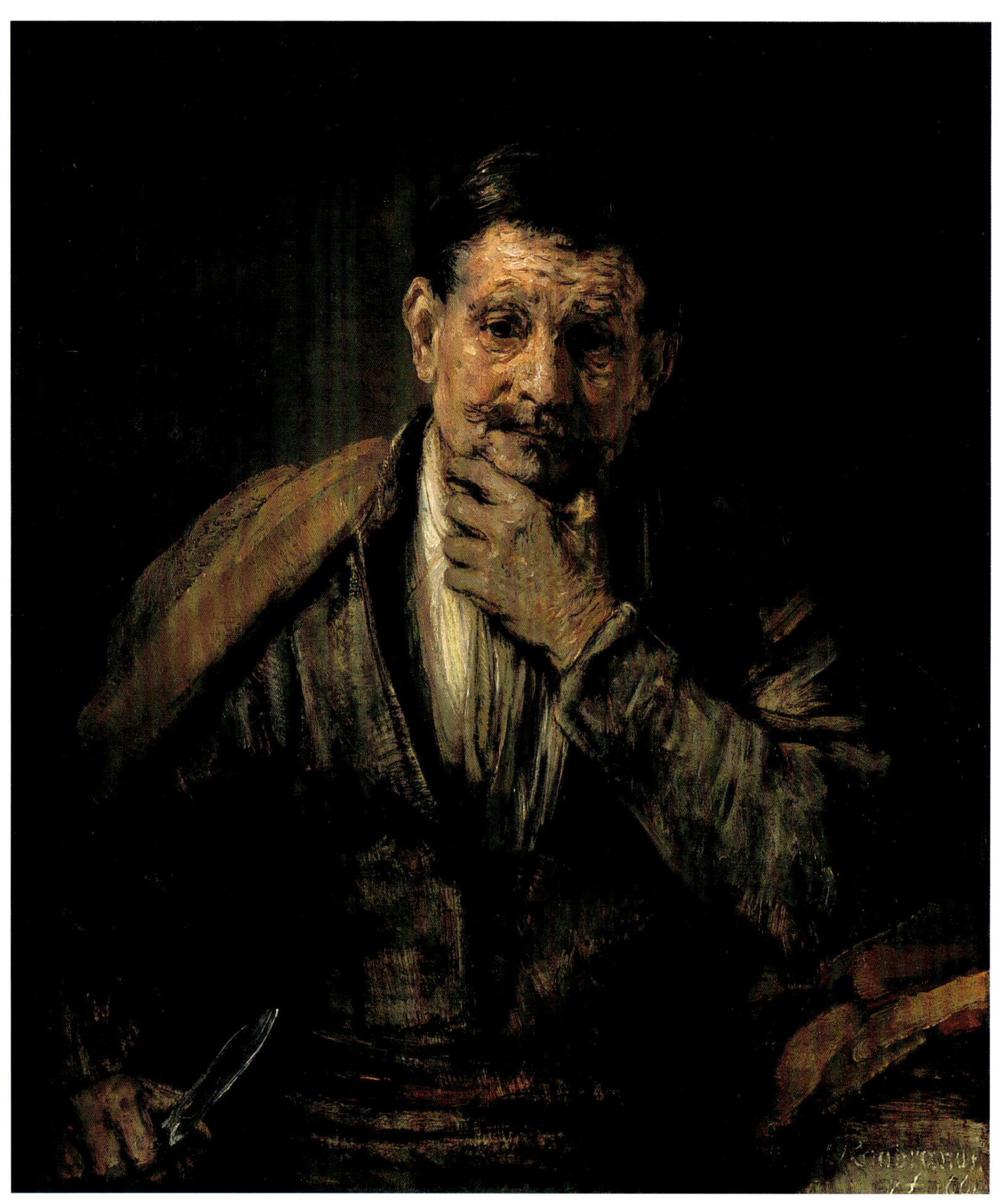

The Apostle Bartholomew, 1661
oil on canvas, 86.7 × 75.6 (34 1/8 × 29 3/4)
The J. Paul Getty Museum, Los Angeles

As in *The Evangelist Matthew and the Angel* (cat. 7) and *The Apostle James the Major* (cat. 9), Rembrandt used a range of brushwork to convey the solemn profundity of his subject. Bartholomew's torso is remarkable for the relatively thin application of paint. While the short, thick, impasted strokes that sculpt the face of Bartholomew are perhaps most similar to those in the face of Matthew, the broken, unblended brushwork is not duplicated among others in the group (fig. 2). The left hand, though textured, is less densely painted than the face. Here, the skin has a looser quality that, combined with its drab tonality, hints at advanced age or even death. The centrality of the hand and the compelling description of the skin, therefore, allude to the saint's ultimate sacrifice by flaying. By contrast, the right hand, which holds the knife, is merely indicated with patchy strokes of red and ocher.

While the frankness of Rembrandt's portrayal has appealed to the modern sensibilities of succeeding periods, it has also served to obscure the subject. The painting was treated as a genre piece when it was engraved in the eighteenth century, first by Richard Houston while part of the holdings of the collector and occasional *marchand-amateur* John Blackwood, under the title *Rembrandt's Cook,* 1757, and later by Charles Phillips, as *The Assassin.*[2] Richard Payne Knight, an enthusiastic collector of Rembrandt's work who also owned the *Rest on the Flight into Egypt* (Br. 540) and the then-famous *Holy Family* (Br. 568), both now considered studio works, probably displayed *The Apostle Bartholomew* in the Adams interior of his Shropshire residence, Downton Castle. Whether he recognized its subject or knew Sir Joshua Reynolds' painting (cat. 3) is unknown. *The Apostle Bartholomew* was exhibited in the late nineteenth century by Payne Knight's descendants with the title *Rembrandt's Cook* or *Man with a Knife,* before Adolf Rosenberg's tentative identification as *Saint Bartholomew (?).*[3] Wilhelm von Bode, recognizing the interplay of portrait and historical subject in this canvas, reasoned "that Rembrandt... intended to characterize his sitter as the Apostle, St. Bartholomew, by the knife in his hand seems to me improbable, in view of the pronounced portrait-like character of the sitter."[4] After the 1929 London exhibition, Sir Joseph Duveen, who had tried unsuccessfully to acquire the picture from the Boughton-Knight family some years earlier, described it as "'Rembrandt St. Bartholomew'... painted in Rembrandt's best year, namely 1661, but most depressing in colour being almost of a monochrome browny grey colour, and the subject is also objectionable."[5] The identification of the subject as Saint Bartholomew was not firmly established until the Rembrandt exhibition of 1956.[6]

Rembrandt's awareness of and familiarity with Mennonite values may explain the artist's conception of the saint. Thieleman Jansz van Braght's *Martyrs' Mirror,* which appeared in 1660, offers a vivid description of the saint's life, emphasizing his preaching in faraway heathen lands, his conversion of leading figures, and his resolute acceptance of his fate (see also Wheelock essay). The tenets of the Mennonite faith included a tradition of directness and appeal to the common man, and an appreciation of ordinary individuals of extraordinary faith. Here, Rembrandt achieved a unique elision of the everyday with the spiritual, creating, in effect, a new exemplar. ATW

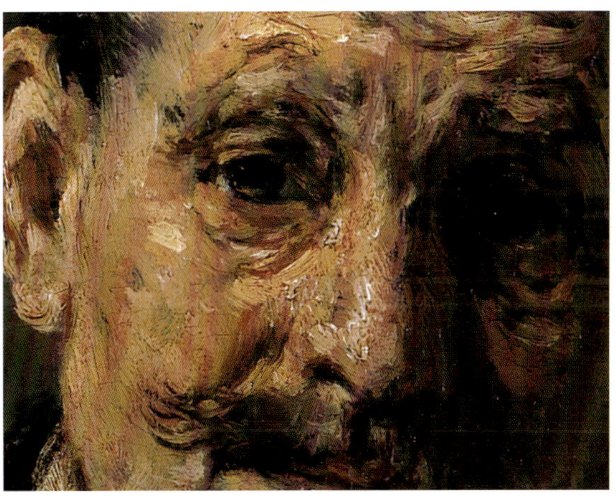

2
Rembrandt van Rijn
The Apostle Bartholomew
brushwork, left eye
(detail, cat. 8)

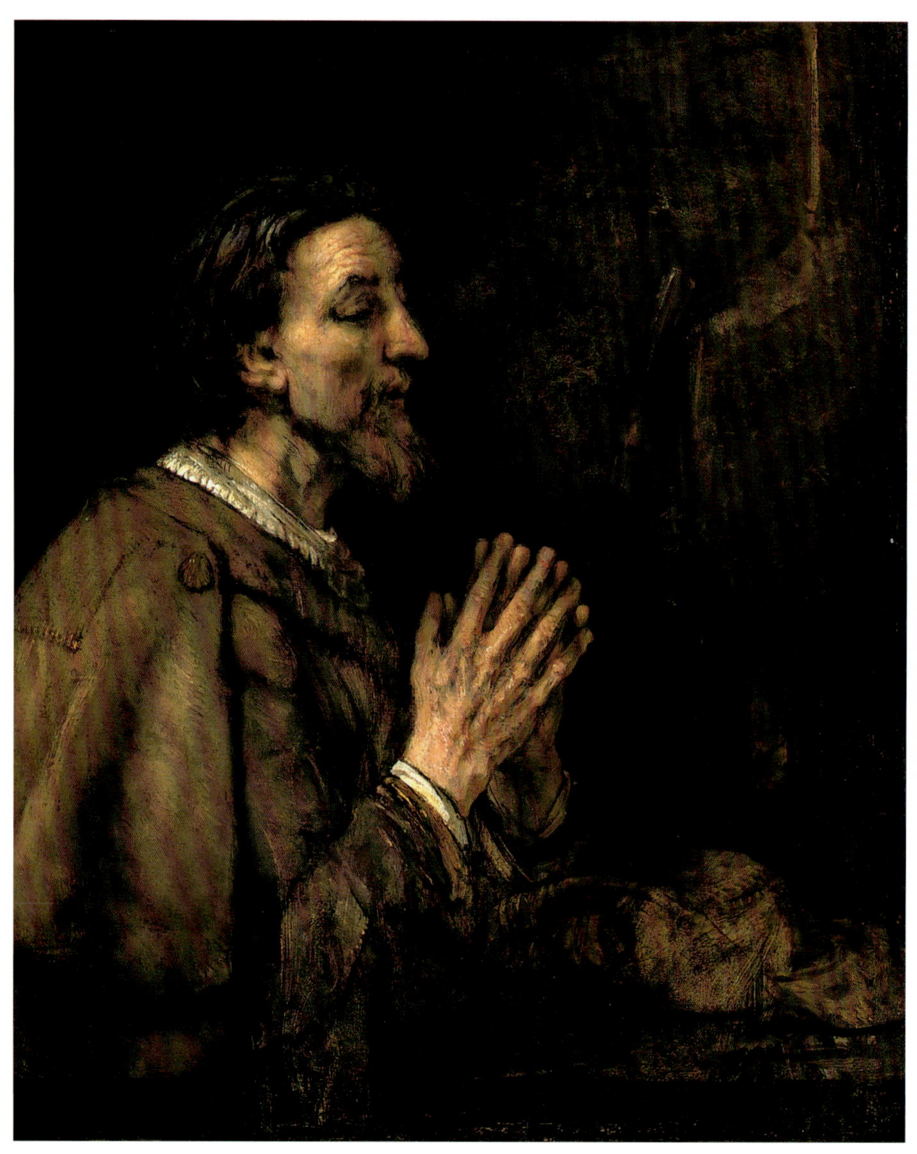

The Apostle James the Major, 1661
oil on canvas, original canvas: 92.1 × 74.9 (36 ¼ × 29 ½)
Private collection

9 The Apostle James the Major

A pilgrim is depicted in profile, at half-length, and turned to the viewer's right. His dark-brown, matted hair is parted in the middle, and he has a drawn and weathered face, a thin, projecting beard, and large hands that are clasped in prayer. His long fingers are splayed, extended stiffly, and interlocked at the tips. Over a shirred white shirt he wears a heavy brown cloak with a short cape, which is fastened at the right shoulder with a scallop. The sleeves of his cloak are worn and there is a patch on his cape. His coarsely stitched hat rests on the table, its broad brim upturned and fastened by a second shell. The pilgrim's wooden staff, burnished from miles of use, rests against a stone wall behind him.

Among the first to publish the work, both Émile Michel and Wilhelm von Bode regarded the subject as an anonymous pilgrim, but Cornelis Hofstede de Groot identified him as Saint James, which has been accepted by virtually all later authors. Saint James (the Major) was a fisherman of Galilee, the brother of Saint John the Evangelist, and an apostle.[1] He was among the men closest to Christ and was present with Saints Peter and John at both the Transfiguration and the Agony in the Garden. The historical James was tried in Jerusalem and executed in AD 44 by Herod Agrippa. His martyrdom is reported in the scriptures (Acts 12:2). Yet much of his persona is dependent not upon the Bible or history but on a series of legends dating from the Middle Ages that tell of his mission to Spain and burial there. His supposed tomb was discovered around the ninth century at Compostela, which had become a pilgrimage site next in importance only to Jerusalem and Rome by the eleventh century. From the thirteenth century onward, Saint James was often depicted as a pilgrim with a staff, wearing a cloak and broad-brimmed hat with the pilgrim's attribute, the scallop shell. Naturally a great favorite among Spanish painters, he also was often shown with a thin beard and dark-brown hair parted in the middle and falling to either side, in the manner of images of Christ.

This painting is one of a group of images by Rembrandt, several also signed and dated 1661, of half-length apostles and evangelists that are among the most soulful and brooding of all the master's works. While most of Rembrandt's paintings of apostles and evangelists depict the sitter frontally or in three-quarter profile, *The Apostle James the Major* is exceptional in being shown in strict profile. As Albert Blankert noted, Rembrandt rarely rendered figures in either portraits or history paintings in profile view, and then sometimes only because it was dictated by the terms of a commission.[2] Most of his profile images were executed during the early 1630s, among them the *Young Woman* of 1632 (Nationalmuseum, Stockholm), and *Saskia* of 1633-1634 (Staatliche Kunstsammlungen, Kassel); we also include the *Flora* of c. 1654-1655 (The Metropolitan Museum of Art, New York).[3] In his early history paintings, such as *Belshazzar's Feast* of c. 1634-1635, the use of this device enabled him by design to call visual attention to the protagonist in the action.[4] His early etchings also include head studies (*tronijen*) in profile.[5] He only returned to the practice of depicting historical figures in profile twenty years later with his *Man in Armor* of 1655 (Art Gallery and Museum, Glasgow).[6] Profile views often figure among his twenty-one copies after Moghul miniatures from the mid-1650s.[7] Significantly for the present work, in several

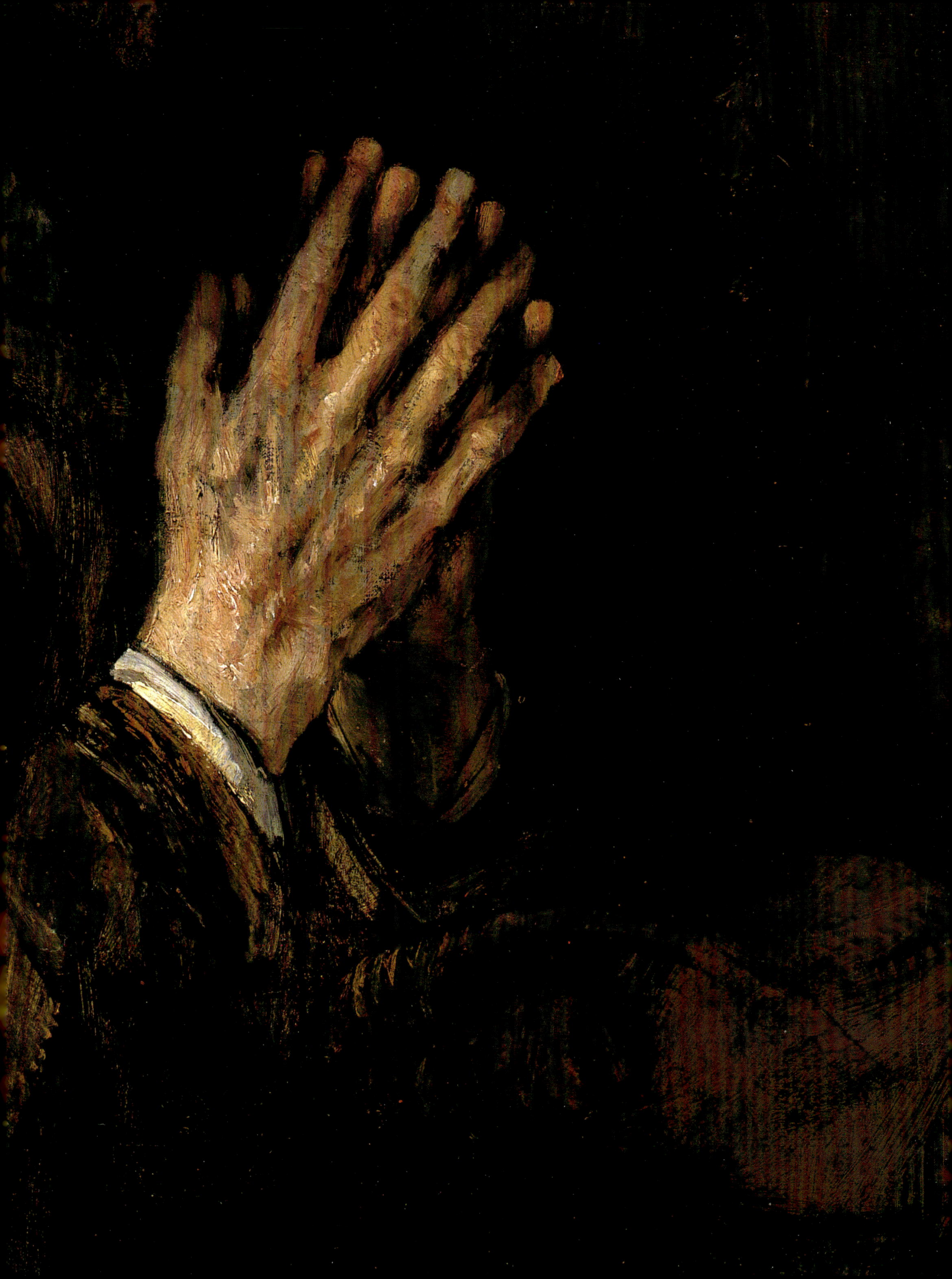

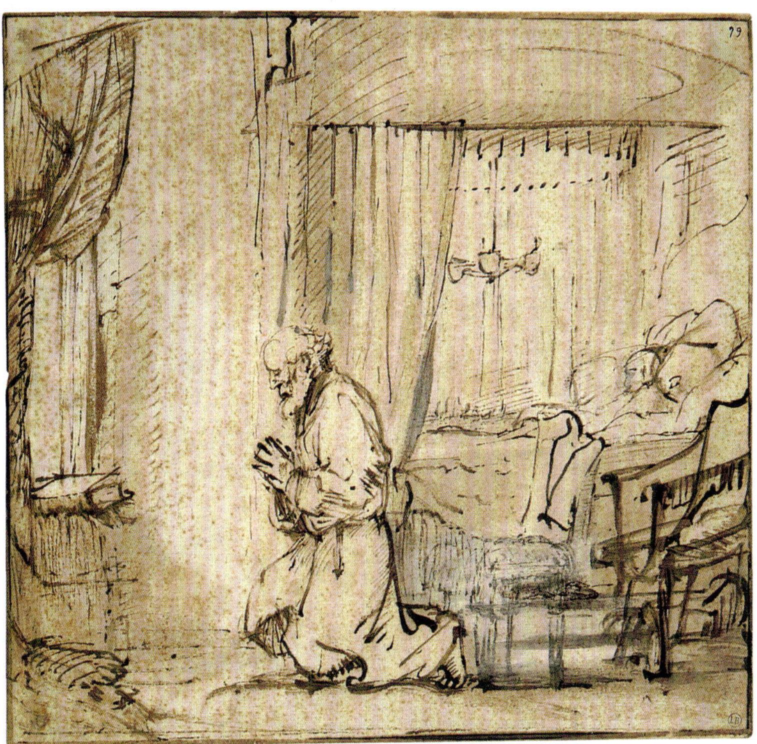

1
Rembrandt van Rijn
The Apostle Peter's Prayer before the Raising of Tabatha
c. 1654–1655, reed pen and wash, Musée Bonnat, Bayonne

drawings from these years, figures in prayer are also shown in profile; see, for example, *The Apostle Peter's Prayer before the Raising of Tabatha* (Acts 9:40) (fig. 1).[8]

The profile view of Saint James in prayer has the effect of recalling time-honored, iconic images of figures in attitudes of devotion, not simply praying saints and other devotees in altarpieces, but also their donors; Otto Benesch observed that Saint James "reminds us...of a donor in a Gothic panel painting."[9] The pose surely contributes to Rembrandt's success in capturing what von Bode praised as "the pilgrim's personality, his ascetic features and the fervid devotion that fascinated the master."[10] The locus of that devotion is concentrated in the saint's joined hands — those tented, fanned, and bristling fingers, fairly trembling with faith and fervor, which offer the external embodiment of all the electrifying passion of his interior devotion.[11] **PCS**

10 The Apostle Simon

This image of Saint Simon represents an apostle about whom, as is the case with Saint Bartholomew, little is known. He is described in the Gospel of Luke (Luke 6:15) as Simon the Zealot, but nothing more is said of him in the Bible. According to the *Golden Legend,* however, after the death of Christ Simon traveled through Syria and Mesopotamia, where he and Saint Jude preached the message of the Gospel. Rembrandt conceived of Saint Simon as a physically powerful patriarch with reddish-brown beard and loose, graying curls, which the artist scratched out with the blunt end of the brush. Looking downward, quietly withdrawn as though preoccupied with his thoughts, Simon rests his left hand on the horizontal handle of a large cross saw, the symbol of his martyrdom.[1]

In this painting Rembrandt effectively used largely monochrome colors to reinforce the scene's deeply brooding mood. The somber tonalities of the apostle's loosely draped brown cloak, and those of the freely brushed background, create a subdued ambiance that resonates with the saint's worldly and spiritual concerns.[2] Rembrandt contrasted these areas, where he suggested the saint's emotions through rushing brushstrokes, with the stark horizontal and vertical forms that define the saw upon which Simon rests his arm. These strong, angular shapes seem to anchor the saint's thoughts to the reality of his impending martyrdom, which, to judge from the familiar manner in which he holds the saw under his arm, he has accepted with resignation and equanimity.

The model who sat for this work had also sat some four years earlier for Rembrandt's equally brooding painting *The Apostle Bartholomew* (cat. 3). In both instances, Rembrandt emphasized the man's physical strength by casting light not only on his massive head but also on his large and strong hands. Rembrandt's Saint Simon is a laborer rather than a scholar, a man in whose hands a saw looks more comfortable than a pen. Simon thus served a specific function in the group of apostles and evangelists that Rembrandt created in 1661 — he is shown as a rugged individual, less aesthetic than Saint James, less contemplative than Saint Bartholomew, less conflicted than Saint Paul, and less inspired than Saint Matthew. Of all the apostles, he was the one who could speak directly to the common man and who could communicate emotionally in ways that the others could not.

This painting, which came to light in England only in the late 1940s, has strengthened the conviction, first articulated by Frederik Schmidt-Degener in 1919 and by Wilhelm R. Valentiner in 1920, that Rembrandt conceived of a loosely organized series of apostles and evangelists in the late 1650s and early 1660s.[3] Saint Simon is a figure only rarely encountered in Dutch and Flemish art, and then exclusively as part of an apostle series, as those by Peter Paul Rubens (see fig. 1) and Anthony van Dyck. As Ludwig Münz has noted, moreover, this painting and *The Evangelist Matthew and the Angel* (cat. 7) share an intriguing characteristic that draws them even closer together than their similar subjects, canvas sizes, and painting techniques. Each work features a black, painted framing edge that denotes the composition's parameters.[4] As this edge is missing along the top edge of *The Apostle Simon,* it is probable that the painting has been slightly trimmed in this dimension.

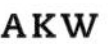

AKW

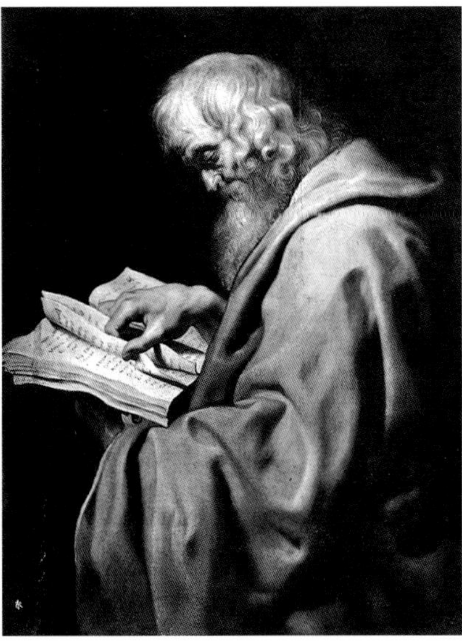

1
Sir Peter Paul Rubens
The Apostle Simon
c. 1610, oil on panel, Museo del Prado, Madrid

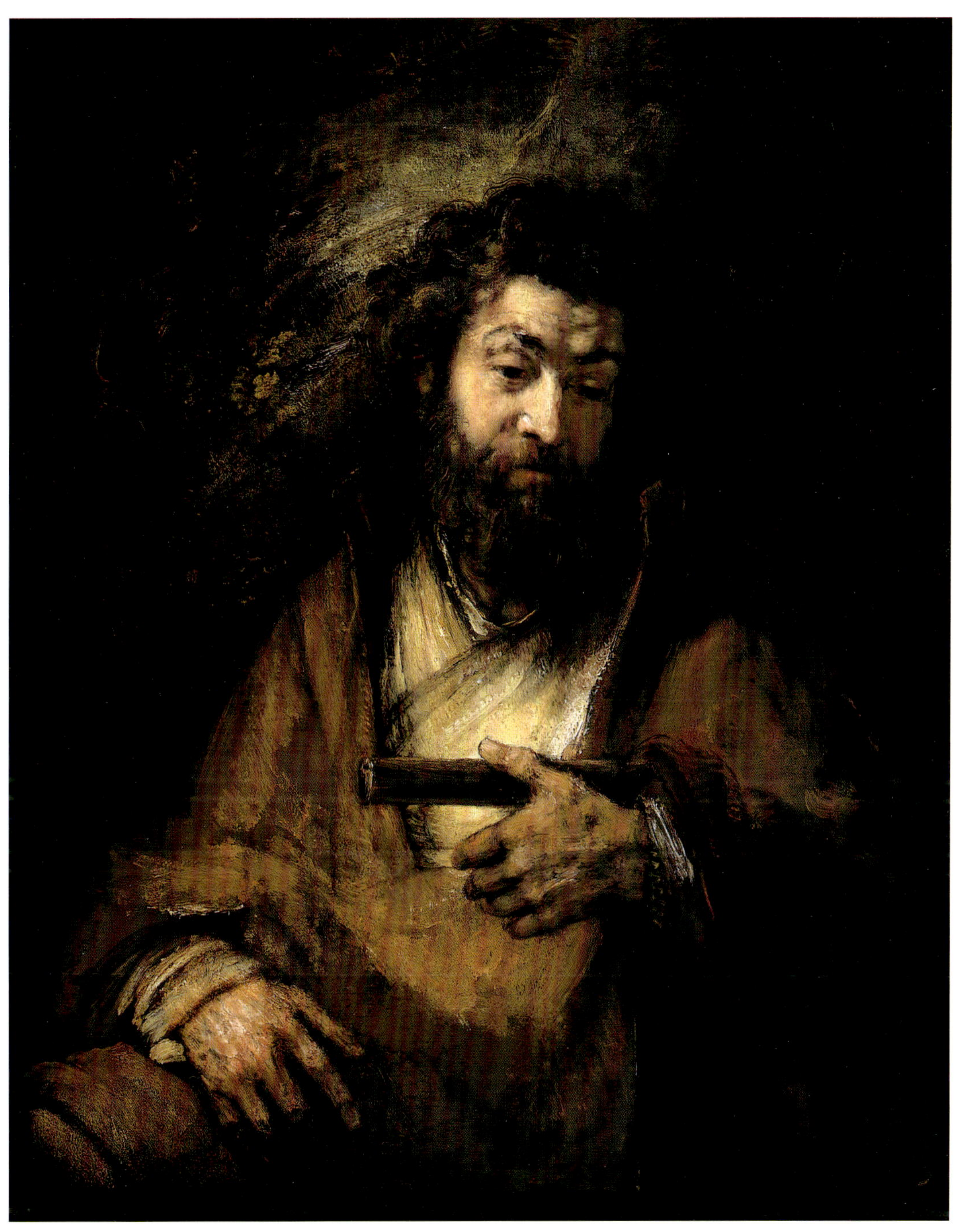

The Apostle Simon, 1661
oil on canvas, 98.3 × 79 (38 11/16 × 31 1/8)
Kunsthaus Zürich,
Stiftung Prof. L. Ruzicka

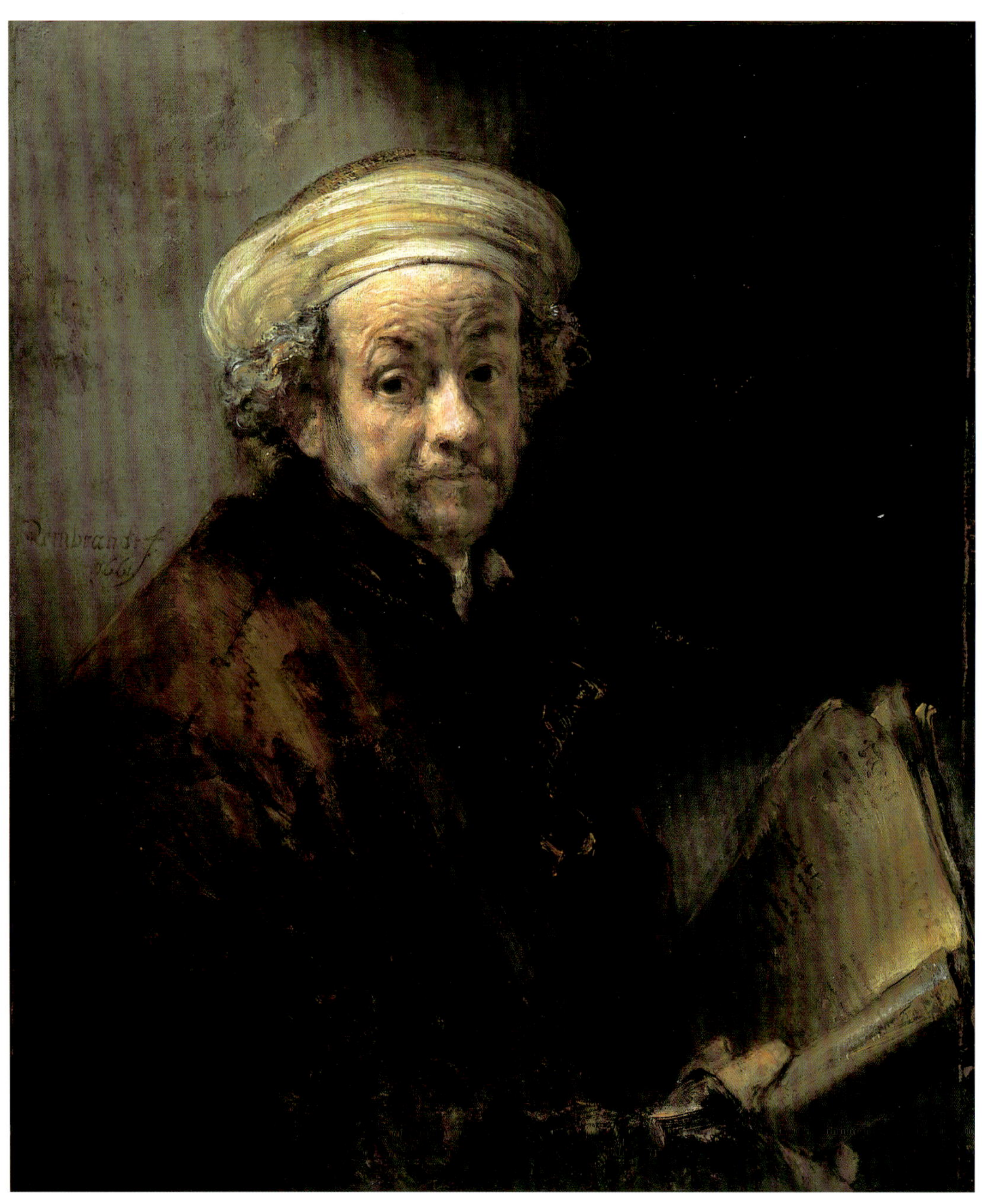

Self-Portrait as the Apostle Paul, 1661
oil on canvas, 91 × 77 (35 $^{13}/_{16}$ × 30 $^{5}/_{16}$)
Rijksmuseum, Amsterdam

11 Self-Portrait as the Apostle Paul

In this painting, the culmination of Rembrandt's depictions of apostles and evangelists, the artist explicitly acknowledges his personal identification with Saint Paul, who is for him the most important of these historical figures. As in the paintings of the apostle in Washington (cat. 2) and London (cat. 4), Rembrandt here defines this historical persona with his attributes — a manuscript, indicative of Paul's role as a preacher of the Gospel, and a sword, symbol of his martyrdom. This painting, however, is fundamentally different from the other images of the apostle. Far from being a quiet and contemplative individual, peering out but looking inward, Rembrandt as Saint Paul stares directly at the viewer, engaging us with his open and somewhat quizzical expression. In contrast to its placement in the other paintings, the apostle's text is no longer considered just by him alone but is turned toward the viewer, as though being offered for our personal review. Finally, the sword of Saint Paul's martyrdom rests not against the wall but protrudes from his doublet, a boldly assertive statement about the dire consequences of his apostolic teachings.[2]

The Rembrandt/Saint Paul in this painting seems quite unheroic, even though light shines brilliantly on his face and white headpiece. His features are swollen and misshapen, his nose is too large, his chin too weak. The hair that protrudes over his ears from his white turban-shaped hat is scraggly, as are his soft beard and mustache. Adding to the quizzical character of his expression is the broad manner in which Rembrandt executed the face, where rough brushstrokes filled with a variety of flesh tones suggest but do not precisely define features such as the eyes, nose, and mouth. Yet we are drawn to this head, not only by the engagement of Rembrandt's gaze, but also by the impasto of the paint and the focus of the light. In contrast, the pages of the manuscript that Rembrandt/Saint Paul reveals to us are dimly lit, with a text too undefined to read.[3]

How is one to explain the wide-open eyes and raised eyebrows of Rembrandt's/Paul's expression, and the artist's unusual placement of the saint's attributes?[4] The Paul represented here does not give the impression of a formidable thinker, one capable, even when confined to the four walls of a prison cell, of articulating the powerful words that formulated essential Christian tenets following the death of Christ.[5] It is equally difficult to imagine him as a leader of men, one whose commanding presence helped spread the Gospel in his missions to Asia Minor, Cyprus, Macedonia, and Achaea. Rather, the apostle Paul with whom Rembrandt identified was that flawed human, the man who once was Saul, the man who somehow, on the way to Damascus, had found favor in God's eye. He had received the gift of grace that he did not deserve, and the realization of that gift continued to bewilder and amaze him until his dying days.[6]

Without a specific written explanation from the artist, it is impossible to determine the full range of associations Rembrandt felt with Saint Paul and the reasons he painted this *portrait historié* at this stage of his life. Whatever psychological and spiritual identifications he may have felt with the apostle himself, Paul's message about the supremacy of grace over law must have resonated with the artist. Throughout his life, and particularly in the mid-to-late 1650s, Rembrandt seems to have felt constricted by the law, whether municipal or religious (see Wheelock essay), and felt no less beholden to artistic "laws." It was with good reason that Adriaen Pels described Rembrandt in 1681 as the "foremost heretic in the art of painting."[7] Thus, at a period when he was busily engaged in depicting apostles and evangelists, it seems almost inevitable that he would create this profound visual expression of his own quest to understand both the mysteries of life and the Christian message.

This painting was among the core paintings that Frederik Schmidt-Degener, Wilhelm R. Valentiner, and Otto Benesch identified as belonging to their proposed series of apostles and evangelists.[8] It is, in fact, rather similar in dimensions to *The Evangelist Matthew and the Angel* (cat. 7), *The Apostle Bartholomew* (cat. 8), *The Apostle Simon* (cat. 10), and *The Apostle James the Minor (?)* (cat. 12), all of which date to the same year. Curiously, Rembrandt outlined all five paintings with a sort of framing device: scratched lines defining the parameters of the painting exist on all sides of this work, whereas black, painted borders appear on the other four works.[9] No early provenance information provides any evidence that these paintings, or any of the paintings associated with this purported series, ever hung together. AKW

SCHOOL OF REMBRANDT VAN RIJN

12 The Apostle James the Minor(?)

A young man is viewed half-length and almost frontally. His reddish-blond hair, parted in the middle, falls to his shoulders, and he has a thin beard and mustache. He gazes serenely out at the viewer with large, dark eyes. Over a white chemise he wears an ample russet-colored cloak, and he rests both hands on a staff or club. Over the back of his head falls a short black veil with a red fringe. Behind the figure, to the right, is a stout column with the suggestion of a plaque or inscription at the top. The object just above the figure's hands has mistakenly been interpreted as "the Tau-shaped stick of a pilgrim,"[1] but it is in fact a fastener for the man's garment.[2]

The subject of the picture has been much discussed. The traditional identification of the figure as Christ, offered at least as early as 1838 by John Smith, who titled the work *The Savior,* has been widely accepted by most twentieth-century scholars, including Wilhelm R. Valentiner, who believed that the picture formed part of an apostle series.[3] In 1956 Otto Benesch, who also identified the figure as Christ, developed the poetic idea of Christ as a divine pilgrim. He described the figure as "Christ the teacher in the Synagogue, wearing a black headcloth, standing beside a heavy inscribed tablet. His face is radiant hazy pink and his reddish hair turns into pure gold. The figure conveys the feeling of the magical and strange. Not only is Christ's garment that of a traveler from a distant Eastern land but his type is foreign, aloof, belonging to another world, which is always to Rembrandt the world of the Spirit."[4] Benesch's interpretation of the figure is reflected in the title given this painting at the Metropolitan Museum of Art: *Christ with a Pilgrim's Staff.*[5] A differing interpretation was given by Hans-Martin Rotermund, who also wrote about this painting in 1956. Rotermund asserted that the model did not conform to Rembrandt's Christ-type, in large part because the figure seems to have blond hair.[6] He concluded that the figure was a Jewish pilgrim and suggested that the column in the background recalled the columns of the Portuguese Jewish Synagogue in Amsterdam.[7] Despite Rotermund's assertion, the figure's youthful appearance and shoulder-length hair, parted in the middle, do conform to Rembrandt's other images of Christ (see cat. 6, fig. 1).[8]

In fact, little about the figure's costume confirms his identity as a pilgrim. While he wears a traveler's heavy cape or cloak, he has neither the broad-brimmed hat nor the shell that appears as a pilgrim's attribute in *The Apostle James the Major* (cat. 9), and his staff is not as tall as those traditionally carried by pilgrims. Moreover, nothing in the setting suggests a site on the road to Emmaus where the Risen Christ appeared to his disciples as a pilgrim. Nevertheless, H. von Einem and others, including most recently Walter A. Liedtke, have claimed that the present work depicts the Risen Christ, likening it to the painting in Munich (cat. 6).[9] Yet the picture from the Alte Pinakothek depicts Christ bare-chested, still wearing his winding cloth like a royal mantle and crowned with a halo, which was probably added by a later hand and augments the work's devotional conception. The Munich painting is a far more hieratic work than the present one, which has none of the attributes of the Salvator Mundi or of Christ as the Man of Sorrows.

Wilhelm von Bode suggested long ago that the figure might depict not Christ but the Apostle James the Minor, a view that was fully endorsed by Christian Tümpel and acknowledged as a possibility by Christopher Wright, although none elaborated on its justification.[10] The variability of the saint's attributes seemed to defy certainty.[11] The account of the saint's appearance and martyrdom in Jacobus de Voragine's *Golden Legend (Legenda Aurea)* of the late thirteenth century, however, lends considerable support to this identification.[12] James was the son of Alpheus, the brother of Simon, and one of the Twelve Apostles. He is mentioned by Saint Paul (Galatians 1:19) and Flavius Josephus, but Jacobus de Voragine offers the fullest account, explaining that James was also known as the "Brother of the Lord." "Brother" could at the time refer to any male relation, and of course did not imply in this case a true sibling but reportedly was a sobriquet inspired by James' resemblance to Christ, which was so complete that they were often mistaken. The *Legend* goes on to claim that Christ's tormentors so feared seizing James by mistake that they ordered Judas to point out Jesus. After Paul's imprisonment and the transfer to Rome, the Pharisees turned their wrath upon James, summoning him to the pinnacle of the temple and asking him to renounce his faith and to order his followers to deny Jesus as the Messiah. When James volubly refused, he was thrown from the roof of the Temple, stoned, and finally killed by a blow to the head with a fuller's club.[13] James was also known as "James the Just," for his abstemious piety and administrative probity in his own life as the first Bishop of Jerusalem.

According to the *Legend*, the consequences of the martyrdom of James were dire and long-lasting: they entailed the destruction of Jerusalem and the dispersal of the Jews, to which the author devotes his only report in his account of James the Minor. Since the hilt of the staff or club upon which the present figure rests his hands is obscured and its full length incalculable, we cannot say positively whether it is a fuller's club, which was the object of James' martyrdom. Because of the figure's physical resemblance to Rembrandt's traditional Christ-type, and because the column at the back evokes the temple of the Pharisees, it seems probable that the painting depicts James the Minor.

The painting has long had its admirers. John Smith called it "a work of transcendent merit," and the author of the Codrington Sale in 1843 praised it as "a capital piece of great merit, full of dignity and expression."[14] It was accepted as the work of Rembrandt until the dealer and collector, Daan Cevat, suggested in 1966 that it was "not entirely by Rembrandt," and Joos Bruyn of the Rembrandt Research Project suggested it might be by Rembrandt with studio participation.[15] The first published rejection of the picture was made by Maryan Ainsworth in 1982.[16] Ainsworth states that technological inconsistencies in the buildup of the paint suggested that it was not by the master himself but by an artist familiar with the artist's techniques and style. Since then the work has been defended, by Christopher Brown and Tümpel, among others, as an autograph original.[17]

While the painting makes a noble and monumental impression overall, the brushwork is not as assured and descriptive as Rembrandt's. It has painterly flourishes and even specific techniques associated with the late Rembrandt, notably the use of the butt-end of the brush to enliven the figure's hair as well as the passage of his right shoulder. The wet-over-wet manner of painting, and the rubbing out and scratching into the paint in details, such as the apostle's white chemise and cloak, are also techniques found in Rembrandt's work. The result, however, is more a superficial display of bravura than a purposeful defining of form. Large expanses of unmodulated form go flaccid, especially in strong light, and in the shadowed areas we detect weak, even unintelligible parts. While some of the painterly techniques have been associated with Rembrandt's gifted late pupil, Arent de Gelder, the specific artist's hand has not been identified.[18] Interestingly, black, painted edges, similar to those seen in cats. 7, 8, and 10, are evident at the top and right sides. PCS

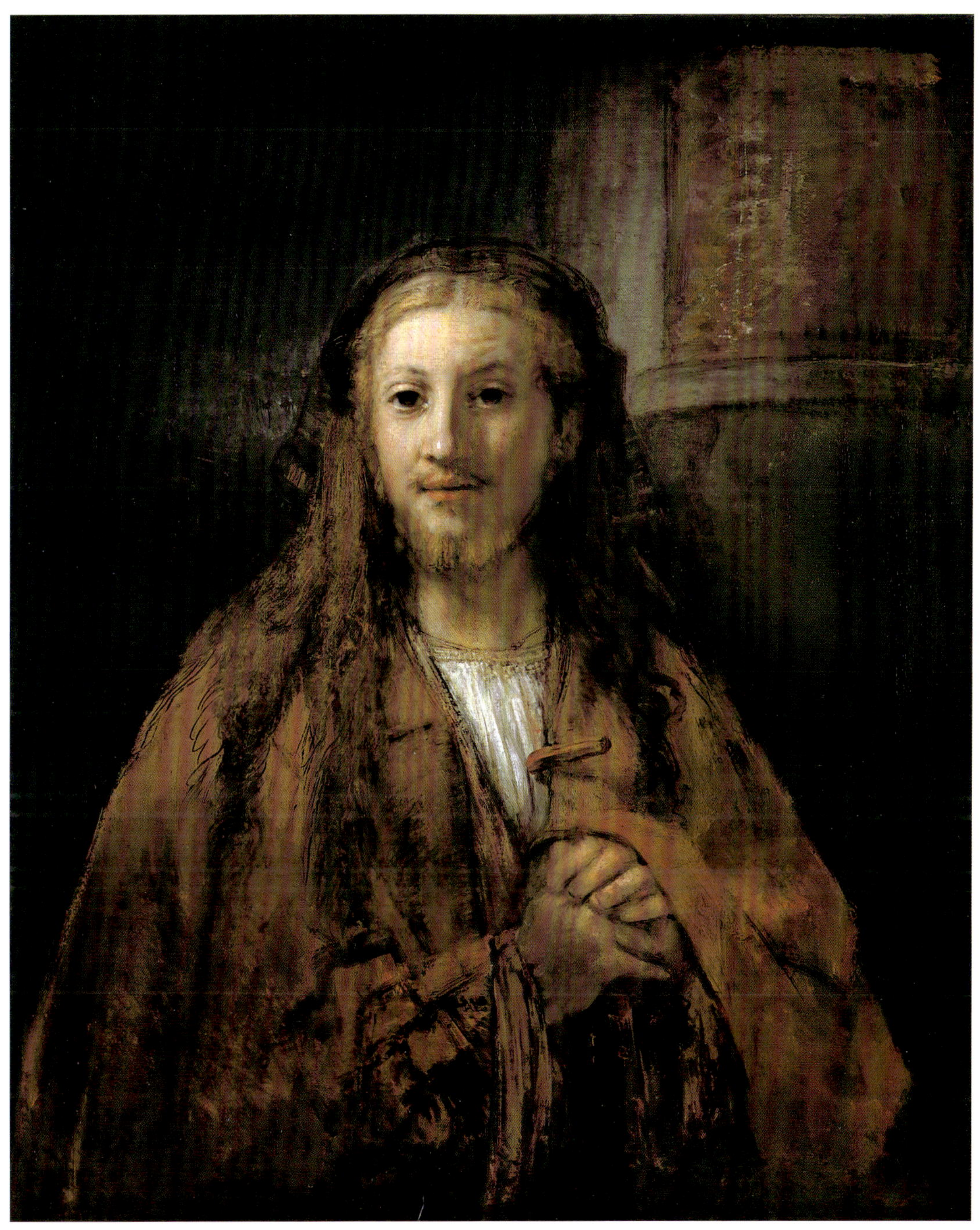

The Apostle James the Minor(?), 1661
oil on canvas, 95.3 × 82.6 (37 ½ × 32 ½)
Lent by The Metropolitan Museum of Art,
The Jules Bache Collection, 1949

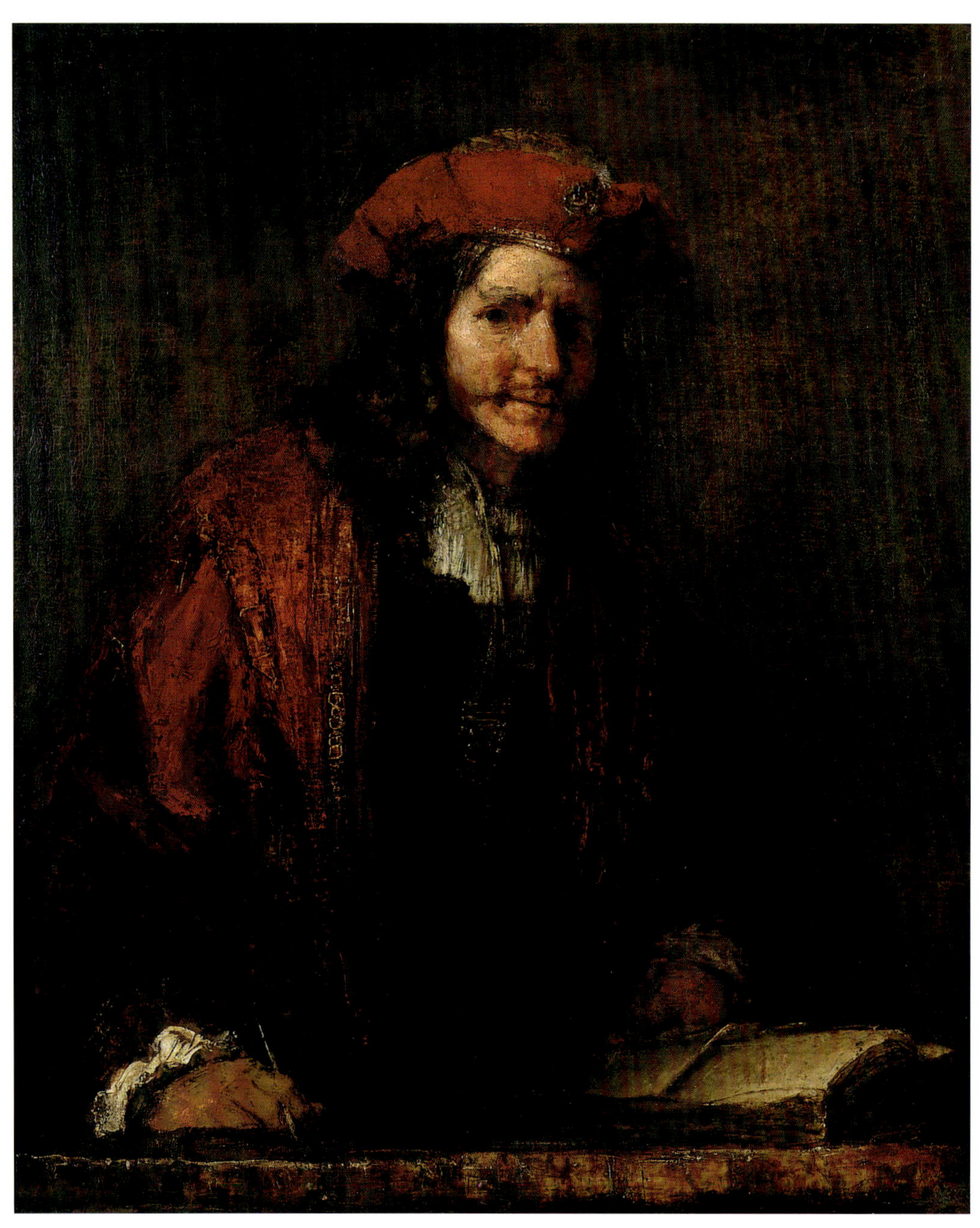

Man in a Red Cap (An Evangelist?), 1660
oil on canvas, 102 × 80 (40 3/16 × 31 1/2)
Museum Boijmans Van Beuningen, Rotterdam

13 Man in a Red Cap (An Evangelist?)

A gentleman with a pencil-thin mustache and shoulder-length brown hair is viewed half-length behind a desk with a book or ledger. He wears a red beret with a gold band and decoration at the crown, a rust-colored tabard over a black cloak, and a white shirt with collar and ample cuffs. In his right hand, which rests atop a small book, he holds a quill pen; his left hand is placed on a second, larger, open book. The low viewpoint that brings the edge of the table almost to eye level makes the pyramidal figure seem to rise dramatically above us.

John Smith described the painting simply as a portrait of a gentleman painted in a "free and bravura manner," but during most of the nineteenth century the figure was identified as an accountant or clerk, no doubt because of his books, quill pen, robes, and the desktop in the immediate foreground.[1] Cornelis Hofstede de Groot first identified him as "The Evangelist, also known as the Accountant."[2] This notion was developed by Wilhelm R. Valentiner, who described the figure as representing Saint Luke in his proposed series of evangelists and apostles, an idea that was subsequently followed by Christian Tümpel.[3] Otto Benesch believed that the evangelist was Saint John, who counts among his attributes a book or scroll.[4]

Jeroen Giltaij and Guido Jansen were the first to question the attribution to Rembrandt, citing "anomalies in the rendering of the man's face" and "weaknesses in the paint application and fall of light"; they demoted the painting to the product of an artist in Rembrandt's circle.[5] Since then, Ernst van de Wetering of the Rembrandt Research Project has reopened the possibility that the painting is by the master himself or by a pupil.[6] As Horst Gerson first cautioned, the problem in resolving the picture's attribution largely stems from its condition.[7] The paint surface has been extensively abraded, with the consequence that many of its details and glazes have been obliterated. Giltaij and Jansen observed that we can gauge the extent to which the form has been lost by comparing the picture to the image in a mezzotint after the work (fig. 1), executed in 1765 by the British artist William Humphrey (1740–1810). At that time the painting was in the possession of the renowned English artist and art theorist, Sir Joshua Reynolds (who also owned *The Apostle Bartholomew,* cat. 3).[8] Many of the details of the figure's robes, particularly the elaborate decoration in the garment cascading over his shoulder, his beret, and features of his face and hands, have been lost.

1
William Humphrey
after Rembrandt
Man in a Red Cap (An Evangelist?)
1765, mezzotint,
Collection Rijksbureau voor Kunsthistorische Dokumentatie (RKD),
The Hague

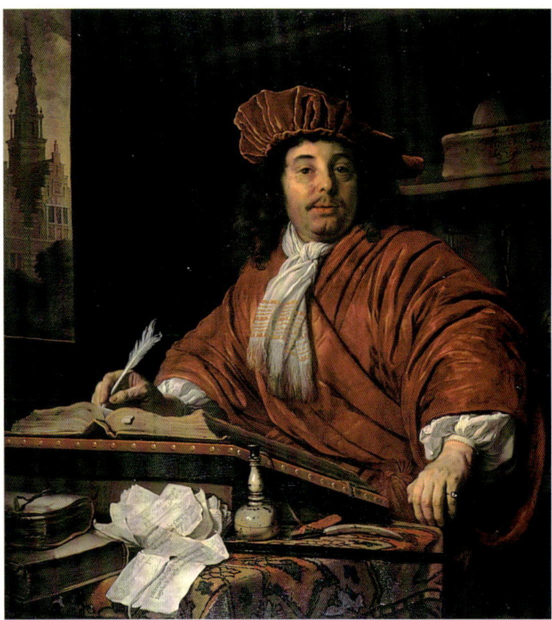

2
Bartholomeus
van der Helst
Portrait of
Daniel Bernhard
1669, oil on canvas,
Museum Boijmans
Van Beuningen,
Rotterdam

Challenging the view of the subject as a historical figure, Giltaij argued that there was nothing in the costume, gestures, or attributes of the figure to regard the image as anything other than the portrait of a professional, either a businessman or scholar.[9] He compares the figure seated at his desk with books and papers, with his red beret, ample housecoat, and rich linen, to Bartholomeus van der Helst's *Portrait of Daniel Bernhard* (fig. 2). Bernhard was a businessman, ship owner, and juror. Consequently, Giltaij titled the present work *Portrait of a Magistrate* and, without explanation, dated the painting several years later (c. 1665) than is customary. While the date need not be adjusted, the observation that the figure seems to have portrait features, a view seconded by Van de Wetering, raises the possibility that it may be a *portrait historié,* like the *Self-Portrait as the Apostle Paul* (cat. 11).[10] **PCS**

14 The Virgin of Sorrows

An elderly woman is viewed half-length and frontally, her arms crossed before her and her head inclined slightly to the left. She wears a long, dark mantle and a heavy headdress over a white, pleated garment. The atmosphere is dark and tenebrous; the light falls softly from the upper left, dramatically highlighting the white wimple encircling the woman's head and the abundant white fabric descending from its gathering at her neck. The shadowed features of her face register a weary sorrow.

When the painting was catalogued in 1778 and 1793, it was described simply as "a woman with a chaplet" and an "old devotee." Subsequently she was described as an old nun (*nonne*), presumably because her costume was interpreted as a white habit covered with a brown mantle. This identification is seemingly supported by the rosary in her right hand. The lower edge of the canvas, however, has a later addition on which all but the top of the rosary is painted; thus it, too, is probably an addition by a later hand.[1] Upon closer inspection the woman's costume differs from the modest habits worn by nuns, or by their lay sisters known in Holland as *begijnen* or *klopzusters*, in the seventeenth century. The headdress, in fact, is no modest hood of unrelieved brown but a subtle, splendidly colored garment glinting with gold and amber.

The painting, with its single figure, frontal and half-length format, and the dark but richly decorated mantle contrasted with a white garment beneath, most closely resembles Rembrandt's *An Old Woman Reading* of 1655 (fig. 1). Julia Lloyd Williams also likened the Virgin's pose, bent slightly at the waist with her arms wreathed before her and one hand on her bosom, to the presumed *Hendrickje Stoffels* (cat. 5).[2] She further pointed out the resemblance to Rembrandt's etching,

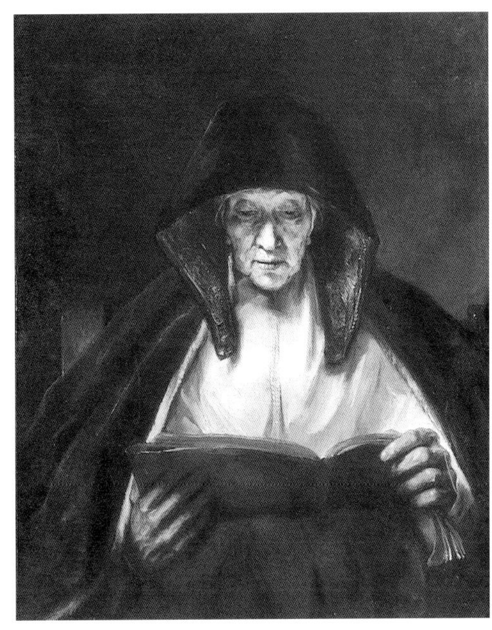

1
Rembrandt van Rijn
An Old Woman Reading
1655, oil on canvas, Collection of The Duke of Buccleuch and Queensberry KT, Drumlanrig Castle

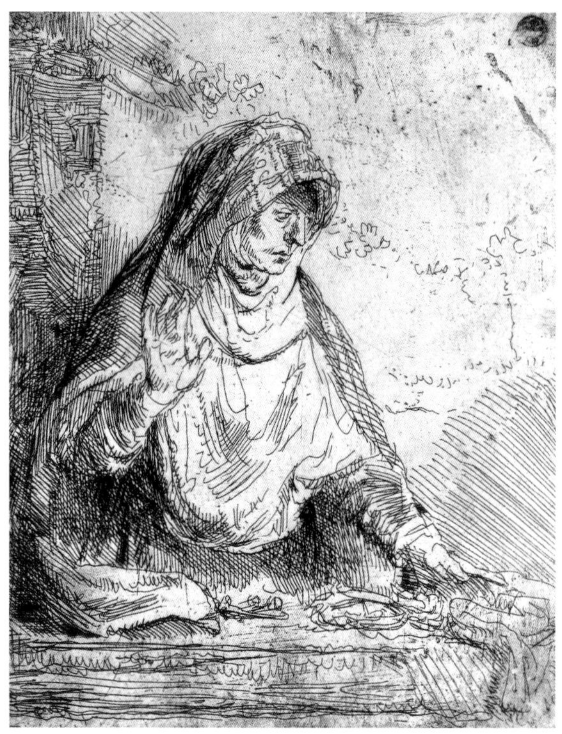

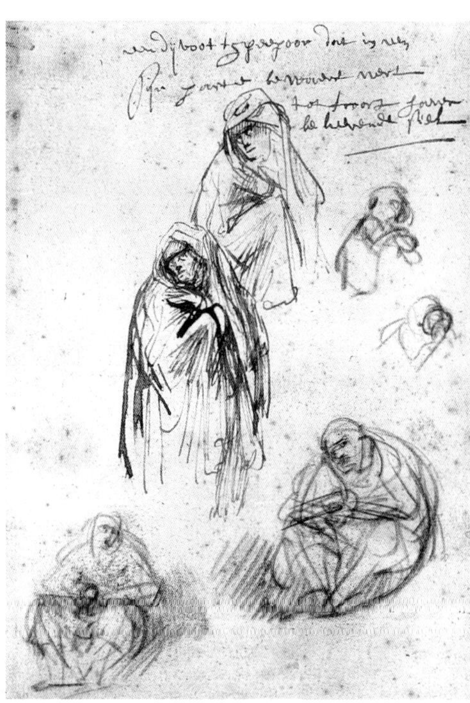

2
Rembrandt van Rijn
The Virgin with the Instruments of the Passion
c. 1652, etching and drypoint, The British Museum, London

3
Rembrandt van Rijn
Studies of the Mater Dolorosa and other Mourners
c. 1637, pen and ink and chalk on paper, Rijksprentenkabinet, Amsterdam

executed perhaps a decade earlier, of *The Virgin with the Instruments of the Passion* (fig. 2). This work also shows an isolated figure of Mary in half-length, clad in a dark mantle with a white wimple, but with one hand raised, and the nails of the cross as well as the crown of thorns of the Passion placed before her.

Wilhelm R. Valentiner was the first to suggest that the painting represents the Virgin of Sorrows (*Mater Dolorosa*), although she is not portrayed with the instruments of the Passion.[3] The *Mater Dolorosa* is a traditional iconic image of Mary, depicted in isolation but inspired by her anguish among other grieving mourners at the Crucifixion or lamenting the dead body of Christ once it had been removed from the cross. The Virgin's sorrow was regarded as the fulfillment of Simeon's prediction to her at the presentation of her infant son in the temple that "a sword shall pierce thy heart" (Luke 2:35). The *Mater Dolorosa* had been treated earlier by Titian — an artist whom Rembrandt held in the highest esteem — as a pendant to an *Ecce Homo*, an archetypal image of the suffering Christ (see cat. 5, figs. 2, 3).[4]

A drawing by Rembrandt of 1637 includes two studies of the mourning Virgin in a sheet of studies for the *Entombment,* from the series of Passion scenes that Rembrandt painted for Frederick Hendrick (Alte Pinakothek, Munich) (fig. 3). This drawing is of special interest here because Rembrandt inscribed it with a phrase that captures the spiritual significance of the grieving mother of Christ. The inscription reads: "een dijvoot thr(?)eesoor dat in een fijn harte bewaert wert tot troost harer beleevende siel" (A devout treasure that is kept in one's heart for the consolation of her compassionate soul). Thus he suggests that Christ resides in Mary's heart as a blessed treasure to comfort her soul, which is filled with emotion.[5] In a famous letter to Constantijn Huygens, Rembrandt explained that the project had been delayed by his effort to imbue the scenes with "the most natural emotion" (*naetuereelste beweechgelickheijt*).[6]

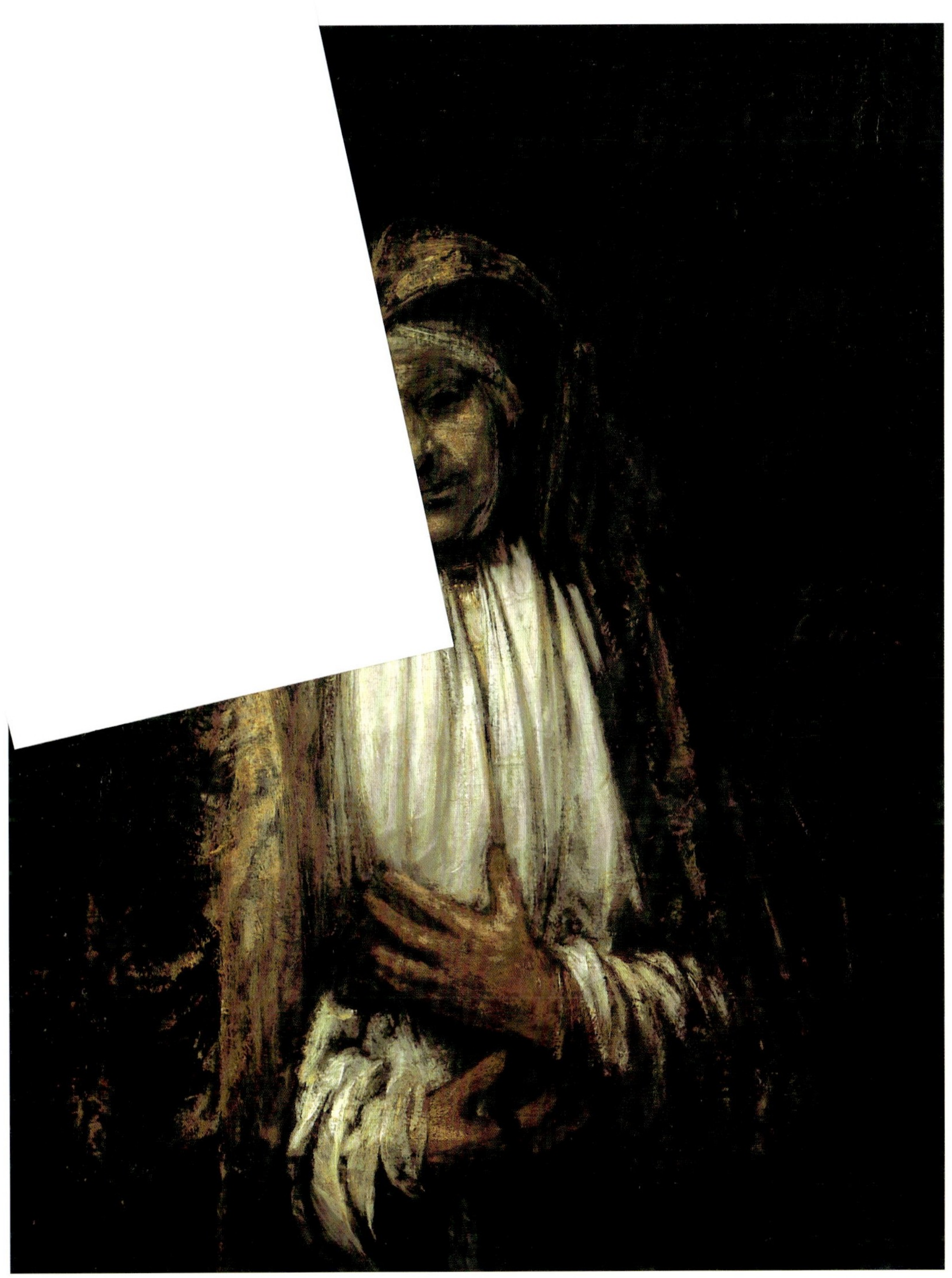

The Virgin of Sorrows, 1661
oil on canvas, 107 × 81 (42 ⅛ × 31 ⅞)
Musée Départemental d'Art Ancien
et Contemporain, Épinal

While this image seems related to the half-length, single figures Rembrandt executed around 1661 of saints and of Christ, the relationship remains obscure. Christ was included in series of apostles by Peter Paul Rubens and others, yet the Virgin Mary was not. The Virgin appears in print series of apostles (see cat. 5, fig. 4), yet no painted series with her image are known. It is iconographically conceivable that she would be paired with the *Christ* (cat. 15), or with *The Resurrected Christ* (cat. 6) if the latter work's unusual oval format was originally rectangular. The rosary was an accepted feature of the iconography of the *Mater Dolorosa* as one of the "Mysteries" of the Virgin. As Julia Lloyd Williams pointed out, it was included in a print by Lucas van Leyden of c. 1520, showing the Virgin in a pose similar to that of the present work; Lloyd Williams' further suggestion, however, that the addition at the bottom of the canvas with the repainted rosary may replicate a lost detail of the original is highly speculative.[7]

We need not assume with Valentiner that Rembrandt's hieratic "Catholic" works, such as this painting, were executed only for the export market. Rembrandt's monumental *Holy Family* of c. 1633 (Alte Pinakothek, Munich) (Br. 544), for example, seems to have been owned by Marten Soolmans (1613-1641) and Oopjen Coppit (1611-1689), who were members of the Reformed Church and whose full-length pendant portraits were executed by Rembrandt in 1634 (Rothschild Collection, Paris).[8] The study of the Virgin's expressions probably was also part of the training in Rembrandt's studio. Among the *tronijen* (head studies) by other artists listed among Rembrandt's possessions in 1656 was "A head of Mary by the same," namely the artist's son and pupil, Titus van Rijn (1641-1668).[9] PCS

15 Christ

Christ is shown half-length and turned slightly to the viewer's left. His long brown hair descends to his shoulders, and he has a full beard and mustache, high cheekbones, and a long, straight nose. He inclines his head slightly and crosses his hands at the wrists upon his chest. An ample brown cloak covers his reddish-brown garment. A sweeping curve at the lower right may indicate that he is seated, and the suggestion of an architectural pier is faintly visible at the left. Christ's gaze seems unfocused, but directed obliquely and meditatively into the distance; his expression is earnest and solemn, with a hint of sadness. Extensive overpaint throughout the figure's costume, most conspicuously in his left sleeve and strengthened left hand, but also in Christ's beard and hair, makes it difficult to read the image properly, but it remains a noble conception, and the salient features of Christ's face and expression remain relatively intact.

When the painting was in the Pushkin Museum in Moscow, thieves cut the central image out from the rectangular canvas into a jagged oval form, perhaps indicating that the picture was once installed in a frame with an oval aperture. While the present frame is modern, there is no evidence that the canvas was ever deliberately fashioned as an oval, as in the case of *The Resurrected Christ* (cat. 6). A photographic diagram (fig. 1) was circulated by the director of the museum, Nicolai Ilich Romanov, in an attempt to recover the painting and other stolen works, including pictures attributed to Correggio and Carlo Dolci. The reduced dimensions of the dismembered oval were recorded as 89 by 66 centimeters. The central section was eventually recovered and sewn back into the original before the picture was sold to the Hyde Collection in 1933.[1] The picture's proportions had already been altered before

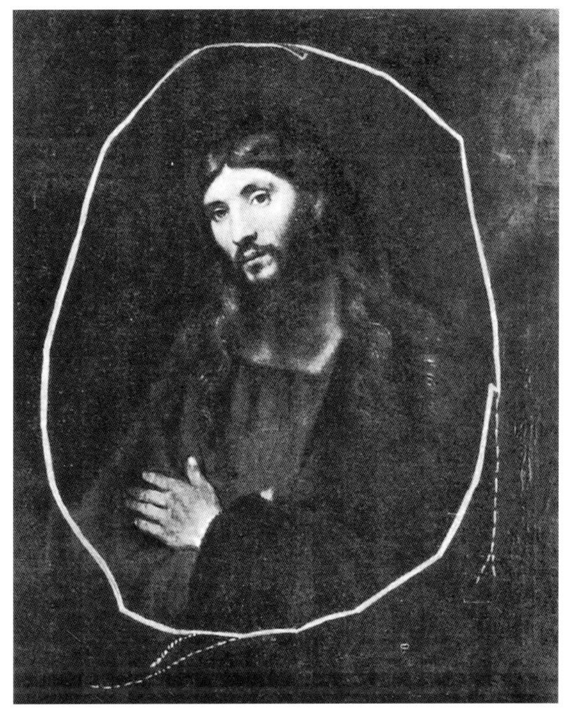

1
Photo-diagram of cat. 15, circulated by the Pushkin Museum after the work was dismembered in a theft, Rijksbureau voor Kunsthistorische Documentatie (RKD), The Hague

it was stolen, since an old relining extended Rembrandt's canvas by about 6 to 7 centimeters on each side and by a centimeter or two at the top and bottom.[2] The remains of the original canvas measure approximately 103 by 76 centimeters.[3]

Residing in Glens Falls, this painting has not been as familiar to twentieth-century and contemporary specialists as other works by Rembrandt from this period, but all authors, with the exception of Christian Tümpel, have accepted it as an autograph work by the master.[4] Seymour Slive, in particular, praised the artist's "incredible power of invention" in the work and related it to a series of small head studies of Christ by Rembrandt and his pupils.[5] The model in these various works also resembles the figure of Christ in Rembrandt's *Christ at Emmaus* of 1648 (Musée du Louvre) and the famous etching known as the *Hundred Guilder Print* (see cat. 7, fig. 1).[6] While the series of head studies of Christ traditionally has been dated to the late 1640s, two of the panels that most specialists accept as by Rembrandt, namely the works in Berlin (see cat. 6, fig. 2) and in the Fogg Art Museum (fig. 2), have recently been established through dendochronological examination to date from c. 1656.[7] The model in these works seems to have been painted from life and closely resembles the figure in the Hyde Collection's painting; thus, while the two panels are not strictly preparatory to the present work, they could have been studies that culminated in the final canvas exhibited

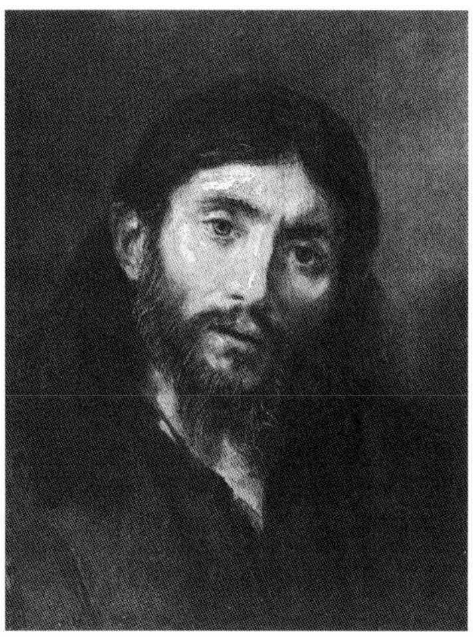

2
Rembrandt van Rijn
Christ
c. 1656, oil on panel, Fogg Art Museum, Harvard University Art Museums, Gift of William A. Coolidge

here. The artist's inventory of 1656 included two entries described as "A head study [*tronie*] of Christ by Rembrandt," as well as an unattributed painting that is of interest in this context because it is described as "A head of Christ, a study from life."[8]

While the present undated work is traditionally thought to have been executed in c. 1661, it has been implausibly dated as early as 1650 by Otto Benesch, and to c. 1655-1657 by James K. Kettlewell, who further speculated that the picture may have been executed in two campaigns some years apart.[9] Technical examination during the treatment in 1976 suggested that the picture was completed in an earlier form with a somewhat different palette and a slightly varied design; for example, x-rays reveal that Christ's arms were not originally crossed but that his left arm and hand were extended lower on the right. Given the new evidence of a later dating of the Cambridge and Berlin panels (see fig. 2), and the stylistic resemblance in the handling of paint in the present work both to *The Apostle Bartholomew* of 1657 (cat. 3) and *The Apostle Simon* of 1661 (cat. 10), a dating of c. 1657-1661 may be proposed.

As we have seen, Wilhelm R. Valentiner originally proposed that the present work and an image of the Virgin Mary (cat. 14) were part of a series of evangelists and apostles Rembrandt conceived around 1661.[10] Peter Paul Rubens provided a precedent for an apostle series that included an image of Christ in the series he painted for the Duke of Lerma in 1610-1612 (Museo del Prado, Madrid).[11] In that series, however, Christ was depicted nude, holding the cross, not clothed and meditative as in the present work. Rembrandt and a close follower executed two other half-length images of Christ during this period, *The Resurrected Christ* of 1661 by the master (cat. 6) and *The Apostle James the Minor (?)* (but frequently identified as Christ) by a follower, also inscribed "Rembrandt" and dated 1661 (cat. 12). All the images of Christ by Rembrandt, his students, and his followers adhere fairly closely to a description of Christ quoted by the Rembrandt pupil Samuel van Hoogstraten from an apocryphal letter by Lentulus (see cat. 6).

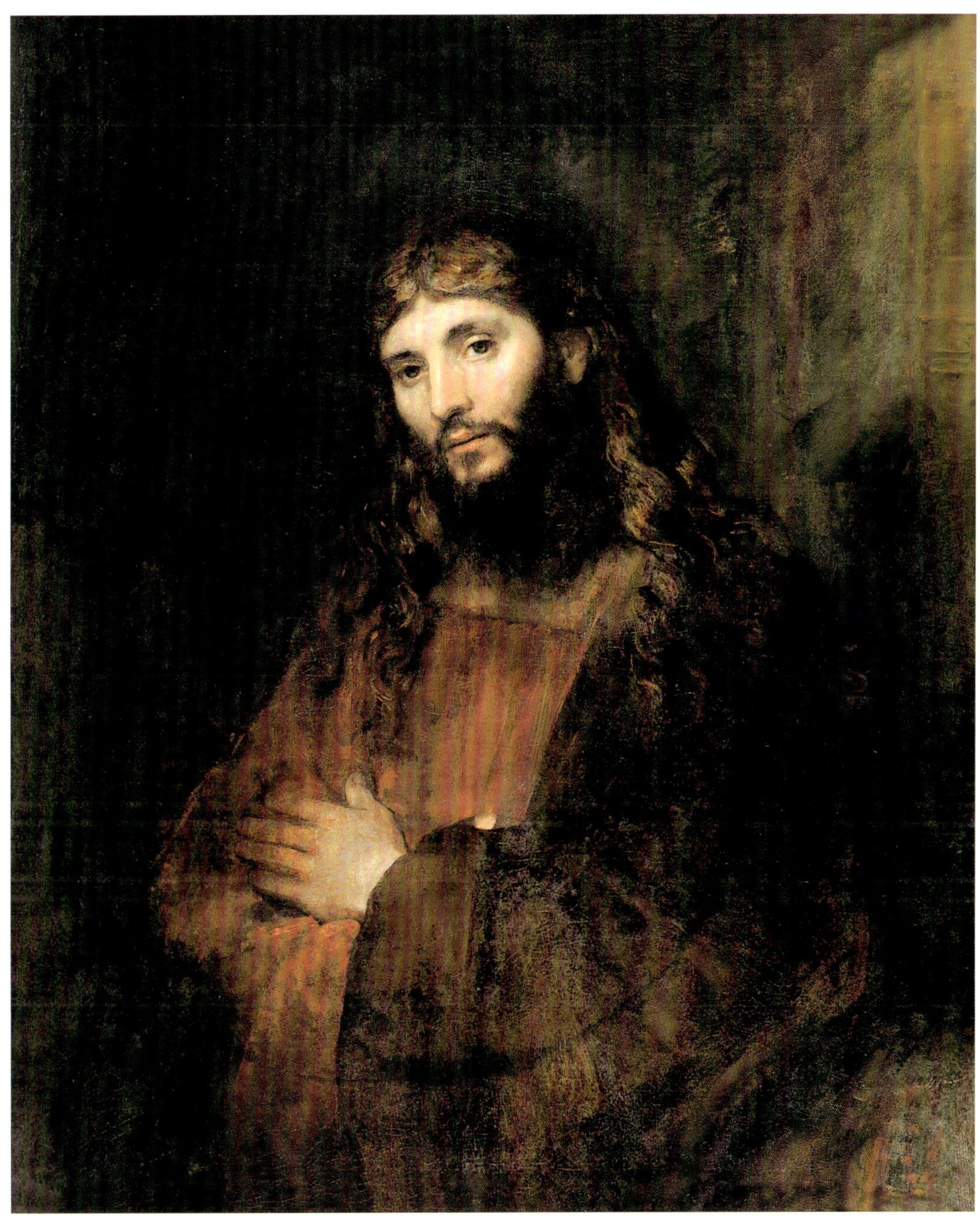

Christ, c. 1657-1661
oil on canvas, 109.2 × 90.2 (43 × 35 1/2)
The Hyde Collection, Glens Falls, New York

It has repeatedly been assumed that Rembrandt used Jews as models not only for secular images (cat. 1) but also for his religious subjects, including his images of Christ. Most observers have concurred in observing Semitic features in the model for the work described here and the smaller head studies. Michael Zell has examined Rembrandt's relationship to the Jews and highlighted the beliefs and writings of one of the artist's Jewish patrons, Rabbi Manasseh Ben Israël.[12] In his mystical publication, *Piedra gloriosa de la Estatua de Nebuchadnesar* (1655), for which Rembrandt made six etchings, the rabbi repeatedly invoked a rapprochement between Jews and Christians that seems to have arisen out of the author's involvement with "Philosemites"— a group of Christian theologians who sought reconciliation and understanding between Christians and Jews. Zell further observes that Rembrandt's religious paintings from the 1650s often allude to Christ's renewal of Mosaic Law, underscoring the unity of the Old and New Testament, thus suggesting the painter's own exposure to the tenets of Philosemitism. Set against the topical religious issues of his time and the beliefs of his patron, the sympathy with which the artist depicted his Jewish subjects and models takes on an added dimension.

Notwithstanding these ideas and practices, Gary Schwartz has pointed out that the public's reaction to Rembrandt's paintings of Christ as a Jew in the seventeenth century may not have been universally positive.[13] This at least is the implication of a poem inscribed by the poet Jan Vos on a painting of Christ after a Jew. The picture was created by the Rembrandt pupil Govert Flinck for Joris de Wijze, who was a notary, playwright, art collector, and patron of, among other artists, Emanuel de Witte: "All that lacks is speech but Govaert Flinck refused / To paint an open mouth, despite de Wijze's plea. / For this Christ would not speak of Christ except in blasphemy. / The heart is not reflected by the face that shines at you. / You ask how come? Because the model was a Jew."[14] PCS

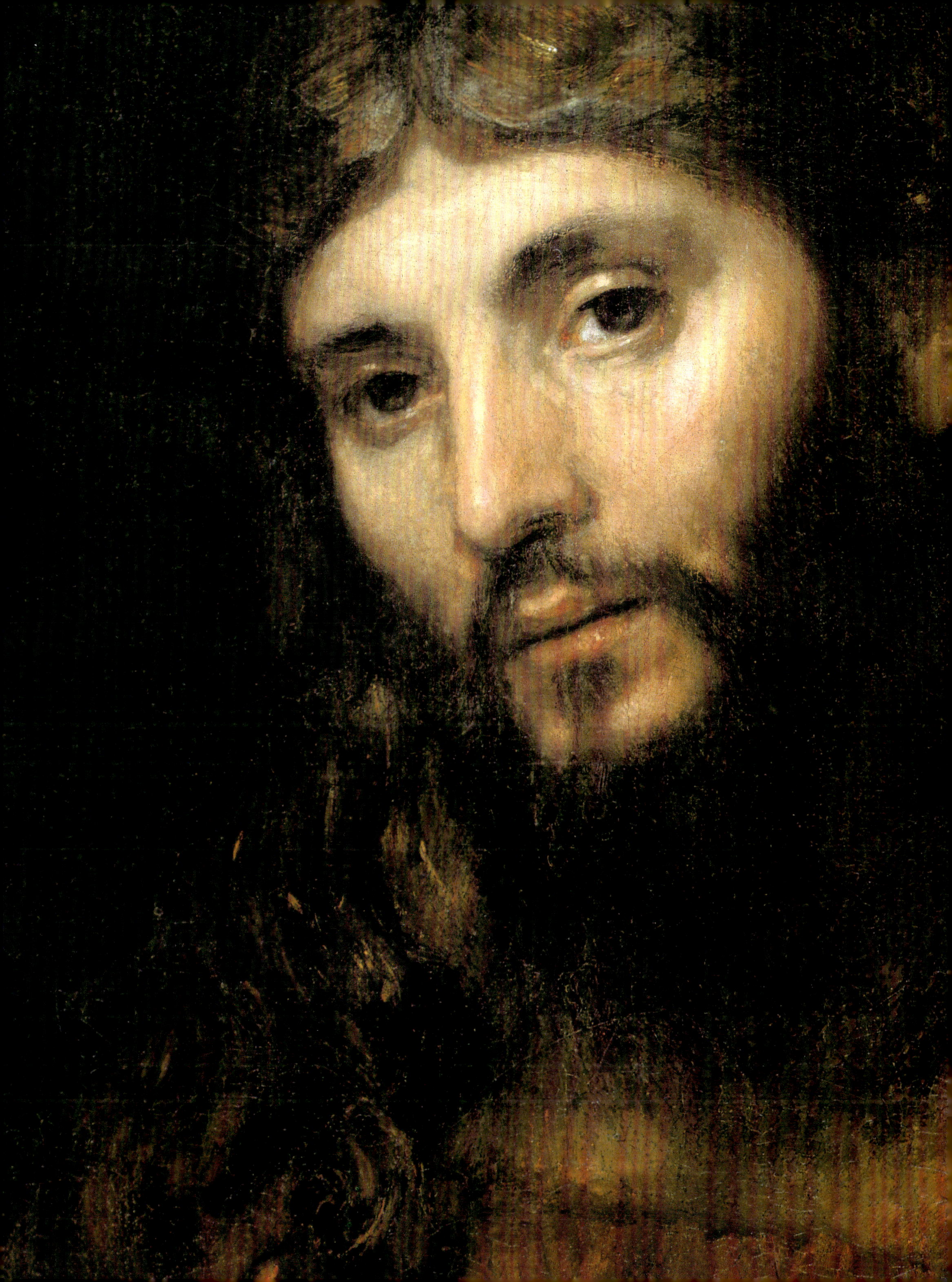

16 Monk (Saint Francis?) Reading

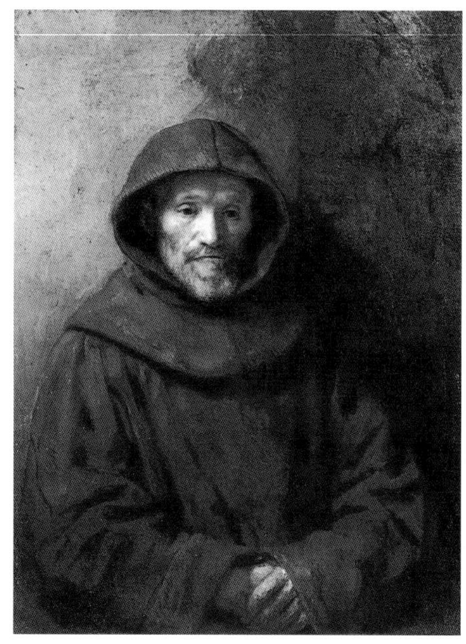

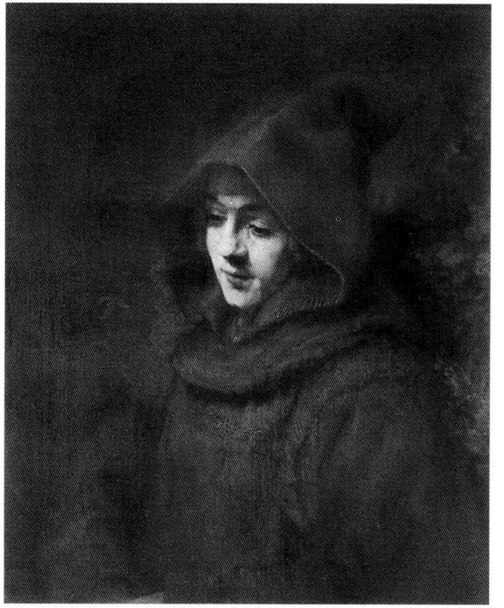

An elderly man with a full white beard, in a monk's habit, reads a paper or pamphlet that he holds in his left hand. His heavy brown garment, crudely stitched, hangs loosely on his frame, and the habit's ample peaked cowl shadows his face. His head is inclined as he reads, his shoulders are relaxed, and his right arm rests on the arm of his chair. A shaft of bright light illuminates the fold of the paper and highlights the base of the reader's left thumb and index finger, implying that the unseen side of the paper is fully illuminated from above. The undifferentiated dark background and the narrowly focused beam of light suggest a spare, cell-like setting with a single aperture to daylight. The monk's attitude of unselfconscious repose, combined with the light's beamed focus on the written word, emphasizes his concentration on his reading.[1]

Notwithstanding the fact that all Catholic religious orders, monasteries, and clerical celibacy had been banned in Protestant Holland, Rembrandt depicted two other half-length figures wearing a monk's habit at this period of his career. *A Franciscan Friar,* dated 165(5?), presents another older bearded man with folded hands staring off into space as if in mediation (fig. 1). The third image shows a young man dressed as a Capuchin monk. The model, who is thought to be the artist's son, Titus, with crossed hands and lowered eyes, is seen before a background suggestive of vegetation (fig. 2). Wilhelm R. Valentiner included all three of these paintings in his discussion of a hypothetical series of apostles, suggesting that they belonged to a smaller series of evangelists and holy men.[2]

The date on the present work was recorded as 1660 until Wilhelm von Bode deciphered it as 1661.[3] This date was subsequently accepted until 1997, when the authors of the catalogue for the exhibition

1
Rembrandt van Rijn
A Franciscan Friar
165(5?), oil on canvas, The National Gallery, London

2
Rembrandt van Rijn
Titus van Rijn in a Monk's Habit
1660, oil on canvas, Rijksmuseum, Amsterdam

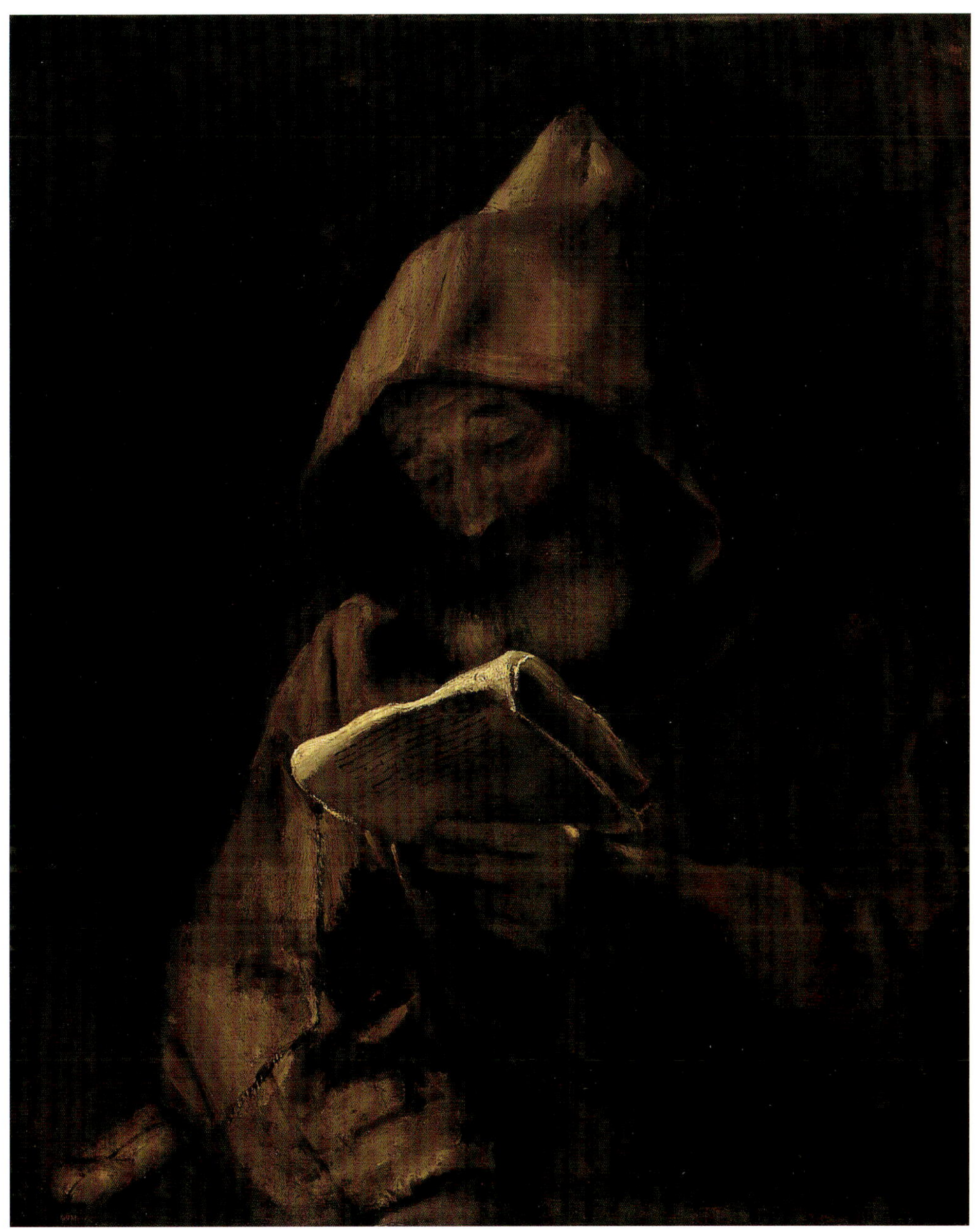

Monk (Saint Francis?) Reading, 1661
oil on canvas, 82 × 66 (32 5/16 × 26)
Sinebrychoff Art Museum, Helsinki

in Melbourne and Canberra stated that no date was discernible. Like the *Franciscan Friar,* the present work has suffered from abrasion and has lost details and subtleties of the artist's original brushwork.[4] There is no reason, however, to question the painting's attribution to Rembrandt, as Christian Tümpel did in 1986.[5]

The figure has usually been described as a monk, sometimes of the Franciscan order, or as a friar of the Capuchin order, a branch of the Franciscans.[6] In the earliest known description of the painting, in the 1759 Comte de Vence catalogue, the work was titled *St. Francis,* while in the 1761 Comte de Vence catalogue the figure was called a *Priest of the Franciscan Order.*[7] Kurt Bauch and Tümpel regarded all three of Rembrandt's paintings of monks as depictions of Saint Francis, a description that Carel Vosmaer had earlier applied to the present work.[8]

Saint Francis (c. 1182–1226) founded the order of the Franciscans, who make vows of poverty, chastity, and obedience. Francis died at the young age of forty-four and was described by his earliest biographer, Thomas of Celano, as of slight build, having an unkempt beard and poor eyesight. He is usually depicted with a brown or gray habit, wearing a girdle with three knots that signify the Franciscan vows. Nevertheless, as Cornelis Hofstede de Groot and Tümpel both observed, the figure in the present painting appears to be older than the traditional representation of Saint Francis.[9] Moreover, there is no evidence of his most distinguishing feature, the stigmata.[10] Tümpel likened the work to Rembrandt's etching of *Saint Francis beneath a Tree Praying*, dated 1657, which is traditionally titled *Saint Francis Praying* and depicts an older, bearded man in a monk's habit kneeling in prayer in the foreground before a statue of the Crucifix.[11] Prior to 1751, however, when catalogued by Edme-François Gersaint, the etching was assumed to be a depiction of Saint Jerome, and it is not certain that the monk in this print is Saint Francis.[12] One must similarly conclude that little evidence exists to support the painting's identification as Saint Francis beyond his costume and humble and pious attitude. **PCS**

17 Saint Bavo

A bearded, middle-aged man with long hair is viewed full-face, life-size, and half-length. He wears a broad red beret with a black border and a white ostrich feather and holds a jessed falcon on his gloved left hand. With large, dark eyes the man stares into the distance beyond the viewer, his expression abstracted and vaguely melancholy. A black mantle draped over his shoulders features a decorative border, and a prominent gold cross hangs from a chord upon his chest. He tucks the thumb of his right hand into the girdle around his waist. Looming behind him is a horse whose head rears at the right and whose saddle appears at the left beside the head of a boy, perhaps a page or equerry who attends the rider. So shallow and compressed is the monumental composition that Wilhelm R. Valentiner likened it to an antique sculpted relief.[1]

Although neither signed nor dated, the painting has always been accepted as by Rembrandt except by Christian Tümpel, who questioned it without offering an explanation.[2] On stylistic grounds, the painting should date from the early 1660s and can be compared with the dated works of 1661; Albert Blankert and Jeroen Giltaij suggest a somewhat later dating, c. 1662-1665.[3] More challenging is the identification of the subject. In early sales the painting was simply titled *The Falconer,* but Valentiner suggested that the figure might represent the popular medieval knight, Count Floris V of Holland (1257-1296). Beloved by his people, Count Floris was imprisoned and ultimately murdered at Muiden Castle by his former friends and associates, Gerard van Velsen and Gysbrecht van Amstel, who lured him there with the promise of a falcon hunt.[4] In the seventeenth century the story was one of the best-known episodes of medieval Dutch history and had been immortalized in the theatrical tragedy, *Gerard van Velsen* (1612), by the poet P. C. Hooft, who was himself the sheriff of Muiden and the occupant of its castle.[5] Given the prominence of the falcon hunt in the count's capture, he was often depicted holding a falcon, as, for example, by Jan Janszn Orlers in his chronicle of the history of Leiden (1641).[6]

In a note first recorded by Tümpel, however, Hans Kaufmann proposed that the subject was Saint Bavo, an interpretation that was developed by Björn Fredlund, director of the Göteborg Museum of Art.[7] Born to a noble family in Haspengouw, Bavo lived in the seventh century. He abandoned a life of dissipation in Ghent to become a penitent hermit dwelling in the woods. Later, he became the patron saint of Saint Baaf Cathedral in Ghent, as well as the patron saint of the cathedral of Saint Bavo and of the bishopric and city of Haarlem, which had close trading ties with Ghent. Bavo often was portrayed as a warrior in armor, with a plumed hat, holding a falcon. The latter detail alludes both to his aristocratic status, since falconry was restricted to the nobility in the Netherlands, and to a legendary episode in his youth when he was condemned to death for stealing a falcon but escaped his fate. A print of

Saint Bavo by Cornelis de Visscher after Pieter Soutman, dated 1650 (fig. 1), closely resembles the present figure, with his plumed hat, robe, prominent cross, and falcon; only the sword and armor are missing. Still another print by Leendert van der Cooghen, dated 1664, also depicts Saint Bavo as an armored warrior with a falcon.[8] Thus Fredlund suggested that if the figure were indeed Saint Bavo, he would be depicted at the moment of his conversion, when he suddenly realized with profound remorse the waste and error of his former life. Notwithstanding the identification's acceptance in recent literature, Fredlund was reluctant to identify the figure as Saint Bavo, in part because x-rays show that Rembrandt initially intended to portray the falconer with a large collar rather than a cape, but more importantly because his depiction is utterly inconsistent with traditional Roman-Catholic conventions of representing the saint.[9] As Albert Blankert observed, the same could be said of Rembrandt's apostles *Matthew, Bartholomew,* and *James the Major* from this period (cats. 7-9), figures that include attributes from the medieval Catholic tradition but are otherwise unrecognizable as saints.[10]

Blankert further observed that an expert on falconry, Wim Huyskens, had noted that the bird depicted is not one of the species used in hunting, that its hood and laces are incorrect, and that it is perched in the wrong position. Apparently Rembrandt was not familiar with the finer points of the sport, nor presumably were his patrons. As Cornelis Hofstede de Groot first observed, the model for the falconer seems to be the same as in Rembrandt's *Aristotle Contemplating the Bust of Homer* (see cat. 2, fig. 3), as well as in other images from the late 1650s (cats. 1, 2) and early 1660s.[11] **PCS**

1
Cornelis de Visscher
after Pieter Soutman
Saint Bavo
1650, engraving,
Rijksprentenkabinet,
Amsterdam

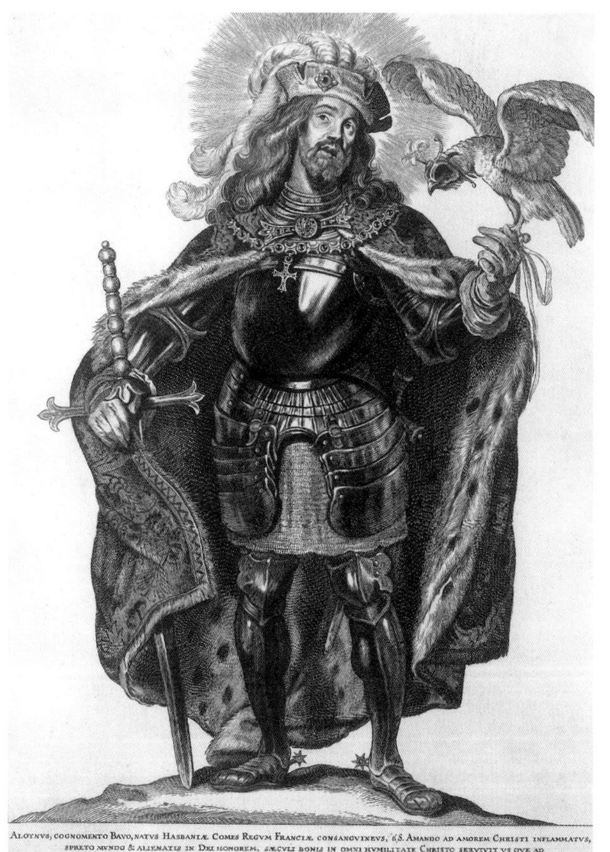

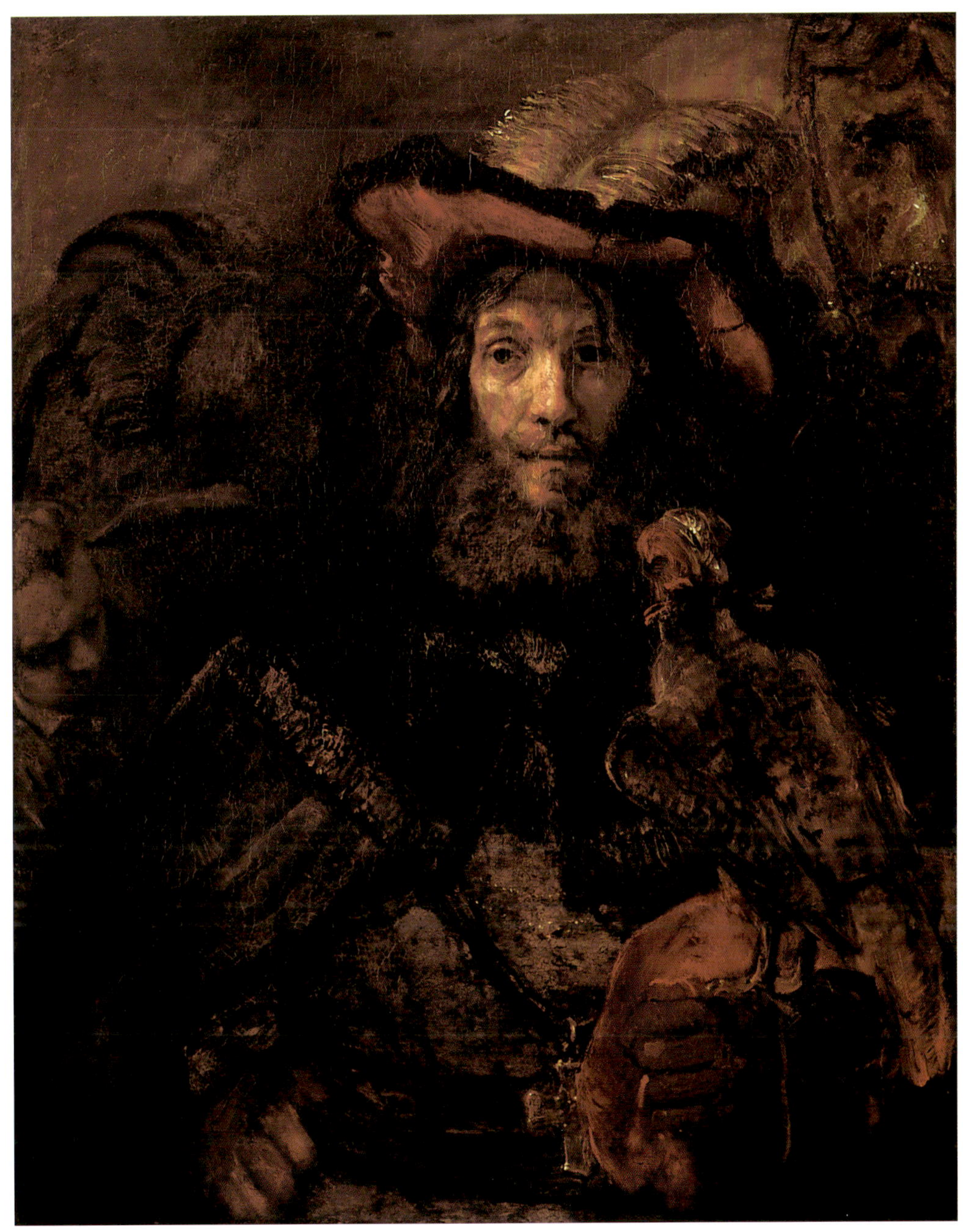

Saint Bavo, c. 1662–1665
oil on canvas, 98.5 × 79 (38 3/4 × 31 1/8)
Göteborgs Konstmuseum,
Göteborg, Sweden

1 A Bearded Man in a Cap

165(7?), oil on canvas, 78 × 66.5 (30 11/16 × 26 3/16)
The National Gallery, London 190

Inscription

Signed and dated at left, below the level of the shoulder: *Rembrandt. f. 165( );* the last figure in the date is covered by a pentimento of the outline of the right arm

Provenance

Collection of the Duke of Argyll, London, before 1781; (sale, Christie's, London, 25-26 May 1798, no. 104); Jeremiah Harman, Woodford, by 1836; (sale, Christie's, London, 17-18 May 1844, no. 23); to Henry Farrer for the National Gallery, London

Exhibitions

London 1945, no. 27; London 1988, no. 14

Literature

Smith 1829-1842, 7 (1836): 126, no. 351; 152, 459; Smith 1884, 4: 1566, no. 42; von Bode/Hofstede de Groot 1897-1906, 6 (1901): 170, no. 469; Hofstede de Groot 1907-1927, 6 (1916): 214-215, no. 392; Rosenberg 1909, 563, no. 440; Benesch 1956, 340; MacLaren 1960, 316-317, no. 190; Bauch 1966, 12, no. 218; Gerson 1968, 401; Bredius/Gerson 1969, 571, no. 283; Charrington/Alexander 1983, 146, no. 184; Schwartz 1985, 308; Tümpel 1986a, 406, no. 142; MacLaren/Brown 1991, 1: 335-336, no. 190; Wheelock 1995, 244, fig. 3

Notes

1 See the technical description in London 1988, 112, no. 14; and MacLaren/Brown 1991, 1: 335.

2 Schwartz 1985, 284; Zell 2002.

3 Bredius/Gerson 1969, 569, no. 259A.

4 See London 1988, 112.

2 The Apostle Paul

c. 1657, oil on canvas, 131.5 × 104.4 (51 3/4 × 41 1/8) National Gallery of Art, Washington, Widener Collection 1942.9.59

Inscription

Signed on desk at right: *Rembrandt f*

Provenance

Johan van Schuylenburg, The Hague; (sale, The Hague, 20 September 1735, no. 31); Marquis de Livois [d. 1790], Angers; (sale, Angers, 1791, no. 65); Gamba; (sale, Paris, 17 December 1811, no. 26); Ferdinando Marescalchi, Bologna, by 1824; Sir George Hayter; (sale, Christie & Manson, London, 3 May 1845, no. 82); M. le comte de Pourtalès-Gorgier, Paris; (sale, "son hotel," Paris, 27 March-4 April 1865, no. 182); Lord Wimborne [formerly Sir Ivor Guest, 1835-1914], Canford Manor, Dorsetshire; (Arthur J. Sulley & Co., London); Peter A.B. Widener, Elkins Park, Pennsylvania, by 1912; inheritance from estate of Peter A.B. Widener by gift through power of appointment of Joseph E. Widener, Elkins Park; gift 1942 to National Gallery of Art, Washington

Exhibitions

British Institution 1841, no. 71 (as *Portrait of Cornelius Pietersz Hooft*); Washington 1969, no. 17

Literature

Smith 1829-1842, 9 (1842): 800, no. 30; von Bode/Hofstede de Groot 1897-1906, 6 (1901): 29-30, 174, no. 382; Hofstede de Groot 1907-1927, 6 (1916): 124, no. 178; Widener 1931, 62; Bredius 1935, 26, no. 612; Benesch 1956, 338-339; Bauch 1966, 12, no. 223; Gerson 1968, 378, no. 295; Bredius/Gerson 1969, 613, no. 612; Haak 1969, 298; Halewood 1982, 118-120; Schwartz 1985, 310, no. 351; Sutton 1986, 313; Tümpel 1986a, 421, no. A16; Wheelock 1995, 241-247; London and The Hague 1999, 213-214

Notes

1 This entry is largely taken from Wheelock 1995, 241-247.

2 For the most reasoned assessment of the attribution of this painting, see Ary Bob de Vries, Magdi Toth-Ubbens, and W. Froentjes, *Rembrandt in the Mauritshuis,* Alphen aan den Rijn, 1978, 148-165. The authors argue that the painting was executed at two distinct periods, about 1655 and about 1660-1665.

3 See also Rembrandt's *A Bearded Man,* 1661, in the Hermitage, Saint Petersburg, inv. no. 751 (Bredius/Gerson 1969, 573, no. 309) (cat. 1, fig. 1).

4 No commission, however, is recorded for this painting. See Wheelock 1995, 245, for a discussion of the x-radiographs of the painting, which indicate that the canvas has been irregularly cut at the corners and has been trimmed at the top and bottom.

5 For the technique of *A Bearded Man in a Cap,* see London 1988, 112, no. 14.

6 For these analyses, see Wheelock 1995, 245-246.

7 Technical evidence supporting this hypothesis is discussed in Wheelock 1995, 245-247. However, it should be noted that cross sections taken near the edges of the painting during the conservation treatment on the painting in 2000-2001 did not reveal differences in the ground layers within and without the oval shape visible in the x-radiographs. Thus, the technical reasons for this oval shape remain uncertain.

8 No intervening varnish layer, for example, was found between the paint layers. I would like to thank Susanna Griswold and Melanie Gifford for discussing these issues with me.

9 Benesch 1956, 338-339, first noted the complementary relationship of the two paintings.

3 The Apostle Bartholomew

1657, oil on canvas, 122.7 × 99.7 (48 3/8 × 39 1/4) The Putnam Foundation, Timken Museum of Art, San Diego, 51.001

Inscription

Signed and dated, center left: *Rembrandt f. 1657*

Provenance

Jonathan Richardson, London; (sale, London, 4 March 1747, lot 49) to William Fauquier; Dr. Robert Bragge (sale Prestage, London, 9 February 1757, lot 48) to Sir Joshua Reynolds, London; the Count de Laval, Jean Charles François Laval de la Loubrerie; his daughter, Princess Ekaterina Ivanova Troubetskaia; her daughter, Elisaveta Sergeevna Davydoff; her grandson, Vassili Vassilievich Davydoff; (Thos Agnew & Sons, London, and Duveen Brothers, New York); (Henry Goldman, New York); acquired by the Putnam Foundation, 1952

Exhibitions

Detroit 1925, no. 22; Detroit 1930, no. 59; New York 1950, no. 18; Toronto 1951, no. 10; Melbourne and Canberra 1997, no. 17

Literature
von Bode 1912, 505–508; Hofstede de Groot 1907–1927, 6 (1916): 120, no. 169; Valentiner 1920/1921, 89; Weisbach 1926, 577–578, 626; Benesch 1956, 338, fig. 1; Rosenberg 1964, 118, no. 106; Bauch 1966, 12, no. 217; Gerson 1968, 379, no. 296; Bredius/Gerson 1969, 613, no. 613; Mongan and Mongan 1983, 66–67, 122–123, no. 23; New Haven 1983, 113; Schwartz 1985, 310, no. 352; Tümpel 1986a, 399, no. 80; Broun 1987, 45–47, no. 4; New York 1995, 2: 31; Wheelock 1995, 244; San Diego 1996, 90–94, no. 16

Notes
1 See Matthew 10:3; Mark 3:18; Luke 6:14.

2 Benesch 1956, 338. For the Berlin painting, also see Bredius/Gerson 1969, 571, no. 284.

3 Wheelock 1995, 244–245.

4 Broun 1987, 45–47.

5 Hofstede de Groot 1907–1927, 6 (1916): 120; Mongan and Mongan 1983, 70.

4 An Elderly Man as the Apostle Paul

165(9?), oil on canvas, 102 × 85.5 (40 1/8 × 33 5/8)
The National Gallery, London 243

Inscription
Signed and dated at right, at the level of the head: *Rembrandt/165(9?)*

Provenance
Collection of N.W. Ridley Colborne [later Lord Colborne] by 1815; Lord Colborne Bequest, 1854

Exhibitions
British Institution 1815, no. 33; British Institution 1832, no. 48; British Institution 1843, no. 101; British Institution 1851, no. 19; London 1947, no. 70; London 1988, no. 15

Literature
Smith 1829–1842, 7 (1836): 125–126, no. 348; von Bode/Hofstede de Groot 1897–1906, 6 (1901): 152, no. 460; Hofstede de Groot 1907–1927, 6 (1916): 172–173, no. 291; Bauch 1966, 12, no. 224; Gerson 1968, 379; Bredius/Gerson 1969, 573, no. 297; Haak 1969, 298; Van Regteren Altena 1973, 186–187; Schwartz 1985, 310, no. 353; Tümpel 1986a, 399, no. 81; Chapman 1990, 125; MacLaren/Brown 1991, 1: 337–339, no. 243; London and The Hague 1999, 213–214; Zell 2002, 111–112

Notes
1 As noted in London 1988, 116–119, Rembrandt did alter the shape of the sitter's white collar.

2 It should be mentioned, however, that Horst Gerson in Bredius/Gerson 1969, 573, no. 297, remarks upon weaknesses in the image (particularly around the hands) that he attributes either to abrasion or to the fact that it is an old copy. Nevertheless, his concerns are unwarranted, and there is no reason to question the attribution of this work.

3 Christopher Brown in MacLaren/Brown 1991, 1: 338, no. 243, considers it unlikely that the painting is a portrait. In any event, as he notes, I.Q. van Regteren Altena's suggestion that the sitter is the poet Joost van den Vondel is unconvincing. See Van Regteren Altena 1973, 186–187.

4 Münz 1948, 64, was the first scholar to associate this painting with the postulated apostle series. His suggestion was followed by Bauch 1966, 12, no. 224.

5 As noted in London 1988, 116, the scene depicted is based, in reverse, on Rembrandt's etching. The roundel in the upper right has been so abraded that it is no longer possible to determine if it contained a religious scene.

6 MacLaren/Brown 1991, 1: 339, note 5, also mentions that the Sacrifice of Abraham is recommended as a subject appropriate for accompanying a figure of Faith in the Dutch version of Cesare Ripa's *Iconologia* by Dirck Pietersz Pers (*Iconologia of Uijtbeeldinghe[n] des Verstants...* [Amsterdam, 1644], 147): "In 't verschiet wordt Abraham mede gestalt, alwaer hy sijnen Soone wilde offeren."

5 Hendrickje Stoffels (as the Sorrowing Virgin?)

1660, oil on canvas, 78.4 × 68.9 (30 7/8 × 27 1/8)
Lent by The Metropolitan Museum of Art, Gift of Archer M. Huntington, in memory of his father, Collis Potter Huntington, 1926, 26.101.9

Inscription
Signed and dated at right: *Rembrandt/f 1660*

Provenance
Collection of the Cotoner family [marqués de la Cenia], Palma de Mallorca, 1880; Gift of Archer M. Huntington, in memory of his father, Collis Potter Huntington, 1926

Exhibitions
New York 1909, no. 103; Amsterdam 1952, no. 147; New York 1995, 2: no. 16; Edinburgh and London 2001, no. 127; Frankfurt and Kyoto 2003, no. 36

Literature
von Bode/Hofstede de Groot 1897–1906, 6 (1901): 108, no. 438; Hofstede de Groot 1907–1927, 6 (1916): 339, no. 720; Rosenberg 1964, 98–99; Bauch 1966, 26, no. 522; Gerson 1968, 435, no. 382; Bredius/Gerson 1969, 557, no. 118; Ainsworth et al. 1982, 72–76; Schwartz 1985, 294, no. 327; Tümpel 1986a, 411, no. 189; London 1988, 106

Notes
1 Liedtke in New York 1995, 2: 78–80, no. 16, questions the reliability of the signature and date, and proposes a period of execution for the work from c. 1654 to 1660. Nevertheless, as Giltaij argues in Frankfurt and Kyoto 2003, 190, no. 36, the painting fits comfortably in the context of Rembrandt's works from 1660 and exhibits no evidence of reworking over such a long period of time.

2 Ainsworth et al. 1982, 72–76, have determined through a study of autogradiography that Hendrickje's face was originally conceived as thinner along the cheeks and jaw than it currently is. Her blouse was also open at the breast.

3 For the relationship between Rembrandt's *Woman at an Open Door (Hendrickje Stoffels?)* and a portrait of a courtesan by Palma Vecchio, see Berlin, Amsterdam, and London 1991, 249, 270.

4 Rosenberg 1964, 98–99.

5 New York 1995, 2: 78–80, no. 16.

6 See New York 1995, 2: 80.

7 For images of these paintings see Wethey 1969, 1: figs. 96–101.

8 This summary is based on Hall 1974, 29–30.

9 The early provenances of these two works are not known, and it is not possible to determine if they were sold together or as part of a larger group. It seems probable that they were painted for an export market. *The Resurrected Christ* was first recorded in the collection of the dean of Mainz Cathedral in the late eighteenth century, while *Hendrickje Stoffels* was first recorded in 1880 in a collection from Mallorca.

6 The Resurrected Christ

1661, oil on canvas, 78.5 × 63 (31 × 24 3/4)
Bayerische Staatsgemäldesammlungen, Alte Pinakothek, Munich 6471

Inscription
Signed and dated: *Rembrandt f. 1661* (perhaps a later inscription)

Provenance
From the collection of Hugo Franz [d. 1779], dean of Mainz Cathedral, count of Eltz

Exhibitions
Amsterdam 1898, no. 112; Schaffhausen 1949, no. 140; Washington and Cincinnati 1988, no. 39; Frankfurt and Kyoto 2003, no. 38

Literature
von Bode/Hofstede de Groot 1897–1906, 6 (1901): 9, 64, no. 416; Hofstede de Groot 1907–1927, 6 (1916): 116–117, no. 157; Valentiner 1920/1921, 221; Benesch 1956, 351; Bauch 1966, 13, no. 240; Gerson 1968, 425, no. 360; Bredius/Gerson 1969, 615, no. 630; Benesch 1970, 1: 190–203; Schwartz 1985, 285, no. 321; Alte Pinakothek 1986, 426, no. 6471; Tümpel 1986a, 399, no. 87

Notes

1 For Rembrandt's etching *Christ Appearing to the Apostles,* see Clifford S. Ackley in Boston and Chicago 2003, 230, 326, no. 152. I would like to thank Sohee Kim for drawing my attention to this comparison.

2 Van Hoogstraten 1678, 105, trans. Schwartz 1985, 284. For a further discussion of the impact of this image of Christ on Rembrandt's work, see Knipping 1974, 2: 446–450.

3 Alte Pinakothek 1986, 426. See, for example, Peter Paul Rubens' *Christ Triumphant over Sin and Death,* c. 1614 (Musée des Beaux-Arts, Strasbourg), in David Freedberg, *Rubens: The Life of Christ after the Passion (Corpus Rubenianum Ludwig Burchard 7)* (London, Oxford, and New York, 1984), 61–63, no. 12, repro.

4 Jeroen Giltaij in Frankfurt and Kyoto 2003, 198, no. 38, notes that these distortions are visible in x-radiographs of the painting. He also suggests that the painting has been cut in such a manner that the image is tilted slightly to the left.

5 Bredius/Gerson 1969, 606, no. 552. Schwartz 1985, 170, notes that Rembrandt painted this work for the Mennonite collector Ameldonck Leeuw (1604–1647), who was a cousin of Govert Flinck. Sohee Kim has pointed out to me that in this picture, as in the Munich work, Rembrandt depicted Christ's wound on his left side instead of the right, which is the standard iconographical approach.

6 Valentiner 1920/1921, 221.

7 The Evangelist Matthew and the Angel

1661, oil on canvas, 96 × 81 (37 13/16 × 31 7/8)
Musée du Louvre, Paris 1738

Inscription
Signed and dated, center right:
Rembrandt f. 1661

Provenance
At the residence of the Comte d'Angiviller, Paris [possibly on loan from the royal collection]; seized during the French Revolution on 4 July 1794; probably purchased by Louis XVI; exhibited at Luxembourg Palace between about 1800 and 1820, and at the Château de Compiègne between 1874 and 1901

Exhibitions
Paris 1955, no. 10; Stockholm 1956, no. 38; Moscow-Leningrad 1965, 36; Paris 1970, no. 182; Berlin, Amsterdam, and London 1991, 47; Stockholm 1992, no. 61; Melbourne and Canberra 1997, no. 22

Literature
Lavallée 1804–1815, 8 (1812): 7; Villot 1852, 406; von Bode/Hofstede de Groot 1897–1906, 7 (1902): 104, no. 521; Hofstede de Groot 1907–1927, 6 (1916): 122, no. 173; Valentiner 1920/1921, 219–222; Benesch 1956, 343; Valentiner 1956, 400; Bauch 1966, 13, no. 231; Gerson 1968, 424, no. 359; Bredius/Gerson 1969, 613, no. 614; Benesch 1970, 197; Brejon de Lavergnée, Foucart & Reynaud 1979, 110; Strauss and Van der Meulen 1979, 480; Foucart 1982, 83–88; Schwartz 1985, 311; Tümpel 1986a, 399–400, no. 88

Notes

1 See, among others, Rosenberg 1964, 201–205; and Amsterdam and London 2000, 253–261, no. 61.

2 For these three works, see Gerson/Bredius 1969, 583–584, no. 409; 607, no. 562; 611, no. 594.

3 For these four studies, see Gerson/Bredius 1969, 573, nos. 302–305. The attribution of these works has been a matter of some discussion. Although they were once viewed as preliminary studies by Rembrandt for Saint Matthew in the Louvre painting, most are now generally considered to be workshop productions (Gerson accepted only Br. 304 as being by the master). My impression is that these works were painted from the model in a Rembrandtesque style rather than being free adaptations of the figure in Rembrandt's Louvre painting. For a discussion of one of these works, see Wheelock 1995, 333–336.

4 As discussed by Albert Blankert in Melbourne and Canberra 1997, 161.

5 For Coppenol's life, see H. F. Wijnman, "Mr. Lieven van Coppenol, schoolmeester, Calligraaf," *Jaarboek Amstelodamum* 30 (1933), 92–187.

6 See, for example, the engraving by Johannes Sadeler I after Maarten de Vos of *Saint Matthew,* c. 1585, in his series Christ, the Virgin, and the Twelve Apostles, Hollstein 1949–, 21–22, nos. 317–324.

7 See Christopher White, *Rembrandt as an Etcher: A Study of the Artist at Work* (New Haven, Conn., 1999), 165–168, pls. 217–220.

8 W. A. Visser 'T Hooft, *Rembrandt and the Gospel* (London, 1957), 87, argues that Coppenol's standing with the Mennonites was not good in 1658 because of the scandalous nature of his personal life. Nevertheless, his own beliefs may have remained intact. Whatever the case, Rembrandt exerted a great deal of time and energy on this print.

9 Otto Hophan, *The Apostle* (Westminster, Md., 1962), 164–165.

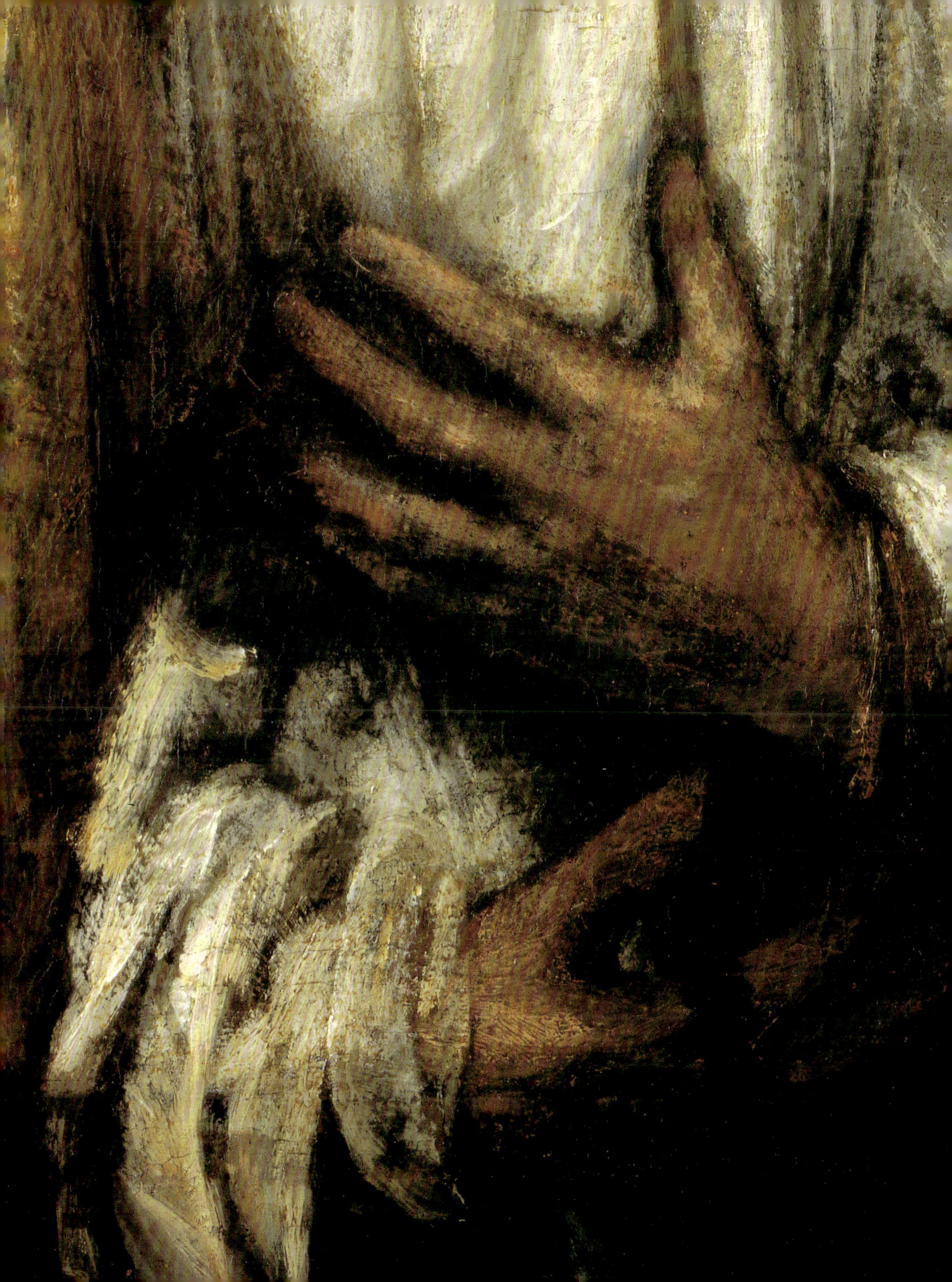

130, no. 190; Valentiner 1920/1921, 221; Bauch 1966, 13, no. 232; Bredius/Gerson 1969, 573, no. 307; Schwartz 1985, 314; Tümpel 1986a, 400, no. 92 (as Rembrandt [?])

Notes

1 Rembrandt was always especially acute in his observation of people absorbed in reading; see, for example, his *Old Woman Reading,* 1631 (Rijksmuseum, Amsterdam), his drawing of an *Old Man Reading,* c. 1661 (Nationalmuseum, Stockholm), and his etchings of *Jan Six,* 1647, and *Saint Jerome Reading in an Italian Landscape,* 1653. For the Amsterdam painting, see Bredius/Gerson 1969, 553, no. 69; for the Stockholm drawing, see Benesch 1973, 5: 308, no. 1150, fig. 1446; for the etchings, see White and Boon 1969, 1: 136, no. B285, and 57, no. B104.

2 Valentiner 1920/1921, 221.

3 See von Bode/Hofstede de Groot 1897-1906, 6 (1901), 198, no. 483.

4 See the various reports of its changing state recorded in Melbourne and Canberra 1997, 157, notes 6, 7, 9.

5 Tümpel 1986a, 400, no. 92.

6 See Smith 1829-1842, 7 (1836): 57, no. 132, who described him as a Franciscan monk, and Hofstede de Groot 1907-1927, 6 (1916): 129-130, no. 190, who described him as a Capuchin.

7 See Melbourne and Canberra 1997, 157.

8 See Bauch 1966, 13, no. 232; Tümpel 1986a, 400, no. 92; and Vosmaer 1877, 561.

9 Hofstede de Groot 1907-1927, 6 (1916): 129-130, no. 190; Tümpel 1986a, 400, no. 92.

10 Tümpel claimed to see evidence of the wounds of the stigmata on the hands of the youth depicted in *Titus van Rijn in a Monk's Habit* (fig. 2), but even less is visible of the youth's hands in that picture than in this work. See Tümpel 1986a, 400, no. 92.

11 Tümpel 1986a, 400, no. 92. For the etching see White and Boon 1969, 1: 58, no. B107.

12 As noted in Melbourne and Canberra 1997, 157, note 21.

17 Saint Bavo

c. 1662-1665, oil on canvas, 98.5 × 79 (38 ¾ × 31 ⅛)
Göteborgs Konstmuseum, Göteborg, Sweden, 698

Provenance

Lord Coventry, London; (sale, George, Paris, 7 June 1853, no. 14 [as *Le Fauconnier*]); J. S. Gilkinet (sale, Paris, 18 April 1863, lot 85, no. 35); Erik Brodin, Stockholm (Paris, 1921); (Bukowski auction house, Helsinki, 1921); acquired from Bukowski and presented to the Göteborgs Konstmuseum in 1921

Exhibitions

Stockholm 1956, no. 42; Amsterdam and Rotterdam 1956, no. 91; Stockholm 1992, no. 62; Melbourne and Canberra 1997, no. 24; Frankfurt and Kyoto 2003, no. 42

Literature

Vosmaer 1877, 581; Hofstede de Groot 1908-1927, 6 (1916): 171-172, no. 287; Valentiner 1921, xxvii, no. 24 (as "attributed to" Rembrandt); Valentiner 1923, 105 (as Rembrandt); Benesch 1935, 267; Valentiner 1948, 122-129; Gantner 1959, 97-102; MacLaren 1960, 316; Gantner 1964, 177-183; Bauch 1966, 13, no. 242; Van Regteren Altena 1967, 71; Gerson 1968, 429, no. 370; Bredius/Gerson 1969, 574, no. 319; Schwartz 1985, 314; Tümpel 1986a, 400, no. 93

Notes

1 Valentiner 1948, 124.

2 See Tümpel 1986a, 400, no. 93.

3 See cats. 6-12, 14, 16. For Blankert, see Melbourne and Canberra 1997, 168-172, no. 24; for Giltaij, see Frankfurt and Kyoto 2003, 214-216, no. 42.

4 Valentiner 1948, 124-125.

5 The story was retold in works by Joost van den Vondel, Phillip von Zesen, and others.

6 Valentiner 1948, 126, fig. 5.

7 Tümpel 1971, 20, note 2; see Hans Kaufmann in Stockholm 1992, 210-213, no. 62.

8 See Melbourne and Canberra 1997, 170, fig. 24d.

9 See Fredlund's entry in Stockholm 1992, 210-213; Frankfurt and Kyoto 2003, 214-216, no. 42.

10 Melbourne and Canberra 1997, 171.

11 A very weak painting in the Statens Museum for Kunst in Copenhagen that also depicts a bearded man with a broad beret and cape with a cross, but no falcon, was attributed by Valentiner to Rembrandt and likewise identified as Count Floris (for the image, see Bauch 1966, 13, no. 243, called *The Crusader*). While it could be inspired by the Göteborg painting, it is certainly not by Rembrandt.

Provenance

Collection of the Princes of Salm, 1778, no. 142, and 1793, no. 16; appropriated for the Préfecture at Épinal when the previously independent principality of Salm was appropriated in 1793 for France during the Revolution; entered the museum's collection in 1829

Exhibitions

Rome 1928, no. 100; Amsterdam and Rotterdam 1956, 1: 184–185, no. 90; Paris 1970, no. 183; Épinal 1993, no. 28; Edinburgh and London 2001, no. 137A

Literature

Laurent 1829, no. 56; Michel 1893, 395, 562; von Bode/Hofstede de Groot 1897–1906, 7 (1902): 84, no. 511; Hofstede de Groot 1907–1927, 6 (1916): 129, no. 189; Valentiner 1920/1921, 221; Bauch 1966, 15, no. 283; Gerson 1968, 428, no. 367; Bredius/Gerson 1969, 581, no. 397; Schwartz 1985, 314, pl. 360; Tümpel 1986a, 399, no. 85

Notes

1 See Friedrich Winckler, "Echt, Falsch, Verfälscht," *Kunstchronik* 10 (1957): 143–144; Bauch 1966, 15, no. 283; and the comments in 1970 of Madeleine Hours, conservateur des Musées Nationaux de France, recorded in Edinburgh and London 2001, 260, no. 137A note 6.

2 Edinburgh and London 2001, 236, no. 137A.

3 Valentiner 1920/1921, 221.

4 See Wethey 1969, 1: pls. 96, 97.

5 For discussion, see Schatborn 1985, 18–19, no. 7.

6 See Slive 1953, 36.

7 Edinburgh and London 2001, 236, no. 137A.

8 For the *Holy Family,* see Bredius/Gerson 1969, 605, no. 544. For the portraits of Soolmans and Coppit, see Bredius/Gerson 1969, 564, no. 199; 576, no. 342.

9 Strauss and Van der Meulen 1979, 381, doc. 1656/12.

15 Christ

c. 1657–1661, oil on canvas, 109.2 × 90.2 (43 × 35 ½)
The Hyde Collection, Glens Falls, New York
1971.37

Provenance

Cardinal Joseph Fesch [Napoleon's minister in Rome] 1845; DeForcade, Paris, 1873; Charles Sedelmeyer, Paris; Bamberger, Paris; Count Alexander Orloff Davidoff, Petrograd; A.S. Pushkin State Museum, Moscow; purchased from the Soviet Union in 1933

Exhibitions

Vienna, 1873; Palais du Corps Legislatif, Paris, 1874; Moscow, Museum of Fine Arts, c. 1930; New York 1939, no. 308, pl. 69; New York 1942, no. 49; Montreal 1944, no. 44; Cambridge 1948, no. 10

Literature

von Bode 1883, 522; Dutuit 1885, 54; Michel 1893, 443, 445, 567; von Bode/Hofstede de Groot 1897–1906, 6 (1901): 62, no. 415; Hofstede de Groot 1907–1927, 6 (1916): 118, no. 162; Valentiner 1920/1921, 221; Benesch 1956, 348; Rotermund 1956, 233–234; Valentiner 1956, 400; Slive 1965, 406–417; Gerson 1968, 428, no. 368; Bredius/Gerson 1969, 614–615, no. 628; Kettlewell 1968, 4, 6; Kettlewell 1981, xii, 108–111, no. 51; Schwartz 1985, 285, 315; Tümpel 1986a, 421, no. A 22 (as Workshop of Rembrandt); New York 1995, 2: 124, note 7

Notes

1 Two subsequent conservation treatments were undertaken by William Suhr in 1958 and by Morton Bradley Jr. in 1977; in the latter case the picture unfortunately was relined on aluminum, which contributes to its flattened appearance today.

2 The painting's dimensions before the theft were given as 108 x 87 cm.

3 It is possible that the vertical edges had been trimmed before the picture was enlarged. Gerson in Bredius/Gerson 1969, 614, briefly noted the dismemberment and abuse: "The figure was once cut irregularly out of the original canvas; it has suffered by this operation and by rubbing all over, but is still a fine interpretation of an ideal image of Christ."

4 Tümpel 1986a, 421, no. A22, "as Workshop."

5 Slive 1965, 407.

6 For the Louvre painting, see Bredius/Gerson 1969, 609, no. 578.

7 For the images, see Bredius/Gerson, 614, no. 624 and 624A; also see New York 1995, 1: 120.

8 Strauss and Van der Meulen 1979, 361, nos. 115 and 118; for the unattributed head ("Een Cristus tronie nae 't leven"), see Strauss and Van der Meulen 1979, 383, no. 326. See also Slive 1965, 407.

9 Benesch 1956, 348; Kettlewell 1981, 109–110.

10 Valentiner 1956, 400.

11 Rubens' original is lost, and the best of several copies is in the National Gallery of Canada.

12 Zell 2002, particularly 58–99.

13 Schwartz 1985, 284.

14 For the translation of the poem, see Schwartz 1985, 284.

16 Monk (Saint Francis?) Reading

1661, oil on canvas, 82 × 66 (32 5/16 × 26)
Sinebrychoff Art Museum, Helsinki 1410

Inscription

Signed and dated at center right, above the shoulder: *Rembrandt f 1661*

Provenance

Comte de Vence, Paris (sale, Paris, 9–17 February 1761, no. 47); Earl of Wemyss, Gosford House, Scotland (1835–c. 1915); Hjalmar Linder Collection, London; acquired in 1920

Exhibitions

Amsterdam and Rotterdam 1956, 1: no. 85; Stockholm 1956, no. 37; Melbourne and Canberra 1997, no. 20

Literature

Comte de Vence, 1759, 24; Smith 1829–1842, 7 (1836), 57, no. 132; Vosmaer 1877, 561; Michel 1893, 444; von Bode/Hofstede de Groot 1897–1906, 6 (1901), 198, no. 483; Hofstede de Groot 1907–1927, 6 (1916), 129–

fig. 150; Eisler 1927, 50; Duveen Brothers 1941, no. 202; Allen 1945, 4: 73; Benesch 1956, 351; Rotermund 1956, 230; Valentiner 1956, 390; Bauch 1966, 13, no. 241; Bredius/Gerson 1969, 615, no. 629; von Einem 1972, 357–358; Ainsworth et al. 1982, 92–95, 101, pls. 64, 65; Tümpel 1986a, 399, no. 86; New York 1995, 1: 126–128, 37, 2: 128–130, no. 37; Wright 2000, 172–173, fig. 156

Notes

1 See Yokahama, Fukuoka, and Kyoto 1986, 136, no. 12.

2 Note the opposing buttonhole. See New York 1995, 2: 126–128, note 4.

3 See Smith 1829–1842, 7 (1836): 32–33, no. 78; Valentiner 1920/1921, 221; and Valentiner 1956, 390.

4 Benesch 1956, 351.

5 See New York 1995, 1, 2: no. 37.

6 Rotermund 1956, 230. Rotermund cited Eisler 1927, 50, who also puzzled over the unusual representation of Christ. See also Allen 1945, 4: 73.

7 Rotermund 1956, 230.

8 Christ appears with reddish-blond hair in Rembrandt's *Christ and the Woman Taken in Adultery*, 1644 (The National Gallery, London) (Bredius/Gerson 1969, 608, no. 566), and in a painting by one of Rembrandt's followers, *The Christ and the Woman of Samaria*, 1655 (The Metropolitan Museum of Art, New York) (Bredius/Gerson 1969, 610, no. 589).

9 von Einem 1972, 357–358; Liedtke in New York 1995, 2: 128–130, no. 37.

10 See von Bode/Hofstede de Groot 1897–1906, 6 (1901): 66, no. 417; Tümpel 1986a, 399, no. 86; Wright 2000, 172–173, fig. 156.

11 His attribute is sometimes a book with or without a staff or club. For examples, see Decimal Index to the Art of the Lowlands (D.I.A.L.) 11 I 57, specifically Hendrik Goltzius' engraving (B. 52), and Goltzius' and Anton Wierix's prints after two designs by Maarten de Vos, depicting the saint standing before scenes of his own martyrdom, respectively, Hollstein 1949–, 8, Goltzius no. 355 (II), and von Wurzbach 1906–1911, 2 (1911): 880.

12 See *The Golden Legend of Jacobus de Voragine*, trans. Granger Ryan and Helmut Ripperger (New York, 1969), 261–269.

13 A bat used to pound wool in the textile's finishing process.

14 See Smith 1829–1842, 7 (1836): 32–33.

15 See New York 1995, 2: 128.

16 Ainsworth et al. 1982, 92–95, 101. Ainsworth credited Egbert Haverkamp-Begemann for raising doubts about the attribution.

17 For Brown's assessment, see Yokohama, Fukuoka, and Kyoto 1986, 136, no. 12; also see Tümpel 1986a, 399, no. 86.

18 See Hubertus von Sonnenburg in New York 1995, 1: 126.

13 Man in a Red Cap (An Evangelist?)

1660, oil on canvas, 102 × 80 (40 3/16 × 31 1/2)
Museum Boijmans Van Beuningen, Rotterdam 2113

Provenance

J. A. Sichterman (possibly sale, Groningen, 20 August 1764, lot 232); Sir Joshua Reynolds [1732–1792], by 1765; (sale, Christie's, London, 17 March 1795, lot 50); William Hardman, Manchester; (sale, Winstanley and Sons, Manchester, 19 October 1838, lot 52); Thomas Green, London (sale, Christie's, 20 March 1874, lot 93); Mrs. Owen Roe (sale, London, 1889); (Charles Sedelmeyer, Paris); P. C. Hanford, Chicago; (E. Fischof Gallery, New York); Charles Schwab, Pittsburgh, 1920; (Lord Duveen of Millbank, New York); (D. Katz, Dieren); gift of the Vereeniging Rembrandt and 100 Friends of the Museum, 1937

Exhibitions

London 1889, no. 166; New York 1909, no. 104; London 1929, no. 85; Detroit 1930, no. 69; Amsterdam 1935, no. 31; Rotterdam 1938, no. 127, fig. 144; Basel 1948, no. 28; Dijon 1950, no. 32; Zurich 1953, no. 126, fig. 124; Rome 1954, no. 124, fig. 28; Stockholm 1956, no. 39; San Francisco, Toledo, and Boston, 1966, no. 38; Tokyo and Kyoto, 1968, no. 51; Brussels 1971, no. 86; Leningrad 1986, no. 29; Rotterdam 1988, no. 26; Melbourne and Canberra 1997, no. 32; Bergamo 2000, no. 24; Frankfurt and Kyoto 2003, no. 44

Literature

Smith 1829–1942, 7 (1836): 102, no. 275; suppl. 9 (1842): 795, no. 9; von Bode/Hofstede de Groot 1897–1906, 7 (1902): 114, no. 526; von Wurzbach 1906–1911, 2 (1910): 410 (as attributed to C. Fabritius); Hofstede de Groot 1907–1927, 6 (1916): 127, no. 185; Valentiner 1920/1921, 219, 221; Weisbach 1926, 578; Eisler 1927, 45, fig. 17; Benesch 1935, 66; Bauch 1966, 13, no. 248; Gerson 1968, 427, no. 363; Bredius/Gerson 1969, 613, no. 618; Schwartz 1985, 312; Tümpel 1986a, 400, no. 89; London and The Hague 1999, 214, note 235

Notes

1 Smith 1829–1942, 7 (1836): 102, no. 275; suppl. 9 (1842): 795, no. 9.

2 Hofstede de Groot 1907–1927, 6 (1916): 127, no. 185.

3 See Valentiner 1920/21, 219–222; Valentiner 1956, 400; and Tümpel 1986a, 400, no. 89.

4 Benesch 1935, 66.

5 Rotterdam 1988, 82, no. 26.

6 See Bergamo 2000, 162–164, no. 24.

7 Gerson in Bredius/Gerson 1969, 613, no. 618.

8 Testimony to the faithfulness of the print, in terms of recording the quality of the image in the mid-eighteenth century, was its receipt of first prize from the Society for the Encouragement of the Arts.

9 Frankfurt 2003, 222–224, no. 44.

10 See London and The Hague 1999, 214, note 235.

14 The Virgin of Sorrows

1661, oil on canvas, 107 × 81 (42 1/8 × 31 7/8)
Musée Départemental d'Art Ancien et Contemporain, Épinal 1828.37

Inscription

Signed and dated, center right:
Rembrandt f. 1661

10 The Apostle Simon

1661, oil on canvas, 98.3 × 79 (38 11/16 × 31 1/8)
Kunsthaus Zürich, Stiftung Prof. L. Ruzicka, R. 26

Inscription
Signed and dated on the saw: *Rembrandt f. 1661*

Provenance
Sir Offley Wakeman, Bart., St. Margaret near Shrewsbury, Shropshire, by 1945; Sir Alexander Walker, Troon near Ayr, Scotland, by 1948; (Marshall Spink, London), Ruzicka-Stiftung, Zurich, in 1949

Exhibitions
Schaffhausen 1949, no. 140a; Zurich 1949, no. 26; Amsterdam and Rotterdam 1956, no. 88

Literature
Münz 1948; Benesch 1956, 346-345; Bauch 1966, 13, no. 237; Gerson 1968, 426, no. 362; Bredius/Gerson 1969, 613, no. 616A; Haak 1969, 298; Schwartz 1985, 312; Tümpel 1986a, 399, no. 84

Notes

1 Simon was reputedly martyred in Persia by being sawed in half.

2 Münz 1948, 64, suggests that the figure is situated in a landscape with a tree in the background.

3 See the essay by Wheelock, which discusses Schmidt-Degener 1919 and Valentiner 1920/1921. *The Apostle Simon* was first published by Ludwig Münz (Münz 1948), who had been alerted of its existence by Sir Kenneth Clark.

4 Münz 1948, 67. Black, painted edges are also visible along the top and right sides of the painting *The Apostle James the Minor(?)* (cat. 12) as well as around *The Apostle Bartholomew* (cat. 8), and scratched lines surround the *Self-Portrait as the Apostle Paul* (cat. 11).

11 Self-Portrait as the Apostle Paul

1661, oil on canvas, 91 × 77 (35 13/16 × 30 5/16)
Rijksmuseum, Amsterdam SK.A.4050

Inscription
Signed and dated at left, next to the shoulder: *Rembrandt f. / 1661*

Provenance
Probably Everhard Jabach (1607/1612-1695) collection, Paris.[1] Nicolas Vleughels (1668-1737), Rome; by inheritance to Marie-Therèse Gosset; Cardinal Neri Maria Corsini (1685-1770), Rome, by 1750; Corsini Palace, Rome; William Buchanan, London, 1807; Lord Kinnaird, Rossie Priory by Dundee; I. de Bruyn and Mrs. I. de Bruyn-van der Leeuw, Spiez and Muri (near Bern), 1936, promised to Rijksmuseum in 1949, acquired 1961

Exhibitions
Amsterdam and Rotterdam 1956, no. 86; London and The Hague 1999, no. 81

Literature
Smith 1829-1842, 7 (1836): 86, no. 209; 91, no. 230; von Bode/Hofstede de Groot 1897-1906, 7 (1902): 64, no. 501; Hofstede de Groot 1907-1927, 6 (1916): 282, no. 575; Schmidt-Degener 1919, 266; Valentiner 1920/1921, 221; Schmidt-Degener 1928, 39; Münz 1948, 64; Benesch 1956, 353; Bauch 1966, 18, no. 338; Gerson 1968, 444; Bredius/Gerson 1969, 552, no. 59; Haak 1969, 299-300; Wright 1982, 33/94, no. 55; Schwartz 1985, 353; Tümpel 1986a, 409, no. 175; Chapman 1990, 9, 35, 63, 105, 120-127, 129; Berlin, Amsterdam, and London 1991, 284-286; Wheelock 1995, 242; Zell 2002, 111-112

Notes

1 This suggestion is made in London and The Hague 1999, 51, where it is noted that number 123 in the 1695 inventory of his collection lists "a portrait of Rembrandt, with a white cloth wrapped around his head, in half-length, life-sized, by himself."

2 Chapman 1990, 126, suggests that the sword is not only exclusively suggestive of the apostle's martyrdom, but also of his statement in Ephesians 6:17, "the sword of the Spirit, which is the word of God."

3 Van Thiel 1969, 1b, suggests that the letters forming the title of the uppermost page of the open manuscript, which appear to be in Hebrew, read "EFESIS," a presumed reference to Paul's Epistle to the Ephesians. Chapman 1990, 126, 168, note 104, however, has argued that the text is not sufficiently legible to reach this conclusion.

4 The authors of the entry on the painting in London and The Hague 1999, 213, interpret the expression as being primarily "pensive."

5 In London and The Hague 1999, 213, it is noted that bars of a window were revealed in the darkened background at the right when the painting was conserved in 1990-1991.

6 For a discussion of two sermons by the Remonstrant preacher, Willem Teellinck, which emphasizes the importance of Paul's self-questioning nature for his message about the importance of grace, see Chapman 1990, 126-127.

7 Slive 1953, 102, 210-211, Appendix E. Pels expressed his opinion in *Gebruik en misbruik des tooneels* (Amsterdam, 1681), 35-36.

8 Schmidt-Degener 1919, 266; Valentiner 1920/1921, 221; Benesch 1956, 353.

9 See London and The Hague 1999, 214, for a discussion of the scratches along the edges of this painting.

SCHOOL OF REMBRANDT VAN RIJN

12 The Apostle James the Minor(?)

1661, oil on canvas, 95.3 × 82.6 (37 1/2 × 32 1/2)
Lent by The Metropolitan Museum of Art, The Jules Bache Collection, 1949 49.7.37

Inscription
Signed and dated, center right: *Rembrandt f. / 1661*

Provenance
Sir C. Bethel Codrington, Bart, London; (sale, Christie's, London, 12 May 1843, no. 65); (Charles J. Nieuwenhuys, London); Baron van Mecklenburg, Paris; (sale, Paris, 11 December 1854, no. 15); Count Eduard Racynski, Ragolin, Poland; Jules Bache, New York

Exhibitions
Amsterdam 1898, no. 114; London 1929, no. 127; Yokohama, Fukuoka, and Kyoto 1986, no. 12; New York, 1995, no. 37

Literature
Smith 1829-1842, 7 (1836): 32-33, no. 78; von Bode/Hofstede de Groot 1897-1906, 6 (1901): 66, no. 417; Hofstede de Groot 1907-1927, 6 (1916): 118-119, no. 164; Weisbach 1926, 498,

8 The Apostle Bartholomew

1661, oil on canvas, 86.7 × 75.6 (34 1/8 × 29 3/4)
The J. Paul Getty Museum, Los Angeles
71.PA.15

Inscription

Signed and dated, lower right:
Rembrandt. f. 1661

Provenance

John Blackwood, London, by 1757; Richard Payne Knight [1751–1824], Downton Castle, Hereford, probably by c. 1809; by inheritance to his brother, Thomas Andrew Knight [1759–1838], Downton Castle; by descent to his daughter, Charlotte Rouse-Boughton; inherited by her son, Andrew Johnes Rouse-Boughton-Knight [1826–1909], Downton Castle, 1856; by descent to his son, Charles Andrew Rouse-Boughton-Knight, 1909; inherited by his grandson, Major William Mandeville Peareth Kincaid-Lennox, Downton Castle; (sale, Sotheby's, London, 27 June 1962, no. 10) to J. Paul Getty, Sutton Place, Surrey; gift to the museum, 1971

Exhibitions

London 1882, no. 234; London 1899, no. 99; London 1912, no. 52; London 1929, no. 52; Birmingham 1934, no. 152; London 1948, no. 3; Amsterdam and Rotterdam 1956, 1: no. 87; Minneapolis 1972, no. 43

Literature

Smith 1829–1842, 7 (1836): 128, no. 359; Vosmaer 1877, 361, 562; von Bode 1883, 581, no. 154; Dutuit 1885, 43, no. 434; Michel 1893, 482–483; von Bode/Hofstede de Groot 1897–1906, 6 (1901): 10, 78, no. 508; Rosenberg 1909, 456; Hofstede de Groot 1907–1927, 6 (1916): 119–120, no. 168; Valentiner 1920/1921, 221; Benesch 1956, 345–346, no. 10; Slive 1962, 486–487; Getty 1965, 31, 113–119; Bauch 1966, 13, no. 235; Lee 1967, 299, 301; Gerson 1968, 427, no. 366; Bredius/Gerson 1969, 613, no. 615; Haak 1969, 298; Fredericksen 1972, 88–89, no. 117; New Haven 1983, 49, 113, no. 113; Schwartz 1985, 313, no. 359; Tümpel 1986a, 399, no. 83; Melbourne and Canberra 1997, 144–145

Notes

1 For the Baltimore painting, see Melbourne and Canberra 1997, 146–149, no. 18.

2 New Haven 1983, 49.

3 Rosenberg 1909, 456.

4 von Bode/Hofstede de Groot, 7 (1902): 10.

5 Extract of a letter from Paris to New York, 29 January 1929. Series II, Papers and Correspondence, Box 277, folder 8. Duveen Brothers Records, 1876–1981, bulk 1909–1964, Getty Research Institute, Research Library, acc. no. 960015.

6 Amsterdam and Rotterdam 1956, 1: 178–179, no. 87.

9 The Apostle James the Major

1661, oil on canvas, original canvas: 92.1 × 74.9 (36 1/4 × 29 1/2)
Private collection

Inscription

Signed and dated, lower right:
Rembrandt f. 1661

Provenance

(Possibly sale of the heirs of Caspar Netscher, A. Schoutman et al., The Hague, 15 July 1749, lot 122 [as *A Pilgrim Praying*]); collections the MacKenzies of Kintore; Sir John Charles Robinson, London; Consul Edmund Friedrich Weber, Hamburg, 1872; (Charles Sedelmeyer Gallery, Paris, 1895); (Maurice Kann, Paris, 1901); (Duveen Gallery, Paris); (Reinhardt Galleries, New York, 1913); John North Willys, Toledo, Ohio; Isabel van Wie Willys [formerly Mrs. John N. Willys], New York (sale, Parke-Bernet, New York, 25 October 1945, no. 16); Billy Rose, New York; Oscar B. Cintas, Havana and New York; Mr. and Mrs. Stephen Carlton Clark by 1955

Exhibitions

Detroit 1930, no. 67; New York 1939, no. 309; New York 1950, no. 24; Boston 1992, no. 121; Melbourne and Canberra 1997, no. 21; Boston and Chicago 2003, no. 216

Literature

Woermann 1891, 32; Rosenberg 1892, 168; Michel 1903, 374; von Bode/Hofstede de Groot 1897–1906, 6 (1901): 202, no. 485; Hofstede de Groot 1908–1927, 6 (1916): 121, no. 170; Flint 1925, 366, 368; Valentiner 1931, no. 152; Benesch 1956, 346; Bauch 1966, 13, no. 236; Gerson 1968, 425; Bredius/Gerson 1969, 613, no. 617; Schwartz 1985, 313; Tümpel 1986a, 399, no. 82; Boston 1992, 198–199, no. 121

Notes

1 Michel 1893, ill. 162, 163; von Bode/Hofstede de Groot 1897–1906, 6 (1901): 202, no. 485; Hofstede de Groot 1908–1927, 6 (1916): 121, no. 170

2 Melbourne and Canberra 1997, 158–159; for example, his *Portrait of Amalia van Solms,* 1632 (Musée Jacquemart-André, Paris), had an existing pendant in profile of the sitter's husband, Prince Frederick Hendrick (Huis ten Bosch, The Hague), by Gerrit van Honthorst, which Rembrandt was required to complement in his design; see Bredius/Gerson 1969, 555, no. 99; *Corpus* 1982–, 2: 249–255, no. A61.

3 For *Young Woman,* see Bredius/Gerson 1969, 77, no. 85, and *Corpus* 1982–, 2: 158–165, no. A49; for *Saskia,* Bredius/Gerson 1969, 555–556, no. 101, and *Corpus* 1982–, 2: 422–439, no. A85; for *Flora,* Bredius/Gerson 1969, 557, no. 114.

4 Bredius/Gerson 1969, 598, no. 497, and *Corpus* 1982–, 3: 124–133, no. A110.

5 See, for example, *Bald-Headed Man in Profile Right; The Artist's Father(?)* in White and Boon 1969, 1: 139–140, 2: 249, no. B292.

6 Bredius/Gerson 1969, 609, no. 480. In this instance, however, the image is not portrayed in the same direct profile as in earlier such portraits (see notes 2, 3).

7 See, for example, Ben. 1190–1197 in Benesch 1973, 5: 320–323.

8 A half-length image in three-quarter view of *Praying Apostle* in the Cleveland Museum of Art (see Wheelock essay, fig. 1) has been attributed to Rembrandt and linked in the past to the group of evangelists and apostles, but its soft and tentative execution leaves little doubt that it is by a later follower or imitator. For fig. 1, see Benesch 1973, 5: 263, no. 949.

9 Benesch 1956, 346.

10 von Bode/Hofstede de Groot 1897–1906, 6 (1901): 29.

11 Strips of canvas that extend the painting at the left (2 in.) and at the top (3/4 in.) were added at some later date. These strips of canvas and their later painted additions have been masked out in the illustration here and in the recent reframing of the painting.

Bibliography, Exhibitions, and Appendix

Bibliography

Ainsworth et al. 1982
Ainsworth, Maryan Wynn, et al. *Art and Autoradiography: Insights into the Genesis of Paintings by Rembrandt, Van Dyck, and Vermeer.* New York, 1982.

Allen 1945
Allen, J. L. "The Museum's Rembrandts." *The Metropolitan Museum of Art Bulletin* 4 (1945): 73.

Alte Pinakothek 1986
Alte Pinakothek Munich: Explanatory Notes on the Works Exhibited. Munich, 1986.

Baldwin 1983
Baldwin, Robert. "Christ's Sublime Humility as Model for Style in Northern Renaissance and Baroque Religious Painting." Ph.D. diss., Harvard University, 1983.

Bauch 1966
Bauch, Kurt. *Rembrandt: Gemälde.* Berlin, 1966.

Benesch 1924
Benesch, Otto. "Rembrandts 'Falkenjäger.'" *Wiener Jahrbuch für Kunstgeschichte* 3 (1924): 115–118.

Benesch 1935
Benesch, Otto. *Rembrandt: Werk und Forschung.* Vienna, 1935.

Benesch 1954–1957
Benesch, Otto. *The Drawings of Rembrandt.* 6 vols. London, 1954–1957.

Benesch 1956
Benesch, Otto. "Worldly and Religious Portraits in Rembrandt's Late Art." *The Art Quarterly* 19 (Winter 1956): 335–355.

Benesch 1970
Benesch, Otto. *Otto Benesch Collected Writings.* Eva Benesch, ed. 2 vols. London and New York, 1970.

Benesch 1973
Benesch, Otto. *The Drawings of Rembrandt: A Critical and Chronological Catalogue.* 6 vols. Enlarged and ed. by Eva Benesch. London, 1973.

Blankert 1973
Blankert, Albert. "Rembrandt, Zeuxis and Ideal Beauty." In *Album Amicorum J. G. van Gelder.* Ed. J. Bruyn, J.A. Emmens, E. de Jongh, and D.P. Snoep. The Hague, 1973, 32–39.

von Bode 1883
Bode, Wilhelm von. *Studien zur Geschichte der holländischen Malerei.* Braunschweig, 1883.

von Bode 1912
Bode, Wilhelm von. "Neu entdeckte und wiedererstandene Gemälde von Rembrandt." *Der Cicerone* 4 (July 1912): 505–508.

von Bode/Hofstede de Groot 1897–1906
Bode, Wilhelm von. *The Complete Work of Rembrandt...* Assisted by Cornelis Hofstede de Groot. 8 vols. Paris, 1897–1906.

Bredius 1935
Bredius, Abraham. *Rembrandt Gemälde.* Vienna, 1935.

Bredius 1936
Bredius, Abraham. *The Paintings of Rembrandt.* London, 1936.

Bredius/Gerson 1969
Bredius, Abraham. *Rembrandt: The Complete Edition of His Paintings.* Revised by Horst Gerson. London, 1969.

Brejon de Lavergnée, Foucart & Reynaud 1979
Brejon de Lavergnée, Arnauld, Jacques Foucart, and Nicole Reynaud. *Catalogue sommaire illustré des peintures du Musée du Louvre: Ecoles flamande et hollandaise.* Paris, 1979.

Broun 1987
Broun, Francis. "Sir Joshua Reynolds' Collection of Paintings." Ph.D. diss., Princeton University, 1987.

Calvin 1989
Calvin, John. *Institutes of the Christian Religion.* Trans. Henry Beveridge. Grand Rapids, Mich., 1989.

Chapman 1990
Chapman, H. Perry. *Rembrandt's Self-Portraits: A Study in Seventeenth-Century Identity.* Princeton, 1990.

Charrington/Alexander 1983
Charrington, John. *A Catalogue of the Mezzotints after, or Said to Be after, Rembrandt.* Cambridge, 1923. Revised by David Alexander in *Rembrandt in Eighteenth-Century England* [exh. cat., Yale Center for British Art] (New Haven, 1983), Appendix C, 119-149.

Comte de Vence 1759
Catalogue des tableaux du cabinet de monsieur le Comte de Vence. Paris, 1759.

Comte de Vence 1761
Remy, R. *Catalogue raisonné des tableaux, dessins, originaux et estampes, du feu M. le Comte de Vence.* Paris, 1761.

***Corpus* 1982-**
Bruyn, Josua, et al. *A Corpus of Rembrandt Paintings.* 3+ vols. The Hague, Boston, and London, 1982-.

Crenshaw 2000
Crenshaw, Paul. "Rembrandt's Bankruptcy." Ph.D. diss., New York University, 2000.

Crenshaw 2002
Crenshaw, Paul. "Rembrandt's Declaration of Bankruptcy." In *Rethinking Rembrandt.* Ed. Alan Chong and Michael Zell. Zwolle, 2002.

Dijkstra et al. 2002
Dijkstra, Jeltje, et al. *De schilderijen van Museum Catharijneconvent.* Utrecht and Zwolle, 2002.

Dudok van Heel 1991
Dudok van Heel, Sebastian. "Rembrandt van Rijn (1606-1669): A Changing Portrait of the Artist." In Berlin, Amsterdam, and London 1991, 50-67.

Dudok van Heel 2001
Dudok van Heel, S.A.C. "Rembrandt: His Life, His Nursemaid and the Servant." In Edinburgh and London 2001, 19-28.

Dutuit 1885
Dutuit, Eugène. *Tableaux et dessins de Rembrandt.* Paris, 1885.

Duveen Brothers 1941
Duveen Brothers. *Duveen Pictures in Public Collections of America.* New York, 1941.

von Einem 1972
Einem, H. von. "Bemerkungen zum Christusbild Rembrandts." *Das Münster* 25 (1972): 349-360.

Eisler 1927
Eisler, Max. *Der alte Rembrandt.* Vienna, 1927.

Flint 1925
Flint, Ralph. "John N. Willys Collection." *International Studio* 80 (February 1925): 363-374.

Foucart 1982
Foucart, Jacques. *Les Peintures de Rembrandt au Louvre.* Paris, 1982.

Fredericksen 1972
Fredericksen, Burton B. *Catalogue of the Paintings in the J. Paul Getty Museum.* Malibu, 1972.

Friedlaender 1967-1976
Friedlaender, Max J. *Early Netherlandish Painting.* 14 vols. Leiden and Brussels, 1967-1976.

Gantner 1959
Gantner, Joseph. "Rembrandts 'Falkenier' in Göteborg — ein letztes Echo aus dem 'Abendmahl' des Leonardo." *Festschrift Karl M. Swoboda zum 28. Januar 1959.* Vienna, 1959, 97-102.

Gantner 1964
Gantner, Joseph. *Rembrandt und die Verwandlung klassischer Formen.* Bern, 1964.

Gerson 1968
Gerson, Horst. *Rembrandt Paintings.* Trans. from the German edition, *Rembrandt Gemälde.* Ed. Gary Schwartz. New York, 1968.

Getty 1965
Getty, J. Paul. *The Joys of Collecting.* New York, 1965.

Haak 1969
Haak, Bob. *Rembrandt: His Life, His Work, His Time.* London, 1969.

Halewood 1982
Halewood, William H. *Six Subjects of Reformation Art: A Preface to Rembrandt.* Toronto, 1982.

Hall 1974
Hall, James. *Dictionary of Subjects & Symbols in Art.* New York, 1974.

Heppner 1935
Heppner, A. "Moses zeigt die Gesetztafeln bei Rembrandt und Bol." *Oud Holland* 52 (1935): 241-251.

Hofstede de Groot 1907-1927
Hofstede de Groot, Cornelis. *A Catalogue Raisonné of the Works of the Most Eminent Dutch Painters of the Seventeenth Century...* 8 vols. London, 1907-1927. Trans. from the German edition, *Beschreibendes und kritisches Verzeichnis der Werke der hervorragendsten holländischen Maler des XVII. Jahrhunderts.* 10 vols. Esslingen and Paris, 1907-1928.

Hollstein 1949-
Hollstein, F.W.H. *Dutch and Flemish Etchings, Engravings, and Woodcuts, ca. 1450-1700.* 58+ vols. Amsterdam, 1949-.

Van Hoogstraten 1678
Hoogstraten, Samuel van. *Inleyding tot de Hooge Schoole der Schilderkonst anders de Zichtbaere Werelt...* Rotterdam, 1678 (reprint, Utrecht, 1969).

Houbraken 1753
Houbraken, Arnold. *De groote schouburgh der Nederlantsche konstschilders en schilderessen.* 3 vols. The Hague, 1753 (reprint, Amsterdam, 1980).

Kettlewell 1968
Kettlewell, James K. *Rembrandt's Christ in Thirteen Paintings and One Etching.* Glens Falls, N.Y., 1968.

Kettlewell 1981
Kettlewell, James K. *The Hyde Collection Catalogue.* Glens Falls, N.Y., 1981.

Kirschbaum 1968-
Kirschbaum, Engelbert, ed. *Lexikon der Christlichen Ikonographie.* 8 vols. Rome, Freiburg, Basel, and Vienna, 1968-.

Knipping 1974
Knipping, John B. *Iconography of the Counter Reformation in the Netherlands.* 2 vols. Leiden, 1974.

Lammertse 2002
Lammertse, Friso. "Van Dyck's Apostles Series, Hendrick Uylenburgh and Sigismund III." *The Burlington Magazine* 144 (March 2002): 140–146.

Laurent 1829
Laurent, J. A. *1er catalogue du musée départemental, comprenant la collection Salm et la collection Choiseul.* Épinal, 1829.

Lee 1967
Lee, Sherman. "Rembrandt: *An Old Man Praying.*" *The Bulletin of the Cleveland Museum of Art* (December 1967): 295–301.

MacLaren 1960
MacLaren, Neil. *National Gallery Catalogue: The Dutch School.* London, 1960.

MacLaren/Brown 1991
MacLaren, Neil. *National Gallery Catalogue: The Dutch School, 1600–1900.* 2 vols. Revised and expanded by Christopher Brown. London, 1991.

Van Mander 1604
Mander, Karel van. *Het schilderboek.* Haarlem, 1604. 2nd ed. Amsterdam, 1618 (reprint, Utrecht, 1969).

Van Mander/Miedema 1994
Mander, Karel van. *The Lives of the Illustrious Netherlandish and German Painters.* Intro. and trans. Hessel Miedema. 6 vols. Doornspijk, 1994.

Michel 1893
Michel, Émile. *Rembrandt: Sa vie, son oeuvre, et son temps.* Paris, 1893.

Michel 1903
Michel, Émile. *Rembrandt, His Life, His Work and His Time.* New ed. London and New York, 1903. Trans. from the French edition, *Rembrandt: Sa vie, son oeuvre, et son temps.* Paris, 1893.

von Moltke 1938/1939
von Moltke, Joachim Wolfgang. "Jan de Bray." *Marburger Jahrbuch für Kunstwissenschaft* 11/12 (1938/1939): 421–523.

Mongan and Mongan 1983
Mongan, Agnes, and Elizabeth Mongan. *European Paintings in the Timken Art Gallery.* San Diego, 1983.

Münz 1948
Münz, Ludwig. "A Newly Discovered Late Rembrandt." *The Burlington Magazine* 90 (1948): 64–67.

Nadler 2003
Nadler, Steven. *Rembrandt's Jews.* Chicago and London, 2003.

Van Regteren Altena 1969
Regteren Altena, I. Q. van. *Miscellanea.* Amsterdam, 1969.

Van Regteren Altena 1973
Regteren Altena, I. Q. van. "Rembrandts Persönlichkeit." In *Neue Beiträge zur Rembrandt-Forschung.* Ed. Otto v. Simson and Jan Kelch. Berlin, 1973, 176–187.

Rosenberg 1892
Rosenberg, Adolf. "Kleine Mitteilungen." *Zeitschrift für bildende Kunst* 27 (1892): 168.

Rosenberg 1909
Rosenberg, Adolf. *Rembrandt: Des Meisters Gemälde* (Klassiker der Kunst 2). Stuttgart and Berlin, 1909.

Rosenberg 1964
Rosenberg, Jakob. *Rembrandt: Life and Work.* Revised from first edition 1948. London, 1964.

Rotermund 1956
Rotermund, Hans-Martin. "Wandlungen des Christus-Typus bei Rembrandt." *Wallraf-Richartz Jahrbuch* 18 (1956): 197–237.

Schama 1999
Schama, Simon. *Rembrandt's Eyes.* New York, 1999.

Schatborn 1985
Schatborn, Peter. *Tekeningen van Rembrandt, zijn onbekende leerlingen en navolgers/Drawings by Rembrandt, His Anonymous Pupils and Followers.* Catalogue of the Dutch and Flemish Drawings in the Rijksprentenkabinet, Rijksmuseum, Amsterdam. Vol. 4. The Hague, 1985.

Schmidt-Degener 1919
Schmidt-Degener, Frederik. "Rembrandt en Vondel." *De Gids* 83 (1919): 222–275.

Schmidt-Degener 1928
Schmidt-Degener, Frederik. "Rembrandt und der holländische Barock." *Studien der Bibliothek Warburg* 9. Leipzig and Berlin, 1928.

Schwartz 1985
Schwartz, Gary. *Rembrandt: His Life, His Paintings.* New York, 1985. Trans. from the Dutch edition, *Rembrandt, zijn leven, zijn schilderijen.* Maarssen, 1984.

Slatkes 1992
Slatkes, Leonard J. *Rembrandt: Catalogo completo dei dipinti.* Florence, 1992.

Slive 1953
Slive, Seymour. *Rembrandt and His Critics, 1630–1730.* Chicago, 1953.

Slive 1962
Slive, Seymour. "Realism and Symbolism in Seventeenth-Century Dutch Painting." *Daedalus* 91 (1962): 469–500.

Slive 1965
Slive, Seymour. "An Unpublished Head of Christ by Rembrandt." *The Art Bulletin* 47 (December 1965): 406–417.

Smith 1829–1842
Smith, John. *A Catalogue Raisonné of the Works of the Most Eminent Dutch, Flemish, and French Painters.* 9 vols. London, 1829–1842.

Smith 1884
Smith, John Chaloner. *British Mezzotinto Portraits.* 4 vols. London, 1884.

Strauss and Van der Meulen 1979
Strauss, Walter L., and Marjon van der Meulen. *The Rembrandt Documents.* New York, 1979.

Sumowski 1979–
Sumowski, Werner. *Drawings of the Rembrandt School.* Ed. and trans. Walter L. Strauss. 10 + vols. New York, 1979–.

Sumowski 1983–1994
Sumowski, Werner. *Gemälde der Rembrandt-Schüler.* 6 vols. Landau, 1983–1994.

Sutton 1986
Sutton, Peter C. *A Guide to Dutch Art in America.* Washington, 1986.

Van Thiel 1969
Van Thiel, Pieter J. J. "Zelfportret als de Apostel Paulus: Rembrandt van Rijn (1606-1669)." *Openbaar Kunstbezit* 13 (1969): 1a-1b.

Timken 1996
Timken Museum of Art: European Works of Art, American Paintings, and Russian Icons in the Putnam Foundation Collection. San Diego, 1996.

Tümpel 1971
Tümpel, Christian. "Ikonographische Beiträge zu Rembrandt: Zur Deutung und Interpretation einzelner Werke. II." *Jahrbuch der Hamburger Kunstsammlungen* 16 (1971): 20-38.

Tümpel 1986a
Tümpel, Christian. *Rembrandt.* Trans. into French by Jacques and Jean Duvernet, Léon Karlson, and Patrick Grilli. Paris, 1986.

Tümpel 1986b
Tümpel, Christian. *Rembrandt: Mythos und Methode.* Antwerp, 1986.

Urbach 1983
Urbach, Susan. "Preliminary Remarks on the Sources of the Apostle Series of Rubens and Van Dyck." *Canadian Art Review (RACAR)* 10 (1983): 5-22.

Valentiner 1920/1921
Valentiner, Wilhelm R. "Die Vier Evangelisten Rembrandts." *Kunstchronik und Kunstmarkt* 56 (1920/1921): 219-222.

Valentiner 1921
Valentiner, Wilhelm R. *Rembrandt: Wiedergefundene Gemälde (1910-1920)* (Klassiker der Kunst 27). Stuttgart and Berlin, 1921.

Valentiner 1923
Valentiner, Wilhelm R. *Rembrandt: Wiedergefundene Gemälde (1910-1920)* (Klassiker der Kunst 27). Revised, 2nd ed. Stuttgart, Berlin, and Leipzig, 1923.

Valentiner 1931
Valentiner, Wilhelm R. *Rembrandt Paintings in America.* New York, 1931.

Valentiner 1948
Valentiner, Wilhelm R. "Rembrandt's Conception of Historical Portraiture." *Art Quarterly* 11 (1948): 117-135.

Valentiner 1956
Valentiner, Wilhelm R. "The Rembrandt Exhibitions in Holland." *Art Quarterly* 19 (1956): 390-403.

Villot 1852
Villot, Frédéric. *Notice des tableaux exposés dans les galleries du Musée national du Louvre: Écoles allemande, flamande et hollandaise* 2. Paris, 1852.

Vlieghe 1972
Vlieghe, Hans. *Saints 1* (Corpus Rubenianum Ludwig Burchard 8). London and New York, 1972.

De Voragine
De Voragine, Jacobus. *The Golden Legend.* Trans. William Granger Ryan. 2 vols. Princeton, 1993.

Vosmaer 1877
Vosmaer, C. *Rembrandt: Sa vie et ses oeuvres.* The Hague, 1877.

Weisbach 1926
Weisbach, Werner. *Rembrandt.* Berlin and Leipzig, 1926.

Van de Wetering 1997
Wetering, Ernst van de. *Rembrandt: The Painter at Work.* Amsterdam, 1997.

Van de Wetering 2000
Wetering, Ernst van de. "Remarks on Rembrandt's Oil-Sketches for Etchings." In Amsterdam and London 2000, 36-63.

Wethey 1969
Wethey, Harold E. *The Paintings of Titian.* 3 vols. London, 1969.

Wheelock 1995
Wheelock, Arthur K. *Dutch Paintings of the Seventeenth Century.* The Collections of the National Gallery of Art Systematic Catalogue. Washington, 1995.

White 1999
White, Christopher. *Rembrandt as an Etcher: A Study of the Artist at Work.* 2 vols. New Haven, 1999.

White and Boon 1969
White, Christopher, and Karel G. Boon. *Rembrandt's Etchings: An Illustrated Critical Catalogue.* 2 vols. Amsterdam, London, and New York, 1969.

Widener 1931
Paintings in the Collection of Joseph Widener at Lynnewood Hall. Intro. Wilhelm R. Valentiner. Elkins Park, Pa., 1931.

Wishnevsky 1967
Wishnevsky, Rose. "Studien zum *'portrait historié'* in den Niederlanden." Ph.D. diss., Ludwig-Maximilians-Universität. Munich, 1967.

Woermann 1891
Woermann, Carl. "Meisterwerke Niederländischer Maler in der Galerie Weber zu Hamburg." *Die Graphischen Künste* 14 (1891): 29-36.

Wright 1982
Wright, Christopher. *Rembrandt Self-Portraits.* London and Bedford, 1982.

Wright 2000
Wright, Christopher. *Rembrandt.* Paris, 2000.

von Wurzbach 1906–1911
Wurzbach, Alfred von. *Niederländisches Künstler-Lexikon.* 3 vols. Vienna and Leipzig, 1906-1911.

Zell 2002
Zell, Michael. *Reframing Rembrandt: Jews and the Christian Image in Seventeenth-Century Amsterdam.* Berkeley, Los Angeles, and London, 2002.

Zwarts 1926
Zwarts, Jac. "Haham Saul Levy Morteyar en zijn portret door Rembrandt." *Oud Holland* 43 (1926): 1-17.

Exhibitions

Amsterdam 1898
Schilderijen bijeengebracht ter gelegenheid van de inhuldiging van Hare Majesteit Koningin Wilhelmina. Stedelijk Museum.

Amsterdam 1935
Rembrandt tentoonstelling. Rijksmuseum.

Amsterdam 1952
Drie eeuwen portret in Nederland. Rijksmuseum.

Amsterdam and Jerusalem 1991
Het Oude Testment in de schilderkunst van de Gouden Eeuw. Joods Historisch Museum and Israel Museum (catalogue by Christian Tümpel).

Amsterdam and Kassel 2001
The Mystery of the Young Rembrandt. Museum het Rembrandthuis and Staatliche Museen Kassel (catalogue by Ernst van de Wetering and Bernhard Schnackenburg).

Amsterdam and London 2000
Rembrandt, the Printmaker. Rijksmuseum and The British Museum (catalogue by Erik Hinterding, Ger Luijten, and Martin Royalton-Kisch).

Amsterdam and Rotterdam 1956
Rembrandt tentoonstelling ter herdenking van de geboorte van Rembrandt op 15 juli 1606: Schilderijen. 3 vols. Rijksmuseum and Museum Boymans, 1956.

Basel 1948
Rembrandt Ausstellung. Galerie Katz.

Bergamo 2000
La Luce del Vero: Caravaggio, La Tour, Rembrandt, Zurbarán. Galleria d'Arte Moderna e Contemporanea.

Berlin, Amsterdam, and London 1991
Rembrandt: The Master & His Workshop: Paintings. Altes Museum, Rijksmuseum, and The National Gallery (catalogue by Christopher Brown et al.).

Birmingham 1934
Commemorative Exhibition of the Art Treasures of the Midlands. City of Birmingham Museum and Art Gallery.

Boston 1992
Prized Possessions: European Paintings from Private Collections of Friends of the Museum of Fine Arts, Boston. Museum of Fine Arts, Boston (catalogue by Peter C. Sutton).

Boston and Chicago 2003
Rembrandt's Journey: Painter, Draftsman, Etcher. Museum of Fine Arts, Boston, and Art Institute of Chicago (catalogue by Clifford S. Ackley et al.).

British Institution 1815/1832/1841/1843/1851
Graves, Algernon. *A Century of Loan Exhibitions 1813-1912.* 5 vols. London, 1913-1915.

Brussels 1971
Rembrandt en zijn tijd. Paleis voor Schone Kunsten.

Cambridge 1948
Rembrandt: Paintings and Etchings. Fogg Art Museum, Harvard University.

Detroit 1925
Loan Exhibition of Dutch Paintings of the Seventeenth Century. The Detroit Institute of Arts.

Detroit 1930
The Thirteenth Loan Exhibition of Old Masters, Paintings by Rembrandt. The Detroit Institute of Arts (catalogue by Wilhelm R. Valentiner).

Dijon 1950
De Jérôme Bosch à Rembrandt, peintures et dessins du Musée Boymans de Rotterdam. Musée de Dijon.

Dordrecht and Cologne 1998
Arent de Gelder (1645-1727): Rembrandts Meisterschüler und Nachfolger. Dordrechts Museum and Wallraf-Richartz-Museum.

Edinburgh and London 2001
Rembrandt's Women. National Gallery of Scotland and Royal Academy of Arts (catalogue by Julia Lloyd Williams).

Epinal 1993
La Collection des Princes de Salm. Musée Départemental d'Art Ancien et Contemporain (catalogue by Bernard Huin).

Frankfurt and Kyoto 2003
Rembrandt Rembrandt. Städelsches Kunstinstitut und Städtische Galerie and Kyoto National Museum (catalogue by Jeroen Giltaij).

Leningrad 1986
Meesterwerken van de Westeuropese schilderkunst uit de XVI-XIX eeuw uit de verzameling van het Museum Boymans-van Beuningen. The State Hermitage Museum.

London 1812
Winter Exhibition. Royal Academy.

London 1882
Winter Exhibition. Royal Academy.

London 1889
Exhibition of Old Masters. Winter Exhibition. Royal Academy.

London 1899
Winter Exhibition. Royal Academy.

London 1929
Exhibition of Dutch Art 1450-1900. Royal Academy.

London 1945
Arts Council Dutch Paintings Exhibition. Arts Council.

London 1947
An Exhibition of Cleaned Pictures (1936-1947). The National Gallery.

London 1948
Exhibition of Fine Paintings by Old Masters. Leger Galleries.

London 1988
Art in the Making: Rembrandt. The National Gallery (catalogue by David Bomford et al.).

London and The Hague 1999
Rembrandt by Himself. The National Gallery and Royal Cabinet of Paintings Mauritshuis (catalogue by Ernst van de Wetering, Volker Manuth, and Marieke de Winkel).

Melbourne and Canberra 1997
Rembrandt: A Genius and His Impact. National Gallery of Victoria and National Gallery of Australia (catalogue by Albert Blankert et al.).

Minneapolis 1972
The J. Paul Getty Collection. The Minneapolis Institute of Arts.

Montreal 1944
Five Centuries of Dutch Art. The Art Association of Montreal.

Moscow-Leningrad 1965
V'stavka kartin zapadnoevropejski chudoznikov. The State Hermitage Museum.

New Haven 1983
Rembrandt in Eighteenth-Century England. Yale Center for British Art (catalogue by Christopher White et al.).

New York 1909
The Hudson-Fulton Celebration: Catalogue of a Collection of Paintings by Dutch Masters of the Seventeenth Century. The Metropolitan Museum of Art (catalogue by Wilhelm R. Valentiner).

New York 1939
Catalogue of European Paintings and Sculpture from 1300-1800, Masterpieces of Art. New York World's Fair (catalogue by George Henry MacCall and Wilhelm R. Valentiner).

New York 1942
Paintings of the Great Dutch Masters of the Seventeenth Century. Duveen Galleries (catalogue by George Henry McCall and Adriaan J. Barnouw).

New York 1950
A Loan Exhibition of Rembrandt at Wildenstein. Wildenstein & Co.

New York 1995
Rembrandt/Not Rembrandt. The Metropolitan Museum of Art. 2 vols. (vol. 1, Hubert von Sonnenburg; vol. 2, Walter Liedtke et al.).

Paris 1955
Rembrandt: Etude photographique et radiographique. Musée du Louvre.

Paris 1970
Le siècle de Rembrandt: Tableaux hollandais des collections publiques françaises. Musée du Petit Palais (catalogue by Jacques Foucart et al.).

Rome 1928
Mostra di Capolavori della Pittura Olandese. Galleria Borghese.

Rome 1954
Mostra di pittura olandese del siecento. Palazzo delle Esposizioni.

Rotterdam 1938
Meesters uit vier eeuwen 1400-1800. Museum Boymans.

Rotterdam 1988
Een gloeiend palet: Schilderijen van Rembrandt en zijn school (A Glowing Palette: Rembrandt and His School). Museum Boymans-van Beuningen (catalogue by Jeroen Giltaij and Guido Jansen).

San Francisco, Toledo, and Boston 1966
The Age of Rembrandt. Palace of the Legion of Honor, Toledo Museum of Art, and Museum of Fine Arts, Boston.

Schaffhausen 1949
Rembrandt und seine Zeit. Museum zu Allerheiligen.

Stockholm 1956
Rembrandt. Nationalmuseum.

Stockholm 1992
Rembrandt och hans tid: Människan i centrum (Rembrandt and His Age: Focus on Man). Nationalmuseum (catalogue by Görel Cavalli-Björkman).

Tokyo and Kyoto 1968
The Age of Rembrandt. Dutch Painting and Drawing in the 17th Century. The National Museum of Western Art and Municipal Museum.

Toronto 1951
Rembrandt Exhibition. Toronto Art Museum.

Washington 1969
Rembrandt in the National Gallery of Art, Washington, DC. National Gallery of Art.

Washington 1990
Anthony van Dyck. National Gallery of Art (catalogue by Arthur K. Wheelock Jr., Susan J. Barnes, and Julius S. Held).

Washington and Cincinnati 1988
Masterworks from Munich: Sixteenth- to Eighteenth-Century Paintings from the Alte Pinakothek. National Gallery of Art and Cincinnati Art Museum (catalogue by Beverly Louise Brown and Arthur K. Wheelock Jr.).

Washington, Detroit, and Amsterdam 1980
Gods, Saints, and Heroes: Dutch Painting in the Age of Rembrandt. National Gallery of Art, The Detroit Institute of Arts, and Rijksmuseum (catalogue by Albert Blankert et al.).

Yokohama, Fukuoka, and Kyoto 1986
Rembrandt and the Bible. Sogo Museum of Art, Fukuoka Art Museum, and Kyoto National Museum of Art (catalogue by Christopher Brown et al.).

Zürich 1949
Gemälde der Ruzicka-Stiftung. Kunsthaus Zürich.

Zürich 1953
Holländer des 17. Jahrhunderts. Kunsthaus Zürich.

Appendix
The Apostles and Evangelists

The Original Twelve Apostles
Andrew
Bartholomew
James (the Major)
James the Minor
John
Judas Iscariot
Jude (Thaddaeus)
Matthew
Peter (also referred to as Simon Peter)
Philip
Simon the Zealot
Thomas

Other Apostles
Matthias
Paul (Paul is considered an adjunct to the Twelve Apostles; reference is often made to the Twelve Apostles and Paul)

The Evangelists
John (apostle and evangelist)
Luke
Mark
Matthew (apostle and evangelist)

Apostles and Evangelists: Historical and Iconographic Considerations

Evangelists are commonly defined as preachers of the Gospel. In large measure the principal roles of the apostles and evangelists can be understood by simply translating the words from the original Greek. Apostle (*apostolos*) denotes one who acts as a delegate or messenger, while evangelist (*euangelistēs*) means one who proclaims good news. When placed within the context of the early Christian church, these terms refer to the small group of emissaries who were either chosen by Christ or appointed in his name and who, by means of the spoken and written word, succeeded in disseminating his teachings. The apostles also witnessed the Resurrection and formed the foundation of the church. Today, theologians and historians of church history often espouse widely differing views on issues relating to the precise nature of the activities and writings of the apostles and evangelists.

No consistent iconography had developed by the early seventeenth century for either the physical appearance of the individual apostles or their attributes. Hence, it is sometimes difficult to identify specific apostles in images from the period. The following sketches provide a brief overview of the apostles' lives and note their most frequently depicted attributes.

Apostles Chosen by Christ

Andrew
A fisherman and an older brother of the Apostle Peter, Andrew was the first to follow Christ. According to tradition, he spread the Gospel in the Northern countries, as far as southern Russia. He was crucified in Patros, Greece. Andrew's attribute is the transverse cross bearing his name.

Bartholomew
According to legend, Bartholomew spread the Gospel in Asia, India, and Armenia. He was flayed alive and is usually depicted with a flaying knife and, in some cases, with his skin draped over his arm.

James the Major
Son of the fisherman Zebedee, James is the older brother of the Apostle John. Along with Peter and James the Minor, he was one of the three apostles closest to Christ and was present at the Transfiguration and the Agony in the Garden. James was tried in Jerusalem and eventually decapitated by order of Herod Agrippa. James the Major is typically portrayed as a pilgrim, and his attribute is the pilgrim's staff.

James the Minor
James, son of Alpheus and Mary Cleophas, half-sister of the Virgin, was called "the Minor" to distinguish him from the Apostle James the Major. After Peter departed for Rome, James became head of the Christian church in Palestine as bishop of Jerusalem. He was stoned in Jerusalem for spreading Christ's message. His attribute is a club.

John
Both an apostle and an evangelist, John was the son of Zebedee and Salome, and the brother of the Apostle James the Major. One of Christ's beloved disciples, he was present at the Last Supper and the Crucifixion. John cared for the Virgin Mary after Christ's Crucifixion and preached in Judaea after the Virgin's death. Exiled by the Roman Emperor Domitian to the island of Patmos, he received the vision of the Apocalypse. He is the author of the Gospel of John, along with the first, second, and third books of John. The last to write his Gospel, he did so roughly sixty-three years after the Ascension. Consequently, his writings are believed to contain much that had been omitted in the work of the other three evangelists. His attributes are the eagle and a book.

Judas Iscariot

One of the Twelve Apostles, Judas carried the disciples' money box and betrayed Christ for thirty pieces of silver. After Christ's arrest by the Roman authorities, Judas was pained by guilt and returned the money to the priests. He eventually committed suicide by hanging himself. Judas is often associated with murky yellow tones, and his attribute is a demon resting on his shoulder.

Jude (Thaddeus)

Jude, son of Alphaeus, was given the surname Thaddeus to distinguish him from Judas Iscariot. Legend says that he evangelized in Syria and Mesopotamia with the Apostle Simon. He was martyred with a sledge hammer. He is depicted both as an old and as a young man, and his attribute is the halberd, a shafted weapon.

Luke

An apostle and one of the four evangelists, Luke was born at Antioch in Syria and was a physician by training. He wrote the third Gospel and the Acts of the Apostles. More than the other evangelists, he carefully recorded the activities of Paul, whom he accompanied on missionary sojourns for many years in Greece and Italy. After Paul's death Luke traveled to Greece, where he continued to preach and later died. According to legend, he was also an artist and painted a portrait of the Virgin Mary. His attributes are the winged ox and a book.

Mark

Mark was an apostle and one of the four evangelists, yet little is known about his early life before he met Paul, often considered the greatest of all missionaries. Mark traveled to Rome, to villages along the Adriatic, and to Egypt and Libya. He founded the church in Alexandria and became its first bishop. Arrested on Easter for having celebrated mass, he was dragged through the streets with a rope tied around his neck and was eventually martyred by clubbing. He was the writer of the Gospel of Mark, and his most common attribute is the winged lion.

Matthew

The Apostle Matthew, also called Levi, was the son of Alphaeus and the brother of the Apostle James the Minor. He was a tax collector before he was called by Christ to become an apostle. He preached the Gospel in Ethiopia, and a tradition says he was martyred in Parthia. Matthew, first among the evangelists to record the Holy Gospel of Christ, completed his writing roughly six years after the Ascension. If he does not appear in the guise of a tax collector, shown with a purse, he is represented as an evangelist with an angel, engaged in the act of writing. Another attribute was a T-square because of the factual character of his Gospel.

Matthias

Not originally one of the Twelve Apostles, Matthias was called to be an apostle after the betrayal of Judas Iscariot. He is often portrayed enveloped by a "beam of divine splendor," which, by pointing to him, signified his appointment as an apostle. According to legend he evangelized in Armenia, where he suffered his martyrdom. His attribute is a lance or an ax.

Paul

Although not originally one of the Twelve Apostles, Paul became one of the most important followers of Christ. Born at Tarsus and named Saul, Paul was a Roman citizen. On his way to Damascus, Paul was thrown from his horse and was struck blind for three days by an intense light. After his recovery, he converted and received the new name of Paul. He became one of the most ardent apostles and evangelized through Asia Minor and Greece. Imprisoned in Rome, Paul was beheaded with a sword, which, along with the Bible, is his attribute.

Peter (also referred to as Simon Peter)

Born in Galilee to a fisherman, Peter was one of the most beloved disciples of Christ. Christ appointed Peter an apostle and gave him the name Cephas, meaning rock. Peter spread the Gospel in Asia Minor, centering his activities on Antioch. According to tradition, he founded the Christian community in Rome and became the first pope of the Roman church. He was eventually imprisoned in Rome and crucified hanging upside down. Peter is generally portrayed as an older man with a short beard. His attributes are the Bible and a pair of keys.

Philip

Little is known about Philip, who was born in Bethsaida in Galilee. According to legend, he evangelized in Galatia in Turkey. Philip was crucified upside down in Hierapolis. He is generally depicted with loaves of bread for his purported role in the feeding of the five thousand, and his attribute is the Latin cross fastened to the top of a staff or reed.

Simon the Zealot

Simon is believed to have evangelized throughout Syria, Mesopotamia, and even in the British Isles with the Apostle Jude (Thaddeus). He was martyred in Persia by being cut in two with a saw, which became his attribute.

Thomas

Also called Didymas (the twin), Thomas was a fisherman in Galilee. He is known particularly for doubting that Christ rose from the Dead. Thomas is thus often shown, as directed by Christ, inserting his fingers into Christ's wound. According to tradition, Thomas went to Babylon and founded the first Christian church. He also preached the Gospel in Persia and India, where he was martyred with a lance. His attribute is a builder's rule, a reference to his belief that faith builds wealth in heaven, or sometimes his attribute is a spear.

Adapted from *Images of the Saints* [exh. cat., Montreal Museum of Fine Arts] (Montreal, 1965); Stefano Zuffi, ed., *Saints in Art* (Los Angeles, 2003); Clara Erskine Clement, *Christian Symbols and Stories of the Saints* (Boston, 1886, and Detroit, 1971); and *www.Biblepath.com.*

Index

Photographic Credits

Every effort has been made to locate the copyright holders for the photographs used in this book.

Rembrandt's Apostles and Evangelists

fig. 1, Jörg P. Anders; fig. 2, Scala/Art Resource, N.Y.; fig. 4, Bildarchiv Preussischer Kulturbesitz/Art Resource, N.Y., photo Jörg P. Anders; fig. 8, © 2004, Museum of Fine Arts, Boston; fig. 9, © The Cleveland Museum of Art, 2002; fig. 14, © The State Hermitage Museum, St. Petersburg; fig. 19, Alinari/Art Resource, N.Y.; fig. 20, Scala/Art Resource, N.Y.

Rembrandt's Apostles: Pillars of Faith and Witnesses of the Word

fig. 1, © Ursula Edelmann; fig. 5, Alinari/Art Resource, N.Y.; fig. 8, Prudence Cuming Associates Limited, photo © The Israel Museum, Jerusalem; fig. 10, Bildarchiv Preussischer Kulturbesitz/Art Resource, N.Y., photo Jörg P. Anders; fig. 13, © Réunion des Musées Nationaux/Art Resource, N.Y., photo Gérard Blot; fig. 14, © Réunion des Musées Nationaux/Art Resource, N.Y.

Rembrandt and the *Portrait Historié*

fig. 1, © Réunion des Musées Nationaux/Art Resource, N.Y., photo C. Jean; fig. 4, Erich Lessing, Art Resource, N.Y.; fig. 5, Rheinisches Bildarchiv, Köln; fig. 6, © Foto Marburg/Art Resource, N.Y.

Catalogue

cat. 1, © The National Gallery, London; fig. 1, © The State Hermitage Museum, St. Petersburg

cat. 2, photo Lorene Emerson; fig. 2, Erich Lessing/Art Resource, N.Y.; fig. 3, All rights reserved, The Metropolitan Museum of Art

cat. 3, fig. 2, All rights reserved, The Metropolitan Museum of Art

cat. 4, © The National Gallery, London

cat. 5, © The Metropolitan Museum of Art; fig. 1, Bildarchiv Preussischer Kulturbesitz/Art Resource, N.Y., photo Jörg P. Anders; fig. 2, Art Resource, N.Y.; fig. 3, © Alinari/Art Resource, N.Y.; fig. 4, All rights reserved, The Metropolitan Museum of Art

cat. 6, © Blauel/Gnamm-Artothek; fig. 3, Scala/Art Resource, N.Y.

cat. 7, © Réunion des Musées Nationaux/Art Resource, N.Y., photo Herve Lewandowski; fig. 2, The Montreal Museum of Fine Arts, Brian Merrett

cat. 8, fig. 1, © Jannes Linders

cat. 9, © 2003 Museum of Fine Arts, Boston; fig. 1, © Réunion des Musées Nationaux/Art Resource, N.Y.

cat. 10, © Kunsthaus Zürich. All rights reserved; fig. 1, © Alinari/Art Resource, N.Y.

cat. 12, © 1995 The Metropolitan Museum of Art

cat. 13, Tom Haartsen

cat. 14, Bernard Prud'homme; fig. 1, Tom Scott; fig. 2, © Rijksmuseum-Stichting, Amsterdam

cat. 15, Joseph Levy; cat. 1, RKD; fig. 2, © 2004 President and Fellows of Harvard College

cat. 16, Central Art Archives/Jouko Könönen